VOICES IN COURT

THE MACMILLAN COMPANY
NEW YORK · CHICAGO
DALLAS · ATLANTA · SAN FRANCISCO
LONDON · MANILA
IN CANADA
BRETT-MACMILLAN LTD.
GALT, ONTARIO

VOICES IN COURT

A Treasury of the Bench, the Bar, and the Courtroom

Edited by WILLIAM H. DAVENPORT

THE MACMILLAN COMPANY
New York   1958

Library of Congress catalog card number: 58–10918

The Macmillan Company, New York
Brett-Macmillan Ltd., Galt, Ontario

Printed in the United States of America

Foreword

This anthology is the end product of an assembly line of circumstances. The process began in 1954 with an experimental course in legal literature at the University of Southern California conducted then and since by myself. The course was suggested by Dean Kingsley and Associate Dean Evans of the Law School, who, together with a faculty committee, had felt the need of a broader cultural base for students specializing in law. The course attracted attention from the local press and *Time* (April 26, 1954), and hundreds of letters came in from all over the globe requesting bibliographies of readings for lawyers.

This response led to my writing articles for the *Journal* of the State Bar of California, the *Journal of Legal Education,* and the American Bar Association *Journal.* I was asked to write reviews in the field of legal literature for the *Law Review* of the University of Chicago, the *Law Library Journal,* and others. Further recognition came from the annual review of the law published at New York University and from the American Association of Law Libraries, which invited me to speak on "Law and Literature Once Again" at its annual banquet meeting at Colorado Springs in June, 1957.

Since the bibliography of legal literature continues to grow (see the American Bar Association *Journal* for September, 1957), it was inevitable that out of this should come a book, and this is it. At first I had planned to include plays and even poetry by authors whose names are household words; but I have left these for another day, if at all, because the material was familiar and expected, and because of the unusual interest of so much that came to my attention that deserved, if I may say so, to be better known. This collection is directed at lawyers, judges, men of law in any capacity, and laymen interested in the law. Essays, formal and informal; biography, letters, decisions, short stories, cases, trials, cross-examinations, history, and lectures are among the types and subtypes of material represented. I hope that the reading process will be entertaining and profitable for the many members of the legal profession and their friends.

An anthology is more than snipping and pasting, although it may seem just that to the inexperienced. In the correspondence, phone calls, conferences, research, reading, writing, photocopying, and general brooding which are part of the picture, an editor is in constant need of help. I owe much to Mr. R. L. De Wilton, Assistant Editor in Chief, and Mr. Cecil Scott, Senior Editor, of The Macmillan Company for patient understanding and advice. They represent the proverbial "without whose help" collaborators. In addition, and with apologies to those inadvertently omitted, I wish to thank the following for various kinds of assistance: my wife, Isobel;

Riley Paul Burton, law librarian, and his staff, of the University of Southern California; Dudley Stephenson of the Los Angeles County Law Library; Hewlett Cox, practicing attorney, Los Angeles; Dean Kingsley and Dean Evans of the University of Southern California School of Law; Professor Eleazer Lecky of the Department of English, University of Southern California; Professor Paul Bowerman of the California Institute of Technology; Mr. Maynard Smith; Professor Elliot Cheatham of the School of Law, Columbia University; and Messrs. Brown and Thayer of the Honnold Library, Claremont, California.

Los Angeles and Claremont, California

October, 1957   WILLIAM H. DAVENPORT

Contents

FOREWORD   v

SECTION I: THE LAWYER

THE ADVOCATE, from *It's Your Law*   2
  Charles P. Curtis

HOLMES PREPARES FOR THE BAR, from *Yankee from Olympus*   26
  Catherine Drinker Bowen

LINCOLN THE LAWYER, from *Abraham Lincoln: The Prairie Years*   43
  Carl Sandburg

THE JIM WHEAT MURDER CASE, from *You May Take the Witness*   58
  Clinton Giddings Brown

KNIGHT WITH THE RUEFUL COUNTENANCE (Profile of Lloyd Paul
    Stryker)   71
  Alexander Woollcott

THE SOLICITOR AND THE WILL, from *Confessions of an Un-Common
    Attorney*   78
  Reginald L. Hine

ART IN DIRECT EXAMINATION, from *Day in Court*   86
  Francis L. Wellman

LAW AND LETTERS, from *Law and Other Things*   99
LAW AND LANGUAGE, from the same   106
  Lord Macmillan

SECTION II: THE JUDGE

JEFFREYS, THE HANGING JUDGE, from *History of England*   120
  Thomas Babington Macaulay

LORD MONBODDO AND LORD BRAXFIELD, from *Some Old Scots Judges*   137
  W. Forbes Gray

LETTER TO JOSEPH STORY, from *An Autobiographical Sketch*   161
  John Marshall

MARBURY VERSUS MADISON, from *The Life of John Marshall*   174
  Albert J. Beveridge

THE NEW SUPREME COURT, from *Roger B. Taney*   195
  Carl Swisher

UNITED STATES OF AMERICA V. ONE BOOK CALLED *ULYSSES*   218
  John Woolsey

THE JUDICIAL TEMPERAMENT, from *Homilies and Recreations*   224
  John Buchan

HOLMES AND BRANDEIS DISSENTING, from *Brandeis: A Free Man's Life* 228
  Alpheus Thomas Mason

FULLER'S INCREASING INFLUENCE ON THE COURT, from *Melville
    Weston Fuller*   240
  Willard L. King

CHIEF JUSTICES I HAVE KNOWN, from *Of Law and Men*   250
  Felix Frankfurter

TROUBLE WITH THE VOLSTEAD ACT, from *A Judge Comes of Age*   269
  John C. Knox

THE FUTURE OF WISDOM IN AMERICA   277
  Learned Hand

LAW AND LITERATURE   283
  Benjamin N. Cardozo

OLD JUDGE AND YOUNG LAWYER, from *The Just and the Unjust*   297
  James Gould Cozzens

SECTION III: THE COURTROOM

TRIAL OF SIR WALTER RALEGH, from *The Lion and the Throne*   308
  Catherine Drinker Bowen

THE DEVIL AND DANIEL WEBSTER   330
  Stephen Vincent Benét

BARDELL V. PICKWICK, from *The Pickwick Papers*   342
    Charles Dickens

"BLEAK HOUSE" AND THE PROCEDURE OF THE COURT OF CHANCERY,
    from *Charles Dickens as Legal Historian*   363
    William S. Holdsworth

PHINEAS FINN AWAITS TRIAL, or CHAFFANBRASS ON THE LAW, from
    Phineas Redux   378
    Anthony Trollope

MADAME LUNEAU'S CASE   388
    Guy de Maupassant; translated by Ernest Boyd

THE BACCARAT CASE, from *Notable Cross-Examinations*   392
    Edward Wilfrid Fordham

THE TRIAL OF OSCAR WILDE: First Trial, Second Day, from *The
    Trials of Oscar Wilde*   403
    H. Montgomery Hyde

THE SEDDON CASE, from *For the Defence: The Life of Edward
    Marshall Hall*   418
    Edward Marjoribanks

THE MANNER OF CROSS-EXAMINATION, from *The Art of Cross-
    Examination*   438
THE CROSS-EXAMINATION OF MRS. REGINALD VANDERBILT, from
    the same   446
    Francis L. Wellman

THE REPUTATION OF THE DEAD, from *Hatred, Ridicule, or Contempt*   459
    Joseph Dean

SECTION IV: THE LAW

ON THE LAW, from *Of Experience*   476
    Michel de Montaigne; translated by E. J. Trechmann

UNJUST LAWS, from *On the Duty of Civil Disobedience*   483
    Henry David Thoreau

THE PROFESSION OF THE LAW   494
THE PATH OF THE LAW   496
    Oliver Wendell Holmes

The Case of the Speluncean Explorers   514
    Lon L. Fuller

The Criminal Law, from *A Mencken Chrestomathy*   539
    H. L. Mencken

The Growth of Substantive Law, from *Men and Measures in
    the Law*   545
    Arthur T. Vanderbilt

Language, Legal & Literary   562
    John Mason Brown

A List of One Hundred Legal Novels   572
    John H. Wigmore

Index by Authors   587

Section I

THE LAWYER

The Advocate*

CHARLES P. CURTIS

To whom does the lawyer owe his loyalty? Just what are the ethics of the legal profession? Many a layman would like to know. Not a few practitioners of the art of advocacy must themselves wonder now and then whether they have the right answers. Charles P. Curtis, the author of It's Your Law, *from which the following selection has been taken, has attempted in an unusually frank manner, by exposition and example, to arrive at the truth. Born in Boston in 1891, educated at Groton and Harvard, Mr. Curtis was admitted to the bar in 1919. He has held numerous trusteeships and directorships, and from 1924 to 1935 was a member of the Harvard Corporation. He is the author of several books, among them, in collaboration with Ferris Greenslet,* The Practical Cogitator.

The Adversary Process

Justice is a chilly virtue. It is of high importance that we be introduced into the inhospitable halls of justice by a friend. I think we neglect the fact that the first function of the lawyer, and the first great purpose of the devotion which a lawyer owes to his client, is the overcoming of this feeling of unfriendliness. The first duty of the bar is to make sure that everyone who feels the need of a friend in court shall have one, and I am not talking only of the poor and indigent. They obviously need a friend, and a good judge will fill the need if the bar does not. Nor only of those whose cause we detest. A proper sense of advocacy will take care of them, and I will speak of that in its place. I mean everyone, including those who seem least to need a friend, those who have the most respect for the law and who are usually the least familiar with it and the most fearful.

But if the devotion a lawyer owes to his client were no more than friendliness, if it were simply to serve the purpose of taking the chill off justice, there would be no more to say. We make greater demands upon our lawyers than that. They must be not only our friends. They must be our champions. For the way we administer justice is by an adversary proceeding, which is as much as to say, we set the parties fighting. This has been so for some

* From *It's Your Law,* by Charles P. Curtis, copyright, 1954, by The President and Fellows of Harvard College. Reprinted by permission of the publishers, Harvard University Press.

2

time; in fact, according to Max Radin, since about the fourth or the fifth century B.C. in Rome, when, Radin says, the judge's task changed from determining the truth to the umpiring of a competition. "At a certain special stage in the history of Western society," Radin said, "the way in which it was done was to call upon the judge to umpire a contest. His task was not to determine truth, but to decide who had the best of a competition—a competition that was not originally one of argument, though it soon became one. The place and time of this event can be set with fair probability at Rome somewhere in the fifth or fourth centuries B.C. . . . For many modern lawyers it is difficult to conceive of a trial as anything else, although the words 'trial' and 'verdict' might have called attention to the fact that these things professed to be something quite different."

This is still largely true. There is the story of the two prizefighters, who had been witnesses in a case and went in and stood in the back of the courtroom where Chief Justice Lemuel Shaw was presiding, as great a judge as his son-in-law, Herman Melville, was a writer. Two blue-black jaws dropped in admiration, and one said, not so much to the other as to himself, "Christ, what a referee!"

Lemuel Shaw was the Chief Justice of Massachusetts a hundred years ago—not so very long in the life of the law—but only a few years ago Mr. Justice Jackson of the United States Supreme Court said, in an opinion on the right of one lawyer to force his opponent to disclose some papers, "A common law trial is and always should be an adversary proceeding." And in the course of a discussion of Trial Tactics sponsored by the American Bar Association in 1951, Lon Hocker of St. Louis, a distinguished trial lawyer, followed this by adding, "If there is any message which I can leave with a younger trial lawyer, this is the one I yearn most to impart: the trial of a lawsuit is an adversary business." I'll quote Mr. Hocker again later.

I find it quite impossible to understand trial by ordeal, where justice apparently used to be put to the touch of a small miracle, but anyone who has been anywhere near a piece of determined litigation will readily understand trial by battle.

"One other method of proof was one introduced into England by the Normans, and this was trial by battle. In civil cases it was not fought between the parties themselves, but between their respective champions. . . . We very soon find from the rolls that there was a professional band of champions who undertook business all over the country; courts would arrange the dates of battle so that the champions could fit in their engagements conveniently. Some very great landowners, such as the larger monasteries, were so constantly involved in litigation that they maintained their own full-time champions. But in criminal cases battle was a much more serious affair. It lay when a private person brought a criminal charge against another, and was fought by the accuser and accused in person. It was deadly; if the defeated defendant was not already slain in the battle he was immediately hanged on the gallows which stood ready."

There are some subjects of litigation in which the adversary proceeding is an admirable way of administering justice. One wise judge implied as much when Charles E. Wyzanski said, "A political libel suit is the modern substitute for ordeal by battle. It is the means which society has chosen to induce bitter partisans to wager money instead of exchanging bloody noses." But litigation by an adversary proceeding is the way we cut the knot of many disputes in which it is disastrously inappropriate. Divorces, the custody of children, will contests, almost any kind of dispute which springs from family or equally intimate dissension—there a broken bone is more easily mendable. And it is intolerably too often true that a criminal trial turns into an adversary proceeding. "Criminal justice is concerned with the pathology of the body politic. In administering the criminal law, judges wield the most awesome surgical instruments of society. A criminal trial, it has been well said, should have the atmosphere of the operating room. The presiding judge determines the atmosphere. He is not an umpire who enforces the rules of a game, or merely a moderator between contestants. If he is adequate to his functions, the moral authority which he radiates will impose the indispensable standards of dignity and austerity upon all those who participate in a criminal trial."

What, then, is the justification for this approach to justice, other than the fact we are several centuries used to it and aside from the fact that spectators in small communities and newspaper readers in cities enjoy the spectacle? It seems to me that the justification of the adversary proceeding is the satisfaction of the parties, and not our satisfaction, except as we too are prospective litigants. This is a rational justification of the adversary approach to justice. Along this line, what the law is trying to do is give the algebraic maximum of satisfaction to both parties. This is a crude, but indeed it is not a bad, definition of the justice which the adversary proceeding provides. The law is trying to do justice between the parties for the parties rather than for us, trying to give them their own justice so far as possible and so far as compatible with what may be distinguished as our justice.

It is necessary, to be sure, to apply the general terms of what we regard as justice to their particular case. For we too must be satisfied. We are prospective customers. But the difference is not great. They are some of us, and they are much influenced by what we regard as just. The law pays more attention to the satisfaction of the needs of the parties in the particular case than it does to our ideas about justice in general. The law takes the position that we ought to be satisfied if the parties are; and it believes that the best way to get that done is to encourage them to fight it out, and dissolve their differences in dissension. We are still a combative people, not yet so civilized and sophisticated as to forget that combat is one way to justice.

We even try to delude ourselves into thinking that combat is the best way. The fact is, the adversary process is an indispensable alternative to the best way to what we may hope to be a wise as well as a just decision. I mean a few candid people pooling their minds on a problem, and not so much arguing with each other as eliciting each other's arguments.

I am afraid this is too flattering a description of our other way to justice, that parties settle their disputes privately and at their own expense; and yet there is a great deal to be said for settlement as a way of administering the law, granted, of course, that a judgment after a trial is a constant alternative. It might even be said that one of the great functions of our courts is to be just that, no more than a constant alternative, to make it certain that the discount in the discounted law which is applied in settlements shall be figured on true value and not on some arbitrary sum. Certainly a great many more cases are settled than tried. No one knows how many because there is no way of defining a case that has not been brought.

Negotiations for settlement are themselves judicial proceedings. Each attorney sits in judgment on the contentions of the other, comparing them with his own prophecies of what a judge would do, as the judge in turn would prophesy what the court of appeal will do. The evidence consists in the claims of each attorney discounted to the prophecy of the other. The negotiations are, indeed, the proceedings of a court of preliminary instance; and they have the virtue of being conducted in private, with each party less committed to his own contentions, and less embittered by the other's. A settlement ends, if it is successful, in a compromise instead of a judgment. Compromise is as often the better part of justice as prudence is the better part of valor, more often than we who are used to the adversary processing of justice are likely to think. But your lawyer is no less your champion in a settlement out of court than he is your champion in the battle in court.

The devotion and the fidelity which a lawyer owes to his client is great enough to strew quandaries and perplexities in the way of his relations with his clients which seem to me to be peculiar to his profession. At any rate, these perplexities offer us by far the best, indeed so far as I know, the only approach to some understanding of the chief function of the lawyer in the law, which is advocacy. And the heart of advocacy, as with other things of the spirit, lies in its ethics.

A Lawyer's Loyalties

I want first of all to put advocacy in its proper setting. It is a special case of vicarious conduct. A lawyer devotes his life and career to acting for other people. So too do the parson and the priest, and, in another way, the banker. The banker handles other people's money. The parson and the priest handle other people's spiritual aspirations. A lawyer handles other people's troubles.

But there is a difference. The loyalty of a clergyman runs, not to the particular parishioner whose joys or troubles he is busy with, but to his church; and the banker looks to his bank. It is the church or the bank on whose behalf they are acting, which serves the communicant or the borrower. Thus their loyalties run in a different direction from a lawyer's.

So too when a lawyer works for the government, his loyalties, like the clergyman's, hang on a superior peg. It is fiction to say that he has the government for his client. The government is too big. It absorbs him. He is a part of it.

Likewise the general counsel for a corporation. His identification with his client is all but complete. Taft, in some lectures at the Albany Law School, referring to work in the legal department of a corporation, said, "Such employment leads to a lawyer's becoming nothing more than an officer of the corporation as closely identified with it as if he was the president, the secretary or the treasurer." Indeed, he usually is a director or a vice-president.

Not so the lawyer in private practice. His loyalty runs to his client. Not the court? you ask. Does not the court take the same position as the church or the bank? Is not the lawyer an officer of the court? Why doesn't the court have first claim on his loyalty? No, in a paradoxical way. The lawyer's official duty, required of him indeed by the court, is to devote himself to the client. He has two masters, and it is sometimes hard to say which comes first. There are occasions when our system of justice seems to give the nod to the client.

Lord Brougham, in his defense of Queen Caroline in her divorce case, told the House of Lords, "I once before took occasion to remind your Lordships, which was unnecessary, but there are many whom it may be needful to remind, that an advocate, by the sacred duty which he owes his client, knows in the discharge of that office but one person in the world—that client and no other. . . . Nay, separating even the duties of a patriot from those of an advocate, and casting them if need be to the wind, he must go on reckless of the consequences, if his fate it should unhappily be to involve his country in confusion for his client's protection."

Lord Brougham was a great advocate, and when he made this statement he was arguing a great case, the divorce of Queen Caroline from George IV before the House of Lords. Plainly he was exerting more than his learning and more than his legal ability. Years later he explained this to William Forsyth, the author of a book on lawyers called *Hortensius*, who had asked him what he meant. Before you read Brougham's reply, let me remind you that the king, George IV, was the one who was pressing the divorce which Brougham was defending, and that George had contracted a secret marriage, while he was heir apparent, with Mrs. Fitzherbert, a Roman Catholic. Brougham knew this, and knew too that it was enough to deprive the king of his crown under the Act of Settlement. Brougham wrote:

"The real truth is, that the statement was anything rather than a deliberate and well-considered opinion. It was a menace, and it was addressed chiefly to George IV, but also to wiser men, such as Castlereagh and Wellington. I was prepared, *in case of necessity,* that is, in case the Bill passed the Lords, to do two things—first, to resist it in the Commons *with the country at my back;* but next, if need be, to dispute the King's title, to show he had forfeited the crown by marrying a Catholic, in the words of the Act, 'as if he were naturally dead.' What I said was fully understood by Geo. IV; perhaps by the Duke of Castlereagh, and I am confident it would have prevented them from pressing the Bill beyond a certain point."

Lord Brougham's menace has become the classic statement of the loyalty which a lawyer owes to his client, perhaps because, being a menace, it is so extreme. And yet the Canons of Ethics of the American Bar Association are scarcely more moderate. "The lawyer owes 'entire devotion to the interest of the client, warm zeal in the maintenance and defense of his rights and the exertion of his utmost learning and ability,' to the end that nothing be taken or be withheld from him, save by the rules of law, legally applied."

How entire is this devotion and how warm is this zeal? How much *alter* do they together put in the lawyer's *ego?* How far from himself do they draw a lawyer? How much less than himself, as a patriot and a citizen and an individual, do they require a lawyer to be? These are hard questions, as hard to ask as I think they are hard to answer.

The Canon has no difficulty with its answer, "But it is steadfastly to be borne in mind that the great trust of a lawyer is to be performed within and not without the bounds of the law. The office of attorney does not permit, much less does it demand of him for any client, violation of law or any manner of fraud or chicane. He must obey his own conscience and not that of his client."

That's all very well and easily said, but acting for others is in a different category of behavior than acting for yourself and I think its ethics are different. Let me examine this proposition with some care and in some detail.

The person for whom you are acting very reasonably expects you to treat him better than you do other people, which is just another way of saying that you owe him a higher standard of conduct than you owe to others. This goes back a long way. It is the pre-platonic ethics which Socrates disposed of at the very outset of the *Republic;* that is, that justice consists of doing good to your friends and harm to your enemies. A lawyer, therefore, insensibly finds himself treating his client better than others; and therefore others worse than his client. A lawyer, or a trustee, or anyone acting for another, has lower standards of conduct toward outsiders than he has toward his clients or his beneficiaries against the outsiders. He is required to treat outsiders as if they were barbarians and enemies. The more devotion and zeal the lawyer owes to his client, the less he owes to others when he is acting for his client. It is as if a man had only so much virtue, and the more he gives to one, the less he has available for anyone else. The upshot is that a man whose business it is to act for others finds

himself, in his dealings on his client's behalf with outsiders, acting on a
lower standard than he would if he were acting for himself, lower than any
standard his client himself would be willing to act on, lower in fact than
anyone on his own.

You devote yourself to the interests of another at the peril of yourself.
Vicarious action tempts a man away from himself. Men will do for others
what they are not willing to do for themselves—nobler as well as ignoble
things. What I want to do now is to illustrate this in the practice of law
by a number of perplexing situations. They raise ethical problems, but none
of them, I think, has a simple right or wrong answer, and I know of no
canons of ethics or morals which lead to any answer. How could there be
when they ignore the cause of the perplexity, which is the difference between acting for another and acting for yourself?

I will give you a personal case. I was a trustee under a will. My co-trustee
was away, and had left me with the duty of trying to sell a piece of real
estate. I got an offer of $50,000 which I agreed orally to accept. They left
to draw up the agreement for me to sign, but before they had it ready I
received a cash offer of $55,000. So I was on the spot, for under the Statute
of Frauds, as any lawyer knows, I was not legally bound on an oral contract
to sell real estate.

I didn't know quite what to do. I called up the purchaser and the broker
and told them to bring their lawyer with them. And I said to them, "I have
received an offer of $55,000, and either you are going to make me an offer
of $55,000 cash or I am going to take up that offer and go back on my
word, which I gave you. Unless you," then I turned to the lawyer, "can
show me out of the correspondence that I am bound under the Statute of
Frauds." By way of peroration I added, "If you want to call me a son of a
bitch, do, because I am going to do just that, and I heartily agree that I am
a son of a bitch to do it."

I didn't like it. They were very angry. Their lawyer was no help. He had
the correspondence, but he didn't point to anything I had written which
legally bound me.

I went back to my office, turned my file over to one of my partners, and
said, "Am I bound under the statute?" My partner took the file, came back
the next day, and to my great relief, he had spelled enough out of the
correspondence to convince me that I was bound. I called up the lawyer
and laughed at him somewhat, and everyone was happy; except that no
one complimented me and no one expressed any disagreement with what I
had called myself.

I did not enjoy the situation, but I was confident that I had done right.
Years later Professor Austin W. Scott, who has written the one and only
best book on trusts and trustees, told me there was an English case I ought
to read. It was not so long ago—1950—in London. Mrs. Simpson—not the
one you think—rented a house in London and decided she wanted to buy it.

She offered the owners, who were three trustees, 6,000 pounds, and they agreed. All the terms of the sale were agreed to, except who should pay the expenses of the sale, which amounted to 142 pounds. At that point, one of the several beneficiaries of the trust, a Canon Buttle, also offered 6,000 pounds. Mrs. Simpson then agreed to pay the expenses. This made hers the better offer, and a contract of sale was drawn up, signed by Mrs. Simpson, and signed by one, only one, of the three trustees. Canon Buttle promptly offered 6,500 pounds, which made his the better offer. The trustees informed the canon that they felt that the sale to Mrs. Simpson could not properly be cancelled and Canon Buttle brought suit against them, to require them to sell the property to him for 6,500 pounds, substantially more than the 6,142 pounds which was Mrs. Simpson's offer.

Was the canon right? This is what Judge Wynn-Parry said. "The trustees felt in a position of great embarrassment. They felt in honour bound to proceed with the proposed sale to Mrs. Simpson. . . . They felt that all considerations of commercial morality required that they should proceed with the contract." Let me interrupt to remind you that two of the three trustees had not signed it and that it had not yet been delivered to the lady. The judge went on, "My view is that the trustees and their solicitors acted on an incorrect principle. The only consideration which was present to their minds was that they had gone so far in the negotiations with Mrs. Simpson that they could not properly, from the point of view of commercial morality, resile from those negotiations."

Fortunately, these sad stories usually have a happier ending than you expect. Mrs. Simpson raised her offer to 6,600 pounds, and everyone, including Canon Buttle, felt better. It would have been interesting to have sat in on the conversations which we may suppose were held between the good canon and the solicitors for the trustees, while the churchman argued for the strict law and the lawyers argued for the principles of morality. But the law was against the lawyers and against the conscience of the trustees, as it was against mine.

The ethical problems of a lawyer are not so simple as the canon, either canon for that matter, thinks.

Duties and Dangers in Advocacy

I will give you an extreme case, for an extreme case is the best test of a hard problem. May it ever become the duty of a lawyer to tell a lie for his client? Does a lawyer's duty to his client, the duty which is enjoined upon him by law and by the obligations of his profession, include telling a lie in his client's behalf?

On my answer to this question, I have had critical help. Some of it came from lawyers who angrily denied that a lawyer should ever tell a lie. Their angry denials shed a somewhat lurid light on the problem, but it was helpful for it made me reconsider my answer. Less lurid and more illuminating criticism came from the more reasoned denials, but the most illumination came from those who knew there was a problem and recognized its difficulties. I have profited by all these criticisms, but my answer remains the same as what I wrote in 1951 in the article in the *Stanford Law Review* which brought them to me. They have led me to clarify some ambiguities and correct some misstatements, but they have not changed my conclusion that the problem exists and that there are occasions when it does become a lawyer's duty to lie for his client, rare as they are, in this extreme case of his devotion to his client.

Perhaps I have done wrong to use the word, lie. I wish I could think of a better word. There are devout theologians who understand what I mean as mental reservations or restrictions, but I am not talking to them, nor do I need to. They know that the Eighth Commandment enjoins more than veracity and that we can be false in our relations to others as well as false in our relation to the truth, as we see it. The only objection to the word, lie, is that it has only three letters, one less, and so the more offensive, than those ugly four-letter words. I am sorry if it gives offense, but I can think of no other which fits the extreme case I am going to talk about.

At the other extreme stands candor. A lawyer whose conscience required him to be as candid and ingenuous for his clients in his practice as he was for himself would be disbarred almost before he knew it. And quite rightly, for he would be betraying his clients and if all lawyers were equally candid, it would make an end of our adversary system of justice.

Suppose, at a pretrial hearing, the judge should ask one of the lawyers if he had authority to settle the case for any less than what he had just demanded and the other lawyer had refused. Certainly the judge had no right to ask such an unconscionable question, but we are supposing he did. Does the lawyer simply decline to answer? His client had authorized him to settle for substantially less, but only if his lawyer thought he could not get more. The lawyer thought he could get more and that was what he was trying to do.

If he simply declines to answer, isn't he in effect by clear implication, telling the other lawyer that he would take less if he can't get more, and thus put it out of his power to get any more? And note that what this unhappy, and angry, lawyer would be telling his opponent by declining to answer the judge was not true until he declined to answer. Until then he had no authority to settle for less because he thought he could get more. He made it true by declining to answer.

I suggest that our lawyer would do better by answering the judge with a flat denial, "No, that is the least I am authorized to settle for." This would be something less than candid, but it would be the truth so long as he thought he could get it, for his client authorized him to settle for less only if he thought he couldn't. It would be a true statement, but not a true answer to the judge's question, for he was assuming that the other lawyer wasn't going to pay more. What a tangled web we weave, when we find we must deceive!

What does the poor lawyer do then? He goes right to the judge's chambers without the other lawyer, insists on seeing him alone, and explains. This may be hard to do, unless the judge has had a twist of conscience. Otherwise our lawyer goes to another judge, and relieves his conscience without betraying his client.

Let me tell you the story of Sam the Lookout as a parable. It was told to me as a true story, but that does not make it any the less good as a parable. I know no relation more like the relation between a lawyer and his client than that between a seaman, captain or sailor, and his ship. Sit in with a distinguished New York lawyer who was once called over to a conference of admiralty lawyers with the crew of a ship which had been in a collision. The lawyers were going over the testimony which the members of the crew would give at the approaching trial. Finally they came to Sam, the lookout, and the Captain, who was asking the questions, turned to him and said, "You, of course, were up in the eyes on the forecastle keeping a sharp lookout." The seaman squirmed in his chair, twisted his cap, and said, "The truth is, Captain, I was in the head having a smoke." The lawyers leaned forward, but the Captain turned to reassure them. "That's all right, gentlemen, he'll testify that he was keeping a sharp lookout. Won't you, Sam?" "No," said Sam, "I guess I can't do that."

And then, this lawyer said, such a storm of indignation burst over Sam as he had never seen. The Captain and the rest of the crew cursed him for betraying his ship. Let him go to the head if he had to. Let him even have his smoke if he must. But when he did let him also take the consequences. The collision was not his fault, they agreed. The fog may have been too thick for him to have seen the other vessel in time, but was he now going to let his own ship down? If he left his post on his own affairs, he had no right to make the ship pay the penalty. What if it was perjury? He'd taken that risk. Not the ship, but he, had taken the risk of perjury.

The admiralty lawyers sat back and listened. They recognized that there were peculiarities in the ethics of the sea which were distinctly not a part of admiralty law. The meeting broke up with Sam still obstinately refusing to do what, the Captain insisted, any good seaman ought to know he was in honor bound to do.

I tried to find a situation in which a lawyer is in duty bound to lie for his client. I asked an eminent and very practical judge. He told me he hoped I was joking. I went to two leaders of the bar, both ex-presidents of bar associations. One said, "No, I don't believe there is such a situation." The other said, "Why, of course, there are." But he has not yet given me one.

Finally I thought I had one. It was the case of a lawyer who, I felt very sure, had lied to me when he told me that he did not represent a certain man. As secretary of the Grievance Committee of the Bar Association at the time, I was trying to find out whether this man had been blackmailed by some other lawyers. I went to this lawyer and asked him. If he had admitted to me that he had represented this man, I should have been pretty sure that the man had indeed been blackmailed, for I knew that he had not gone to his regular counsel, but to a different lawyer, in order to keep the whole affair secret. The lawyer told me he did not even know the man.

I recall thinking then that this lawyer was doing just right by lying to me, but my lawyer went on to make the same denial to the Grievance Committee, and later, when the Bar Association brought proceedings for his disbarment, in the course of those proceedings, persisted in his denial before the court itself. He was not disbarred, but he was subsequently reprimanded and suspended.

It was inadmissible for him not to tell the truth to the court. A lawyer's duty to his client cannot rise higher than its source, which is the court. I think he did right to lie to me, but I don't think he should have lied to the Grievance Committee as well, for it had a right to ask him. With me he was properly playing for time to see what it was all about, for I had no obvious authority.

It may be that it all depends on whether your lawyer is asked the question by someone who has a right to ask it. If he has no right to ask and if simple silence would, or even might, lead him to the truth, then, I believe your lawyer is in duty bound to lie. For the truth is not his, but yours. It belongs to you, and he is bound to keep it for you even more vigorously than if it were only his own. He must lie, then, beyond the point where he could permissibly lie for himself.

A lawyer is called on the telephone by a former client who is unfortunately at the time a fugitive from justice. The police want him, and he wants advice. The lawyer goes to where his client is, hears the whole story, and advises him to surrender. Finally he succeeds in persuading him that this is the best thing to do and they make an appointment to go to police headquarters. Meanwhile the client is to have two days to wind up his affairs and make his farewells. When the lawyer gets back to his office, a police inspector is waiting for him, and asks him whether his client is in town and where he is.

What does the lawyer do? What should he say? I have had three interesting suggestions. The best, if it would work, was for the lawyer to say, "Don't you wish you knew!" or something like that. But what if it didn't work, and the police inspector insisted? In that case, says James E. Harpster, the lawyer would be "morally bound to answer the policeman truthfully. For it seems to us that the police have the right to know the whereabouts of wanted criminals." I wonder. Criminals have rights too, and one of them is the right to counsel. The problem is not so easy.

The most authoritative suggestion came from the chairman of the Committee on Professional Ethics of the American Bar Association, Mr. Henry S. Drinker. In his learned and able, as well as authoritative, reply to my article in the *Stanford Law Review*, which was published in the next number, in April 1952, Mr. Drinker says, "When the police officers asked the lawyer, there was no necessity for him to lie. He should have said: 'If I knew, my duty as a lawyer would forbid my telling you.'" The clear implication is that he did not know, and I don't see that Mr. Drinker's reply is very different from what I think the lawyer should have said, which is simply, "I don't know." But he did know. He had just come from where his client was and his client had agreed to meet him two days later.

It was certainly not the lawyer's duty to disclose his client's whereabouts. Whatever others may think, lawyers will agree to that. Mr. Drinker's Committee on Professional Ethics has been quite definite about it. It once had the following facts presented to it: A lawyer's client was a fugitive from justice. He jumped bail, forfeited his bond, and a warrant was issued for his arrest. The lawyer learned in confidence from the client's relatives where he was and advised his client to give himself up, which eventually he did. But he refused to tell the police. The question asked was whether it was "the duty of the attorney to disclose to the prosecuting authorities the whereabouts of a fugitive client."

The Committee was of the opinion: "It is in the public interest that even the worst criminal should have counsel, and counsel cannot properly perform their duties without knowing the truth. To hold that an attorney should reveal confidential information which he has obtained, by virtue of his professional employment from members of the family of the criminal, would prevent such frank disclosure as might be necessary to a proper protection of the client's interest."

Now, if there was no other way of keeping his client's secret, I believe the lawyer had better be false to the truth than false to his client. The Committee on Professional Ethics, as you see, comes perilously close to agreeing with me.

Sometimes we forget that veracity is only a part of honorable behavior. When we isolate telling the truth and put it on its own pinnacle, we neglect the larger problem. On one occasion the British Cabinet met and decided to devalue the pound the next day. When the meeting was over, the newspaper men asked Sir Stafford Cripps, the Chancellor of the Exchequer, whether the pound was going to be devalued. He said, No. The next day, after the announcement, one of the London papers called it "the immaculate deception." Sir Frederick Pollock wrote Holmes, "I never heard of any real authority for any such proposition as that one owes full disclosure of the truth to all men at all times." Holmes replied, "You know that G. Washington cannot tell a lie business was a fiction in a popular life of him by an itinerant parson."

A lawyer is not faced with the question whether he may find it his duty to lie, not for a client, but to a client, as a physician must sometimes lie to his patient. Dr. Lawrence J. Henderson made, so far as I know, the only sensible observations on this duty of a physician. He took the position that to speak of telling the truth, the whole truth, and nothing but the truth to a patient is absurd, because it is quite impossible. He cited cancer. If a physician tells his patient that he has cancer, it is a stimulus to which there will be a response in the patient's circulatory, respiratory, and nervous system. In other words, the physician can't tell him without affecting the very condition which the physician is not only called upon to diagnose, but to cure. "I suggest, therefore," Henderson says, "that if you recognize a duty of 'telling the truth to the patient,' you range yourself outside the class of biologists with lawyers and philosophers." No, a lawyer is not a biologist, nor is a lawyer retained to minister to his client's moral health. So the lawyer must tell the truth, all of it, to his client.

A parson will lie for his parishioner, a priest for his penitent, a physician for his patient. You would lie to protect your wife or your child. There are others with whom you are intimate enough, close enough, to lie for, when you would not lie for yourself. At what point do you stop lying for them? I don't know and you are not sure.

To every one of us come occasions when we don't want to tell the truth, not all of it, certainly not all of it at once, when we want to be something less than candid, a little disingenuous. Indeed, to be candid with ourselves, there are times when we deliberately and more or less justifiably undertake to tell something less or even something different, not the whole truth. Complete candor to anyone but ourselves is a virtue that belongs to the saints, and to those who have no other responsibilities. Even when we do want to tell the truth, all of it ultimately, we see no reason why we should not take our own time, tell it as skillfully and as gracefully as we can. Most of us doubt our own ability to do this as well by and for ourselves as another could do, so we go to a lawyer. He will make a better fist of it than we can.

I don't see why we must not come out roundly and say that one of the functions of a lawyer is the disagreeable duty of choosing between being false to his client or false to the truth. On rare occasions, as I think I have shown, I believe it is his duty to prefer his client to the truth, and if need be to tell a lie. Happily they are few and far between, only when his duty gets him into a corner or puts him on the spot. Day in, day out, a lawyer can be as truthful as anyone. But not so ingenuous.

A lawyer is required to be disingenuous. He is required to say things which he does not believe in. In the higher brackets of generality, he has to be freed from his own beliefs and prejudices, for they are irrelevant unless pressed into service for the client. But his insincerity does not extend to the particular. The farther what he says descends toward the particular, the more truthful he must be, except, as I have been arguing, in respect to particulars which do not belong to him because they are his client's secrets. Barring these, when he is talking for his client, a lawyer is absolved from veracity down to a certain point of particularity.

I have said that a lawyer may not lie to the court. But it may be a lawyer's duty not to speak. Let me give you a case from the autobiography of one of the most distinguished and conscientious lawyers I or any man have ever known, Samuel Williston. In his autobiography, he tells of one of his early cases. His client was sued in some financial matter. The details of the claim are not important. Mr. Williston, of course, at once got his client's letter file and went through it painstakingly, sorting, arranging, and collating it. The letters, we may well believe, told the whole story, as they usually do in such a case. Trial approached, but the plaintiff's lawyers did not ask for the file or that the letters be produced. "They did not demand their production and we did not feel bound to disclose them." At the close of the trial, "In the course of his remarks the Chief Justice stated as one reason for his decision a supposed fact which I knew to be unfounded. I had in front of me a letter that showed his error. Though I have no doubt of the propriety of my behavior in keeping silent, I was somewhat uncomfortable at the time."

We may share his discomfort, but there is no doubt of the propriety of his behavior. I want to quote Mr. Hocker again. He went on from what he said about a trial being an adversary business to say this:

"A trial lawyer who unnecessarily discloses the contents of his file to his adversary is as much a traitor to his client as is the general traitor to his country who discloses his plan of battle to the enemy. Play your cards from close to the vest, never volunteer damaging information which you are not obliged to disclose, obtain all of the information you can extract from the other side of the case, never yield a significant advantage. By this I do not mean to suggest that a trial lawyer should be cantankerous or disagreeable. If you know that you will be obliged to produce your client for a deposition or for a medical examination, there is no sense in requiring the opposition to obtain a court order. What you know he can get by the process, and what cannot hurt you, you might as well give him with a pleasant smile and good grace. Where there is a reasonable doubt as to whether your opponent can get dangerous information, refuse with a pleasant smile and good grace, but refuse. Ask no favors of your opponent, lest this oblige you to grant one that may pinch. If you are not a fighter by disposition you should hire a fighter to try your cases."

I don't know whether Mr. Williston or Mr. Hocker want any confirmation of the rectitude of their conduct, but the Committee on Professional Ethics of the American Bar Association stands behind them, five to two. A local bar association recently put up just such a situation to the committee. An attorney is in court with his client, who has been convicted, when he comes up for sentence. The clerk, or whoever it is that has the criminal records, tells the judge that this man has no record, and the judge then puts him on probation. As a matter of fact, he has a record, and his attorney knows it. Is it the attorney's duty to speak up?

A careful casuist might want to know the source of the attorney's knowledge. Did the defendant tell him, or how else did he learn? We may assume that his knowledge came to him in the course of his professional relations with his client. Let that pass. The crucial question seemed to a majority of the committee to be whether the defendant's attorney has any reason to understand that the judge is relying on him to corroborate or correct the clerk's statement. If so, the majority of the committee thought that the attorney should ask the judge to excuse him from answering and not to rely on his personal knowledge. It is, of course, possible that the judge would leave it at that. This would depend on the circumstances, and probably on the lawyer's demeanor and the overtones in his voice. However, the majority of the committee ruled that "If the lawyer is quite clear that the court does not rely on him as corroborating, by his silence, the statement of the clerk or of his client, the lawyer is not, in our opinion, bound to speak out." If he did, we will agree, so much the less lawyer he.

You will note that Williston was the attorney for the defendant in the case. The other attorney, who was trying to make a case for the plaintiff, had the burden of proof. If he had found a damaging letter in his client's file, or if Williston's client had been bringing instead of defending the suit, what then? Quite a different situation would be presented, such is our adversary system of justice. If the ugly fact belongs to the plaintiff's case, it must go in with it; and if it is so ugly that it spoils the case, then either the plaintiff must withdraw his case or his lawyer must withdraw from it. The point is, and the reason for this difference between the claim and the defense is, simply that, unless a lawyer presents all the available relevant facts, he would be presenting a different case to the court than the one which his client brought to him. A will without its codicil is not the testament. A contract without an amendment is not the agreement. But here we come to the edge of a technical precipice. What is matter of defense? Some things are strictly the business of the defendant to bring up, if he chooses. You bring suit for divorce on the ground of adultery. You tell your lawyer that you have condoned your husband's offense by living with him after you learned of it. The court may very well deny you a divorce because you have, as the law says, condoned his adultery. I am using the word in its technical sense. You may or may not have forgiven him. Need your lawyer bring out the fact that you have forgiven your husband? Or should that be left for him to bring up?

The Twenty-second Canon of Professional Ethics states that "The conduct of the lawyer before the Court and with other lawyers should be characterized by candor and fairness." This is all very well, but Williston, when he sat there with the letter in front of him, was being faithful to his client, and uncomfortable that he could not be candid with the court. If I ask you which of two girls you love the most, you are in effect declining to answer when you say, "Both." Lawyers say that the adversary process gives the court priority over the client in matters of law and the client a priority over the court in matters of fact. The distinction is familiar enough to lawyers, and it is a useful distinction once we know what they mean by it, as I will try to make clear later. The point I want to make now is that the relations which a lawyer has with his client on one hand and his court on the other are somewhat bigamous.

Here is what Williston went on to say in his autobiography. "One of the troublesome ethical questions which a young trial lawyer is confronted with is the extent to which he is bound to disclose to the court facts which are injurious to his client's case. The answer is not doubtful. The lawyer must decide when he takes a case whether it is a suitable one for him to undertake and after this decision is made, he is not justified in turning against his client by exposing injurious evidence entrusted to him. If that evidence was unknown to him when he took the case, he may sometimes withdraw from it, but while he is engaged as counsel he is not only not obliged to disclose unfavorable evidence, but it is a violation of his duty to his client if he does so." And Williston concluded, ". . . doing something intrinsically regrettable, because the only alternative involves worse consequences, is a necessity in every profession."

It was a question, he said, of moral compromise, and he referred to a passage in Lecky's *The Map of Life*. This passage is worth quoting:

"But at best there must be many things in the profession from which a very sensitive conscience would recoil, and things must be said and done which can hardly be justified except on the ground that the existence of this profession and the prescribed methods of its action are in the long run indispensable to the honest administration of justice."

"I must be cruel, only to be kind," said Hamlet, on his way to his mother. And so likewise a lawyer has to tell himself strange things on his way to court. But they are strange only to those who do not distinguish between truth and justice. Justice is something larger and more intimate than truth. Truth is only one of the ingredients of justice. Its whole is the satisfaction of those concerned. It is to that end that each attorney must say the best, and only the best, of his own case.

This is not the method we have used in other endeavors, with not only more, but with conspicuous success. But the law has other things than success to think about. It must give the losing party, and his friends and his sympathizers, as much satisfaction as any loser can expect. At least the most has been said for him. The whole has been shaken out into the sun, and everyone concerned is given a feeling akin to the feeling of security which you get when you have told yourself the worst before you make a decision.

The administration of justice is no more designed to elicit the truth than the scientific approach is designed to extract justice from the atom.

Advocacy requires a lawyer to start with something to be proved, and this is as true of facts as it is of propositions of law. When he goes to interview a witness as well as when he goes to the law library, he goes to get something. He will waste a lot of time if he goes with an open mind. He must, of course, first formulate the issue in his mind, but he does this only to make it the easier to find what lies on his side of the issue. He fixes on the conclusion which will best serve his client's interests, and then he sets out to persuade others to agree.

Judges do the same thing, but not on purpose. They find themselves reaching a decision before they know just how they got there. Raeburn Green has spoken of this phenomenon. He says,

"We are told by authorities of diverse experience—Mr. Justice Cardozo, Mr. Radin and Signor Calamandrei—that the course of judicial reasoning is frequently backward, from conclusion to premise. It is a course which (as has been pointed out) is familiar to the practicing lawyer, whose client often presents him with a conclusion ready-made, and who must then search for whatever premises can be discovered or developed, to support that conclusion. It is no doubt true also that the judicial practice of taking a vote following the oral argument, leaving the opinion to be written later, is frequently conducive to the inverted process.

"When the whole structure is complete in the opinion, it is naturally difficult to detect whether the roof was first erected or the supporting pillars. One would think that Mr. Justice Brandeis must have almost invariably proceeded in the orthodox fashion, from premise to conclusion, and that Mr. Justice Holmes must in some cases have proceeded in this fashion and in others in the reverse; but the fact may have been quite otherwise. For not only is the opinion deceptive, but there can also be dispute as to what is a conclusion and what is a premise. One man's premise may be another's conclusion; and every premise which is not an absolute is itself the conclusion of some syllogism, however long forgotten."

Now it is quite true that our thinking is done on an alternating current, so to speak, from induction to deduction and reverse. A process which we do not clearly understand—at least no philosopher has yet explained it— induces a tentative conclusion from which we proceed deductively. This is an intellectual process. We can watch deduction work, which we cannot do with the inductive phase, and so we call it intuitive, by which we mean only that we cannot watch it work. It is none the less a fact, as Cardozo, whom Green cites, and others in other lines of work have recognized.

In *Paradoxes of Legal Science*, Cardozo writes,

"For the creative process in law, and indeed in science generally, has a kinship to the creative process in art. Imagination, whether you call it scientific or artistic, is for each the faculty that creates. There are successive stages of preparation, incubation and illumination described with so much insight by Graham Wallas in his analysis of the art of thought. Learning is indeed necessary, but learning (to paraphrase what has been said of Keats) is the springboard by which imagination leaps to truth. The law has its piercing intuitions, its tense, apocalyptic moments. We gather together our principles and precedents and analogies, even at times our fictions, and summon them to yield the energy that will best attain the jural end. If our wand has the divining touch, it will seldom knock in vain. So it is that the conclusion, however deliberate and labored, has often the aspect in the end of nothing but a lucky find. 'When I once asked the best administrator whom I knew,' writes Mr. Wallas, 'how he formed his decisions, he laughed, and with the air of letting out for the first time a guilty secret, said: "Oh, I always decide by feeling. So and so always decides by calculation, and that is no good." When, again, I asked an American judge, who is widely admired both for his skill and for his impartiality, how he and his fellows formed their conclusions, he also laughed, and said that he should be stoned in the street if it were known that, after listening with full consciousness to all the evidence, and following as carefully as he could all the arguments, he waited until he "felt" one way or the other.' He had elided the preparation and the brooding, or at least had come to think of them as processes of faint kinship with the state of mind that followed. 'When the conclusion is there,' said William James, 'we have always forgotten most of the steps preceding its attainment.' "

The same thing is true of physicians. Lawrence J. Henderson said, "More often than not, skillful diagnosticians reach a diagnosis before they are aware, or at any rate, conscious, of the grounds that justify their decision. If asked to explain the reasons for the diagnosis, they often clearly show by their behavior that they are obliged to think them out, and that to do so is an awkward task. This is true of doctors, of lawyers, and of men of affairs." And it is equally true of the investment analyst and advisor, according to one of the best of them. In *Security Analysis*, Graham has an appendix in which he compares his work with the work of a physician in the light of Henderson's remarks, finding an analogy between the patient and the security. I think we may take what Henderson says as common to all pursuits in which the discipline is not capable of being strict and the pursuit not completely successful.

This is an unconscionably long assertion of the inexplicable. So far as the lawyer is concerned, a single remark from a scientist should content you. Charles Darwin said, "How odd it is that anyone should not see that all observation must be for or against some view if it is to be of any service!" You have to be as eager in your thinking as in anything else. In other words, you have to be an advocate. Of course, I recognize that this demands a counterweight of candor to yourself. But neither eagerness nor advocacy makes candor to yourself impossible. And equilibrium is easier as well as more stable between two distant and opposed forces than when anything, big or little, is precariously balanced on the center of the seesaw.

I was once chairman of a commission to recommend revisions in the workmen's compensation law of Massachusetts. We opened our deliberations with a meeting which was open to the public. A man spoke up from the back of the hall and said he was glad that the chairman was impartial. He was referring to the fact that the other members of the commission were drawn from labor and management. I brightened at the compliment, however obvious, and thanked him. I assured him that I was indeed impartial, at any rate for the time being. I had, I said, the pure impartiality of complete ignorance, and I hoped that it would not last. I hoped that it would be gone before we had to make our report.

There are those who admire what they call objectivity, and journalists, in their asceticism, as well as lawyers are properly interested. The Nieman Fellows at Harvard held a symposium a few years ago on the question of whether a newspaperman could interpret the news and still retain his objectivity. One of the symposiasts pointed out that objectivity could be "carried to the point of unintelligibility." He gave an example—I forget what it was—of what he called "strictly factual" writing, and said, "And so it is. There is no slant, no bias, no prejudice. You just can't understand it."

Karl Llewellyn has shrewdly pointed out the consequence of having the conclusion given to you and predetermined. It requires lawyers to rely solely upon the power of persuasion. No authority. Only persuasion. He says, "Now the advocate is the one peculiar thinker about problems whose *conclusion is always given*. On this, his only choice is whether he will refuse to take the case, either because he does not like the case or because he cannot find premises to support it. *If* he takes it, even to work on, he starts his thinking *by trade necessity* with his conclusion. What direct relevance has judicial or counsellor's predictive thinking to such a peculiar thought-process? Other thinkers seek for the conclusion. But the emphasis, for advocates' thinking, is and must be always: *given* my conclusion, how can I develop a *persuasive* line of premise, and how can I *persuade* my premises into *acceptance by the tribunal?*"

Lawyers have great respect for authority perhaps just because they exercise none. They argue to the court and to the jury. They advise their clients, and their clients need not take their advice. There are other lawyers. Indeed there are other advisers. A good lawyer is so persuasive that we forget that he has no more authority over a client than he has over the court. A successful businessman, an executive, on the other hand, gets so used to authority, even over his board of directors, that he forgets the skills of persuasion. This is the businessman's great handicap in politics. A congressional committee has little, very little, in common with a board of directors, or even a majority stockholder. It is only the executive who has been brought up through the sales department who retains even the rudiments of the art of persuasion.

You will not think me irreverent, nor, I hope, presumptuous, if I offer you Plato's Supreme Craftsman as analogous. He was not omnipotent. He was not coercive. He was persuasive. Plato's "final conviction," Whitehead says, "towards the end of his life," was "that the divine element in the world is to be conceived as a persuasive agency and not as a coercive agency. This doctrine should be looked upon as one of the greatest intellectual discoveries in the history of religion. . . . The alternative doctrine, prevalent then and now, sees either in the many gods or in the one God, the final coercive forces wielding the thunder."

The Guilty Client

The problem presented to a lawyer when he defends a man he knows is guilty or takes a case he knows is bad is perplexing only to laymen. Brandeis said, "As a practical matter, I think the lawyer is not often harassed by this problem, partly because he is apt to believe at the time in most of the cases that he actually tries, and partly because he either abandons or settles a large number of those he does not believe in."

It is profoundly true that the first person a lawyer persuades is himself. A practicing lawyer will soon detect in himself a perfectly astonishing amount of sincerity. By the time he has even sketched out his brief, however skeptically he started, he finds himself believing more and more in what it says, until later, when he starts arguing the case before the court, his belief is total; and he is quite sincere about it. You cannot very well keep your tongue in your cheek while you are talking. He believes what he is saying in a way that will later astonish himself as much as now it does others.

Not that he cares how much we are astonished. What he does care about is whether we are persuaded, and he is aware that an unsound argument can do much worse than fall flat. For it may carry the implication that he has no better one. He will not want to make it unless he really has no better.

This sort of self-sown sincerity, however, is not deep-rooted; and it had better not be, if what Justice Darling said was true. "I think," he said, "that most Counsel would be better advocates did they content themselves with simulating the belief instead of actually embracing it. The manifest appearance of a believer is all that is wanted; and this can well be acted after a little study, and will not interfere with that calmness of judgment which it is well to preserve in the midst of uncertainties, and which does not appear to be consistent with much faith." "Better advocates," Justice Darling says, not better men. I trust you understand that I am drawing a distinction which I have no doubt Justice Darling would draw too, and equally emphatically. I am talking about cases, not about causes. I am not talking about the integrity and righteousness on which our best hopes hang. This is vicarious zeal and enthusiasm, not one's own belief. To be truly honest, you've got to be honest, not only with yourself, but also for yourself. At some time or other, you stand alone. We are bipeds, which means we must stand on our own two feet, not on the four feet we may make with another.

This is more than a domestic problem. It strikes close to the best the bar can do for the community, as the bar very well knows. The trouble is, there is also the right of a lawyer to take only the cases he wants to take. It is the same problem of reconciling two confronting rights which festers in racial discrimination. There is the right to choose whom you prefer to employ confronting the right to a job on something better than the color of your skin. Likewise a lawyer's right to choose his clients confronts a free man's right to counsel. The bar, as I say, is wholly aware of this. Just this year, the foremost bar association we have, the Association of the Bar of the City of New York, made this matter clear. Its Committee on the Bill of Rights, whose chairman is George S. Leisure, said this,

"A principal duty of the bar is to see that no accused lacks counsel because his person is infamous or his cause detested. When a member of the bar defends a client who is publicly abhorred, the bar expects that representation none the less to be vigorous, competent and responsible in every way. The bar regards that lawyer as fundamentally independent of his client and therefore holds him accountable to it for guiding his client's cause by its standards of professional conduct. Public misapprehension of the duty threatens its performance. The prevalence of the error, too often reflected in our local press, which confuses professional obligation with personal belief, will deter lawyers from representing unpopular clients. The organized bar should act to dispel such misunderstanding, and should support against criticism arising from it those lawyers who, guided by the profession's standards, follow its most honored tradition and help discharge its most essential responsibility."

The classical solution to a lawyer taking a case he knows is bad is Dr. Johnson's. It is perfectly simple and quite specious. Boswell asked Johnson whether as a moralist Johnson did not think that the practice of the law, in some degree, hurt the nice feeling of honesty.

"What do you think," said Boswell, "of supporting a cause which you know to be bad?"

Johnson answered, "Sir, you do not know it to be good or bad till the Judge determines it. I have said that you are to state facts fairly; so that your thinking, or what you call knowing, a cause to be bad, must be from reasoning, must be from your supposing your arguments to be weak and inconclusive. But, Sir, that is not enough. An argument which does not convince yourself, may convince the Judge to whom you urge it: and if it does convince him, why, then, Sir, you are wrong, and he is right."

Dr. Johnson ignored the fact that it is the lawyer's job to know how good or how bad his case is. It is his peculiar function to find out, for otherwise he can't make it look better. Dr. Johnson's answer is sound only in cases where the problem does not arise. It is not the lawyer, but the law, that does not know whether his case is good or bad. The law is trying to find out, and so wants everyone defended and every debatable case tried. To this end, the law tries to make it easy for a lawyer to take a bad case, whether it's bad in the relevant sense of looking hopeless, or bad in the irrelevant sense of being unpopular, perhaps even deliberately made offensive by the capering of some Congressional Committee.

In England, the law goes so far as to make it the duty of a barrister to take the case of any client who properly and adequately retains him. In this country we lay that duty upon the bar as a whole, and so we don't try to do more than make it as easy as we can for a lawyer to take a bad case. One of the ways the bar helps itself to perform this duty is the Canon of Ethics which says, "It is improper for a lawyer to assert in argument his personal belief in his client's innocence or in the justice of his cause." It is called improper just so that the lawyer may feel that he does not have to. This, I think, must be its only purpose, for it is honored in no other way, as you will agree if you have ever heard a lawyer argue a case which he has chosen to turn into a cause. How else would you have your lawyer argue any case to a jury or a constitutional case to the Supreme Court?

Listen to George Wharton Pepper's peroration to his argument to the Supreme Court on a constitutional question. Having argued in the most precise terms that the AAA is unconstitutional, he proceeds most eloquently to express his own personal belief in the justice of his cause. "My time is fleeting and I must not pause to sum up the argument I have made. . . . But I do want to say just one final and somewhat personal word. I have tried very hard to argue this case calmly and dispassionately, and without vehement attack upon things which I cannot approve, and I have done it thus because it seems to me that this is the best way in which an advocate can discharge his duty to this Court. But I do not want your Honors to think that my feelings are not involved, and that my emotions are not deeply stirred. Indeed, may it please Your Honors, I believe I am standing here today to plead the cause of the America I have loved; and I pray Almighty God that not in my time may 'the land of the regimented' be accepted as a worthy substitute for 'the land of the free.'"

To be sure, constitutional law is less law than it is politics and statesmanship. As if the best of the one was not as good as the other! But here is a canon which calls improper something which the most proper lawyers do. I suggest that its only purpose is to relieve lawyers of the necessity of expressing their opinion, so that they may never need express it unless they want to express it, and keep it to themselves whenever they choose. The canon gives a lawyer an excuse when his client wants him to espouse a cause, when all the lawyer wants to take is a case.

No, there is nothing unethical in taking a bad case or defending the guilty or advocating what you don't believe in. It is ethically neutral. It's a free choice. There is a Daumier drawing of a lawyer arguing, a very demure young woman sitting near him, and a small boy beside her sucking a lolly-pop. The caption says, "He defends the widow and the orphan, unless he is attacking the orphan and the widow." It is hanging in my office. It was given to me by a lady whose case I did not want to take.

I am not being cynical. We are not dealing with the morals which govern a man acting for himself, but with the ethics of advocacy. We are talking about the special moral code which governs a man who is acting for another. Lawyers in their practice—how they behave elsewhere does not concern us—put off more and more of our common morals the farther they go in a profession which treats right and wrong, vice and virtue, on such equal terms. Some lawyers find nothing to take its place. There are others who put on new and shining raiment.

I will give you as good an example as I know that a lawyer can make a case as noble as a cause. I want to tell you how Arthur D. Hill came into the Sacco-Vanzetti case. It was through Felix Frankfurter, and it is his story. Frankfurter wrote some of it in the newspapers shortly after Arthur's death, and he told it to me in more detail just after the funeral.

When the conviction of Sacco and Vanzetti had been sustained by the Supreme Judicial Court of Massachusetts, there was left an all but hopeless appeal to the federal courts, that is, to the Supreme Court. "It was at this stage," Felix Frankfurter said, "that I was asked if I would try to enlist Arthur Hill's legal services to undertake a final effort on behalf of the men, hopeless as it seemed, by appeal to the Federal law."

Frankfurter called Arthur Hill up and said that he had a very serious matter to discuss with him. "In that case," said Arthur Hill, "we had better have a good lunch first. I will meet you at the Somerset Club for lunch and afterwards you will tell me about it." They lunched together at the Somerset Club, then after lunch crossed Beacon Street and sat on a bench in Boston Common overlooking the Frog Pond. And Frankfurter asked Arthur Hill if he would undertake this final appeal of the Sacco-Vanzetti case to the Supreme Court.

Arthur Hill said, "If the president of the biggest bank in Boston came to me and said that his wife had been convicted of murder, but he wanted me to see if there was any possible relief in the Supreme Court of the United States and offered me a fee of $50,000 to make such an effort, of course I would take the retainer as would, I suppose, everybody else at the bar. It would be a perfectly honorable thing to see whether there was anything in the record which laid a basis for an appeal to the Federal Court.

"I do not see how I can decline a similar effort on behalf of Sacco and Vanzetti simply because they are poor devils against whom the feeling of the community is strong and they have no money with which to hire me. I don't particularly enjoy the proceedings that will follow, but I don't see how I can possibly refuse to make the effort."

Arthur Hill took it as a law case. To him it was a case, not a cause. He was not the partisan, he was the advocate. I want to add just one other thing, which Arthur Hill said to me, years later. It sets a sort of seal upon his conduct in the case, as a case, and not a cause. I used to meet him fairly often walking downtown, because we both often stopped at the Boston Athenaeum and we would go on downtown together. One morning I was stupid enough to ask him an indiscreet question. I had expressed my own opinion on the guilt or innocence of Sacco and Vanzetti. I said I thought that on the whole it seemed to me probable that they had been guilty, and asked Arthur what he thought. Arthur looked at me—it was years later, twenty years later—smiled, and said, "I have never said, and I cannot say, what I think on that subject because, you see, Charlie, I was their counsel."

I met Judge Thayer once. This, too, was some years after the trial. We were in his chambers in Boston settling an automobile accident case then on trial before him. We were all standing, and he was standing between me and the window, so that when I looked out the window behind him I saw the top of the Charlestown Jail where the death house was in the background of a sort of living portrait of Judge Thayer framed by the window. I wasn't thinking anything much about it until I realized that Judge Thayer was no longer talking about our case, but strutting up and down and boasting that he had been fortunate enough to be on the bench when those sons of bitches were convicted. I had a chill, and I comforted and warmed myself over thoughts of Arthur Hill.

I have talked lovingly about the practice of the law. I have spoken unsparingly, as I would to another lawyer. In a way the practice of the law is like free speech. It defends what we hate as well as what we most love. For every lawyer whose conscience may be pricked, there is another whose virtue is tickled. Every case has two sides, and for every lawyer on the wrong side, there's another on the right side. I don't know any other career that offers an ampler opportunity for both the enjoyment of virtue and the exercise of vice, or, if you please, the exercise of virtue and the enjoyment of vice, except possibly the ancient rituals which were performed in some temples by vestal virgins, in others by sacred prostitutes.

Holmes Prepares for the Bar*

CATHERINE DRINKER BOWEN

Few readers interested in the law need any introduction to Oliver Wendell Holmes (1841–1935), Justice of the Supreme Court of the United States. After distinguishing himself at Harvard for his literary ability, he served with great gallantry in the Civil War, being wounded three times and miraculously surviving. After his regiment was mustered out in July, 1864, Holmes prepared for the bar in spite of the gloomy warnings of his famous father that a lawyer could not become a great man. He became successively member of the Harvard law faculty, the Supreme Court of Massachusetts and, in 1902, of the highest tribunal in the land. When Holmes retired in 1932, he had built a great reputation for the character of his opinions. Known as the Great Dissenter, but often a great affirmer, he was justly famous as a liberal, and had a generally yeasty effect on the history of American jurisprudence. For a picture of Holmes and Brandeis, see page 228. For an example of his own writing see Section IV.

Of the many studies of Holmes, that by Catherine Drinker Bowen (Yankee from Olympus) *is the best known, perhaps because of its success in play and motion-picture form. Mrs. Bowen has painted successive portraits of Holmes, John Adams and, most recently, Sir Edward Coke (see page 308). She has long held an interest in the law, for, as she said in part in an address to the Brandeis Society in 1951, "The lawyer and the writer . . . can be classified under one genus, Articulate Man. . . . Between writer and lawyer there is a sameness, a sympathy." The sympathy emerges charmingly in the following sketch of law school and bar examination as they were in the last century.*

September, 1864 . . . A young man walks up the steps of Dane Hall on Harvard Square, up between the white columns, through the wide doors, and takes his seat in the lecture room of Judge Joel Parker. He is eager, but he is also more than a little confused. He is by no means sure of himself. He has only the stubborn, hazy conviction that the law is what he is going to do next and do with all his might. Within the boundaries of this conviction he is slated for hours, days, years of doubt and bitter uncertainty.

Law student, Holmes had written with a flourish three years ago in his army identification papers. On his return from the war in July of 1864 he would have liked to go over to Cambridge immediately and enroll in the Law School. But he hesitated. It was a serious step. Was the law really his objective in life—not merely the "starting point" he had called it in his class autobiography? There was one other possibility: philosophy, with the eventual goal a professorship at Harvard. Since his undergraduate days and the prize essay on Plato, Holmes's passion for philosophy had grown steadily deeper. Metaphysics, dialectics, formal logic, theories of government and theories of sovereignty: these things fascinated him. And in 1864, these were the things that lay behind the law.

The question was, should such knowledge be pursued with only itself as goal, or was it better to have a focus, a boundary, some clinical application outside the classroom such as a money-making law practice that brought a man up against the world and the living problems of the world? Mr. Robert Morse, who had a very good law practice on Pemberton Square, said Wendell was born for the law.

Wendell received this statement with skepticism. The only thing he felt born for was to use his powers to the full. Even more clearly than when he was in the army, Holmes recognized that his powers were intellectual, that he was an "internal" man, to whom ideas were more interesting than things. For three years, he had lived a life as external as it would be possible to live. He had slept on the ground, had killed men with his own hand, saved men's lives by his own hand. Now he was free, and the life of pure scholarship beckoned. But if he embraced it, if he followed in the footsteps of such a man as Emerson, might he not, at forty, find himself dwelling in a cloud land of pure speculation, his own vital force dilute in this rarefied region?

All his youth he had looked up to Emerson as the wisest man he knew. When you were young you found your hero, never doubting that you could pattern yourself upon him, follow after him. But life changed you. Or at least, the things that happened brought you to yourself. Behind Emerson's highest flights of writing, behind his most magnetic utterances, one could discern always a moral purpose. Not a narrow purpose; of all men Emerson was most tolerant.

But examining himself, Holmes felt no such crusader's impulse. Merely, he desired to use his brain, drive it to its fullest capacity. He desired to examine and understand the laws of social being, the pattern men followed in their lives. In the law, if one dug far enough, would not one find recorded all the customs of mankind? In Wendell Holmes's day, anthropology did not exist as a science or as a study. Neither did sociology. Political economy existed—but it was a dry subject, filled with statistics. What had Carlyle called it? *The dismal science.*

You heard stories of great men and how they chose their professions.

Jeremy Bentham as a young man had examined himself severely to see if he had a *genius* for anything. The answer had come clearly—"a genius for legislation." Bentham had followed that voice and because of it the course of English history had changed and was still changing. But were these stories true, about great men? Did not luck have a lot to do with it? It seemed to Wendell Holmes that success in a chosen profession depended as much upon luck as upon logic.

At home he said nothing of his plans, aware that his father had long ago studied the law and hated it. Dr. Holmes liked philosophy no better, having the scientist's mistrust for abstract speculation. It seemed to him that lawyers went about solving their problems—and what dreary problems!—in a manner both unreal and devious. He had a quotation from Gulliver about lawyers that he loved to air. "*It is a maxim among . . . lawyers, that whatever hath been done before may legally be done again: and therefore . . .*" Recollection of it kept Wendell's lips sealed. He had no wish to be preached at concerning the uselessness of lawyers and philosophers in a hard, practical world.

"What are you going to do?" Dr. Holmes asked continually. "What about science? Science is the coming thing. What about teaching? It's true the professor's chair has an insulating quality that cuts it off from contact with reality. I've said that rather well in the *Autocrat*. But combined with writing or some more practical application, teaching is a very satisfactory way to make a living."

He had talked until his wife cautioned him to be still, let Wendell alone, give him a chance for a rest and a few months' vacation before making his decision. If the war was not over by spring the boy would probably re-enlist whether he was physically fit or not. Let him have a winter free of responsibility. Give him time to look round, get flesh on his bones, heal up his nervous system.

On the first of August, Holmes was mustered out of the Twentieth Regiment in a ceremony on the Common with the other three-year men. He carried the title of Lieutenant Colonel, brevetted for "gallant and meritorious service at the battle of Chancellorsville." Afterward the Regiment marched around Faneuil Hall behind the brass band, ending up at the Apollo Gardens for beer and an excellent supper provided by the Citizens' Committee. Wendell sat by Captain Magnitzky, from Germany, who had enlisted as a private a month after reaching this country and served right through the war. Wendell was immensely fond of him. "Do not look so troubled," Magnitzky told him now. "You have done your part. You were a good soldier, Colonel Holmes. And you were not born for it. In six months, eight months, if we do not beat the Rebels you can perhaps re-enlist. Now it is time for you to forget soldiering and be a scholar. It is time for you to do for a little while the things you were born to do."

A few days later, Holmes went out to Concord to see Emerson. In the warm summer afternoon the two sat under the elms, talking earnestly. Emerson said nothing definite. He never gave advice, having too much respect for a man's freedom. He talked eloquently, passionately, about his beliefs, about the world that lay ahead after this war and the part a young man might take in rebuilding that world. Holmes was stirred. But traveling home by the cars in the summer twilight, he knew that Emerson had not reached him as once he would have reached him. About it all there had been something remote. Wendell's teeth needed a harder bite, something tougher to cut on. "You are a lawyer," Dr. Johnson had said to—somebody or other. "*Lawyers know life practically. A bookish man should always have them to converse with. They have what he wants.*"

Next morning Holmes knocked on the door of his father's study. "I am going to the Law School," he said without preamble.

Dr. Holmes looked up from his desk. "What is the use of that?" he said. "What's the use of that, Wendell? A lawyer can't be a great man."

The remark was instinctive. But if he had tried, Dr. Holmes could not have devised a statement more provocative to his son. *A lawyer can't be a great man.* To Wendell the statement combined a paternal cocksureness concerning the universe and its arrangements with a bland assurance that any son of Dr. Oliver Wendell Holmes could be a great man if he started out right. The words struck home, pointed, steel-shafted. If there had been doubts, they were resolved now. Wendell would go over to Cambridge and sign his name on the rolls at Dane Hall, not for a starting point but as a profession that would last a lifetime. . . .

His father looked at him sharply. Had Wendell heard what Dean Swift had to say about lawyers? Before Wendell could reply, Dr. Holmes reached for a book on his desk. "Here!" he said. "Gulliver is talking to the Houyhnhnms. '*It is a maxim among these lawyers, that whatever hath been done before, may legally be done again: and therefore they take special care to record all the decisions formerly made against common justice, and the general reason of mankind. These, under the name of precedents, they produce as authorities, to justify the most iniquitous opinions; and the judges never fail of directing accordingly.*'"

Highly pleased with the aptness of the allusion, the doctor returned *Gulliver* to its place. Uncle John, he continued, had tried the law and abandoned it. Had Wendell discussed a law career with Uncle John?

Wendell had, but he saw no reason for telling his father about it. Uncle John did not hate the law, he merely laughed at it. "So," Uncle John had said, "you will be nursemaid to the ambulatory will, with all its little codicils running around after it? . . . Wendell, it does not matter what career you choose. If a man is adequate in native force he probably will be happy, no matter what fate has in store for him. I think you have that adequacy. There is no reason why you should not apply it to the law as well as to anything."

Wendell Holmes did not repeat this to his father. Leaving the book-lined study, leaving Gulliver and Dr. Holmes, he went over to Cambridge and signed his name in the rolls. . . . But his father's words went with him. *A lawyer can't be a great man.* When he was ninety, Wendell Holmes would quote that phrase, adding that his father had kicked him upstairs into the law and he supposed he should be grateful.

But what Dr. Holmes had said about the law was not, Wendell knew in all fairness, dictated wholly by the personal prejudice of a man who had tried a profession and failed. There was tradition behind his remark. Not so very long ago, America had despised lawyers. Colonial America had looked upon them as mere tradesmen who earned a questionable living by cleverness and chicanery. Paid attorneys were barred from the courts, rigidly restricted as to fees and procedure. Later, lawyers rose to power simply because America desired to fit the English common law to its own local needs, and lawyers were the only men who could do it. Lawyers drafted the Constitution. John Adams was trained in the law. So were Jefferson, Madison, Monroe, John Quincy Adams. With truth, Burke had remarked in Parliament that the American Union was governed by lawyers.

Even so, the public was slow to separate statesmen from lawyers and continued to mistrust the latter. The American law had had of necessity a slow growth. The grandfather of one of Holmes's classmates—James Kent Stone—became Chancellor of New York in 1814. For the nine years that Chancellor Kent held office, not a single decision or opinion of his American predecessors was cited to him or even suggested. Now in 1864 the traditional English material, worked over for a hundred years, was becoming available in its American form. The Harvard Law School was not yet fifty years old; it had amounted to little until Judge Story had come there in '29, determined that a lawyer should have training beyond the customary apprenticeship in a lawyer's office. Two years of such apprenticeship—unless you were lucky enough to get into the office of a man of genius—usually resulted in nothing more than a good scrivener's handwriting.

But it was hard to alter custom. In 1864, the Harvard Law School was conducted very much like a lawyer's office. The three lecturers had all been practising lawyers; they shared the outlook of their day as to how their various subjects should be taught. They were all elderly men who never heard of teaching law by the case system or indeed by any system other than giving the student a text to read and commenting on it. As the life of the law lies in its application, this system was not only dull but remote. There were no requirements for admission. It was not necessary to be a college graduate or take an examination. The student could enter at any time during the winter, sit down with the others and try to catch up. When Holmes signed the register he paid exactly what a student in a law office paid: one hundred dollars for the year. At the end of eighteen months he would receive, without examination, a certificate called LL.B. which would not, of course, admit him to the bar.

Wendell Holmes had no complaint to make concerning this system. How could he, when nothing existed with which to compare it? He had read a fair amount of social theory: Montesquieu and Plato, Hume, Locke, Hobbes, John Mill, Spencer. Long ago, Thomas Jefferson had advised the law student to make all knowledge his province, to read the natural sciences, history, *belles-lettres*, criticism, rhetoric, oratory—and read from dawn until bedtime. It was a program to appeal to Wendell Holmes. Profession of the law was not a way to make money on Court Street. The law was a door opening into knowledge. It was a window, opening out on all mankind.

Sitting in Judge Parker's lecture room on a bright day of September, Holmes took out his notebook as the Judge began to speak. It was a large class; the war had not caused college enrollments to fall off. The last undergraduate class at Harvard had in fact been much larger than Wendell's own class of '61. George Morison sat just across the aisle, Sedgwick next to him; both Boston men. Peter Olney, Robert Lincoln. Strange to be a student once more—to sit, notebook in hand, waiting for the professor's voice. What an impressive-looking man Judge Parker was! Senior professor of the Law School, he had been Chief Justice of New Hampshire. His black eye shot lightning, his features were strong, he carried himself very straight. When he strode through the room and onto the platform he looked as if he were going to walk right on through the other side. He was sixty-nine; he had lectured at the school for sixteen years. A good fight was meat and drink to Parker. He was much concerned with politics and for the past two years had bitterly condemned Lincoln's use of wartime powers. Everyone knew what Judge Parker had said to the president of Dartmouth. "Sir!" roared Parker. "This modern education is all a humbug!"

President Lord had only sighed. "Judge Parker," he replied, "it is."

There was no other way to converse with Judge Parker. His knowledge of the law was vast. It was also exact, formal, and involved to the point of obscurity. Holmes had been warned not to try to understand Parker's lectures. Just get what he said into a notebook and then learn it by heart. Wendell had been scornful of this. He was no undergraduate trying to skim through college. He was a man of twenty-three who had been to the wars and desired knowledge.

But after the first twenty minutes of Joel Parker, Holmes was not so scornful of his adviser. He could not make sense of one word the Judge was saying. Holmes glanced around. Everyone else had stopped writing too. Morison looked dazed, Sedgwick's eye was glassy. Only Peter Olney leaned forward, intent, frowning. Was this the frown of understanding or the anxious pucker that goes with hopeless incomprehension? Holmes hoped it was the latter. Only last night, Harry James had told him that he had sat through an entire winter of lectures at the Law School without under-standing a single word. Then he had joyfully abandoned the law. Father, Uncle John, Harry James . . . not stupid men. . . .

At home that night Wendell Holmes was unusually silent. Next day Professor Parsons lectured. And Professor Parsons, fortunately, was a dif-ferent matter altogether. At sixty-seven, Parsons seemed years younger than Judge Parker. He was ruddy-cheeked and big. He liked to tell a good story and he was interested in many things outside the law—the *Free Press* which he had edited for years; Swedenborgianism, to which he was almost as ardent a convert as Mr. Henry James the elder. Parsons hated the more technical parts of the law, such as pleading and property, and did not hesi-tate to say so. His father had been Chief Justice of Massachusetts, his own book on contracts was getting ready its fifth edition and was so much used in the courts that a student was heard to ask if there was a statute making Parsons an authority. Even so he seemed more *litterateur* than lawyer. Holmes was drawn to him immediately.

Parsons always gave his first lecture of the year on the ethics of the pro-fession and it always opened with the same words. The students grinned with anticipation: *"If a young lawyer pays for his sign the first year and his office rent the next, he can tell himself he is doing very well."* . . .

The third professor, Emory Washburn, was a strikingly handsome man in his early sixties. In the early days of the war Holmes had been much impressed by seeing him march up and down, gun on shoulder, guarding Cambridge Arsenal with his students. Like the other two professors, Wash-burn was descended from a long line of patriots. He himself had been state Senator, Judge, Whig Governor of the Commonwealth. This summer Holmes had twice seen him walking behind soldiers' funerals in the uniform of the Home Guard. The bushy gray eyebrows and side whiskers of the former Governor looked strange under a private's cap, and somehow touch-ing. "Oh, I like to help when I can," Washburn said. He was the best lec-turer in the school, he could breathe life even into Coke on Littleton and the dreadful logic of Fearne on Contingent Remainders. When he laughed you could hear him across the Yard, and the students loved him. Holmes said it was Washburn who taught him the meaning of the phrase, *enthu-siasm of the lecture room*. Non-law students, seen mounting the steps of Dane Hall, explained that they were going in to hear Washburn talk law for a while.

So far, so good. Under teachers of first-rate minds, strong characters and contagious personalities, Holmes could start off with enthusiasm. He lived at his father's house on Charles Street, going back and forth to Boston in the crowded horsecars over the West Bridge, carrying large brown books to study at home—Spence and Fearne and Austin. Austin's *Jurisprudence* was new. Its second edition, published in London in 1861, had taken sudden fire from discussion of the impending Reform Bill. Austin was a Utilitarian.

Lawyers said his book attempted to untangle law from ethics, to separate old theories of political sovereignty from the historical foundations of society. But the book made very unpleasant reading. Later, in London, Frederick Pollock said that Austin "dogmatized overmuch," and with typical Pollockian candor declared the author to be "uncouth and excessive," his literary manner so repulsive that even at his most accurate it was difficult to believe what he said.

Not all the books Holmes studied were British. From the Law School itself came some of the best ones: Story's commentaries, Greenleaf on Evidence, Stearns on Real Actions, Parsons on Contracts. For American jurisprudence Holmes had a book he liked: Walker's *Introduction to American Law*. It was, he said afterward, one of the two books that gave him a glimpse of what he was seeking—the law in its general, historical aspect. The other was the first volume of Spence's *Equitable Jurisdiction*.

Timothy Walker, a student at the Law School under Judge Story, had written his book as a very young man, apologizing in the preface because somebody older and wiser had not written it instead. In it he examined American law from the Bill of Rights to Civil Procedure, discussed the conflict of laws and from state to state quoted case and precedent to support him. The student was advised to shun delights and live laborious days. "Genius without toil," Holmes read on page nineteen, "may, to some extent, distinguish a man elsewhere; but here he must labor, or he cannot succeed. No quickness of intuition can supply the place of patient investigation. A clear mind might determine at once what the law ought to be, but actual inspection alone can determine what the law is."

Wendell Holmes did not spurn this investigation. He reveled in it, pursued it mightily. In the students' law club—the Marshall Club, it was called—he argued cases with Olney and Lincoln. At home he continued the argument until his father, rebelling, said if Wendell went on talking law he would get out his fiddle and play against him right here in the library.

> Come you of the law, who can talk, if you please,
> Till the man in the moon will allow it's a cheese.

Did Wendell remember, his father demanded, those very apt lines from his poem written long ago for the Berkshire Jubilee? Wendell laughed. How much pleasanter his father was to get on with, now that the decision was made and he was actually committed to the law! Wendell had not looked forward to living at home. After being a captain in the army, how could he submit even outwardly to his father's authority? Yet he had no choice. He had no money, he was twenty-three. It was his business to get through Law School as cheaply as possible.

Neddy was a sophomore at Harvard, he came home only for holidays. Wendell's sister Amelia was twenty-one—a tiny, brisk creature, very congenial with her father. But Mrs. Holmes's pleasure in having her eldest son once more under her roof was extreme. It touched Dr. Holmes, made him suddenly more tolerant. When Mrs. Holmes heard Wendell's voice she came quickly into the room and sat down, watching him with an expression of such bright pleasure that Wendell turned instinctively, addressing the rest of his remarks to her. Once, while Wendell was speaking, his father got up and, putting an arm over his wife's shoulder, patted her gently, then left the room.

Mrs. Holmes was interested in every detail her son brought home from the Law School. She did not want to talk about the war, she said. She had had enough of war. Wendell had earned the right to use his mind. Let him use it then, while the chance was given him. The Rebels were not beaten; God knew what lay ahead. Mrs. Holmes was especially interested in the Marshall Club debates. Wendell had a talent for speaking, she said. Dr. Holmes did not agree, but for once he kept silence. The law was a bowl of sawdust; Wendell had undertaken to swallow it down. Let him swallow it then. His father wished him well. But what exactly was that phrase? *Sawdust without butter* . . . Some English barrister had said it to a young aspirant. *"If you can eat sawdust without butter, young man, you will be a success in the law."* He must look the phrase up, have it ready for Wendell next time the boy began to orate on the virtues of jurisprudence over against medicine, as a mind trainer.

John Ropes, coming in one evening, found Wendell sparring with his father and was hugely amused. At the end of October he wrote John Gray that Wendell seemed well and happy and had just written a sonnet for the *Transcript*—"really strong and good," Ropes added.

Actually, the sonnet sounds like bad Matthew Arnold. But compared with most of the poems in the papers and magazines of the period, it was sterling work. In the same issue was a poem called "A Sea-Shell." "Cool lips of shell, sing, sea-shell warm and sweet!" . . . Even the *Atlantic Monthly* gave space, under the name of poetry, to effusions so sentimental one is astonished to see the famous names appended to them.

Wendell published his sonnet anonymously. He had loved Henry Abbott, it was good to relieve himself of the burden of debt to a comrade-at-arms:—

H. L. A.

Twentieth Massachusetts Volunteers

He steered unquestioning nor turning back,
Into the darkness and the unknown sea;
He vanished in the starless night, and we
Saw but the shining of his luminous wake.
Thou sawest light, but ah, our sky seemed black,
And all too hard the inscrutable decree,
Yet noble heart, full soon we follow thee,
Lit by the deeds that flamed along thy track. . . .

To Holmes, out of the war himself, it seemed particularly terrible to see soldiers' funerals along the streets. Day after day the muffled drums, the slow processions over Beacon Hill. The war news itself was very favorable. Atlanta captured, Jubal Early routed in Virginia. It was a good thing, too, with a Presidential election only a few weeks off. If news from the front had continued bad, Lincoln supporters would have had a hard time putting a stop to the premature peace talk. Faneuil Hall in September had been the scene of a tremendous Democratic rally. Orators reminded the people that four years of war had failed to save the Union—and that Lincoln started the war.

On the Republican side, George Shattuck was very active. Holmes liked to see him in the public forum, vigorous, confident, with his handsome gray head, his skillful oratory of the trial lawyer. As election day approached, victory looked safe for Lincoln. Higginson was home, honorably discharged from the army, looking white and wobbly, but campaigning passionately for Lincoln. On November 8, a day of rain and wind, it was decided. "Lincoln will walk the course, God bless him!" Professor Asa Gray of Harvard wrote his friend, Charles Darwin. "Homely, ungainly Lincoln is the representative man of the country." By the middle of December, Sherman was within five miles of Savannah. It began to look as though the end were in sight. News from the front was almost pushed off the newspapers by advertisements of new petroleum and coal companies. In the early mornings Wendell saw smartly turned out broughams lining the sidewalks downtown. Ladies in furs, waiting for the brokers' offices to open so they might be first in line.

One evening in December, Mr. Robert Morse stopped in to see Wendell. He had a proposition to make. How would Wendell like to come into his office for the rest of the winter, part time of course, and see a little practical application of all this theory he was reading in Cambridge? Might do him good to handle a real writ, acquire a practical conviction of the difference between assumpsit and trover. After all, lawyers weren't made in libraries. The old apprentice system had had its points.

Wendell did not hesitate. Next Monday afternoon he sat on a high stool behind a desk in Barrister's Hall and copied wills, deeds, trusts, for three hours. He could not pretend it was invigorating work. But as the weeks wore on he was continually surprised at the speed with which Morse moved when a question was brought to him. At law school it had seemed that such questions would require weeks of argument, reference, and cross reference before a decision was reached. It left Wendell open-mouthed, he told the family at supper, to see the swift certainty with which a master of his business turned it off.

Dr. Holmes, helping himself to butter from the dish on the table, paused, knife in hand. "*Sawdust!*" he murmured. "*Sawdust without butter.*" He looked up. The old gleam was in his eye. "Wendell, have you heard what the English judge said to the young man who asked how a person could recognize a real vocation for the law?"

Under the table Neddy kicked his brother swiftly. Across the table Amelia watched, her brown eyes quick as a bird's. Mrs. Holmes poured Wendell's tea, handing it to him serenely. Wendell looked at his mother; their eyes met without expression.

"No, Father," Wendell said gravely. "I haven't heard. What did the judge say to the young man who wanted to be a lawyer?"

Wendell Holmes, returning to Boston in September, 1866, expected somehow to find the whole face of nature changed. What had happened to him was important, exciting. Like many a returning traveler he never doubted the excitement would be reflected everywhere.

But it was not reflected. Here at home, things were remarkably the same. Dr. Holmes went off to Grove Street every day to lecture. He had ceased—mercifully—to play the violin, but he was writing a new novel and burned to talk about it. Neddy, a senior at Harvard, came home over the week ends. Amelia was brisk and cheerful, helping her mother with the housekeeping, going to her Sewing Circle and to such festivities as the season afforded.

The supper table listened for a night or two to the elder brother's adventures abroad, then turned eagerly to its own affairs. They had been to Nahant in the summer, in a cottage near Longfellow and Agassiz. Dr. Holmes had suffered his usual Nahant asthma. The Indians had been a real nuisance, coming in swarms for the fishing, pitching their dirty tents right against the Lodges' hedge over on the Point.

Ben Butler down in Washington wanted to impeach the President, Neddy interposed. But of course, Wendell never had been interested in politics. In England, had he continued his absurd habit of not reading the newspapers? . . . "Your grandfather, Judge Jackson, never read the newspapers," Mrs. Holmes said quickly. "At least; during the three years he was reading law I know he never looked at a paper. He told me himself."

Dr. Holmes laughed. Wendell would never lack a champion while his mother lived, he said. . . . But even his esteemed father-in-law, Judge Jackson, had the defects of his qualities. Would the Judge's daughter permit him to recall the contemporary estimate of her father?

"I remember very well," Mrs. Holmes replied serenely. "You have often reminded me. 'Law knowledge, 100 per cent adequate. Political knowledge, 30 per cent. Classical knowledge, 10 per cent. Talent, 80. Integrity, 100. Practice of law, 100 . . .'" Mrs. Holmes paused, smiling. "Wit, 0," she finished.

Never mind about Grandfather Jackson, Neddy went on. Even if Wendell didn't read newspapers, he would be interested in what was going on in Boston. Laboring men here and all over the country were combining against their employers. The Eight-hour Movement was the talk everywhere. Cousin Wendell Phillips had thrown himself into it, and orated away on platforms about how ten hours of work ruined a man's soul. There had been a printers' strike in Boston during the summer. There seemed to be an actual trend toward Federal socialism. Somebody had even suggested publishing income returns in the newspapers. It would be a sad day when our government ceased to protect the privacy of individuals. But anyway, a boss blacksmith told the commissioners at the State House that a man working only eight hours could be of more value to an employer than one who worked ten. He said when a man got too tired he used tobacco and liquor. Pure nonsense of course. A harness maker had stood up and said he couldn't fail to notice that the men who worked shorter hours were always more intelligent. . . . What did John Mill in London say about the Eight-hour Movement?

Nobody waited for Wendell's reply. Fourteen chapters of his new novel were finished, Dr. Holmes said eagerly. *The Guardian Angel,* he was going to call it. It was a kind of sequel to *Elsie Venner,* on the same theme of heredity. But he was taking a hard crack at the old-fashioned hell-fire type of clergy. Dr. Bellamy Stoker, the villain of the story, had three sermons on hell—his *sweating* sermon, his *fainting* sermon, and his *convulsion-fit* sermon. He hadn't made that up, the doctor added quickly. He had got it from an actual instance in a town in Maine back in his lecture-circuit days. The *Atlantic* probably would publish the novel serially.

"You had better be careful," Wendell told his father. "There was trouble enough about *Elsie* and the *Autocrat*. People will be calling you a Freethinker all over again."

Dr. Holmes rubbed his small hands delightedly. "In New England they weld iron bands around the sapling elms to keep them within bounds. Your Uncle John and I, Wendell, were banded with iron in our youth. My books help me to get the iron of Calvinism out of my soul."

"Uncle John," Neddy said irrelevantly, "only goes abroad so he can have the extreme pleasure of coming back to Boston. In Venice he used to go every day to some perfectly commonplace spot and stand there. He said it reminded him of the junction of Broadway and Cambridge Streets in Cambridge. . . . Mr. Appleton told me."

Boston people were hopelessly provincial, Dr. Holmes said genially. Had Wendell noticed it, after being abroad? As he had once written Motley, your Boston man carries the Common in his head as a unit of space, the State House as the standard of architecture, and measures off men in Edward Everetts as with a yardstick. He himself had often been accused of provincialism. But he was not at all sure, for a literary man, that it was a weakness.

"They are still trying to name the new hotel," Amelia said, complacently pursuing her own line of conversation. "It is nearly finished and it is enormous. It will have a passenger elevator as big as a room. They cannot decide between The Hub Hotel and Everett House. Father, if they name it The Hub you will have to be godfather and assist at the christening. Wasn't it you who called Boston the hub of the universe?"

Neddy fixed his sister with a cold eye. Quite a long time ago he had asked his brother a question about the eight-hour day. Was it never possible, he asked, to get an answer from this family before somebody started their irrelevant *chatter?*

Looking around the table, Wendell was amused. He had no slightest intention of telling this supper table what John Mill thought about the Eight-hour Movement. He had already told Fanny Dixwell, before he had been home forty-eight hours, every word Mill had said. Fanny did not interrupt a man to tell stories of her own. She listened attentively, her comments and questions intelligent. This family could not hold its peace for two consecutive moments. Yet, listening now to their talk, Wendell recognized, with the fresh eye of the returned traveler, that his family, while undoubtedly irritating, was very far from dull. This was not the wit of London dinner tables, but whatever it was, it had life. *Provinciality!* There was something good about it, something vigorous and plain.

"Mother!" Wendell said suddenly. His strong voice came out easily above the rest. "Did you hear what Saint Peter said to the Boston man at the pearly gates?" *

Surprisingly, the table was silent, waiting.

On a Monday morning, Holmes went down to Court Street to the office of Chandler, Shattuck and Thayer. Mr. Shattuck greeted him with enormous heartiness. Peleg Chandler, the senior partner, came out. Gray whiskers grew all around under his chin; his wing collar came up to his ears. He shook Wendell's hand. "How is your father?" he said. "No candidate from this office ever failed a Bar examination, my boy." He bowed slightly and disappeared.

George Shattuck winked. It would take a half-wit to fail the Bar examination, he said. If Holmes had sat three years in this office he would be admitted without examination. As it was, he had been to Law School instead, and the Commonwealth took no account of law schools. "Make sure you don't know too much," Shattuck said. "The examiners don't like smart young men from the Law School. I've known them to fail a man because he tried to show off. I've also known them to drive a nice little bargain, promising not to ask the candidate any question he couldn't answer if the candidate would do the same by them."

A client came in. George Shattuck vanished. Holmes stood at a loss, looking at the rows of familiar brown books on the shelves. A heavy film of dust lay over most of them. There was dust on the long windows. In the

* Answer: *"You won't like it here."*

street below, a market dray rumbled past, and from the wharf near by a
steamer whistle sounded.

The inner door opened. James Bradley Thayer came out. He was ten
years older than Holmes. He had got his LL.B. at Harvard in '56. Rumor
said he was aiming for a professorship at the Law School. He wore his fine
dark hair rather long, he had the dreamy, gentle eye of the scholar. Shattuck, it appeared, had turned over the student end of the office to Thayer.
"Sit down," Thayer said. "Now, what are you after, Holmes? Admission to
the Bar or perhaps a trifle more education with it? No thinking will be
required at the Court House. Judge Shaw used to make them think, but the
rules are changed. Only memory is required. . . . But they can lay it on
pretty thick, in spite of what Shattuck says. If you get old Asaph Churchill
he is partial to Coke. Wasn't Churchill in college with your father? Do you
know the rule in Shelley's Case?"

That autumn, Holmes's card at the Athenaeum listed *Coke on Littleton,*
Austin's *Jurisprudence,* Stephen's history of English criminal law, Gibbon,
Humboldt, Mill's *Logic* again, Bracton's *Relation to the Roman Law,* Montesquieu's *Spirit of the Laws.* Holmes was fascinated by Montesquieu.
Here was a lonely scholar, sitting in a library—yet his book had done as
much to remodel the world as any material product of the eighteenth
century. Montesquieu was an authority for the writers of the *Federalist.* He
was the precursor of Burke, of modern political economy, of Adam Smith
and the Mills.

Sitting in the outer room of Chandler, Shattuck and Thayer, the *Esprit
des Lois* open on his knee, Holmes was struck anew with the awful power
of ideas to change a world. Montesquieu commanded the future more
surely from his study than Napoleon from his throne. A valid idea was
worth a regiment any day. The man of action has the present, yes—but
does not the thinker control the future?

Perhaps a man had to fight in a war to find that out. When you were
twenty it was the Henry Abbotts, the Caspar Crowninshields—external men
all—who seemed to rule the world.

But this picture Montesquieu drew of the government of England—was
it valid? Montesquieu divided it into three distinct parts, the legislative,
executive, judicial. Surely that was a fiction, even two centuries ago!
Holmes got up, knocked on Thayer's door. . . . "Find out for yourself,"
Thayer said. "Read Bagehot. How well do you know Stephens on English
criminal law? Have you read Reeves?"

An enormous impatience began to possess Wendell Holmes. He could
not find what he wanted fast enough. On his card at the Athenaeum appeared Bagehot on *The English Constitution,* Argyll's *Reign of Law,* Gladstone's *Reform Speeches,* McCosh on *Mill's Philosophy.* Holmes read Lecky,
Phillimore's *Principles and Maxims of Jurisprudence,* Forsyth's *History of
Trial by Jury,* Reeves's *History of English Law,* Palgrave's *English Com-*

monwealth. It seemed no more than a drop in the bucket of knowledge. His age had begun to worry him. He was nearly twenty-six. He had lost three years by the war. Men younger than he were well along now in law offices, done years ago with such puerilities as Bar examinations.

"When will you come up for examination?" Dr. Holmes asked just before Christmas. He had asked at least three times in the past month. "In the January term of Court," Wendell replied.

It was, actually, the twenty-seventh of February before George Shattuck wrote the conventional letter of recommendation, testifying to his good moral character. Holmes took it to the courthouse. His petition was filed. Asaph Churchill and Charles W. Huntington were appointed his examiners.

On a Wednesday morning, by appointment, Holmes walked up a flight of dark stairs to Mr. Churchill's office. He felt more curious than apprehensive. "Good morning, Holmes," Churchill said. "How is your father? We were at college together. Afterward, I believe he was not so successful at law as at writing verse. . . . You gentlemen from the Law School have the advantage of us. Huntington, here, and I got our law the hard way, in a lawyer's office."

Behind Churchill, Charles Huntington grinned broadly. He was a much younger man, graduate of Harvard in '54, but he had not been to Law School. Asaph Churchill motioned Holmes to be seated across the big desk. He put on his glasses. His face was serious but Holmes was conscious that Churchill was enjoying himself. "We might as well begin," Churchill said. "Huntington, with your permission . . . Now, Holmes, who owns the land between high and low water mark?"

"In Massachusetts and nowhere else," Holmes replied with equal gravity, "the land belongs to the owner of the adjoining land. . . ."

An hour later, Holmes walked out on Court Street. He felt exhilarated. They had let him off too easily, he thought. After one or two routine questions, the three had simply sat and talked law. But it was not bad fun, being examined for the Bar. He could have got through with a third of his knowledge, a fifth of it. There were six hundred lawyers in Boston. Had they all slipped through so easily?

He turned in at 4 Court Street. George Shattuck whacked him on the shoulder. "Did you know the rule in Shelley's Case, my boy?" he said. "Chandler will take you to court Monday to be sworn in. Like to go myself, but I have a client coming. This will call for celebration. Come to my house Monday evening. Bring Ropes and Gray. I will ask Parkman and Warner and Green. I have a receipt for a new gin toddy. There is nothing better for drinking the healths of newborn counsellors at law."

Monday morning was dark and gusty, with a threat of rain. Peleg Chandler, his ears entirely hidden inside his shirt collar, walked to the courthouse with Holmes. It was barely a block, on the same side of the street. The pillared granite portico was dark and high. Holmes always entered the place with a quick sensation, not so much of excitement as recognition. This courthouse was a part of him, of his background and childhood. Here Judge Loring had sentenced the runaway slaves, Sims and Burns. Manacled to these very benches, they had waited the verdict. Up these wide granite stairs, Higginson had led the mob that tried to rescue Sims. Holmes had been eight years old. He had stood at his bedroom window on Montgomery Place, three blocks away. There had been shouts, feet running on Tremont Street. . . .

Entering the wide doorway with Peleg Chandler, Holmes did not think of these things. Merely, he was conscious of them. They were part of him, and what he was about to do would make these remembered things, this dark high hallway, even more a part of him. . . .

Holmes and Chandler were early. Court sat at nine-thirty. Behind the Judge's Bench the new oaken panels shone yellow in the gaslight. There were five lawyers in court, they sat facing the Bench. Holmes recognized two of them; they nodded to him. Peleg Chandler walked back and took his seat with the spectators.

Judge Lord came in, thrust back his coattails, and sat down, looking toward Holmes, who sat alone on the petitioners' bench. Lord was nearsighted; he raised his bearded chin, his face straining slightly toward Holmes.

". . . and God save the Commonwealth and this Honorable Court," the crier finished.

There was a rustling of papers among the members of the Bar. The Clerk stood up. His voice was loud, monotonous: "The Court will attend to the taking of the oath."

Holmes came forward. It was like graduation, like walking up for your diploma, like the Brevet-Colonelship given him three years ago on the Common. It was absurd to feel so solemn. But Holmes did feel solemn. He liked ceremony. You did your work, and someone in a black gown handed you a piece of paper, bowed to you. . . .

The five lawyers stood up, so did the spectators. The room was silent. Holmes swore true faith and allegiance to the Commonwealth, swore to support the Constitution of Massachusetts and of the United States. Then with his hand on the Bible he took the Attorneys' Oath:—

I solemnly swear that I will do no falsehood nor consent to the doing of any in Court; I will not wittingly or willingly promote or sue any false, groundless or unlawful suit, nor give aid or consent to the same; I will delay no man for lucre or malice; but I will conduct myself in the office of an attorney within the Courts according to the best of my knowledge and discretion, and with all good fidelity as well to the Courts as my clients. So help me God.

Judge Lord smiled, inclined his head. "Come and sign the Bar Book," Peleg Chandler said. It was in the next room, on a high desk against the wall. At the bottom of the page was room for one more name. There were twelve names inscribed in this January term of court. Most of them, Holmes noted, were from the Law School. Horace Graves, Josiah Bellows . . .

Holmes signed his name carefully. There was no flourish to the way he did it. Peleg Chandler peered over his shoulder. "Horace Graves," he read. "Promising fellow, Graves. I knew his father. Well well, Holmes! You can have a sign on your door now. Be sure you bring us in some clients."

For Peleg Chandler, this was unusually facetious. Holmes put down the pen, turned, and followed Shattuck's senior partner to the door. On the portico, rain drove through the pillars, wind blew back the skirts of Chandler's overcoat. Turning up his coat collar, Holmes descended the steps and followed Peleg Chandler down the gray slope of Court Street.

A week later, the secretary of the class of '61, Harvard University, received a small card in the mail:—

OLIVER WENDELL HOLMES, JR. [it read]
Counsellor at Law
4 Court Street, Boston.

Lincoln the Lawyer*

CARL SANDBURG

Lincoln and Carl Sandburg go well together. Both represent the Midwest, have a knowledge of the good earth and a respect for labor, can tell a yarn with the right folk-crackle; both have strength and wisdom, and in both there is the same homespun quality. The five brief chapters that follow show what it was like to be a young lawyer in the 1830's and 1840's.

Springfield with its 1,500 inhabitants in 1837 was the big town of Sangamon County, selling to the 18,000 people of the county a large part of their supplies, tools, groceries, handling grain, pork, beef, and produce, with stores, churches, schools, banks, newspapers, courts, lawyers, offices of government, taverns, saloons, places of entertainment. It was a city, its people ready to say there was no more wilderness in that part of the country; the land had been surveyed and allotted.

The farm women who came to town wore shoes where they used to go barefooted; the men had changed from moccasins to rawhide boots and shoes. Farmers no longer spent time killing deer, tanning the hide and making leather breeches to tie at the ankles: it was cheaper and quicker to raise corn and buy pantaloons which had come from Massachusetts over the Ohio or the Mississippi River or the Great Lakes. Stores advertised "velvets, silk, satin, and Marseilles vestings, fine calf boots, seal and morocco pumps, for gentlemen," and for ladies "silks, bareges, crepe lisse, lace veils, thread lace, Thibet shawls, lace handkerchiefs, fine prunella shoes."

Carriages held men riding in top-boots and ruffled silk shirts, and women in silks and laces. It was civilization which Abraham Lincoln, twenty-eight years old, saw as he rode into Springfield that March day in 1837—to be a lawyer. Its people were mostly from Kentucky, coming by horse, wagon, and boat across country not yet cleared of wolves, wildcats, and horse thieves. And there were in Sangamon County 78 free negroes, 20 registered indentured servants, and 6 slaves.

The centre of the town was a public square, with the courthouse, jail, stores, churches, banks, harness-makers, and blacksmiths lined about the

* From *Abraham Lincoln: The Prairie Years*, Volume I, by Carl Sandburg, copyright, 1926, by Harcourt, Brace and Company, Inc.; renewed by Carl Sandburg. Reprinted by permission of the publishers.

square. The streets and sidewalks were plain black Illinois soil underfoot, except for gravel here and there for dry footing in rain or snow, and stones and sticks for street crossings.

Lincoln pulled in his horse at the general store of Joshua Speed. He asked the price of bedclothes for a single bedstead, which Speed figured at $17.00. "Cheap as it is, I have not the money to pay," he told Speed. "But if you will credit me until Christmas, and my experiment as a lawyer here is a success, I will pay you then. If I fail in that I will probably never pay you at all." Speed said afterward: "The tone of his voice was so melancholy that I felt for him. I looked up at him and thought that I never saw so gloomy and melancholy a face in my life." Speed offered to share his own big double bed upstairs over the store. Lincoln took his saddlebags upstairs, came down with his face lit up and said, "Well, Speed, I'm moved."

His meals he had arranged to take with Bill Butler, one of the "Long Nine," who said Lincoln could put his feet under the table at the Butler home as long as he wanted to; they wouldn't worry about the board bill. He joined Stuart, and their professional card read, "J. T. Stuart and A. Lincoln, Attorneys and Counsellors at Law, will practice conjointly, in the Courts of this Judicial Circuit—Office No. 4 Hoffman's Row upstairs. Springfield, April 12, 1837."

In his new copy of Webster's dictionary, he wrote, to see how it would look, on the flyleaf, "A. Lincoln, Esq., Attorney and Counselor-at-Law."

The county courtroom was on the lower floor of a two-story building in Hoffman's Row. Upstairs, over the courtroom, was the law office of the new firm of Stuart & Lincoln: a little room with a few loose boards for bookshelves, an old wood stove, a table, a chair, a bench, a buffalo robe, and a small bed.

Stuart was running for Congress, so Lincoln handled all of the law practice in range of his ability. His first case was one he had helped work on during the previous year, defending David Wooldridge, in a suit brought by James P. Hawthorn. Hawthorn claimed Wooldridge was to furnish him two yoke of oxen to break up twenty acres of prairie sod-ground; also he claimed Wooldridge was to allow him to raise a crop of corn or wheat on a certain piece of ground; and Wooldridge had failed him in both cases.

Furthermore, Hawthorn claimed damages because Wooldridge struck, beat, bruised, and knocked him (Hawthorn) down; plucked, pulled, and tore large quantities of hair from his head. Also because with a stick and his fists he struck Hawthorn many violent blows and strokes on or about the face, head, breast, back, shoulders, hips, legs, and divers other parts of the body, and because he had with violence forced, pushed, thrust, and gouged his fingers into Hawthorn's eyes.

Such were the allegations on assumpsit and trespass vi et armis, including also replevin action demanding return of a black and white yoke of steers, one black cow and calf, and one prairie plow. Lincoln's first move was to bring up a board bill for eight months which Hawthorn owed Wooldridge, amounting at $1.50 a week to $45.75. Also, for the same eight months, he had used a wagon and team for which he should pay $90.00 besides a cash loan of $100.00. The case never came to trial. Peacemakers settled it out of court. The plaintiff and defendant divided the court costs. In the record Lincoln spelled wagon "waggon" and prairie "prairy."

Between law cases he kept up his political fences, writing such letters as this to John Bennett at Petersburg:

SPRINGFIELD, August 5, 1837.

DEAR SIR:

Mr. Edwards tells me you wish to know whether the act to which your town incorporation provision was attached, passed into a law. It did. You can organize under the general incorporation law as soon as you choose.

I also tacked a provision on to a fellow's bill to authorize a relocation of the road from Salem down to your town; but I am not certain whether or not the bill passed; neither do I suppose I can ascertain before the laws will be published. If it is a law, Bowling Green, Bennet Abell, and yourself are appointed to make the change.

No news. No excitement except a little about the election of Monday next. I suppose, of course, our friend, Dr. Henry, stands no chance in your "diggings."

Your friend and humble servant,
A. LINCOLN.

Mrs. Joseph Anderson, a widow, came into the office of Stuart & Lincoln, to ask if they could help her. She had come to Springfield to sell ten acres of land left by her husband, but she found that General James Adams claimed the ten acres had been signed over to him by her husband for a debt he owed General Adams as a lawyer. Lincoln worked on the case, searched the records, and then published a handbill opening with the statement: "It is well known to most of you, that there is existing at this time, considerable excitement in regard to Gen. Adams's titles to certain tracts of land, and the manner in which he acquired them."

He then went into a tissue of facts to show that Adams had falsified documents in order to swindle "a widow woman" out of ten acres of land. General Adams wrote a reply which filled six newspaper columns, and Lincoln returned with a one-column answer analyzing affidavits offered by Adams, saying they were "all false as hell," and adding: "In conclusion I will only say that I have a character to defend as well as Gen. Adams, but I disdain to whine about it as he does."

When Adams again filled six newspaper columns with his defense, Lincoln commented: "Let it be remembered that when he first came to this country he attempted to impose himself upon the community as a lawyer, and actually carried the attempt so far, as to induce a man who was under a charge of murder to entrust the defense of his life in his hands, and finally took his money and got him hanged. Is this the man that is to raise a breeze in his favor by abusing lawyers? If he is not himself a lawyer, it is for the lack of sense, and not of inclination. If he is not a lawyer, he *is* a liar, for he proclaimed himself a lawyer, and got a man hanged by depending on him."

His scorn of Adams was put into a clear lingo. "It is true I have no children nor *kitchen boys;* and if I had, I should scorn to lug them in to make affidavits for me."

He declared further newspaper argument closed. "Farewell, General. I will see you again at Court, if not before—when and where we will settle the question whether you or the widow shall have the land."

In the trial he won for Mrs. Anderson her ten acres of land, shortly after which an editorial supposed to have been written by Lincoln was published in the *Sangamo Journal,* containing a copy of an indictment found against Gen. Adams in Oswego County, New York, in 1818, the crime charged being forgery of a deed. "A person of evil name and fame and of a wicked disposition," was the *Journal's* allusion to Adams, who at the August election had been chosen probate justice of the peace.

The affair with General Adams was taken by some people as a noisy rumpus that could have been conducted more decently by Lincoln, while others held it as a sign that chivalry was alive, even if it came in drab blue jeans, with a grin.

Veiled accusations were published in the *Illinois Republican,* a Democratic newspaper, that Lincoln's friend, Dr. A. G. Henry, the acting commissioner in charge of the construction work on the new Statehouse, was hornswoggling the taxpayers; a committee of Whigs marched on the editorial rooms of the newspaper; warnings and threats were exchanged; it was said that among the Democratic leaders who got their hair mussed was Stephen A. Douglas, reported to be the writer of the unsigned articles attacking Dr. Henry.

Lincoln helped organize a mass meeting where he offered a resolution pointing at Dr. Henry as being accused of "squandering uselessly and wastefully the public money" appropriated for the Statehouse. Therefore, said Lincoln's resolution, a committee of seven should be appointed to investigate whether the work under Dr. Henry was "progressing in the most economical and judicious manner." The committee was appointed and did its duty in a report vindicating the Whig commissioner, Lincoln's friend.

It was a year with branches thickening out into the air, struggling for fresh lines for the run of the sap.

The young lawyer and politician could look out from the office window on the main street and the public square, with freedom to read what could be read in the passers-by, the forms and faces, the doctor going to a birth, the hearse leading a burial party, children going to school, the town drunk-ard dragged by the town constable, bankers, landowners, squatters, car-penters, well-diggers, washerwomen, Kentuckians, Virginians, Yankees, French-Canadians, Pennsylvania Dutch, Irish, and Germans—passers-by.

Past the window of the law office of Stuart & Lincoln came farmers hauling corn, wheat, potatoes, and turnips, in wagons; the axles creaked; husky voices bawled at the yokes of steers while the whip thongs lashed and cracked.

Droves of hogs came past, in muddy weather wallowing over their knees, the hair of their flanks spattered, their curls of tails flipping as they grunted onward to sale and slaughter.

And there were horses, and men riding and driving who loved horses. It was a horse country. They too were passers-by—roans, grays, whites, black horses with white stockings, sorrels with a sorrel forelock down a white face, bays with a white star in the forehead.

In a letter to Levi Davis, Esq., of Vandalia, Lincoln wrote one April day, "We have generally in this Country, Peace, Health, and Plenty, and no News."

One day Lincoln had dipped a pen in an ink-bottle and written the words, "State of Illinois, Sangamon County and Circuit—of the July term of the Sangamon Circuit Court in the Year of Our Lord One Thousand Eight Hundred and Thirty-Nine." And he had since dipped his pen and written the same words, changing only the date, dozens of times, and he knew if he lived he would write them thousands of times. He could almost write those words in his sleep. Likewise with the form he scratched off, reading, "I do hereby enter myself as security for costs in this cause, and acknowledge myself bound to pay, or cause to be paid, all costs which may accrue in this action either to the opposite party or to any of the officers of this court in pursuance of the laws of this state." He could repeat that, almost, back-ward.

Money came to his hands, fees, of which half must go to Stuart. He wrote a memorandum, such as "I have received five dollars from Deed of Macon, five from Lewis Keeling, five from Andrew Finley, one half of which belongs to Stuart and has not been entered on the books."

"Safety" was the anxious key word in one letter. "I am unwilling to make any conveyance until I see the assignments and original certificate. If Mr. Underhill will bring that certificate I will do all an honorable man should do. It is not money, but safety, I desire." And closing the letter he repeated, "If Mr. Underhill will come and bring the certificate I will do all in safety I can."

A caller came one day, representing the United States Government and its Post Office Department. The caller wanted to ask about a certain number of dollars and cents that had come into the hands of Lincoln as postmaster at New Salem. Lincoln stepped to a corner of the office, dug out a sack and counted the money in it, the exact amount asked for by the inspector, who took the money, gave a receipt, and went away satisfied.

His grocery days were an advantage to Lincoln in the case where the Hickox brothers had sold flour to the defendant as "good, merchantable, superfine flour," against which Lincoln pleaded that "twenty barrels were *not* at the time of sale, good, merchantable, superfine flour, but, on the contrary, greatly inferior in quality."

In one of his first murder cases, tried in Hancock County, Lincoln failed to save William Fraim, who was convicted on April 25, 1839, and, by court order, hanged by the neck till dead, just twenty-three days later.

Murderers, horse thieves, scandalmongers, and slanderers came at various times and poured out their stories amid the walls of the Stuart & Lincoln law office. There came bothered and puzzled people.

George Stockton walked in one day and told how a cooking-stove was spoiled a hundred dollars' worth, he guessed; and Lincoln brought suit against Tolby for that amount of damages to "a cooking-stove." But he had many quiet hours when there was little business, because there was little crime. In the office record of expenses he made an entry, "Lincoln paid for wood . . . $.50," and "Lincoln paid for saw . . . $2.25." If not busy at law practice, he was sawing wood.

A boatload of corn coming down the Sangamon River ran onto a fish-trap dam, and sprang a leak so that the corn was wet. On being unloaded the corn got rained on and further damaged. Lincoln brought suit for the owners of the boat and the corn against the fish-trappers for obstructing the navigation of the Sangamon River and unlawfully damaging the boat and the corn as property.

One hot summer day Harvey Ross came; in order to prove ownership of his farm at Macomb he had to have the testimony from a witness near Springfield. Court had closed for six months, Lincoln explained, but they would go out to Judge Thomas's farm a mile east and see what he could do. Lincoln took off his coat, laid it on a chair, and with a bundle of papers in one hand and a red handkerchief for wiping sweat off, in the other hand, he and the witness walked out to the Thomas farm, asking the way and taking the short cuts.

The judge's wife said the judge had gone to the north part of the farm, where he had a tenant house, to help his men put up a corncrib. If they went the main road it would be a half-mile, but if they cut across the corn-field it would be only a quarter-mile, Mrs. Thomas said; and on Lincoln asking her to show them the path she came out of the house and pointed to where the short cut led across the cornfield from their barn.

They struck out Indian-file, Lincoln with a bundle of papers in one hand and a red handkerchief in the other, till they came to where the judge and his men were raising logs to make a corncrib and hogpen. Lincoln put the case to the judge, who looked over the papers, swore in the witness, and, with pen and ink from the tenant house, signed the documents.

All were in shirt-sleeves, and Lincoln remarked it was a kind of shirt-sleeve court they were holding. "Yes," laughed the judge, "a shirt-sleeve court in a cornfield."

The main business being over, Lincoln asked the judge if he didn't want some help in rolling up the logs. The judge guessed two of them were pretty heavy and he could stand a little help. So Lincoln and Ross pitched in and helped, and when Ross offered to pay the judge for his services the judge said he guessed the helping with the logs was pay enough.

On the road back to Springfield Lincoln could have told Ross some of the stories passing among lawyers and judges, of the man, for instance, charged with sheep-killing, who was asked by the court, "Are you guilty or not guilty?" And the man wouldn't answer. The court kept at him, and at last said, "You must do something—what do you do?" The man answered, "I stands mute," and, pushed further, would only answer, "I stands mute." On trial the case was decided against him, but he was told he could carry it higher up to the Court of Errors. And he murmured, "If this here ain't a court of errors, I'd like to know where you kin find one!"

In the case of a defendant charged with mistreating a livery-stable horse, a witness testified, "When his company rides fast he rides fast, and when his company rides slow he rides slow." "I want to know," said the important lawyer for the other side, "how he rides when he is alone." "W-e-l-l," said the witness, a slow talker, "I—never—was—with—him—when—he—was—alone; so—I don't know."

And there was a case told among lawyers of a defendant, losing, who stood up and called the court unjust, corrupt, and false. He was fined ten dollars for contempt of court, and handed the clerk a twenty-dollar bill. "I can't change this," said the clerk. "Never mind about the other ten dollars," came the hot reply, "I'll take it out in contempt!"

Two farmers, Samuel Wycoff and Dennis Forrest, came to see Lincoln one day. Each owned a quarter-section of land in Township Fourteen North of Range Six, West, in Sangamon County. They had a dispute concerning a small strip of land, each claiming it. And they agreed in writing to submit their dispute "to the arbitrament of Abraham Lincoln, who is to hear the evidence and thereupon decide which is the owner of the disputed land, and what line is hereafter to be the dividing line." Furthermore, "We hereby mutually bind ourselves in the penal sum of five hundred dollars, as liquidating damages, to abide by the decision he shall make, and each to give and allow the other peaceable possession and enjoyment of his own side of the line so to be designated."

Two weeks later Lincoln handed the two farmers, who had come to him instead of a court, his decision, reading: "In pursuance of agreement, having fully heard the evidence, I decide that the land in dispute between Wycoff and Forrest belongs to said Wycoff, and that the old United States Surveyor's line, beginning at the West end thereof, and running thence Easterly as marked through the timber by said U. S. Surveyor, so far as the timber extends, and continuing the same course as so marked, the proper distance to reach the East side of the lands of said Wycoff and Forrest above described, shall hereafter be the dividing line between the said lands of the parties."

Once a jury picked by the Menard County sheriff got filled up with men of whom Lincoln said: "I would like to throw the whole panel out, for I know every single one of them; but I can't object to a man among them." It was a murder case, with Lincoln called in as a prosecutor. Two brothers named Denton had got into a dispute with a brother-in-law named Brown. They fought with axes; Brown was killed; the Dentons were the only witnesses.

During the trial, which lasted a week, Lincoln felt sure the jury wouldn't convict; he left the questioning of witnesses and the final plea to the jury with another prosecutor. And, as it happened, the jury freed the Dentons. Lincoln had sensed from the first that it would be uphill work to convict with that particular jury—and Lincoln never made much of a record when called in as a prosecutor.

Fine points in justice came before him. He pressed a claim of John Warner against John Calhoun, who had been his chief when he was a surveyor; he questioned Calhoun as to transfers and assignments of property. Then there was the case of Nancy Green, who had loaned $200.00 and got a note for it, but couldn't collect. She put it in Lincoln's hands. He had to collect it from Mentor Graham, the New Salem schoolmaster who had helped Lincoln learn the science of surveying and had loaned Lincoln books. Lincoln sued Graham, won the suit, but didn't force immediate payment. What he asked was that the schoolmaster should do his best to pay the woman. This was the second suit Lincoln won for Nancy Green, the first being a dissolution of her marriage-bond with Aaron Green.

He took a case to the supreme court, and wrote Marshall, his Shawneetown friend: "At the request of Mr. Eddy, I got the judgment reversed. This was no business of yours, and I now only ask, as a favor of you, that if Mr. Eddy is well, you say to him I would like to have the little fee in the case, if convenient."

In the divorce case of Samuel Rogers *vs.* Polly Rogers, Lincoln represented the husband and advised that no charge of adultery be made. In the development of the case he filed an affidavit: "A. Lincoln being first duly sworn says that he was employed as counsel in the case of Samuel Rogers *vs.* Polly Rogers for a Divorce; that he, the affiant, drew up the complainant's bill; that said complainant at that time told this affiant that he could prove that the said defendant had been guilty of adultery with one William Short while she was living with said complainant; but that affiant advised said complainant not to make the charge in his bill as there was other sufficient grounds upon which to obtain a divorce, to-wit, absence of more than two years." In effect, Lincoln was ready to help his client get a divorce, but was not willing to make an unnecessary public record against the woman in the case.

In the same year Thomas McKibben came to Lincoln down in Coles County. Jonathan Hart had called McKibben a horse thief. Lincoln brought court action against Hart for slander, demanding $2,000.00 damages. The case was tried; McKibben was awarded $200.00; Lincoln was paid a fee of $35.00. And old Thomas Lincoln, the father of Abraham Lincoln, living in his log cabin out from Charleston, came in to town and was handed the $35.00, as required by Abraham Lincoln, who had left instructions with the clerk of the court thus to deliver the money to his father and get a receipt.

In Lincoln's Springfield office was an account book marked "Day Book of Lincoln & Herndon," in one place, and in another "Lincoln & Herndon's Fee Book." The fees in 180 cases for the year 1846 were entered, mostly by Lincoln; one fee was $2.50; two were $3.00; in 64 cases the charge was $5.00; in five, $7.00; in 63, $10.00; in five, $50.00; in one, $100.00; and in the remainder from $15.00 to $25.00. One entry read, "Scott *vs.* Busher (for Def't). To attending case in Menard Cir. Court if it ends where it is. Paid $20." Another case, tried before a justice of the peace, was recorded, "Negro *vs.* Robert Smith (for Deft.). To attending case of Negro Bob. J. P. $5.00."

His reputation was spreading as a man and lawyer of whom people said, "He'll be fair and square." He couldn't talk just to be talking. At a political meeting, where an orator was speechifying splendiferously with arms uplifted, and with a voice bawling and ranting neither fact nor argument, Lincoln turned to friends and said in an undertone, "Cut his galluses and let him go up!"

Lincoln couldn't talk against time if there was nothing to talk about. His quitting-time, for speaking, came earlier than for other lawyers. With nothing to say, he was dumb. In a criminal case he tried with Usher F. Linder, the two of them agreed that in the strategy of the case each should make the longest speech possible, and go on talking till he was used up. And, as Linder told it afterward, Lincoln's performance ran out of wind at the end of an hour, while he, Linder, rambled on in a three-hour speech to the jury.

A doctor at Matamora, Robert C. Lamson, said that he had learned from Lincoln, who had stayed overnight at his house several times, that it was a healthy habit to tell other people all he positively knew about one thing or a few things, and to say nothing at all about things he wasn't sure of. Of a patient doomed to pass away, Lamson used to remark, "He's got the can't-help-its," a phrase he said he had picked up from hearing Lincoln use it.

Homely phrasings of Lincoln often lingered and were repeated. The lawyer Bagby at Pekin told Lincoln of a lawsuit with a highly educated minister as the important witness. And the minister had an extra-fine sense of the distinctions and definitions of words. Bagby found the witness would not testify positively to things which Bagby knew that the witness knew. "I think so" and "I believe so" were the answers. Finally Bagby asked, "What do you mean by the expression 'I think'?" The witness answered at once, "That, sir, is the knowledge I have of my recollection of things of which I am not positively certain." He was then asked, "What do you mean by the expression, 'I believe'?" To which he just as smoothly answered, "That is the faith I have in the existence of objects of which I have a distinct recollection." Which made Lincoln chuckle, "He came out of the same hole he went in at."

Passions, deaths, reputations, the incessant and shifting forces of life, the stuff of the plays of Shakespeare and the books of Boccaccio and Rabelais, plain tales of life's surprises, put the stain of their designs on the parchments of Lincoln's law practice. Among his clients were descendants of Cain and Abel, of David and Bathsheba, of prodigal sons, of virgins who brought oil or came empty-handed.

Lincoln petitioned the supreme court for a rehearing in the case of Patterson *vs.* Edwards, which was a suit between two women in which one charged the other was the mother of a negro child. In a closely reasoned brief, the argument of Lincoln dwelt on allegations. "The words alleged are: 'Mrs. Edwards has raised a family of children by a negro, and I can prove it.' If we change the language from the second person, past tense, as detailed by the witnesses, to the first person, present tense, as spoken by Mrs. Patterson, the words proved by Mrs. Seymour to have been spoken by Mrs. Patterson are: 'I did tell Julius Scoville that Mrs. Edwards has had children by a negro, and all her children are negroes.'" He discussed whether in law it is sufficient to prove words equivalent to those identically charged. "While we understand words amounting to the *identical* charge alleged, as being, in the sense of the law, not *merely equivalent* words, but *the* words alleged, notwithstanding a slight literal or verbal variance—we insist that a variance to be material in the law must be a variance in *sense*. If we are right in this, we ask, 'Is there any difference *in sense* between saying a woman has *raised* children by a negro, and saying she *had* children by a negro?'"

In as simple a manner as though he were addressing a jury of farmers, he presented certain points to the supreme court. "On the question of arrest of judgment this court declared that the words, 'Mrs. Edwards has raised a family of children by a negro' do not, 'in their plain and popular sense, or in common acceptation, *necessarily* amount to a charge of adultery.'

Wherein these words vary from, or fall short of such a charge, the opinion does not state. Whether the court believe that these words do not mean that Mrs. Edwards had raised a family of children, of whom she was the *mother*, and a negro was the *father;* or whether, admitting this, the court believe she may have been the wife of the negro, and therefore, may have borne children by him without adultery, the opinion shows nothing from which we can judge. Until the decision of this court, we had never supposed there could be a rational doubt that these words would be construed by all who might hear them, as the declaration construes them. We have thought, and still do think, that if twelve plain men should enter this room and each, out of the hearing of the others, should be told these words, not one of them would fail to attach to them the very meaning that the declaration attaches to them." Then, saying, "But we may be mistaken," he branched out into old and new rules in courts, and a train of judicial decisions bearing on the construction of words of doubtful meaning.

In the July term, A.D. 1845, in the Sangamon circuit court, Lincoln and Herndon represented Jonathan and Susan Miller, who were defendants against charges of slander brought by William and Martha Ann Beaty. In Lincoln's handwriting, the plea opened: "And the said defendants come and defend the wrong and injury, when, where, etc., and say the said Susan is not guilty in manner and form as the said plaintiffs, in their said declaration have alleged, and of this, they, the said defendants, put themselves upon the county, etc. And for further plea in this behalf the said defendants (now disclaiming all intention of affirming the truth of the supposed slanderous words in the said declaration mentioned) say plaintiffs *actio non,* because they say that at time of the supposed speaking of the supposed slanderous words in the said declaration mentioned, by the said Susan, she, the said Susan did speak the said words, in the connection following, and not otherwise, that is to say: 'I' (the said Susan, meaning) 'have understood that Mrs. Beaty' (the said Martha Ann meaning) 'and Dr. Sullivan were seen together in Beaty's' (the said William's, meaning) 'stable, one morning, very early, in the very act'—'It certainly is a fact'—'Jo Shepherd can prove it by two respectable witnesses'—'Mrs. Beaty' (the said Martha Ann, meaning) 'and Dr. Sullivan were seen in the very act'—'They' (the said Martha Ann and the said Dr. Sullivan, meaning) 'were caught in the very act'—'Old Mr. Vandergrift' (one Thomas Vandergrift, meaning) and the said Thomas (by the hearers, then and there being understood to be meant) 'told Mr. Miller' (the said Jonathan, meaning) 'so at the tanyard.' And the said defendants aver, that before the speaking of the words aforesaid, to wit on the (blank) day of May, A.D. 1845, at the county aforesaid, the said Thomas Vandergrift did speak and tell said words as aforesaid to the said Jonathan—and so the said defendants say that she, the said Susan, did speak the said words in the said declaration mentioned, as lawfully she might, for the cause aforesaid. And the said defendants are ready to verify;

wherefore they pray judgment, etc." In the document written by Lincoln and Herndon in the case, two replications follow, each of about the same length, one written by Herndon, the final one by Lincoln.

In the year 1843 a man named Robert Matson came from his home in Bourbon County, Kentucky, and bought a large tract of land in Coles County, Illinois, not many miles from the cabin of Thomas Lincoln in that county. Matson started farming his land, naming it Black Grove farm, bringing with him his slaves from Kentucky to plant and gather the crops. When the harvests were over he took the negroes back to Kentucky, working his Illinois land with a different gang of slaves each year.

One free negro, Anthony Bryant, stayed in Illinois from year to year, acting as foreman or overseer for Matson, studying the Bible at odd times, learning to spell his way slowly through some of the chapters. In the year 1847 Bryant's slave wife and four children were brought from Kentucky, and put to work on the Matson farm.

Matson's housekeeper, Mary Corbin, who was more than a housekeeper to him, one day exploded with anger and spoke terrible words to Jane Bryant, the wife of Anthony. "You're going back to Kentucky," shrieked Mary Corbin, "and you're going to be sold way down South in the cotton fields."

Anthony Bryant heard what seemed to be a death sentence on his wife, and drove as fast as horseflesh would let him to the village of Oakland, two miles away. There he talked to Hiram Rutherford, a young doctor from Pennsylvania, and Gideon M. Ashmore, from the Duck River country of Tennessee. And in the middle of that night Anthony Bryant, his wife and one child, on horseback, and three children on foot, arrived at the Ashmore home in Oakland. They stayed at the Ashmore home several days while Robert Matson and his friend, Joseph Dean, argued and threatened. Then Matson went before William Gilman, justice of the peace, swore that the negro woman and her children were his property, and they were arrested and locked up in the county jail at Charleston.

Squire Gilman heard the arguments of Orlando B. Ficklin for the negroes, and of Usher F. Linder for Matson. The squire decided he didn't have authority on the question of freedom or slavery for the negroes, and turned the prisoners back into the hands of the sheriff. After the Bryant woman and her children had spent forty-eight days in jail, the sheriff, A. G. Mitchell, put into the hands of lawyers a bill to be collected from Matson. The main item read, "To keeping and dieting five negroes forty-eight days at 37 cents each per day, $107.30."

Next, Matson was arrested and convicted, the charge being that he had lived unlawfully with Mary Corbin, a woman not his wife. After that Matson brought an action against Rutherford and Ashmore, claiming damages for the unlawful seizure and holding of his property, negro slaves.

The main action came when Matson went into circuit court, demanding the release of his property on grounds of habeas corpus and calling for $2,500.00 damages from Rutherford, valuing the slaves at $500.00 apiece. When the summons in the case was served on Rutherford, he rode to Charleston, found Abraham Lincoln sitting tilted in a chair on the tavern veranda, interrupted as Lincoln had finished telling one story and was going to start on another, and they went to one side for a talk.

As Rutherford told his troubles, he noticed Lincoln growing sober, sad, looking far off, shaking his head in a sorry way. "At length, and with apparent reluctance, Lincoln answered that he could not defend me, because he had already been counselled with in Matson's interest," said Rutherford, later. "This was a grievous disappointment and irritated me into expressions more or less bitter in tone. He seemed to feel this, and endeavored in his plausible way to reconcile me to the proposition that, as a lawyer, he must represent and be faithful to those who counsel with and employ him. I appeared not to be convinced, retorting that 'my money was as good as any one's else.' Although thoroughly in earnest I presume I was a little hasty."

A few hours later Lincoln sent a message to Rutherford, and followed the first message quickly with a second. "The interview and my quick temper," said Rutherford, "made a deep impression on Mr. Lincoln, I am sure, because he dispatched a messenger to me with the information that he had sent for the man who had approached him in Matson's behalf, and if they came to no more decisive terms than at first he would probably be able to represent me. In a very brief time this was followed by another message, that he could now easily and consistently free himself from Matson and was, therefore, in a position if I employed him to conduct my defense. But it was too late; my pride was up, and I plainly indicated a disinclination to avail myself of his offer. Instead, I employed Charles H. Constable, a lawyer who had emigrated to Illinois from Maryland, a classical scholar, fluent and ready in debate, and of commanding physical presence. Ashmore made terms with Orlando B. Ficklin, a Kentuckian, who had won renown as a lawyer."

The case came to trial before Judges Willson and Treat, of the supreme court of the state, with Lincoln and Usher F. Linder as counsel for Matson. Farm hands went on the witness stand for Matson and swore he had told them at the time he brought the slaves to his Illinois land that he didn't intend to keep them there permanently.

It seemed as though Matson's lawyers expected to win by showing that Matson had no plans for permanently locating slaves in Illinois. And yet, when Lincoln presented his statements for Matson, they sounded like a searching inquiry into the cold facts and the elemental justice of the case, rather than an argument for a plaintiff. A Coles County lawyer, D. F. McIntyre, got the impression that Lincoln was clumsy at handling the case in favor of his client. He made no attack on the defense, no attempt to batter down the points of the opposition, and practically gave his case away by the outright admission that if the Kentucky slave owner had brought his slaves to Illinois for the purpose of working them and using them as slaves on the Coles County farm, the negroes were thereby entitled to freedom. McIntyre noted that Lincoln said the whole case turned on one point. "Were these negroes passing over and crossing the State, and thus, as the law contemplates, *in transitu,* or were they actually located by consent of their master? If only crossing the State, that act did not free them, but if located, even indefinitely, by the consent of their owner and master, their emancipation logically followed. It is, therefore, of the highest importance to ascertain the true purpose and intent of Matson in placing these negroes on the Black Grove farm."

McIntyre noted further: "When Mr. Lincoln arose to make the closing argument, all eyes were fixed upon him. Every person in the court room was curious to hear what reasons he could or would assign, in behalf of this slave holder, to induce the court to send this mother and her four children back into lives of slavery. But strange to say Lincoln did not once touch upon the question of the right of Matson to take the negroes back to Kentucky. His main contention was that the question of the right of the negroes to their freedom could only be determined by a regular habeas corpus proceeding."

Judge Willson leaned forward over the bar and asked: "Mr. Lincoln, your objection is simply to the form of the action by which, or in which this question should be tried, is it not?" "Yes, sir."

Then came the high point of the day for Lincoln. Judge Willson asked: "Now, if this case was being tried on issue joined in a habeas corpus, and it appeared there, as it does here, that this slave owner had brought this mother and her children, voluntarily, from the State of Kentucky, and had settled them down on his farm in this State, do you think, as a matter of law, that they did not thereby become free?" And Lincoln answered, "No, sir, I am not prepared to deny that they did."

Linder then argued, for Matson, that slaves were chattel property, the Federal Constitution protected such property, and it could not lawfully be taken from him. But the court decree on October 17, 1847, declared Jane Bryant and her four children "are discharged from the custody as well of the Sheriff as of Robert Matson and all persons claiming them as slaves, and they shall be and remain free from all servitude whatever to any person or persons from henceforward and forever."

And Matson quietly slipped away toward the Wabash River, quit the county, and without paying Lincoln his fee. Rutherford saw Lincoln leave Charleston for the next county on the circuit. "As he threw across the animal's back his saddlebags, filled with soiled linen and crumpled court papers, and struck out across the prairie, he gave no sign of any regret because, as a lawyer, he had upheld the cause of the strong against the weak." Thus spoke Rutherford, who had put up the barriers after Lincoln had gone the limit trying to break into the case on the side he preferred.

As Lincoln straddled his gray mare and rode in the October prairie haze, he might have recalled the remark he once made to a lawyer who had asked him to go in on a case he didn't believe in, and he had said: "You'll have to get some other fellow to win this case for you. I couldn't do it. All the while I'd be talking to that jury I'd be thinking, 'Lincoln, you're a liar,' and I believe I should forget myself and say it out loud."

The Jim Wheat Murder Case*

CLINTON GIDDINGS BROWN

Every now and then a case comes along in court which attracts attention not because of its sensationalism or the fine points of law involved but simply because it is heart-warming and human. Such is the story of little Lige which follows.

The author, Clinton G. Brown, is a retired trial lawyer living in San Antonio, Texas. He began to practice in 1906 and usually defended corporations in personal-injury damage suits. He became District Attorney of Bexar County in 1913 and served two terms as Mayor of San Antonio from 1914 on, resigning to serve in France. In 1955 Mr. Brown found time to set down his reminiscences in a volume entitled You May Take the Witness, *a work which combines tough legal experience, humor, sentiment, and rich folk background.*

I have mentioned earlier that in the matter of promoting sentiment and sympathy, I was always on the wrong side of the docket. I was the lawyer for the big rich company against the little man. (I was well paid for it, but I sure did work hard to hold the job. However, after I joined the firm bills never worried me any more, but I am sorry to say I did not save much money. I had a good time spending it, though.)

I don't believe I could have stood up under the responsibility of being the little man's lawyer all the time. I hated very much to lose a verdict for any company we represented in court, but I knew that such losses were figured in as a regular percentage of corporation operating expenses. Losing a case was not a terrible disaster to a company, though it was often a disaster to my vanity.

But suppose I am the lawyer for the plaintiff. He comes to me for help. He is relying on me alone. I investigate the case, believe that the company was at fault for the accident, and know that my man is badly hurt. He has a wife and kids, and on account of his injury will never be able to hold down his old job again. Suppose I make a mistake in trying his case. Suppose I forget something. Suppose I do *one little thing* the wrong way, and that causes him to lose his case. His case is not "a percentage of operating expenses." His case is everything. I do not believe I could have stood up under it. I would have worried myself to death.

When I was district attorney, I learned something about criminal law, and after I got out of the Army and started practicing law again, before I joined the firm, I did have a few clients who had been charged with murder—but a *very* few. I just couldn't take that either, and so I made it a rule when a man charged with murder wanted to hire me to be his lawyer, I would send him to some good criminal lawyer. Suppose in the trial I made a mistake that caused his electrocution or caused him to go to the pen for life! No, I just couldn't do it. I realize that saying so is an admission of weakness, but the weakness is there, it always has been there, and it always will be there.

But then old Jim Wheat killed a white man.

When I was a boy Jim Wheat worked as our yard man for several years. He always helped me with my chickens and pigeons and we became great friends. But one time he did something that displeased my father (I never did understand what it was), and my father felt he had to discharge him.

In the little room where he had lived, next to the stable, I watched him put his stuff in a sack, and then I followed him down the driveway to the double gates. When he shook my hand and said, "Well, good-by, Clint," I just could say, "Well, good-by, Jim,"—and he was gone.

Jim went back to Luling and got a job on a farm. The first Thanksgiving he sent us a fine big turkey, addressed to my mother, and for Christmas she sent him a Christmas present worth a whole lot more than the turkey, and this exchange of gifts, of about the same respective values, was repeated annually until my mother's death. After that I lost track of him for many years, though I did hear that he had married and was sharecropping a small farm near Luling. And then one day I got a letter from him.

Old Jim Wheat had killed a white man, and in the whole wide world, he had nobody to help him but me and his little eleven-year-old grandson, who lived with him on the farm near Luling. His wife was dead. His children were all dead.

Jim was not a big man. After the killing, to get him away from the mob, the sheriff of that county had handcuffed him to two big deputies, right hand and left hand, and shipped him over to Giddings for safekeeping. There was a very kindhearted deputy sheriff at the jail in Giddings (and it's strange indeed for a deputy to be that kindhearted), who wrote down what Jim dictated in a letter and sent it to me.

I still have that old file and that letter. When I was writing this book I read the letter over and realized that it was very long and had many repetitions in it, and several times I tried to shorten it, but finally I decided just to put it all in for what it is worth.

Dear Mr. Clint Brown: I am Jim Wheat. I am the colored man that used to work for your papa as yard man when you all lived on Ninth Street. I guess you will remember me when I say I used to throw down to you the best and most ripest figs when I was picking figs for breakfast, and I showed you how to take care of your chickens and your pigeons.

Mr. Clint I am in awful bad trouble. I killed a white man up at Luling and they brought me over to Giddings to keep the crowd from hanging me. Please help me Mr. Clint. Last year I got my wagon and my plow and my good span of six year old mules all paid for and you can get maybe a hundred dollars for them. I will give them all to you. I haven't got nobody else to help me but just you and my grandson. He is eleven years old and his name is Lige. I mended a whole string of fence for Mr. Walters and he said he would pay me $7.00 if I mended the fence. I mended it good and next Saturday after I got through mending the fence I went over to his house to get my $7.00. He told me I did not drive the staples in hard enough. I went back and covered the whole string of fence and drove in every single staple just as hard as any living man in the world could drive them in and then I went back to his house to get my $7.00 but he wouldn't pay me. He said the barb wires were all loose on the fence and he wasn't going to pay out his good money for a bad job like that. So I took Lige along and we tightened up the wires on the fence as good as we could but we couldn't tighten them up so very much because I had drove in the staples so hard. I went back to see Mr. Walters late the next evening to try to get my $7.00 and Lige went with me, and Mr. Walters was out behind the barn trying to shoot some rats that were gnawing a hole in his corn crib. When he saw us he called me some bad names and I knew he was drunk. He was plumb drunk. He called me some more bad names and told me to get off of his land. He said he was tired of fooling with me and he didn't owe me one cent. He said I ruined his fence instead of mending it and he said if he couldn't get rid of me one way he would get rid of me another way and he started to raise up his shotgun. I snatched up a hatchet that was laying right there on the ground by the barn wall and flung it at him hard and the sharp part of the hatchet caught him right in the middle of the front part of his head and killed him deader than a door nail. The people up at Luling wanted to hang me but the Sheriff sent me over to Giddings. The man who is writing this letter for me is very nice to me. His name is Mr. John Jones. He is a deputy sheriff here. If you come down here to see me Mr. Clint Mr. John Jones will show you where my cell is. Please come down here to see me Mr. Clint. My little grandson Lige is at the colored Protestant's Orphans home in Luling. If you can come down to see me Mr. Clint a pint of gin and a plug of Big Bale chewing tobacco sure would come in handy. Please come down here to see me Mr. Clint.

From your old colored friend,
Jim Wheat

P. S. Mr. Clint I want to tell you something else I forgot to tell you in the main part of my letter. Another colored man was in the same cell with me that first day up at Luling and he told me it said in the newspaper that I took my hatchet and went over to Mr. Walters house and beat him to death. But Mr. Clint that ain't so. It just ain't so. I did not even have a hatchet. That hatchet I flung at Mr. Walters was his own hatchet. When he started to aim at me with that shotgun his hatchet was laying right there on the ground right next to the barn wall and I snatched up his hatchet and flung it at him hard. But it was his own hatchet. It was not my hatchet. Lige was the only one who saw the whole business and Lige knows it was not my hatchet. I have got nothing but a hammer and a old saw and a axe. About three years ago I had a good hatchet but I was cutting up fire wood down by the river and broke the handle on my hatchet and I just flung the head down on the ground and left it laying right there on the ground but I knew where I flung it down and a few days later it rained some and the water looked like good cat-fish water and she was up about a foot and moving pretty pert and I needed a good sinker to hold my line down and there was the head of my hatchet laying right there on the ground where I flung it down and I took a stick and knocked the end of the handle out of the hole and it made a sure enough good heavy sinker but that night she rose about six feet and it was not a cat that broke my line because I had a sure enough good line but my line must have got caught on some drift wood because in the morning it was broke off and the head of my hatchet was gone. You see Mr. Clint it was not my hatchet that I flung at Mr. Walters. I didn't even have a hatchet. How could I fling my hatchet at him when my hatchet was somewhere on the bottom of the river. It took us all of Mr. John Jones spare time for two days to write this letter to you and Mr. John Jones says it don't make no difference to him what name a bottle has got on it just so it is a quart instead of a pint and if you do come down here to help me Mr. Clint please don't forget about that pint of gin and that plug of Big Bale chewing tobacco I asked you about and please come down here to help me Mr. Clint. Please come down here to help me.

From your old colored friend,
Jim Wheat

I guess some money-makers would say I was a damned fool, but when I read that letter from Jim I canceled all engagements and lit out for Giddings, hell-bent for breakfast. On the way through Luling I picked up Lige, the grandson, and after I got to Giddings I picked up a quart of good stuff for the deputy sheriff and two pints of good gin and four hunks of Big Bale chewing tobacco for Jim, and the four of us went into a huddle in Jim's cell, and the stake was—shall old Grandpappy Jim live or die? They all counted on me to save him. (God help me! God help me!)

I knew Jim and Lige and I would be loyal to the cause, but how about this deputy sheriff? He seemed to like Jim but I had to be sure. I couldn't take a chance. I approached the problem directly. I asked Jim to excuse us a minute and went out into the hall with Mr. Jones.

"Mr. Jones, why are you so interested in Jim Wheat?"

"Well," he said, "I tell you. There is just something I like about old Jim. And another thing is that my folks have always lived in the South, and we have been with the colored people so long that we know something about the difference between the bad ones and the good ones. I think old Jim is a good one and I believe he is telling the truth. I'd like to help him if I can. That's why I took up all that time writing that long letter."

"O.K. Shake," I said, and from the look in his eyes and from his handshake I was satisfied.

I told them that the first thing I was going to do was try to get Jim out on bail, and then I'd try to get a change of venue. I explained that the law is that if it can be shown to the satisfaction of the judge that the sentiment in the county where the crime was committed is such that it is probable that a fair trial cannot be had in that county, the judge, in his discretion, may transfer the case to another county for trial. I told them I would attend to that part of the campaign. I asked Jim for the names of a few of the smartest, best-informed Negroes in Luling. I wasn't planning to use them as witnesses, I just wanted to talk to them to get the low-down.

I made arrangements to pay Mr. John Jones six dollars every Sunday that he could go over to Luling. That did not interfere with his regular job as a deputy sheriff; it would just be money on the side. I told Jim I did not want his plow, wagon, and mules and that I was the lawyer for the S. P. and had a free pass over all the railroads in Texas and could come down to Luling or Giddings any time I wanted to without it costing me a cent, and that I would be his lawyer for nothing and try to help him out all I could, and he would not owe me one cent.

That broke poor old Jim down, and he cried and sobbed like a baby and kept on saying, "God bless you, Mr. Clint, God bless you, Mr. Clint," and little Lige chimed in too, and walled his white eyes around and the tears were just streaming down his shiny little black face, and he kept saying, "He wus goin' a shoot Grandpappy. He was goin' a shoot Grandpappy." It embarrassed me so much that I said I had to go to the toilet, and I went out in the hall and stood by the barred window and the cool breeze blew on my face, and all of a sudden, I knew how to try that lawsuit. Just let them alone! Just let them alone—if you try to give them *any* instructions you might cramp their style. Just let them alone. Just let them alone.

I told Mr. Jones to go up to Luling next Sunday and stir around and learn the sentiment of the people about Jim Wheat and the dead man. I told him not to go "undercover" but to come right out and say he was employed by Jim Wheat and me. I planned to spend the next week end in Luling, too.

Jim told me that Mr. Wright, the president of the Luling National Bank, had known him a long time, because he always kept his money in that bank when he had any, and sometimes borrowed a few dollars from the bank and always paid it back; and he told me he always bought his grocery supplies and feed from Mr. Slick's General Store, and that Mr. Slick was a good merchant and stocked a good line of stuff and always gave you fair weight on the scales if you were careful enough to stand right close to the scale and look right at it, and Jim said there was nothing against Mr. Slick except he loved his right eyeball a little less than he loved a dollar. A trial lawyer must pick up every little straw that floats by within reaching distance.

I asked my father if he knew Mr. Wright, and he said Mr. Wright was one of the best friends he had in the banking business in southwest Texas, and he gave me a nice letter of introduction. He also told me that he knew young Mr. Hamilton, cashier of the bank, and that Mr. Hamilton was ambitious and wanted to move to a bigger city and had been trying to get a job with my father at the Alamo National Bank. I filed that straw for future reference.

Next Saturday morning I handed my letter of introduction to Mr. Wright in Luling. He was very cordial, and he introduced me to Mr. Hamilton. I realized from Mr. Hamilton's attitude toward me that Mr. Hamilton had caught the point (important to Mr. Hamilton), that I was the son of J. N. Brown, president of the Alamo National Bank in San Antonio. Mr. Wright said he admired my father very much and thought he was the best banker in all of southwest Texas. He invited me to go to the Methodist Church with him Sunday morning and to have Sunday dinner at his home. On Sunday he introduced me to the preacher, and I told the preacher I was a Methodist, but I did not tell him I was such a back-sliding Methodist that I had not been to church in ten years, except to weddings and funerals. He had a large congregation that morning, and upon inquiry I learned that he had many friends in town and was very highly regarded.

All that day I did not mention to Mr. Wright what I had in mind, because I thought it would be discourteous to try to mix business with pleasure, and I wanted him to get to know me. But it was no secret of course that I was Jim Wheat's lawyer in the murder case.

Monday morning I went to the bank without kid gloves on. Mr. Hamilton was in Mr. Wright's private office. I told them Jim wasn't eating anything and was just pining away in the cell over at Giddings and that I had to get him out of jail. I asked them to sign his bond. They did so, and I had Jim and Lige back with the mules and the pig and the turkeys and chickens before sundown that next Wednesday.

A few weeks later I went to Giddings again to go into a huddle with Mr. Jones, the deputy sheriff. (I'm proud to say that the town was named after the man I was named after, my great-uncle, Colonel DeWitt Clinton Giddings. My mother used to tell me about him when I was a boy. He had come to Texas from Pennsylvania, and in 1852 began to practice law in Brenham, Texas. Though he wasn't in favor of secession, he served in the Confederate Army as a lieutenant colonel in the 21st Texas Cavalry. In 1870 he accepted the Democratic nomination to the Forty-second Congress, but there followed quite a hassle with his carpetbag opponent, who was backed by the governor. He finally uncovered a lot of rascality on the part of the carpetbagger, and the House of Representatives declared Colonel Giddings entitled to the Congress seat. Later on he was a banker in Brenham, and he was three times a delegate to the Democratic National Convention.)

Mr. Jones had spent two Saturday afternoons and Sundays in Luling, and from what he had heard about how Jim Wheat was regarded and how the dead man was regarded, and from what I had heard in my own rounds, I decided not to apply for a change of venue and to play the final game on our own home grounds. The threat of a lynching seemed to have cooled off.

I kept wishing that I had some good reason for continuing the case until the second term of court, became a little water under the bridge has never yet harmed a defendant in a criminal case, but the district attorney, who was fat, pompous, and ambitious, had set the case for trial as the first one on the criminal docket at the next term of court. There was nothing I could do about it, so I concentrated on rounding up some good character witnesses for Jim and on plans for picking a jury and trying the case.

Mr. Wright at the bank said he would be glad to testify that he had known Jim Wheat for many years and knew his general reputation in the community of being a peaceful and law-abiding citizen. Mr. Hamilton was a cinch, and the preacher at the colored Methodist Church was a cinch; that made three, but I wanted to back them up with the preacher from the white Methodist Church and with Mr. Slick, the owner of the general store. If Mr. Slick did not testify he would be conspicuous by his absence, because Jim had traded with him for so many years. But I nosed around and found out that the dead man had traded there too and had friends among Mr. Slick's other customers, and so I was afraid I might not be able to land Mr. Slick.

I picked my character witnesses, not for quantity, but for quality. I guess I could have had fifty character witnesses, some black and some white, but I did not want too many. If you put too many witnesses on the stand and every one of them says the same thing, the jury will stop paying attention to any of them after a while.

I asked the preacher of the colored Methodist Church to take a committee and visit the preacher of the white Methodist Church and ask him to please help Jim any way he could, being sure to tell him that Jim attended services regularly and was a regular financial contributor. After this preliminary missionary work had had time to take root, I visited the white preacher and told him that Mr. Wright was going to testify in Jim's favor. So he was a cinch. That made four.

But how about Mr. Slick, the grocer? Remembering what Jim had told me about Mr. Slick's right eye, I concocted a little scheme that I hoped might entice Mr. Slick to help us. I told Jim to go to Mr. Slick and tell him that since he got into this trouble he had had to spend all of his cash, and to give Mr. Slick a chattel mortgage on his mules and his crop to cover his future grocery bill and other purchases. I suggested that Jim run his bill up as high as he could by buying nonperishable stuff, but not to run it up high enough to make Mr. Slick suspicious. Jim told me about a week later that for several years he had needed a new set of harness awful bad, and a few days after he gave Mr. Slick the mortgage he bought a complete new double set of harness from him, and his bill was already bigger than it ever was before. I figured that Mr. Slick loved money more than he did mules, and if Jim were electrocuted he would have mules on his hands instead of money. So, when I dropped in on Mr. Slick a few days before the trial, bought a carton of Lucky Strike cigarettes, and told him that I hoped he would join Mr. Wright (Mr. Hamilton having informed me that Mr. Slick always had a considerable account at the bank on the promissory note side of the docket), Mr. Hamilton, and the two preachers in testifying as to Jim's good reputation, he was a cinch. He said he would be glad to do so and had wondered why I hadn't asked him before. I didn't tell him why I hadn't asked him before.

Five character witnesses; that was enough.

The case was to be called for trial Monday, but Saturday Lige fell out of a big pecan tree and broke his leg. I got the case continued for three months until the next term of court. We were in the outfield. Strike-a-one.

But finally we had to try it. I decided to use my challenges to get any poor white trash off of the jury, because they don't like good, hard-working colored people. I wanted jurors who knew Jim and who had known the dead man; I didn't want the dead man's relatives or warm personal friends. With the aid of tips from Mr. Hamilton, I got on the jury several men who owed money to the Luling National Bank, because Mr. Wright was going to testify in Jim's favor. I also got all the Methodists I could.

The State proved, beyond any question, that Jim Wheat had killed Mr. Walters.

Lige was my first witness.

I remember that his feet did not touch the floor as he sat in the witness chair, his shoes were highly polished, his shirt was nice and clean and stiffly starched, he had gotten a new haircut, his little black face was shiny from soap and water, his perfect teeth were very white, and his eyes were as bright as diamonds.

If a child is so young and ignorant that he does not comprehend the sanctity and obligation of an oath, the judge should rule that he is not qualified to testify. The opposing lawyer has a right when a child is put on the stand to find out, before he can testify, if he comprehends the sanctity and obligation of an oath. I knew this, and at first I thought maybe I had better explain it to Lige a little, but I decided to let him alone. I thought (and hoped) that he would be able to take care of himself better without any instructions from me.

After Lige was sworn and had stated his age, that his name was Elijah Wheat, and that he was Jim Wheat's grandson, the district attorney rose and said:

"May it please the Court, the State demands the privilege of testing this witness to ascertain if he comprehends the sanctity and obligation of an oath."

"You have that right," said the judge. "Proceed."

"Your name is Elijah Wheat?" asked the district attorney.

"Yes, sir, it sure is, but everybody calls me Lige."

(The court reporter in the transcript did not attempt to reproduce the dialect of the witness.)

"You say you are eleven years old?"

"Yes, sir, eleven years old, going on twelve."

"Do you comprehend the sanctity and obligation of an oath?"

"Excuse me, Mister, but is you talking to me?"

"Yes, of course I'm talking to you."

"Well, I sorry, Mister, but I don't know what you are talking about."

The judge: "Mr. District Attorney, please phrase your inquiry in simpler language."

"Yes, sir. All right, Your Honor. Do you know what an oath is?"

"Sure. I knows what an oat is."

"Well, what is an oath?"

"Well, I tell you. I knows lots of oats but I don't want to say none of them right here where all these nice white folks can hear me."

"Listen to me. Yes, I'll make it simple, Judge. Tell me, what is an oath?"

"Please, Mister Judge, do I have to tell him what a oat is?"

The judge: "Yes, Lige, go ahead and tell him."

"Well, then, if I has to say it, I has to say it. If a white man gets mad at me and calls me a 'goddam stinking little black nigger son-of-a-bitch,' why, that's a oat."

There was some laughter, the judge rapped with his gavel, and Lige looked embarrassed and worried. I wanted badly to get up and try to coach him from the sidelines, but I held myself down.

"Do you know who God is?" the district attorney asked.

"Do I know who God is? You asking me do I know who God is? I sure do. That's one thing I *do* know."

"Well, who is God?"

Lige looked over at old Jim and asked in a loud whisper, "Must I tell him, Grandpappy?"

"Sure, Lige, go on and tell him as good as you can."

Lige did not look at the district attorney. He looked at the wall across the courtroom and said in a lower, slower voice,

"God is my kind father in Heaven, and he takes me by the hand when I am tired and leads me down to a nice cool river and shows me a soft, smooth, grassy place to sleep, and he sees every good thing I do and every bad thing I do, but I don't know what God's got to do with this killing."

"Do you read the Bible?"

"No, sir, Grandpappy can read better than me and he reads it to me every night. Sometimes I am so tired I get sleepy but I always wakes up when he starts reading anything about the animals, and I hear the preacher reading it every Sunday at the Methodist Sunday School."

"If you hold up your hand and swear to tell the truth, so help you God, and then tell a lot of lies, what is going to happen to you?"

"I'll burn up in hell so quick it'll make your head swim."

At this juncture the judge frowned at the district attorney, and ruled, in a voice that was somewhat harsh,

"This boy is qualified to testify."

I had one surprise for the State. I proved by the local scoutmaster and some little Kodak pictures that, at my request and when I offered a ten-dollar cash prize to the diver who could find it, the scoutmaster had taken his Boy Scout troop out to Jim's place, and Jim had shown them where he had lost the head of his old hatchet, and they had dived and dived for more than an hour until finally one of the boys came up with it and got the prize. I put the head of Jim's old rusty hatchet and the Kodak pictures on the table where all the jury could look at them for the rest of the trial.

All of my witnesses stood up just fine. But the best of all were Lige and Jim. I had given them absolutely no instructions. I just let them alone.

Old Jim was just wonderful—calm, dignified, and respectful but not humble, and everybody who heard him knew that every single word that came from his lips was the absolute truth. And Lige! Well, the truth is that this pencil is too dull for me to try to describe Lige and his testimony. Lige was more than wonderful; he was superb! After all my years of trial work, Lige remains to this day the best and most effective witness I ever saw on the witness stand.

The jury stayed out only twenty-two minutes and brought in a verdict of "Not Guilty."

I had not eaten any lunch because I had to make my speech in the afternoon, and after the verdict came in I was so tired I was not hungry and just felt like I wanted to lie down somewhere on a good bed and go to sleep and sleep for a week.

Mr. John Jones had driven his Ford over for the trial. I told him I was not going home that night and that I wanted to go out to Jim's place and rest up a little, and I asked him to borrow a tent and two cots and some blankets from the sheriff. We put Jim and Lige, the tent, the cots, and the blankets in the back seat and drove over to Mr. Slick's General Store. On the way a good many people, white and black, smiled and waved at us, and it made old Jim very happy, and it made me happy, too.

We bought a good supply of solid refreshments from Mr. Slick, and did not charge them to Jim's mule mortgage. I paid cash, and did not even glance at the scale while Mr. Slick was weighing out the stuff, and I bought a good supply of all-day suckers for Lige. We went next to the liquor store, and laid in a good supply of liquid refreshment, as well as smoking and chewing tobacco, twelve bottles of pink soda water for Lige, and two hundred pounds of ice. We pitched our tent on the river bank, not far from Jim's cabin, and Lige soon collected wood and had a good fire going.

Somebody has said that you may forget the statuary and cathedrals and scenery you have seen on a journey, but you will probably remember the time when you put your legs under the table, across from your good friend, at the little wayside inn, and had something good to eat and something good to drink. That trial happened a good many years ago, but I remember to this day exactly what I had for supper at old Jim's campfire that night.

We ate off tin plates and drank out of tin cups. From the cabin Lige brought a straight chair for Mr. John Jones, and Jim brought me a most comfortable, weak-legged old rocking chair. Jim and Lige sat on a log, to do the cooking and keep the fire going.

They would not let us get up. They waited on us as if we were kings. As soon as I got comfortable in my rocking chair, the first thing I had was a long toddy, with very little sugar in it, a little ice, and a sprig of mint. And then I had another one.

For salad we each had a nice cool tomato, not cut in slices to make it look pretty, but cut in quarters so a man could eat it without most of the best part spilling out, and we had a wonderful salad dressing, made out of nothing but salt. The second course consisted of three cans of Campbell's vegetable soup, warmed up to a nice heat but not hot enough to burn your tongue off.

A broiler looking as if it used to be the bottom part of a stationary engine was propped up on four rocks, one at each of its corners, over a little separate fire, and Jim said the fire was made out of nothing but hickory wood, because that would make the broiled sausages taste better. Jim got the hickory coals spread out good and the link sausages spread out good on top of the broiler, turned the long fork over to Lige, and started making the coffee.

After Jim got the coffee going, he said, "Lige, you listen to me. If you let those sausages burn up, I'll take the hide off of you," and Lige said.

"I'm watching them good, Grandpappy. I got my eagle eye glued tight on every single one of them."

So then we had link pork sausages, broiled over a hickory fire, and seasoned from a big jar of Mr. Slick's best sweet-pickle relish, and we had fresh baker's bread, hot coffee, and for dessert, all-day suckers. For my dessert I had another long toddy, which was consumed in a leisurely manner.

Lige did most of the talking that night. He and Jim used the dialect of country colored people, and, although I have been around colored people since I was born, I will not try here to reproduce their dialect, because I am afraid I cannot do it well enough. On account of the excitement of the verdict, and the proper amount of solid and liquid refreshment, I remember some of the conversation to this very day.

With a sausage in one hand and two pieces of baker's bread in the other, and his mouth so full he could hardly speak, Lige said,

"This sausage sure is good. Grandpappy sure knows how to cook good. He can cook anything so it tastes good, but the best thing he can cook is squirrel stew. When he wants to cook a squirrel stew he gets some onions and some Irish potatoes and I goes over to Mr. Black's house and borrows his twenty-two rifle off of him. I sure can knock 'em down good if I ever get this eagle eye on 'em. I knocks 'em down and Grandpappy cooks 'em, and he always puts in plenty of black pepper."

Here Jim interrupted. "Lige, keep your mouth shut. You're doing all the talking. Get yourself up off of this log and give Mr. Clint and Mr. John Jones some more sausages."

From snatches of conversation I had heard between Jim and Lige around the fire I know that Lige was puzzled about why the district attorney had asked him about God. After we were all through supper, Lige came back to the fire after taking the tin plates to the cabin, put another piece of wood on the fire, sat down by Jim on the log, and with a bottle of pink soda water in one hand he took a red all-day sucker out of his mouth with the other, and said in a hoarse whisper,

"Mr. Clint, what did the judge mean when he said, kinder mean-like, 'This boy is qualified to testify'? Is it something like crucify? Is they going to do something to me for saying that bad oat right there in front of everybody? The judge told me to say it, but maybe he didn't know how dirty it was going to be."

I motioned for Lige to come over and sit down by me. I leaned his shoulder against my knee and patted his kinky head and explained as well as I could all about the obligation of an "oat," and after a while he got so sleepy he could hardly hold his head up, and old Jim picked him up and carried him to the cabin.

Next day at about four o'clock when we got back to Luling I told Mr. Jones to take us to Mr. Slick's store and I ushered them all into the hardware department. I told old Jim to pick out the best new hatchet in the store and that I was going to give it to him for a present.

I took Lige by the hand and led him down to the big showcase where there were all kinds of guns on exhibition. We didn't go fast. We admired the deer rifles and the single-barrel and double-barrel shotguns, and finally we got down to the corner where they had the .22 rifles on display, new and secondhand. I bought Lige the best brand-new single-shot .22 rifle that they had in the store, and a good ramrod, and a good canvas case to keep the rifle in so it would not get rusty, and a can of gun oil, and one hundred cartridges, fifty longs and fifty shorts. When Lige stood there in the aisle of that country store, with the rifle in his right hand and the ramrod in his left, the oil can and the one hundred cartridges in his pockets, and the canvas case across one shoulder, and finally realized that they were his very own, his very own, he could not say a word. For the first time in his life Lige was absolutely speechless.

I dipped in next door to the liquor store and bought a last quart of good stuff for Mr. John Jones and had them wrap it up in four or five bags so it would look like a bag of potatoes that this peace officer was carrying home.

As the wheels of the train began to turn, I waved through the window to the Three Musketeers on the platform, and Mr. John Jones waved his bag of potatoes, old Jim waved his new hatchet, and dear little Lige waved his rifle in his right hand and his ramrod in his left. Then I settled back in the corner of the seat and went to sleep.

That was a wonderful case.

Knight with the Rueful Countenance*

(Profile of Lloyd Paul Stryker)

ALEXANDER WOOLLCOTT

Lloyd Paul Stryker (1885–1955) was one of the best known criminal lawyers in New York. He was educated at Hamilton College and was admitted to the bar in 1909. Among his writings are a life of Andrew Johnson (1929), Courts and Doctors (1932), and a biography of Thomas Erskine (1947). The Art of Advocacy was published in 1954, the year before his death.

Alexander Woollcott (1887–1943) first became widely known as dramatic critic for the New York World. Later his book reviews and short pieces for the New Yorker, as well as his radio work as the Town Crier from 1929 to 1942, enormously extended his audiences.

Not so long ago—it was some years after the house of cards fell down in 1929—a widow with a grievance came on from St. Louis in quest of a champion. Fortified with a letter of introduction from the old family lawyer, she gained access even to a hushed and innermost sanctum in one of the more imposing of our law firms. A multitude of clerks, young law-school graduates, and stenographers milled and murmured on the outer ramparts. But this was the office of a partner. It was a sympathetic and silver-haired member of the New York bar who received her and who, for the purposes of this cautious narrative, shall be known as Mr. A. To Mr. A she told her story.

It seemed that when her husband died, a life-long friend of his had volunteered to help her with all the vexing little problems of investment which had so suddenly and so frighteningly overwhelmed her. A banker chap, this friend was privy to such mysteries. Besides, he had been poor, dear John's roommate at Williams and best man at their wedding. Why, he had even stood up as godfather when Junior was christened. Yet now it began to look as if Junior might be unable to finish *his* course at Williams, for, under Godpapa's tender fiduciary care, the family fortune had dwindled to nothing.

Furthermore, all the available data tended to suggest that Godpapa had invested this widow's mite in securities belonging to his firm and with a neat little profit to the firm at that. Dear, dear, that was naughty of Godpapa. Did she have any remedy at law? Yes, an action would lie. And Mr. A would take her case? No—this with genuine regret—no, that would be impossible.

It was not without some pensive pacing of the thick beige carpet that Mr. A told her why. You see, one of his many partners happened to have this very banking house of Godpapa's for a client and even if there were not this complicating coincidence, he himself was retained annually by several private bankers who, and not unreasonably, would resent his taking the intimate knowledge of banking practice he had thereby acquired and using it for the discomfiture of a neighbor. Indeed, he could think of no considerable law firm in all the city which, while recognizing the justice of her grievance, would not feel, for one reason or another, a similar embarrassment.

The widow from St. Louis grew acrid. Was there no such thing in New York as an independent lawyer? Apparently she must go looking for one who had no partners and no clients. Yes, Mr. A agreed, and furthermore a lawyer of such experience and standing that he could take on a formidable antagonist. With heavy St. Louis sarcasm the widow said she assumed Mr. A could name her a dozen such to choose from. No, but he could name her one. For the life of him he couldn't think of two. Just one. For her convenience he wrote out the name and address of that one on a slip of paper—Lloyd Paul Stryker, 40 Wall Street.

"If you can get Stryker interested," Mr. A explained, as he escorted his visitor to the door, "he'll take your case and enjoy it. You see, he likes fights and has a distaste for bankers." The visitor brightened up at the prospect of meeting someone after her own heart. "Has he been swindled, too?" she asked hopefully. "No," said Mr. A with a reminiscent smile, "he just dislikes bankers instinctively."

By the way, Mr. Stryker did take that case, putting on for the purpose a first-rate imitation of a dragon-slayer, and won it hands down—even unto the Court of Appeals. But that is another story. *This* story is merely an attempt at a likeness of one who is a curious mixture of Clarence Darrow, Demosthenes, the late Abe Levy, St. George, William Sylvanus Baxter, Jr., and a bull of Bashan. It will be read the more charitably by those who recall that a profile is a portrait with some of the features only half visible and some of them not visible at all.

Some glimpses of this fabulous mixture in action will be available to sightseers next week in the Court of General Sessions. Come early and bring your lunch. Also, in case counsel for the defence really gets going, bring some cotton wool to put in your ears. For on Monday, if the schedule is adhered to, one James J. Hines must, for the second time, stand his trial under a conspiracy indictment which, in effect, charges him with having been the broker through whom the scoundrels of the policy racket bought their immunity from prosecution. And once again Lloyd Stryker will defend him.

It will be remembered that the first attempt to lay this district leader by the heels was halted midway one day in September when, despite several stern admonitions from the bench, the District Attorney so persisted in a certain line of questioning that Justice Pecora declared a mistrial. This ruling evoked from the laity (editorial writers included) an extraordinary amount of unenlightened comment. But none of it revealed so befuddled an understanding of the very theory of the law as did the widespread wonder that a lawyer of Mr. Stryker's standing had been willing to appear in such a cause at all. Among the people with whom he grew up and in all the better golf clubs where, with unflagging ardor, he swings an indifferent niblick, he must have been conscious of raised eyebrows and even, in extreme cases, of a few rather pointed shudders. An illuminating instance of just such behavior is examined in that part of the new biography of Elihu Root where Professor Jessup deals with the trial of a somewhat earlier Tammany chieftain named Tweed. It is a familiar American attitude which always puzzles the English, who, whenever a barrister has come majestically to the defence in enough gaudy murder cases, are quite likely to give him a knighthood. The contrary disposition in this country, in so far as it makes any sense at all, would seem to imply that whereas even a Bruno Hauptmann, when on trial for his life, is entitled to the services of a lawyer, he is surely not entitled to the services of a good one. As a healthful exercise in self-examination, it is hereby suggested to the aforesaid shudderers that they look into their hearts and ask themselves whether they would even have winced if, instead of representing Hines, Mr. Stryker had gone into court in behalf of Richard Whitney.

However, the whole point of raising this ethical question here is for the opportunity of saying that in this instance it is purely academic. In the trial about to reëngage his attention, Mr. Stryker believes absolutely in the stainless innocence of his snow-white client. Anyone who has known Mr. Stryker well could tell you that. There is no doubt about it whatever. You see, Lloyd Stryker always does believe in the innocence of his clients.

The cynical will too hastily assume that such faith must be a purchasable article. But Mr. Stryker need not take any case unless he is genuinely interested and, whatever his preliminary doubts, once he plunges in, his client not only can do no wrong but never could have done any. Wherefore it is safe to assume that by this time the aforesaid Hines in his lawyer's eyes (and possibly to his own surprise) is not only innocent of the specific crime of which he stands accused and a cruelly wronged citizen but so rare a blend of all the virtues as to be almost indistinguishable from St. Francis of Assisi.

What is really at work here in behalf of Hines is a unique capacity for violent partisanship. That capacity was in full flower when, a few years ago, Mr. Stryker devoted no small part of his prodigious energy to writing the life of Andrew Johnson. His vivid and engrossing biography of that luckless man is 824 pages of passionate special pleading in which Stanton and Sumner and Thaddeus Stevens and Ben Butler all appear as such slimy, black-hearted villains that any reader reared on the old saying about there being two sides to every question instinctively hurries to the nearest reference library for a little sobering corrective.

In 1929, President Coolidge named Stryker to a judgeship and those to whom he is dear must be glad that, through a freakish prank of fate, the nomination miscarried. No doubt Stryker would have brought sound learning, ripe experience, and incorruptible honor to the Federal Court. Probably he would even have striven to be judicial. But this uncongenial effort would, it is certain, have led to his early death from apoplexy—right there on the bench, in the climax of some trial.

His ardor of championship derives from a genuine relish for combat as such. Lloyd Stryker might be identified as that member of the New York bar who not only has no partners and (in the sense that he is not a kept lawyer) no clients but who, all things being equal, would rather go to trial than not. In these days such a one is a rare bird. The practice of settling out of court has so gained ground of late that many a noted lawyer can hardly remember when last he underwent the disconcerting experience of trying a case before a jury. Furthermore, it may be guessed that among the many excellent reasons which dictate a settlement in any case is the unconfessed one that, for personal reasons, the counsel involved would a little rather not submit to ordeal by combat. Once down in that dusty and unpredictable arena, the most disturbing things might happen to them. It is too much like running for office. Much pleasanter to be appointed to something. But Stryker has no such reluctance. While, in the interest of his client, he often does settle out of court, the fact that in his heart of hearts he would rather not gives him a tremendous advantage when it comes to bargaining.

A good trial lawyer, says Francis Wellman in his classic work on cross-examination, is the outcome of a generation of witnesses, and Lloyd Stryker owes his present eminence to thirty years of courtroom experience. Thirty years of facing men in groups of twelve. First he faced them in this county as a young and fuming assistant on the staff of District Attorney Whitman —fuming with impatience because his daily chore of prosecuting the obscenities which the late Anthony Comstock used to round up so happily was just marking time for one who meant to be Chief Justice or something. These thirty years of trial work were not even altogether interrupted by the war, because, both at Camp Upton when the 77th Division was in training and later in France, where he served as a lieutenant in the artillery, he defended many an officer in court-martial proceedings. Indeed, on one occasion in the Baccarat sector, the charges of negligence against one exhausted young shavetail were hastily withdrawn by command of divisional headquarters when the rumor ran along the grapevine about the disquieting defence Lieutenant Stryker had thought up for him. Then, after the war, he faced juries in every county of this commonwealth when, as a member of Whiteside & Stryker (which firm represented the Medical Society of the State of New York), he so far conquered his distaste for the physical as to master the mysteries of anatomy. Thus equipped, he ranged from Owego to Oswego, from Ballston Spa to Batavia, defending such local medicos as might be sued for malpractice.

His flood of trial work has increased rather than diminished ever since—in 1930—he decided to give up being a Republican (he who had been brought up in the shadow of Elihu Root and James Schoolcraft Sherman and who had once been secretary of the Union League Club) and while he was in this mood for a *vita nuova* decided also to chuck all retainers, refuse all partners, and go it alone. Sometimes a case of his gets into the newspapers—the defence of District Attorney Geoghan of Brooklyn in the hearing at Albany, for example; or that abortive relief investigation which at least enriched the language with the word "boon-doggling;" or his immensely enjoyable encounter with the New York County Medical Society in its brush with that genius in orthopedic surgery, Dr. Fred H. Albee. But the general reader, of course, hears nothing of the run-of-the-mill cases which tax Stryker most.

Out of his adventures in medical jurisprudence he compiled his *Courts and Doctors,* a unique and indispensable textbook, but compared with his cherished life of Johnson he sets no store by it because, you see, it was born of his everyday activities and on those it is characteristic of him to look with disfavor, whatever they may be. Here—or somewhere near here—is the key to the rueful countenance which is this knight's habitual expression. Here, perhaps, is the answer to the conundrum presented by a man who, to the mystification of his neighbors, manages somehow to combine an infectiously melancholy manner with an insatiable and glowing zest for living. It may seem fanciful to suggest that the melancholy is born of the zest. Yet consider an episode of which the scene is Weimar and the time a day in 1897. With his mother and sisters, Master Lloyd was being exposed to a cultural year in Germany. As a great treat he was taken through the stables of the Crown Prince, from which adventure he came back to the *pension* weeping bitterly. It took some time to find out why. Yes, the stables were wonderful. *Und die Pferde? Ja, sie waren grossartig.* Then what was the trouble? Well, it had just been borne in on him that he could never be Crown Prince.

Even now kindred realizations fill with rue the days of one who—in addition to his present career and all at the same time, mind you—would so like to be an English country gentleman and a really good historian such as the late George Otto Trevelyan and Senator from New York and principal tenor at the Metropolitan. It is literally true that when Lloyd Stryker saw *Libel* he came away from the theatre in a state of fathomless gloom because he had not written it. Sometimes an observer, catching him at lunch at the University Club and noting on his face an expression of utter despair, has reported around town that some case of Stryker's must be going wrong, when the chances are that the great counsellor's thoughts had really been preoccupied by the Blue Hill Troupe. That club of amateurs would be reviving *The Pirates of Penzance* this winter. Just his luck to end up in the chorus again when, if, there were any justice in this world, they would give him the rôle of Frederic, of whom, it will be remembered, the Pirates, as the curtain rises, are warbling thus:

> *Here's good luck to Frederic's ventures!*
> *Frederic's out of his indentures.*

If Stryker likes to sing and, whenever possible, to sing at the top of his lungs, it is only one of the many respects in which he endearingly recalls his father, the late Melancthon Woolsey Stryker, a colorful and endlessly surprising divine, who, in 1892, was called from a Presbyterian pulpit in Chicago to the presidency of Hamilton College. Dr. Stryker was a really superb speaker and it was among his grimmer determinations to make a speaker of this, his younger son, if it killed him (the said son). In the big barn behind the presidential mansion on College Hill, Lloyd in his high-school days was drilled and drilled until he wept from irritation and exhaustion. Even before he entered Hamilton, therefore, he had rung most of the welkins in Oneida County.

There is now no more effective speaker at the New York bar—resourceful, various, dramatic. In his opening speech at the first Hines trial he gave a good account of himself. It may be recalled that the ventilator in the courtroom kept up a competitive rattle which sometimes rendered Mr. Dewey inaudible to everyone except the jurors, who were, after all, the listeners that mattered. Next day, after its vivid report of Stryker's opening, the New York *Times* said:

When he stopped talking the court-room crowd once more became aware of the whirring and buzzing of the air-conditioning apparatus which drowned out Mr. Dewey's words for those in the back rows. No one was conscious of the droning sound while Mr. Stryker was speaking.

That would have pleased his father.

Since he has always had enough vitality for ten men—and still has, despite the fact that he is now a grandfather of several years' standing—

it is one of Stryker's weaknesses as a speaker that he sometimes lets his feelings run away with him and indulges in sonorous periods which can be heard for blocks. When the fit is on him he would, were he speaking in Madison Square Garden, brush aside the amplifier as a crutch needed only by weaklings.

One day last month, in the course of an argument before the Circuit Court of Appeals, even the bench protested. The argument was in the Weiss case, wherein the prosecution in the lower court had relied on evidence obtained by wire-tapping, a detective process which the late Justice Holmes in a dissenting opinion had once characterized as "dirty business." Mr. Stryker quoted that dissent with approval. "Dirty, dirty business," he said, and, finding the phrase sweet to his lips, he kept repeating it with mounting enthusiasm until the courthouse shook and one of the judges, managing somehow to make himself heard, called down, "Don't make so much noise; I can hear you."

This rebuff was followed by one of those moments of aching silence during which no one in the courtroom breathed. Then, ever so quietly, Mr. Stryker made answer, thereby having the last word. Let him also have it here.

"I am very sorry," he said, "that the tone of my voice should have been such as to annoy Your Honor. I regret it. Perhaps my fault lies in the fact that I have never yet been able to encounter outrage with complacence. Nor have I yet attained that poise which would enable me to speak in the quiet tones of equanimity about an effort to strip an American citizen of his liberty by perjured testimony. And yet I have one consolation. As I think back to that little Boston State House in February, 1761, when James Otis before a hostile court thundered against the Writs of Assistance, I am satisfied that he too on that occasion raised his voice."

The Solicitor and the Will*

REGINALD L. HINE

Many British men of law are also devoted to literature, history, and the fine arts. Such a man was Reginald Hine, a highly respected family solicitor living in the little town of Hitchin, in the beautiful county of Hertfordshire. But Hine was also an antiquarian with a sense of humor and a tendency to philosophize. He possessed the same love of curiosa as Sir Thomas Browne and Robert Burton in the seventeenth century. Historian and solicitor, a Fellow of the Society of Antiquaries and a Fellow of the Royal Historical Society, Hine wrote with mellow warmth, and was one of the best raconteurs in the legal profession.

Not many find humor in death. In the following pages, however, Hine completely avoids the mortuary note, and concentrates with delightful effect on the gentle art of dying.

To any old-fashioned person like myself there is much to miss and deplore in the form and subject-matter of modern testaments. One felt happier, legally and religiously, about wills that opened with the hallowed invocation: "In the name of God. Amen." . . . But what can you do, in this irreligious age, with people who are doubtful if they possess a soul to be bequeathed or saved? If we solicitors were to ask for instructions on such a matter they would smile.

Another change for the worse is the gradual displacement of the old family-solicitor-executor by the bank trustee and the public trustee. No doubt there is an advantage in having a trustee who does not die, and who never would play ducks and drakes with the estate. And one must admit there was an atom of truth in the old rhyme:

> Women be forgetful, children be unkind,
> Executors are covetous and take what they can find.

But in the office of a personal representative what you need is not a cold, correct official, an impeccable machine, but a human being, even if he be a fallible mortal, someone who has been the confidant of the testator and his household, the repository of the family secrets, the trusted adviser and friend. If he has seen the deceased through all the troubles and trials of a lifetime, surely he is the best person to see him into the next world, and watch over the interests of his widow and the children. Besides, bank trustees and the public trustee insist on having every detail of the executorship considered in London town; they are not at beck and call, on any daily and hourly emergency, like the solicitor in the next street.

And again, what distant official would dream of carrying out all the hundred-and-one requests and secret trusts confided to a family executor and friend? I am thinking of the pledges I have given to many a dying person to make sure, when the end came, that life was really extinct. I have been asked to place love letters, tresses of hair, and even food, in the coffins of my clients. I promised a lady, whose husband had deserted her, that she should be buried in her wedding dress. I promised a poet that he should be laid to rest with his unpublished poems as a pillow for his head. I have seen the light come back into a dying woman's eyes as I undertook to look after her Shetland ponies and her cats. I have committed breaches of trust finding homes for pets I had been directed to destroy. I have taken many a last message—the secret of a lifetime—to a parson or a priest.

Like every family solicitor, I have gone through hundreds of thousands of papers—some of them very private papers—not consigning them in a blind hurry to the everlasting bonfire, but dealing with them in the way the testator would like best. And once, having found an unfinished manuscript—and there is no more pitiful sight to a man of letters—I completed the work in the style of the deceased and published it posthumously. These are things that no bank trustee or public trustee, even if capable, could fairly be asked to undertake.

In nearly every town, there are to be found friendly and trustworthy people—quite apart from solicitors—willing to act as executors, and something more than executors, in delicate matters of this kind. At Hitchin, a hundred years ago, a certain John Morgan was much in demand for the purpose, because, as parish clerk, he could see the funeral through; as a printer, he could prepare the black-edged memorial cards; and, as a poet, he was always willing to throw in a "copy of verses" for the relations, e.g., "Lines on the very sudden and affecting death of Miss Laura Stanton of Hitchin which took place there on Saturday, January 21, 1832, after a short but severe illness, aged 20. Written on the day of her funeral." He certainly earned his reward: "I give to my friend John Morgan for his trouble my best Nite Gown and my Bigest Boots." Unfortunately, I do not possess Morgan's talent in elegiac verse. But, at the risk of becoming a professional necrologist, I have composed many "personal impressions," and "character sketches" of my client-friends to supplement the formal obituary notices printed in local papers. So many of them have deserved a good remembrance, and of "the last sad offices" it is the one I have liked best to do.

Then, too, in modern will-making, it seems a pity to resort as much as we do to general terms. I suppose one should be pleased to simplify, to shorten. Anything to avoid prolixity and tautology. But "all that my personal estate," "all my furniture and personal belongings," "all my personal chattels as defined by section 55, I (x), of the Administration of Estates Act, 1925"—how dull and unspecific and unsatisfying such formal phrases be—especially in wills, which ought to express the testator's wishes, as far as can legally be allowed, in his self-chosen words. Besides, the legatee likes to know, on the face of the will, just what he is getting. And pieces of furniture too—though classed as goods and chattels—have a life, a personality, of their own. In a poem on *Solitude* my friend Harold Monro wrote of these so-called inanimate objects with understanding:

> The large and gentle furniture has stood
> In sympathetic silence all the day
> With that old kindness of domestic wood.

But there is more in it than kindness. In course of time, standing and serving us generation after generation, these miscalled "pieces" become friends of the family, and ought, with a loving particularity, to be mentioned by name in the will. How often do I turn aside from our bleak and precedent-prepared modern testaments, and dip into my glorious collection of Hitchin wills in medieval, Stuart, and Georgian days, when beds and coffers and tables, "silver sponys," "platterys and pewter dyshes," saucers and candlesticks, and even warming-pans, were handed down to children and grandchildren with tender care as though each prized possession were an heirloom.

So likewise—and even to a later period—was it with the doublets, gowns, kirtles, and cloaks with which our forefathers arrayed themselves when they were "in the body." Agnes Hemmyng (1533) gives "to Thomas my girdell of friers knottys, and to Robert the girdell I was married in." Elizabeth Joyce enriches her sister-in-law with "my best beaver hatt, my Damaske gowne, and Damaske petticoat of a sea-green colour." Mary Corrie (1762) passes on to brother George "a Bible and a pair of sheets." Mary Swain, spinster, of Preston hamlet (1764), has no one to love and very little to leave: "To my niece Mary Swain my best stays and my worst, together with the nut-meg-grater and the jack and spit. To May Doggett my second-best stays, my red cloake, and a frying pan." The beginning of modern generalization can be seen in the will of Margaret Albury (1800), who, if only she had been more specific, would have saved a deal of trouble: "My books to be divided amongst the family as they can agree, but I hope there will bee no words, and pray dont sell none of my books."

Years ago, at the end of a lecture that I had delivered on medieval England to a village audience, a fine old country couple came up to me and said: "Muster 'Ine, we proper fancied what you said about them 'dieval wills, and if you dunt moind the missus and me 'ud loike to 'ave ouren dun arter ther same fashun." For a moment I was taken aback. It rather looked as though I had been touting for business. So I hurried my new clients out of the hall, had a whispered conversation in the porch, and then the three of us, linking arms for safety in the dark, jogged down the lane to their cottage so that I could make an inspection of their treasures. They had been quite right in their "feelings." Along with the tawdry trinkets, the oleographs, the hand-stitched scriptural texts, and the terrible photographs, there were some admirable pieces: a Dutch dower-chest, a Welsh dresser, a red-lacquer corner-cupboard, a copy of the Breeches Bible, and a portrait of John Bunyan that looked like an original. Having taken instructions how to share these amongst the sons and daughters, I inquired about grandchildren, and learnt that there was but one. "What can we do for Hannah?" I asked. The old man scratched his head. But the old woman looked suddenly bright. "I have it," she declared, "I have it. You mentioned bells, sir, in your talk." "Yes, indeed I did," I replied, "I told you about Edward Pryor, barber-surgeon, who died wondering what he could do to amuse his little girl when he was dead and gone, and how he slipped into his will: 'I give my daughter Mary bells for a child to play with.'"

"That's it," she broke in, "that's the very thing." And with that she flew to the corner cupboard, and fetched out a miniature set of hand-bells, made at Biggleswade of all unmusical places. We tried playing *The Bailiff's Daughter of Islington* upon them, with very poor results.

"But Hannah will do better," I declared. And then, muddling up my modern and medieval notes, and drinking to their long life in nauseous cowslip wine, likely to shorten my own, I took my leave.

Yet another change in will-making has been brought about by the Inheritance (Family Provision) Act of 1938, which has curbed the freedom of husbands and wives to cut one another, and the children, off with the proverbial shilling. In future there must be a "reasonable provision for dependents." The Court, however, "shall have regard to the *conduct* of the dependents, and to any other matter the Court may consider *relevant*." It is those two words in italics that have worked the mischief. They have thrown open the flood gates of "divers unhappy differences" and bitter family feuds. In cases likely to be affected by the Act some solicitors advise that a Statutory Declaration should be prepared of even date with the will. But I hold the view that the relevant considerations, justifying a testator in cutting out his near-yet-not-dear ones, should be embodied in the will. There they operate with more force and solemnity; and no great harm is done, because the respectable Probate, Divorce, and Admiralty Division takes care to exclude any scandalous matter from the grant. In the mere will, therefore, you can be as scandalous as you please. Certainly, the testator has no scruples. By the time the will is opened he will be safely shut up in his coffin. Meantime, with malice prepense, he is resolved to have his fling. Sitting at your table, he will pour out the gall and wormwood of a lifetime, dictating—relevant or irrelevant—the shameful incriminating charges that are to be recorded.

Here I will cite nothing from modern instances; the Act is far too recent. But there were wills being made after this fashion long ago; and with time as the great healer, there is no harm in quoting from them. Here, for example, is a clause from the 1869 will of a Hitchin solicitor, Thomas Gorham Pierson, declaring that "my wife Christiana Jane, having withdrawn herself from me without my consent, and petitioning for a separation on at best trifling grounds, and having rendered to me next to no assistance, but on the contrary proved herself to have been very artful, designing, provocative, grasping, and overbearing, she deserves and I desire that she may have nothing more than she can legally obtain for her life."

There is nothing so implacable and incurable as hatred between husband and wife; it will flare up even on a death-bed. Once upon a time I went to see an old, old Quaker die, and it was an experience I am not likely to forget. Like many a birthright member of this select society, he had a religion within a religion; it was that of ancestor worship. Year in and year out, he worked away at the family pedigree, and pored over the family letters. From Joseph Besse's *Sufferings of the Quakers* (1650–89), and from Quaker minute-books, he knew to a day how long his forbears had spent in "the stronghouse" for their faith, and to a farthing how much had been taken from them by distress, that the "hireling-priest" might have his "wages." True, he had spared time to marry, and some further time to beget children. But this was done simply to add to the pedigree. He did not love them. In return, they hated him. So inhuman was he, so little concerned about *their* sufferings that, one after another, they left him to follow their own "creaturely activities."

As no one answered the door, I walked in. Such was the silence, I wondered if the crotchety old housekeeper had "walked out." Knowing my way up the stairs, I opened a landing door, and there was the old man propped up on two pillows, his eyes wide open and staring into space. The room itself was indescribable, littered with bottles of unavailing physic, the debris of two or three days' meals and ablutions, dust and dirty linen everywhere. The windows were hermetically sealed. There was a heavy smell as of oncoming dissolution. On the floor beside the bed were bundles of title-deeds and account books; and on the bed itself, to be within reach to the very end, were the boxes of family letters.

All the thirty years I had known him the old man had possessed a deathly pallor (had he not been living always with the dead?). But now the face had gone as white as the snow-white billy-goat beard; and to crown all he

had donned a white night-cap or death-cap with grotesque lappets standing out like horns above each side of his head.

Slowly and painfully his wits travelled back from the eighteenth to the
twentieth century. And at last a gleam of recognition and of pleasure flashed
into the eyes. He even smiled, for, in an attempt to chaff him back to life,
I had reminded him of the day, sixty years before, when attired in a frock-
coat and a top-hat he had ridden round and round Hitchin market-place
on the back of an elephant. But the smile soon waned. There was no time
to lose. Above all, he wanted to entrust me with those letters: "You and I,
Hine, you and I, are the only ones who care." With that, a dark shadow
drifted across his face, and the eyes glowed with fury as he thought of
those who ought to have cared. There was a lull, an ominous, un-Quakerly
silence, a silence before a storm. Then, summoning his reserves of strength,
he sat up straight in bed and, looking for all the world like an Old Testament patriarch, he cursed his wife by her names and he cursed his children
by their names, cursed them one and all, and went on cursing. It seemed
such a piteous, indeed wicked, way to die that I could bear it no longer.
I took up the letters, and tiptoed out of the room, followed down the stairs
by the raving incantation of those curses.

Many a long year has passed since then. But neither God nor man has
provided me with the leisure to edit and publish those family papers as the
old Quaker expected me to do. Whenever I come upon them in my study,
I wonder if he has any power—from wherever he may be—to lay a curse
on me.

Let me turn to another death-bed scene, one that I was not privileged to
witness for myself, but which I had at first hand from a professional man
who was present. In this particular case the dying client was a considerable
landed proprietor. But his wife had committed the unpardonable sin. She
had failed in the one thing needful, viz. to provide him with male heirs.
Instead, she had given birth to a succession of daughters whom he never
wanted. When at last she died, he was anxious, but almost too old, to re-
marry and to beget sons. There were written proposals in a shaky hand;
but the letters were intercepted by the daughters. He was foiled and furi-
ous. Then he, too, was summoned to that world where, as it is said, we
neither marry nor are given in marriage. The rector, the family, the lawyer,
the agent, were hoping for a quiet and godly end, for in his time the squire
had been a good churchman, and in support of the Tractarian Movement
had written many a pious and learned pamphlet.

But it was not to be.

"James," he commanded, "fetch me my Wellington boots."

"The master must be crazy," said the butler to himself, but the habit of
unquestioning obedience was too strong. He did as he was told. Then,
glowering upon the assembled company, the old man took hold of each

heavy Wellington by the thong, mustered every ounce of available energy, paused awhile for breath, then hurled the boots at the heads of his daughters as they stood beside the bed.

"I hate you all," he screamed, sank back upon the pillows, and expired.

At one time I meditated writing a monograph on Hitchin death-bed scenes; and the mention of "boots" reminds me of one that would certainly have been included. It can be told truthfully in the very words of the niece who communicated it to me: "Years passed by, and William grew so frail and feeble that he could not take off his boots. So he went to bed in his boots. Months passed. Still more feeble he grew, and unable to take off his clothes. So he went to bed in his clothes. Then came his sister and said: 'This will not do, William. Thee must have a night-nurse, the doctor shall order thee one to-day.'

"The sick man shook his head. 'Never,' he expostulated, 'sooner than have a night-nurse would I die.' And the next afternoon, at four o'clock, just as the night-nurse tapped upon the door, the obstinate old man yielded up the ghost, and slept with his fathers, clothes and boots and all."

In the hour of death, as in the hours of life, women can be ministering angels. Yet not all men believe them to be so. I remember visiting the death-bed of a clergyman who—like William—would not have a woman near him in the house. It was a baffling, piteous, rather sinister case, for the client was suffering from the third and last of his strokes, and could neither speak nor move. Yet I could tell from his eyes, and from the fumbling of his hands, that he wanted me to find something, or to do something urgently before he died. Yet with all my questioning and prompting I could not interpret his dumb anguish; and he slipped out of this world with his message undelivered. It was only when I went through the papers in his bedroom that I came upon the clue. There it was—a horrible collection of obscene photographs that, ever since his days were numbered, he must have been longing to destroy. As I burnt them, and as I thought what agony of conscience the parson must have endured, the dreadful warning of Oscar Wilde sprang into my mind: "He who lives more lives than one more deaths than one must die."

It seems to me that the art of dying is fast dying out. Nowadays, few people, be they Christians or pagans, die "according to plan"; whereas, in the eighteenth century, it was almost an article of religion to pass out of this life in a manner befitting. If you read the four volumes of *Piety Promoted*, collecting testimonies and death-bed sayings of Quaker elders and ministers (some of them Hitchin people) from 1657 to 1854, you will come to the conclusion that their affecting last words must have been long and carefully rehearsed. Though they disdained all the arts of living, they were past masters in the art of dying. Over the death-bed scenes of other people there is an exasperating uncertainty. At school, for example, I was made to copy out the pathetic utterance of William Pitt: "Oh, my country! how I leave my country!" When I left school I was told that he had said nothing of the kind, that his last words were: "I think I could eat one of Bellamy's veal pies." What and where is truth? Such doubts and misgivings made me the more careful about my references when I was writing the lives and deaths of my Hitchin worthies and unworthies, many of whom made a good, and some a glorious, end.

It was testified of Thomas Shillitoe that, as he neared the farther shore, he caught sight of a better land and cried out joyfully: "Mine eyes have seen Thy salvation and Thy glory; when shall I feel Thy presence?" The same authentic vision was vouchsafed to another Quaker minister, Thomas Thompson: "To them that may Enquire concerning my end," he exclaimed, "let them know that I die in the Faith that saves and triumphs over death and hell, finding no cloud in my way, but perfect peace with God, the presence of whose glory is with me." The Rev. Samuel James, pastor of the Baptist church that Bunyan himself had founded, died with a triumphant and radiant expression and with the cry of "Victory, Victory" upon his lips. There is a quieter note, but no less confident, in the valediction of Samuel Spavold: "The truth," he assured those who stood about his bed, "the truth is a precious thing; it is worth seeking for." Then, taking each of them by the hand in turn, he said: "Farewell, I love you, I love you all."

It is only the elect who can die in a manner so sanctified. Of the great majority it must be confessed that the world and all its cares were with them to the end. In the delirium of his last moments John Hawkins, the solicitor of Portmill Lane, was stammering over the speech that he had written for the annual meeting of the Hitchin Friendly Institution. The last words of Frederick Peter Delmé-Radcliffe were touched by no commiseration for himself, but for his physician who would soon be losing the best patient on his books. "Ah! doctor," he said chaffingly, "you've killed the goose that laid the golden eggs." As for my old friend Kit Nash, the female poacher, she too died in character. It had to be in the workhouse, but the master was a sportsman and an understanding friend. Knowing her ruling passion, strong in death, he went out and bought her a pheasant; and as she lay in bed, reciting from an unfailing memory the parable of the prodigal son, she would run her fingers over and over the soft and silken feathers, blessedly content. It was a fine end to a fine old poacher.

Art in Direct Examination[*]

FRANCIS L. WELLMAN

Alexander Woollcott in his profile of Stryker (see page 71) refers to "Wellman's classic work on cross-examination." But Francis L. Wellman (1854–1942) wrote other volumes besides the Art of Cross Examination; *among them are* Gentlemen of the Jury *and* Day in Court, *and from the last named a chapter is here reprinted. After taking his degree at Harvard, Wellman was admitted to the Massachusetts bar in 1880. Subsequently he became corporation counsel for the City of New York, a post he held for eight years, and assistant district attorney for four years—in addition to carrying on the duties of general practice.*

The material which follows is somewhat in the nature of a primer for young lawyers; it consists of advice on the art of direct examination. However, a liberal sprinkling of humorous anecdote and brief digressions into the philosophy of experience warm and illuminate the pages.

As to the examination-in-chief of the advocate's own witnesses, of course it is impossible within the limits of one chapter to give a systematic and scientific exposition of the entire subject. We must assume, therefore, that the advocate has become entirely familiar with the rules of evidence before entering upon the trial, and I must content myself with indicating some of the arts employed by great advocates and making a few suggestions which my experience has impressed upon me as important to be kept in mind when conducting the examination-in-chief.

The impression prevails quite generally in the profession that the direct examination of witnesses requires far less skill than the cross-examination.

I am inclined not to agree with this view, and it is a matter of regret that so little attention is paid to the examination-in-chief, while many arts are exercised to produce effects in cross-examination.

I presume this is owing largely to the fact that cross-examination is so much more engaging to the spectators and its results are so much more quickly perceived by them.

The subtle arts and consummate skill of an examination-in-chief are seldom apparent to the mere spectator, however it may be appreciated by

[*] Reprinted from *Day in Court*, copyright, 1910, by The Macmillan Company, by the kind permission of Mrs. Ethel Wellman.

86

the lawyers engaged in the case, who may be able to recognize with what ingenuity and tact the desired facts have been elicited and the weak points suppressed or at least not clearly revealed.

Is it not far easier to propound cross-questions which will put a man in an unattractive position before an audience than to so conduct his direct examination as to make him show himself to the greatest possible advantage?

Many an idle boy has broken painted windows, but no one but an Albert Dürer could have made them!

If the direct examination is properly and skilfully conducted, the impression thus made by an honest witness is more lasting than any argument of counsel. The vivid story of a single witness told in a winning way will leave a first impression upon a juror's mind that no eloquence can efface.

It is no easy matter for an advocate to get his own evidence properly before a court and jury.

It is an important fact for him to remember that cases are often won or lost by the straightforward statements of the parties themselves, and the natural homely way they sometimes have of putting things.

A builder was suing for extra work done on a dwelling. The defence was that everything had been paid for as originally contracted, but that much of the work had not been done according to agreement. An expert was called as defendant's witness. He testified that the house was six inches lower than called for by the specification; that the windows were on weights instead of opening out like French windows on hinges, and that there were other material defects in workmanship. Item by item had to be carefully scrutinized. There was a chimney too short, a cornice defective, etc. The jurors were much worried and confused. Finally, defendant herself, an illiterate woman, took the witness-stand in her own behalf. She knew nothing of books or architecture or plans, but "she was sure the plaintiff had made the house entirely contrary to his bargain, for he promised that the windows should reach clear to the floor. She remembered telling the plaintiff, Mr. Walker, so, and explaining to him that if they had a death in the family and wanted to take a coffin out on the porch, French windows would open like a door and let it out without cramping it in a narrow hall and bruising the edges of the coffin all up." This graphic description settled the question with the jury, and the woman went away happy.

One more instance will suffice to fix this important fact in the mind, and these anecdotes will serve not only as illustrations, but give a little refreshment from the more tiresome rules and suggestions for the advocate's work.

A German had fitted up a fine barber-shop with mahogany sideboards, gilded mirrors, etc., and a tenant just above him had let the water-basin run over during the night, causing the plaster to drop and spatter all over the new furniture in the barber-shop below.

When told about it, the tenant made light of it, and when asked to make it good, he replied, "Oh, you go to hell." Therefore the barber brought suit in a justice's court before a jury. On the trial the barber was the only witness in his own behalf and stated to the jury with great candor what had been said by the tenant. When the lawyer prompted him by asking, "and what did *you* say?" he replied, "*I said, I vill not go to hell, I vill go to law,*" and then rising to his feet he said, "*und, shentlemen, dot vas schust so bad as to go to hell.*" He won a fine verdict by saying the right thing in the right way.

One of the first objects in the examination of witnesses, both on direct and cross, should be brevity. By his opening speech the advocate has clearly defined the issues between himself and his opponent. In his examination of the witnesses it should be his effort to adhere as closely as possible to these issues.

It is in this part of his work that the superior talent of the good trial lawyer in modern times is the most strikingly displayed. Cases take entirely too long to try, and the issues thereby get needlessly confused.

Modern trials should be conducted more as a matter of business, the one object being to ascertain the truth of the matter in controversy and in the shortest time possible, and not to display the talents of the lawyers on one side or the other.

The advocate should select and arrange his evidence so that the development of his case will be interesting to his hearers. He should strive to keep the jury ever alert. He should remember that nowadays cases are practically won as they go along and not by the arguments of counsel after the testimony is completed.

There is a great fascination for jurors in a well-planned trial that leads them to constant discovery of new facts as if they were developed almost unawares.

The jury should be made to feel that the advocate at least believes in his own case.

He should speak clearly and distinctly, mindful that he is engaged in a matter of importance and let his art conceal art.

I am inclined to put clearness, simplicity, and brevity before everything else in the conduct of a case in court, including the examinations of witnesses and the attempt to keep the salient facts ever prominent before the jury.

An advocate should always use the simplest language possible. It is better understood both by his witnesses and his jury.

He should preserve ever a calm, cool, deliberate, self-possessed, dignified demeanor. Calmness is shown by not growing petulant over little defects, in a kindly and courteous behavior toward witnesses, and in a quiet dignity which gives the idea of reserve force.

Any nervousness or petulance is immediately noticed by the jury and is apt to embarrass and disquiet his witness as well.

He should convey to his witness the impression that he is strong enough to prevent him from stumbling or falling. This confidence is created by the manner and demeanor of the advocate, by the form in which he frames his questions, and the manner in which he asks them.

One mind communicates to another its feelings and emotions, and there is without doubt a well-defined wireless telegraphy going on all the time between a skilful examiner and his witness.

The very first thing that should be done is to put his witness at ease. If he wants to realize the embarrassment of a witness as he mounts the witness-stand, let an advocate step up there (in imagination) for a moment himself, sit down, and look into the "sea of upturned faces,"—the three or four hundred strange eyes, eager with curiosity, that are gazing into his own.

Few witnesses can fail to experience embarrassment, even trepidation, under such circumstances; and at the start it is extremely difficult for them to collect their thoughts and give their evidence in a natural way and not become confused and contradict themselves.

What wonder that a witness, however truthful and intelligent, should take the oath as a witness with trepidation, akin to fear,—especially when he discovers the opposing counsel ready to cross-examine him as a hostile witness and turn his evidence to ridicule, if possible, or to his own discredit.

A man who had presided over many trials, Chief Justice Burke, having been summoned as a witness, said to one of his friends: "The character of a witness is new to me, Philips; I am familiar with nothing here. The matter on which I came is most important; I need all my self-possession, and yet I protest to you I have only one idea, and that is, *Lord Brougham cross-examining me.*"

Many may remember the almost historic reply of Henry Ward Beecher in the Tilden-Beecher case when William Fullerton, who was cross-examining him, shouted at him, "Why don't you answer my question?" *"Because I am afraid of you,"* replied Beecher.

How can the advocate best overcome this embarrassment on the part of his witnesses?

Each witness should be properly introduced to the jury. It is during this introduction that the witness can be made to feel the gentle hand on the rein.

A few simple, unimportant questions should be put in a modulated, reassuring tone of voice. The witness sees that the advocate is at his ease and takes courage.

"You said your name was John Doe—I believe?

"You live on 14th Street, do you not?

"What number, if you please?"

This is simple enough, and the witness, almost without any thought, replies, "No. 314."

Q. "How long have you lived in the one house?"

A. "Fifteen years."

Q. "And with your wife and children?"

A. "Yes."

Q. "You are in the manufacturing business, I believe?"

A. "Yes."

Q. "What position do you hold?"

A. "General manager."

Q. "How long have you been employed there?"

A. "Twenty years."

Q. "Then you must have started as an apprentice?"

A. "I did, at the work-bench."

Q. "And were gradually promoted?"

A. "Yes—I became foreman of the shop, and then superintendent of the factory."

The witness is at ease. Even rather proud of himself. The jury think well of him. The advocate can now safely proceed to the important work he has in hand.

Contrast this style of examination with the less orderly system which is so prevalent in our courts.

Examiner (in loud, harsh voice). "What is your name, Madam?"

Witness (timidly). "Mary Jones."

Lawyer. "Can't hear you, please speak louder."

Court interferes. "Madam, you must speak loud enough for that gentleman over there (pointing to the twelfth juror) to hear you."

(Witness looks at the twelve staring men and becomes even more embarrassed.)

Lawyer. "Where do you reside?"

(Witness doesn't *"reside"* anywhere that she knows of. So the court helps out with the suggestion, "Ask her where she *lives*."

Witness (almost inaudibly). "14th Street."

Lawyer. "Please speak up."

(Court officer now takes a hand and shouts in her ear, "Speak louder, Madam.")

Lawyer. "Do you live on the East Side?"

Witness (embarrassed). Nods her head.

Now the *stenographer can't hear her or see the nod,* so he addresses her and asks her to *please speak her answers* as he is writing and can't see her if she shakes her head.

This completes the confusion of the witness for she suddenly realizes that everything she says and even every nod of her head is being *recorded* by somebody.

Lawyer. "Are you acquainted with the *plaintiff?*"

(Witness hesitates and can't answer. She has never been in court before and doesn't know plaintiff from defendant, even if she was *"acquainted"* with either one of them.)

Lawyer (with a ray of intelligence). "Do you *know* your next-door neighbor, Mrs. Smith, who is sitting at the table by my side?"

This elicits a ready "Yes, sir."

Then the counsel dives right at the *heart of his case.*

Q. *"Do you remember the 5th of November, 1905?"*

This completely upsets the witness. She cannot, in all probability, even remember the day of the month she is testifying in, much less the 5th of November, 1905, though she may remember all about the occurrences of that day.

If trying to get at the date of her birth, the lawyer might just as well ask her, "Do you remember the 5th of June, 1875?" (the day she was born), and yet this inquiry of a witness, whether she remembers a certain day, is one of the most common of the many errors committed almost daily in our courts.

By this time our lady witness under such a style of examination has become completely discredited with the jury by her apparent stupidity, and little credit will be given to anything she may afterwards say. And all through the fault of the lawyer conducting her examination.

Imagine this same witness taken in hand by an experienced advocate, and again note the contrast.

This time the advocate takes his stand at the further end of the jury-box. The witness, answering from such a distance, naturally raises her voice without having her attention distracted by a command to do so.

Q. "I believe you said your name was Mary Jones?"

A. "Yes, sir."

Q. "And you live at No. 16 East 14th Street?"

A. "Yes, sir."

Q. "How long have you known this lady sitting by my side, Mrs. Smith, the plaintiff in the case?"

A. The answer comes readily enough—"Some ten years."

Q. "Do you remember some years ago being at her house when there was a conversation about an accident that had occurred the night before, in front of her house?"

A. "Yes."

Q. "I don't suppose you remember the date of that conversation, but can you remember about what year it was?"

A. The witness answers naturally, "About three years ago."

Q. "And in the fall of the year?"

A. "Yes."

Q. "Who was there besides yourself"—and the witness will now, likely enough, go on and remember minutely the whole occurrence.

Such questions as these would now naturally follow:—

"State to the jury what occurred?" "State what next occurred?" "What was said, if anything?" "What was done?" "Go on and tell the jury in your own words what happened in your presence?"

As soon as the witness gets thoroughly at ease and started, the fewer interruptions, the better. He should be permitted to tell his own story as far as possible, but the advocate should always register in his own mind the important facts and see that they are all clearly brought out.

Thus it can readily be seen how his thorough preparation for trial and his intimate knowledge of his case and of his witnesses, which we have already discussed, will now come to his assistance.

The advocate should always be on the alert to restrain his own witness if he wanders from his subject, and not wait for him to be rebuked by the court, for this may entirely disconcert his witness. If, however, such rebuke comes, as it not infrequently does, a few simple commonplace questions will allow him to recover from his embarrassment and continue with his story.

The advocate should avoid technical terms, as well as long, fine, or high-sounding words. These only confuse the witness and distract the attention of the jury from the story he is wresting from the witness.

The more neatly a question is put, the better, for it has to be understood not only by the witness but by the jury as well.

It will be necessary for the advocate to train himself to handle his own witnesses of various kinds, such as the stupid witness, the diffident witness, and, hardest of all, the over-zealous one, the witness who insists upon proving too much. Here is a type of man he is bound to hold in check. He should never let him tell his own story, for the witness will thereby usually prepare himself for slaughter at the hands of the cross-examiner. The effort should be to keep such a witness well to the point and compel him to answer only such questions as are asked. An old lawyer's advice in regard to this kind of a witness is to "get rid of him as soon as possible."

A stupid witness will require all an advocate's patience and good temper.

Some witnesses are not capable of a train of thought on any subject. They can observe no order of events whatsoever, and their ideas are confused even as to time. All that can be done with such witnesses is to direct them simply to answer the questions put to them, and then confine the questions to the isolated facts it is desired to show by them. A display of anger to such a witness only adds to his confusion. He should be encouraged by looks and expressions of approval. Questions should be framed to meet his difficulties. By observing his answers, and with a little ingenuity, an advocate can readily frame questions to fall in with his degree of intelligence.

Judge Jeffries once mistook one of these apparently stupid witnesses, and having taken quite a dislike to the man (who had been testifying in his court, and who happened to have a very long beard), finally broke out with the remark that if his conscience was as long as his beard, he must have a very vacillating one; to which the witness quickly replied, "My Lord, if you measure consciences by beards, you have none at all."

With a witness who is discovered to be adverse, one who, as the phrase goes, tries to "throw you" on the witness-stand, the method and manner should be entirely different from that employed with a merely stupid witness. The adverse witness should be led to show his bias as soon as possible. The rules of evidence will then allow a resort to leading questions. Advantage should be taken of them, and the witness artfully led to make the admissions wanted. While the advocate is not allowed to discredit him directly, as he is his own witness, yet if he once succeed in exposing the bias of the witness, what little he can induce him to say in his favor will be doubly effective with the jury, and he can prove by other witnesses the material facts that he has denied, even though the effect would be to indirectly discredit him.

If his evidence is unfavorable and the advocate exhibits the slightest sign of displeasure, he will only add to the bad effect, as there are sure to be men on the jury who form their opinions of the nature and character of the testimony chiefly by the effect which it may appear to produce upon the counsel; whereas, if, after an unfavorable answer, the counsel abandon the witness entirely, he still more intensifies the damage done, and gives the impression of complete demoralization.

The statement should be calmly received and the inquiry quietly turned to some new, but unimportant matter, and an attempt made to tone down and soften the adverse impression made.

The advocate should not examine any witness as though he were catechising him. He should frame his questions as though he were a companion anxious to hear the story the witness is willing to tell, and as if it were all new to him, not as if he had heard it all before and were merely rehearsing it for the benefit of the jury.

The most elementary rule of evidence in connection with the examination-in-chief is that leading questions shall not be put to your own witness (a leading question being such a one as suggests the answer). It is often excessively difficult to adhere strictly to this rule.

It is properly applicable only to such questions as relate to the *matter at issue,* although it is commonly thought to refer to all questions that suggest the answer. If it were rigidly enforced, trials would be ridiculously prolonged, and it is the practice of all experienced trial judges to allow lawyers to put leading questions almost entirely until the real issue in the case is reached. One no longer says "What is your name?" "Where do you live?" "What is your business?" But "Mr. Brown, I understand you live at No. 6 Madison Avenue, and are in the real estate business with offices at 125 Broadway?" and so on. Thus by quick stages we come to the more important part of the case.

Not long ago I was employing this method of leading a witness quickly to the real issues in a case in a trial conducted before a Supreme Court judge, quite fifteen years my junior, when he stopped me by a rather peremptory direction not to lead my witness. I was taken quite aback by his tone and meekly remarked that I feared I did not quite know what a leading question was. To this the judge replied, superciliously, "A leading question, Mr. Wellman, is one that suggests the answer." The learned justice had remembered this much from his law-school days, but had forgotten, if he ever knew, that the rule against leading questions applies only to matters material to the issue and not to such preliminary inquiries.

I was placed in a most humiliating position before the jurors by this youthful rebuke, but made no attempt at an effective retort. I was reminded, however, of a rejoinder that Curran once made to an English judge who expostulated at the proposition of law Curran was arguing before him and exclaimed, "If that is the law, Mr. Curran, I may *burn* my law books," to which Curran tartly replied, "Better *read* them, my Lord."

One also recalls the retort made by a leader of the Boston Bar (a man distinguished for his learning) to the presiding judge of the full bench, who had stopped him in his argument with the brusque remark: "That is not the law, counsellor." With fine suavity of manner the counsel replied: "I beg your honor's pardon, it *was* the law before your honor spoke."

Perhaps, however, my own method of making no real reply but accepting the rebuke was the wiser course to pursue, as I am a believer in the wisdom and propriety of showing the greatest courtesy toward the Bench; and then one never can forget the story of the man who told his neighbors in great excitement about how his dog would go out each night and bark and bark at the moon, and when asked, "And then what happened?" he replied: "Oh, nothing, nothing at all; the moon went right on just as it always had!"

On another occasion a judge from one of the up-state circuits of our Federal Courts nearly adjudged me in contempt of court because I started out with all my witnesses by leading questions when interrogating them about their residence, their occupation, and how they happened to come from other cities to testify in our courts, etc.

The learned justice nearly broke the learned bench, so hard did he pound it with his gavel as he ordered me to sit down and desist from such a practice, a practice which in no wise injures the cause of truth but saves an immense amount of time otherwise wasted.

Had I been arraigned for contempt upon this occasion (and it was but a few years ago) I should long to have been represented by some one resembling Mr. John Clark, afterward the distinguished Lord Eldon, who was remarkable when at the English Bar for the *sang froid* with which he treated the judges.

On one occasion a junior counsellor, on hearing their Lordships give

judgment against his client, exclaimed that he was surprised at such a decision. This was construed into a contempt of court and he was ordered to
attend at the Bar next morning. Fearful of the consequence he consulted
his friend John Clark, who told him to be perfectly at ease, for he would
apologize for him in a way that would prevent any unpleasant result. Accordingly, when the name of the delinquent was called, John Clark arose
and thus addressed the assembled tribunal: "I am very sorry, my Lords,
that my young friend has so far forgotten himself as to treat your honorable
Bench with disrespect; he is extremely penitent and you will kindly ascribe
his unintentional insult to his ignorance. You must see at once that it did
originate in ignorance, for he said he was 'surprised' at the decision of your
Lordships; now if he had not been very ignorant of what takes place in
this court every day, had he known you but *half* so long as I have done, *he
would not be surprised at anything you did!*"

When, however, the main issues of the case are reached, the rule against
leading questions (with few exceptions) is strictly adhered to, and very
properly so.

Some lawyers put the clearly inadmissible question which suggests the
answer, and though it is ruled out, perhaps with a rebuke from the court,
the witness nevertheless has caught the idea. This is disreputable practice.

There are, however, several legitimate ways of assisting the witness's defective memory. One method is to ask him to repeat the whole story over
again. Perhaps his second recital contains the part he omitted at the first
but makes some new omission, and thus is secured the testimony wanted,
but at the same time the witness is proved to be a man of poor memory.

A better way is to so frame the question that it shall contain a part of
the forgotten sentence, but otherwise applied, as, for example, by referring
to some collateral circumstance which would recall the forgotten phrase.
This can be legitimately done if the advocate is quick-witted enough, and
thereby readily save the situation.

Every advocate is in honor bound not to transgress the rule against
"leading questions" when it really comes to important matters, but it is
sometimes extremely difficult. Indeed, there are cases in which the court,
in its discretion, may permit him to ask leading questions in the interests
of justice, so that important testimony may not be lost. Suppose, for instance,
a witness is giving his memory of a long conversation he overheard between
the parties to an action, and, as often happens, leaves out of his narrative
perhaps what, in law, amounts to the most important part.

In vain the advocate tries not to lead him. He asks, "Have you given all
the conversation?" "Was that all that was said?" The witness remembers
no more. The memory of the witness has been exhausted by direct questions, and then the court may properly permit him to lead the witness so
far as to ask the witness whether anything was said about so and so (with-

out suggesting what was said), and thus call his attention to the matter which the witness has inadvertently overlooked, and thus save very important testimony which would otherwise be lost.

So too, when it is discovered that a witness is hostile, the court, as already intimated, may permit leading questions to be put, because the reason for the rule against them no longer exists.

In other words, the rule against putting leading questions to your own witness is based upon the tendency of the human mind to adopt the suggestion of the person or side that it desires to aid and to quickly respond to any hint of what is wanted to assist the party making the suggestion. Hence, in the case of a hostile witness obviously the reason for the rule is gone.

A very common fault to be observed almost every day in our courts upon direct examination is that of pressing the witness too far. Counsel become so enamoured with a favorable answer that they seem to want to hear it again and again. It is a pretty good rule to remember to "let well enough alone."

Harris gives an interesting example of this rule. A junior counsel was conducting a case before Mr. Justice Hawkins. The fact seemed pretty clear upon the bare statement of the prosecution. "Are you quite sure of this fact?" "Yes," said the witness. "Quite?" inquired the counsel. "Quite," said the witness. "You have no doubt?" persisted the counsel, thinking that he was making assurance doubly sure. "Well," said the witness, "I haven't much doubt, because I asked my wife." Mr. Justice Hawkins: "You asked your wife in order to be sure in your own mind?" "Quite so, my Lord." "Then you had some doubt before?" "Well, I may have had a little, my Lord." This ended the case, because the whole question turned upon the absolute certainty of the witness's mind.

If an adversary is examining in chief, an advocate should be ever on the watch for improper questions. I do not refer to leading questions alone, but to those vastly more numerous ones that violate some rule of evidence.

If one observes a skilful and rather unfair examiner handle his witnesses when opposed only by some beginner, it is amazing what an amount of inadmissible testimony he adroitly imports into the case, owing to the fact that his opponent is unfamiliar with the rules of evidence; whereas to an experienced advocate the rules of evidence become so familiar that a question that violates one of them is as quickly discerned by him as a discord would be by a trained musician.

The following criminal case, reported by Harris, serves as an excellent example of the folly of intrusting the examination-in-chief to inexperienced hands.

The prisoner had committed an atrocious murder, and the main evidence against him was the dying declaration of his victim—his wife. It is a well-known rule of evidence that any dying declaration made in the absence of the prisoner can only be received in evidence after independent proof that the declaration was made with the *full consciousness* and expectation of approaching death.

The doctor who attended the wife was called as a witness to prepare the way for the dying declaration, which, if allowed in evidence, would undoubtedly have hanged the prisoner.

The young prosecuting attorney asked, "Did she *fear* death?" "No," said the doctor. The lawyer stared in astonishment at the witness, who was perfectly cool, as most doctors are in the witness-box, and who made no effort to assist the district attorney. The ingenious young counsellor, however, repeated the question. "Did she *fear* death?" Answer: "Oh dear no, not at all." The judge: "You cannot put the statement in evidence; the witness may step down"; then turning to the jury, "and you, gentlemen, cannot find a verdict of guilty."

The blank look on the face of the counsel, the sagacious smile of the judge, who evidently thought the right question would be put next, the quick perceptive glance of the witness who stood leaning on the witness-box with his hands carelessly folded—all this is graphically described by Harris, who was present.

The answer of the doctor was true so far as it went, for the woman did not *fear* death, but it was also true, that she was *conscious* of approaching death, and if this had been brought out by the proper question, the dying declaration could have been made admissible.

One of the most pernicious habits in a trial is that of making constant objections to evidence on trivial matters. It is a very common fault among young advocates. The lawyer who is constantly shouting out "we object," "we object," without solid ground for his objection is in reality losing his case as fast as he possibly can, as well as befogging and delaying the trial and annoying the presiding judge.

The objecting and objectionable young lawyer imagines he is displaying his knowledge of evidence and proving himself smart. The jury, on the other hand, only get the idea that there must be some very damaging evidence which he is trying to keep from their ears, and as the truth is what they are after, they have little patience with anybody who tries to hide it from them.

A rule I would urge upon young advocates is "never to be moved to anger by anything, however provoking, and however you may appear, for policy's sake, to be in a passion."

Colton says that the "intoxication of anger, like that of the grape, shows us to others but hides us from ourselves; unnerves us and unmans us, and in every way unfits us for the business of the courts, especially if the trial is a difficult one."

An advocate should not be disconcerted if his women witnesses lose their tempers in the witness-box, for the rules of evidence happen to be peculiarly repressive of feminine conversation.

In closing this chapter I have but one suggestion more, and that is in regard to the examination of the parties to the suit—the clients. Here should be pursued quite a different method, even though it allow them a very loose rein.

It is often a clever move to interrogate a party to a suit—known to be honest—on matters which the advocate knows him to be uncertain, although he can readily prove them by some one else. The client will answer that "He couldn't be certain enough about that to swear to it." When, afterwards, the fact is proved independently of him, every one will think better of him for being so scrupulously careful in speaking of a matter which might perhaps be vital to his chance of winning his case.

Parties very properly feel that they are the chief actors in the drama and are more or less proud of having brought so many people together to hear and decide their wrongs; then, too, it is they who pay the advocates for their time. The parties' appreciation of their own supreme importance reminds me of the story of the highwayman, of whom it is related, that when the chaplain, on the way to the scaffold, said he feared they would be late, the condemned one answered, "Never trouble about that, sir; they can't begin without us."

Law and Letters[*]

LORD MACMILLAN

"For quotable good things, for pregnant aphorisms, for touchstones of ready application, the opinions of the English judges are a mine of instruction and a treasury of joy." This generous acknowledgment of his English colleagues by Justice Cardozo will be found later in this volume in an essay which is itself distinguished by the beauty of its style. Nevertheless it is doubtful if anyone but a distinguished British jurist such as Lord Macmillan could have written what follows, so gracefully does it carry the weight of its learning, so captivating is its assumption that other lawyers share its author's high convictions. Law and Letters *was an address delivered at the Meeting of the American Bar Association in 1930.*

Lord Macmillan of Aberfeldy learned his law in Scotland at the Universities of Edinburgh and Glasgow and at his death in 1952 was a Lord of Appeal.

I am happy to have this opportunity of acknowledging in person the distinction which you conferred on me when in 1924 you elected me an honorary member of the American Bar Association, thus enabling me to-day to enjoy the privilege of addressing you as one of yourselves. But indeed a lawyer can never feel himself a stranger at a gathering of the members of his profession in whatever quarter of the globe, for I am convinced that there is no profession which binds its members in a closer fraternity. It is not for nothing that in the law we call each other brethren. We may not succeed in attracting the same measure of popular affection as do certain of the other professions. Nevertheless our services to the community are indispensable and I suspect are valued much more highly than it is customary to avow.

If I were to seek for the explanation of the bond which binds in brotherhood the servants of the law throughout the world, I venture to think that I should find it in our common devotion to a great ideal, the promotion of the orderly progress of civilisation. The famous orders of chivalry in the middle ages dedicated their lives and labours to some noble cause. We in these modern and more prosaic days have no less need, we have indeed more

* Reprinted from *Law and Other Things*, 1937, by Lord Macmillan, by permission of the Cambridge University Press.

need, of a similar inspiration, and the cause to which we are devoted is
truly a worthy one—that justice and truth shall prevail throughout the world.
Amidst the daily drudgery of court and office we are apt to lose sight of
the lofty aims of our profession. Occasions such as this enable us to recap-
ture the enthusiasm of our high calling, to realise afresh the great and vital
interests which are committed to us and in the glow of mutual encouragement and good fellowship to rekindle ideals which, when we separate once
more on our several ways, will long continue to illumine our daily path
of duty.

I read recently that the great Chief Justice of the United States Supreme
Court, John Marshall—*clarum et venerabile nomen*—wore during his life
an amethyst ring with the motto *Veritas Vincit* engraved upon it. No minister of the law ever observed more loyally the lesson of that daily reminder.
Steadfastly and unswervingly, through good report and through evil report,
he pursued the even tenor of his way and proved to the world once more
that truth is great and must prevail. His memory is revered not only here
in his own country but wherever the law is practised, and his noble judgments will ever continue to echo down the corridors of time. To me, as a
Scotsman, it is of peculiar interest that the Chief Justice should have
adopted this talisman, for the words *Veritas Vincit* are the motto of the
famous Scottish family of the Keiths, the Earls Marischal of Scotland, whose
name is associated with many of the most stirring and romantic episodes
of my native land. His right to wear it came to him from his maternal grandfather, the Reverend James Keith, a member of this historic Scottish family
who fled to Virginia to escape the consequences of his participation in the
Jacobite rebellion. Thus Marshall could count among his ancestors Sir
Robert Keith, the commander of the Scottish horse at Bannockburn in 1314,
George Keith, the fifth Earl, a famous scholar and diplomatist who in 1593
founded and endowed Marischal College in the University of Aberdeen,
and William, the seventh Earl, who saved the regalia of Scotland by concealing them in his castle at Dunnottar. If heredity counts for anything, it
is not surprising that John Marshall, coming from such a stock, found himself equally at home in the camp and in the Courts and won distinction in
each. And now I must tell you that over the doorway into the law library
in the Old Parliament House where the Law Courts meet in Edinburgh
there is hung the standard of the Earl Marischal of Scotland which was
carried at the fateful battle of Flodden Field in 1513 and which bears em-
broidered on it, along with the Keith arms, those self-same words—*Veritas
Vincit*. Thus the advocates of the Scottish Bar have ever before their eyes
the same admonition which the great Chief Justice of the United States
adopted as the key-note of his life work.

There are other pleasant links between the Chief Justice and Scotland
besides the fact that some of our best Scottish blood ran in his veins, for
he received his first tutoring from a young emigrant Scottish divine, James

Thompson, who lived for a year in his father's house, while his second instructor was the Reverend Archibald Campbell, who belonged to a Glasgow family of Virginian merchants and was an uncle of the poet Thomas Campbell, the well-known author of *The Pleasures of Hope*. In the school which Campbell started in Westmoreland County, Virginia, he no doubt imparted to his young pupil the sound classical teaching which he had himself imbibed at a Scottish University. I note, too, that among the earliest books which the Chief Justice bought were the *Lectures on Rhetoric* of the famous Professor Hugh Blair of Edinburgh University and the *Principles of Equity*, a treatise written by the Scottish judge, Lord Kames.

The name and fame of John Marshall lead me easily to the theme on which I should like to say a few words to you to-day, namely, the association between law and letters, for, as I shall show, he exemplified that association in a conspicuous degree. I am convinced, as he was convinced, that no lawyer is justly entitled to the honourable and conventional epithet of "learned" if his learning is confined to the statutes and the law reports. It is the province of the lawyer to be the counsellor of persons engaged in every branch of human activity. Nothing human must be alien to him. "You are a lawyer," said Dr. Johnson to Mr. Edwards; "Lawyers know life practically. A bookish man should always have them to converse with. They have what he wants." Equally the man of letters has what the lawyer wants, for if he is to fulfil his rôle usefully and wisely he must have a mind not merely stored with the precedents of the law but possessing that width of comprehension, that serenity of outlook and that catholicity of sympathy which can nowise be so well acquired as from consort with the great masters of literature. In such company is found the corrective for the narrowness of mere professionalism. The lawyer does well from time to time to lift his eyes from his desk and look out of the window on the wider world beyond. There can be a too sedulous devotion to the textbooks of the law and I do not commend the example of Chief Baron Palles, who is said to have taken Fearne on *Contingent Remainders* with him for reading on his honeymoon.

Fortunately the law has always been on excellent terms with the Muses. You have only to read the biographies of our great judges and advocates of the past to realise how versed in letters most of them were, and what solace and inspiration they drew from that source. Take Chief Justice Marshall himself. Before he was twelve years of age he had copied out every word of Pope's *Essay on Man* and committed his favourite passages to memory. He bought Mason's *Poems* about the same time as he acquired Blackstone's *Commentaries,* and among his other early purchases were Chesterfield's *Letters,* the *Life of Clarendon,* Machiavelli's *Works* and translations of Æschines' *Orations* and Demosthenes *On the Crown*—a sufficiently varied intellectual diet. When he was seventy-one years of age he read the whole of Jane Austen's novels, of which he made this perspicacious estimate in a letter to his colleague Joseph Story—"Her flights are not lofty. She does not soar on eagle's wings, but she is pleasing, interesting, equable and yet amusing." In a letter written in 1829 he said: "The plan of my life I had formed for myself to be adopted after my retirement from office is to read nothing but novels and poetry." Alas, in his case, as in that of so many others who have looked forward all their lives to the delights which they have promised themselves on retirement, this happy time never came, for he died six years later still in harness.

Abraham Lincoln in his early days had even greater difficulties to surmount in the pursuit of learning than John Marshall. I may properly call him also as a witness to my plea, for although his greatest triumphs were in the realm of statesmanship he was also an accomplished lawyer. As a boy "he read," we are told by his stepmother, "every book he could lay his hands on and when he came across a passage that struck him he would write it down on boards, if he had no paper, and keep it there until he did get paper. Then he would rewrite it, look at it, repeat it. He had a copybook, a kind of scrapbook, in which he put down all things and thus preserved them." Lincoln diligently borrowed such books as were to be found in the neighbourhood of his early home in Indiana. They were not many, but they included *Robinson Crusoe, Æsop's Fables,* Bunyan's *Pilgrim's Progress,* Weems's *Life of Washington* and a *History of the United States,* while Shakespeare and Burns were his favourite poets. With these he mitigated the perusal of the *Revised Statutes of Indiana,* in those days happily not so bulky as now. Thus Lincoln acquired his marvellous command of clear-cut simple English which reached its perfection of combined brevity and beauty in the dedicatory speech at Gettysburg and the great Second Inaugural. His happy gift of style is illustrated not only in resounding aphorisms, such as the famous "He who would be no slave must consent to have no slave," but also enabled him in more colloquial moments to coin innumerable delightful sayings. Thus when speaking of his difficulties in the organisation of recruits, he said that he felt like "a man trying to shovel a bushel of fleas across a barn floor." Again when he was besieged by office seekers while his own position was highly precarious, he complained that his task was like letting rooms at one end of his house while the other end was on fire. And yet again when he was reproached for the stern measures which war necessitated, he asked—"Would you prosecute it in future with elder-stalk squirts charged with rose water?"

I have given you evidence of the debt which two of the greatest American lawyers and statesmen owed to literature. May I in turn say something of the connection of the Bar of Scotland with the world of letters, for nowhere have law and literature been more closely related? I cannot say how far this may have been due to the fact that the Scottish Bar has for two and a half centuries lived in daily contact with the famous Advocates' Library, the greatest library which ever belonged to any professional body in the world. Founded in 1682 by the famous, some would say notorious, Lord Advocate, Sir George Mackenzie of Rosehaugh—that "noble wit of Scotland" as Dryden called him—it had grown to over three-quarters of a million books and pamphlets, not including its priceless collection of manuscripts, when in 1925 the Faculty handed it over as a free gift to the nation, beyond all comparison the greatest literary benefaction in our country's history. With such resources at hand to inspire them, the Bar of Scotland have always lived in an atmosphere of what used to be called polite learning. It should not be forgotten that Sir Walter Scott was a practising Scottish advocate, and for many years held office as a Sheriff or Country Court Judge and as Clerk of the Court of Session, the Scottish Supreme Court. He was a lawyer of no mean attainments and his pen was not solely devoted to poetry and romance. I suppose I am one of the few people of this generation who have read his official disquisition on the technical subject of jury trials. In *Guy Mannering*, Sir Walter has stated my thesis for me in his own inimitable way. You remember the visit which Colonel Mannering pays to the study of his counsel, Mr. Pleydell, in the High Street of Edinburgh. "The library into which he was shown," we read, "was a well-proportioned room, hung with a portrait or two of Scottish characters of eminence by Jamieson, the Caledonian Vandyke, and surrounded with books, the best editions of the best authors and in particular an admirable collection of classics. 'These,' said Pleydell, 'are my tools of trade. A lawyer without history or literature is a mechanic, a mere working mason; if he possesses some knowledge of these he may venture to call himself an architect.' "

I enjoy for the moment the privilege which the lawyer is so rarely accorded of being as irrelevant as I please and I cannot refrain from referring here to a literary link with the past which may interest you. The late Archbishop of Canterbury told me that Sir Walter tried out his *Tales of a Grandfather* by reading them over to the Archbishop's mother, Mrs. Davidson, then a little girl of seven, and according to her verdict retained or rejected what he had written. Dining at Grillion's Club one evening only a year or two ago I sat between the Archbishop and Lord Finlay, who in turn told me that he was reading the *Tales of a Grandfather* to his own little granddaughter. So the ages are bridged.

Another Scottish advocate of our own day has attained a literary fame second only to Sir Walter's. It cannot be said that R. L. Stevenson had much professional association with the Bar to which he was called as a contemporary of Lord Dunedin, who is with us here to-day. Yet he found the inspiration of some of his best writing in the legal life of Edinburgh, whose characteristic flavour no one appreciated better than he. There is general agreement that his masterpiece was his unfinished *Weir of Hermiston*, in which he gives us with amazing insight and infinite gusto a portrait of a Scottish judge of the old school. I could mention many other names; Lord Jeffrey, for instance, the pungent Edinburgh reviewer who is perhaps best remembered for the petulant "This will never do" with which he greeted the publication of Wordsworth's *Excursion*, and Aytoun, the author of the *Bon Gaultier Ballads* and the *Lays of the Scottish Cavaliers*, who confessed that although he followed the law he never could overtake it. But I content myself with reminding you that the two greatest biographies in the English language—Boswell's *Life of Johnson* and Lockhart's *Life of Scott*—were written by members of the Scottish Bar. So we may accept with becoming modesty Dr. Johnson's reluctant tribute—"The Scotch write English wonderfully well!"

The fine scholarship of the Bench and Bar of England is traditional. It has exhibited itself perhaps less in actual contributions to literature than in the professional sphere. The deliverances of the judges of England in the leading cases of the law are distinguished by the highest qualities of literary craftsmanship, witness the historic judgments in which Lord Mansfield enunciated the principles of the common law in their application to commerce, the commanding brevity of Jessel, Master of the Rolls, the elegant irony of Lord Bowen, and those delightful passages in which Lord Macnaghten contrived to illumine with humanity and humour the most accurate exposition of the technical doctrines of the law. Of him it could certainly never be said, as was said of another Law Lord, that he was not only dull himself but the cause of dullness in others. The compilers of anthologies have at last discovered how much admirable literary matter is concealed within the unpromising covers of the Law Reports, and in a recent volume of selections of the best English prose will be found two passages from judgments of Lord Sumner, that incomparable master of the English language, whose retirement from the judiciary even his inadequate successor may be permitted to lament.

While literature for its own sake has always possessed a special attraction for the members of our profession, I venture to suggest that its study has a utilitarian side also. Words, the spoken and the written word, are the raw material of the lawyer's trade, and the possession of a good literary style which enables him to make effective use of that material is one of the most valuable of all professional equipments. Such a style is often a natural gift, but even where it is not so bestowed it may be acquired by study and by practice. We may all at least aspire to such a style as, we are told, characterised the judgments of a well-known American judge—"clear, compact and complete, carrying no immaterial discussions and losing no weight through grammatical leaks or rhetorical cracks." For the attainment of a good English style there is no discipline so admirable as the reading of the Bible, a statement appropriate for a son of the Scottish manse which I take leave to endorse as a Lord of Appeal. I have been pleased to observe in the advertisement columns of the *Journal* of the American Bar Association the Bible finding a place among the notices of legal publications. It is there commended to purchasers "bound in high-quality buckram that looks well with other books in your law library. Every lawyer in active practice," says the advertiser, "needs it . . . you'll find it a wonderful help in your practice." I respectfully agree, though I am not quite sure that we mean exactly the same thing. It was Daniel Webster who said—"I have read the Bible through many times and now make it a practice to read it through once every year. It is a book of all others for lawyers as well as divines; and I pity the man who cannot find in it a rich supply of thought and of rules of conduct." In that delightful and friendly series of letters which those two veteran combatants, Adams and Jefferson, exchanged in their old age and which fortunately has been preserved for our edification, I find Adams on Christmas Day 1813 confessing to his correspondent—"The Bible is the best book in the world. It contains more of my little philosophy than all the libraries I have seen." I am for the moment, however, thinking of the Bible purely as literature, and I am very sure that those who have learned to drink from that well of English undefiled have sought the best source of literary inspiration. If to this you add some generous draughts from the Pierian spring of the classics, you can never descend to the mean vulgarity which characterises so much of the writing of the present day.

There is no reason why legal arguments or judicial judgments should not be expressed in good English. There is every reason why they should. The advocate who can impart a literary flavour to his address adds to its persuasiveness and attraction; "Nor pleads he worse who with a decent sprig of bay adorns his legal waste of wig." Exotic flowers of oratory are not suitable adornments for our modern Law Courts, but the Temple has never disdained to deck its plots with the classic blossoms of the English flower garden. It is of even more vital importance that those who sit in judgment should have a mastery not only of law but of letters, so that they may be able to use with ease and freedom—and I should like to add, with distinction —the vehicle of language in which their decisions must be conveyed. The draftsman comes to take a joy in his sheer craftsmanship. I venture to think that there are few higher intellectual pleasures than success in the task of expressing an argument or a conclusion in just precisely the right language, so that the thought is caught and poised exactly as we would have it. Clear thinking always means clear writing and clear writing is always good writing.

And so I come back to the point from which I set out that alike for the preservation of our position as a learned profession and for the promotion of efficiency in the art we practise, it is essential that the lawyer should be steeped in literature and keep his mind constantly refreshed and renewed by contact with the great thinkers of the past. So only can he attain to true eminence.

Law and Language*

LORD MACMILLAN

Law and Language *was delivered to the law students of Birmingham in 1931.*

To the legal profession, above all others, words and their meanings are a matter of supreme concern. The lawyer, indeed, may not unfairly be described as a trafficker in words. They are his staple, his stock-in-trade, and the annual turnover of the profession must far outstrip the almost astronomical figures of the Bankers' Clearing House. For all day and every day the lawyer is using words, whether he is framing a conveyance or a contract, advising a client about his affairs, arguing a case, writing a judgment or opinion, preparing the report of a decision—judges, counsel and solicitors are constantly making use of words, written or spoken, and are constantly endeavouring by the use of words to convey their meaning to others.

I do not pause to consider whether the service rendered to the community by dealers in words is as valuable as that which is rendered by those who follow the more creative callings, the architect, the shipbuilder, and the like. "Words," we are reminded, "are the daughters of earth, things are the sons of heaven." But this at least is certain, that it is of the utmost importance for the lawyer, if he is to perform adequately his duty to his clients and to the public, that he should possess a special skill in the use of language. It is not, of course, with words in themselves that he is concerned, as is the etymologist and, to some extent, the literary artist. For him "it is not necessary," as Vice-Chancellor Kindersley said (in construing the word "money" in a will), "to go into the derivation of the word, for that sort of reasoning would not assist in the administration of justice." For the lawyer the importance of words lies in the fact that they are the vehicle of the law. In statutes, reports, and textbooks he finds the law in static form set out in words; in judgment, argument and draft he seeks to express the law in dynamic form, again in words. For the formulation, the exposition and the application of law the only medium is language, and success or failure in these endeavours is dependent on the skill and precision with which the lawyer handles his medium.

* Reprinted from *Law and Other Things*, 1937, by Lord Macmillan, by permission of the Cambridge University Press.

The surprising thing is that so little conscious and systematic study is in these days devoted by the legal profession to the art of the right use of language. In classical times it was otherwise. In Greece and Rome much time and much thought were given to the technique of words, and the schools of the grammarians were the training ground of the lawyer. We can still learn much from the precepts of the Attic orators and the treatises of Cicero and Quintilian.

The art of words is a difficult art and a fine art, and the practice of it brings pleasure as well as profit. It is not, however, the aesthetic aspect of language that is of primary interest to the lawyer, though Sir Frederick Pollock is right when he says that not even the draftsman of an ordinary lease can produce really good work "unless he has a share of artistic feeling in the eminent sense, and takes a certain artistic pride in the quality of his workmanship apart from the reward he will get for it." It is rather the utilitarian and practical side of the art which interests the practitioner. Let him not dismiss the matter as merely theoretical. It is a matter of business. No experienced lawyer will belittle the importance of accuracy and precision in the record of his transactions and the expression of his arguments, or fail to recognise how indispensable it is to appreciate the exact meaning of the words he uses. It is not inappropriate that the Law Society should have adopted the word "Interpret" as its telegraphic address!

The student of law soon realises that of all things words are the most uncertain and ambiguous. "The greatest sophism of all sophisms," according to Bacon, "is the equivocation and ambiguity of words and phrase." Dryden says the same thing in verse:

> As long as words a diff'rent sense will bear,
> And each may be his own interpreter,
> Our airy faith will no foundation find:
> The word's a weathercock for every wind.

Indeed, such is the imperfection of the human vocabulary that hardly any word has a precise and definite meaning except the terms used in mathematics and the physical sciences. The terminology of the law labours in a special degree under this disability because of the nature of its subject-matter. The infinite diversity of human relationships with which the law has to deal transcends the limited resources of language, which is always trying to overtake the complexities of life and business and reduce them to categories. Hence the paradox presents itself that the science whose main object is the achievement of order is most open to the accusation of indefiniteness and uncertainty in its pronouncements.

It is only the inefficient craftsman, however, who quarrels with his tools. The efficient workman will rather address himself to their mastery. Let me read you the admirable admonition of the author of the famous *Essay on the Human Understanding*. "I know," says Locke in his Epistle to the

Reader, "there are not words enough in any language to answer all the variety of ideas that enter into men's discourses and reasonings. But this hinders not but that when anyone uses any term he may have in his mind a determined idea which he makes it the sign of and to which he should keep it steadily annexed during that present discourse. Where he does not or cannot do this he in vain pretends to clear or distinct ideas: it is plain his are not so; and, therefore, there can be expected nothing but obscurity and confusion where such terms are made use of which have not such a precise determination." Addressed to mankind in general, this exhortation has a very special application to the lawyer. It may be said without exaggeration that at least half the contests of the law have their origin in the ambiguous use of language. The imperfections of the human vocabulary are as lucrative to the legal practitioner as our physical frailties are to the physician. Many of these controversies over words are no doubt inevitable owing to the inherent defects of the instrument which perforce we must use, and cannot be entirely eliminated even by the most skilful, but, on the other hand, much the larger number of them arise from perfectly avoidable slipshodness and want of precision in thought and expression.

The subject of the lawyer's use of language is thus one which may profitably engage our consideration for a little. There is one interesting aspect of it on which I do not propose to enlarge, for it would take me into fields of investigation foreign to my present purpose, but it is worth mentioning. I mean the peculiar virtue attached to the use of certain words as solemnities. In the ceremonial ritual of all peoples in primitive times we know that a mystic potency was attributed to particular words and a whole branch of folklore is devoted to the study of spells and charms. The law has not been entirely free from this tendency. It is in the historical formalities attendant on transactions in real property that the ritual use of special words finds its best illustrations. The element of symbolism was by the nature of things imported into such transactions, for corporeal "traditio" is not possible in the case of land as it is in the case of personal chattels. And with the prescribed legal ceremonial the use of certain words was always associated. The omission of these "words of style," as they are called, was fatal. Let me give an example from the history of Scottish conveyancing. In Scots law from early times there was one word the use of which was indispensable to constitute an effectual transfer of heritable property, and that was the word "dispone." So recently as 1874 the House of Lords had to consider the consequences of its omission, in the case of *Kirkpatrick's Trustees* v. *Kirkpatrick*. It there appeared that Mrs. Kirkpatrick had on 4 March 1867 executed a trust disposition and settlement in which she used in the dispositive clause with regard to certain property the familiar array of words, I "give, grant, assign, convey and make over," but omitted to say "I dispone." The deed was held to be ineffectual to convey her heritable property. Lord Chancellor Cairns bases his judgment on the ground that the deed "has not in it that word of art and style of efficacy according to Scotch law, I mean the word 'dispone,' and it has been held unanimously by all the judges of the Court of Session that as the law stood at the time this deed was executed the want of the word 'dispone' was fatal to the deed as a conveyance of heritable property." This insistence on the use of a particular word to effect a particular legal result is not peculiar to Scots law. The Lord Chancellor goes on to say: "It may appear to be a very technical view to hold the presence or absence of a single word of this kind to be efficacious or fatal in a deed conveying heritable property, but your Lordships must bear in mind that according to the law of England also there are other words, I apprehend, not of greater importance, the presence or absence of which will be found to have an equal effect on the validity of a deed." I am not expert in the mysteries of English conveyancing, but I have no doubt that the Lord Chancellor was thinking of the virtues attached by it to such words as "demise," "heirs and assigns," and so forth. Mrs. Kirkpatrick's omission to "dispone" her property as well as to give, grant, assign, and convey and make it over would not now be visited with the penalty of nullity, for the Conveyancing (Scotland) Act of 1874, enacted by section 27 that "It shall not be competent to object to the validity of any deed or writing as a conveyance of heritage coming into operation after the passing of this Act on the ground that it does not contain the word 'dispone,' provided it contains any other word or words importing conveyance or transference or present intention to convey or transfer." So another good plea has been consigned by the Legislature to the law's lumber room. There are still, however, I believe, cases in which it is as necessary to legal efficacy to use the correct verbal incantation as it was to employ the words "Open Sesame" to cause the door of the treasure cave of the Forty-Thieves to roll back.

The requirement that prescribed words and formulas must be used to achieve certain legal results was not entirely a matter either of mere primitive mumbo-jumbo or of professional pedantry. It had a purpose. It was intended to secure deliberation and certainty. The law said: If you wish to accomplish a particular result, this is the way to do it; if you do it in that way, no question can arise and all the controversies which are so apt to surround questions of intention will be avoided. In Scotland, if you used the word "dispone" you conveyed the property; if you did not, you did not, and there was an end of it. Now under the statute of 1874 any word importing conveyance or transfer will do, but how much vaguer and more open to question is this concession to the linguistic frailty of those who wish to make a grant of their landed property! I confess to being rather an admirer of the discipline which required people to be accurate, precise, and formal in their important transactions and visited departure from the rules with penalties. Lord Cockburn once said: "Words acquire the character of being words of style solely because, from their expressing a thought necessary or usual for the occasion, they can never be safely omitted. 'I hereby dispone' is a piece of style because without it there would be no disposition. When a man reserves power to revoke a deed and says in a subsequent writing, 'I revoke that deed,' the force of these words is surely not weakened by saying that they are so precise, necessary, and conclusive that they have become words of style. No insignificant word ever becomes a matter of style."

I leave this digression on what I may term spell-binding words and return to my main purpose, which is to discuss the general topic of the lawyer's use of words. "Most of the disputes in the world arise from words," said Lord Mansfield. The experience of every practising lawyer will confirm this saying. I know for myself that for the past thirty years and more a great part of my daily business has been to give opinions, to argue or to decide as to the meaning of words. These disputes are by no means always barren logomachies. Great questions of principle may turn upon a word and valuable rights and interests depend on the meaning assigned to it. The difficulty of interpretation arises, as I have said, from the imperfection and inexactitude of language as a vehicle of ideas. If words are the currency of our business, they suffer from the defects which have always affected human currency. Their value in exchange is unstable, and they not only undergo changes in time but at any one moment their precise content is often indeterminable.

One of the great controversies of the law will serve as an illustration. I refer to the determination of the meaning of the word "minerals" in the Clauses Acts, and particularly the Railways Clauses Consolidation Act of 1845. As you know, when a railway company buys land for the construction of its line there is implied in the statutory form of conveyance an exception of the mines and minerals in the land purchased. These remain the property of the vendor. This was, no doubt, designed to save the railway companies the expense of purchasing valuable underlying minerals when all that they required was the use of the surface. There is a code which provides for what is to happen when the owner of the retained minerals wants to work them, and the railway company, if it is afraid that its line may subside if it is undermined, has to pay compensation if it exercises its right of stopping the workings. Hence a whole series of leading cases has arisen in which the railway companies have maintained that particular materials were not minerals, and, consequently, belonged to them under their conveyances, while the landowners on the other hand have contended that these materials were minerals reserved to them which they were entitled to extract or for the non-working of which they must be compensated. The word is an admirable example of ambiguity. There is no definition of it in the statutory code, and, consequently, the Courts have been called upon to adjudicate upon one substance after another. What is to be the criterion? It is obvious that the familiar distinction between animal, vegetable and mineral which sufficed for the parlour games of our youth could afford no adequate guide. Is fireclay a mineral or merely part of the ordinary substance of the earth? Is building sandstone a mineral or like ordinary stones and rock part of the common structure of the ground? To the former question the House of Lords answered that fireclay was a mineral, to the latter, that sandstone was not a mineral. Other cases have arisen about whinstone, china clay, brick clay, and so forth. The criterion ultimately prescribed by the House of Lords was that those things are minerals which are so described in "the vernacular of the mining world, the commercial world, and landowners." This may be a practical test and probably as good as any that could be devised, but it obviously relegated each case to be determined by evidence of usage. And it gave rise to another interesting question. If vernacular usage is to be the test we know that such usage varies from one generation to another. As at what date are we to ascertain the usage? The point came up in a litigation between the Marquis of Linlithgow and the North British Railway. A canal which subsequently came to be owned by the railway company was constructed in the early part of last century partly through Lord Linlithgow's lands and traverses the well-known Linlithgow shale field. The statute authorising the construction of the canal was passed in 1817 long before the Clauses Acts, but its terms gave rise to the same question as I have just indicated. The landowner desired to work out the oil shale under the canal or to be paid for it as a mineral, while the railway company maintained that it belonged to them as part of the land conveyed to them. Possession of the land was taken by the original canal undertakers in 1818, but no conveyance was actually executed till 1862. Here were the makings of a first-class controversy. If vernacular usage was to be the test, was it to be the vernacular of 1817 when the Act was passed, or the vernacular of 1818 when possession was taken, or that of 1862 when the conveyance was executed, or that which was current when the question came before the Courts? The question was critical, for mineral oil became known as a commercial commodity only after Young's famous patents, the pioneer patents of the great modern oil industry, were taken out in the 'fifties of last century. Before that time shale was regarded merely as rubbish and of no value to anyone. A most interesting body of evidence on the history of mineral oil extraction was collected, and I remember Professor Gregory, the well-known geologist, furnished a remarkable reconstitution of the state of geological science at different periods on the subject of the properties of shale. The Scottish Courts held that the crucial date was the date of the actual transference of possession in 1818, and that at that date shale was not known as a mineral in the vernacular of the mining world, the commercial world, and landowners. The case went to the House of Lords, but there the interesting questions to which I have alluded were not dealt with, for in their disappointing way they found another ground in the terms of the statute for deciding the matter in favour of the railway company. There could be no better example of the uncertainty of language for, as you have seen, it was not merely a question of ascertaining the meaning of a term but a question as well of determining the date at which the meaning was to be ascertained.

Probably the most notorious instance of the difficulty of interpreting even the simplest words is to be found in the famous case of *Powell* v. *Kempton Park Race Course Co., Ltd.,* where the controversy related to the meaning of a "place opened, kept or used" for the purposes prohibited by the Betting Act, 1853. The locality—I must not say place—under discussion was a railed-in enclosure adjoining a race course, to which enclosure the public were admitted on payment of an entrance fee and to which bookmakers resorted for the purpose of their business. Such an array and such a division of eminent judicial minds has seldom been seen. Taking all the Courts which considered this momentous question, I find on the one hand Lord Russell of Killowen, L.C.J., Rigby, L.J., Lord Davey and Lord Hobhouse in favour of finding that the enclosure came within the scope of the Act, while of the contrary and prevailing opinion were Lord Esher, M.R., Lindley, Lopes, A. L. Smith and Chitty, L.JJ., Lord Chancellor Halsbury and Lords Watson, Macnaghten, Morris, Shand and James of Hereford. The Lord Chancellor in his judgment sets out the statutory words that required to be construed in an analytical table, and deals with the problems which each word raises. In Lord James of Hereford's speech a good example of the process of interpretation is exhibited. "There must," says his Lordship at p. 194, "be a defined area so marked out that it can be found and recognised as 'the place' where the business is carried on and wherein the bettor can be found. Thus, if a person betted on Salisbury Plain there would be no place within the Act. The whole of Epsom Downs or any other race course where betting takes place would not constitute a place; but directly a definite localisation of the business of betting is affected, be it under a tent or even movable umbrella, it may be well held that a 'place' exists for the purposes of a conviction under the Act." The enclosure in question, his Lordship went on to say, might therefore physically speaking under certain conditions constitute a place, but even if so he held that it was not opened, kept, or used for the purpose of the owners, occupiers, or users of it betting with persons resorting thereto.

Many other examples of this uncertainty in the meaning of words will occur to you. The undiscriminating use of the conjunctive "and" and the disjunctive "or" has given rise to many a contest and Jeremy Bentham devotes to the ambiguities of the latter monosyllable some devastating criticism. "May" and "shall" have almost a legal literature of their own. The amount of money which has been spent in trying to ascertain what is an "accident" within the meaning of the Workmen's Compensation Acts must now have reached a surprising total. The arguments and disquisitions on this topic enshrined in the law reports are an excellent commentary on my thesis. The question readily lends itself to metaphysical subtleties, and the whole theory of chance and design is involved. The layman is always exhorting the lawyer to use ordinary language which the people can understand, and when this legislation was first introduced we were assured that it was expressed in simple terms which would reduce litigation to a minimum. You see the result of this endeavour in the endless disputes which have arisen in the Courts over such apparently straightforward words as "wages," "suitable employment," "able to earn," "incapacity," and the like in which this so-called commonsense legislation abounds. An interesting contrast is afforded by the Succession Duty Act, 1853, one of the most technical enactments in the statute book, which has earned high praise as an almost perfect example of the legislative art. So logical is its structure and so precise is its use of language, that the number of reported cases to which it has given rise is remarkably small considering the important interests it affects. But it is not easy reading.

Only last week you may have noticed reported in adjoining columns of *The Times* two cases in the King's Bench Division in one of which the question was what was meant by the word "cream" in a statute, while in the other the question was what was meant by the apparently tautological expression "non-working holidays" in a charter party. In the former the Court held that Messrs. J. Lyons and Co., Ltd., who had sold certain articles with the label "Lyons' Swiss Rolls, Chocolate Sponge (Cream Filled)," had not contravened a statute which forbids the sale, under a description including the word "cream," of any substance purporting to be cream unless the substance *is* cream. In the latter case Roche, J., expressed the view that the mere fact that work might possibly be done on a holiday did not turn that day into a working holiday but that a working holiday was a holiday on which men worked without any substantial addition to their ordinary wages; in other words, the kind of holiday with which we lawyers are only too painfully familiar.

Thus every day we see the Courts engaged in elucidating the meaning of the English language. These problems are likely to increase rather than to diminish in number in view of the growing tendency of the Legislature to enter upon regions which were formerly regarded as outside its province and to regulate every incident and transaction of our daily lives. The modern legislator, concerning himself with all the day-to-day affairs of the social life of the people, cheerfully imports into the statute book the inaccurate and colloquial language of the street and the market-place with only the most casual appreciation of what he is doing, and so we have questions as to whether catering is a trade, and as to whether a chemist who sells Lysol in an automatic machine at the door of his shop is conducting this business himself. So complicated and various is our daily life that the Legislature which would seek to regulate its every activity would require to be endowed with superhuman knowledge and imagination in order to provide for every case, and even with these gifts it would find human language inadequate for its purpose. Whatever may be our political views, it is consoling to reflect that the increasing intervention of Parliament in the life of the people by means of imperfectly framed statutes will, at any rate, save many lawyers from swelling the ranks of the unemployed.

I fear, indeed, that the tasks which are being set to our highly skilled Parliamentary draftsmen in these days are becoming more than they can perform, for it is only possible to frame an intelligible and workable statute when its promoters have a clear and definite idea of what it is that they wish to express in the language of enactment, and such clear and definite ideas are far from being commonly possessed by the promoters of much of our modern legislation. Witness the recent breakdown in Parliament of a Bill which sought to amend the law of trade disputes. The learned Attorney-General proposed what he described as "simple words." They included the expression "the primary object" of a strike or lock-out; indeed the pivotal words of the Bill were these words: "the primary object." I doubt if any words more difficult of judicial interpretation and application could be found in the dictionary, and yet it was proposed to use them in a matter in which precision and certainty are pre-eminently desirable. The Attorney-General's happy quotation from *Through the Looking-Glass* in the earlier part of his speech—a quotation which is also prefixed to Stroud's *Judicial Dictionary*—seems to me peculiarly apposite to his own proposal. " 'When *I* use a word,' Humpty Dumpty said, in rather a scornful tone, 'it means just what I choose it to mean, neither more nor less.' 'The question is,' said Alice, 'whether you *can* make words mean so many different things.' "

In much less exalted spheres this problem of attaining precision in the use of language equally presents itself. Suppose you are trying to draw up the rules for a students' union or a tennis club. You probably proceed to provide that members may introduce as guests persons belonging to their families. Then the trouble begins. What is a member's family? Does it mean his children, as when you say of a man that he has no family? Or does it mean those who live in family with the member, which may include his sisters, his cousins, and his aunts, or any one else who happens to reside under the same roof with him? Does it include his grandparents and his grandchildren? And so on and so on. This is not travesty. Those of you who have tried your hand at such tasks will have more sympathy, perhaps, with the unhappy Parliamentary draftsman who is required to produce over-night a measure for the better regulation of the ice-cream trade or some of the other lofty topics of jurisprudence with which the Legislature nowadays busies itself. He has to remember in Mr. Justice Stephen's words that "it is not enough to attain to a degree of precision which a person reading in good faith can understand; but it is necessary to attain, if possible, to a degree of precision which a person reading in bad faith cannot misunderstand. It is all the better if he cannot pretend to misunderstand it."

As I have indicated, one of the chief functions of our Courts is to act as an animated and authoritative dictionary. It is for the Courts, we are told, to say what the statute or the contract means. The words used by one set of persons have to be interpreted by another set of persons. It is a difficult task enough, and perhaps none the less so that one of the cardinal rules is that you must not ask the person who used a particular word what he meant by it. The testator who leaves his "books" to a public library cannot be asked if he meant by that word to include his valuable stamp collection for the best of all reasons that he is now beyond the reach of examination, even if his evidence were otherwise admissible. And in construing an Act of Parliament the legislators who passed it cannot be asked to state on oath what they meant by particular words in it—for which they must often be devoutly thankful. Even the debates which have preceded the enactments of a statute must not be looked at, however surreptitiously. At least they must not be referred to in Court.

The extent of the task thus laid upon the Courts, and upon those who have to advise the public outside the Courts, may be gauged from the four admirable volumes of Stroud's *Judicial Dictionary,* a work already mentioned, for which we have all reason to be grateful, and which I wish was regularly brought up to date, for if you will look at the *Annual Digest* under "Words" you will see that every year adds new judicial interpretations to the English language. In the *English and Empire Digest* some 120 columns of the index are devoted to "Words and Phrases."

How is this duty of interpretation to be performed? "Is not the judge bound to know the meaning of all words in the English language?" asked Baron Martin, judiciously adopting the rhetorical and non-committal interrogative, in *Hills* v. *London Gas Light Co.,* to which he added the merciful qualification: "or if they are used technically or scientifically to inform his own mind by evidence and then to determine the meaning?" Happily, we are not left entirely without guidance, for certain rules have been formulated for our assistance, though these rules themselves, being in turn expressed in words, are not always certain in their application.

There is first of all what has been termed the Golden Rule that in construing all written instruments the grammatical and ordinary sense of the words is to be adhered to unless that would lead to some absurdity or some repugnance or inconsistency with the rest of the instrument, in which case the grammatical and ordinary sense of the words may be modified so as to avoid that absurdity and inconsistency, but no further. This rule, originally formulated by Burton, J., afterwards received the high imprimatur of Lord Wensleydale, and has been again and again approved. It is a rule of good sense and sounds impressive, but, like another gold standard of which we hear much in these days, it may be criticised as effecting less than it professes. For the grammatical and ordinary sense of a word may vary, as we have seen in the case of so common a word as "family," and may also be different at different times, as we have seen in the case of the word "minerals." And how is the judge to know what is the grammatical and ordinary sense of every word? Fortunately he is permitted to consult the dictionary, and no work is more appreciated in the Courts than Murray's monumental *New English Dictionary*. But even its aid often fails him, for it presents an embarrassing choice of meanings in many instances.

I could spend much time in discussing the various canons of interpretation which have been devised to aid the process of ascertaining the meaning of words. There is the famous *ejusdem generis* rule which prescribes that when you find an enumeration of specific items followed by general words you must examine the specific items to see if they belong to a genus or class, and if they are found to do so then the general words must be read as confined to other items of the same genus or class. If the expression to be construed were "dogs, cats and other animals," the genus might be said to be domestic animals, and the phrase would be reasonably read as excluding lions and tigers, though they are also animals. The rule fails, however, where the enumeration of the specific items is so heterogeneous as to disclose no common genus.

Another rule is embodied in the words *noscitur sociis,* which I may render by the jingle "words of a feather flock together." The meaning of a word is to be judged by the company it keeps. This is really a particular case of the general rule of interpretation which directs us to read all passages in a writing as controlled by their context. Divorced from their context both words and sentences may be made to mean something very different from what their authors intended, as we can see in the extracts which politicians quote from their opponents' speeches or publishers quote from the reviews in the Press.

A famous canon is afforded by the logical principle *expressio unius est exclusio alterius,* of which Coke also gives the alternative form *expressum facit cessare tacitum.* Of this rule, Lopes, L.J., said: "It is often a valuable servant but a dangerous master." It is based on the fact that every affirmation implies a negation, every frontier excludes what it does not include. Illustrations of its application may be found, for example, where a statute which prescribes a particular method of doing something is held to prohibit by implication all other methods, and where a specific enumeration of items evidently intended to be exhaustive is held to exclude all items not specifically enumerated.

I must not fail to notice a method of interpretation much favoured by the Legislature, whereby the draftsman of a statute provides in an interpretation section a special dictionary of the terms employed in the measure. Some of these efforts in modern times are not a little surprising, and we find Parliament telling us that quite familiar words are for the purpose in hand to be deemed to include the most unexpected things. "These interpretation clauses," says Crompton, J., "are often the parts of the Act most difficult to be understood." But they are a useful expedient if they are framed with a due regard to the advice given by Lord Thring in his work on *Practical Legislation*. "Definitions," he says, "require to be carefully considered, as a misuse of them is a frequent cause of ambiguity. It should be recollected that a word once defined preserves its meaning throughout the whole Act—a truism frequently overlooked in practice. A word should never be defined to mean something which it does not properly include—e.g., 'piracy' ought not to be defined to include 'mutiny,' and so forth. The fewer the definitions the better, and, as a general rule, the draftsman should endeavour to draw his Act without definitions and insert them only when he finds that they are absolutely necessary. The proper use of definitions is to include or exclude something with respect to the inclusion or exclusion of which there is a doubt without such a definition, and no attempt should be made to make a pretence of scientific precision by defining words of which the ordinary meaning is sufficiently clear and exact for the purpose of the Act in which they are used." This is sound advice, and I could wish it were more often observed.

And then, of course, the Interpretation Act, 1889, must always be borne in mind with its famous enactment that "words importing the masculine gender shall include females and words in the singular shall include the plural and words in the plural shall include the singular," besides a host of other definitions, all carefully guarded with the prefatory warning "unless the contrary intention appears."

But it is superfluous to set out all the aids which have been devised for our assistance, for they may be found collected, discussed, and illustrated in that most fascinating of legal textbooks—I use the epithet advisedly—Beal's *Cardinal Rules of Legal Interpretation*. As regards the special department of statute law, we have also the classic treatises of Maxwell and Hardcastle, the latter now known by the name of its editor, Craies, while Norton on *Deeds* is an admirable guide in its own province. To these I refer you, and I can promise you that you will find them good reading, which cannot be said of many law books.

From the earliest times the technical terms of our art have been gathered and explained in law dictionaries, a form of compilation now largely superseded by our digests and encyclopaedias. One of the earliest of these dictionaries is Skene's *De Verborum Significatione*, of which my edition is dated 1681. It professes to be an exposition of the "Termes and Difficill Wordes conteined in the Foure Buikes of Regiam Majestatem and uthers, in the Acts of Parliament, Infeftments; and used in Practique of this Realme; with Diverse Rules and Common Places or Principalles of the Lawes." There is much curious and forgotten lore in its pages. I am glad to see that Mr. Cowley, the County Librarian of Lancaster, has undertaken the preparation of a bibliography of such works. In a recent issue of the *Law Journal* he gave a preliminary list and appealed for assistance in his enterprise, which I hope he will receive. His list included several law dictionaries previously unknown to me, but it omitted Skene, and, rather remarkably, the well-known work of Dr. John Cowell, sometime the King's Majesty's Professor of the Civil Law in the University of Cambridge, who published in the seventeenth century his monumental volume entitled *The Interpreter or Book containing the Signification of Words, wherein is set forth the true meaning of all or the most part of such words and terms as are mentioned in the Law Writers or Statutes of this victorious and renowned Kingdom requiring any Exposition or Interpretation: a work not only profitable but necessary for such as desire thoroughly to be instructed in the knowledge of our Laws, Statutes, or other antiquities.* The worthy professor sets a high standard for us. "Indeed," he says in his Address to the Reader, "a Lawyer professeth true Philosophy, and therefore, should not be ignorant (if it were possible) of either beasts or fowls or creeping things nor of the trees from the Cedar in Lebanon to the Hyssop that springeth out of the wall."

It is not, however, with the technical words of our craft that I am so much concerned. These have attained a reasonable scientific precision. It is for a more accurate and scholarly use by the practising lawyer of our ordinary vocabulary in his daily work that I plead. We have a matchless inheritance in our mother tongue, and a great tradition in its use handed down from the Bible and Shakespeare through a long list of masters to our own day. Let us see to it that we do not suffer it to be debased in our time, and that in our generation the legal profession shall continue to merit the proud distinction of being pre-eminently the learned profession.

Section II

THE JUDGE

Jeffreys, the Hanging Judge*

THOMAS BABINGTON MACAULAY

"The prince of literary rogues who always preferred the tale to the truth, and smirched or glorified great men and garbled documents according as they affected his drama." † *Such is Winston Churchill's verdict on Thomas Babington Macaulay from whose History of England our portrait of Judge Jeffreys is taken. Yet few would challenge Macaulay's estimate of Lord Jeffreys as the most dissolute and infamous judge ever to wear ermine, or fail to be captivated in the reading of his pages by the great Victorian's style.*

Nature is never more capricious than in the coloring which she lavishes on her beasts of prey. Jeffreys is no exception. His portrait by Sir Godfrey Kneller shows a countenance of striking physical beauty, worthy of a Captain or Knight or Man at Arms. His preferment by King James II he may have owed to his handsome face, but it is more likely that his vengeful sovereign knew that Jeffreys was the man for the Bloody Assizes, the royal vengeance on the survivors of the Duke of Monmouth's Rebellion. Lord Jeffreys' fortunes turned to dust on the accession of William III and he died in the Tower at the early age of forty-one of a combination of drink and disease.

The person selected was Sir George Jeffreys, Chief Justice of the Court of King's Bench. The depravity of this man has passed into a proverb. Both the great English parties have attacked his memory with emulous violence; for the Whigs considered him as their most barbarous enemy, and the Tories found it convenient to throw on him the blame of all the crimes which had sullied their triumph. A diligent and candid inquiry will show that some frightful stories which have been told concerning him are false or exaggerated; yet the dispassionate historian will be able to make very little deduction from the vast mass of infamy with which the memory of the wicked judge has been loaded.

He was a man of quick and vigorous parts, but constitutionally prone to insolence and to the angry passions. When just emerging from boyhood,

* From *History of England*.

† Winston Churchill: *A Roving Commission*, copyright, 1930, 1939 by Charles Scribner's Sons.

he had risen into practice at the Old Bailey bar, a bar where advocates have always used a license of tongue unknown in Westminster Hall. Here, during many years, his chief business was to examine and cross-examine the most hardened miscreants of a great capital. Daily conflicts with prostitutes and thieves called out and exercised his powers so effectually that he became the most consummate bully ever known in his profession. All tenderness for the feelings of others, all self-respect, all sense of the becoming, were obliterated from his mind. He acquired a boundless command of the rhetoric in which the vulgar express hatred and contempt. The profusion of maledictions and vituperative epithets which composed his vocabulary could hardly have been rivaled in the fish-market or the beargarden. His countenance and his voice must always have been unamiable; but these natural advantages—for such he seems to have thought them—he had improved to such a degree that there were few who, in his paroxysms of rage, could see or hear him without emotion. Impudence and ferocity sat upon his brow. The glare of his eyes had a fascination for the unhappy victim on whom they were fixed; yet his brow and eye were said to be less terrible than the savage lines of his mouth. His yell of fury, as was said by one who had often heard it, sounded like the thunder of the judgment day. These qualifications he carried, while still a young man, from the bar to the bench. He early became common sergeant, and then recorder of London. As judge at the city sessions he exhibited the same propensities which afterward, in a higher post, gained for him an unenviable immortality. Already might be remarked in him the most odious vice which is incident to human nature, a delight in misery merely as misery. There was a fiendish exultation in the way in which he pronounced sentence on offenders. Their weeping and imploring seemed to titillate him voluptuously; and he loved to scare them into fits by dilating with luxuriant amplification on all the details of what they were to suffer. Thus, when he had an opportunity of ordering an unlucky adventuress to be whipped at the cart's tail, "Hangman," he would exclaim, "I charge you to pay particular attention to this lady! Scourge her soundly, man! Scourge her till the blood runs down! It is Christmas; a cold time for madam to strip in! See that you warm her shoulders thoroughly!" He was hardly less facetious when he passed judgment on Ludowick Muggleton, the drunken tailor who fancied himself a prophet. "Impudent rogue!" roared Jeffreys, "thou shalt have an easy, easy, easy punishment!" One part of this easy punishment was the pillory, in which the wretched fanatic was almost killed with brickbats.

By this time the heart of Jeffreys had been hardened to that temper which tyrants require in their worst implements. He had hitherto looked for professional advancement to the Corporation of London. He had therefore professed himself a Roundhead, and had always appeared to be in a higher state of exhilaration when he explained to popish priests that they were to be cut down alive, and were to see their own bowels burned, than when he passed ordinary sentences of death. But, as soon as he had got all that the city could give, he made haste to sell his forehead of brass and his tongue of venom to the court. Chiffinch, who was accustomed to act as broker in infamous contracts of more than one kind, lent his aid. He had conducted many amorous and many political intrigues, but he assuredly never rendered a more scandalous service to his masters than when he introduced Jeffreys to Whitehall. The renegade soon found a patron in the obdurate and revengeful James, but was always regarded with scorn and disgust by Charles, whose faults, great as they were, had no affinity with insolence and cruelty. "That man," said the king, "has no learning, no sense, no manners, and more impudence than ten carted street-walkers." Work was to be done, however, which could be trusted to no man who reverenced law or was sensible of shame; and thus Jeffreys, at an age at which a barrister thinks himself fortunate if he is employed to lead an important cause, was made Chief Justice of the King's Bench.

His enemies could not deny that he possessed some of the qualities of a great judge. His legal knowledge, indeed, was merely such as he had picked up in practice of no very high kind; but he had one of those happily-constituted intellects which, across labyrinths of sophistry and through masses of immaterial facts, go straight to the true point. Of his intellect, however, he seldom had the full use. Even in civil causes his malevolent and despotic temper perpetually disordered his judgment. To enter his court was to enter the den of a wild beast, which none could tame, and which was as likely to be roused to rage by caresses as by attacks. He frequently poured forth on plaintiffs and defendants, barristers and attorneys, witnesses and jurymen, torrents of frantic abuse, intermixed with oaths and curses. His looks and tones had inspired terror when he was merely a young advocate struggling into practice. Now that he was at the head of the most formidable tribunal in the realm, there were few indeed who did not tremble before him. Even when he was sober, his violence was sufficiently frightful; but, in general, his reason was overclouded, and his evil passions stimulated by the fumes of intoxication. His evenings were ordinarily given to revelry. People who saw him only over his bottle would have supposed him to be a man gross indeed, sottish, and addicted to low company and low merriment, but social and good-humored. He was constantly surrounded on such occasions by buffoons, selected, for the most part, from among the vilest pettifoggers who practiced before him. These men bantered and abused each other for his entertainment. He joined in their ribald talk, sang catches with them, and, when his head grew hot, hugged and kissed them in an ecstasy of drunken fondness. But, though wine at first seemed to soften his heart, the effect of a few hours later was very different. He often came to the judgment seat, having kept the court waiting long, and yet having but half slept off his debauch, his cheeks on fire, his eyes staring like those of a maniac. When he was in this state, his boon companions of the preceding night, if they were wise, kept out of his way, for the recollection of the familiarity to which he had admitted them inflamed his malignity, and he was sure to take every opportunity of overwhelming them with execration and invective. Not the least odious of his many odious peculiarities was the pleasure which he took in publicly browbeating and mortifying those whom, in his fits of maudlin tenderness, he had encouraged to presume on his favor.

The services which the government had expected from him were performed, not merely without flinching, but eagerly and triumphantly. His first exploit was the judicial murder of Algernon Sidney. What followed was in perfect harmony with this beginning. Respectable Tories lamented the disgrace which the barbarity and indecency of so great a functionary brought upon the administration of justice; but the excesses which filled such men with horror were titles to the esteem of James. Jeffreys, therefore, after the death of Charles, obtained a seat in the cabinet and a peerage. This last honor was a signal mark of royal approbation; for, since the judicial system of the realm had been remodeled in the thirteenth century, no chief justice had been a lord of Parliament.

Guildford now found himself superseded in all his political functions, and restricted to his business as a judge in equity. At council he was treated by Jeffreys with marked incivility. The whole legal patronage was in the hands of the chief justice; and it was well known by the bar that the surest way to propitiate the chief justice was to treat the lord keeper with disrespect.

At Winchester the chief justice first opened his commission. Hampshire had not been the theater of war; but many of the vanquished rebels had, like their leader, fled thither. Two of them, John Hickes, a Non-conformist divine, and Richard Nelthorpe, the lawyer who had been outlawed for his share in the Rye House Plot, had sought refuge at the house of Alice, widow of John Lisle. John Lisle had sat in the Long Parliament and in the High Court of Justice, had been a commissioner of the great seal in the days of the Commonwealth, and had been created a lord by Cromwell. The titles given by the Protector had not been recognized by any government which had ruled England since the downfall of his house; but they appear to have been often used in conversation even by Royalists. John Lisle's widow was therefore commonly known as the Lady Alice. She was related to many respectable, and to some noble families, and she was generally esteemed even by the Tory gentlemen of her county; for it was well known to them that she had deeply regretted some violent acts in which her husband had borne a part, that she had shed bitter tears for Charles the First, and that she had protected and relieved many Cavaliers in their distress. The same womanly kindness which had led her to befriend the Royalists in their time of trouble would not suffer her to refuse a meal and a hiding-place to the wretched men who now entreated her to protect them. She took them into her house, set meat and drink before them, and showed them where they might take rest. The next morning her dwelling was surrounded by soldiers. Strict search was made. Hickes was found concealed in the malt-house, and Nelthorpe in the chimney. If Lady Alice knew her guests to have been concerned in the insurrection, she was undoubtedly guilty of what in strictness is a capital crime; for the law of principal and accessory, as respects high treason, then was, and is to this day, in a state disgraceful to English jurisprudence. In cases of felony, a distinction, founded on justice and reason, is made between the principal and the accessory after the fact. He who conceals from justice one whom he knows to be a murderer, though liable to punishment, is not liable to the punishment of murder; but he who shelters one whom he knows to be a traitor is, according to all our jurists, guilty of high treason. It is unnecessary to point out the absurdity and cruelty of a law which includes under the same definition, and visits with the same penalty, offenses lying at the opposite extremes of the scale of guilt. The feeling which makes the most loyal subject shrink from the thought of giving up to a shameful death the rebel who, vanquished, hunted down, and in mortal agony, begs for a morsel of bread and a cup of water, may be a weakness, but it is surely a weakness very nearly allied to virtue; a weakness which, constituted as human beings are, we can hardly eradicate from the mind without eradicating many noble and benevolent sentiments. A wise and good ruler may not think it right to sanction this weakness, but he will generally connive at it, or punish it very tenderly. In no case will he treat it as a crime of the blackest dye. Whether Flora Macdonald was justified in concealing the attainted heir of the Stuarts, whether a brave soldier of our own time was justified in assisting the escape of Lavalette, are questions on which casuists may differ; but to class such actions with the crimes of Guy Faux and Fieschi is an outrage to humanity and common sense. Such, however, is the classification of our law. It is evident that nothing but a lenient administration could make such a state of the law endurable. And it is just to say that, during many generations, no English government, save one, has treated with rigor persons guilty merely of harboring defeated and flying insurgents. To women especially has been granted, by a kind of tacit prescription, the right of indulging, in the midst of havoc and vengeance, that compassion which is the most endearing of all their charms. Since the beginning of the great civil war, numerous rebels, some of them far more important than Hickes or Nelthorpe, have been protected against the severity of victorious governments by female adroitness and generosity; but no English ruler who has been thus baffled, the savage and implacable James alone excepted, has had the barbarity even to think of putting a lady to a cruel and shameful death for so venial and amiable a transgression.

Odious as the law was, it was strained for the purpose of destroying Alice Lisle. She could not, according to the doctrine laid down by the highest authority, be convicted till after the conviction of the rebels whom she had harbored. She was, however, sent to the bar before either Hickes or Nelthorpe had been tried. It was no easy matter in such a case to obtain a verdict for the crown. The witnesses prevaricated. The jury, consisting of the principal gentlemen of Hampshire, shrank from the thought of sending a fellow-creature to the stake for conduct which seemed deserving rather of praise than of blame. Jeffreys was beside himself with fury. This was the first case of treason on the circuit, and there seemed to be a strong probability that his prey would escape him. He stormed, cursed, and swore in language which no well-bred man would have used at a race or a cockfight. One witness named Dunne, partly from concern for Lady Alice, and partly from fright at the threats and maledictions of the chief justice, entirely lost his head, and at last stood silent. "Oh, how hard the truth is," said Jeffreys, "to come out of a lying Presbyterian knave." The witness, after a pause of some minutes, stammered a few unmeaning words. "Was there ever," exclaimed the judge, with an oath, "was there ever such a villain on the face of the earth? Dost thou believe that there is a God? Dost thou believe in hell fire? Of all the witnesses that I ever met with, I never saw thy fellow." Still the poor man, scared out of his senses, remained mute, and again Jeffreys burst forth: "I hope, gentlemen of the jury, that you take notice of the horrible carriage of this fellow. How can one help abhorring both these men and their religion? A Turk is a saint to such a fellow as this. A pagan would be ashamed of such villainy. Oh, blessed Jesus! What a generation of vipers do we live among." "I can not tell what to say, my lord," faltered Dunne. The judge again broke forth into a volley of oaths. "Was there ever," he cried, "such an impudent rascal? Hold the candle to him, that we may see his brazen face. You, gentlemen, that are of counsel for the crown, see that an information for perjury be preferred against this fellow." After the witnesses had been thus handled, the Lady Alice was called on for her defense. She began by saying, what may possibly have been true, that though she knew Hickes to be in trouble when she took him in, she did not know or suspect that he had been concerned in the rebellion. He was a divine, a man of peace. It had, therefore, never occurred to her that he could have borne arms against the government; and she had supposed that he wished to conceal himself because warrants were out against him for field preaching. The chief justice began to storm. "But I will tell you. There is not one of those lying, sniveling, canting Presbyterians but, one way or another, had a hand in the rebellion. Presbytery has all manner of villainy in it. Nothing but Presbytery could have made Dunne such a rogue. Show me a Presbyterian, and I'll show thee a lying knave." He summed up in the same style, declaimed during an hour against Whigs and Dissenters, and reminded the jury that the prisoner's husband had borne a part in the death of Charles the First, a fact which was not proved by any testimony, and which, if it had been proved, would have been utterly irrelevant to the issue. The jury retired, and remained long in consultation. The judge grew impatient. He could not conceive, he said, how, in so plain a case, they should even have left the box. He sent a messenger to tell them that, if they did not instantly return, he would adjourn the court and lock them up all night. Thus put to the torture, they came, but came to say that they doubted whether the charge had been made out. Jeffreys expostulated with them vehemently, and, after another consultation, they gave a reluctant verdict of Guilty.

On the following morning sentence was pronounced. Jeffreys gave directions that Alice Lisle should be burned alive that very afternoon. This excess of barbarity moved the pity and indignation even of that class which was most devoted to the crown. The clergy of Winchester Cathedral remonstrated with the chief justice, who, brutal as he was, was not mad enough to risk a quarrel on such a subject with a body so much respected by the Tory party. He consented to put off the execution five days. During that time the friends of the prisoner besought James to show her mercy. Ladies of high rank interceded for her. Feversham, whose recent victory had increased his influence at court, and who, it is said, had been bribed to take the compassionate side, spoke in her favor. Clarendon, the king's brother-in-law, pleaded her cause. But all was vain. The utmost that could be obtained was that her sentence should be commuted from burning to beheading. She was put to death on a scaffold in the market-place of Winchester, and underwent her fate with serene courage.

In Hampshire Alice Lisle was the only victim; but, on the day following her execution, Jeffreys reached Dorchester, the principal town of the county in which Monmouth had landed, and the judicial massacre began.

The court was hung, by order of the chief justice, with scarlet; and this innovation seemed to the multitude to indicate a bloody purpose. It was also rumored that, when the clergyman who preached the assize sermon enforced the duty of mercy, the ferocious mouth of the judge was distorted by an ominous grin. These things made men augur ill of what was to follow.

More than three hundred prisoners were to be tried. The work seemed heavy, but Jeffreys had a contrivance for making it light. He let it be understood that the only chance of obtaining pardon or respite was to plead guilty. Twenty-nine persons, who put themselves on their country and were convicted, were ordered to be tied up without delay. The remaining prisoners pleaded guilty by scores. Two hundred and ninety-two received sentence of death. The whole number hanged in Dorsetshire amounted to seventy-four.

From Dorchester Jeffreys proceeded to Exeter. The civil war had barely grazed the frontier of Devonshire. Here, therefore, comparatively few persons were capitally punished. Somersetshire, the chief seat of the rebellion, had been reserved for the last and more fearful vengeance. In this county two hundred and thirty-three prisoners were in a few days hanged, drawn, and quartered. At every spot where two roads met, on every market-place, on the green of every large village which had furnished Monmouth with soldiers, ironed corpses clattering in the wind, or heads and quarters stuck on poles, poisoned the air, and made the traveler sick with horror. In many parishes the peasantry could not assemble in the house of God without seeing the ghastly face of a neighbor grinning at them over the porch. The chief justice was all himself. His spirits rose higher and higher as the work went on. He laughed, shouted, joked, and swore in such a way that many thought him drunk from morning to night; but in him it was not easy to distinguish the madness produced by evil passions from the madness produced by brandy. A prisoner affirmed that the witnesses who appeared against him were not entitled to credit. One of them, he said, was a papist, and the other a prostitute. "Thou impudent rebel," exclaimed the judge, "to reflect on the king's evidence! I see thee, villain, I see thee already with the halter round thy neck." Another produced testimony that he was a good Protestant. "Protestant!" said Jeffreys; "you mean Presbyterian. I'll hold you a wager of it. I can smell a Presbyterian forty miles." One wretched man moved the pity even of bitter Tories. "My lord," they said, "this poor creature is on the parish." "Do not trouble yourselves," said the judge, "I will ease the parish of the burden." It was not only on the prisoners that his fury broke forth. Gentlemen and noblemen of high consideration and stainless loyalty, who ventured to bring to his notice any extenuating circumstance, were almost sure to receive what he called, in the coarse dialect, which he had learned in the pot-houses of White Chapel, a lick with the rough side of his tongue. Lord Stawell, a Tory peer, who could not conceal his horror at the remorseless manner in which his poor neighbors were butchered, was punished by having a corpse suspended in chains at his park gate. In such spectacles originated many tales of terror, which were long told over the cider by the Christmas fires of the farmers of Somersetshire. Within the last forty years, peasants in some districts well knew the accursed spots, and passed them unwillingly after sunset.

Jeffreys boasted that he had hanged more traitors than all his predecessors together since the Conquest. It is certain that the number of persons whom he executed in one month, and in one shire, very much exceeded the number of all the political offenders who have been executed in our island since the Revolution. The rebellions of 1715 and 1745 were of longer duration, of wider extent, and of more formidable aspect than that which was put down at Sedgemoor. It has not been generally thought that, either after the rebellion of 1715, or after the rebellion of 1745, the house of Hanover erred on the side of clemency; yet all the executions of 1715 and 1745 added together will appear to have been few indeed when compared with those which disgraced the Bloody Assizes. The number of the rebels whom Jeffreys hanged on this circuit was three hundred and twenty.

Such havoc must have excited disgust even if the sufferers had been generally odious; but they were, for the most part, men of blameless life, and of high religious profession. They were regarded by themselves, and by a large proportion of their neighbors, not as wrong-doers, but as martyrs who sealed with blood the truth of the Protestant religion. Very few of the convicts professed any repentance for what they had done. Many, animated by the old Puritan spirit, met death, not merely with fortitude, but with exultation. It was in vain that the ministers of the Established Church lectured them on the guilt of rebellion and on the importance of priestly absolution. The claim of the king to unbounded authority in things temporal, and the claim of the clergy to the spiritual power of binding and loosing, moved the bitter scorn of the intrepid sectaries. Some of them composed hymns in the dungeon and chanted them on the fatal sledge. Christ, they sang while they were undressing for the butchery, would soon come to rescue Zion and to make war on Babylon, would set up his standard, would blow his trumpet, and would requite his foes tenfold for all the evil which had been inflicted on his servants. The dying words of these men were noted down; their farewell letters were kept as treasures; and, in this way, with the help of some invention and exaggeration, was formed a copious supplement to the Marian martyrology.

A few cases deserve special mention. Abraham Holmes, a retired officer of the Parliamentary army, and one of those zealots who would own no king but King Jesus, had been taken at Sedgemoor. His arm had been frightfully mangled and shattered in the battle; and, as no surgeon was at hand, the stout old soldier amputated it himself. He was carried up to London and examined by the king in council, but would make no submission. "I am an aged man," he said, "and what remains to me of life is not worth a falsehood or a baseness. I have always been a Republican, and I am so still." He was sent back to the west and hanged. The people remarked with awe and wonder that the beasts which were to drag him to the gallows became restive and went back. Holmes himself doubted not that the Angel of the Lord, as in the old time, stood in the way, sword in hand, invisible to human eyes, but visible to the inferior animals. "Stop, gentlemen," he cried, "let me go on foot. There is more in this than you think. Remember how the ass saw him whom the prophet could not see." He walked manfully to the gallows, harangued the people with a smile, prayed fervently that God would hasten the downfall of anti-Christ and the deliverance of England, and went up the ladder with an apology for mounting so awkwardly. "You see," he said, "I have but one arm."

Not less courageously died Christopher Battiscombe, a young Templar of good family and fortune, who, at Dorchester, an agreeable provincial town proud of its taste and refinement, was regarded by all as the model of a fine gentleman. Great interest was made to save him. It was believed through the west of England that he was engaged to a young lady of gentle blood, the sister of the sheriff; that she threw herself at the feet of Jeffreys to beg for mercy; and that Jeffreys drove her from him with a jest so hideous that to repeat it would be an offense against decency and humanity. Her lover suffered at Lyme piously and courageously.

A still deeper interest was excited by the fate of two gallant brothers, William and Benjamin Hewling. They were young, handsome, accomplished, and well connected. Their maternal grandfather was named Kiffin. He was one of the first merchants in London, and was generally considered as the head of the Baptists. The chief justice behaved to William Hewling on the trial with characteristic brutality. "You have a grandfather," he said, "who deserves to be hanged as richly as you." The poor lad, who was only nineteen, suffered death with so much meekness and fortitude, that an officer of the army who attended the execution, and who had made himself remarkable by rudeness and severity, was strangely melted, and said, "I do not believe that my lord chief justice himself could be proof against this." Hopes were entertained that Benjamin would be pardoned. One victim of tender years was surely enough for one house to furnish. Even Jeffreys was, or pretended to be, inclined to lenity. The truth was, that one of his kinsmen, from whom he had large expectations, and whom, therefore, he could not treat as he generally treated intercessors, pleaded strongly for the afflicted family. Time was allowed for a reference to London. The sister of the prisoner went to Whitehall with a petition. Many courtiers wished her success; and Churchill, among whose numerous faults cruelty had no place, obtained admittance for her. "I wish well to your suit, with all my heart," he said, as they stood together in the ante-chamber; "but do not flatter yourself with hopes. This marble," and he laid his hand on the chimney-piece, "is not harder than the king." The prediction proved true. James was inexorable. Benjamin Hewling died with dauntless courage, amid lamentations in which the soldiers who kept guard round the gallows could not refrain from joining.

Yet those rebels who were doomed to death were less to be pitied than some of the survivors. Several prisoners to whom Jeffreys was unable to bring home the charge of high treason were convicted of misdemeanors, and were sentenced to scourging not less terrible than that which Oates had undergone. A woman, for some idle words such as had been uttered by half the women in the districts where the war had raged, was condemned to be whipped through all the market-towns in the county of Dorset. She suffered part of her punishment before Jeffreys returned to London; but, when he was no longer in the west, the jailers, with the humane connivance of the magistrates, took on themselves the responsibility of sparing her any further torture. A still more frightful sentence was passed on a lad named Tutchin, who was tried for seditious words. He was, as usual, interrupted in his defense by ribaldry and scurrility from the judgment seat. "You are a rebel; and all your family have been rebels since Adam. They tell me that you are a poet. I'll cap verses with you." The sentence was, that the boy should be imprisoned seven years, and should, during that period, be flogged through every market-town in Dorsetshire every year. The women in the galleries burst into tears. The clerk of the arraigns stood up in great disorder. "My lord," said he, "the prisoner is very young. There are many market-towns in our county. The sentence amounts to whipping once a fortnight for seven years." "If he is a young man," said Jeffreys, "he is an old rogue. Ladies, you do not know the villain as well as I do. The punishment is not half bad enough for him. All the interest in England shall not alter it." Tutchin, in his despair, petitioned, and probably with sincerity, that he might be hanged. Fortunately for him, he was, just at this conjuncture, taken ill of the small-pox and given over. As it seemed highly improbable that the sentence would ever be executed, the chief justice consented to remit it in return for a bribe which reduced the prisoner to poverty. The temper of Tutchin, not originally very mild, was exasperated to madness by what he had undergone. He lived to be known as one of the most acrimonious and pertinacious enemies of the house of Stuart and of the Tory party.

The number of prisoners whom Jeffreys transported was eight hundred and forty-one. These men, more wretched than their associates who suffered death, were distributed into gangs, and bestowed on persons who enjoyed favor at court. The conditions of the gift were that the convicts should be carried beyond sea as slaves, that they should not be emancipated for ten years, and that the place of their banishment should be some West Indian island. This last article was studiously framed for the purpose of aggravating the misery of the exiles. In New England or New Jersey they would have found a population kindly disposed to them, and a climate not unfavorable to their health and vigor. It was therefore determined that they should be sent to colonies where a Puritan could hope to inspire little sympathy, and where a laborer born in the temperate zone could hope to enjoy little health. Such was the state of the slave-market that these bondmen, long as was the passage, and sickly as they were likely to prove, were still very valuable. It was estimated by Jeffreys that, on an average, each of them, after all charges were paid, would be worth from ten to fifteen pounds. There was, therefore, much angry competition for grants. Some Tories in the west conceived that they had, by their exertions and sufferings during the insurrection, earned a right to share in the profits which had been eagerly snatched up by the sycophants of Whitehall. The courtiers, however, were victorious.

The misery of the exiles fully equaled that of the negroes who are now carried from Congo to Brazil. It appears, from the best information which is now accessible, that more than one fifth of those who were shipped were flung to the sharks before the end of the voyage. The human cargoes were stowed close in the holds of small vessels. So little space was allowed that the wretches, many of whom were still tormented by unhealed wounds, could not all lie down at once without lying on one another. They were never suffered to go on deck. The hatchway was constantly watched by sentinels armed with hangers and blunderbusses. In the dungeon below all was darkness, stench, lamentation, disease, and death. Of ninety-nine convicts who were carried out in one vessel, twenty-two died before they reached Jamaica, although the voyage was performed with unusual speed. The survivors, when they arrived at their house of bondage, were mere skeletons. During some weeks coarse biscuit and fetid water had been doled out to them in such scanty measure that any one of them could easily have consumed the ration which was assigned to five. They were, therefore, in such a state, that the merchant to whom they had been consigned found it expedient to fatten them before selling them.

Meanwhile, the property both of the rebels who had suffered death, and of those more unfortunate men who were withering under the tropical sun, was fought for and torn in pieces by a crowd of greedy informers. By law, a subject attainted of treason forfeits all his substance; and this law was enforced after the Bloody Assizes with a rigor at once cruel and ludicrous. The broken-hearted widows and destitute orphans of the laboring men whose corpses hung at the cross-roads were called upon by the agents of the Treasury to explain what had become of a basket, of a goose, of a flitch of bacon, of a keg of cider, of a sack of beans, of a truss of hay. While the humbler retainers of the government were pillaging the families of the slaughtered peasants, the chief justice was fast accumulating a fortune out of the plunder of a higher class of Whigs. He traded largely in pardons. His most lucrative transaction of this kind was with a gentleman named Edmund Prideaux. It is certain that Prideaux had not been in arms against the government, and it is probable that his only crime was the wealth which he had inherited from his father, an eminent lawyer who had been high in office under the Protector. No exertions were spared to make out a case for the crown. Mercy was offered to some prisoners on condition that they would bear evidence against Prideaux. The unfortunate man lay long in jail, and at length, overcome by fear of the gallows, consented to pay fifteen thousand pounds for his liberation. This great sum was received by Jeffreys. He bought with it an estate, to which the people gave the name of Aceldama, from that accursed field which was purchased with the price of innocent blood.

He was ably assisted in the work of extortion by the crew of parasites who were in the habit of drinking and laughing with him. The office of these men was to drive hard bargains with convicts under the strong terrors of death, and with parents trembling for the lives of children. A portion of the spoil was abandoned by Jeffreys to his agents. To one of his boon companions, it is said, he tossed a pardon for a rich traitor across the table during a revel. It was not safe to have recourse to any intercession except that of his creatures, for he guarded his profitable monopoly of mercy with jealous care. It was even suspected that he sent some persons to the gibbet solely because they had applied for the royal clemency through channels independent of him.

Some courtiers nevertheless contrived to obtain a small share of this traffic. The ladies of the queen's household distinguished themselves preeminently by rapacity and hard-heartedness. Part of the disgrace which they incurred falls on their mistress, for it was solely on account of the relation in which they stood to her that they were able to enrich themselves by so odious a trade; and there can be no question that she might, with a word or a look, have restrained them; but, in truth, she encouraged them by her evil example, if not by her express approbation. She seems to have been one of that large class of persons who bear adversity better than prosperity. While her husband was a subject and an exile, shut out from public employment, and in imminent danger of being deprived of his birthright, the suavity and humility of her manners conciliated the kindness even of those who most abhorred her religion; but when her good fortune came, her good nature disappeared. The meek and affable duchess turned out an ungracious and haughty queen. The misfortunes which she subsequently endured have made her an object of some interest; but that interest would be not a little heightened if it could be shown that, in the season of her greatness, she saved, or even tried to save, one single victim from the most frightful proscription that England has ever seen. Unhappily, the only request that she is known to have preferred touching the rebels was that a hundred of those who were sentenced to transportation might be given to her. The profit which she cleared on the cargo, after making large allowance for those who died of hunger and fever during the passage, can not be estimated at less than a thousand guineas. We can not wonder that her attendants should have imitated her unprincely greediness and her unwomanly cruelty. They exacted a thousand pounds from Roger Hoare, a merchant of Bridgewater, who had contributed to the military chest of the rebel army. But the prey on which they pounced most eagerly was one which it might have been thought that even the most ungentle natures would have spared. Already some of the girls who had presented the standard to Monmouth at Taunton had cruelly expiated their offense. One of them had been thrown into a prison where an infectious malady was raging. She had sickened and died there. Another had presented herself at the bar before Jeffreys to beg for mercy. "Take her, jailer," vociferated the judge, with one of those frowns which had often struck terror into stouter hearts than hers. She burst into tears, drew her hood over her face, followed the jailer out of court, fell ill of fright, and in a few hours was a corpse. Most of the young ladies, however, who had walked in the procession were still alive. Some of them were under ten years of age. All had acted under the orders of their schoolmistress, without knowing that they were committing a crime. The queen's maids of honor asked the royal permission to wring money out of the parents of the poor children, and the permission was granted. An order was sent down to Taunton that all these little girls should be seized and imprisoned. Sir Francis Warre, of Hestercombe, the Tory member for Bridgewater, was requested to undertake the office of exacting the ransom. He was charged to declare in strong language that the maids of honor would not endure delay; that they were determined to prosecute to outlawry, unless a reasonable sum were forthcoming; and that by a reasonable sum was meant seven thousand pounds. Warre excused himself from taking any part in a transaction so scandalous. The maids of honor then requested William Penn to act for them, and Penn accepted the commission; yet it should seem that a little of the pertinacious scrupulosity which he had often shown about taking off his hat would not have been altogether out of place on this occasion. He probably silenced the remonstrances of his conscience by repeating to himself that none of the money which he extorted would go into his own pocket; that if he refused to be the agent of the ladies, they would find agents less humane; that by complying he should increase his influence at the court, and that his influence at the court had already enabled him, and might still enable him, to render great services to his oppressed brethren. The maids of honor were at last forced to content themselves with less than a third part of what they had demanded.

No English sovereign has ever given stronger proofs of a cruel nature than James the Second; yet his cruelty was not more odious than his mercy; or, perhaps, it may be more correct to say that his mercy and his cruelty were such that each reflects infamy on the other. Our horror at the fate of the simple clowns, the young lads, the delicate women, to whom he was inexorably severe, is increased when we find to whom and for what considerations he granted his pardon.

The rule by which a prince ought, after a rebellion, to be guided in selecting rebels for punishment is perfectly obvious. The ring-leaders, the men of rank, fortune, and education, whose power and whose artifices have led the multitude into error, are the proper objects of severity. The deluded populace, when once the slaughter on the field of battle is over, can scarcely be treated too leniently. This rule, so evidently agreeable to justice and humanity, was not only not observed, it was inverted. While those who ought to have been spared were slaughtered by hundreds, the few who might with propriety have been left to the utmost rigor of the law were spared. This eccentric clemency has perplexed some writers, and has drawn forth ludicrous eulogies from others. It was neither at all mysterious nor at all praiseworthy. It may be distinctly traced in every case either to a sordid or to a malignant motive, either to thirst for money or to thirst for blood.

In the case of Grey there was no mitigating circumstance. His parts and knowledge, the rank which he had inherited in the state, and the high command which he had borne in the rebel army, would have pointed him out to a just government as a much fitter object of punishment than Alice Lisle, than William Hewling, than any of the hundreds of ignorant peasants whose skulls and quarters were exposed in Somersetshire. But Grey's estate was large, and was strictly entailed. He had only a life interest in his property, and he could forfeit no more interest than he had. If he died, his lands at once devolved on the next heir. If he were pardoned, he would be able to pay a large ransom. He was therefore suffered to redeem himself by giving a bond for forty thousand pounds to the lord treasurer, and smaller sums to other courtiers.

Sir John Cochrane had held among the Scotch rebels the same rank which had been held by Grey in the west of England. That Cochrane should be forgiven by a prince vindictive beyond all example, seemed incredible; but Cochrane was the younger son of a rich family; it was therefore only by sparing him that money could be made out of him. His father, Lord Dundonald, offered a bribe of five thousand pounds to the priests of the royal household, and a pardon was granted.

Samuel Storey, a noted sower of sedition, who had been commissary in the rebel army, and who had inflamed the ignorant populace of Somersetshire by vehement harangues in which James had been described as an incendiary and a poisoner, was admitted to mercy; for Storey was able to give important assistance to Jeffreys in wringing fifteen thousand pounds out of Prideaux.

None of the traitors had less right to expect favor than Wade, Goodenough, and Ferguson. These three chiefs of the rebellion had fled together from the field of Sedgemoor, and had reached the coast in safety; but they had found a frigate cruising near the spot where they had hoped to embark. They had then separated. Wade and Goodenough were soon discovered and brought up to London. Deeply as they had been implicated in the Rye House Plot, conspicuous as they had been among the chiefs of the western insurrection, they were suffered to live, because they had it in their power to give information which enabled the king to slaughter and plunder some persons whom he hated, but to whom he had never yet been able to bring home any crime.

How Ferguson escaped was, and still is, a mystery. Of all the enemies of the government, he was, without doubt, the most deeply criminal. He was the original author of the plot for assassinating the royal brothers. He had written that declaration which, for insolence, malignity, and mendacity, stands unrivaled even among the libels of those stormy times. He had instigated Monmouth first to invade the kingdom, and then to usurp the crown. It was reasonable to expect that a strict search would be made for the arch-traitor, as he was often called; and such a search a man of so singular an aspect and dialect could scarcely have eluded. It was confidently reported in the coffee-houses of London that Ferguson was taken, and this report found credit with men who had excellent opportunities of knowing the truth. The next thing that was heard of him was that he was safe on the Continent. It was strongly suspected that he had been in constant communication with the government against which he was constantly plotting; and that he had, while urging his associates to every excess of rashness, sent to Whitehall just so much information about their proceedings as might suffice to save his own neck, and that, therefore, orders had been given to let him escape.

And now Jeffreys had done his work, and returned to claim his reward. He arrived at Windsor from the west, leaving carnage, mourning, and terror behind him. The hatred with which he was regarded by the people of Somersetshire has no parallel in our history. It was not to be quenched by time or by political changes, was long transmitted from generation to generation, and raged fiercely against his innocent progeny. When he had been many years dead, when his name and title were extinct, his granddaughter, the Countess of Pomfret, traveling along the western road, was insulted by the populace, and found that she could not safely venture herself among the descendants of those who had witnessed the bloody assizes.

But at the court Jeffreys was cordially welcomed. He was a judge after his master's own heart. James had watched the circuit with interest and delight. In his drawing-room and at his table he had frequently talked of the havoc which was making among his disaffected subjects with a glee at which the foreign ministers stood aghast. With his own hand he had penned accounts of what he facetiously called his lord chief justice's campaign in the west. Some hundreds of rebels, his majesty wrote to the Hague, had been condemned. Some of them had been hanged; more should be so; and the rest should be sent to the plantations. It was to no purpose that Ken wrote to implore mercy for the misguided people, and described with pathetic eloquence the frightful state of his diocese. He complained that it was impossible to walk along the highways without seeing some terrible spectacle, and that the whole air of Somersetshire was tainted with death. The king read, and remained, according to the saying of Churchill, hard as the marble chimney-pieces of Whitehall. At Windsor the great seal of England was put into the hands of Jeffreys, and in the next London Gazette it was solemnly notified that this honor was the reward of the many eminent and faithful services which he had rendered to the crown.

At a later period, when all men of all parties spoke with horror of the bloody assizes, the wicked judge and the wicked king attempted to vindicate themselves by throwing the blame on each other. Jeffreys, in the Tower, protested that, in his utmost cruelty, he had not gone beyond his master's express orders; nay, that he had fallen short of them. James, at Saint Germain's, would willingly have had it believed that his own in-

clinations had been on the side of clemency, and that unmerited obloquy
had been brought on him by the violence of his minister; but neither of
these hard-hearted men must be absolved at the expense of the other. The
plea set up for James can be proved under his own hand to be false in fact.
The plea of Jeffreys, even if it be true in fact, is utterly worthless.

Lord Monboddo and Lord Braxfield*

W. FORBES GRAY

Jeffreys was an Englishman. The pair who follow, Lord Monboddo and Lord Braxfield, were Scots. Scotland has its separate law, and Scottish law has its own traditions. It is interesting to contrast Braxfield, the original of "Weir of Hermiston," with his English counterpart, Jeffreys. Uncouth, dissipated, and provincial though Braxfield was, he had powers of industry and a knowledge of the law that put him head and shoulders above Jeffreys. Lord Monboddo, with his eccentricity, his love of the great, and his devotion to the classics, could be a product of no place except Scotland. For further anecdotes of these and other famous Scottish judges, the reader is referred to Lord Cockburn's Memorials of his Time.

Lord Monboddo (1714–1799)

James Burnet, Lord Monboddo, one of the most extraordinary men who ever sat on the judgment seat—"a character rarely to be met with in common life; being fitter for a comedy or novel than anything else"—was born in 1714 of a family more ancient than opulent. His paternal ancestors could be traced back to the days of King Robert the Bruce, and were the owners of the Deeside property of Leys. His father, James Burnet, was the proprietor of a small estate in Kincardineshire, known as Monboddo, in the unpretentious and somewhat dilapidated mansion-house of which the future judge first saw the light. Burnet's lineage on the maternal side was also distinguished, his mother being the only daughter of Sir Arthur Forbes, Bart., of Craigievar.

Of the parents there are few personal details. The father was a strong Jacobite and, along with many other landed gentlemen, got into trouble in connection with the Rebellion of 1715. He was present at the battle of Sheriff-muir, and one incident, recorded by Ramsay, of Ochtertyre, shows him in rather an amiable light. An English officer, who had been stunned by a fall from his horse, perceiving, on his recovery, a gentleman on horseback near him, said: "Sir, I am your prisoner." "No," answered the other (who saw the

* From the book *Some Old Scots Judges* by W. Forbes Gray. Published by E. P. Dutton, 1914. Reprinted by permission of the publishers, and by Constable, London.

137

King's troops approaching), "I am your prisoner." "If that be the case," said the officer, "dismount, and I will protect you." Burnet of Monboddo accordingly walked, while the officer rode his horse, and brought him safely to Stirling Castle.

Burnet received his first schooling from a Robert Milne, designated in the family archives "Tutor to Monboddo's bairns." Monboddo, however, does not seem to have rated the tutor's gifts very highly, for in 1722 we find him writing a doleful letter to his spouse from Edinburgh, expressing doubts as to the efficacy of home tuition, and gravely assuring her that "Jamie will be lost" if she does not send him to a proper school. The advice was taken, and "Jamie" was despatched forthwith to the parish school of Laurencekirk, where he was taught by Thomas Ruddiman who, in later years, shone as a prince among Latin grammarians and as Keeper of the Advocates' Library, an office in which he was succeeded by no less a person than David Hume. Ruddiman was an apt teacher, a scholar, and, if all reports be true, a gentleman. But, notwithstanding these excellent qualifications, Monboddo had still gloomy forebodings that "Jamie" was in danger of being "lost." The result was that the boy was early recalled from the parish school, and home tuition was given another trial—this time under Dr. Francis Skene.

Under his new tutor Burnet made satisfactory progress, and imbibed that love of Greek literature and philosophy which was to become the ruling passion of his life. Skene remained at Monboddo until his appointment to the Chair of Philosophy in King's College, Aberdeen. Thither his pupil followed him. He is even said to have lived under his tutor's roof; but, however that may be, it is certain that, inspired by Skene and Principal Blackwell, the latter one of the most ardent champions of Greek study in Scotland, Burnet became an enthusiastic disciple of Aristotle and Plato, and a contemner of Bacon, Locke, Newton, Hume, and other mere moderns.

Having graduated Master of Arts at Aberdeen University, he removed to Edinburgh, where he began to equip himself for the Scottish Bar. He afterwards went to Holland to learn the maxims of the great Dutch jurists (which then had great weight in the Parliament House), to see the world, and to converse with strangers of figure and fashion. Monboddo, in after years, prided himself not a little upon the fact that he had spent three years studying Civil Law at Groningen, and never lost an opportunity of advocating a similar education for all promising Scottish lawyers.

Returning to Scotland, he happened to arrive in Edinburgh on the day when the notorious Captain Porteous expiated his crime on a dyer's pole in the Grassmarket. When about to retire to rest, Burnet's curiosity was aroused by a tumultuous crowd hurrying along the thoroughfare beneath his window. Instead of going to bed, he made his way to the street, where his scantily clad condition and the nightcap which he wore added a touch of humour to a situation tragic in the extreme. Speedily becoming entangled with the crowd, he soon found himself in the Grassmarket, where he was an involuntary witness of the scene which Scott has painted in indelible colours in his *Heart of Midlothian*. Burnet was so shocked by what he saw that he passed a sleepless night, and next morning seriously meditated leaving Edinburgh as a place unfit for a civilized being to live in. Better counsels prevailed, however, for on learning how Porteous had come by his miserable end, he heroically resolved to hazard his life among the turbulent populace of the Scottish capital.

Burnet became an advocate in 1737 and, with a true sense of the fitness of things, went to reside in Advocates' Close. Here he practised the simple life, partly because briefs were few, and partly because his capacity for convivial enjoyment was limited. One good story has come down to us of those days when Burnet's plight seems to have been that suggested by the cheerless line in Johnson's *London*:

> Slow rises worth by poverty dépress'd.

He was junior counsel for the Laird of Stracathro and the tacksman of the Edzell fishings in an action which they had brought against Mr. Scott of Brotherton with reference to the construction of certain "cruive fishings" near the mouth of the North Esk. The cruives had to be inspected, and Burnet, in doing this, fell into a deep pool. Efforts were made to rescue him, but Scott, the defender, thought this a work of supererogation. "Let him alone," he cried, "the young man wants to go to the bottom of the cause." Burnet, however, was saved, and did get to the bottom of the cause, though in a different way from what the defender in the case expected.

As a young man, Burnet sedulously attended social entertainments of all kinds, and in fashionable society he speedily rose to honour. There was no more familiar figure at the assemblies in Bell's Wynd, where he generally appeared in a suit of white velvet. Adorned in this garb, which he thought might well have become the person of the Chancellor of France, he would dance a minuet in truly Dutch style, to the delight of the ladies, and to the no small satisfaction of himself. He was unfailing, too, in his devotion to theatricals, though, as will be shown later, his ideas of the drama were decidedly peculiar. When West Digges and the captivating Mrs. Ward appeared in the Edinburgh playhouse, Burnet was nightly in attendance, and found scope for his energies in handing the ladies to their seats. He was also fond of hunting and other manly exercises.

The outbreak of the Jacobite rebellion in 1745 brought about a temporary cessation of business in the Court of Session, and Burnet, loathing civil strife, hurried off to London to cement a number of literary and philosophical friendships. In the Metropolis, which, in later life, he visited annually, he mixed in the best society, his company being much sought after by wits, men of letters, and fashionable ladies. Indeed, he knew almost everybody worth knowing, not excepting the King. Among his most intimate London acquaintances were Thomson, the poet of the *Seasons,* in whose house at Richmond he passed many a pleasant hour; David Mallet, that notorious literary adventurer who changed his name "from Scotch Malloch to English Mallet," and tried to filch from Thomson the honour of having written "Rule, Britannia"; and Dr. John Armstrong—frugal, taciturn, splenetic— who divided his time between a lucrative medical practice and the Muses, cultivating the latter with profit to himself, if not with advantage to the human race.

Burnet was also intimate with a group of law lords, including the great Thurlow, who is remembered by Fox's jest, "No man was so wise as Thurlow looked," and the greater Mansfield, one of the finest intellects that ever added lustre to the King's Bench. Then there was Mrs. Montagu, "a faded beauty, a wit, a critic, an author of some fame" who "might have been admired by the first order of minds, had she not been greedy of more praise than she was entitled to." It was at Mrs. Montagu's that Burnet met Hannah More, whom he exasperated by defending slavery because the Ancients did so, and by maintaining that Home's *Douglas* was the greatest of tragedies. Nor must we forget Mrs. Garrick, of whom he saw a good deal in the days of her widowhood. The lady still retained her beauty and charm of manner, so much so that the eccentric judge—now a widower of some years' standing—fell deeply in love with her. Twice the widower offered marriage to the widow, and twice it was politely declined.

Last, but not least, Burnet basked in the sunshine of royal favour. George III became quite interested in the Scottish judge, and frequently welcomed him at the Court of St. James. One day Burnet was walking on the terrace at Windsor Castle, when the King, recognising him, desired him to be called. "My Lord," said His Majesty with much affability, "how did you travel from Scotland?" "On horseback, please your Majesty." "That was too much at your time of life, and in the late bad weather, when even my dragoon officers took chaises; but, tell me, does your lordship call a wheel-carriage a *box?*" "Sire," replied Monboddo, "I am afraid I gave it a worse name; for I called it a *close box.*"

Burnet won his legal spurs in the Douglas Cause, which began in 1762. This, by far the most famous of Scottish lawsuits of the eighteenth century, centred in a very small point, regarding which, however, the evidence was extremely conflicting, namely, "whether Archibald Stewart was or was not the son of Sir John Stewart of Grandtully and Lady Jane Douglas, sister of the Duke of Douglas." The case created immense interest and excitement, as upon it hung the succession to the extensive estates of the last Duke of Douglas, for which there were several claimants.

"Briefed" on behalf of the Duke of Queensberry, Burnet acquitted himself so well as to make his elevation to the Bench inevitable. His industry and success in collecting evidence amazed his friends and disconcerted his opponents. Thrice did he visit France for this purpose, where his mastery of the language, a legacy of the Groningen days, was of great service. The Paris lawyers employed in the case were not very hopeful of success, and actually drafted a letter to the Duke of Queensberry counselling withdrawal, but Burnet would not hear of his client being so easily vanquished, and the letter was destroyed. Subsequent events fully justified the line he took. The pleadings lasted no fewer than thirty-one days, Burnet sustaining his part brilliantly all the while. It is true that the Court of Session, by the casting vote of the Lord President, decided against him; but when the case was taken to the House of Lords, where sat Camden and Mansfield, the Douglas side won an easy victory. So ably did Burnet plead his case that the Supreme Court of Appeal, without a vote, reversed the decision of the Scottish judges, who had decided that Archibald Stewart was not the son of Sir John Stewart.

The death in 1767 of Andrew Fletcher, Lord Milton, created a vacancy among the ordinary Lords of Session, and Burnet became his successor, assuming the title of Lord Monboddo. As the Douglas Cause was not yet finally decided, efforts were made to delay the appointment, and not unnaturally, for Burnet's elevation at that moment meant that he would be placed in the invidious position of being called upon to pronounce judgment in a case in which he had played a leading part as an advocate. Burnet, it must be confessed, acted in this matter neither with discrimination nor delicacy, for he allowed the Duke of Queensberry, who was not slow to appreciate the advantage of transforming the man who had pled his cause into being its judge, to go to the King, and secure his appointment. Surely no judge was ever placed in a more embarrassing position than was Monboddo, for on the first occasion on which he appeared in his judicial capacity, the Douglas Cause came up for disposal.

But however inauspicious was the beginning of Monboddo's judicial career, it was fully atoned for. He is credited with having been not only a master of legal principle, but a wise, independent, impartial, and learned judge. Monboddo would probably have subscribed to the dictum of the American orator, "One man with God is a majority." Certainly, he often differed from his brethren, and found himself in a minority of one; but it says much for his soundness as a lawyer that his judgments were seldom, if ever, reversed by the House of Lords. Paradoxical Monboddo was in his books and in his talk, but he seems to have kept this dubious accomplishment under rigorous restraint while on the Bench.

Not less creditable is the fact that he was instrumental to some extent in getting rid of the "law's delay." One notable improvement instituted by him in a court in which circumlocution had become almost a fetish, was the substitution of what is known, in legal terminology, as "hearings" for "pleadings." Monboddo might have become a judge in the Court of Justiciary, but he declined all overtures, because the duties would have interfered with the pursuit of his Greek studies in the vacation.

The personality of Monboddo is puzzling beyond all belief. He was typically Scottish in his shrewdness, wit, thrift, and "dourness," but there was also a quixotic element in his nature which unmistakably differentiated him from the normal type of Scotsman. He was not exactly winsome, yet it would be a perversion of truth to say that he had no heart. A staunch if candid friend, an excellent host, a lover of cultivated society, an honest advocate of respectability in high places, and a latitudinarian churchman, Monboddo sat under his own vine and fig tree, none daring to make him afraid.

It cannot be said that he was prepossessing, looking, says Chambers, "rather like an old stuffed monkey dressed in a judge's clothes, than anything else. His face, however, 'sicklied o'er' with the pale cast of thought, bore traces of high intellect." His manners were brusque; his habits plain, methodical, and frequently odd. He was abstemious, which is saying much, orgies being then in fashion. He was a thorough-going champion of sunlight and fresh air, which his contemporaries rigidly economised; and he unfeignedly believed that cleanliness was next to godliness, a doctrine more honoured in the breach than in the observance by his neighbours.

It was his custom, summer and winter, to take a cold bath on rising, usually at a very early hour. When staying at his Kincardineshire seat, he enjoyed this luxury in a structure erected for the purpose at some distance from the mansion, and near a running stream which supplied the water. He took a light dinner about noon, but considerably neutralised his excellent system of hygiene by making his supper the heaviest meal of the day. Before retiring to rest he indulged in an air-bath, and then did homage to the Ancients (for whom he considered no sacrifice too great), by applying to his body a lotion composed of rose-water, olive oil, saline, aromatic spirit, and Venetian soap. Besmeared with this formidable concoction, he slept the sleep of the just.

It has been well said that Monboddo earned more fame by his eccentricities than by his acuteness and learning. Unquestionably, he both said and did very odd things—things so odd as to give rise to serious apprehension regarding his sanity. He called forth more ridicule than any other public character of his time. The vagaries of Adam Smith (and they were singular enough) were insignificant compared with the oddities of Monboddo. The queer sayings and doings of this judge were not excrescences, the offspring of affectation; they were part of the man himself. Monboddo could no more do obeisance to tradition and conventionality than he could admit that Shakespeare was a great dramatist, or David Hume an influential philosopher. And this obliquity of conduct and speech, simply because it was innate, has always weighed most in the popular judgment of Monboddo. Whimsical people are often tantalising, but no one can say they are ever dull.

To chronicle all the stories about this crotchety man would be impossible, and even if it could be done no good purpose would be served, but one or two may be retailed as characteristic. What would be said nowadays of a judge who dispensed justice not from the Bench, but from the well of the court? This Monboddo invariably did. Several reasons have been given for his singular conduct. It is said that when he made his first appearance as a judge, he felt the awkwardness of his situation in connection with the Douglas Cause, and, with doubtful expediency, sought relief from a wounded conscience by delivering his "opinion" from the well of the court. Cockburn says that some slight had made Monboddo resolve never to sit on the same bench with Lord President Dundas. He, however, adds that by sitting at the clerk's table, Monboddo was enabled to get easily in and out of the court, a more likely reason, for "whenever there was a pause he was sure to slip off, gown and all, to have a talk in the Outer House."

But Chambers gives another version. The story goes that his lordship once embroiled himself in an action respecting a horse which he had committed when sick to a farrier, with instructions to give the animal a certain medicine. The farrier, thinking to improve the occasion, administered, along with the medicine, a liberal dose of treacle, no doubt surmising that a horse was as fond of its medicine being made palatable as a child. Unfortunately, the horse died next morning, and the farrier found himself the unhappy victim of a prosecution at the hands of Monboddo, who pleaded his own cause at the Bar. He lost the case, however, and became, Chambers alleges, "so enraged in consequence at his brethren, that he never afterwards sat with them upon the bench, but underneath, amongst the clerks."

In Butler's *Hudibras* there is a line which says:

Great on the bench, great in the saddle.

These words might be fitly applied to Monboddo. He despised a carriage for two reasons. First, because he thought it was degrading to be dragged at the tails of horses instead of being mounted on their backs; and, secondly, because carriages were not in universal use among the Ancients. One wonders what would have been Monboddo's attitude had he lived in this era of motor cars and aeroplanes. The truth is that, apart from his partiality for classical habits, he was very fond of horses. No one delighted more than he in the pleasures of the chase. Mounted on Alburac, his favourite nag, he would scour the country in all weathers. And he was proud of the performance. He told Ramsay of Ochtertyre once that, in a journey from Dalhousie Castle to Monboddo, he had met but one traveller who, to avoid the blast, rode with his face to the tail.

His annual journeys to London were invariably made on horseback. These equestrian performances continued until he was upwards of eighty years of age. On his last journey he took ill, and it was with great difficulty that a friend, who had overtaken him on the road, persuaded him to enter a carriage, which sorely touched his dignity as well as cast a slur upon the Ancients. But he was ill at ease, and, on the following day, he again mounted Alburac, and arrived in Edinburgh without further mishap.

In May 1785, Monboddo was in the court of the King's Bench when a rumour that the building was falling caused a general stampede. The Scottish judge, however, took the matter very coolly, as the following extract from a contemporary newspaper sufficiently testifies: "In the curious rout of the lawyers' corps, it is singular that the only person who kept his seat was a venerable stranger. Old Lord Monboddo, one of the Scots judges, was in the court of the King's Bench, and being short-sighted and rather dull in his hearing, he sat still during the tumult, and did not move from his place. Afterwards, being questioned why he did not bestir himself to avoid the ruin, he coolly answered 'that he thought it was *an annual ceremony* with which, as an alien to our laws, he had nothing to do!'"

When the colonel in *Guy Mannering* informs Mr. Pleydell that the usual hour of supper will be anticipated, the latter gaily expresses his delight, and remarks, "I am of counsel with my old friend Burnet. I love the *cœna*, the supper of the Ancients." The allusion is to Monboddo's custom of entertaining his friends to what he called "learned suppers," in imitation of the Ancients. These took place fortnightly at his residence in St. John Street. Here of an evening would gather as choice a company of intellectual aristocrats as could be found anywhere, for the colloquial fare was as substantial as the repast. The supper was usually at an early hour, and had all the variety and abundance of the chief meal of the day, Monboddo, in his unquenchable enthusiasm for the Ancients, being intent on reviving as much of the glory of the Attic banquets as was possible in an unattractive house in murky Edinburgh. The table was strewn with roses, for did not Horace love to have it so at his beautiful home among the Sabine hills? Similarly, the master of the feast would garland his flasks of excellent Bordeaux, as Anacreon was wont to do at the court of Polycrates of Samos. And as the sumptuous feast proceeded, Monboddo, who loved to unbend after the labours of the day to a select and admiring company, would discourse upon many things ancient and modern with wit, vivacity, and learning, or would expound some of his eccentric theories regarding the savage state or the diminution of the human race with an ingenuity and eloquence which might have been expended in a better cause.

While Monboddo's conversational powers were exhibited to most advantage at the suppers of the Ancients, his brilliant dialectical skill was in evidence at the meetings of the Select Society. There he met foemen worthy of his steel who by argument, and, occasionally, by sarcasm, sought to demolish his most cherished ideas. But he usually proved more than a match for his antagonists. On one occasion he had an animated encounter with Wedderburn who, in after years, found his way to the Woolsack. The future Lord Chancellor had ventured to say something derogatory to the Ancients which, immediately, brought Monboddo to his feet. "Mr. Preses," he said, "the Ancients roasted *above* the fire; the Moderns roast *before* the fire; but methinks this young gentleman would fain roast without any fire at all!"

An ingenious though unsound philosopher, a scholar whose knowledge was extensive rather than profound, a trafficker in paradox, and a man of letters whose judgment ran counter to that of most of his contemporaries, Monboddo had his full share of the trials of the man who is misunderstood. And like most misunderstood men, he made not a few enemies, partly by his intellectual singularity, and partly by a certain acerbity towards those who happened to differ from him. He quarrelled with Hume, whose "wretched philosophy" he could not abide; he despised his colleague, Kames, and, with perhaps a touch of jealousy, made light of his metaphysics; and he had no love for Dr. Johnson because, among other reasons, he had not "genius enough to comprehend the beauties of Milton," and held very unorthodox views concerning the Ancients.

Foote said of Monboddo that he was "an Elzevir edition of Johnson"— a pretty compliment, though some, perplexed as to whether Foote really meant what the phrase usually implies, have asserted that he was only thinking of a pocket edition. Be that as it may, Monboddo and Johnson could forget their feuds, and meet as gentlemen. Boswell, however, was not at all sure on this point, and believing for once that discretion is the better part of valour, he cautiously "sounded" Monboddo as to whether a visit from Johnson, who was then trudging to the Hebrides, would be acceptable.

It was the vacation, and the judge was as usual living in the guise of a farmer on the ancestral estate. Thither Boswell despatched a letter announcing that Johnson had, with touching magnanimity, expressed a wish to "go two miles out of his way to see Lord Monboddo." Boswell's wish was gratified. Lexicographer and judge met, and if they did not fall upon each other's neck nor always return the soft answer which turns away wrath, they, on the whole, spent a pleasant time, and parted better friends than they were when they met.

Boswell gives a fairly full and graphic description of the interview: "Lord Monboddo received us at his gate most courteously; pointed to the Douglas arms upon his house, and told us that his great-grandmother was of that family. 'In such houses (said he) our ancestors lived, who were better men than we.' 'No, no, my lord (said Dr. Johnson). We are as strong as they, and a great deal wiser.' This was an assault upon one of Lord Monboddo's capital dogmas, and I was afraid there would have been a violent altercation in the very close, before we got into the house. But his lordship is distinguished not only for 'ancient metaphysics' but for ancient *politesse* . . . and he made no reply."

"His lordship," Boswell continues, "was drest in a rustic suit, and wore a little round hat; he told us, we now saw him as Farmer Burnet, and we should have his family dinner, a farmer's dinner. He said: 'I should not have

forgiven Mr. Boswell, had he not brought you here, Dr. Johnson.'" The ice
once broken, the two men talked genially concerning many topics in which
they had a common interest, and soon became conscious that they were not
so far apart after all. Both, of course, spoke highly of Homer. "Johnson:
'He had all the learning of his age. The shield of Achilles shows a nation in
war, a nation in peace; harvest sport, nay stealing.' Monboddo: 'Ay, and
what we (looking to Boswell) would call a Parliament House scene; a
cause pleaded.' Johnson: 'That is part of the life of a nation at peace. And
there are in Homer such characters of heroes, that the united powers of
mankind ever since have not produced any but what are to be found there.'
Monboddo: 'Yet no character is described.'"

Then the conversation turned to history. "Monboddo: 'The history of
manners is the most valuable. I never set a high value on any other history.'
Johnson: 'Nor I; and therefore I esteem biography, as giving us what comes
near to ourselves, what we can turn to use.' Boswell: 'But in the course of
general history, we find manners. In wars we see the dispositions of people,
their degrees of humanity, and other particulars.' Johnson: 'Yes; but then you
must take all the facts to get this; and it is but a little you get.' Monboddo:
'And it is that little which makes history valuable.'"

Monboddo and Johnson then sharpened their wits on such subjects as
the decay of learning, the attainments of bishops, and the momentous problem as to whether a savage or a London shopkeeper had the best existence,
the judge characteristically casting his vote for the savage. Johnson subsequently examined his host's son, Arthur, in Latin, an ordeal which the youth
seems to have stood fairly well. It remains to be added that Johnson ate
a hearty dinner, and that the judge suspected him of gourmandism.

It would have been surprising had Monboddo escaped the unpopularity
which ever awaits the man whose tongue is not only sharp but indiscreet.
He rushed in where angels fear to tread. His likes and dislikes he expressed
with the utmost freedom, regardless of consequences. Candour is a virtue,
but if not linked to prudence it may do endless havoc. Monboddo and
Kames, between whom there was no love lost, once found themselves at
Gordon Castle as guests of Jane, Duchess of Gordon. For this great lady
Monboddo had much respect. "Sir," he once remarked to a friend, "her
Grace has a brilliancy and radiance about her like the rays round the head of
an apostle!"—clumsy but genuine appreciation which ill accorded, however,
with the incident about to be mentioned. Discussing his favourite topic—
the Ancients—Monboddo remarked to the Duchess that few Moderns could
write with elegance. It was suggested that Kames (who was present) was
at least one exception to the rule. But Monboddo, with amazing tactlessness,
declined to admit the exception. Kames, who thought himself as good as any
Ancient, was, of course, highly offended. Happily, the noble hostess, not
relishing the prospect of a literary duel in her drawing-room, adroitly re-

lieved a desperate situation by proposing that the protagonists should dance
a reel with her.

Monboddo's domestic life was clouded by bereavement. In 1760 he married Miss Farquharson, a relative of Marshal Keith, but the lady died in
giving birth to her third child. Then his only son was taken at an early age,
and, in 1790, his second daughter, who was the light of his eyes and the
pride of his heart, fell a victim to consumption. Her remarkable beauty
was the talk of Edinburgh; and she is supposed to have been the person who
was elegantly praised in one of the papers of the *Mirror* as rejecting the
most flattering offers of marriage in order that she might tend her father in
his old age. Burns, who met her on the occasion of his first visit to Edinburgh, surrendered at once to her charms. "Well," said his friend Geddes to
him when he arrived back in his native Ayrshire, "and did you admire the
young lady?" "I admired God Almighty more than ever. Miss Burnet is
the most heavenly of all His works," was the unhesitating reply. Writing
later to William Chalmers, the bard explained that "Fair B——is heavenly
Miss B., daughter of Lord Monboddo, at whose house I have had the honour
to be more than once. There has not been anything nearly like her, in all
the combinations of beauty, grace, and goodness, the great Creator has
formed, since Milton's Eve on the first day of her existence."

It would have been strange, indeed, if Burns had not followed up such
superlative laudation by singing the praises of Monboddo's fair daughter
in verse. Accordingly, there is the well-known allusion to her in the "Address
to Edinburgh":

> Fair Burnet strikes th' adoring eye,
> Heav'n's beauties on my fancy shine;
> I see the Sire of Love on high,
> And own His work indeed divine!

Miss Burnet's death, however, impelled the poet to try something more
ambitious, and after several months' "hammering," he produced the fine
elegy of seven stanzas beginning:

> Life ne'er exulted in so rich a prize
> As Burnet, lovely from her native skies;
> Nor envious Death so triumph'd in a blow
> As that which laid th' accomplish'd Burnet low.

Even Clarinda was forced to acknowledge the bewitching beauty of Monboddo's daughter. To "dear Sylvander," she wrote: "Miss Burnet sat just behind me. What an angelic girl! I stared at her, having never seen her so near.
I remembered you talking of her, etc. What felicity to witness her 'softly
speak and sweetly smile!' How could you celebrate any other Clarinda! Oh,
I would have adored you, as Pope of exquisite taste and refinement, had you

loved, sighed, and written upon her for ever!" Whatever foibles Clarinda may have had, certainly jealousy was not one of them.

The death of his beloved daughter was a blow from which Monboddo never recovered. It is said that, after she died, his son-in-law covered her portrait to spare the old man's feelings. "Quite right—quite right," said Monboddo, casually looking up from his book. "Never," says Ramsay, "did Lord Monboddo appear in a more advantageous light. . . . He bore his loss like a hero and a Christian, returning to his studies and duties seemingly with increased ardour." Monboddo survived his daughter for nine years. Shortly before his own death, which occurred at his house in Edinburgh on May 26, 1799, he said to Dr. Gregory, his medical adviser and friend: "I know it is not in the power of Art to cure me: all I wish is euthanasia—a happy death." And euthanasia he got, for he died in harness.

Monboddo was fortunate in many things—fortunate in possessing a fine intellect, a sound heart, and a good conscience. But his estimable qualities and his undoubted learning were buried beneath as ludicrous a mass of crotchets and idiosyncrasies as ever were credited to a man outside of bedlam. Ridicule was his only portion during his lifetime, and it has not forsaken his memory—so hard is the way of the man who habitually trades in paradox. Of Monboddo's writings something will be said in the next chapter; but here, having regard solely to his personality, there is little to cavil at in the inflated lines which Dr. H. W. Tytler, author of *Pædstrophia*, wrote in memory of his friend:

> If wisdom, learning, worth, demand a tear,
> Weep o'er the dust of great Monboddo here;
> A Judge upright, to mercy still inclined;
> A generous friend, a father fond and kind;
> His country's pride, for skill in Grecian lore,
> And all Antiquity's invalued store.

Lord Braxfield (1722–1799)

To Lord Braxfield belongs the unenviable reputation of being the most execrated judge in the annals of Scottish jurisprudence. Even Lord Advocate Mackenzie, whose cruelty to the Covenanters earned him the sobriquet of "Bluidy Mackenzie," was a scholar, a poet, and, some say, a gentleman; but the most ardent apologist for Braxfield is compelled to admit that his good qualities are not easily discoverable.

> Men's evil manners live in brass; their virtues
> We write in water.

The latter part of the Shakespearian dictum hardly applies to the "Hanging Judge," for the most charitable view of his career leads only to the conclusion that his virtues, if he ever had any, were distinctly elusive. He is popularly regarded as the counterpart of the "infamous Jeffreys"; but this hardly does him justice. When Cockburn dubbed him "the Jeffreys of Scotland," he was thinking more of his flagrant conduct in connection with the sedition trials of 1793–94 than of his general character. Braxfield, it must be acknowledged, was a shade better than the English judge. He was a sound and able lawyer, which Jeffreys was not, and he was no sycophant, which Jeffreys was. Nevertheless, no one who has studied in contemporary records the judicial part which he played at a critical period in Scottish affairs, and is familiar with the word-portrait which Cockburn drew from the life, can have any doubt that he came dangerously near being destitute of principle and character. Unscrupulous, tyrannical, coarse, dissipated, illiterate, he was morally almost featureless. He had a hard heart, a tainted mind, a cross-grained, domineering nature, and an uncouth exterior. A noble aspiration or a lofty motive he was incapable of appreciating. Without faith, without hope, without charity, he moved continually in a world of sordid interests and ignoble purposes.

Let it be admitted that Cockburn's ultra-Whiggism did colour to some extent his portrait of Braxfield, but the broad lineaments of the notorious Lord Justice-Clerk are unquestionably there. And what a repulsive portrait it is! "Strong built and dark, with rough eyebrows, powerful eyes, threatening lips, and a low growling voice, he was like a formidable blacksmith. . . . Illiterate and without any taste for refined enjoyment, strength of understanding, which gave him power without cultivation, only encouraged him to a more contemptuous disdain of all natures less coarse than his own. Despising the growing improvement of manners, he shocked the feelings even of an age which, with more of the formality, had far less of the substance of decorum than our own. Thousands of his sayings have been preserved, and the staple of them is indecency; which he succeeded in making many people enjoy, or at least endure, by hearty laughter, energy of manner, and rough humour."

The genius of Stevenson has familiarised an immense public with the odiousness of Braxfield's character—a public that Cockburn could not reach. The prototype of Weir of Hermiston was, as every one knows, no other than the redoubtable judge who sat at the head of the criminal court of Scotland in the closing years of the eighteenth century. "Mind you," wrote Stevenson in 1892 from far Vailima, "I expect *The Justice-Clerk* (afterwards changed to *Weir of Hermiston*) to be my masterpiece. My Braxfield is already a thing of beauty and a joy for ever, and, so far as he has gone, *far* my best character." Of course, Stevenson, for the purposes of romance, added touches to his portraiture which are not to be found in the original; but as his description was mainly based on Cockburn's account, and from what he could glean from the Raeburn canvas, it is indisputable that the general characteristics of Weir of Hermiston faithfully reflect those of the truculent Braxfield. This judge had a strange fascination for Stevenson, to whom he makes more than one reference in his writings. Readers of *Virginibus Puerisque* will recall his graphic account of the impressions made upon him by the "Hanging Judge's" portrait when he saw it for the first time at the Raeburn Exhibition in Edinburgh in 1876.

Born in 1722, Robert Macqueen was mainly indebted to himself for his advancement in life, "being a man of no family and very small estate." His paternal grandfather was gardener to Charles, Earl of Selkirk, and his son, John Macqueen, the father of the judge, was bred a writer, to qualify him to be a baron-bailie to the Earl. He prospered in business, was sheriff-substitute of the Upper Ward of Lanarkshire, and in due season became the owner of a small property in the county, from which the future judge derived his legal title. His wife also belonged to Lanarkshire, being a daughter of John Hamilton of Gilderscleugh. Robert was the eldest son.

The family being large, and the means to support them small, John Macqueen could not afford to entertain exalted notions respecting the future of his children. Robert got a good, but not an expensive education, the father's intention being that he should succeed him. No stories have come down to us to show what manner of boy young Macqueen was when attending the grammar-school of Lanark, but at Edinburgh University, where he afterwards studied civil law, he seems to have created a favourable impression. At all events, there is the testimony of a class-fellow, Dr. Erskine, who affirms that the civil law students "would have fought for Robbie Macqueen, whose honesty and good nature made him a general favourite."

Macqueen's ambition at first was to be a Writer to the Signet, and for some time he was an apprentice to an Edinburgh practitioner. When next we hear of him, he is in his father's office in Lanark. Here he came into contact with Dundas, afterwards the second President of that name, whose wife owned the estate of Bonnington. Dundas was struck by Macqueen's shrewdness and legal abilities, and urged him to qualify for the Scottish Bar. The advice was taken, and Macqueen set himself seriously to study for his new vocation. His industry was unflagging, and his enthusiasm great, and in 1744 he found himself wearing the gown of an advocate.

For a number of years he had the ordinary fate of young members of the Bar in having little to do, but gradually agents began to discover his merit, "which was not inaptly compared to a rough diamond." When his friend, Dundas, became Lord Advocate, he was made one of his deputes, an office which, if it yielded little money, at least gave a young barrister an opportunity of showing of what stuff he was made. Macqueen had been a careful student of feudal law, and when the litigation arising out of the forfeitures consequent upon the Jacobite rebellion of 1745 came before the Court, he,

as one of the counsel for the Crown, was found to be the right man in the
right place. His extensive and accurate knowledge, and his clear and forcible
exposition of the many complicated points at issue, called forth general
admiration.

His good sense and sound law, his candour, his unfailing instinct for
what was relevant, made both judges and agents overlook his ungainly
presence, his rustic manners, his broad dialect, and his vulgarisms. Macqueen had none of the art of the rhetorician, indeed despised it. He mainly
relied upon a vigorous understanding, a thorough mastery of legal principle,
and the sheer driving power of a strong virile personality. Many brilliant
lawyers there were at the Bar at this time, but ere long he was the rival
of the foremost of them. When at the height of his fame he is reputed to
have pled from fifteen to twenty causes in a single day. Boswell's lines in
the "Court of Session Garland" is a reminder, too, that he was a proficient
draughtsman.

> However, of our cause not being ashamed,
> Unto the whole Lords we straightway reclaimed;
> And our petition was appointed to be seen,
> Because it was drawn by Robbie Macqueen.

Macqueen's success at the Bar, conspicuous though it was, was eclipsed
by his success in the tavern. Many outside Parliament House knew him to
be a great lawyer, but many more recognised him as a great drinker. He
early joined the claret-drinking, card-playing fraternity, and soon rose to
be the ideal type of boon companion—coarse, boisterous, dissipated—a man
who swore without provocation, "like an ensign of the last age in his teens,"
and who, when in high spirits and in congenial company, would exclaim
in dubious English, "What a glorious thing is it to speak nonsense!" As
Stevenson says, "He was a convivial man, a lover of wine, and one who
shone peculiarly at tavern meetings." But though these drinking-bouts were
neither infrequent nor slight, they seem hardly to have impaired his powers
of work. "Bacchus," says Cockburn, "had never an easy victory over
Macqueen." He is credited with having thriven on a "stintless regimen of
beef, brandy, and claret," being firmly persuaded that a point of law will
be more easily studied after drinking a bottle of the favourite beverage
than by abstemiousness. It is a novel doctrine, but Macqueen seemed to
lend countenance to the idea that it was true.

The character of this man appears to be almost humanly inscrutable.
It defies all ordinary standards of comparison. His father is said to have
been at much pains to give him a religious upbringing, and he himself,
despite his deep potations and his love of strong expletives, took credit for
being "a sincere Christian." He would have indignantly repudiated any
suggestion to the contrary. Of religion, Ramsay of Ochtertyre deliciously
remarks, "he retained all along a due sense, being thoroughly persuaded

of its truth, though it did not always produce suitable fruits or make him set a watch on his lips."

He was illiterate to a degree hardly conceivable in a person occupying his exalted position. He had no interest in literature, or art, or philosophy. With the writings of the Dutch jurists he was tolerably familiar, and for the works of Lord Stair he showed all the reverence he possessed, but it is doubtful whether he ever read a book which did not bear directly upon his professional labours. He fully imbibed the spirit of Prior's lines:

> From ignorance our comfort flows,
> The only wretched are the wise.

The intellectual lustre of the Edinburgh of his day meant nothing to him. He preferred the joviality of the tavern to the learned talk of Monboddo's supper parties. While Kames was struggling hard to get his countrymen to speak and write "English undefiled," Braxfield was glorying in the vernacular and perpetrating the most outrageous Scotticisms. His humour was broad, but his speech was broader. "Hae ye ony coonsel, man?" said he to Maurice Margarot, when placed at the bar on a charge of sedition. "No," was the laconic reply. "Dae ye want to hae ony appointit?" continued the judge. "No," said Margarot sarcastically, "I only want an interpreter to make me understand what your lordship says." When Jeffrey, fresh from Oxford, began his career at the Scottish Bar, his speech gave his lordship much trouble. "The laddie," he remarked wittily, "has clean tint his Scotch and fund nae English."

After more than thirty years' exacting but eminently successful work as a pleader, Macqueen, in 1776, was raised to the Bench with the title of Lord Braxfield. This post he accepted only after the earnest solicitation of his old friend Dundas, for though it brought him honour, it implied substantial pecuniary loss. Four years later, he succeeded Lord Auchinleck, the father of Johnson's biographer, as a Lord of Justiciary. The appointment was not allowed to pass unnoticed. In the same year there was published an anonymous "Letter to Robert Macqueen, Lord Braxfield, on his Promotion to be one of the Judges of the High Court." Cockburn attributes this senseless pamphlet, for such it was, to Boswell. If he was really the author—and it is not difficult to imagine him in that capacity—then the publication may be set down as one of those "blazing indiscretions" for which the renowned biographer was so famous. Apart from the fact that he was the son of the retiring judge, it was highly presumptuous, if not something worse, to lecture the judges of the criminal court on their partiality, indecorum, and carelessness, as the writer of this pamphlet did in terms neither wise nor moderate. Moreover, it was surely very improper to address the "Letter" to Braxfield, who as yet had had no opportunities of committing the judicial sins complained of. The only construction that can be put upon the writer's action is that he was taking time by the forelock and warning Braxfield against a course of conduct to which his past record showed him peculiarly liable.

But whatever the explanation of this epistle, we may be sure that it did not hurt the new judge's feelings nor injure his prospects. As at the Bar so on the Bench, his forceful personality carried all before it. In 1788 he became Lord Justice-Clerk, in which capacity his most notorious deeds were done. It is impossible to understand what Braxfield was as a judge unless due allowance is made for his abnormal character—a character devoid of nearly every judicial virtue. He was coarse and jocular when he ought to have been dignified and circumspect; vindictive when he ought to have been dispassionate; cruel when he ought to have been just; boisterous and domineering when he ought to have been serenely calm.

"Judges," says Bacon, "ought to be more learned than witty; more reverend than plausible; and more advised than confident." Braxfield ran counter to all three injunctions. He was a sort of swashbuckler of the Bench. It is true that he once declared (what is usually assumed on the part of a judge), "I am one of those who are always for giving fair-play to panels"; but this most excellent rule he honoured more in the breach than in the observance. He bullied prisoners, he bullied witnesses, he bullied young advocates if he thought them "Bar flunkies" (his term for fops), and, at times, he bullied his colleagues.

"It is impossible," writes Cockburn, "to condemn his conduct as a criminal judge too gravely, or too severely. It was a disgrace to the age. A dexterous and practical trier of ordinary cases, he was harsh to prisoners even in his jocularity, and to every counsel whom he chose to dislike. . . . It may be doubted if he was ever so much in his element as when tauntingly repelling the last despairing claim of a wretched culprit, and sending him to Botany Bay or the gallows with an insulting jest; over which he would chuckle the more from observing that correct people were shocked."

And all the specimens of his lordship's *obiter dicta* that have been chronicled, bear out this amazing indictment by one who was himself a judge. Braxfield was indeed a "terror of the law." Lockhart, in his *Life of Scott*, reports him as having said to an eloquent culprit at the bar: "Ye're a vera clever chiel, man, but ye wad be nane the waur o' a hangin'." When Muir, the political reformer, was being tried, Braxfield, parting with the last vestige of judicial honour, whispered to the father of Francis Horner (one of the Edinburgh Reviewers), as he entered the jury-box, "Come awa, Maister Horner, come awa, and help us to hang ane o' thae d—— scoondrels." At a time when the procedure in criminal cases was more a mystery than it is now, and the line to be taken often seemed doubtful, Braxfield at all events was ready for any emergency. "Hoot! jist gie me Josie Norrie (a clerk of court well up in forms and precedents) and a gude jury, an' I'll do for the fallow"—a typical example of his lordship's best judicial manner.

In ribaldry and coarseness, Braxfield would have offended the Lord

Chesterfield of that day, a man by no means squeamish, if we are to judge by those flagitious letters he wrote to his son. Even the most sacred things were not immune from his ridicule. In one of the sedition trials, the prisoner, Gerrald, ventured to remark that all great men had been reformers, "even our Saviour Himself." "Muckle He made o' that; He was hangit" was the profane reply of the man who prided himself upon being a "sincere Christian." On another occasion two young advocates, looking considerably the worse for a protracted orgy, were about to plead before his lordship when they were admonished in the following fashion: "Gentlemen, ye maun jist pack up yer papers and gang hame, for the tane o' ye's riftin' punch, and the ither's belching claret, and there'll be nae gude got oot o' ye the day."

And where claret was concerned, Braxfield's opinion was not to be traduced. Being entertained once at Douglas Castle, and observing that port was the only wine produced after dinner, his lordship, with his customary rudeness, asked his host if "there was nae claret in the castle?" "I believe there is," was the reply, "but my butler tells me it is not good." "Let's pree't," said the senator. The claret having been produced and pronounced excellent, Braxfield, wishing to show that he was not ignorant of ecclesiastical phraseology, proposed that as a *fama clamosa* had gone forth against the wine, the parish minister (who was present) should "absolve" it. But his lordship had been a little foolhardy. "I know," said the clergyman, "that you are a very good judge in cases of civil and criminal law; but I see you do not understand the laws of the Church. We never absolve till after three appearances."

In the same year that Braxfield became Lord Justice-Clerk, he was called upon to play the principal judicial part in the trial of the notorious Deacon Brodie, who, for a time, was highly successful in his dual position of town councillor by day and burglar by night. In this, with the single exception of the Douglas Cause, the most famous Scottish trial of the eighteenth century, Braxfield was thoroughly in his element. It was a case well fitted to call forth all his sinister powers, and he made the most of his opportunities. Four other judges sat beside him, but he alone controlled the case.

John Clerk (afterwards Lord Eldin) was counsel for George Smith, one of the Deacon's confederates, and with this young and brilliant advocate Braxfield had several encounters. Clerk, it must be confessed, was rash and pugnacious, and just the type of man to ruffle the not too equable temper of the Lord Justice-Clerk. In the first encounter Clerk did not figure well. In language not very respectful, he charged the Court with admitting improper evidence. He was, of course, reproved, but he persisted in impugning the judgment of the Court, and in asserting that the jury were to judge of the law as well as the facts. "Sir, I tell you," exclaimed the infuriated Braxfield, "that the jury have nothing to do with the law, but to take it *simpliciter* from me." "That I deny," was Clerk's insolent answer. The Court was indignant, but Clerk held his ground, and once more affirmed that the jurors were judges of the whole case. "You are talking nonsense, sir," roared Braxfield. "My lord, you had better not snub me in this way," was the instant reply, whereupon his lordship merely said, "Proceed—gang on, sir." There followed more interruptions, and a tactful counsel would certainly have been more deferential, but Clerk never believed that discretion is the better part of valour. So he went on: "Gentlemen of the jury, I was just saying to you, when this outbreak on the Bench occurred, that you were the judges of the law and of the facts in this case." Braxfield: "We cannot tolerate this, sir. It is an indignity to this High Court—a very gross indignity, deserving of the severest reprobation." But Clerk would either address the jury in his own way, or not speak at all. Whereupon the Lord Justice-Clerk called upon the counsel for the prisoner, Brodie, to proceed with his address; but the latter shook his head, as if declining to do so. The climax had now been reached. Braxfield was about to charge the jury when Clerk, starting to his feet, and raising a defiant fist to the Bench, shouted, "Hang my client if you daur, my lord, without hearing me in his defence!" These words produced a great sensation, and the judges immediately retired to hold a consultation. On returning to the court, the Lord Justice-Clerk requested Clerk to resume his speech, which he did without further interruption.

Braxfield's address to the prisoners in passing sentence of death revealed the protean essence of his character. He was surely the last man in the world to reprove the vices of the age, and to point to the consolations of religion, but this he did in the case of Deacon Brodie. Here are his hypocritical words: "It is much to be lamented that those vices, which are called gentlemanly vices, are so favourably looked upon in the present age. They have been the source of your (Brodie's) ruin; and, whatever may be thought of them, they are such as assuredly lead to ruin. I hope you will improve the short time which you have now to live by reflecting upon your past conduct, and endeavouring to procure, by a sincere repentance, forgiveness for your many crimes. God always listens to those who seek Him with sincerity." Not bad for a man who could make the Founder of Christianity the subject of a jest!

The most memorable episode in Braxfield's career—the episode which exhibits more clearly than any other his real characteristics, both personal and professional—was the part he played in the trials of Muir, Skirving, Margarot, and others who were charged with sedition in 1793–94. The judicial aspect of the matter, and particularly Braxfield's conduct, was exhaustively investigated by Cockburn in his *Examination of the Trials for Sedition in Scotland* (2 vols., 1888). It would not be difficult to convict Cockburn of bias. He was a staunch Whig, he himself was counsel for three prisoners who were tried for sedition in 1817–19, and he had the good fortune to live in later times when a loftier standard of ethics prevailed on the Bench. These circumstances were almost bound to influence his judgment, and influence it they did. To call the Lord Justice-Clerk "a coarse and dexterous ruffian" was to betray a spirit which suggested anything but judicial serenity. Such a phrase Cockburn surely ought not to have used. But when every allowance has been made for his Whiggism, it cannot be said that his severe condemnation of Braxfield's methods is unmerited. The harsh, censorious, and avowedly partisan conduct of the Lord Justice-Clerk as revealed by the records of these trials is almost incredible to a person living in the twentieth century.

An attempt has been made to palliate Braxfield's wrongdoing by contending that such a judge as he was needed to curb the lawless spirit of the time. Braxfield may have crushed the lawless spirit; he certainly did not administer justice. Even when the trials were proceeding his judicial conduct was strongly criticised. The attention of Parliament was drawn to the matter, and Lord Advocate Dundas was compelled to inform him that representations had been made against the legality of the sentences on Muir and Palmer. But the Lord Justice-Clerk was utterly unrepentant. He affirmed that the sentences were legal, and gratuitously urged that the royal clemency should not be extended to either prisoner.

Only one influential voice was raised in Braxfield's defence—Lord Mansfield's. Unfortunately, it did not, on this occasion, count for much since Mansfield admitted that he had no personal acquaintance with Braxfield, though he had "long heard the loud voice of fame that speaks of him as a man of pure and spotless integrity, of great talents, and of a transcendent knowledge of the laws of his country."

How this man of "pure and spotless integrity" comported himself in the sedition trials of 1793–1794, we shall see presently. Meanwhile, it may be noted that Braxfield was a political partisan of the deepest dye. He was a disciple of Dundas, to whose "nod every man owed what he got, and looked for what he wished." And Dundas stood for a Toryism which spelt political degradation, and the triumph of the forces of reaction. Accordingly, Whigs, Radicals, French Revolutionists, and "siclike enemies o' the King and Constitution" were Braxfield's pet aversion. If he did not exactly hold with Dr. Johnson that "the first Whig was the Devil," he certainly made it his business both on and off the Bench to see that the "Whig dogs" did not get the best of it. Where politics were concerned, it was impossible to look for justice from Braxfield. "Bring me prisoners, and I'll find you law" was his attitude during a period of intense political excitement. "His blamableness in these trials," says Cockburn, "far exceeds that of his brethren. They were weak; he was strong. They were frightened; he was not. They followed; he, the head of the Court, led."

Braxfield's ruling principle in the sedition trials was to obtain a conviction, and having obtained it, to impose a sentence that would strike terror in the hearts of his political adversaries. The ethical sense had become so atrophied that he was prepared to go to any length. Had not Dundas, who trembled lest the Lord Justice-Clerk's zeal for Toryism should carry him too far, counselled moderation, the situation might have been worse. But even as it stands, Braxfield's record is very black. Never, it may be confidently asserted, had the Scottish judiciary sunk so low, never had political passion so blinded judges who ought to have risen superior to all party feeling.

In the trial of Thomas Muir (1793), Braxfield accused the prisoner of trying to overturn "our present happy Constitution—the happiest, the best, and the most noble Constitution in the world." Furthermore, he proclaimed the novel doctrine that to promote parliamentary reform was to be guilty of sedition. He also fulminated against the French as "monsters of human nature." "Mr. Muir might have known that no attention could be paid (by Parliament) to such a rabble (the advocates of political reform). What right had they to representation? . . . A government in every country should be just like a corporation; and, in this country, it is made of the *landed interest, which alone has a right to be represented.*"

This extraordinary outburst was severely commented upon in Parliament, but so many conflicting interests were at work that the judge was neither censured nor asked to retract. When the jury unanimously found Muir guilty, Braxfield expressed his high approval of the verdict, declared that "transportation was the proper punishment," and "only hesitated whether it should be for life or for a term of fourteen years." In such fashion was justice administered in Scotland in the closing years of the eighteenth century.

An equally violent display of political rancour occurred in connection with the trial of William Skirving (1794), Braxfield more than hinting that he expected the jury to acquit themselves as good party-men. All opposition to the predominant political mood of the hour was sedition. "I say, gentlemen, that the greatest union in this nation is necessary to support us under a war with a neighbouring nation, consisting of the most profligate monsters that ever disgraced humanity." This tirade Braxfield wound up as follows: "It would be very difficult for me to conceive it possible that this man, now at the bar, can be found not guilty." The jury did not misinterpret his meaning, and poor Skirving received the penalty of political contumacy.

Of all the political prisoners brought before Braxfield, Maurice Margarot gave, perhaps, the most trouble. During his trial (1794) a scene occurred to which it would be difficult to find a parallel in legal history. Margarot was no poltroon. Quite early in the trial he proved himself more than a match for the formidable Braxfield. Learning that the court was being filled with people who had paid the doorkeepers for admission, he demanded that the court should be open to all comers. "That you have no business with," was Braxfield's answer. Margarot said no more, but on entering upon his defence, he again threw down the gauntlet. The scene which then took place was so extraordinary that the passage-at-arms between the prisoner and the Lord Justice-Clerk may well be reproduced in full.

Margarot. Now, my lord, comes a very delicate matter indeed. I mean to call upon my Lord Justice-Clerk; and I hope that the questions and the answers will be given in the most solemn manner. I have received a piece of information which I shall lay before the Court in the course of my questions. First, my lord, are you on oath?

Braxfield. State your questions, and I will tell you whether I will answer them or not. If they are proper questions I will answer them.

Margarot. Did you dine at Mr. Rochead's at Inverleith in the course of last week?

Braxfield. And what have you to do with that, sir?

Margarot. Did any conversation take place with regard to my trial?

Braxfield. Go on, sir.

Margarot. Did you use these words: "What should you think of giving him (Margarot) a hundred lashes together with Botany Bay," or words to that effect?

Braxfield. Go on. Put your questions if you have any more.

Margarot. Did any person—did a lady say to you that the mob would not allow you to whip me? And, my lord, did you not say that the mob would be the better for losing a little blood? These are the questions, my lord, that I wish to put to you at present in the presence of the Court. Deny them, or acknowledge them.

The consternation which this encounter—surely one of the most extraordinary that ever took place between a judge of the High Court and a prisoner—produced, may be more easily imagined than described. Braxfield appealed to his colleagues as to whether he should answer the questions; but, amazing to relate, all replied that they were irrelevant, and ought not to be answered. A more despicable piece of sophistry can hardly be conceived. Braxfield, at all events, knew that Margarot's questions were not only relevant, but that the story which gave rise to them was true. In a rash moment he had uttered the sentiments mentioned by Margarot at Mr. Rochead's house, and a lady had indiscreetly repeated them. In point of fact, his lordship never sought to deny the story. Moreover, at the subsequent trial of Joseph Gerrald, an offer was made to establish its truth by evidence independent of Braxfield, but the Court refused to allow the matter to be gone into—"a proceeding which," as Cockburn remarks, "it is difficult to reconcile with any hypothesis except one."

Gerrald's trial came on in March 1794, and was conducted with all the severity and want of fair-play which had been displayed in the trials of Muir, Skirving, and Margarot. Judging by Braxfield's summing-up, Gerrald's offence seems to have been one of nationality rather than of sedition. "Gentlemen," said his lordship, "Gerrald has no relation, nor the least property, in this country, but comes here to disturb the peace of the country, as a delegate from a society in England, to raise sedition in this country. I say he appears to me to be much more criminal than Muir, Palmer, and Skirving, because they were all natives of this country." This statement was both irrelevant and untrue—irrelevant inasmuch as the circumstances of these men were not before the jury (Palmer had not even been tried before Braxfield), untrue, because Palmer, at any rate, was an Englishman.

Braxfield's valiant efforts to stem the rising tide of democratic sentiment gained him many friends who had no reason to be dissatisfied with the state of things which existed under the Dundas regime. But it was otherwise with the great mass of the people. The political animosity of Braxfield and his colleagues, and the remorseless way in which they transported men whose chief offence was that they were "Friends of the People," roused the most unruly passions. For a time Braxfield was quite as unpopular as Mansfield had been during the Gordon riots, though for a very different reason. In this very brief catalogue of virtues, courage occupied a prominent place. There was nothing clandestine about Braxfield. The man who told the Radicals to their faces that "they would a' be muckle the better o' being hangit" might be lamentably indiscreet, but was certainly no coward. As an instance of his great nerve, it is recorded that after the sedition trials were over, which was generally about midnight, he would walk to his house in George Square, alone and unprotected.

What kind of a domestic life Braxfield led it is impossible to say, but from what is known of his public character and of his habits, it is permissible to assume that the family circle would not be the brighter for his presence. He was twice married. His first wife, by whom he had two sons and two daughters, was a daughter of Major James Agnew of the 7th Dragoon Guards, and niece of Sir Andrew Agnew, Bart., of Lochnaw, Wigtownshire. He married, secondly, Elizabeth, daughter of Robert Ord, Lord Chief Baron of the Exchequer of Scotland, by whom he had no issue.

When Braxfield paid his addresses to this lady, he did so in a thoroughly business-like fashion. Having satisfied himself as to her suitability, he called upon her, and announced his mission with a brevity and point which all suitors will admire, though few can emulate. "Lizzy, I am looking out for a wife, and I thought you just the person that would suit me. Let me have your answer, off or on, the morn, and nae mair aboot it." It is pleasant to add that the lady was quite as business-like. Next day she returned a favourable answer, and the marriage took place with the minimum of delay. Ramsay of Ochtertyre relates an anecdote of this lady upbraiding her husband for niggardliness. The story is to the effect that Lord Hailes and Braxfield were once entering a town where a circuit court was to be held, when Mrs. Macqueen remarked upon the shabbiness of their equipage compared with that of Hailes. "It is a shame," she said, "to have horses of different colours." "Never mind that, my dear," said her partner, "have we not a dog that he wants?"

Braxfield was a near neighbour of the father of Sir Walter Scott, the former residing at 28 and the latter at 25 George Square. Between the two families there appears to have been considerable intimacy; and it is interesting to recall that Scott's thesis on *The Title of the Pandects concerning the Disposal of the Dead Bodies of Criminals,* written in connection with his admission to the Faculty of Advocates, was dedicated to Braxfield—a tribute, no doubt, to the Lord Justice-Clerk's Toryism, which Scott shared to the full.

In his declining years Braxfield, no longer equal to the exacting pleasures of the tavern, became enamoured of the life of a country gentleman. Much of his leisure was passed at his Lanarkshire seat, "which he loved the more that he had gathered birds' nests there in his boyish years." As a landed proprietor he did remarkably well. He devoted much time and attention to farming with excellent financial results, he improved and extended Braxfield, and he purchased "several valuable estates at a time when land was comparatively cheap."

From his seventieth year onwards, Braxfield suffered much from ill-health, and for more than twelve months prior to his death he was unable to attend the Parliament House. He died at his town residence in 1799, and was buried at Lanark. "Regardless of the threats and invectives of a misled populace, Braxfield," wrote a contemporary, "discharged his duties with a manly firmness of mind, well-tempered intrepidity of conduct, and a wise and faithful application of the law, that must make his memory ever be gratefully remembered by his country." That so unrighteous a judge should have been graced with so fine an epitaph is one of the travesties of human life. "He has carried more sound law with him than he has left upon the Bench" observed one of his ablest professional rivals on learning of his death. Posterity will prefer to think of Braxfield the lawyer rather than of Braxfield the judge, or of Braxfield the man.

Letter to Joseph Story *

JOHN MARSHALL

*It would be superfluous to add a note to the famous "autobiographical let-
ter" from Marshall to Joseph Story which immediately follows were it not
for the fact that modesty on the part of Marshall prompted him to gloss
over some of the facts. John Marshall (1755–1835) was born in Virginia,
served in the Revolution, became a lawyer in the informal manner of the
day, was successively a state assemblyman, congressman, and Secretary
of State under John Adams. He also found time to write a life of Washington.*

*As Chief Justice, Marshall did more than any other man to establish
the dignity of the Court. He looked upon the Constitution as the be-all and
end-all of legal procedure in the United States. In the case of Marbury v.
Madison (see page 174) he made history when the Court set aside an Act of
Congress on constitutional grounds.*

MY DEAR SIR:

The events of my life are too unimportant, and have too little interest
for any person not of my immediate family, to render them worth communicating or preserving. I felt therefore some difficulty in commencing
their detail, since the mere act of detailing, exhibits the appearance of
attaching consequence to them;—a difficulty which was not overcome till
the receipt of your favour of the 14th inst. If I conquer it now, it is because
the request is made by a partial and highly valued friend.

I was born on the 24th of Septr. 1755 in the county of Fauquier at that
time one of the frontier counties of Virginia. My Father possessed scarcely
any fortune, and had received a very limited education;—but was a man to
whom nature had been bountiful, and who had assiduously improved her
gifts. He superintended my education, and gave me an early taste for history and for poetry. At the age of twelve I had transcribed Pope's essay on
man, with some of his moral essays.

There being at that time no grammar school in the part of the country
in which my Father resided I was sent, at fourteen, about one hundred
miles from home, to be placed under the tuition of Mr. Campbell a clergy-

* From *An Autobiographical Sketch by John Marshall*, edited by John Stokes Adams,
University of Michigan Press, Ann Arbor, 1937. Reprinted by permission.

161

man of great respectability. I remained with him one year, after which I was brought home and placed under the care of a Scotch gentleman who was just introduced into the parish as Pastor, and who resided in my Father's family. He remained in the family one year, at the expiration of which time I had commenced reading Horace and Livy. I continued my studies with no other aid than my Dictionary. My Father superintended the English part of my education, and to his care I am indebted for anything valuable which I may have acquired in my youth. He was my only intelligent companion; and was both a watchful parent and an affectionate instructive friend. The young men within my reach were entirely uncultivated; and the time I passed with them was devoted to hardy athletic exercises.

About the time I entered my eighteenth year, the controversy between Great Britain and her colonies had assumed so serious an aspect as almost to monopolize the attention of the old and the young. I engaged in it with all the zeal and enthusiasm which belonged to my age; and devoted more time to learning the first rudiments of military exercise in an Independent company of the gentlemen of the county, to training a militia company in the neighbourhood, and to the political essays of the day, than to the classics or to Blackstone.

In the summer of 1775 I was appointed a first lieutenant in a company of minute men designed for actual service, who were assembled in Battalion on the first of September. In a few days we were ordered to march into the lower country for the purpose of defending it against a small regular and predatory force commanded by Lord Dunmore. I was engaged in the action at the Great Bridge; and was in Norfolk when it was set on fire by a detachment from the British ships lying in the river, and afterwards when the remaining houses were burnt by orders from the Committee of safety.

In July 1776 I was appointed first Lieutenant in the 11th Virginia regiment on continental establishment; and, in the course of the succeeding winter marched to the north, where, in May 1777, I was promoted to the rank of Captain. I was in the skirmish at iron hill where the Light Infantry was engaged; and in the battles of Brandy Wine, German town, and Monmouth.

As that part of the Virginia line which had not marched to Charleston was dissolving by the expiration of the terms for which the men had enlisted, the officers were directed to return home in the winter of 1779–80, in order to take charge of such men as the legislature should raise for them. I availed myself of this inactive interval for attending a course of law lectures given by Mr. Wythe, and of lectures of Natural philosophy given by Mr. Madison then President of William and Mary College. The vacation commenced in July when I left the university, and obtained a license to practice law. In October I returned to the army, and continued in service until the termination of Arnolds invasion after which, in February 1781, before the invasion of Phillips, there being a redundancy of officers, I resigned my commission.

I had formed a strong attachment to the young lady whom I afterwards married; and, as we had more officers than soldiers, thought I might without violating the duty I owed my country, pay some attention to my future prospects in life.

It was my design to go immediately to the bar; but the invasion of Virginia soon took place, and the courts were closed till the capitulation of Lord Cornwallis. After that event the courts were opened and I commenced practice.

In the spring of 1782 I was elected a member of the legislature; and, in the autumn of the same year was chosen a member of the Executive Council. In January 1783 I was married to Miss Ambler the second daughter of our then Treasurer, and in April 1784 resigned my seat at the Council board in order to return to the bar. In the same month I was again elected a member of the legislature for the county of Fauquier of which I was only a nominal resident having resided actually in Richmond as a member of the Council. Immediately after the election I established myself in Richmond for the purpose of practicing law in the superior courts of Virginia.

My extensive acquaintance in the army was of great service to me. My numerous military friends, who were dispersed over the state, took great interest in my favour, and I was more successful than I had reason to expect. In April 1787, I was elected into the legislature for the county in which Richmond stands; and though devoted to my profession, entered with a good deal of spirit into the politics of the state. The topics of the day were paper money, the collection of taxes, the preservation of public faith, and the administration of justice. Parties were nearly equally divided on all these interesting subjects; and the contest concerning them was continually renewed. The state of the Confederacy was also a subject of deep solicitude to our statesmen. Mr. James Madison had been for two or three years a leading member of the House of Delegates, and was the parent of the resolution for appointing members to a general Convention to be held at Philadelphia for the purpose of revising the confederation. The question whether a continuance of the Union or a separation of the states was most to be desired was some times discussed; and either side of the question was supported without reproach. Mr. Madison was the enlightened advocate of Union and of an efficient federal government; but was not a member of the legislature when the plan of the constitution was proposed to the states by the General Convention. It was at first favorably received; but Mr. P. Henry, Mr. G. Mason, and several other gentlemen of great influence were much opposed to it, and permitted no opportunity to escape of inveighing against it and of communicating their prejudices to others. In addition to state jealousy and state pride, which operated powerfully in all the large states, there were some unacknowledged motives of no inconsiderable influence in Virginia. In the course of the session, the unceasing efforts of the enemies of the constitution made a deep impression; and before its close, a great majority showed a decided hostility to it. I took an active part in the debates on this question and was uniform in support of the proposed constitution.

When I recollect the wild and enthusiastic democracy with which my political opinions of that day were tinctured, I am disposed to ascribe my devotion to the union, and to a government competent to its preservation, at least as much to casual circumstances as to judgement. I had grown up at a time when a love of union and resistance to the claims of Great Britain were the inseparable inmates of the same bosom;—when patriotism and a strong fellow feeling with our suffering fellow citizens of Boston were identical;—when the maxim "united we stand, divided we fall" was the maxim of every orthodox American; and I had imbibed these sentiments so thoroughly that they constituted a part of my being. I carried them with me into the army where I found myself associated with brave men from different states who were risking life and everything valuable in a common cause believed by all to be most precious; and where I was confirmed in the habit of considering America as my country, and congress as my government. I partook largely of the sufferings and feelings of the army, and brought with me into civil life an ardent devotion to its interests. My immediate entrance into the state legislature opened to my view the causes which had been chiefly instrumental in augmenting those sufferings, and the general tendency of state politics convinced me that no safe and permanent remedy could be found but in a more efficient and better organized general government. The questions too, which were perpetually recurring in the state legislatures, and which brought annually into doubt principles which I thought most sound, which proved that everything was afloat, and that we had no safe anchorage ground, gave a high value in my estimation to that article in the constitution which imposes restrictions on the states. I was consequently a determined advocate for its adoption, and became a candidate for the convention to which it was to be submitted.

The county in which I resided was decidedly antifederal, but I was at that time popular, and parties had not yet become so bitter as to extinguish the private affections.

A great majority of the people of Virginia was antifederal; but in several of the counties most opposed to the adoption of the constitution, individuals of high character and great influence came forward as candidates and were elected from personal motives. After an ardent and eloquent discussion to which justice never has been and never can be done, during which the constitution was adopted by nine states, the question was carried in the affirmative by a majority of eight voices.

I felt that those great principles of public policy which I considered as essential to the general happiness were secured by this measure & I willingly relinquished public life to devote myself to my profession. Indeed the county was so thoroughly antifederal, & parties had become so exasperated, that my election would have been doubtful. This however was not my motive for withdrawing from the legislature. My practice had become very considerable, and I could not spare from its claims on me so much time as would be necessary to maintain such a standing in the legislature as I was desirous of preserving. I was pressed to become a candidate for congress; and, though the district was unequivocally antifederal I could have been elected because that party was almost equally divided between two candidates who were equally obstinate and much embittered against each other. The struggle between the ambition of being engaged in the organization of the government, and the conviction of the injury which would be sustained by my private affairs was at length terminated in the victory of prudence, after which the federalists set up and elected Colonel Griffin, who obtained rather more than one third of the votes in the district which constituted a plurality.

Colonel Griffin named me to General Washington as the attorney for the district, an office which I had wished, but I declined accepting it because at that time the circuit courts of the United States were held at two distinct places far apart, and distant from the seat of government where the superior courts of the state sat. Consequently I could not attend them regularly without some detriment to my state practice. Before this inconvenience was removed the office was conferred on another gentleman.

In December 1788 the legislature passed an act allowing a representative to the city of Richmond, and I was almost unanimously invited to become a candidate. The city was federal. I yielded to the general wish partly because a man changes his inclination after retiring from public life, partly because I found the hostility to the government so strong in the legislature as to require from its friends all the support they could give it, and partly because the capitol was then completed, and the courts and the legislature sat in the same building, so that I could without much inconvenience [leave?] the bar to take part in any debate in which I felt a particular interest.

I continued in the assembly for the years 1789 & 1790 & 1791, during which time almost every important measure of the government was discussed, and the whole funding system was censured; that part of it especially which assumes the state debts was pronounced unconstitutional. After the session of 1791 I again withdrew from the assembly, determined to bid a final adieu to political life.

The arrival and conduct of Mr. Genet excited great sensation throughout the southern states. We were all strongly attached to France—scarcely any man more strongly than myself. I sincerely believed human liberty to depend in a great measure on the success of the French revolution. My partiality to France however did not so entirely pervert my understanding as to render me insensible to the danger of permitting a foreign minister to mingle himself in the management of our affairs, and to intrude himself between our government and people. In a public meeting of the citizens of Richmond, some of the earliest if not the very first resolutions were passed expressing strong disapprobation of the irregular conduct of Mr. Genet, our decided sense of the danger of foreign influence, and our warm approbation of the proclamation of neutrality. These resolutions, and the address to the President which accompanied them, were drawn and supported by me.

The resentments of the great political party which led Virginia had been directed towards me for some time, but this measure brought it into active operation. I was attacked with great virulence in the papers and was so far honoured in Virginia as to be associated with Alexander Hamilton, at least so far as to be termed his instrument. With equal vivacity I defended myself and the measures of the government. My constant effort was to show that the conduct of our government respecting its foreign relations were such as a just self-respect and a regard for our rights as a sovereign nation rendered indispensable, and that our independence was brought into real danger by the overgrown & inordinate influence of France. The public & frequent altercations in which I was unavoidably engaged gradually weakened my decision never again to go into the legislature, & I was beginning to think of changing my determination on that subject, when the election in the spring of 1795 came on.

From the time of my withdrawing from the legislature two opposing candidates had divided the city, the one was my intimate friend whose sentiments were very much those which I had entertained, and the other was an infuriated politician who thought every resistance of the will of France subserviency to Britain, and an adhesion to the coalition of despots against liberty. Each election between these gentlemen, who were both popular, had been decided by a small majority; & that which was approaching was entirely doubtful. I attended at the polls to give my vote early & return to the court which was then in session at the other end of the town. As soon as the election commenced a gentleman came forward and demanded that a poll should be taken for me. I was a good deal surprized at this entirely unexpected proposition & declared my decided dissent. I said that if my fellow citizens wished it I would become a candidate at the next succeeding election, but that I could not consent to serve this year because my wishes & my honour were engaged for one of the candidates. I then voted for my friend & left the polls for the court which was open and waiting for me. The gentleman said that he had a right to demand a poll for whom he pleased, & persisted in his demand that one should be opened for me—I might if elected refuse to obey the voice of my constituents if I chose to do so. He then gave his vote for me.

As this was entirely unexpected—not even known to my brother who though of the same political opinions with myself was the active & leading partisan of the candidate against whom I had voted, the election was almost suspended for ten or twelve minutes, and a consultation took place among the principal freeholders. They then came in and in the evening information was brought me that I was elected. I regretted this for the sake of my friend. In other respects I was well satisfied at being again in the assembly.

Throughout that part of the year which followed the advice of the senate to ratify Mr. Jays treaty, the whole country was agitated with that question. The commotion began at Boston and seemed to rush through the Union with a rapidity and violence which set human reason and common sense at defiance. The first effort was to deter the President from ratifying the instrument—the next to induce Congress to refuse the necessary appropriations. On this occasion too a meeting of the citizens of Richmond was convened and I carried a series of resolutions approving the conduct of the President.

As this subject was one in which every man who mingled with public affairs was compelled to take part, I determined to make myself master of it, and for this purpose perused carefully all the resolutions which were passed throughout the United States condemning the treaty and compared them with the instrument itself. Accustomed as I was to political misrepresentation, I could not view without some surprize the numerous gross misrepresentations which were made on this occasion; and the virulent asperity, with which the common terms of decency in which nations express their compacts with each other, was assailed. The constitutionality of the treaty was attacked with peculiar vehemence, and, strange as it may appear, there was scarcely a man in Virginia who did not believe that a commercial treaty was an infringement of the power given to Congress to regulate commerce. Seven other articles of the treaty were pronounced unconstitutional; but, on the particular ground of commerce, the objectors believed themselves to be invulnerable.

As it was foreseen that an attempt would be made in the legislature to prevent the necessary appropriations, one or two of my cautious friends advised me not to engage in the debate. They said that the part which it was anticipated I would take, would destroy me totally. It was so very unpopular that I should scarcely be permitted to deliver my sentiments, and would perhaps be treated rudely. I answered that the subject would not be introduced by me; but, if it should be brought before the house by others, I should undoubtedly take the part which became an independent member. The subject was introduced; and the constitutional objections were brought forward most triumphantly. There was perhaps never a political question on which any division of opinion took place which was susceptible of more complete demonstration, and I was fully prepared not only on the words of the constitution and the universal practice of nations, but to show on the commercial proposition especially, which was selected by our antagonists as their favorite ground, that Mr. Jefferson, and the whole delegation from Virginia in Congress, as well as all our leading men in the convention on both sides of the question, had manifested unequivocally the opinion that a commercial treaty was constitutional. I had reason to know that a politi-

cian even in times of violent party spirit maintains his respectability by
showing his strength; and is most safe when he encounters prejudice most
fearlessly. There was scarcely an intelligent man in the house who did not
yield his opinion on the constitutional question. The resolution however
was carried on the inexpediency of the treaty.

I do not know whether the account given of this debate, which was
addressed to some members of Congress in letters from Richmond, and was
published, was written by strangers in the gallery or by some of my partial
friends. Be this as it may my arguments were spoken of in such extravagant
terms as to prepare the federalists of Congress to receive me with marked
attention and favour, the ensuing winter when I attended in Philadelphia
to argue the cause respecting British debts before the supreme court of the
United States. I there became acquainted with Mr. Cabot, Mr. Ames, &
Mr. Dexter & Mr. Edgewic, of Massachusetts, with Mr. Wadsworth of
Connecticut and with Mr. King of New York. I was delighted with these
gentlemen. The particular subject which introduced me to their notice was
at that time so interesting, and a Virginian who supported with any sort of
reputation the measures of the government was such a *rara avis*, that I was
received by them all with a degree of kindness which I had not anticipated.
I was particularly intimate with Ames, & could scarcely gain credit with
him when I assured him that the appropriations would be seriously opposed
in Congress.

It was about or perhaps a little after this time that I was invited by
General Washington to take the office of Attorney General of the United
States. I was too deeply engaged in the practice in Virginia to accept this
office, though I should certainly have preferred it to any other.

I continued in the assembly though I took no part in the current business.
It was I think in the session of 1796–97 that I was engaged in a debate
which called forth all the strength and violence of party. Some Federalist
moved a resolution expressing the high confidence of the house in the virtue,
patriotism, and wisdom of the President of the United States. A motion was
made to strike out the word "wisdom." In the debate the whole course of
the administration was reviewed, and the whole talent of each party was
brought into action. Will it be believed that the word was retained by a
very small majority. A very small majority in the legislature of Virginia
acknowledged the wisdom of General Washington.

When the cabinet decided on recalling Mr. Monroe from France, the
President invited me to succeed him. But I thought my determination to
remain at the bar unalterable, and declined the office. My situation at the
bar appeared to me to be more independent and not less honorable than
any other, and my preference for it was decided.

In June 1797 I was placed by Mr. Adams, then President of the United
States, in the commission for accommodating our differences with France,
and received a letter requesting my attendance in Philadelphia in order to

receive the communications of the government respecting the mission previous to my embarcation. It was the first time in my life that I had ever hesitated concerning the acceptance of office. My resolution concerning my profession had sustained no change. Indeed my circumstances required urgently that I should adhere to this resolution because I had engaged with some others in the purchase of a large estate the arrangements concerning which were not yet made. On the other hand I felt a very deep interest in the state of our controversy with France. I was most anxious and believed the government to be most anxious for the adjustment of our differences with that republic. I felt some confidence in the good dispositions which I should carry with me into the negotiation, and in the temperate firmness with which I should aid in the investigations which would be made. The subject was familiar to me, and had occupied a large portion of my thoughts. I will confess that the *eclat* which would attend a successful termination of the differences between the two countries had no small influence over a mind in which ambition, though subjected to controul, was not absolutely extinguished. But the consideration which decided me was this. The mission was temporary, and could not be of long duration. I should return after a short absence, to my profession, with no diminution of character, &, I trusted, with no diminution of practice. My clients would know immediately that I should soon return & I could make arrangements with the gentlemen of the bar which would prevent my business from suffering in the meantime. I accepted the appointment and repaired to Philadelphia where I embarked for Amsterdam. I found General Pinckney at the Hague, and we obtained passports from the Minister of France at that place to secure our passage in safety to Paris. While at the Hague intelligence was received of that revolution which was effected in the French government by the seizure of two of the Directory and of a majority of the legislature by a military force acting under the orders of three of the Directory combined with a minority of the councils. This revolution blasted every hope of an accommodation between the United States and France.

On reaching Paris General Pinckney and myself communicated our arrival to Mr. Talleyrand & expressed a wish to suspend all negotiation till our colleague should be united with us. In a week or ten days Mr. Gerry joined us, and we immediately addressed ourselves to the minister. The failure of our attempts at negotiation is generally known. A journal which I kept exhibits a curious account of transactions at Paris. As soon as I became perfectly convinced that our efforts at conciliation must prove abortive I proposed that we should address a memorial to Mr. Talleyrand in which we should review fully the reciprocal complaints of the two countries against each other, and bring the whole controversy, at least our view of it before the French government in like manner as if we had been actually accredited. My motive for this was that if the memorial should fail to make its due impression on the government of France, it would show the sincerity

with which we had laboured to effect the objects of our mission, and could
not fail to bring the controversy fairly before the American People and
convince them of the earnestness with which the American government
sought a reconciliation with France. General Pinckney concurred with me
in sentiment and we acted most cordially together. I found in him a sensible
man, and one of high and even romantic honour. Mr. Gerry took a different
view of the whole subject. He was unwilling to do anything, and it was with
infinite difficulty we prevailed on him to join us in the letter to the minister
of exterior relations. It was with the same difficulty we prevailed on him
to sign the reply to this answer of the minister. We were impatient to hasten
that reply from a fear that we should be ordered to leave France before it
could be sent. We knew very well that this order would come and there
was a trial of skill between the minister and ourselves, (Genl. Pinckney &
myself) he endeavouring to force us to demand our passports, we endeavouring to impose on him the necessity of sending them. At length the passports came and I hastened to Bordeaux to embark for the United States.
On my arrival in New York I found the whole country in a state of agitation
on the subject of our mission. Our dispatches had been published and their
effect on public opinion had fully equalled my anticipations.

I returned to Richmond with a full determination to devote myself entirely to my professional duties, and was not a little delighted to find that
my prospects at the bar had sustained no material injury from my absence.
My friends welcomed my return with the most flattering reception, and
pressed me to become a candidate for Congress. My refusal was peremptory,
and I did not believe it possible that my determination could be shaken.
I was however mistaken.

General Washington gave a pressing invitation to his nephew, the present
Judge, & myself, to pass a few days at Mount Vernon. He urged us both
very earnestly to come into Congress & Mr. Washington assented to his
wishes. I resisted, on the ground of my situation, & the necessity of attending to my pecuniary affairs. I can never forget the manner in which he
treated this objection.

He said there were crises in national affairs which made it the duty of a
citizen to forego his private for the public interest. We were then in one
of them. He detailed his opinions freely on the nature of our controversy
with France and expressed his conviction that the best interests of our
country depended on the character of the ensuing Congress. He concluded
a very earnest conversation, one of the most interesting I was ever engaged
in, by asking my attention to his situation. He had retired from the Executive department with the firmest determination never again to appear in a
public capacity. He had communicated this determination to the public,
and his motives for adhering to it were too strong not to be well understood. Yet I saw him pledged to appear once more at the head of the

American army. What must be his convictions of duty imposed by the present state of American affairs?

I yielded to his representations & became a candidate. I soon afterwards received a letter from the Secretary of state offering me the seat on the bench of the supreme court which had become vacant by the death of Judge Iredell; but my preference for the bar still continued & I declined it. Our brother Washington was intercepted in his way to Congress by this appointment.

My election was contested with unusual warmth, but I succeeded, and took my seat in the House of Representatives in Decr. 1799. There was a good deal of talent in that Congress both for and against the administration, and I contracted friendships with several gentlemen whom I shall never cease to value. The great number of them are no more.

In May 1800, as I was about to leave Philadelphia (Though Congress was still in session) for the purpose of attending the courts in Richmond, I stepped into the war office in order to make some enquiries respecting patents for some of my military friends, and was a good deal struck with a strange sort of mysterious coldness which I soon observed in the countenance of Mr. McHenry, the secretary of war, with whom I had long been on terms of friendly intimacy. I however prosecuted my enquiries until they brought me into conversation with Mr. Fitzsimmons the chief clerk who congratulated me on being placed at the head of that department, and expressed the pleasure it gave all those who were engaged in it. I did not understand him, and was really surprized at hearing that I had been nominated to the senate as secretary of war. I did not believe myself to be well qualified for this department, and was not yet willing to abandon my hopes of reinstating myself at the bar. I therefore addressed a letter to Mr. Adams making my acknowledgements for his notice of me, and requesting that he would withdraw my name from the senate, as I was not willing openly to decline a place in an administration which I was disposed cordially to support. After writing this letter I proceeded immediately to Virginia.

Mr. Adams did not withdraw my name, & I believe the nomination was approved. I had not been long in Virginia when the rupture between Mr. Adams and Mr. Pickering took place, and I was nominated to the senate as secretary of state. I never felt more doubt than on the question of accepting or declining this office. My decided preference was still for the bar. But on becoming a candidate for Congress I was given up as a lawyer, and considered generally as entirely a political man. I lost my business alltogether, and perceived very clearly that I could not recover any portion of it without retiring from Congress. Even then I could not hope to regain the ground I had lost. This experiment however I was willing to make, and would have made had my political enemies been quiet. But the press teemed with so much falsehood, with such continued and irritating abuse of me that I could not bring myself to yield to it. I could not conquer a stubbornness of temper which determines a man to make head against and struggle with injustice. I felt that I must continue a candidate for Congress, and consequently could not replace myself at the bar. On the other hand the office was precisely that which I wished, and for which I had vanity enough to think myself fitted. I should remain in it while the party remained in power; should a revolution take place it would at all events relieve me from the competition for Congress without yielding to my adversaries, and enable me to return once more to the bar in the character of a lawyer having no possible view to politics. I determined to accept the office.

I was very well received by the President, and was on very cordial terms with all the cabinet except Mr. Wolcot. He at first suspected that I was hostile to the two exsecretaries, & to himself, because they were all three supposed to be unfriendly to the President to whom I was truely attached. My conduct soon convinced him however that I had no feeling of that sort, after which I had the satisfaction of finding myself on the same cordial footing with him as with the rest of the cabinet.

On the resignation of Chief Justice Ellsworth I recommended Judge Patteson as his successor. The President objected to him, and assigned as his ground of objection that the feelings of Judge Cushing would be wounded by passing him and selecting a junior member of the bench. I never heard him assign any other objection to Judge Patteson [sic], though it was afterwards suspected by many that he was believed to be connected with the party which opposed the second attempt at negotiation with France. The President himself mentioned Mr. Jay, and he was nominated to the senate. When I waited on the President with Mr. Jays letter declining the appointment he said thoughtfully "Who shall I nominate now"? I replied that I could not tell, as I supposed that his objection to Judge Patteson remained. He said in a decided tone "I shall not nominate him." After a moments hesitation he said "I believe I must nominate you." I had never before heard myself named for the office and had not even thought of it. I was pleased as well as surprized, and bowed in silence. Next day I was nominated, and, although the nomination was suspended by the friends of Judge Patteson, it was I believe when taken up unanimously approved. I was unfeignedly gratified at the appointment, and have had much reason to be so. I soon received a very friendly letter from Judge Patteson congratulating me on the occasion and expressing hopes that I might long retain the office. I felt truely grateful for the real cordiality towards me which uniformly marked his conduct.

I have my dear Sir been much more minute and tedious in detail than the occasion required, but you will know how to prune, condense, exclude, and vary. I give you the materials of which you will make some thing or nothing as you please—taking this only with you, that you will be sure to gratify me by pursuing precisely the tract you had marked out for yourself, & admitting nothing which may overload the narrative according to the original plan. Do not insert any thing from the suspicion that I may look for it because I have introduced it into my narrative.

It would seem as if new and perplexing questions on jurisdiction will never be exhausted. That which you mention is one of the strongest possible illustrations, so far as respects the original act, of the necessity in some instances of controuling the letter by the plain spirit of the law. It is impossible that a suit brought by the U. S. can be within the intention of the exception. There is however great difficulty in taking the case out of the letter. The argument you state is very strong and I am much inclined to yield to it. As no private citizen can sue in a district court on a promissory note I am much inclined to restrain the exception to those district courts which have circuit court jurisdiction. But the difficulty is I think removed by the act of the 3d of March 1815 and by the decision of the last term. I speak of that decision however from memory as I have not yet received 12th Wheaton.

Farewell—with the highest respect & esteem

I am yours

J MARSHALL

Marbury Versus Madison*

ALBERT J. BEVERIDGE

Albert J. Beveridge (1862–1927) was born in Ohio, grew up on an Illinois farm, and became senator for Indiana at the age of thirty-six. Although Beveridge had two terms as senator and was an organizer of the Progressive party, he did not continue to hold office. His four-volume life of John Marshall has become a classic in its field. He also left an unfinished life of Lincoln.

The headnote to the autobiographical letter from Marshall to Story (see page 161) mentions the famous case of Marbury v. Madison. "A law repugnant to the Constitution is void," wrote Marshall. The word "then" in the first line of the selection which follows means 1803.

A case was then pending before the Supreme Court the decision of which might, by boldness and ingenuity, be made to serve as the occasion for that tribunal's assertion of its right and power to invalidate acts of Congress and also for the laying-down of rules for the guidance of all departments of the Government. This was the case of Marbury *vs.* Madison.

Just before his term expired, President Adams had appointed forty-two persons to be justices of the peace for the Counties of Washington and Alexandria in the District of Columbia. The Federalist Senate had confirmed these nominations, and the commissions had been signed and sealed, but had not been delivered. When Jefferson was inaugurated he directed Madison, as Secretary of State, to issue commissions to twenty-five of the persons appointed by Adams, but to withhold the commissions from the other seventeen.

Among the latter were William Marbury, Dennis Ramsay, Robert Townsend Hooe, and William Harper. These four men applied to the Supreme Court for a writ of mandamus compelling Madison to deliver their commissions. The other thirteen did not join in the suit, apparently considering the office of justice of the peace too insignificant to be worth the expense of litigation. Indeed, these offices were deemed so trifling that one of Adams's appointees to whom Madison delivered a commission resigned, and five others refused to qualify.

* From Albert J. Beveridge, *Life of John Marshall,* published by Houghton Mifflin Company. Reprinted by permission of the publishers.

When the application of Marbury and his associates came before Marshall he assumed jurisdiction, and in December, 1801, issued the usual rule to Madison ordering him to show cause at the next term of the Supreme Court why the writ of mandamus should not be awarded against him. Soon afterward, as we have seen, Congress abolished the June session of the Supreme Court; thus, when the court again convened in February, 1803, the case of Marbury *vs.* Madison was still pending.

Marshall resolved to make use of this unimportant litigation to assert, at the critical hour when such a pronouncement was essential, the power of the Supreme Court to declare invalid acts of Congress that violate the Constitution.

Considering the fact that Marshall was an experienced politician, was intimately familiar with the political methods of Jefferson and the Republican leaders, and was advised of their purposes, he could not have failed to realize the probable consequences to himself of the bold course he now determined to take. As the crawling months of 1802 wore on, no signs appeared that the Republican programme for overthrowing the independence of the Judiciary would be relinquished or modified. On the contrary, the coming of the new year (1803) found the second phase of the Republican assault determined upon.

At the beginning of the session of 1803 the House impeached John Pickering, Judge of the United States District Court for the District of New Hampshire. In Pennsylvania, the recently elected Republican House had impeached Judge Alexander Addison, and his conviction by a partisan vote was assured. Already the Republican determination to remove Samuel Chase from the Supreme Bench was frankly avowed.

Moreover, the Republicans openly threatened to oust Marshall and his Federalist associates in case the court decided Marbury *vs.* Madison as the Republicans expected it would. They did not anticipate that Marshall would declare unconstitutional that section of the old Federalist Judiciary Act of 1789 under which the suit had been brought. Indeed, nobody imagined that the court would do that.

Everybody apparently, except Marshall and the Associate Justices, thought that the case would be decided in Marbury's favor and that Madison would be ordered to deliver the withheld commissions. It was upon this supposition that the Republican threats of impeachment were made. The Republicans considered Marbury's suit as a Federalist partisan maneuver and believed that the court's decision and Marshall's opinion would be inspired by motives of Federalist partisanship.

There was a particular and powerful reason for Marshall to fear impeachment and removal from office; for, should he be deposed, it was certain that Jefferson would appoint Spencer Roane of Virginia to be Chief Justice of the United States. It was well known that Jefferson had intended to appoint Roane upon the death of Chief Justice Ellsworth. But Ellsworth had resigned in time to permit Adams to appoint Marshall as his successor and thus thwart Jefferson's purpose. If now Marshall were removed, Roane would be given his place.

Should he be succeeded by Roane, Marshall knew that the great principles of Nationalism, to the carrying-out of which his life was devoted, would never be asserted by the National Judiciary. On the contrary, the Supreme Court would become an engine for the destruction of every theory of government which Marshall held dear; for a bolder, abler, and more persistent antagonist of those principles than Spencer Roane did not exist. Had he become Chief Justice those cases in which Marshall delivered opinions that vitalized the Constitution would have been decided in direct opposition to Marshall's views.

But despite the peril, Marshall resolved to act. Better to meet the issue now, come what might, than to evade it. If he succeeded, orderly government would be assured, the National Judiciary lifted to its high and true place, and one element of National disintegration suppressed, perhaps destroyed. If he failed, the country would be in no worse case than that to which it was rapidly tending.

No words in the Constitution gave the Judiciary the power to annul legislation. The subject had been discussed in the Convention, but the brief and scattering debate had arisen upon the proposition to make the President and Justices of the Supreme Court members of a Council of Revision with power to negative acts of Congress. No direct resolution was ever offered to the effect that the Judiciary should be given power to declare acts of Congress unconstitutional. In the discussion of the proposed Council of Revision there were sharp differences of opinion on the collateral question of the right and wisdom of judicial control of legislative acts. But, in the end, nothing was done and the whole subject was dropped.

Such was the record of the Constitutional Convention when, by his opinion in Marbury *vs.* Madison, Marshall made the principle of judicial supremacy over legislation as much a part of our fundamental law as if the Constitution contained these specific words: the Supreme Court shall have the power to declare invalid any act of Congress which, in the opinion of the court, is unconstitutional.

In establishing this principle Marshall was to contribute nothing new to the thought upon the subject. All the arguments on both sides of the question had been made over and over again since the Kentucky and Virginia Resolutions had startled the land, and had been freshly stated in the Judiciary debate in the preceding Congress. Members of the Federalist majority in most of the State Legislatures had expressed, in highly colored partisan rhetoric, every sound reason for the theory that the National Judiciary should be the ultimate interpreter of the Constitution. Both Federalist and Republican newspapers had printed scores of essays for and against that doctrine.

In the Virginia Convention of 1788 Marshall had announced as a fundamental principle that if Congress should pass an unconstitutional law the
courts would declare it void, and in his reply to the address of the majority
of the Virginia Legislature he had elaborately, though with much caution
and some mistiness, set forth his views. Chief Justice Jay and his associates
had complained that the Judiciary Act of 1789 was unconstitutional, but
they had not had the courage to announce that opinion from the Bench.
Justices Iredell and Paterson, sitting as circuit judges, had claimed for the
National Judiciary the exclusive right to determine the constitutionality of
laws. Chief Justice Jay in charging a grand jury, and Associate Justice
Wilson in a carefully prepared law lecture, had announced the same conclusion.

Various State judges of the Federalist faith, among them Dana of Massachusetts and Addison of Pennsylvania, had spoken to like effect. At the
trial of Callender Marshall had heard Chase deliver the opinion that the
National Judiciary had the exclusive power to declare acts of Congress
unconstitutional. Jefferson himself had written Meusnier, the year before
the National Constitution was framed, that the Virginia Legislature had
passed unconstitutional laws, adding: "I have not heard that in the other
states they have ever infringed their constitution; . . . *as the judges would
consider any law as void* which was contrary to the constitution."

Just as Jefferson, in writing the Declaration of Independence, put on
paper not a single new or original idea, but merely set down in clear and
compact form what had been said many times before, so Marshall, in his
opinion in Marbury *vs*. Madison, did nothing more than restate that which
had previously been declared by hundreds of men. Thomas Jefferson and
John Marshall as private citizens in Charlottesville and Richmond might
have written Declarations and Opinions all their lives, and to-day none
but the curious student would know that such men had ever lived. It was
the authoritative position which these two great Americans happened to
occupy and the compelling emergency for the announcement of the principles they expressed, as well as the soundness of those principles, that have
given immortality to their enunciations.

Learned men have made exhaustive research for legal decisions by which
Marshall's footsteps may have been guided, or which, at least, would
justify his conclusion in Marbury *vs*. Madison. The cases thus discovered
are curious and interesting, but it is probable that Marshall had not heard
of many of them. At any rate, he does not cite one of them in the course
of this opinion, although no case ever was decided in which a judge needed
so much the support of judicial precedents. Neither did he know anything
whatever of what was said on the subject in the Constitutional Convention,
unless by hearsay, for its sessions were secret and the Journals were not
made public until 1819—thirty years after the Government was established,
and sixteen years after Marbury *vs*. Madison was decided. Nor was Marshall

informed of the discussions of the subject in the State Conventions that ratified the Constitution, except of those that took place in the Virginia Convention.

On the other hand, he surely had read the Judiciary debate in Congress, for he was in the Capital when that controversy took place and the speeches were fully reported in the Washington press. Marshall probably was present in the Senate and the House when the most notable arguments were made. More important, however, than written decisions or printed debates in influencing Marshall's mind was *The Federalist,* which we know he read carefully. In number seventy-eight of that work, Hamilton stated the principle of judicial supremacy which Marshall whole-heartedly adopted in Marbury *vs.* Madison.

"The interpretation of the laws," wrote Hamilton, "is the proper and peculiar province of the courts. A constitution is, in fact, and must be regarded by the judges, as a fundamental law. It therefore belongs to them to ascertain its meaning, as well as the meaning of any particular act proceeding from the legislative body. If there should happen to be an irreconcilable variance between the two, . . . the Constitution ought to be preferred to the statute, the intention of the people to the intention of their agents."

In this passage Hamilton merely stated the general understanding of nearly all the important framers of the Constitution. Beyond question, Marshall considered that principle to have been woven into the very fiber of the Nation's fundamental law.

In executing his carefully determined purpose to have the Supreme Court formally announce the exclusive power of that tribunal as the authority of last resort to interpret the Constitution and determine the validity of laws by the test of that instrument, Marshall faced two practical and baffling difficulties, in addition to those larger and more forbidding ones which we have already considered.

The first of these was the condition of the Supreme Court itself and the low place it held in the public esteem; from the beginning it had not, as a body, impressed the public mind with its wisdom, dignity, or force. The second obstacle was technical and immediate. Just how should Marshall declare the Supreme Court to be the ultimate arbiter of conflicts between statutes and the Constitution? What occasion could he find to justify, and seemingly to require, the pronouncement as the judgment of the Supreme Court of that opinion now imperatively demanded, and which he had resolved at all hazards to deliver?

When the Republicans repealed the Federalist Judiciary Act of 1801, Marshall had actually proposed to his associates upon the Supreme Bench that they refuse to sit as circuit judges, and "risk the consequences." By the Constitution, he said, they were Judges of the Supreme Court only; their commissions proved that they were appointed solely to those offices;

the section requiring them to sit in inferior courts was unconstitutional. The other members of the Supreme Court, however, had not the courage to adopt the heroic course Marshall recommended. They agreed that his views were sound, but insisted that, because the Ellsworth Judiciary Act had been acquiesced in since the adoption of the Constitution, the validity of that act must now be considered as established. So Marshall reluctantly abandoned his bold plan, and in the autumn of 1802 held court at Richmond as circuit judge. To the end of his life, however, he held firmly to the opinion that in so far as the Republican Judiciary Repeal Act of 1802 deprived National judges of their offices and salaries, that legislation was unconstitutional.

Had the circuit judges, whose offices had just been taken from them, resisted in the courts, Marshall might, and probably would, have seized upon the issue thus presented to declare invalid the act by which the Republicans had overturned the new Federalist Judiciary system. Just this, as we have seen, the Republicans had expected him to do, and therefore had so changed the sessions of the Supreme Court that it could not render any decision for more than a year after the new Federalist courts were abolished.

Certain of the deposed National judges had, indeed, taken steps to bring the "revolutionary" Republican measure before the Supreme Court, but their energies flagged, their hearts failed, and their only action was a futile and foolish protest to the very Congress that had wrested their judicial seats from under them. Marshall was thus deprived of that opportunity at the only time he could have availed himself of it.

A year afterward, when Marbury *vs.* Madison came up for decision, the entire National Judiciary had submitted to the Republican repeal and was holding court under the Act of 1789. This case, then, alone remained as the only possible occasion for announcing, at that critical time, the supervisory power of the Judiciary over legislation.

Marshall was Secretary of State when President Adams tardily appointed, and the Federalist Senate confirmed, the forty-two justices of the peace for the District of Columbia, and it was Marshall who had failed to deliver the commissions to the appointees. Instead, he had, with his customary negligence of details, left them on his desk. Scarcely had he arrived at Richmond, after Jefferson's inauguration, when his brother, James M. Marshall, wrote him of the plight in which the newly appointed justices of the peace found themselves as the result of Marshall's oversight.

The Chief Justice replied: "I learn with infinite chagrin the 'development of principle' mentioned in yours of the 12th,"—sarcastically referring to the Administration's conduct toward the Judiciary,—"& I cannot help regreting it the more as I fear some blame may be imputed to me. . . .

"I did not send out the commissions because I apprehended such as were for a fixed time to be completed when signed & sealed & such as depended on the will of the President might at any time be revoked. To withhold the commission of the Marshal is equal to displacing him which the President, I presume, has the power to do, but to withhold the commissions of the Justices is an act of which I entertaind no suspicion. I should however have sent out the commissions which had been signed & sealed but for the extreme hurry of the time & the absence of Mr. Wagner [Clerk of the State Department] who had been called on by the President to act as his private secretary."

Marshall, it thus appears, was thoroughly familiar with the matter when the application of Marbury and his three associates came before the Supreme Court, and took in it a keen and personal interest. By the time the case came on for final disposition the term had almost half expired for which Marbury and his associates had been appointed. The other justices of the peace to whom Madison had delivered commissions were then transacting all the business that required the attention of such officials. It was certain, moreover, that the Administration would not recognize Marbury and his associates, no matter what Marshall might decide. In fact, these appointees must have lost all interest in the contest for offices of such slight dignity and such insignificant emoluments.

So far, then, as practical results were concerned, the case of Marbury *vs.* Madison had now come to the point where it was of no consequence whatever to any one. It presented only theoretical questions, and, on the face of the record, even these were as simple as they were unimportant. This controversy, in fact, had degenerated into little more than "a moot case," as Jefferson termed it twenty years later.

At the hearing it was proved that the commissions had been signed and sealed. One witness was Marshall's brother, James M. Marshall. Jefferson's Attorney-General, Levi Lincoln, was excused from testifying as to what finally became of them. Madison refused to show cause and denied, by utterly ignoring, the jurisdiction of the Supreme Court to direct or control him in his administration of the office of Secretary of State.

Charles Lee, former Attorney-General, counsel for the applicants, argued the questions which he and everybody else thought were involved. He maintained that a mandamus was the proper remedy, made so not only by the nature of the relation of the Supreme Court to inferior courts and ministerial officers, but by positive enactment of Congress in the Judiciary Law of 1789. Lee pointed out that the Supreme Court had acted on this authority in two previous cases.

Apparently the court could do one or the other of two things: it could disavow its power over any branch of the Executive Department and dismiss the application, or it could assert this power in cases like the one before it and command Madison to deliver the withheld commissions. It was the latter course that the Republicans expected Marshall to take.

If the Chief Justice should do this, Madison undoubtedly would ignore the writ and decline to obey the court's mandate. Thus the Executive and Judicial Departments would have been brought into direct conflict, with every practical advantage in the hands of the Administration. The court had no physical means to compel the execution of its order. Jefferson would have denounced the illegality of such a decision and laughed at the court's predicament. In short, had the writ to Madison been issued, the court would have been powerless to enforce obedience to its own mandate.

If, on the contrary, the court dismissed the case, the Republican doctrines that the National courts could not direct executives to obey the laws, and that the Judiciary could not invalidate acts of Congress, would by acquiescence have been admitted.

No matter which horn of the dilemma Marshall selected, it was hard to see how his views could escape impalement. He chose neither. Instead of allowing his cherished purpose of establishing the principle of supervisory power of the Judiciary over legislation to be thus wounded and perhaps fatally injured, he made the decision of this insignificant case—about which the applicants themselves no longer cared—the occasion for asserting that principle. And he did assert that principle—asserted it so impressively that for more than a century his conclusion has easily withstood repeated assaults upon it, which still continue.

Marshall accomplished his purpose by convincing the Associate Justices of the unconstitutionality of that section of the Ellsworth Judiciary Act of 1789 which expressly conferred upon the Supreme Court the power to issue writs of mandamus and prohibition, and in persuading them to allow him to announce that conclusion as the opinion of the court. When we consider that, while all the Justices agreed with Marshall that the provision of the Ellsworth Judiciary Law requiring them to sit as circuit judges was unconstitutional, and yet refused to act upon that belief as Marshall wanted them to act, we can realize the measure of his triumph in inducing the same men to hold unconstitutional another provision of the same act—a provision, too, even less open to objection than the one they had sustained.

The theory of the Chief Justice that Section 13 of the old Judiciary Law was unconstitutional was absolutely new, and it was as daring as it was novel. It was the only original idea that Marshall contributed to the entire controversy. Nobody ever had questioned the validity of that section of the statute which Marshall now challenged. Ellsworth, who preceded Marshall as Chief Justice, had drawn the act when he was Senator in the First Congress; he was one of the greatest lawyers of his time and an influential member of the Constitutional Convention.

One of Marshall's associates on the Supreme Bench at that very moment, William Paterson, had also been, with Ellsworth, a member of the Senate Committee that reported the Judiciary Act of 1789, and he, too, had been a member of the Constitutional Convention. Senators Gouverneur Morris of New York, William S. Johnson of Connecticut, Robert Morris of Pennsylvania, William Few of Georgia, George Read and Richard Bassett of Delaware, and Caleb Strong of Massachusetts supported the Ellsworth Law when the Senate passed it; and in the House James Madison and George Wythe of Virginia, Abraham Baldwin of Georgia, and Roger Sherman of Connecticut heartily favored and voted for the act. Most of these men were thorough lawyers, and every one of them had also helped to draft the National Constitution. Here were twelve men, many of them highly learned in the law, makers of the Constitution, draftsmen or advocates and supporters of the Ellsworth Judiciary Act of 1789, not one of whom had ever dreamed that an important section of that law was unconstitutional.

Furthermore, from the organization of the Supreme Court to that moment, the bench and bar had accepted it, and the Justices of the Supreme Court, sitting with National district judges, had recognized its authority when called upon to take action in a particular controversy brought directly under it. The Supreme Court itself had held that it had jurisdiction, under Section 13, to issue a mandamus in a proper case, and had granted a writ of prohibition by authority of the same section. In two other cases this section had come before the Supreme Court, and no one had even intimated that it was unconstitutional.

When, to his great disgust, Marshall was forced to sit as a circuit judge at Richmond in the winter of 1802, a case came before him that involved both the validity of the Republican Repeal Act and also the constitutionality of that provision of the Ellsworth Judiciary Law requiring justices of the Supreme Court to sit as circuit judges. This was the case of Stuart vs. Laird. Marshall held merely that the plea which raised these questions was insufficient, and the case was taken to the Supreme Court on a writ of error. After extended argument Justice Paterson delivered the opinion of the court, Marshall declining to participate in the decision because he had "tried the cause in the court below."

At the same term, then, at which Marbury vs. Madison was decided, and immediately after Marshall's opinion in that case was delivered, all the justices of the Supreme Court except the Chief Justice held "that practice and acquiescence under it [the Judiciary Act of 1789] for a period of several years, commencing with the organization of the judicial system . . . has fixed the construction. It is a contemporary interpretation of the most forcible nature. This practical exposition is too strong and obstinate to be shaken or controlled. Of course, the question is at rest, and ought not now to be disturbed."

But the exigency disclosed in this chapter required immediate action, notwithstanding the obstacles above set forth. The issue raised by the Republicans—the free hand of Congress, unrestrained by courts—must be settled at that time or be abandoned perhaps forever. The fundamental consideration involved must have a prompt, firm, and, if possible, final answer.

Were such an answer not then given, it was not certain that it could ever be made. As it turned out, but for Marbury *vs.* Madison, the power of the Supreme Court to annul acts of Congress probably would not have been insisted upon thereafter. For, during the thirty-two years that Marshall remained on the Supreme Bench after the decision of that case, and for twenty years after his death, no case came before the court where an act of Congress was overthrown; and none had been invalidated from the adoption of the Constitution to the day when Marshall delivered his epochal opinion. So that, as a matter of historical significance, had he not then taken this stand, nearly seventy years would have passed without any question arising as to the omnipotence of Congress. After so long a period of judicial acquiescence in Congressional supremacy it seems likely that opposition to it would have been futile.

For the reasons stated, Marshall resolved to take that step which, for courage, statesmanlike foresight, and, indeed, for perfectly calculated audacity, has few parallels in judicial history. In order to assert that in the Judiciary rested the exclusive power to declare any statute unconstitutional, and to announce that the Supreme Court was the ultimate arbiter as to what is and what is not law under the Constitution, Marshall determined to annul Section 13 of the Ellsworth Judiciary Act of 1789. In taking such a step the Chief Justice made up his mind that he would sum up in final and conclusive form the reasoning that sustained the principle.

Marshall resolved to go still further. He would announce from the Supreme Bench rules of procedure which the Executive branch of the Government must observe. This was indispensable, he correctly thought, if the departments were to be harmonious branches of a single and National Government, rather than warring factions whose dissensions must in the end paralyze the administration of the Nation's affairs.

It was not, then, Marshall's declaring an act of Congress to be unconstitutional that was innovating or revolutionary. The extraordinary thing was the pretext he devised for rendering that opinion—a pretext which, it cannot be too often recalled, had been unheard of and unsuspected hitherto. Nothing but the emergency compelling the insistence, at this particular time, that the Supreme Court has such a power, can fully and satisfactorily explain the action of Marshall in holding this section void.

In his opinion the Chief Justice spoke of "the peculiar delicacy of this case, the novelty of some of its circumstances, and the real difficulty attending the points which occur in it." He would follow, he said, the points of counsel in the order in which they had been made. Did the applicants have a right to the commissions? This depended, he said, on whether Marbury had been appointed to office. If so, he was entitled to the commission which was merely the formal evidence of the appointment. The President had nominated him to the Senate, the Senate had confirmed the nomination.

the President had signed the commission, and, in the manner directed by act of Congress, the Secretary of State had affixed to it the seal of the United States.

The President could not recall his appointment if "the officer is not removable." Delivery of the commission was not necessary to the consummation of the appointment which had already been effected; otherwise "negligence, . . . fraud, fire or theft, might deprive an individual of his office." But the truth was that "a copy from the record . . . would be, to every intent and purpose, equal to the original." The appointment of Marbury "vested in the officer legal rights . . . of his country," and "to withhold his commission is an act . . . not warranted by law, but violative of a vested legal right. . . .

"The very essence of civil liberty," continues Marshall, "certainly consists in the right of every individual to claim the protection of the laws, whenever he receives an injury. One of the first duties of government is to afford that protection." Ours has been "emphatically termed a government of laws, and not of men. It will certainly cease to deserve this high appellation, if the laws furnish no remedy for the violation of a vested legal right. . . .

"The act of delivering or withholding a commission" is not "a mere political act, belonging to the executive department alone," but a ministerial act, the performance of which is directed by statute. Congress had ordered the Secretary of War to place the names of certain persons on the pension rolls; suppose that he should refuse to do so? "Would the wounded veteran be without remedy? . . . Is it to be contended that the heads of departments are not amenable to the laws of their country?"

Would any person whatever attempt to maintain that a purchaser of public lands could be deprived of his property because a Secretary of State withheld his patent? To be sure, the President had certain political powers and could appoint agents to aid him in the exercise of them. The courts had no authority to interfere in this sphere of Executive action. For example, the conduct of foreign affairs by the Secretary of State, as the representative of the President, can never be examinable by the courts. But the delivery of a commission to an office or a patent to land was a different matter.

When Congress by statute peremptorily directs the Secretary of State or any other officer to perform specific duties on which "the rights of individuals are dependent . . . he cannot at his discretion sport away the vested rights of others." If he attempts to do so he is answerable to the courts. "The question whether a right has vested or not, is, in its nature, judicial, and must be tried by the judicial authority." The court therefore was empowered to decide the point; and held that Madison's refusal to deliver Marbury's commission was "a plain violation of that right, for which the laws of his country afford him a remedy."

But was this remedy the writ of mandamus for which Marbury had applied? It was, said Marshall; but could such an order be directed to the

Secretary of State? This was a task "peculiarly irksome, as well as delicate," for, he observed, there were those who would at first consider it "as an attempt to intrude into the cabinet, and to intermeddle with the prerogatives of the executive." Far be it from John Marshall to do such a thing. He need hardly "disclaim all pretensions to such jurisdiction." Not "for a moment" would he entertain "an extravagance so absurd and excessive. . . . Questions in their nature political, . . . can never be made in this court." But if the case before him presented only questions concerning legal rights of an individual, "what is there in the exalted station" of the Secretary of State which "exempts him from . . . being compelled to obey the judgment of the law"? The only remaining question, therefore, was whether a mandamus could issue from the Supreme Court.

In such manner Marshall finally arrived at the examination of the constitutionality of Section 13, which, he said, fitted the present case "precisely"; and "if this court is not authorized to issue a writ of mandamus" to Madison, "it must be because the law is unconstitutional, and therefore absolutely incapable of conferring the authority." In reaching this point Marshall employs almost seven thousand words. Fifteen hundred more words are used before he takes up the principle of judicial supremacy over legislation.

The fundamental law of the Nation, Marshall explained, expressly defined the original jurisdiction of the Supreme Court and carefully limited its authority. It could take original cognizance only of specific cases. In all others, the court was given nothing but "appellate jurisdiction." But he omitted the words that immediately follow in the same sentence—"with such exceptions . . . as the Congress shall make." Yet this language had, for fourteen years, apparently been considered by the whole bench and bar as meaning, among other things, that while Congress could *not take from* the Supreme Court original jurisdiction in the cases specifically named in Article Three of the Constitution, Congress *could add* other cases to the original jurisdiction of the Supreme Court.

Marshall was quite conscious of all this, it would seem. In the argument, counsel had insisted that since "the clause, assigning original jurisdiction to the Supreme Court, contains no negative or restrictive words, the power remains to the legislature, to assign original jurisdiction to that court in other cases than those specified." But, reasons Marshall, in answer to this contention, if Congress could thus enlarge the original jurisdiction of the Supreme Court, "the subsequent part of the section is mere surplusage, is entirely without meaning, . . . is form without substance. . . . Affirmative words are often . . . negative of other objects than those affirmed; and in this case, a negative or exclusive sense must be given to them, *or they have no operation at all.*"

That is to say, when the Constitution conferred upon the Supreme Court original jurisdiction in specified cases, it thereby excluded all others—denied to Congress the power to add to the jurisdiction thus affirmatively granted. And yet, let it be repeated, by giving original jurisdiction in cases specifically named, the Constitution put it beyond the power of Congress to interfere with the Supreme Court in those cases; but Marshall asserted that the specific grant of jurisdiction has *"no operation at all"* unless "a negative or exclusive sense" be given it.

Marshall boldly held, therefore, that Section 13 of the Ellsworth Judiciary Act was "not warranted by the Constitution." Such being the case, ought the Supreme Court to act under this unconstitutional section? As the Chief Justice stated the question, could "an act, repugnant to the constitution . . . become the law of the land"? After writing nearly nine thousand words, he now reached the commanding question: Can the Supreme Court of the United States invalidate an act which Congress has passed and the President has approved?

Marshall avowed that the Supreme Court can and must do that very thing, and in so doing made Marbury *vs.* Madison historic. In this, the vital part of his opinion, the Chief Justice is direct, clear, simple, and convincing. The people, he said, have an elemental right to establish such principles for "their future government, as . . . shall most conduce to their own happiness." This was "the basis on which the whole American fabric had been erected." These "permanent" and "fundamental" principles, in the instance of the American Government, were those limiting the powers of the various departments: "That those limits may not be mistaken, or forgotten, the constitution is written. To what purpose are powers limited . . . if these limits may, at any time, be passed by those intended to be restrained?"

If Congress or any other department of the Government can ignore the limitations of the Constitution, all distinction between government of "limited and unlimited powers" is done away with. To say that "acts prohibited and acts allowed are of equal obligation" is to deny the very purpose for which our fundamental law was adopted. "The constitution controls any legislative act repugnant to it." Congress cannot alter it by legislation. All this, said Marshall, was too clear to admit of discussion, but he proceeded, nevertheless, to discuss the subject at great length.

There is "no middle ground." The Constitution is either "a superior paramount law" not to be changed by legislative enactment, or else "it is on a level with the ordinary legislative acts" and, as such, "alterable" at the will of Congress. If the Constitution is supreme, then an act of Congress violative of it is not law; if the Constitution is not supreme, then "written constitutions are absurd attempts, on the part of the people, to limit a power in its own nature illimitable." Three times in a short space Marshall insists that, for Congress to ignore the limitations which the Constitution places upon it, is to deny the whole theory of government under written constitutions.

Although the contention that the Judiciary must consider unconstitutional legislation to be valid was "an absurdity too gross to be insisted on," Marshall would, nevertheless, patiently examine it. This he did by reasoning so simple and so logical that the dullest citizen could not fail to understand it nor the most astute intellect escape it. But in the process he was tiresomely repetitious, though not to so irritating an extent as he at times became.

If two laws conflict, the courts must decide between them. Where the Constitution and an act of Congress apply to a case, "the court must determine which . . . governs [it]. This is of the very essence of judicial duty. . . . If, then, . . . the constitution is superior to any ordinary act of the legislature," the Judiciary must prefer it to a mere statute. Otherwise "courts must close their eyes on the constitution," and see only the legislative enactment.

But to do this "would subvert the very foundation of all written constitutions." It would be to "declare that an act which . . . is entirely void, is yet . . . completely obligatory," and that Congress may do "what is expressly forbidden." This would give to the legislature "a practical and real omnipotence, with the same breath which professes to restrict their powers within narrow limits." It would be "prescribing limits, and declaring that those limits may be passed at pleasure." This "reduces to nothing" both the letter and the theory of the Constitution.

That instrument expressly extends the judicial power to cases "arising under the constitution." Must the courts decide such a case "without examining the instrument under which it arises?" If the courts must look into the Constitution at all, as assuredly they must do in some cases, "what part of it are they forbidden to read or to obey?"

Marshall cites hypothetical examples of legislation in direct conflict with the fundamental law. Suppose that Congress should place an export duty on cotton, tobacco, flour, and that the Government should bring suit to recover the tax. "Ought judgment to be rendered in such a case?" Or if a bill of attainder should be passed and citizens prosecuted under it, "must the court condemn to death those victims whom the constitution endeavors to preserve?"

Take, for example, the crime of treason: the Constitution emphatically prescribes that nobody can be convicted of this offense "unless on the testimony of two witnesses to the same overt act, or on confession in open court." The Judiciary particularly are addressed—"it prescribes, directly for them, a rule of evidence not to be departed from." Suppose that Congress should enact a law providing that a citizen might be convicted of treason upon the testimony of one witness or by a confession out of court? Which must the court obey—the Constitution or the act altering that instrument?

Did not these illustrations and many others that might be given prove that the Constitution must govern courts as well as Congress? If not, why does the Constitution require judges "to take an oath to support it"? That solemn obligation "applies in an especial manner to their conduct in their official character." How "immoral" to direct them to take this oath "if they were to be used as the instruments, and the knowing instruments, for violating what they swear to support!" Such contradictions and confusions would make the ceremony of taking the oath of judicial office "a solemn mockery" and even "a crime."

There is, then, said Marshall, no escape from the conclusion "that a law repugnant to the constitution is void," and that the judicial as well as other departments are bound by the Constitution. The application of Marbury and others must therefore be dismissed.

Thus, by a coup as bold in design and as daring in execution as that by which the Constitution had been framed, John Marshall set up a landmark in American history so high that all the future could take bearings from it, so enduring that all the shocks the Nation was to endure could not overturn it. Such a decision was a great event in American history. State courts, as well as National tribunals, thereafter fearlessly applied the principle that Marshall announced, and the supremacy of written constitutions over legislative acts was firmly established.

This principle is wholly and exclusively American. It is America's original contribution to the science of law. The assertion of it, under the conditions related in this chapter, was the deed of a great man. One of narrower vision and smaller courage never would have done what Marshall did. In his management and decision of this case, at the time and under the circumstances, Marshall's acts and words were those of a statesman of the first rank.

His opinion gave fresh strength to the purpose of the Republican leaders to subdue the Federalist Judiciary. It furnished Jefferson and his radical followers a new and concrete reason for ousting from the National Bench, and especially from the Supreme Court, all judges who would thus override the will of Congress. Against himself, in particular, Marshall had newly whetted the edge of Republican wrath, already over-keen.

The trial of John Pickering, Judge of the United States Court for the District of New Hampshire, brought by the House before the bar of the Senate, was now pushed with cold venomousness to what Henry Adams calls "an infamous and certainly an illegal conviction"; and then Marshall's associate on the Supreme Bench, Justice Samuel Chase, was quickly impeached for high crimes and misdemeanors. If the Republican organization could force from its partisans in the Senate a verdict of "guilty" in Chase's case also, Marshall's official head would be the next to fall.

Concerning Marshall's assertion of the power of the National Judiciary to annul acts of Congress and to direct administrative officers in the discharge of their legal duties, Jefferson himself said nothing at the time. But the opinion of the Chief Justice was another ingredient thrown into the caldron of Jefferson's heart, where a hatred was brewed that poisoned the great politician to his latest day.

Many months after the decision in the Marbury case, Jefferson first broke his silence. "Nothing in the Constitution has given them [the Supreme Court] a right to decide for the Executive, more than to the Executive to decide for them," he wrote. "The opinion which gives to the judges the right to decide what laws are constitutional, and what not, not only for themselves in their own sphere of action, but for the Legislature & Executive also, in their spheres, would make the judiciary a despotic branch."

Again, during the trial of Aaron Burr, Jefferson denounced Marshall for his opinion in Marbury *vs.* Madison; and toward the close of his life he returned again and again with corroding words to the subject regarding which, at the moment it arose, he concealed, so far as written words were concerned, his virulent resentment. For instance, seventeen years later Jefferson wrote that "to consider the judges as the ultimate arbiters of all constitutional questions . . . would place us under the despotism of an oligarchy."

But for the time being, Jefferson was quiescent. His subtle mind knew how, in political controversies, to control his tongue and pen. It could do no good for him, personally, to make an outcry now; and it might do harm. The doctrine which Marshall announced had, Jefferson knew, a strong hold on all Federalists, and, indeed, on many Northern Republicans; the bar, especially, upheld it generally.

The Presidential campaign was drawing near, and for the President openly to attack Marshall's position would create a political issue which could win none to the Republican cause not already fighting for it, and might keep recruits from joining the Republican colors. Jefferson was infinitely concerned about his reëlection and was giving practical attention to the strengthening of his party for the approaching contest.

"I am decidedly in favor of making all the banks Republican, by sharing deposits among them in proportion to the [political] dispositions they show," he wrote to his Secretary of the Treasury three months after Marshall's bold assertion of the dignity and power of the National courts. "It is," he continued, "material to the safety of Republicanism to detach the mercantile interests from its enemies and incorporate them into the body of its friends."

Furthermore, Jefferson was, at that particular moment, profoundly troubled by intimate personal matters and vast National complications. He had been trying, unsuccessfully, to adjust our dispute with France; the radical West was becoming clamorous for a forward and even a militant policy concerning the control of the Mississippi River, and especially of New Orleans, which commanded the mouth of that commercial waterway; while the Federalists, insisting upon bold measures, had a fair prospect of winning from Jefferson's support those aggressive and predatory frontiersmen who, until now, had stanchly upheld the Republican standard.

Spain had ceded Louisiana to France upon the condition that the territory never should be transferred to any other government; but neither New Orleans nor any part of Louisiana had actually been surrendered by the Spanish authorities. Great Britain informed the American Government that she would not consent to the occupation by the French of any part of Spain's possessions on the American continent.

Hating and distrusting the British, but also in terror of Napoleon, Jefferson, who was as weak in the conduct of foreign affairs as he was dexterous in the management of political parties, thought to escape the predicament by purchasing the island of Orleans and perhaps a strip on the east side of the Mississippi River.

A series of events swiftly followed the decision of Marbury *vs.* Madison which enthralled the eager attention of the whole people and changed the destiny of the Republic. Three months after Marshall delivered his opinion, Napoleon, yielding to "the empire of circumstances," as Talleyrand phrased it, offered, and Livingston and Monroe accepted, the whole of Louisiana for less than fifteen million dollars. Of course France had no title to sell—Louisiana was still legally owned and actually occupied by Spain. The United States bought nothing more than a pretension; and, by force of propinquity and power, made it a fact.

The President was amazed when the news reached him. He did not want Louisiana—nothing was further from his mind than the purchase of it. The immorality of the acquisition affected him not at all; but the inconvenience did. He did not know what to do with Louisiana. Worse still, the treaty of cession required that the people living in that territory should be admitted into the Union, "according to the principles of the Federal Constitution."

So, to his infinite disgust, Jefferson was forced to deal with the Louisiana Purchase by methods as vigorous as any ever advocated by the abhorred Hamilton—methods more autocratic than those which, when done by others, he had savagely denounced as unconstitutional and destructive of liberty. The President doubted whether, under the Constitution, we could acquire, and was sure that we could not govern, Louisiana, and he actually prepared amendments authorizing the incorporation into the Republic of the purchased territory. No such legal mistiness dimmed the eyes of John Marshall who, in time, was to announce as the decision of the Supreme Court that the Republic could acquire territory with as much right as any monarchical government.

To add to his perturbations, the high priest of popular rights found himself compelled to abandon his adored phrase, "the consent of the governed," upon which he had so carefully erected the structure of his popularity, and to drive through Congress a form of government over the people of Louisiana without consulting their wishes in the least.

The Jeffersonian doctrine had been that the Union was merely a compact between sovereign States, and that new territory and alien peoples could not be added to it without the consent of all the partners. The Federalists now took their stand upon this indefensible ground, and openly threatened the secession at which they had hinted when the Federalist Judiciary Act was repealed.

Jefferson was alive to the danger: "Whatever Congress shall think it necessary to do [about Louisiana]," he cautioned one of the Republican House leaders, "should be done with as little debate as possible." A month earlier he wrote: "The Constitution has made no provision for our holding foreign territory, still less for incorporating foreign nations into our Union. The Executive . . . have done an act beyond the Constitution."

Therefore, he declared, "the less we say about constitutional difficulties respecting Louisiana the better. . . . What is necessary for surmounting them must be done sub-silentio." The great radical favored publicity in affairs of state only when such a course was helpful to his political plans. On other occasions no autocrat was ever more secretive than Thomas Jefferson. Seemingly, however, the President was concerned only with his influence on the destiny of the world.

At first the Federalist leaders were too dazed to do more than grumble. "The cession of Louisiana . . . is like selling us a Ship after she is surrounded by a British Fleet," shrewdly observed George Cabot, when the news was published in Boston. Fisher Ames, of course, thought that "the acquiring of territory by money is mean and despicable," especially when done by Republicans. "The less of it [territory] the better. . . . By adding an unmeasured world beyond that river [Mississippi], we rush like a comet into infinite space."

Soon, however, their dissatisfaction blew into flame the embers of secession which never had become cold in their bosoms. "I am convinced," wrote Uriah Tracy, "that the accession of Louisiana will accelerate a division of these States; whose whenabouts is uncertain, but somewhen is inevitable." Senator Plumer thought that the Eastern States should form a new nation: "Adopt this western world into the Union," he said, "and you destroy at once the weight and importance of the Eastern States, and compel them to establish a separate and independent empire." A few days' reflection brought Ames to the conclusion that "our country is too big for union, too sordid for patriotism, too democratic for liberty." Tapping Reeve of Connecticut made careful inquiry among the Federalists in his vicinity and informed Tracy that "all . . . believe that we must separate, and that this is the most favorable moment."

Louisiana, however, was not the only motive of the foremost New England Federalists for their scheme of breaking up the Republic. As we have seen, the threat of secession was repeatedly made during the Republican assault on the Judiciary; and now, as a fundamental cause for disunion, the Northern Federalists speedily harked back to Jefferson's purpose of subverting the National courts. The Republicans were ruling the Nation, Virginia was ruling the Republicans, Jefferson was ruling all. Louisiana would permanently turn the balance against the Northern and Eastern States, already outweighed in the National scales; and the conquest of the National Judiciary would remove from that section its last protection against the pillaging hands of the Huns and Vandals of Republicanism. So reasoned the Federalists.

What could be done to save the rights and the property of "the wise, the rich and the good"? By what pathway could the chosen escape their doom? "The principles of our Revolution point to the remedy," declared the soured and flint-hearted Pickering. "The independence of the judges is now directly assailed. . . . I am not willing to be sacrificed by such popular tyrants. . . . I do not believe in the practicability of a long-continued union."

For the same reasons, Roger Griswold of Connecticut avowed that "there can be no safety to the Northern States *without a separation from the confederacy*." The Reverend Jedediah Morse of New Hampshire wrote Senator Plumer that "our empire . . . must . . . break in pieces. Some think the sooner the better." And the New Hampshire Senator replied: "I hope the time is not far distant when . . . the sound part will separate from the corrupt."

With the exception of John Adams, only one eminent New England Federalist kept his head steady and his patriotism undefiled: George Cabot, while sympathizing with his ancient party friends, frankly opposed their mad project. Holding that secession was impracticable, he declared: "I am not satisfied that the thing itself is to be desired. My habitual opinions have been always strongly against it."

But the expressions of such men as Pickering, Ames, and Griswold indicated the current of New England Federalist thought and comment. Their secession sentiment, however, did not appeal to the young men, who hailed with joy the opportunity to occupy these new, strange lands which accident, or Providence, or Jefferson had opened to them. Knowledge of this was indeed one cause of the anger of some Federalist managers who owned immense tracts in New England and in the Ohio Valley and wanted them purchased and settled by those now turning their eyes to the alluring farther western country. They saw with something like fury the shifting of political power to the South and West.

The management of the unwelcome Louisiana windfall, the conduct of the National campaign, the alarming reports from New England, left Jefferson no time to rail at Marshall or to attack that "subtle corps of sappers and miners" who were then beginning "to undermine . . . our confederated fabric," as Jefferson declared seventeen years later. For the present the great public duty of exposing Marshall's decision in Marbury *vs.* Madison must be deferred.

But the mills of democracy were grinding, and after he was reëlected certain impeachments would be found in the grist that would make all right. The defiant Marshall would at least be humbled, perhaps—probably —removed from office. But all in good time! For the present Jefferson had other work to do. He himself must now exercise powers which, according to his philosophy and declarations, were far beyond those conferred upon him by the Constitution.

So it came about that the first of Marshall's great Constitutional opinions received scant notice at the time of its delivery. The newspapers had little to say about it. Even the bench and the bar of the country, at least in the sections remote from Washington, appear not to have heard of it, or, if they had, to have forgotten it amid the thrilling events that filled the times.

Because popular interest had veered toward and was concentrated upon the Louisiana Purchase and the renewal of war in Europe, Republican newspapers, until then so alert to discover and eager to attack every judicial "usurpation," had almost nothing to say of Marshall's daring assertion of judicial supremacy which later was execrated as the very parent of Constitutional evil. An empire had been won under Jefferson; therefore Jefferson had won it—another proof of the far-seeing statemanship of "The Man of the People." Of consequence he must be reëlected. Such was the popular logic; and reëlected Jefferson was—triumphantly, almost unanimously.

Circumstances which had shackled his hands now suddenly freed them. Henceforth the President could do as he liked, both personally and politically. No longer should John Marshall, the abominated head of the National Judiciary, rest easy on the bench which his audacity had elevated above President and Congress. The opinion of the "usurping" Chief Justice in Marbury *vs.* Madison should have answer at last. So on with the impeachment trial of Samuel Chase! Let him be deposed, and then, if Marshall would not bend the knee, that obdurate judicial defender of Nationalism should follow Chase into desuetude and disgrace.

The incessant clamor of the Federal past-statesmen, unheard by the popular ear, had nevertheless done some good—all the good it ought to have done. It had aroused misgivings in the minds of certain Northern Republican Senators as to the expediency, wisdom, and justice of the Republican plan to shackle or overthrow the National Judiciary. This hesitation was, however, unknown to the masters of the Republican organization in Congress. The Federalists themselves were totally unaware of it. Only Jefferson, with his abnormal sensibility, had an indistinct impression that somewhere, in the apparently perfect alignment of the Republican forces, there was potential weakness.

Marshall was gifted with no such divination. He knew only the fate that had been prepared for him. A crisis was reached in his career and a determinative phase of American history entered upon. His place as Chief Justice was to be made secure and the stability of American institutions saved by as narrow a margin as that by which the National Constitution had been established.

The New Supreme Court*

CARL SWISHER

Roger B. Taney (1777–1864), Attorney General, Secretary of the Treasury, and Chief Justice of the Supreme Court of the United States, is a logical subject to follow John Marshall, for he followed him in office. Born of a Maryland planter family, Taney graduated from Dickinson, read law, and was admitted to the bar in 1799. He was vigorous in Maryland politics for many years; when his Federalist party collapsed he went over to Jackson. Two issues with which he was concerned—the rights of Negroes and a sound currency—were to play a continuing part in his busy life; he was criticized for his hostile attitude toward the Bank of the United States, and his opinion in the famous Dred Scott case likewise drew fire, but he remained adamant. During the War years, in poor health and virtually bankrupt, he heard his decisions hooted; yet some of these opinions are quoted today.

Carl Swisher calls for sympathy and admiration for this stormy figure. The account of the Charles River Bridge Case in the next few pages will give the reader a sample for judgment. Professor Swisher, who was born in 1897, is a graduate of Pomona; since 1937 he has been on the faculty at Johns Hopkins, where he is Stran Professor of Political Science.

The relatively high prestige which belonged to the Supreme Court of the United States at the time of Taney's appointment had been acquired for the most part during the years when John Marshall was Chief Justice. John Jay, the first Chief Justice, had preferred the position of governor of New York, and resigned from the bench to accept it. Oliver Ellsworth, Marshall's immediate predecessor, had resigned because of his preference for a diplomatic post. Alexander Hamilton, preferring private practice, had refused to accept the position of head of the court. Evidently he had no conception of the way in which that institution could be used to establish his ideas more firmly in the constitutional law of the country. No one, it seems safe to say, had at the time of Marshall's appointment a clear conception of the position of prominence which the court was to take in the federal government.

* From *Roger B. Taney*, by Carl Swisher, copyright, 1935, by The Macmillan Company. Reprinted by permission.

The growth of its prestige was coincident with and a part of the growth of the prestige of the legal profession in the United States. Lawyers and the English common law, which was their principal stock in trade, had been in low repute with the masses at the time of the Revolution. The need for the settlement of innumerable doubtful titles to property in the new country had, however, necessitated much litigation, and necessary litigation had created a demand for trained lawyers. Since the demand for outstanding legal ability was greater than the supply, the aristocrats of the bar were generally in position to choose whom they would serve, and at what price. Clients were individuals, or partnerships, or small corporations, employing legal aid spasmodically as they needed it. With the limited exception of the Bank of the United States, there were no great corporations practically monopolizing the services of the more eminent lawyers. The clients did not have lawyers so much as the lawyers had clients. The Frenchman, De Tocqueville, making a survey of America during the Jackson period, came to the conclusion that the legal profession constituted the only real aristocracy in the United States, the only barrier against the leveling influences of mass rule.

Naturally enough, the clients who employed high-priced lawyers were usually the possessors of substantial amounts of property. It was to protect or to acquire property that lawyers were retained. It is therefore not surprising that lawyers, like clients, were highly property-conscious; that property and legal ability and the rising aristocracy were becoming more and more closely allied; and that the alliance was distrustful of and to a degree hostile to the unpropertied masses, and to those who preached the preservation of human rights as against the rights of property. The rise of the legal profession in the United States, therefore, was coincident with and a part of the rise of a class, within what, in terms of democratic theory, was supposed to be a classless society.

The unfolding of the powers and the development of the reputation of the Supreme Court was a part of the same movement. Chief Justice Marshall's first great judicial opinion, in *Marbury* v. *Madison*, is not immediately relevant, though in claiming for his court the power to determine the constitutionality of acts of Congress he paved the way for the use of that power by his successors to protect property from federal legislation. The more important of his later opinions are usually hailed as providing the basis for strengthening the national government. Such, however, was their immediate purpose in only a limited degree. Most of them do not assert the power of Congress to legislate, or the power of the Federal Executive to administer. They assert, instead, that the states *may not* legislate in a fashion hostile to property. The addition to the strength of the national government is chiefly in the exercise of a veto power by the judiciary.

To choose a few examples, the result of one case was to prevent a state legislature from recapturing property granted away by a corrupt predecessor. Another claimed for the Supreme Court the power to review cases decided by the highest courts in the states when federal questions were involved. Another sanctified the creation by Congress of a national bank, which was essentially a great private financial institution, on the ground that it was an instrumentality of the federal government, and then denied to the states the power to tax the notes of that institution. Another translated corporation charters into contracts which the states were forbidden to impair. Another struck down state bankruptcy laws relieving debtors from obligations incurred before the laws were passed. Another devitalized similar laws applying to obligations incurred after the laws were passed to the extent of holding that the debtor was relieved only in the courts of the state in which the bankruptcy laws were passed. Another went a long way in the direction of the argument of Daniel Webster that the states might not legislate on interstate or foreign commerce even if there was no conflict with an act of Congress. Another denied the right of the states to tax goods which had been imported until after sale or the breaking of the original package. Another killed a state law under which the state borrowed money by issuing notes which were small enough to circulate as money.

So the story goes, in terms of the better known decisions of the Marshall period. He wrote the opinions of the court in all but two of them, and on them the celebrity of John Marshall largely depends. It is true that where the conduct of the external affairs of the United States was involved, as in the acquisition of territory, he interpreted broadly the positive powers of the federal government. Such powers were not at issue, however, in most of the important cases which came before him. The question was as to whether or not the court should so use its prerogative of interpreting the Constitution as to prevent state interference with property, in the enforcement of laws supposed to have been enacted for the public good. In voicing a sturdy "Thou shalt not," the court won from property its vaunted reputation as the guardian of the Constitution, and made itself the kingpin of the lawyer-property alliance.

It is not to be inferred that Marshall was a thoughtful student of John Locke's ideas concerning property, or that he was a glowing apostle of Adam Smith. Marshall did not read widely even in his own field, and he seems to have been almost wholly unlearned outside it. All he did was give persuasive utterance to the prevailing beliefs of the propertied classes of his times, in the terminology of constitutional law. Few or none of his ideas were new. Those which can not be found in the *Federalist* or in other writings of Hamilton were part of the current notions of those people who had property which they wanted protected but otherwise let alone.

The popularity of John Marshall, therefore, and the prestige acquired by the Supreme Court during his régime, resulted largely from the fact that he wrote into constitutional law the beliefs and prejudices of a class, the class, incidentally, from whose records and in terms of whose judgments most of the history of the period has been written. Outside that class he and his court were anything but popular, as is shown by the wrathful outpourings of Thomas Jefferson, Judge Spencer Roane and others during his early years as Chief Justice, and by the criticisms of the partisans of Old Hickory during the Jackson period.

Some of the opposition came doubtless from that ever present group who are critical because property is in the hands of the wrong people, with the implication that the right people are themselves. Some of it came from the holders of one kind of property, who believed that other kinds were being protected and nurtured at their expense, as for example the landholders of the South who saw themselves injured by the manipulations of a national government with pro-industrial and pro-banker leanings. Opposition came likewise from the great debtor and small-property class who had little expectation of achieving great wealth under any régime, and from their doctrinaire friends who rejected the theory that unqualified protection of property produced inevitably the highest possible total of human welfare.

Strong though the opposition was, Marshall so dominated the opinions of his brethren on the court that it was not until near the closing years of his life that a reversal of the trend of decisions was seriously threatened. With the coming of old age, however, he lost some of the captivating persuasiveness by which he had hitherto carried his brethren with him, and opposition within the court became more and more apparent. The accession to power of Jacksonian democracy revealed the strength of the advocates of change, and the prospect that Jackson would fill vacancies on the bench with men of his own point of view suggested the coming of a new order in judicial decisions. Conservatives of course resisted the tendency toward change. Able lawyers who supported it were regarded as little more than renegades —as witness the treatment of Taney—and the blatantly satisfied clamored for the perpetuation of the constitutional interpretations worked out by John Marshall and the Godlike Daniel.

The worst was feared, of course, when Taney, the arch-enemy of the Bank of the United States and critic of the merchant class, with heretical notions as to the interpretation of the Constitution and as to the authority of the court, was chosen as Marshall's successor. Would the court, under his guidance, surrender its guardianship over the rights of property and leave it at the mercy of state legislatures dominated by the masses of the people?

The answer to this question was to come gradually in terms of a long line of decisions on various topics, some related and some highly divergent. Those decisions fall into three major groups. The first group had to do with the interpretation of the rights of corporations, with the question as to whether the court should interpret corporation charters broadly, as it had hitherto interpreted the Constitution itself, or whether, in the interest of the public, they should be interpreted narrowly. The second group of decisions had to do with the interpretation of the commerce clause of the

Constitution. The question was not usually one of whether or not Congress had a certain power over interstate or foreign commerce. It was usually a question as to whether the states could enforce regulatory laws which affected such commerce, but which did not conflict with any act of Congress. The third group of decisions had to do with property in connection with the "peculiar institution" of the South, that is to say, with slavery. It is in terms of the dramatic judicial controversies over these subjects, together with sketches of personal and political backgrounds, that the chapters dealing with Taney's work as Chief Justice are presented.

The Supreme Court was composed of seven members during Taney's first year as its head, and of nine members thereafter. None of the judges resided permanently in Washington. Although one of them occasionally brought his wife with him when he came to the capital each January for the annual term of the court it was more usual to come alone. For many years arrangements had been made in advance for all the judges to live at the same boarding house and take their meals at the same table. This intimate living arrangement, indeed, which made possible the discussion of the work of the court at all hours, may have been largely responsible for the captivating influence which John Marshall exercised over the minds of his brethren. Certain it is that he thoroughly approved of this mode of living, and his many letters mentioning the subject show his desire to have the custom continued as long as he retained his position.

As if by inertia the judges, or those of them who could live peacefully together, continued to live in this fashion for a number of years after Taney's appointment, until a time, around 1850, when because of the presence of wives or for some other reason it was thought best that each should choose his own residence. The cost of living may have added to the attraction of the traditional arrangement, and in addition to the arduousness of long-distance travel may have been a reason for leaving wives at home. Members of the bachelor group could get accommodations for from sixteen to seventeen dollars a week, while a man and wife had to pay forty.

The judges moved about from year to year among the several boarding houses which catered to their trade. In the autumn of 1837 the clerk of the court was in doubt as to whether to choose the accommodations offered by Dawson's on the hill, or those of the Misses Polk. In 1839 Taney was at Elliott's, on Pennsylvania Avenue, as he told his son-in-law in a letter asking for a box of his long, black cigars. In 1841 he lived at Mrs. Turner's, likewise on the Avenue. Accommodations varied greatly in quality, as Taney found to his discomfort. "I have not been fortunate in our boarding arrangements," he wrote in 1840, again to his son-in-law. "My room is very good. I would not desire a better one, but all the rest of the house is more comfortless than you can well imagine. I do not speak of the chambers of the other judges for they are all pretty good, but of the dining room, food, servants &c. &c.

You can imagine nothing more abominably filthy." Yet the woman in charge had just lost her husband, he hastened to say, and had a house full of children. The judges therefore took their evils good humoredly. Nothing must be said against the house to injure its reputation in Baltimore, for he was convinced that the woman did as well as she was able.

Taney received a salary of $5,000 annually, while his colleagues received $4,500. They were paid less than the Secretaries of State, War, and Navy, who received $6,000, and more than the Postmaster General and Attorney General, who received $4,000. In addition to their work in Washington each of the judges had to preside over circuit courts in the several circuits to which they were assigned. The policy of requiring them to ride circuit had long been a source of controversy. The judges and their friends claimed that it was unreasonable to require elderly men, after serving in the Supreme Court, to ride hundreds of miles over rough roads and through rough country to preside over local courts when they ought to be in Washington or elsewhere adding to their knowledge of law.

The opposition replied that an important task of the Supreme Court was the application of local law in cases involving citizens of different states, and that service in the circuit courts provided excellent opportunities for learning about local conditions and local law. It was feared that if the judges established themselves in Washington and lost contact with the circuits they would become more than ever the tools of a national government for interfering with the powers of the states.

Taney held two terms of the circuit court in Baltimore each year, and one each in New Castle and Dover, Delaware. The Delaware terms required strenuous trips by stagecoach over a total of more than three hundred miles. In addition he had to go to Washington each January for the regular term of the Supreme Court, and in August for a vestigial term at which he alone was required to be present. The Washington trip could now be made over the Baltimore and Ohio Railroad, and was not difficult except for the fact that he found the crowded condition of the cars oppressive in winter time.

Difficult as it was, Taney's burden was light as compared with that of his brethren. Whereas he estimated his annual travels at 458 miles, Justice Story listed 1,896 miles, besides innumerable trips from his home in Cambridge to Boston. Justice Barbour, who lived at Richmond, made an estimate of 952 miles. Justice Wayne, who lived in Savannah, found a total of 2,370. Justice Thompson, from Poughkeepsie, estimated at 2,590. Justice McLean, of Richmond, in Ohio, covered 2,500 miles. Justices Catron and McKinley, who were added to the Supreme Court in 1837 and were assigned to new circuits in the West, estimated their prescribed travels at 3,852 and 10,000 miles respectively.

The difficulties of travel were often distressing and at times insuperable. McLean told of a trip through Indiana when the mud was so deep as to be almost impassable to a carriage of any description, on which the mails and passengers had to be conveyed in common wagons. McKinley declared that "upon some of the roads there are no private conveyances; and the time allowed for holding the courts would render it impossible to perform the traveling by any private mode. I have never yet been at Little Rock, the place of holding the court in Arkansas, but from the best information I can obtain it could not be conveniently approached in the spring of the year, except by water, and by that route the distance would be greatly increased." Catron complained that when he had made the trip to Washington, gone back westward down the Ohio River to St. Louis, and returned to Tennessee, he had been away from his home in Nashville for six or seven months.

Taney's judicial duties began on April 8, 1836, when he first presided over the United States circuit court in Baltimore, doubtless under the eyes of many who were eager to see if the advocate and the partisan would be submerged in the judge. Daniel Webster, in a mood of unusual frankness, once expressed doubt as to his own ability to be a judge. He had mixed so much study of politics with the study of law that although he had some respect for himself as an advocate he was not confident of possessing the accuracy and precision which the bench required. Taney may have had similar moments of self-questioning, and, although he must have known as well as Webster that the administration of law could not be completely severed from politics, he did set watch upon all his political utterances and activities which might become known to the public.

He exercised notable self-restraint and shrewd political caution in his charge to the grand jury at the opening of the circuit court. From the time of the organization of the federal courts it had been the custom of the judges to deliver to grand juries long discourses on broad principles of jurisprudence and on the nature of the federal system. Since the federal judiciary had been the stronghold of the Federalist party, the charges had often been resolved into proclamations of party principles, much to the disgust and resentment of the opposition. Taney announced to his first grand jury that he had a few words to say, not in compliance with the custom of delivering charges, of which he disapproved, but to give his reason for dispensing with the usage. He thought the court should enter at once with promptness and industry upon the performance of its duties, disencumbered of all unnecessary forms. The age had passed which called for particular instructions from the court. The intelligence of the jurors was adequate for their duties, and if they needed technical information the district attorney could provide it for them. It was unnecessary that the court should discourse on the wide field of jurisprudence when the only cases for the jury were a few infractions of criminal law. He therefore merely advised that the jury examine testimony with diligence, finding a bill when and only when they were clearly convinced of guilt, remembering that "our liberties and the permanency of our free institutions could only be secured by maintaining the supremacy of the laws, securing to the innocent the enjoyment of their rights, and visiting the violator of the law with the punishment due to his guilt."

Taney was in a sense acting politically in this abnegation of a privilege which had become a tradition with his predecessors. Since it had been exercised largely by Federalists for Federalist purposes, their enemies were on record as opposing it. Taney's gesture of self-restraint was hailed as a Democratic gesture by the spokesmen of the Jackson party. On the other hand it was much less obnoxious to political opponents than a positive assertion of Democratic principles would have been.

Taney and Upton S. Heath, his friend of the bank war period and now a United States district judge, sat together in the circuit court. It was said that Taney presided in a manner courteous but firm, which won the approval of the public and more particularly of the bar. Most of the cases decided were unimportant. In one of them, however, Taney's interpretation of law was significant. The case was a suit by sailors to recover wages from an owner who had lost his freight through an illegal capture, but had won back part of the value of the freight in a suit for damages.

The law of the sea was not particularly friendly to the interests of sailors. It had been molded through its centuries of development not by sailors in the interest of sailors, but by judges whose training and associations generally led them to sympathize with the viewpoint of the propertied classes. They had worked out the principle that "freight is the mother of wages," which meant that sailors were entitled to wages only if the freight carried was delivered, or compensation recovered for it. The principle was justified by the assumption that sailors would not work hard enough and risk their lives for vessel and cargo unless their wages were at stake. A sailor could not even protect his prospect for wages by insurance, for if he were thus assured of compensation he might defend against pirates with abated zeal, or he might wrestle less valiantly in the midst of storms.

Furthermore, if a cargo was lost and the owner was recompensed by insurance, he was under no obligation to pay wages to his sailors. Since the compensation of the owner came from insurance, and since sailors could not insure their wages, the collection of wages from the money paid to this owner would be doing indirectly that which could not be done directly, and would therefore shock the sense of justice possessed by the spokesmen of the law. It would also deplete the purse of the owner, and it might also be bad for insurance companies, in that sailors might not in the future strive hard enough to protect cargoes which were covered by insurance!

In the case before Taney the cargo had been condemned by the British, during the War of 1812, after Spain had illegally permitted it to be captured in her waters. The owner won compensation not in full but in part, and not from an insurance company but from Spain. The owner refused to pay wages, perhaps on the theory that sailors should be taught not to permit cargoes to be captured by the enemies of their country. It is not surprising, in view of his knowledge of the blatant selfishness of mercantile interests, that Taney refused in this case to follow the analogy of the insurance cases, declaring that he could see no principle of justice which required him to do so. Nor is it particularly surprising that he held that the wages must be paid in full even though the owner had not been recompensed in full, and had been put to great expense to make the collection.

In his discussion Taney adhered closely to the legal points involved, and refrained from elaborating on what he called principles of justice. There was nothing startling in the decision itself or in the way in which the opinion was written. Yet there was a suggestion of an emphasis upon the rights of non-propertied people which was alien to the decisions of John Marshall and most of his colleagues, and which bore promise of a new trend in the development of law.

Taney sat with his brethren of the Supreme Court for the first time on January 9, 1837, when he was slightly less than sixty years of age. As if in token of the changing order the semicircular court room in the basement of the Capitol had been redecorated. Back of each of the seven mahogany desks was set a new mahogany armchair covered with velvet. Light sifted feebly through the windows back of the seats of the judges, to melt down upon the cushioned sofas arranged for spectators in the middle of the room. At twelve o'clock Taney and five of his colleagues, Justice Wayne being absent, garbed themselves in the robes of office and took their places, Taney in the central position belonging to the Chief Justice and his associates arranged on either side of him alternately according to seniority.

Taney impressed spectators as tall, narrow of face, with clear black hair and an elasticity of step that hardly suggested his three-score years. There was something of portent, perhaps, in the fact that beneath his official robe he wore ordinary democratic garb, instead of the knee breeches customarily donned by his predecessor for the occasion. He was the first Chief Justice, it was said, to depart from precedent and give judgment in trousers.

Joseph Story, who sat at Taney's right, was two and a half years younger. He was of medium height, slightly portly of build, with expressive features, spectacles on nose, high and broad forehead, and hair that hung down over the collar of his robe. He had been a member of the court since 1811, and had been a closer friend of Marshall's and probably more deeply in sympathy with his ideas than any other of his colleagues. He had undoubtedly coveted the succession for himself, while knowing full well that Andrew Jackson would never confer it upon him. He was a voluminous writer on legal subjects, dabbled in poetry, was a fluent conversationalist, and had great personal charm. He viewed the passing of the old order of things, however, with a despair that shrouded the remaining eight years of his life with gloom.

At Taney's left sat Smith Thompson, sixty-nine years of age, gray-haired, and spare almost to the point of emaciation. He had been a member of the court since 1823, when James Monroe chose him for the position rather than Martin Van Buren, who coveted it. He had recently married a young wife, whom he gallantly attended in the midst of the social life of the capital.

At Story's right sat John McLean, fifty-two years of age, well built, with clear-cut features and an expression suggesting strength of character and of intellect. He had been a member of the court since 1829, when Jackson, seeking to reward him for not supporting John Quincy Adams, his former chief, for the presidency but unwilling to retain him as Postmaster General because of his reluctance to remove old employees to make way for deserving Jacksonians, had offered him the vacant position on the bench. McLean's friends had long ago succeeded in convincing him that he was of presidential timber, and his reputation as a judge had suffered and was to continue to suffer because he was never able to keep that subject out of his mind. He was friendly to Nicholas Biddle and to the Bank of the United States. He aligned himself with the Whigs, although he would probably have willingly led any party strong enough to make him president. In most respects he was probably closer to Story than any other member of the court.

At Thompson's left sat Henry Baldwin, fifty-seven years of age, the logical but emotional and at times intellectually unbalanced Pennsylvanian whom Jackson had appointed in 1830. A reporter, knowing something of Baldwin's reputation, wrote: "I expected to find a little, cross, crabbed old man. He is, on the contrary, a large, full favored, black haired, quaker looking gentleman, of the most prepossessing exterior—industrious, attentive, careful, and I should think, exceedingly agreeable and obliging." He was not always as agreeable or obliging as he seemed, however, as some of his colleagues and as the court reporter, Richard Peters, might have told.

At McLean's right was a vacant seat which would be occupied by James M. Wayne when he arrived from Georgia. Wayne was the youngest, perhaps the handsomest, and socially the most versatile member of the court. He had received his appointment from Jackson in 1835. At Baldwin's left sat Philip P. Barbour, fifty-three years of age, whose appointment and confirmation dated with those of Taney. He was an old-fashioned state-rights Virginian, with many years of political experience and with a brief experience as a federal district judge. He was not impressive in appearance, and he was to be the first of the group to leave the bench, but during the five terms which they served together there is reason for believing that no colleague had closer friendship with Taney than did he.

The meeting of the court on the first day of the term was, as usual, but a matter of form, and was adjourned when Taney had announced that he would begin the call of the calendar on the following day, postponing the calling of cases involving constitutional questions, however, until the entire membership of the court was present. There were about sixty cases on the docket, in only a few of which constitutional questions were involved. These few were the important cases, however, the cases which would give some basis for predicting the changes which the new personnel of the court would make in the trend of constitutional development.

Of these the most important was the Charles River Bridge Case, which had been argued before the Supreme Court six years earlier, but which, because of the absence of judges and lack of agreement among those present, remained yet to be decided. The case had its roots far back in history, yet it had intimate connection with the most controversial constitutional and economic problems of the day. In 1650 the legislature of Massachusetts, assuming the control over public ferries which under the common law belonged to the government, had given aid to the new institution for higher education established at Cambridge by granting to the president of Harvard College the power, by lease or otherwise, to dispose of the ferry which crossed the tidewater Charles River between Charlestown and Boston.

The college had kept the ferry and received the profits from it until 1785. In that year a number of men, setting forth the inconvenience of transportation by ferries over the Charles River, petitioned the legislature to be incorporated for the purpose of erecting a bridge across the river in the place where the ferry was then kept. The petition was granted, and the company was empowered to erect the bridge and to collect tolls from passengers for a period of forty years, during which time two hundred pounds were to be paid annually to Harvard College, in lieu of the profits which might have been received had the ferry not been discontinued. At the end of the forty years the bridge was to become the property of the state, except that the state would still be obligated to make a reasonable annual payment to the college.

The bridge was built, at considerable financial risk to the builders, for because of climatic and soil conditions there were reasonable doubts as to whether a bridge across what was virtually an arm of the sea would remain in place long enough to pay for itself. The bridge was opened to traffic, and so profitable and so convenient did it prove, that as the population of the region increased it was desired to build other bridges in the vicinity. In 1792 the legislature chartered another company to build a bridge across the same river between Cambridge and Boston. The proprietors of the first bridge protested against the building of the second on the ground that it would divert some traffic and revenue from the first, even though it was some distance away. The legislature, without admitting that it was under legal obligation to do so, compensated the proprietors of the first bridge by giving them an added thirty years in which to collect tolls.

The population of Boston and its business with the surrounding country continued to increase, as did the profits of the first bridge, known always as the Charles River Bridge. Shares which had a par value of $333.33 sold in 1805 at $1,650 and in 1814 at $2,080. Whereas the original capitalization had been $50,000, the bridge company in 1823 claimed that the value of its property was $280,000. The time came when few shares of stock were in the hands of the original investors, most of them being held by persons who had bought them at high prices, and who, when the public protested against the continued payment of tolls after profits amounting to far more than the original capital with interest had been earned, claimed that they had the right to returns on their own high investments. The owners of stock, most of them Bostonians, smugly resisted the demands made by the traveling public for concessions in the form of improved services and reduced tolls.

Repeated attempts were made to persuade the legislature to authorize the building of a new bridge closely adjoining the old one, and finally, in a concerted political movement in which the masses organized to protect their own interests as against those of the holders of investment property, the battle was won. The legislature of 1828 chartered a company to build the Warren Bridge, which was to be only sixteen rods from the old bridge on the Charlestown side and fifty rods on the Boston side. The Warren Bridge was to be surrendered to the state as soon as sufficient tolls had been collected to pay for its construction, or in any case within a maximum period of six years from the time at which the collection of tolls was begun. Thereafter its use was to be free to the public. It was obvious that a free bridge which was so close to one which was charging tolls, would get all the traffic, no tolls would be collected on the toll bridge, and the value of the stock of the toll bridge would be destroyed.

The old bridge company attempted unsuccessfully to secure an injunction against the construction of the Warren Bridge, and carried the case to the Supreme Court of the United States on the ground that the act of the legislature chartering the Warren Bridge unconstitutionally impaired the contract in the charter of the Charles River Bridge, by setting up a competitor which prevented it from earning tolls. When the case was argued in 1831 Marshall, Story, and Thompson seem to have agreed with this contention, and Story's opinion was apparently written out; but because of absences and disagreements either on the merits or on jurisdictional questions they were unable to get a decision.

Six years had now passed, and three of the old judges had been replaced by Jacksonian appointees. The Warren Bridge had been erected, had earned in tolls the amount of the cost of its construction, and had been for ten months a free bridge, drawing to itself all the passengers who might otherwise have paid tolls to the old corporation. The outcome was a victory for the traveling public over what were loosely called vested rights. It threatened ominously the defeat of the claims of investors to the bountiful fruits of successful enterprise, provoking the warning that unless capitalists were protected in their winnings they would in the future refuse to invest in desirable but risky enterprises in which their capital might be lost.

Profits, large or small, were, in other words, the just rewards for risk. Law ought to give protection to such rewards. When law was vague, and precedents confusing, conflicting, or nonexistent, judges, in obedience to what were called principles of justice, ought to give full protection to these rights of property.

The controversy over the rights of the Charles River Bridge arose during the period when people were just coming to realize the value of the corporate form for instituting such enterprises as the building of bridges, roads, and canals. The Supreme Court, with Marshall as spokesman, had in 1819 labeled as contracts the grants of privileges and property made in corporate charters, and held that the Constitution forbade their impairment by state legislation. Taney and the other new members of the Supreme Court were not hostile to the creation of public improvements. On the contrary Taney had been among those who were most eager to improve economic conditions in Maryland by building first roads, then canals, and finally railroads.

As a member of the state Senate, however, he had observed the cupidity of those who lobbied for incorporation and for special privileges. He was so convinced of the inefficiency or untrustworthiness of corporations which then seemed large but which today would seem petty, that he advised that the building of the Chesapeake and Ohio Canal be financed and supervised by the government rather than attempted by private enterprise. He admitted a feeling of revulsion at the grasping and short-sighted selfishness of the mercantile classes of the country, and his experience with the Bank of the United States convinced him that moneyed corporations, unless kept within narrowly defined limits, were a menace to the welfare of the country.

On September 5, 1833, about three weeks before he became Secretary of the Treasury, Taney had given a legal opinion concerning issues closely approximating those now before the Supreme Court. The Camden and Amboy Railroad and the Delaware and Raritan Canal companies had persuaded the New Jersey legislature of 1832 to incorporate in charter provisions the agreement that without the consent of these companies no company should for a stated time be incorporated to build a railroad for service between Philadelphia and New York or to compete in any way with the Camden and Amboy. Taney and Judge James Kent of New York, probably Daniel Webster, and possibly other noted lawyers of the day were asked for opinions as to whether one legislature could thus limit the powers of its successor. Kent expressed the opinion, concurred in by Webster, that such a legislative stipulation ought to be sternly construed, "as one that may be exceedingly inconvenient to the public welfare."

Taney admitted that if such a provision was included in a valid contract it must be considered binding under the contract clause of the Constitution. He declared, however, that the power to bind the state not to create corporations to build internal improvements was such an integral part of the power of sovereignty that no legislature could be assumed to have it unless it was specifically conferred by the state constitution. He admitted that others disagreed with him. "But with every respect for the distinguished men who have sanctioned such legislation in the general government, or in the states, I cannot think that a legislative body, holding a limited authority under a written constitution, can by contract or otherwise limit the legislative power of their successors. . . . The existence of such a power in a representative body has no foundation in reason, or in public convenience, and is inconsistent with the principles upon which all our political institutions are founded. For if a legislative body may thus restrict the power of its successors, a single improvident act of legislation may entail lasting and incurable ills on the people of a state. It may compel them to forego the advantage which their local situation affords, and prevent them from using the means necessary to promote the prosperity and happiness of the community." It was his opinion, therefore, that the monopoly provisions of the act of 1832 should have no status when passed upon by the courts, and that a company could legally be chartered to build a competing railroad.

Taney's opinion "made much sensation from its imputed denial of what, without reflection, are apt to be thought not only vested but sacred rights." It revealed an absence of respect for privileges and rights extracted from legislatures by propertied groups which in later years, when such groups had become more firmly entrenched in the economic life of the country, would have done much to blacklist the name of any lawyer, of whatever character and ability, for a position on the Supreme Court. It may, indeed, have been one of the causes of opposition to Taney, although because of the more dramatic aspects of the bank war, it seems to have been pretty much or completely submerged.

In an official opinion given during the preceding year Taney had emphasized a fact which business men were accustomed to ignoring; namely, that when a corporation was formed and special privileges were given the gift was supposed to be for the benefit of the public, and not for the exclusive benefit of the corporations. He emphasized the same fact in 1836, after he was confirmed as Chief Justice, in analyzing for Jackson the act which provided for the rechartering of the banks of the District of Columbia: "Every charter granted by a state or by the United States, to a bank or to any other company for the purposes of trade or manufacture, is a grant of peculiar privileges, and gives to the individuals who compose the corporation, rights and privileges which are not possessed by other members of the community. It would be against the spirit of our free institutions, by which equal rights are intended to be secured to all, to grant peculiar franchises and privileges to a body of individuals merely for the purpose of enabling them more conveniently and effectually to advance their own private interests. No charter could rightfully be granted on that ground. The consideration upon which alone, such peculiar privileges can be granted is the expectation and prospect of promoting thereby some public interest, and it follows from these principles that in every case where it is proposed to grant or to renew a charter the interests or wishes of the individuals who desire to be incorporated, ought not to influence the decision of the government. The only inquiry which the constituted authorities can properly make on such an application, is whether the charter applied for, is likely to produce any real benefit to the community, and whether that benefit is sufficient to justify the grant."

Although the quotation just given had not been made public, enough was known of Taney's attitude and of his own experience and that of two of his colleagues with the Bank of the United States to provoke the belief that the new Supreme Court would read law and precedents with a consideration for the welfare of the general public, and would scrutinize the claims of propertied groups with a critical attitude, which had not characterized Marshall and his colleagues. Six weeks before the court met, Charles J. Ingersoll, in giving his opinion that the State of Pennsylvania had the power to repeal the charter of the Bank of the United States which Biddle and his friends had extracted from the legislature, declared that the decisions of the Supreme Court applying the contract clause of the Constitution had left the whole subject in doubt and difficulty. "By recent appointments there is now a majority of that bench, not involved in these perplexing contradictions, and when these clauses of the Constitution come once more to be considered by the Supreme Court, the public may expect a final harmonious and satisfactory interpretation of them."

The bridge case was to be argued by four Massachusetts lawyers. Warren Dutton and Daniel Webster represented the Charles River Bridge; and Simon Greenleaf, a teacher at Harvard Law School, and John Davis, the Whig senator who had voted to confirm Taney's nomination as Chief Justice, represented the Warren Bridge. The counsel were kept waiting pending the arrival of Justice Wayne, who, according to Greenleaf, had remained at home with Senator Cuthbert to work for the election of a member of Congress. At length, on Thursday January 19, all members of the court were present, and Dutton opened the argument. The era of long arguments before the Supreme Court had not yet ended. Dutton spoke through Thursday, Friday, and into Saturday morning. Greenleaf spoke for two hours on Saturday and three on Monday. Davis spoke during the remainder of the Monday session and for three hours on Tuesday. Webster spoke through the remainder of Tuesday and probably all day Wednesday, and the records show that the case was still before the court on Thursday.

There is no diary to reveal Webster's feelings at the prospect of addressing respectfully and presenting a constitutional argument before the man whom in another capacity he had maligned. It was reported that his speech was a masterly effort of argument and ingenuity, and that painting could have conveyed no better idea of the positions of the bridges than did his description. Greenleaf noted, however, that Webster was very uneasy and moody during the whole defense, and a letter from his son indicates that he predicted that he would lose this case and that it would be his last case before the Supreme Court. Justice Story remarked that Webster's closing was in his best manner, but with a little too much *fierté* here and there. Unfortunately for our interest in such personal matters there seems to be no evidence at all as to Taney's feelings at being addressed by the man whom he had accused of being a "pliant instrument" of the Bank of the United States.

The vital point to be decided by the Supreme Court was the question as to whether the Charles River Bridge charter gave contract rights which were impaired by the act chartering the Warren Bridge. The legislators who had granted the first charter had been faced with such questions as whether one bridge could be successfully and permanently erected, but had given no thought as to what should be done if other parties desired to erect another bridge a few rods away, and in the charter had said nothing at all on the subject. The original grantees now asked the court to hold that exclusive rights to the traffic between Charlestown and Boston were given by implication, while their opponents contended that no rights were given by a charter save those which were conferred in express language.

Counsel on both sides analyzed at length the principles and precedents on the subject of the interpretation of public grants, and the power of government to interfere with them by eminent domain or otherwise, and then turned to what for the public and to a large extent even for the lawyers and the judges were the realities of the case—the effect which the decision would have upon the security of property rights and upon general welfare throughout the country. Dutton declared that in Massachusetts alone the title to more than ten millions of dollars in corporate property would be determined by the decision, for if the decision went against his clients the public might as easily secure legislation which would render valueless the property of other corporations as they had that of the proprietors of the Charles River Bridge.

In a closing plea he warned: "Popular prejudice may be again appealed to; and popular passions excited by passionate declamations against tribute money, exclusive privileges, and odious monopolies: and these, under skillful management, may be combined and brought to bear upon all chartered rights, with a resistless and crushing power. . . .

"I have as much respect for, and confidence in legislative bodies as reason and experience will warrant; but I am taught by both that they are not the safest guardians of private rights. I took to the law; to the administration of the law, and, above all, to the supremacy of the law, as it resides in this court, for the protection of the rights of persons and property, against all encroachments by the inadvertent legislation of the states. So long as this court shall continue to exercise this most salutary and highest of all its functions, the whole legislation of the country will be kept within its constitutional sphere of action. The result will be general confidence, and general security."

Thus counsel for the plaintiffs appealed to the Supreme Court as if its prime function were to act as a super-guardian to the propertied interests of the country. They used a type of appeal which in a later era fell upon highly receptive ears, resulting in the elaboration of a due process clause to curb the activities of state legislatures which were more or less responsive to popular demands. Counsel for the Warren Bridge, on the other hand, with a copy of Taney's Camden and Amboy opinion of September 5, 1833, in their possession, argued that the claim set up was against common right. "They contended that the legislature possessed only limited powers;—that the power of laying taxes, of providing for the common defense, of providing safe and convenient public ways, and of taking private property for public uses, or sacrificing private rights to public necessities, were essential to the existence of all government whatever; and were entrusted to the legislature to be exercised for the public good, and not to be sold or conveyed away; and each legislature must necessarily assemble with the same powers, in these respects, as were held by its predecessors."

The proprietors of the Charles River Bridge were in no worse condition, Davis declared, and had no higher claim to indemnity than other losers by public improvements. Railroads took traffic from highways near which they were built, thus depriving the latter of tolls which had been anticipated, and reducing the value of stages, wagons, and other property. Some communities were deprived of business and the value of their real estate depreciated, but there could be no legal indemnity for such losses, and, since public convenience demanded such improvements, they could not be obstructed from such causes. As a matter of strategy in winning their case, however, and doubtless also for personal reasons, counsel for the Warren Bridge avoided the denunciations of the possessors of vested rights, and the demands for radical legal changes which had characterized the popular movement culminating in the chartering of the Warren Bridge. They avoided everything "peoplish," as Greenleaf expressed it, and argued that the decision which they sought was called for by a correct interpretation of existing law.

On February 14 the decision of the Supreme Court was announced, and on that and the following day three opinions were read. Taney's opinion, for a majority of the court, upheld the claims of the Warren Bridge. McLean attempted to prove that justice was on the side of the Charles River Bridge, but that the Supreme Court had not jurisdiction to decide the case. Story, in an opinion first written six years earlier, swept aside all quibbling on the score of constitutionality, and defended the claims of the Charles River Bridge. Taney passed over as unnecessary to the decision many of the arguments of counsel, held that the case turned exclusively upon the interpretation of a contract, that the contract should be construed narrowly, and that when so construed it did not confer the rights claimed by the plaintiffs. In words ominous to the representatives of entrenched property interests, he declared it to be well settled by the decisions of the Supreme Court that a state law might devest vested rights and yet not violate the Constitution, unless it impaired the obligation of a contract. Relying heavily upon an opinion in a recent English decision and on other cases there cited, he stated the principle that public grants were to be construed strictly, and any ambiguity in the terms of such contracts was to be decided in the interest of the public. Our system of jurisprudence was based on that of England, and there was no good reason for departing from it in this respect.

"The object and end of all government," declared Taney, "is to promote the happiness and prosperity of the community by which it is established; and it can never be assumed, that the government intended to diminish its power of accomplishing the end for which it was created. And in a country like ours, free, active, and enterprising, continually advancing in numbers and wealth; new channels of communications are daily found necessary, both for travel and trade; and are essential to the comfort, convenience, and prosperity of the people. A state ought never to be presumed to surrender this power, because, like the taxing power, the whole community have an interest in preserving it undiminished. And when a corporation alleges, that a state has surrendered for seventy years, its power of improvement and public accommodation, in a great and important line of travel, along which a vast number of its citizens must daily pass; the community have a right to insist, . . . 'that its abandonment ought not to be presumed, in a case, in which the deliberate purpose of the state to abandon it does not appear.'"

The continued existence of a government would be of no great value, Taney believed, if by implications and presumptions it was disarmed of the powers necessary to accomplish the ends of its creation, and the functions it was designed to perform transferred to the hands of privileged corporations. No one would question that the interests of the great body of the people of the state would, in this instance, be affected by the surrender of this great line of travel to a single corporation, with the right to exact toll and exclude competition for seventy years. "While the rights of private property are sacredly guarded," he declared in a sentence sharply revealing his point of view, "we must not forget that the community also have rights, and that the happiness and well being of every citizen depends on their faithful preservation."

Summarizing the provisions of the charter and of subsequent legislation affecting it, Taney declared that it would indeed be a strong exercise of judicial power which would, by a sort of judicial coercion, raise an implied contract and infer it from the nature of the charter. Such a decision would affect conditions of transportation all over the country. In preceding years franchises had been granted to build roads, other franchises had been granted to competitors, canal companies had been chartered and had taken business away from the highways, and railroad companies were taking business both from the highways and from the canals. If the precedent was established of reading monopoly rights into the old charters by implication, modern improvements would be at the mercy of the old corporations.

The country would "be thrown back to the improvements of the last century, and obliged to stand still, until the claims of the old turnpike corporations shall be satisfied; and they shall consent to permit these states to avail themselves of the lights of modern science, and to partake of the benefit of those improvements which are now adding to the wealth and prosperity, and the convenience and comfort, of every other part of the civilized world. Nor is this all. This court will find itself compelled to fix, by some arbitrary rule, the width of this new kind of property in a line of travel; for if such a right of property exists, we have no lights to guide us in marking out its extent, unless, indeed, we resort to the old feudal grants, and to the exclusive rights of ferries, by prescription, between towns; and are prepared to decide that when a turnpike road from one town to another has been made, no railroad or canal, between these two points, could afterwards be established. This court are not prepared to sanction principles which must lead to such results."

Justice Story, dissenting, declared that the opinion which he had originally formed had not been shaken but rather confirmed by the recent argument of the case. Relying not so much upon modern cases as did Taney, but rather upon voluminous researches into the common law of England of centuries past, he sought to establish the claims of the plaintiffs. "I stand upon the old law," he declared; "upon law established more than three centuries ago, in cases contested with as much ability and learning as any in the annals of our jurisprudence, in resisting any such encroachments upon the rights and liberties of the citizens, secured by public grants. I will not consent to shake their title deeds by any speculative niceties or novelties."

As for the effect of the decision of the case upon the prosperity of the country, he saw less danger in the assertion of the legal rights of old turnpike and canal corporations than in the prospect that men of property would refuse to invest in public improvements if the courts showed themselves other than diligent in the protection of vested property rights. Story, like most of the business leaders of the country before and since, adhered to what might be called the seepage theory of economics, to the theory that if government, including the judiciary, was sufficiently zealous and effective in protecting property for the benefit of those who held title to it, those persons would engage in productive enterprise, and a goodly share of the wealth produced thereby would seep down through the otherwise less capable or less fortunate classes of the people, and the country as a whole would prosper.

Taney, with a point of view which had become sharply defined during his experiences in the bank war, but which perhaps in some of its aspects dated back to the time when transatlantic merchants sapped the wealth of rural Maryland by dictating the low prices at which tobacco must be sold if sold at all, had not Story's faith in the seepage of wealth in such a way as to bring about the greatest good of the community. His opinion in this case does not show how far he would have had government interfere with property for the benefit of the community. It demonstrates, however, his intention to resist the use of government for the benefit of vested interests when other groups would be made to suffer thereby; and, to repeat, he saw in this instance possibilities of such suffering which Story, imbued with a different social philosophy, could not or would not recognize.

Two other cases, *Briscoe* v. *The Bank of the Commonwealth of Kentucky* and *New York* v. *Miln,* received with the Bridge case most of the public attention given to the work of the Supreme Court during this term. The first arguments in both of these cases had likewise been made before Chief Justice Marshall. Marshall, speaking for a majority of his court, had held in *Craig* v. *Missouri* that small denomination notes issued by the State of Missouri and circulated as money were bills of credit which the Constitution forbade the states to issue. He had been likewise of the opinion in the Kentucky case that notes issued by a bank owned and controlled by the State were bills of credit, and could not legally be issued. The decision had been left over until the new régime in the court, however, and now McLean, speaking for a majority, read an opinion holding that the notes were not bills of credit, since they were issued by a bank instead of by the State, even though the State owned the bank.

Story's lone dissent reveals starkly the tenaciousness with which he clung to a régime and a personnel which had gone. A majority of the judges who heard the first argument had been of the opinion that the act in question was unconstitutional. "Among that majority was the late *Mr. Chief Justice* Marshall—a name never to be pronounced without reverence." The second argument, he declared, had been upon precisely the same grounds as the former. After explaining at length his reasons for believing the decision to be wrong, he declared that he did so because of his belief that the public had the right to know the opinion of every judge who dissented from the opinion of the court on a constitutional question. "I have another and strong motive," he continued; "my profound reverence and affection for the dead. *Mr. Chief Justice* Marshall is not here to speak for himself; and knowing full well the grounds of his opinion, in which I concurred, that this act is unconstitutional; I have felt an earnest desire to vindicate his memory from the imputation of rashness, or want of deep reflection."

Taney voted silently with the affirmative in the Kentucky case, as he did also in the New York case, in which Story again attempted to preserve the reign of the dead hand. The latter case dealt with important issues of commerce and police powers, in the discussion of which Taney was in the future to find himself many times deeply embroiled. Briefly, the court had to decide whether or not New York could constitutionally require the masters of ships to make reports of such matters as the age, health, and last legal residence of immigrants whom they brought into the country. Counsel argued as to whether such a law was a regulation of foreign commerce, and if so, whether the power of Congress to regulate foreign commerce was exclusive, so as to prevent the enactment of valid state laws on the subject. Barbour, speaking for a majority of the court, held that the act was not a regulation of commerce, but was a police measure such as a state had the power to enact. Thus began in earnest the battle to determine definitions of police and commerce powers which were to be involved in most of the important decisions of the court during the next quarter of a century.

As was to be expected, Democrats and Whigs differed sharply in their appraisals of the work of the court during the term. Democrats approvingly prophesied the restoration of the Constitution, "without shocks or reversals, by such quiet, conciliatory and unassailable adjudications as those pronounced in the cases just mentioned." Taney's opinion in the Bridge case received high praise. "It is a most able document," declared a democratic magazine, "bearing on its face those features for which all the intellectual productions of that distinguished statesman and jurist are remarkable. He clears the very intricate subject before the court of all irrelevant matter, with the unerring instinct of genius; and as he pursues his unbroken chain of clear, logical reasoning, spreads light all around, leaving no cloud to confound or mislead those who may come after him. Indeed the present Chief Justice escapes from irrelevant matter with as much ease as Judge Marshall or the most distinguished of the English judges."

Whigs, on the other hand, were distressed and disapproving. The reporter of a Boston paper, who had listened to the arguments in the important cases and to the opinions as they were delivered by the judges, expressed the belief that the system of constitutional law built up by Marshall and his associates was to be gradually, though not openly and avowedly, enclosed in black lines. Federal restraint would be removed from state legislatures, and investments in corporate property would have no guarantee of legal protection. The tone and character of the decision in the Bridge case, declared the *North American Review*, "chime in with doctrines, which tend, or may be urged, deplorably, to the subversion of the principles of law and property."

A New York newspaper lamented that "the fruit of all the accumulated wisdom and all the profound research and meditation of Jay, Ellsworth, Chase, Marshall, Washington, Story, and Thompson, is to be set at naught by such small lights as have been recently placed on the bench—such shallow metaphysical hair splitters as P. P. Barbour." The editor of the *American Monthly Magazine* was so inarticulately enraged at a Democratic defense of the court that his article was hardly more than a jumble of denunciatory adjectives. The *New York Review,* a leading Whig magazine, lamented of deep shadows cast over fairest and proudest hopes. In reading the decisions of the Supreme Court under the new dynasty, "we perceive at once an altered tone and a narrower spirit, not only in Chief Justice Taney, but even in some of the old associates of Chief Justice Marshall, when they handle constitutional questions. The change is so great and so ominous, that a gathering gloom is cast over the future. We seem to have sunk suddenly below the horizon, to have lost the light of the sun, to hold our way *per incertam lunam sub luce maligna.*"

Daniel Webster, defeated, assured Story that his opinion in the Bridge case left the opposition not a foot nor an inch to stand on. "The intelligent part of the profession will all be with you. There is no doubt of that; but then the decision of the court will have completely overturned, in my judgment, one great provision of the Constitution." He was wrong as to the ultimate position of the bar, for the decision was in time to be fully accepted and approved, but he never changed his own opinion. "When I look back after a long lapse of years," he declared in 1845, "and read the judgment of those judges . . . I must say that I see, or think that I see, all the difference between a manly, honest, and just maintenance of the right, and an ingenious, elaborate, and sometimes half shamefaced apology for what is wrong." He staked his reputation as a lawyer that the decision could not stand.

Chancellor James Kent, of New York, one of the best known jurists in the country, read the decisions of the Supreme Court for the term, and wrote to Story to vent in confidence his grief and mortification. "It appears to me," he declared, "that the court has fallen from its high station and commanding dignity, and has lost its energy, and spirit of independence, and accuracy, and surrendered up to the spirit of the day, the true principles of the Constitution." He had reperused the Bridge case with increased disgust. It violated a great principle of constitutional morality, and destroyed the sanctity of contracts. "Now we feel with a pang the loss of Marshall. Now we sadly realize that we are to be under the reign of little men—a pigmy race and that the sages of the last age are extinguished." As for the Kentucky case, "It absolutely overwhelms me in despair, and I have no hopes left especially when I consider that we have two new judges—very feeble lights added to your bench. . . . I am astonished that Judge Thompson should have deserted you, *but he had married a wife and could not come to the rescue.* I have lost my confidence and hopes in the constitutional guardianship and protection of the Supreme Court."

By the clamor of his Whig friends Story was persuaded that he had the approbation of those persons whose good opinion was worth having. Taney's opinion was not deemed satisfactory, even by those who were not against the decision of the court. Justice Baldwin had published a pamphlet in which he discussed the constitutional issues involved in the important cases of the term, on which he had voted with the majority of the court. Story read it calmly. Chief Justice Marshall had approved the doctrines which he laid down in his *Commentaries,* and by that fact he was quite consoled, even though another judge expressed disapproval.

But though convinced that he was right, he faced the future with sadness. "I am the last of the old race of judges. I stand their solitary representative, with a pained heart, and a subdued confidence. Do you remember the story of the last dinner of a club, who dined once a year? I am in the predicament of the last survivor." He doubted gloomily that in his day any law of a state or of Congress would be declared unconstitutional, and he made up his mind to resign, only to be persuaded by his friends to remain on the bench a while longer. He remained a member of the court for eight years, during which time friction continued between him and most of his colleagues on important constitutional issues, for, although he was younger in years than many of them, he had lost the flexibility of thought and emotion which should have enabled him to adjust more or less happily to the new régime.

The United States of America
v.
One Book Called Ulysses

JOHN M. WOOLSEY

Judge Woolsey's decision "One Book Called Ulysses" has been widely praised and in particular for one sentence: "In respect of the recurrent emergence of the theme of sex in the minds of his characters, it must always be remembered that his locale was Celtic and his season Spring." But Joyce's season was not in fact Spring, since June is Summer in Ireland, and it remains to be proved that the theme of sex emerges more frequently in the city of Dublin than in any other capital city in Europe. Nevertheless, the spirit that informs the judgment is admirable, and readers everywhere owe Judge Woolsey gratitude.

Judge Woolsey (1877–1945) was trained at Yale and Columbia; he helped found the Columbia Law Review. Called to the bar in 1901, he became in 1929 Judge of the United States District Court, Southern New York District, an office he held until 1943.

UNITED STATES DISTRICT COURT
SOUTHERN DISTRICT OF NEW YORK

United States of America, *Libelant* v. One Book called "Ulysses" Random House, Inc., *Claimant*	OPINION A.110-59

On cross motions for a decree in a libel of confiscation, supplemented by a stipulation—hereinafter described—brought by the United States against the book "Ulysses" by James Joyce, under Section 305 of the Tariff Act of 1930, Title 19 United States Code, Section 1305, on the ground that the book is obscene within the meaning of that Section, and, hence, is not importable into the United States, but is subject to seizure, forfeiture and confiscation and destruction.

218

United States Attorney—by Samuel C. Coleman, Esq., and Nicholas Atlas, Esq., of counsel—for the United States, in support of motion for a decree of forfeiture, and in opposition to motion for a decree dismissing the libel.

Messrs. Greenbaum, Wolff & Ernst,—by Morris L. Ernst, Esq., and Alexander Lindey, Esq., of counsel—attorneys for claimant Random House, Inc., in support of motion for a decree dismissing the libel, and in opposition to motion for a decree of forfeiture.

WOOLSEY, J:

The motion for a decree dismissing the libel herein is granted, and, consequently, of course, the Government's motion for a decree of forfeiture and destruction is denied.

Accordingly a decree dismissing the libel without costs may be entered herein.

I. The practice followed in this case is in accordance with the suggestion made by me in the case of *United States v. One Book Entitled "Contraception,"* 51 F. (2d) 525, and is as follows:

After issue was joined by the filing of the claimant's answer to the libel for forfeiture against "Ulysses," a stipulation was made between the United States Attorney's office and the attorneys for the claimant providing:

1. That the book "Ulysses" should be deemed to have been annexed to and to have become part of the libel just as if it had been incorporated in its entirety therein.

2. That the parties waived their right to a trial by jury.

3. That each party agreed to move for decree in its favor.

4. That on such cross motions the Court might decide all the questions of law and fact involved and render a general finding thereon.

5. That on the decision of such motions the decree of the Court might be entered as if it were a decree after trial.

It seems to me that a procedure of this kind is highly appropriate in libels for the confiscation of books such as this. It is an especially advantageous procedure in the instant case because on account of the length of "Ulysses" and the difficulty of reading it, a jury trial would have been an extremely unsatisfactory, if not an almost impossible, method of dealing with it.

II. I have read "Ulysses" once in its entirety and I have read those passages of which the Government particularly complains several times. In fact, for many weeks, my spare time has been devoted to the consideration of the decision which my duty would require me to make in this matter.

"Ulysses" is not an easy book to read or to understand. But there has been much written about it, and in order properly to approach the consideration of it it is advisable to read a number of other books which have now become its satellites. The study of "Ulysses" is, therefore, a heavy task.

III. The reputation of "Ulysses" in the literary world, however, warranted my taking such time as was necessary to enable me to satisfy myself as to the intent with which the book was written, for, of course, in any case where a book is claimed to be obscene it must first be determined, whether the intent with which it was written was what is called, according to the usual phrase, pornographic—that is, written for the purpose of exploiting obscenity.

If the conclusion is that the book is pornographic that is the end of the inquiry and forfeiture must follow.

But in "Ulysses," in spite of its unusual frankness, I do not detect anywhere the leer of the sensualist. I hold, therefore, that it is not pornographic.

IV. In writing "Ulysses," Joyce sought to make a serious experiment in a new, if not wholly novel, literary genre. He takes persons of the lower middle class living in Dublin in 1904 and seeks not only to describe what they did on a certain day early in June of that year as they went about the City bent on their usual occupations, but also to tell what many of them thought about the while.

Joyce has attempted—it seems to me, with astonishing success—to show how the screen of consciousness with its ever-shifting kaleidoscopic impressions carries, as it were on a plastic palimpsest, not only what is in the focus of each man's observation of the actual things about him, but also in a penumbral zone residua of past impressions, some recent and some drawn up by association from the domain of the subconscious. He shows how each of these impressions affects the life and behavior of the character which he is describing.

What he seeks to get is not unlike the result of a double or, if that is possible, a multiple exposure on a cinema film which would give a clear foreground with a background visible but somewhat blurred and out of focus in varying degrees.

To convey by words an effect which obviously lends itself more appropriately to a graphic technique, accounts, it seems to me, for much of the obscurity which meets a reader of "Ulysses." And it also explains another aspect of the book, which I have further to consider, namely, Joyce's sincerity and his honest effort to show exactly how the minds of his characters operate.

If Joyce did not attempt to be honest in developing the technique which he has adopted in "Ulysses" the result would be psychologically misleading and thus unfaithful to his chosen technique. Such an attitude would be artistically inexcusable.

It is because Joyce has been loyal to his technique and has not funked its necessary implications, but has honestly attempted to tell fully what his characters think about, that he has been the subject of so many attacks and that his purpose has been so often misunderstood and misrepresented. For his attempt sincerely and honestly to realize his objective has required him incidentally to use certain words which are generally considered dirty words and has led at times to what many think is a too poignant preoccupation with sex in the thoughts of his characters.

The words which are criticized as dirty are old Saxon words known to almost all men and, I venture, to many women, and are such words as would be naturally and habitually used, I believe, by the types of folk whose life, physical and mental, Joyce is seeking to describe. In respect of the recurrent emergence of the theme of sex in the minds of his characters, it must always be remembered that his locale was Celtic and his season Spring.

Whether or not one enjoys such a technique as Joyce uses is a matter of taste on which disagreement or argument is futile, but to subject that technique to the standards of some other technique seems to me to be little short of absurd.

Accordingly, I hold that "Ulysses" is a sincere and honest book and I think that the criticisms of it are entirely disposed of by its rationale.

V. Furthermore, "Ulysses" is an amazing *tour de force* when one considers the success which has been in the main achieved with such a difficult objective as Joyce set for himself. As I have stated, "Ulysses" is not an easy book to read. It is brilliant and dull, intelligible and obscure by turns. In many places it seems to me to be disgusting, but although it contains, as I have mentioned above, many words usually considered dirty, I have not found anything that I consider to be dirt for dirt's sake. Each word of the book contributes like a bit of mosaic to the detail of the picture which Joyce is seeking to construct for his readers.

If one does not wish to associate with such folk as Joyce describes, that is one's own choice. In order to avoid indirect contact with them one may not wish to read "Ulysses"; that is quite understandable. But when such a real artist in words, as Joyce undoubtedly is, seeks to draw a true picture of the lower middle class in a European city, ought it to be impossible for the American public legally to see that picture?

To answer this question it is not sufficient merely to find, as I have found above, that Joyce did not write "Ulysses" with what is commonly called pornographic intent, I must endeavor to apply a more objective standard to his book in order to determine its effect in the result, irrespective of the intent with which it was written.

VI. The statute under which the libel is filed only denounces, in so far as we are here concerned, the importation into the United States from any foreign country of "any obscene book." Section 305 of the Tariff Act of 1930, Title 19 United States Code, Section 1305. It does not marshal against books the spectrum of condemnatory adjectives found, commonly, in laws dealing with matters of this kind. I am, therefore, only required to determine whether "Ulysses" is obscene within the legal definition of that word.

The meaning of the word "obscene" as legally defined by the Courts is: tending to stir the sex impulses or to lead to sexually impure and lustful thoughts. *Dunlop* v. *United States,* 165 U. S. 486, 501; *United States* v. *One Book Entitled "Married Love,"* 48 F. (2d) 821, 824; *United States* v. *One Book Entitled "Contraception,"* 51 F. (2d) 525, 528; and compare *Dysart* v. *United States,* 272 U. S. 655, 657; *Swearingen* v. *United States,* 161 U. S. 446, 450; *United States* v. *Dennett,* 39 F. (2d) 564, 568 (C. C. A. 2); *People* v. *Wendling,* 258 N. Y. 451, 453.

Whether a particular book would tend to excite such impulses and thoughts must be tested by the court's opinion as to its effect on a person with average sex instincts—what the French would call *l'homme moyen sensuel*—who plays, in this branch of legal inquiry, the same role of hypothetical reagent as does the "reasonable man" in the law of torts and "the man learned in the art" on questions of invention in patent law.

The risk involved in the use of such a reagent arises from the inherent tendency of the trier of facts, however fair he may intend to be, to make his reagent too much subservient to his own idiosyncrasies. Here, I have attempted to avoid this, if possible, and to make my reagent herein more objective than he might otherwise be, by adopting the following course:

After I had made my decision in regard to the aspect of "Ulysses," now under consideration, I checked my impressions with two friends of mine who in my opinion answered to the above stated requirement for my reagent.

These literary assessors—as I might properly describe them—were called on separately, and neither knew that I was consulting the other. They are men whose opinion on literature and on life I value most highly. They had both read "Ulysses," and, of course, were wholly unconnected with this cause.

Without letting either of my assessors know what my decision was, I gave to each of them the legal definition of obscene and asked each whether in his opinion "Ulysses" was obscene within that definition.

I was interested to find that they both agreed with my opinion: that reading "Ulysses" in its entirety, as a book must be read on such a test as this, did not tend to excite sexual impulses or lustful thoughts but that its net effect on them was only that of a somewhat tragic and very powerful commentary on the inner lives of men and women.

It is only with the normal person that the law is concerned. Such a test as I have described, therefore, is the only proper test of obscenity in the case of a book like "Ulysses" which is a sincere and serious attempt to devise a new literary method for the observation and description of mankind.

I am quite aware that owing to some of its scenes "Ulysses" is a rather strong draught to ask some sensitive, though normal, persons to take. But my considered opinion, after long reflection, is that whilst in many places the effect of "Ulysses" on the reader undoubtedly is somewhat emetic, nowhere does it tend to be an aphrodisiac.

"Ulysses" may, therefore, be admitted into the United States.

JOHN M. WOOLSEY
UNITED STATES DISTRICT JUDGE

The Judicial Temperament*

JOHN BUCHAN

John Buchan (1875–1940), first Baron Tweedsmuir, Governor-General of Canada, is perhaps best known to two generations of readers for such adventure stories as The Thirty-Nine Steps *and* Greenmantle. *In the excerpts which follow from one of Buchan's informal essays, we see again that "a great judge must be a great man" and realize again what Lord Macmillan (see page 99) said and meant about the relationship between law and literature.*

We arrive at the last endowment of the great judge—an endowment without which the exercise of the others is apt to be handicapped— I mean the gift of lucid and graceful speech. Without lucidity a judgment will not be understood with that complete accuracy which is necessary in so exact a science as law, and without grace it will not be effectively remembered. Some very great judges have been clear enough, but they have lacked grace, and the result is that they have not had that influence on legal history which they deserved. Eldon is a case in point. He is probably the greatest equity judge, except Hardwicke, that ever lived, but I have yet to meet the man who can read him with pleasure. Take the case of *Wykham* v. *Wykham* (18 Ves. 415), which laid down the distinction between law and equity in the case of contracts—a masterly and epoch-making judgment, but as flat as ditch-water and as ponderous as a tombstone.

It is a fact, I think, that the greatest judges have been usually men of a wide general culture. Such were Hardwicke, Mansfield, Wensleydale, Selborne, Bowen; such very notably in America was Story. There have been exceptions, such as Sir Edward Coke, but they go to prove the rule. Let it be remembered for the encouragement of classical scholars, that Lord Westbury, that ornament of Oxford, obtained his first chance at the Bar because of a brilliant extempore translation of a passage in Pindar at an Oxford *viva voce* examination. A wide culture will beyond doubt be of inestimable advantage to a man when he comes to the preparation of judgments, for no scholar, born with a love of good English, will content himself with the clumsy jargon which sometimes does duty for legal terminology. I am

* From *Homilies and Recreations* by John Buchan, reprinted by permission of the Rt. Hon. Susan Lady Tweedsmuir and Thomas Nelson and Sons, Ltd., Edinburgh.

prepared to maintain that there is a surprising amount of fine literature in the Law Reports. Indeed, I am ready to assert that almost the best prose has been written by men who were not professional men of letters, and who therefore escaped the faded and weary mannerisms of the self-conscious litterateur. As an example I would point to the prose of Cromwell, of Abraham Lincoln, of a dozen explorers like Captain Scott and Captain Boyd Alexander, and of soldiers in the recent war like the Canadian general Sir Arthur Currie. It is the same with the great judges. Mansfield's prose has the massive dignity of the best Georgian manner. Bowen's is often as delicate and careful as an essay of Stevenson's. John Marshall was not, generally speaking, a master of style, as those who have tried to read his *Life of Washington* will bear witness. But he could rise at a great moment to a noble and restrained eloquence, as may be learned from his judgment in *M'Culloch* v. *Maryland.* I have sometimes had an idea of compiling a legal anthology of those judgments which are good literature as well as good law. It would be a fascinating book, and it would put most professional stylists to shame. There is only one rule for good prose, the rule which Newman and Huxley in their different ways enunciated and followed—to set down your exact, full, and precise meaning so lucidly and simply that no man can mistake it. That, and not flowers of rhetoric, has been the aim of the best judges, and small wonder that good prose has been the result.

I am prepared to maintain, too, that in the perfect judicial style there must be both wit and humour on occasion—humour, because unless a man have a sense of the preposterous contrasts of life he will not have the quick eye for reality and the mental perspective which we have postulated; wit, because an argument is often best and most clearly put in those sharp antitheses which we call witty. There will be many examples of both in my anthology. Some of the finest, such as Lord Macnaghten's judgment in the *Gluckstein* case, are too familiar to quote. So are the best of Lord Bowen's. In looking about for an example which might be new to you I have gone to the Scottish Bench—to Lord Robertson, who succeeded Lord Watson, I think, in the year 1900, as the Scottish Lord of Appeal in the House of Lords. He was a brilliant politician, and was said to have been the only man of his time in the House of Commons whom Mr. Gladstone really feared. His political interests distracted his attention a good deal from the law, but when he chose he was an exceptionally able judge, and he was at all times the master of a perfect style. His manner must have been rather like Lord Westbury's, for he had a refined finicking accent and a dulcet voice. Here is an example of the very dry vintage of his wit. It is taken from his judgment in the case of *The Edinburgh Street Tramway Company* v. *The Lord Provost and Magistrates of Edinburgh* (21 R. 704). The question was as to the value of the tramway undertaking based on a calculation of past and future profits.

The argument of the defenders was that "past and future profits" is merely "profits" writ large—for the reason, that time is exhaustively divided into past and future, and that the present is merely an imaginary line between the two. That is, of course, a profound and impressive truth, but there are times and places for everything, and I should hardly have thought a Tramway Act exactly the occasion which Parliament would choose for teaching business men metaphysics unawares —more especially as this statute applies to England as well as to Scotland.

When Lord Westbury fell into disgrace he was replaced on the Woolsack by a virtuous but undistinguished ex-Lord Chancellor, Lord Cranworth. After the appointment he went to Windsor, and the story goes that Queen Victoria took Lady Cranworth for a walk on the terrace after dinner and, laying an affectionate hand on her arm, said, "My dear, do not recent events teach us how much wiser it is to be good than clever?" Gentlemen, there is much more in that saying than a mere pious reflection, especially in relation to the Bench. Mere cleverness is an ineffective thing in most walks of life, and will certainly not by itself make a great judge. For that, intellect is not the only desideratum; certain conspicuous gifts of character are demanded. Do you recall a passage in *Weir of Hermiston* where Stevenson speaks of the satisfactory life of a great lawyer? "As he toiled into the night, he tasted deeply of recondite pleasures. To be wholly devoted to some intellectual exercise is to have succeeded in life; and perhaps only in law and the higher mathematics may this devotion be maintained, suffice to itself without reaction, and find continual rewards without excitement." That is one side of the business—the easy, happy exercise of the intellect among familiar material. But there must be more if a man's work is to be a landmark in the history of Law. The Lord St. Leonards type of judge cuts a considerable figure in the Reports; but, valuable as he is, he does not contribute greatly to the living and organic growth of the Law. For that, a man with a richer and more various nature is needed, a man of a wider and deeper experience of human life. It was a wise saying of the American Mr. Justice Holmes that "the life of the law is not logic but experience." John Marshall was not a great scholar in legal matters. His equipment could not for a moment compare with the wide and profound book-learning of Story. But his mind became a perfect weapon for the judicial task because he never lost touch with the realities of our common life. The great Chief Justice, jugging in a gig along the sandy roads of North Carolina, and after the day in court was done playing quoits with the townsfolk behind the tavern, was in a better way of judicial education than if he had burned the midnight oil over his law books. And how much did not his years as a soldier and a politician contribute to his success?

Dr. Johnson, you remember, angrily withdrew Mansfield from the category of mere lawyers. "Mansfield," he said, "was not a mere lawyer. When he came to town he drank champagne with the wits; he was the friend of

Pope." There is virtue in the distinction. Mansfield was a scholar, a wit, a man of fashion, a statesman who might on two occasions, if he had chosen, have been Prime Minister of England; and with all these things he was the greatest Chief Justice in our history. I am inclined to think that to the higher types of mind and character success is open in any sphere, and that it is only the accident of fate which determines their final destination. I believe that the greatest soldiers have also been great statesmen *in posse*, and that the statesman who steers a country through a crisis could also, with a different training, have led its armies to victory. With the more exalted type of mind there is no specialization *ab origine*. The greatest judge is one who might have been great in politics, in administration, in business, or in war. Which is simply to say that a great judge must be also a great man.

Holmes and Brandeis Dissenting*

ALPHEUS THOMAS MASON

We have already seen something of Holmes (page 26). It is fitting that we also see something of the man with whom his name is so often paired, Louis D. Brandeis (1856–1941). Brandeis was born in Louisville, educated at Dresden and Harvard Law, and called to the bar in 1876. His long practice in Boston, 1879–1916, was marked by participation in many cases involving freight rates, wage-hour disputes, and public utilities. He became known as the People's Attorney. Brandeis was appointed to the Supreme Court in 1916 and retired in 1939; his opinions marked him as a crusading liberal. Catherine Drinker Bowen tells us that "Holmes divided lawyers into kitchen knives, razors, and stings. Brandeis, he said, was a sting."

Brandeis, with his flair for economics and statistics, his sharp mind, his faith in the future, has an able biographer in Alpheus T. Mason, distinguished professor, author, and lecturer. Born in 1899, educated at Dickinson and Princeton, Mason has taught at Princeton since 1923; in 1947 he became McCormick Professor of Jurisprudence. His American Constitutional Law *appeared in 1954.*

"In a few days," Holmes wrote Sir Frederick Pollock, October 21, 1926, "Brandeis who is next to me in age among the judges will be seventy. . . . I think he has done great work and I believe with high motives."

After his first decade on the Court the phrase "Holmes and Brandeis dissenting" had become classic in the progressive fight to liberalize constitutional interpretation. In their work they usually reached the same goal, but they did not travel the same route. In fact, they differed singularly in technique and approach as well as in conception of the scope of judicial review.

THE TWO FRIENDS

Various factors had brought these "liberals" together as friends. They first met in 1879 through Brandeis's law-partner Samuel D. Warren, who had been for a while in Holmes's office. Brandeis and Warren were accustomed in those Boston days to meet Holmes at the Parker House for beer and talk. Later on when Holmes became an Associate Justice of the United States Supreme Court, occasional notes passed between them, and Brandeis called on the Holmeses in Washington from time to time. In early years on the Court they often walked together, and after Holmes became enfeebled by age they took short motor trips in Virginia. "But for all his philosophy," Brandeis commented in 1940, "Holmes worried." Friendship of the younger man, himself free from worry, was a source of great comfort to Holmes.

Brandeis's letters to his wife often referred to hour or half-hour visits at the red brick house, 1720 I Street. There were opinions to talk over or Holmes wished to read one of his literary creations. "I have practiced solitude," Brandeis wrote his wife, February 4, 1923, "save for a call on Holmes this afternoon. He has finished for the printer his introduction to John Wigmore's book and wanted to read it to me." Brandeis was among the first to ride on Holmes's "beautiful elevator," an experience which reminded him of the "sacred precincts of a safe deposit vault."

A marked spirit of camaraderie pervaded Holmes's note written from the Corey Hill Hospital where he recuperated July 1922 from a serious operation. "Your letter went to my heart, and if the unforeseen does not cut in again, you and I will have another run together. I hope to be in shape by the beginning of the term, as usual, but can't be certain till the term comes. Meanwhile, I can't write, but my reading goes from Frost to Kipling. Nothing doing in things intellectual, but gratitude in those more complex matters with which latterly I have grown more familiar."

As the Court became ever more reactionary in its decisions, Taft suspected Brandeis and Holmes of ganging up out of sheer deviltry, thus blighting the Chief Justice's ambition to "amass the Court" and avoid his pet aversion—the 5 to 4 decision. Taft was sure that Brandeis had gotten "the old gentleman" under his magnetic spell. "I think perhaps his age makes him a little more subordinate or yielding to Brandeis, who is his constant companion, than he would have been in his prime," Taft commented. "He is so completely under the control of Brother Brandeis that it gives to Brandeis two votes instead of one." No doubt Taft's habit of gossip and natural distrust of Brandeis's "radicalism" led him to exaggerate, but we do know from Brandeis's letters that on occasion he urged his elder brother to speak out in dissent. "I have interrupted myself at this point," Holmes commented in a letter to Pollock, November 3, 1923, "to consider a case which Brandeis wants me to be ready with a dissent, because it weighs on my mind, and so I am no longer the careless and happy boy that began this." Thus by Brandeis's persistence the choice phrase, the priceless epigrams of Holmes in dissent, that might otherwise have been lost, were achieved for humanity. A shrewd friend has observed of Brandeis: "I wonder if even in his relations with Holmes he was not chiefly concerned with giving."

Holmes himself may have been conscious of yielding somewhat to Bran-

deis's persuasive power. One notes a trace of pride, of independence recon-
quered in his comment to Pollock, February 17, 1928: "I am glad that he
dissents from the only opinion I have to deliver. It will indicate that there
is no pre-established harmony between us." Just as the Northern Securities
case afforded him opportunity to assert his independence of T.R., so *Casey
v. United States* provided an occasion to demonstrate his independence of
his "upward and onward" brother on the bench.

Holmes was fifteen years older than Brandeis, but both had come to intellectual maturity in an age of cultural crudeness and political turmoil. Business enterprise was beginning to crystallize into a structure of corporate
and supercorporate monopoly. Socialist and populist movements had their
hour; labor awakened and organized. As popular sovereignty began to
assert itself in legislation, lawyers and judges decisively interposed the
Constitution, their Constitution, in support of their own social and economic predilections. Both Justices had been sensitively aware of these
dynamic pressures and conflicts; but whereas Holmes (save for his timeless
words in protest against cases "decided upon an economic theory") remained calm and unmoved, Brandeis became militant, emerging as the
People's Attorney.

The Gulf Between

Holmes regarded neither the rise of business combination nor of trade
unionism as unmitigated evil. For him, as for Darwin, struggle was the
law of life. If allowed to go on unhindered, the best in politics, in ideas, in
economics, as in life itself, would survive. Therefore, when lawyers and
judges sought to block change, he branded them "simple-minded men,"
needing "education in the obvious." We too, he said, need to "transcend
our own convictions," to leave room for much that "we hold dear to be
done away with short of revolution by the orderly change of law."

Holmes was fully as harsh in criticizing social reformers (a category in
which he was rather too much inclined to include Brandeis) who were
sure that "wholesale social regeneration" would result from "tinkering with
the institution of property. . . . The notion that with socialized property
we should have women free and a piano for everybody seems to me an
empty humbug."

Holmes's liberalism might perhaps be described as aloof or detached—
not in the sense of unawareness of the crucial social and economic struggles of his day but rather as denoting the deeply rooted naturalism that
drove him to accept monopolies, trade unions, and legislation as part of
the law of social organization, and of life itself. His oft professed humility
would not allow him to take sides or to join with those whose passion for
change was greater than his, or to agree with lawyers and judges who
thought they could thwart change and thus maintain the status quo.

Holmes abjured any and all absolute values. "When I say that a thing is true, I mean," he observed, "that I can't help believing it. . . . I therefore define the truth as the system of my limitations and leave absolute truth for those who are better equipped." Having himself no infallible measure of right and wrong, he upheld programs and policies in legislation even though he personally considered them in error or foolish. As he himself said, "I am so skeptical as to our knowledge about the goodness and badness of laws that I have no practical criterion except what the crowd wants. Personally I bet that the crowd if it knew more wouldn't want what it does—but that is immaterial." One day a friend asked him if he had ever worked out any general philosophy to guide him in the exercise of the judicial function. "Yes," the aged jurist replied. "Long ago I decided that I was not God. When a state came in here and wanted to build a slaughter house, I looked at the Constitution and if I couldn't find anything in there that said a state couldn't build a slaughter house I said to myself, if they want to build a slaughter house, God-dammit, let them build it."

Amid conflicting social forces Brandeis simply could not stand aloof. His uncanny knowledge that man's failure to solve today's problems accentuates and complicates the issues of tomorrow drove him on to take a resolute stand in favor of social control as against the anarchy of private economic power and greed. One with such knowledge and vision simply could not find ease in Holmes's citadel of "enlightened skepticism." Brandeis was passionately convinced that it lay within the power of statesmanship to determine the course of our social development. He held with Holmes that the extension of social control was inevitable, but he knew also that men had the capacity to determine whether such changes were to be along lines of "evolution or of revolution." Failure to heed that responsibility promptly and effectively would, he was certain, seriously limit the alternatives open to statesmanship in the years ahead. Failure to curb the excesses of capitalism would not only insure more extensive and more arbitrary government control, but would in fact jeopardize the very existence of our much vaunted free enterprise.

Thus Brandeis differed fundamentally from both Holmes, the so-called liberal, and Taft, the ultraconservative. Holmes's keen perception of the absurdities and dangers of visionary social reform as well as those of blindly naïve opposition to change drove him to a position of detachment. Taft's lack of education in the obvious, his proved incompetence in dealing with complicated economic issues, his inability to allow that which he held dear to be altered or ended by orderly processes of law, prompted his futile effort to block change. He, unlike Holmes, had in his own mind a measure of truth, of right and wrong; it was absolute as only such abstractions can be; he could and did take sides with complete conviction, blithely unaware of Holmes's wise words: "To rest upon a formula is a slumber that, prolonged, means death."

Brandeis also had a norm or standard to guide his action—knowledge of the conditions out of which modern legislation emerges. That is why his decisions and opinions are alive with deep conviction and carry much heavier wordage than those of Holmes. The latter might uphold state legislation which he detested for no better reason than his belief in the right of legislatures to carry on experiments within their states. Brandeis, on the other hand, while no less ardent in advocacy of legislative experimentation, might well uphold or set aside legislation depending on whether the statute conformed to certain standards of social justice established prima facie by the facts.

No one realized better than the dissenters themselves the chasm separating them. A basic difference as to the role of power in modern industrial society set them apart. Brandeis believed that unrestrained power, as such, and under whatever auspices, was a social menace. As organized and manipulated by monopoly management, it imperiled the rights of employees, entrepreneurs, and consumers; it rivaled and even surpassed the power of the state itself.

Surmising these differences between them, Holmes had written Brandeis as early as April 20, 1919:

Let me not be put in an attitude of opposition when I don't oppose. . . . I agree that wherever a great fortune produces an idler like the chap that shot Stanford White it produces an evil. But that does not seem to me more than an incident, dramatically impressive but not of the first or even great economic importance. The luxuries of the few I believe to be a drop in the bucket. The "sums withdrawn by Capital" that even such able men as Croly talk about seem to me merely the adjustments made by the most competent prophet to the anticipated equilibrium of social desires six months hence. They are not expenditures on luxuries, they are investments—intended to be the most profitable that can be got —and most profitable because they most nearly satisfy the consumer's demands. This adjustment would be as necessary under socialism as under any other system—otherwise the community gets less of what it wants. It never gets or can get as much as it wants. I believe that this man—the poor—now has substantially all there is. . . . Generally speaking I agree with you in liking to see social experiments tried, but I do so without enthusiasm because I believe that it is merely shifting the place of pressure and that so long as we have free propagation Malthus is right in his general view. All of which you know, but I like a moment of leisure to sing my old song over again. I believe it to be responsive in substance, although not so perhaps in form.

Yours ever,
O.W.H.

P.S. You might twit—that it is easy for those who don't appear to philosophize to chide me—I have known some suffering in my day. . . . Philosophy, as an old fellow in a book . . . says of courage, never is proved but always to be proved. I hope, if I am destined to be tried, I shall remember what I quoted yesterday, "They know not what they do."

"It is not far from the mark," Mr. Francis Biddle says of Holmes, "to conclude that his thinking in the field of economics stopped at twenty-five." The important thing, according to Holmes, was to forget money matters, private ownership and control, and consider the more vital question of who consumes the annual product. What difference does it make, he was accustomed to argue, if Rockefeller owns all the wheat in the United States, so long as the wheat is eventually consumed by the people? Private ownership should be viewed not as a terminus but as a gateway; "large ownership means," as he put it, "investment, and investment means the direction of labor toward the production of the greatest returns."

Anyone inclined to consider Holmes and Brandeis as Siamese twin liberals should put these words alongside those uttered by the People's Attorney in his 1911 testimony before the Senate Committee on Interstate and Foreign Commerce. Holmes entertained the naïve eighteenth-century faith that the economic process worked automatically—that the self-seeking drive of the individual results in gain which would somehow redound to the good of all. "For a man so skeptical about philosophic systems he was curiously uncritical," Mr. Biddle has observed, "about the orthodox economic axioms on which he was brought up."

"I know," Holmes himself said, "no way of finding the fit man so good as the fact of winning it [command] in the competition of the market." Industrial magnates whom Brandeis denounced as guilty of unconscionable social wrongs, Holmes admired as having triumphed in the life and death struggle of competition. "I regard a man like Hill [James J., the railroad giant] as representing one of the greatest forms of human power, an immense mastery of economic details, an equal grasp of general principles, and ability and courage to put his conclusions into practice with brilliant success. . . ."

Holmes was naturally unsympathetic toward any government interference with this struggle, this triumph of the fittest. Those government controls which Brandeis strove to win as essential to social justice, Holmes decried as humbug: "I don't disguise my belief that the Sherman Act is a humbug based on economic ignorance and incompetence, and my disbelief that the Interstate Commerce Commission is a fit body to be entrusted with rate-making, even in the qualified way in which it is entrusted."

Obviously to call two men "liberals" who held views so diametrically opposed is to empty this much abused word of all meaning. Holmes was a liberal primarily in the sense that he enforced (as he himself said) "whatever constitutional laws Congress or anybody else sees fit to pass—and do it in good faith to the best of my ability."

It was this tolerance of social change that constituted an important area

of agreement. Both believed in freedom as the way to truth; both understood the essence of politics as involving an unending search for points of
equilibrium, for balance between conflicting social forces. Both saw a more
stable society resulting from struggle and change—an evolution no force
on earth could stop. They agreed that the limits of conflicting social desires
must ultimately be defined, and that this is the essence of government.
They agreed also in holding that no mechanical rule can determine precisely where Aristotle's Golden Mean is to be found, that "government is
not an exact science."

The dissenters parted company, however, as to the factors to be taken
into account when confronted with a specific case. For Holmes the power
factor—that is, legislative majorities—was usually decisive, not because the
dictates of majorities were necessarily right, but because of the futility of
opposing or arguing with a superior force. For him, "wise or not, the
proximate test of a good government is that the dominant power has its
way." Though Brandeis did not ignore the power factor, he did stress knowledge as an auxiliary measure. Nor was Holmes unmindful of the effectiveness of Brandeis's approach. There should be, he said, no "slackening in
the eternal pursuit of the more exact. The growth of education is an increase
in the knowledge of measure . . . ; it is a substitution of quantitative for
qualitative judgments." Although the "worth of the competing social ends
. . . cannot be reduced to number and accurately fixed," it is of "the essence
of improvement that we should be as accurate as we can."

Despite such profession, Holmes himself showed no dominant inclination
to shape economic forces constructively. His contributions to our liberalism
are essentially negative. He not only detected the blindness of conservatives
to the inevitability of change, but also exposed the illusions of reformers
who believe that by changing property, or otherwise revolutionizing institutions, man can surely reach freedom's final goal. Holmes's liberalism
must be measured primarily in terms of his own rare open-mindedness when
most judges were singularly obtuse. He failed to contribute constructively,
not because he did not value facts, not because he was unaware of the
path of progress as hit upon by Brandeis, but because he could not bring
himself to undertake "the eternal pursuit of the more exact." For the factual
studies in which Brandeis reveled, Holmes expressed "fastidious disrelish."
His reaction, amounting almost to inertia, when Brandeis suggested that he
spend a summer investigating the textile industry, is typical:

"Brandeis the other day drove a harpoon into my midriff with reference
to my summer occupations," Holmes wrote Pollock, May 26, 1919. "He said
'you talk about improving your mind, you only exercise it on the subjects
with which you are familiar. Why don't you try something new, study some
domain of fact. Take up the textile industries in Massachusetts and after
reading the reports sufficiently you can go to Lawrence and get a human

notion of how it really is.' I hate facts. I always say the chief end of man is to form general propositions—adding that no general proposition is worth a damn. Of course a general proposition is simply a string for the facts and I have little doubt that it would be good for my immortal soul to plunge into them, good also for the performance of my duties, but I shrink from the bore—or rather I hate to give up the chance to read this and that, that a gentleman should have read before he dies. . . ."

Brandeis read economics as well as Euripides; Holmes read and reread Plato. The results are clearly reflected in their judicial opinions. Holmes is the enlightened skeptic; Brandeis, the militant crusader.

VARIATIONS ON THE LIBERAL THEME

When the Court set aside social legislation, it was enough for Holmes that the dominant power had embarked on experiments not prohibited by the Constitution. The nub of his quarrel with his conservative brethren was that they used the Constitution as a device for enforcing their own prejudices. Said he: "There is nothing that I more deprecate than the use of the Fourteenth Amendment beyond the absolute compulsion of its words to prevent the making of social experiments that an important part of the community desires, in the insulated chambers afforded by the several states, even though the experiments may seem futile or even noxious to me and to those whose judgment I most respect."

Holmes felt no compulsion or responsibility for making his opinions instructive as to the broader social and economic issues. "It rests with counsel," he said on one occasion, "to take the proper steps [to furnish the Court with relevant facts], and if they deliberately omit them, we do not feel called upon to institute inquiries on our own account." Brandeis, on the other hand, in disagreeing with the majority, explored and illumined the entire subject. He was not content to deal merely with the constitutional issue. He must go further and make his opinion both persuasive and informative.

Even when Holmes concurred in Brandeis's weighty opinions, he sometimes grew weary reading them. On one occasion Holmes "knit his brow" over a long opinion, profusely decorated with the usual footnotes as to economic data, trade journals, and committee reports. Beautifully clear and no doubt true, Holmes thought, as he leaned back in his chair; then he wrote on the margin: "This afternoon I was walking on the towpath and saw a cardinal. It seemed to me to be the first sign of Spring. By the way, I concur."

Holmes's and Brandeis's judicial vetoes were not always in agreement. When, for example, Pennsylvania prohibited mining coal in such a way as to cause private dwellings to cave in, Holmes held the law an unconstitutional encroachment on property rights. Brandeis, less concerned for the

sacredness of property, was more willing to allow legislative experimentation.

With an entirely different set of values, the positions of the dissenters
were reversed. When legislatures passed statutes affecting freedom of
thought, speech, and press, or when government agents invaded that right
"most valued by civilized men"—the right "to be let alone"—Brandeis did
not hesitate to interpose his judicial veto, though Holmes sometimes ruled
that the legislature be allowed to experiment. Brandeis could not agree,
contending that such statutes denied the fundamental right of free men
"to strive for better conditions." Thus when Nebraska prohibited German-
language instruction in private, parochial, and public schools, Holmes permitted the dominant power to have its way. To Brandeis, "what the crowd
wants" was in this instance no safe guide, and he voted with the majority
to overthrow the statute.

Brandeis's own decisions were not entirely governed by facts alone. Both
as a lawyer and a judge, the decisive factors were "partly legal, partly sentimental, and partly a recognition of economic rights and a sound social
policy." Certain prejudices and certain special preferences formed a picture
of an ideal society and predetermined his stand. His major prejudice was
against unconfined and irresponsible power—political or economic—whether
it was wielded by Executive or Judiciary, business corporation or trade
union. His fundamental maxim was stated in an early battle for civic
betterment: "Power must always feel the check of power." This he applied
in cases involving power conflicts between the federal government and the
states, between President and Congress.

Another prejudice was exhibited in cases posing the conflict between
property rights and human rights. Brandeis never underestimated the importance and social utility of private property, but he protested strongly
against any tendency to make it dominant over men. This was clearly
shown in *International News Service* v. *Associated Press* where the Court
upheld the Associated Press claim not to have its news items copied so
long as they had "commercial value as news." Brandeis objected to this
ruling as "an important extension of property rights [by judicial decision]
and a corresponding curtailment of the free use of knowledge and ideas."
He observed: ". . . with the increasing complexity of society, the public
interest tends to become omnipresent; and the problems presented by new
demands for justice cease to be simple. Then the creation or recognition
by courts of a new private right may work serious injury to the general
public, unless the boundaries of the right are definitely established and
wisely guarded."

Because the public interest in modern society tends to become omnipresent, Brandeis accorded legislatures wide latitude for their experiments
affecting property and contract, while judicial review was correspondingly

curtailed. He was especially alert to any tendency to create a property right by judicial decision. Thus when the Court settled on a narrowly technical definition of income that would render stock dividends immune from taxation, he penetrated the corporate veil, digging into the motives of management to prove how financiers, with the aid of their lawyers, had devised the stock dividend as a device for retaining profits while actually distributing them. In ruling that stock dividends are not income, the Court in effect flouted the "terse, comprehensive language" of the Sixteenth Amendment. This disinclination to endorse judicial power when used to protect property against government control was not always shared by Justice Holmes. Nor were recognized liberals, such as Judge Learned Hand, always able to agree. But Brandeis's position was solidly in accord with his general doctrine that "in order to preserve the liberty and the property of a great majority of the citizens of a state, rights of property and the liberty of the individual must be remolded, from time to time, to meet the changing needs of society." But this remolding process, as he saw it, must be largely legislative rather than judicial.

Brandeis's quarrel with the majority was not that facts were neglected but rather that the Court so often presumed to decide "as a fact" and without full knowledge whether or not measures were necessary, thus appropriating the "powers of a super-legislature." It is not, he contended, the business of judges to pass on facts but rather "in the light of all facts which may enrich our knowledge and enlarge our understanding" to decide whether the challenged legislation "is so clearly arbitrary or capricious that legislators, acting reasonably could not have believed it to be necessary or appropriate for the public welfare. . . . Knowledge is essential to understanding; and understanding should precede judging. Sometimes, if we would guide by the light of reason, we must let our minds be bold."

WHAT TRUTH—AND WHOSE

Brandeis's methods were soon imitated by conservative justices, who now fortified themselves with their own statistical data, picked and polished. Surely the use and abuse of facts to support opposite conclusions makes it seem not unlikely that facts, like syllogisms, will remain for judges as relatively unimportant in the judicial process. As Holmes said: "The felt necessities of the time, the prevalent moral and political theories, intuitions of public policy, avowed or unconscious, even the prejudices which judges share with their fellow-men, have had a good deal more to do than the syllogism in determining the rules by which men should be governed."

These observations are as applicable to Brandeis as to Butler or Sutherland. In letters to Pollock, Holmes sometimes made a point of saying that much of what Brandeis had written was not only irrelevant but "all wrong." Brandeis, like his conservative colleagues, was inclined by the pressures and drives of his own nature to translate his own economic and social views into the Constitution itself. That Constitution, an embalming fluid of status quo to the conservatives, to him was a fiery sword of freedom.

In this respect Holmes's position was unique. He was about equally skeptical of reforming zealots, who would make a new world in their own small image, and of those who would maintain moss-grown social and economic institutions unaltered. His "enlightened skepticism," and inertia, prompted him to take the hands-off, laissez-faire position, whereas Brandeis's moving knowledge of the economic forces of his day developed in him a sense of urgency. "How can you be so sure," a friend once asked, "that a particular line of action is the right one?" "When you are 51 per cent sure that you are right," he replied, "then go ahead." Skepticism was not so generic in Brandeis, but after years of association with Holmes he too could observe: "The economic and social sciences are largely uncharted seas. . . . Man is weak and his judgment is at best fallible."

Brandeis's approach was more constructive, less esoteric. In Max Lerner's words: "Where Holmes had spoken of philosophy, Brandeis spoke of service to the nation; where Holmes talked abstractly of battle, Brandeis talked pragmatically of reform; where Holmes fashioned graceful phrases, Brandeis quarried in the hard rock of social reality." Then Mr. Lerner adds: "Perhaps by the very fact of his indirections and his lesser urgency Holmes may ironically prove the more enduring voice."

Quite apart from the proved effectiveness of Brandeis's method and the validation of his insight and forecasts, Lerner's hypothesis would seem persuasive only if the comprehension that knowledge confers is turned to anti-social ends. Brandeis did not, indeed could not, find all the answers in his facts, but surely his briefs and opinions were much more than apparatus to support a preconceived policy or specific judicial decision. They led, first of all, to a sharper sense of the questions to be asked. At a time when conservatives saw the Constitution as synonymous with the laissez faire of Herbert Spencer, and Holmes spoke of the fundamental law as embodying no particular economic theory, Brandeis stated the crucial issue as that of reconciling our political democracy with industrial absolutism. Can anyone doubt today that his method meant a tighter grasp on the relevancy of the various possible answers? Can anyone doubt that his command of the facts of industrialism helped produce that sense of "urgency" unknown to liberal Holmes or conservative Taft? Can anyone doubt that such comprehension made for clearer insight into the advantages gained from choosing one answer rather than another? If judges really decide great constitutional questions according to their social and economic opinions, should they not make those opinions as informed as possible?

Brandeis took his stand and accepted full responsibility for action. He demonstrated his belief that man does have a measure of control over his own destiny. He proved that, given leadership, knowledge, persistence, and wide participation in public affairs, man can lay the foundations of a society with more security as well as more leisure, broader social responsibility as well as greater social privilege—in short, a nearer approach than men have ever thought possible to the ideal of an enlarging liberty through a living law.

Fuller's Increasing Influence on the Court*

1890–1892

WILLARD L. KING

Felix Frankfurter (see page 250) has much to say about Melville Weston Fuller (1833–1910); therefore only a brief sketch will be given of the man who became Chief Justice without any previous experience in public office. Fuller was born in Maine and educated at Bowdoin and Harvard Law. His Chicago period, 1856–1888, was marked by brilliant success as a trial lawyer, and offset by tragedy in the death of his wife, the loss of his office and all his papers by fire, and mounting debts. His qualities, however, drew the attention of Cleveland, who, in a political surprise move, raised him to the high office. Fuller remained on the bench for twenty-two years, winning over his formidable colleagues by his humor and courtesy, and introducing ways to cut through the backlog of cases which had threatened to choke the judicial process.

Our selection shows Fuller taking command. In the complete study by Willard L. King ensuing chapters discuss the Income Tax Case, the McKinley Administration, and the Venezuela Boundary Arbitration. King, who was born in 1893, is a Chicago lawyer, educated at Knox and Chicago, and recognized further by honorary degrees. Member of the Illinois bar since 1917, he holds various trusteeships and writes for legal publications.

Fuller's growing command of the Court, his firmness when Field roared but his gentleness and forbearance with the errors of a subordinate like the Reporter, are shown by certain cases decided between 1890 and 1892. In the same period he began to display a daring and resourcefulness in evolving novel legal theories. And his increasing influence with his colleagues frequently gave him majorities for these conceptions.

His first landmark decision was delivered in 1890 in the case of *Leisy* v. *Hardin*. It involved the power of a state to restrict interstate commerce in

* From *Melville Weston Fuller*, by Willard L. King, copyright, 1950, by Willard L. King. Reprinted by permission.

intoxicating liquor. The central fact in Fuller's life was the enormous growth of Chicago—a direct result of interstate commerce. Restrictions on such commerce were odious to him. When he came to the Court, it had recently been decided that a state could not stop an interstate shipment of liquor at the state boundary. But it had also been decided several years before, that a state could forbid the sale of an interstate shipment of liquor after it had arrived. In the *Leisy* case, Fuller persuaded the Court to over-rule this last decision and adopt a rule called the "original-package doc-trine."

The Leisys made beer in Peoria, Illinois, and shipped it in kegs to a relative in Keokuk, Iowa, who sold it there. Under an Iowa liquor-prohibi-tion Act this beer was seized by the city marshal in the original kegs in the hands of the Keokuk Leisy. The Supreme Court, in an opinion by the Chief Justice, held that the Iowa statute as thus applied was an unlawful interference with interstate commerce.

Fuller said that intoxicating liquor was a recognized article of com-merce. Under the interstate commerce clause of the Constitution, a state could not prohibit its entry from another state. But the question remained: When does an interstate shipment cease to be such? At some point articles shipped into a state must become subject to its laws. Fuller then applied for the first time to interstate commerce a rule of thumb which had been sug-gested by Chief Justice Marshall to determine when a foreign importation ended so that a state could tax an imported article despite the constitutional provision against state taxes on imports. Importation does not end, Marshall had said, until the imported goods have become intermingled with the common mass of property in the state. It does not end, he held, while the goods are in the original package in the hands of the importer; and the right to import includes the right to sell. Under this test the city marshal of Keokuk had unlawfully interfered with interstate commerce when he seized these original kegs of beer.

An able dissent from Fuller's opinion in the *Leisy* case was delivered by Justice Gray, who was joined by Justices Harlan and Brewer. The dissenters argued that—Congress being silent on the subject—the states had a right to prevent importations which they thought harmful to the health of their citizens. Fuller responded that a state had no right under that guise to ex-clude entirely a recognized article of commerce. Otherwise a state could exclude any and all importations, and interstate commerce would exist only at the sufferance of the several states. The Constitution was adopted, he said, largely to avoid that condition, and "the magnificent growth and prosperity of the country attest the success which has attended the accom-plishment of that object."

A great clamor arose over this decision from the anti-liquor people, who then had great political power. They forced through Congress an Act to the effect that intoxicating liquor when shipped into a state should become subject to its laws and should not be exempt therefrom because it was in the "original package." Fuller, in the *Leisy* opinion, had repeatedly said that such an Act of Congress would be proper. However, it was clear that Congress could not logically give to the states the power to determine the constitutional scope of interstate commerce. Fuller sustained the new Act by holding that Congress had not delegated such power to the states but had merely divested liquor shipments of their interstate character at an earlier date than that of the original-package rule. Several years later, the Court held that under this Act a state could not interfere with an interstate shipment of liquor prior to its arrival in the hands of the consignee. Only the consignee's right to sell was cut off by the law. The dispute over Fuller's original-package doctrine raged for several years, but he was eventually victorious and the rule became firmly embedded in the law.

The *Leisy* case shows Fuller's pluck in opposing a popular desire in favor of what he thought was a more fundamental need. The case also demonstrates his grit in overruling a prior decision. It indicates his resourcefulness in applying in a new way a doctrine having the sanction of Marshall's great name and transparent reasoning. It proves Fuller's influence on the Court in his ability to lead his colleagues in these strange paths. It shows his moderation through his invitation to Congress to legislate, and the subsequent cases show his adroitness in accepting the legislation in a restricted sense and without destruction of his original theory.

A sequel to the *Leisy* case—*O'Neil* v. *Vermont* caused great trouble inside the Court. O'Neil was convicted of selling liquors in Vermont. He had sent the liquor by express in jugs and flasks from his store in New York to individual customers in Vermont. The shipments were made C.O.D., and the Supreme Court of Vermont held that the express company was therefore O'Neil's agent and that the sales were made by him in Vermont through such agent. Title in the liquors did not pass to the buyer until they were paid for in Vermont. O'Neil was sentenced to pay a fine of some $6,500, and in default of payment he was to be imprisoned for more than fifty-four years.

The Supreme Court of the United States in an opinion by Justice Blatchford dismissed the case on the ground that no federal question had been decided by the Supreme Court of Vermont. The commerce clause had not been mentioned in the trial court. The Supreme Court of Vermont, under its rules, could not, therefore, consider that question. The Vermont court never mentioned the commerce clause in its opinion as to O'Neil, though it did refer to that clause in deciding the cases brought against the express company for condemnation of the liquors.

Justice Field passionately dissented. He insisted that the commerce clause had been brought to the attention of the Supreme Court of Vermont. He pointed out that the arguments of counsel for O'Neil in that court as reported in the official report had expressly referred to that clause.

When he published these opinions, Bancroft Davis, the Reporter, set off this storm anew by the language which he used in the head note for the case. "No point on the commerce clause of the Constitution," he said, was "considered by the Supreme Court of Vermont *or called to its attention.*" Blatchford's opinion had stated that the points made in the trial court were "too general to call the attention" of the Vermont Supreme Court to the commerce clause. Field immediately wrote the Reporter that the italicized words in the head note were not correct. Field's letter is not now available, but in view of his irascibility and his strong feeling in the case, its tone may be well imagined. Davis sent Field's letter to the Chief Justice, who wrote to Field:

"My DEAR MR. JUSTICE FIELD:

"Mr. Davis has sent me a copy of your note to him of the 17th & you must allow me to say that it greatly surprises & pains me.

"The headnote numbered 5 expresses the facts as I understand & have always understood the record in O'Neil v. Vermont in this court. In your vigorous and eloquent dissent you arrive at a different conclusion upon the point but inasmuch as the headnote accords with the opinion of the majority in that regard, I do not see how it can be changed on the ground of being incorrect. It seems to me impossible for any misapprehension to arise on the part of any reader of both opinions and I deeply regret if you feel otherwise.

"Very sincerely & truly yours,
MELVILLE W. FULLER"

Fuller sent a copy of this correspondence to Justice Gray, who responded: "As to the Reporter's headnote in O'Neil v. Vermont, I unhesitatingly concur with you on both points: 1. It accords with the opinion of the court. 2. That is the whole office of a headnote."

In answer to Fuller's letter, Field wrote:

"DEAR MR. CHIEF JUSTICE FULLER:

"Your letter of yesterday's date, respecting the syllabus to the decision in O'Neil v. Vermont, is received. If my note to the Reporter surprises and pains you I regret it but cannot help it. The syllabus is incorrect and the statement that no point on the commerce clause of the constitution was called to the attention of the Supreme Court of Vermont is not correct and no repetition of it will make it so. The report of the case in the Vermont Reports contains a synopsis of the briefs of counsel before that court and shows that the point was expressly taken. . . . The decision in O'Neil v. Vermont and the opinion of the court are, in my judgment, destined to an

unenviable notoriety, greater than has followed any previous decision of
the Supreme Court. . . .

"If my associates, who concurred in that decision and opinion could
read some of the letters I have received on the subject from distinguished
judges, lawyers and legal writers, they would find that I am not alone in
my views but that they are held by some of the ablest intellects of the
country. I should have shown some of these letters to my associates had I
not feared that they would consider that I intended to be rude to them;
so I have refrained. I have selected one of the most moderate in expression
of all of them from the distinguished writer on criminal law, Joel P. Bishop,
Esq., and send a copy of it for your perusal.

"I am

Very respectfully yours,
Stephen J. Field"

Joel P. Bishop was a legal author of some renown in that period. But
he had an "enormous vanity." His letter on this case was afterward published in an anonymous communication to a legal periodical. Bishop's letter
did not mention the commerce clause but abused the Supreme Court for
failing to hold the conviction void under the "due process" clause of the
Constitution.

The Chief Justice responded to Field's letter:

"Dear Judge Field:

"I received yours of the 19th yesterday but delayed acknowledgment
until I could read Mr. Bishop's paper which I return as requested. I am
obliged to you for giving me the opportunity but I do not think it adds
anything to the force of your dissent and it is impertinent in its allusions
to the court though that may be unintentional.

"Very truly yours,
Melville W. Fuller"

A month later Field printed a long letter to the Chief Justice and sent
copies to all of the Justices. "I have often wondered," he said, "how it
happened that you, who I know wish in all cases to be correct, could concur
in the erroneous statement. At last I think I have found out the cause of
your error, and I do only as I would wish to be done by in calling your
attention to what I suppose it to be."

Field said that it was very evident that Blatchford erroneously thought
that only the lawyers for the express company, and not counsel for O'Neil,
had relied on the commerce clause in the Vermont court. Field then quoted
in full the Vermont brief for O'Neil on the commerce clause. It would

appear, however, that Field was mistaken in his inferences from Blatchford's opinion. Blatchford knew that the commerce clause had been mentioned in the brief for O'Neil: he could hardly fail to know that fact, since it had been emphatically stated in the dissenting opinions. Blatchford's point was that the reference to the commerce clause in the brief was not sufficient to give the Supreme Court of Vermont jurisdiction to consider that clause because the subject had not been mentioned in the trial court. The *O'Neil* case shows how difficult Field could be, but it also shows Fuller's patience and firmness in handling him.

The first five to four decision in the Fuller regime did not occur until about three years after his appointment. The case—*Briggs* v. *Spaulding*—involved the liability of directors of an insolvent bank for alleged neglect in permitting the president of the bank to have such control of its affairs that he was enabled, without their knowledge, in a few months' time to wreck the bank. No one knowing Fuller would doubt his answer to this question. He was generous in his judgments of men's conduct, and in order to condemn a director for mere inaction he would require strong evidence. The majority of the Court thought that there was no such evidence in the case, and Fuller wrote the opinion of the Court affirming the Circuit Court's exculpation of these directors. The minority thought that the misconduct of the president of the bank could have been discovered by reasonable diligence on the part of certain of the directors.

There is evidence that Fuller was originally a dissenter in this case and secured a majority for his dissenting opinion. Among the Chief Justice's papers is an undated note from Justice Brown:

"DEAR CHIEF JUSTICE:

"May I ask you to circulate your dissent as soon as you conveniently can. I happen to know that an effort will be made to postpone final adjournment to June 3. To give time to this would be as bad as a continuance to me as I am booked to sail for Europe June 1 and could not possibly be present without breaking up my summer.

"Very truly yours,
H. B. BROWN"

There are reasons to believe that this note refers to an original dissent by Fuller in *Briggs* v. *Spaulding*. He dated the note in his own hand "May 19/91" and carefully preserved it. No dissenting opinion was thereafter delivered by him in any case argued prior to this note. However, the five to four decision in *Briggs* v. *Spaulding* was rendered six days thereafter (May 25, 1891), when the Court adjourned for the term. The case had been argued on March 3, and Fuller perhaps knew when he dated Brown's note and put it away that his "dissent" would be the majority opinion. The dissenting Justices were Harlan, Gray, Brewer, and Brown. And it would seem that only a five to four decision could threaten postponement of Brown's trip to Europe. There was no other close division of the Court at that term or for some time thereafter. Moreover, the dissenting opinion in this case by Justice Harlan bears on its face some evidence that it was originally prepared as a majority opinion. It never refers to the majority opinion and lacks the usual tone of a dissenting opinion.

In this case there was more trouble about the headnote. Fuller corrected the proof sheets of the opinion and sent them to the Reporter in June, 1891. In September, in Chicago, he received a letter from Harlan, who had written the dissent in the case:

"DEAR CHIEF JUSTICE:

"I have read the head-notes in the Bank case. They are awful & are enough to make you & not me sick. There is time to correct them. Make the corrections & send to Banks Brothers & tell them they must be made. It will require some of the opinions of the next term to complete Vol. 141 & hence you have time to have the corrections made.

"Yrs.

JNO. MARSHALL HARLAN"

This letter indicates the affection in which Fuller had come to be held by his colleagues. Here is a case about which Harlan had felt keenly enough to publish a long dissenting opinion—an appeal to posterity against the majority opinion. Yet when he discovered that the effect of Fuller's opinion had been ruined by the headnotes, he at once warned the Chief Justice and suggested the surest method of correction.

Harlan was right. The headnote was badly mangled and made Fuller's reasoning appear ridiculous. But the kindliness of Fuller's letter of correction to the Reporter was characteristic. It is reminiscent of Sir Isaac Newton's gentleness with the little dog that knocked over a candle and thereby burned up Newton's scientific paper on which he had labored for a year.

"CHICAGO
Oct. 8/91

"DEAR MR. DAVIS:

"The closing paragraphs of the head note to Briggs v. Spaulding, 141 U.S. 132 are so inaccurate as to require correction. I think it would be quite as well to omit the summing up entirely but if that can not readily be done, I would like to have the enclosed substituted for the defective matter. Mr. Justice Blatchford improved the notes as far as he went but I do not think he went far enough.

"My opinion in Rogers v. Durant, 140 U.S. 498 is attributed to Mr. Justice Field. If he does not object I do not know that I need to.

"I hope Mrs. Davis & yourself are very well. My eldest daughter, Mrs. Brown, has been lying dangerously ill for some weeks. Her condition was imminently critical last night—This morning, you will be glad to know there are grounds for hope of recovery.

"Very truly yours,
MELVILLE W. FULLER

Hon. J. C. Bancroft Davis"

No correction of the head note was ever made, apparently because Fuller's letter was received too late. If he had written directly to Banks Brothers, the publishers, as Harlan advised, the changes might have been made. Fuller doubtless did not adopt that course through fear of wounding the feelings of the Reporter.

The *Briggs* case illustrates Fuller's compassion for the defendants and his influence with his brethren on the Court. When the Court divided five to four, the majority was more likely to be on his side. This case also indicates in a striking way Harlan's great affection for Fuller. And, more sharply, it shows the Chief Justice's restraint in dealing with the Reporter's errors.

Another case which discloses Fuller's compassion as well as his daring in evolving legal theories is *Boyd v. Nebraska*. It also proves again his power in securing a majority for his ideas. And the subsequent correspondence shows once more the great regard in which his colleagues held him.

The case involved the right of James Boyd to be governor of Nebraska. He had been elected and inaugurated as governor, but the Supreme Court of Nebraska had decided by a two to one vote that he was not a citizen of the United States and therefore not qualified for the office.

Boyd had been born in Ireland and brought to this country as a child by his father in 1844. His father had settled in Ohio and soon thereafter filed his declaration of intention to become a citizen of the United States. But it was alleged that he had not completed his naturalization before his son attained the age of twenty-one, although the father had voted and held political office in Ohio. In 1856 the son had gone to Nebraska, where he had since repeatedly voted and held many elective offices prior to his election as governor in 1890. The father was formally naturalized in Ohio in 1890, and this proceeding provoked the controversy in Nebraska over the son's citizenship. The son claimed that this 1890 naturalization had occurred only because his father was unable to find his citizenship papers issued many years before.

Fuller held that Boyd was a citizen of the United States, regardless of his father's citizenship, because he had been a resident in Nebraska when the Congressional enabling Act was passed and the State admitted into the Union. Those statutes declared that all residents of Nebraska who had filed their declarations of intention to become citizens were citizens of the United States. The son, Fuller said, had acquired an inchoate or potential citizenship by his father's declaration, which placed him in the same category which his father would have occupied had he moved to Nebraska. Furthermore, Fuller held that the son had duly alleged in his answer that his father had been fully naturalized during the son's minority. The Supreme Court of Nebraska had held the contrary.

The first basis on which Fuller put the case was rather bold, for statutes are not usually extended beyond their terms. But he was frankly moved by sympathy for a man who had been a pioneer in the State and had been a member of the legislature, a delegate to two constitutional conventions, mayor of Omaha, and had been fairly elected governor. Harlan, Gray, and Brown concurred in the opinion only on the second basis. This ground was that Boyd had alleged on information and belief that his father had completed his naturalization in strict accordance with the Acts of Congress prior to the time when the son became twenty-one. The Supreme Court of Nebraska had held this allegation insufficient. Fuller pointed out that prior decisions of the Supreme Court of the United States had held that, where a naturalization certificate was lost, a jury might infer citizenship from voting and holding office for a long period of time. Since Boyd alleged these facts, Fuller held his allegation of his father's citizenship to be sufficient.

Fuller secured the concurrence in the decision of every Justice of the Court except Field. Field said that the federal courts had no power to determine a state election contest, that the states had the "absolute power to prescribe the qualifications of all their state officers," and that the decision was an unwarranted invasion of states' rights.

This point was the least vulnerable portion of Fuller's opinion. He had based the federal jurisdiction on the fact that Boyd had claimed to be a citizen of the United States under federal statutes, to which the Nebraska court had not given proper effect. But Fuller's opinion was labored and prolix, while Field's was sparkling and succinct. A week after the opinions were delivered, Justice Gray wrote to Fuller:

"DEAR CHIEF JUSTICE:

"I had in mind to say to you on your return from Richmond (but it escaped my mind yesterday) that Judge Field's dissent in *Boyd* v. *Thayer* is so insidious and plausible to the common mind that I hope you will enlarge upon the question of jurisdiction so as to meet it—which would not be difficult.

"Respectfully & truly yours,
HORACE GRAY"

It is typical of Gray's feeling for Fuller that in a case where Gray was only half-convinced that Fuller was right, Gray was still extremely anxious that the Chief Justice should not be disparaged by Field's dissent.

But whatever changes the Chief Justice made in the opinion in pursuance of this suggestion were quite inadequate. The *Harvard Law Review* in an editorial note condemned the decision for invading the rights of the states and commended the dissenting opinion of Justice Field. Perish the thought that the Harvard law professors were, in the terminology of Justice Gray, persons "of common mind!"

Chief Justices I Have Known*

FELIX FRANKFURTER

Felix Frankfurter was born in Vienna in 1882 and came to the United States in 1894. Educated at the City College of New York and Harvard, he was appointed an assistant United States attorney under Henry Stimson, 1906–1910, and professor in the Harvard Law School from 1914 to 1939, at which point he mounted the bench as Associate Justice of the Supreme Court. Among his many writings are an essay on the Sacco-Vanzetti case, a work on Justice Holmes and the Court, and many collections of edited cases, done in collaboration.

"Chief Justices I Have Known" is a delightful and informative backstage view of five of the six Chief Justices Frankfurter knew. Since he prefaces his reminiscences with appraisals of earlier justices and has a good deal to say about Fuller (also p. 240), his essay has useful summary value; furthermore, Frankfurter speaks of Chief Justice Hughes and others not represented in this volume.

This informal talk was given by Mr. Justice Frankfurter before a group of students and professors at the University of Virginia Law School in Charlottesville on May 12, 1953. A transcript of his remarks, which had been tape recorded, appeared in the *Virginia Law Review* for November 1953 (Vol. 39, p. 883) and is reprinted here, with minor editorial revisions.

I'm told you can't teach an old dog new tricks, but my problem tonight is not to try to indulge in new tricks but to see if I can recall an old trick—talking to a group of people. I must see if I can do what I used to do for twenty-five years—sit in a room and talk with students, fellow students, the difference between whom and myself was merely that I had traveled the road once, or several times, before they did.

Here I am without a note, and therefore we'll just have a chat. This room is larger than the one in which I used to meet with students at the Harvard Law School, but we'll contract the walls and imagine we are sitting around that room, where for twenty-five years I received such stimulus and delight as only the young can give a teacher. It's about as pleasurable a thing as can come to a man in a lifetime.

* From *Of Law and Men*, by Felix Frankfurter, edited by Philip Elman, copyright, 1956, by Harcourt, Brace and Company. Reprinted by permission of the publishers.

I've been told to talk to you about chief justices I've known, and I'll talk just as it lies in my mind.

It is 164 years since the Supreme Court of the United States was established by an act of Congress. During those years there have been, including Fred M. Vinson, the present incumbent, thirteen chief justices. It seems almost incredible, old as I am, that I've known six of them. The mystery is easily resolved by the fact that the term of office of chief justices, if nature is kind, as happily it has been to some of the greatest of them, is longer than that of any other official in our government.

I shall speak to you about five of the chief justices. I shall not say anything, of course, of the chief justice whom I've known longest in service, the present occupant of the seat. But I shall speak of one—Fuller—whom I knew only rather remotely, somewhat platonically as it were, because I never had any personal relations with him. But I saw him on and off, first when I was a student at the Harvard Law School, and eventually when I appeared before him in that wonderful old courtroom in the Capitol, which I think it was almost a desecration of tradition to leave.

The five chief justices of whom I will speak are Fuller, White, Taft, Hughes, and Stone. But, of course, in order that what I say may have something more than merely episodic significance, a few preliminary remarks ought to be made.

The one judicial figure whom even the least informed knows of in the history of the United States is the great Chief Justice John Marshall, of your Commonwealth. It is an interesting fact that although, for essential purposes, the history of our constitutional law almost begins with him, and the significant history of the Supreme Court of the United States begins with him, he was the fourth chief justice. His three predecessors all had very short tenure.

The first was a great man, John Jay. It is not without significance in attempting to understand the then position of the chief justice of the United States, that John Jay resigned the chief justiceship to become governor of New York—not that I underrate the importance of the governorship of New York, either then or now. But it is certainly true that since Marshall's time only a madman would resign the chief justiceship to become governor, let me say, even of Virginia.

Jay's successor, John Rutledge of South Carolina, had the singular distinction of serving only a few months as chief justice by interim appointment. He was rejected by the Senate of the United States, and therefore was not able to continue to occupy the post.

The third chief justice was another eminent man in our history, Oliver Ellsworth, who was the architect of the act that created the federal judicial system. His structure remained, for all practical purposes, unaltered from 1789 to 1869. He was chief justice for only four years. Ill health put an end to his service.

Then came John Marshall. I should say the three greatest chief justices we've had were John Marshall, Roger Taney, and Charles E. Hughes. It is an interesting fact that the first two of these, between them and in immediate succession, served for almost one-half of the 164 years the Court has been in existence. Marshall from 1801 to 1835, and Taney from 1836 to 1864. I emphasize the duration of their service because the length of time during which a chief justice presides over the Court has, of course, a great deal to do with his place in history. Time is one of the most important factors in the realization of a man's potentialities.

Coming to the chief justices whom I have seen in action, about whom professionally I may be allowed to have some judgment, let me come down to 1888 when Grover Cleveland appointed a man who was not known generally to the country at all. I suppose Melville Weston Fuller was a man about whom there was nothing in what newspapermen call the morgues of the leading newspapers in the country. He had no record to speak of, except a professional one. His appointment is a striking illustration of the contingencies of life. And I think he—and I shall speak of others— illustrates the importance of not having a fixed, specific ambition in life. The chances of realizing a specific ambition, the laws of chance, are so much against you that, if I may say so, I do not think any of you should harbor an ambition to become chief justice of the United States. The likelihood that you will realize it—I do not know what the mathematicians, if there be any in this audience, would say—is worth nothing, and the likelihood that you will have an embittered life is very considerable. The thing to do is to have ambition in a certain direction but not to fix it on a point of arrival, an ambition going to general purpose in life and not to the particular form in which that purpose is to be realized.

When Chief Justice Waite died, if a poll had been taken among lawyers and judges to determine the choice of a successor, I do not suppose a single vote would have been cast for Melville W. Fuller, certainly outside Chicago. Indeed, he was not Grover Cleveland's first choice. It was widely believed that a man named Edward J. Phelps of Vermont would become chief justice. He was a leader of the bar. He was a well-known man. He had been minister to Great Britain. But 1888 was a time when the so-called Irish vote mattered more than it has seemed to matter in recent years. Edward J. Phelps, as has been true of other ministers and ambassadors to Great Britain, had made some speeches in England in which he said some nice things about the British people. Patrick Collins, a Democratic leader, then an influential member of the House of Representatives and later mayor of Boston, felt that that wouldn't do. A man who says nice things about the British, he evidently thought, couldn't possibly make a good chief justice of the United States. And since Patrick Collins was a powerful influence in the Democratic party, he advised President Cleveland that if he sent Phelps's name to the Senate, the chances of confirmation might not be very bright. Phelps's name was not sent to the Senate.

Melville Fuller was born in Maine, educated at Bowdoin, and the Harvard Law School. As a young man, after a little political activity in Augusta, Maine, he tried his luck in the beckoning West. He went to Chicago, where he was active as a Democrat. In that way it chanced that Grover Cleveland came to know and respect him. After some maneuvering, Cleveland named Fuller, to the great surprise of the press of the country and even of the profession. Fuller was confirmed, but with a very large vote in opposition. One of the opponents of confirmation was Senator Hoar of Massachusetts, then on the powerful Judiciary Committee, who afterward did the handsome thing by saying how wrong he had been, just as in our day Senator Norris, who had opposed the confirmation of Harlan F. Stone, later publicly expressed his regret.

The point about Fuller was, or rather is, that he was a practicing lawyer, and a lawyer only. I need hardly tell this audience that to me being a lawyer, with the full implications of responsibility and opportunity that the word carries, in a society like ours, in a government of laws under a written Constitution, is a calling second to none. Melville Fuller had held no public office of any kind, unless you call being a member of a constitutional convention public office. He was fifty-five years old when he was appointed to the Supreme Court, and he had not only had no judicial experience, he had had, as I have said, no official experience of any kind. I think Fuller was the only man, with the exception of his immediate predecessor, who came to the chief justiceship so wholly without a record in official public life.

When you deal with a number as small as that of the chief justices of the United States, any inference from one or more cases is statistically not of much validity. I merely point out, parenthetically, that five chief justices came to the office without having had prior judicial experience. I do not want you to draw any inference from that fact which you cannot rationally defend. There is much to be said, and I have not time to say it now, on the general question of the relevance of prior judicial experience as a qualification for membership on the Supreme Court. Perhaps, parenthetically again, I can sum up my own views by saying that prior judicial experience should be neither an essential qualification nor, of course, a disqualification. I think that when the President of the United States comes to select someone to fill a vacancy on the Supreme Court, no single factor should be the starting point in his deliberation. He should not say, "I want a man who has had experience as a judge," or, "I want a man who hasn't had experience as a judge." I shall say more about this in a moment, but to me it is important that if you blot out the names of those who came to the Supreme Court without any prior judicial experience, you blot out, in my judgment, barring only two, the greatest names on its roster.

At all events, Fuller came to the Court as a man who had had wide experience at the bar, and, what is important, wide experience at the bar of the Supreme Court and with the kind of business that came before the Supreme Court in his day. He was a dapper little man. I remember vividly seeing him for the first time. I was a student at the Harvard Law School and he was president of the Harvard Alumni Association. He was introducing the speaker of the day, none other than William H. Taft, who had just returned from the Philippines to become secretary of war. Fuller had silvery locks, more silvery and more—what shall I say?—striking, because he was a little man, than the locks of the former senator from Texas, Tom Connally. He was an extremely cultivated man, which is important. He read the classics. He was a student of history. He had felicity of speech.

Fuller came to a Court that wondered what this little man was going to do. There were titans, giants on the bench. They were powerful men, both in experience and in force of conviction, and powerful in physique, as it happened. For myself, I think all justices of the Supreme Court should be big, powerful-looking men! Certainly those whom he met there, who welcomed him courteously but not hopefully, were as I have described them. (Believe it or not, there is ambition even in the breasts of men who sit on the Supreme Court of the United States. There is a good deal to be said for the proposal of Mr. Justice Roberts that no man should ever be appointed to the chief justiceship from the Court.) At any rate, Fuller met on that Court at least four or five men of great stature. The senior among them was Samuel F. Miller, who had been appointed by Lincoln and whose career, incidentally, is an exciting story of American life. Miller started out as a physician and practiced medicine for ten or twelve-odd years, until he became a lawyer and in very quick order a justice of the Supreme Court. He had great native ability, and was a strong man in every sense. Fuller, if they had had the expression in those days, might have been called an egghead. He was a blueblooded intellectual, and the contrast with Miller was great. Then there was Harlan, a six-foot-three, tobacco-chewing Kentuckian. You did not have to come from Kentucky to chew tobacco in those days. They did it in Massachusetts too. But Harlan was all Kentuckian. And there was a smallish man whom I regard as one of the keenest, profoundest intellects that ever sat on that bench, Joseph Bradley of New Jersey. And there were Matthews of Ohio and a six-foot-five- or six-inch giant from Massachusetts, Horace Gray. Those were the big, powerful, self-assured men over whom Melville Fuller came to preside.

They looked upon him, as I have indicated, with doubt and suspicion, but he soon conquered them. They soon felt that the man who presided over them justly presided over them. He had gentle firmness, courtesy, and charm. He also had lubricating humor. Justice Holmes was fond of telling a story. In his early days, he said, "I'm afraid my temper was a little short." (There could hardly have been two men more different than Mr. Justice

Holmes, who wielded a rapier, and Mr. Justice Harlan, who wielded a battle-ax. A rapier and a battle-ax locked in combat are likely to beget difficulties for innocent bystanders.) Justice Harlan, who was oratorical while Justice Holmes was pithy, said something during one of the Court's conferences that seemed to Holmes not ultimate wisdom. Justice Holmes said he then did something that ordinarily isn't done in the conference room of the Supreme Court. Each man speaks in order and there are no interruptions, because if you had that you would soon have a Donnybrook Fair instead of orderly discussion. But Holmes afterward said, "I did lose my temper at something that Harlan said and sharply remarked, 'That won't wash. That won't wash.'" Tempers flared and something might have happened. But when Holmes said, "That won't wash," the silver-haired, gentle little chief justice said, "Well, I'm scrubbing away. I'm scrubbing away."

Whether you are in a conference room of the Supreme Court, or *en banc* in a court of appeals, or at faculty meetings, or in a law club, the same kind of thing can happen. When men get short of temper, humor is a great solvent. Fuller had that. He presided with great courtesy. He presided with quiet authority unlike Hughes's, of whom I shall speak shortly. He presided with great but gentle firmness. You couldn't but catch his own mood of courtesy. Advocates, too, sometimes lose their tempers, or, in the heat of argument, say things they should not. There was a subduing effect about Fuller. Soon these men, who looked at him out of the corner of their eyes, felt that they were in the presence of a chief whom they could greatly respect. I have the authority of Mr. Justice Holmes, who sat under four chief justices in Massachusetts before he came down to Washington, and under four (Fuller, White, Taft, Hughes) in Washington, that there never was a better presiding officer, or rather, and more important in some ways, a better moderator inside the conference chamber, than this quiet gentleman from Illinois.

Somehow or other the felicity of his pen, more of his tongue but also his pen—if you will read a speech he made on the occasion of the centennial of the founding of this country, reported in 132 United States Reports,—that charm which he had in occasional writings did not manifest itself, or he did not exert it, in his opinions. You cannot tell the quality or the importance of a man on the Supreme Court solely from his opinions. Mr. Justice Van Devanter, in passing, is a striking illustration of that. And so Fuller's opinions will give you nothing of his charming qualities. He is rather diffuse. He quotes too many cases. And generally he's not an opinion writer whom you read for literary enjoyment, though you can profitably read his nonjudicial things for that purpose.

Fuller was invited to leave the Supreme Court, not to become governor of New York, but because Grover Cleveland was very anxious to have him as his secretary of state. An important document in the history of the judiciary, and I think in the history of the law, is Fuller's letter to President

Cleveland stating why a man shouldn't leave the chief justiceship, and, I should add, an associate justiceship, for any political office. He was, as I said, fifty-five years old when he came to the Court. He was chief justice for twenty-two years. The difference in functions between the chief justice and the other members of the Court, is, as Holmes said, mainly on the administrative side, and there never was a better administrator on the Court than Fuller.

I ought to add one thing that seems to me not without interest and not without pleasure to record. I said Fuller was appointed in 1888. That was, let me remind you, a presidential election year. Like every party out of power, the Republicans expected to be returned, as indeed they were. If mere partisanship had ruled, it would not have been difficult to await the result of the election and give the selection of a chief justice to the incoming administration. Instead, the Senate confirmed the Democratic choice of President Cleveland. This broad-minded action reflects honor on all the senators whose votes confirmed Fuller. Especial mention, however, should be made of Senator Shelby M. Cullom of Illinois, who knew Fuller and his qualifications as lawyer and man, and, transcending party considerations, pressed his confirmation. Now, that is a very gratifying thing to one who, like myself, is out of party politics and party attachments—that politicians did not play for position in relation to such a high office.

I must move on. Fuller died in 1910, and the appointment of his successor is a most interesting episode in American history, because Fuller died shortly after President Taft had named Governor Hughes of New York as an associate justice. As a matter of fact, Hughes had not even taken his place when, in the summer, shortly after he was named, Fuller died. President Taft was a great admirer, not unnaturally, of Hughes, who made the decisive campaign speech for Taft in 1908 at Youngstown, Ohio. In offering Governor Hughes the place on the Supreme Court, Taft, with that charming exuberance and forthrightness of his, indicated that Fuller couldn't live forever, and that, of course, he, Hughes, would be the natural choice of Taft for the chief justiceship. He indicated, as much as words can indicate, that he would name Hughes to be chief justice. Then, having doubtless re-read the letter after he signed it, he scribbled under it a postscript, being fully aware of his delightful and generous indiscretion, "Of course, I do not make this as a firm promise," or words to that effect. (I'm not quoting accurately.) Governor Hughes, in accepting the position, told the president that of course he was as free as a bird as far as the chief justiceship was concerned.

Well, a vacancy in the chief justiceship did occur six weeks after this exchange of letters, and everybody expected Hughes to be made chief justice. Hughes took his seat, and it must have been extremely embarrassing for the baby member of the Court to be the heir apparent to the vacant chief justiceship. Some of the older fellows must have disliked the idea.

You know, the notion of a freshman runs all through life—younger brother, younger sister, freshman at college, freshman on the Supreme Court.

By that time—1910—the Court had completely changed. Of the men whom Fuller had found when he went there in 1888, only one survived. That was Harlan. There were very strong men on the Court in 1910. It would be a pathetic Court indeed if there weren't always at least some strong men on it. By 1910 there were some new strong men. When Hughes joined the Court he found there, in addition to Mr. Justice Harlan, that nice birdlike creature with a beard, Mr. Justice McKenna of California. Holmes by that time had been on for eight years. There was Mr. Justice White. There was Mr. Justice Day.

They did not like the idea of having this untried New York governor and politician become chief justice. They drew up a round robin to present to Taft, who had appointed some of them. They saw President Taft, I believe, and indicated that they did not like to have their junior member made chief justice. Mr. Justice Holmes, with his characteristic high honor, refused to join this kind of protest. He was perfectly ready to have Hughes become chief justice.

Taft appointed a member of the Court, a powerful member of the Court, Edward D. White of Louisiana. President Taft was glad to appoint—we are so much removed from 1910 in some ways—White as chief justice because White had been a Confederate. It was not until the 'eighties that a Confederate Southerner had again been put on the Supreme Court. That was Lucius Quintus Cincinnatus Lamar of Mississippi. But to make a Confederate, an ex-Confederate—are Confederates ever "ex"?—chief justice was something that could contribute much, even then, so Taft thought, and I believe rightly, to the cohesion of our national life.

We shall never know the full story of what happened, but within twenty-four hours after the justices called on him there was a change in the mind of Taft, and it was then that White became chief justice. There is the most absurdly contradictory testimony of people who think they do know what happened. Within a half-hour after Taft had summoned Hughes, probably to tell him he was going to be chief justice, he canceled the request that Hughes come. During that time something happened.

Anyhow, White was made chief justice. At the Saturday conference following the sending of White's name to the Senate, Hughes, the junior member of the Court, made what I am told was one of the most gracious speeches of welcome to the new chief justice.

Now let me tell you about Edward D. White. He looked the way a justice of the Supreme Court should look, as I indicated a little while ago. He was tall and powerful. I think a jowl also helps a justice of the Supreme Court, and White had an impressive jowl. He had been a drummer boy in the Confederacy, and that had upon him a very important influence, not only in life, but as a judge—a very profound influence. It is a very interesting thing, but Edward D. White, the Confederate drummer boy, was much more nationalistic, if that phrase carries the meaning I should like it to carry, and was far more prone to find state action forbidden as an interference with federal power, than was Holmes, the Union soldier, who went to his death with three bullets in his body. White was so impressed with the danger of divisiveness and separatism, with the intensification of local interest to the disregard of the common national interest, that again and again and again he found that local action had exceeded the bounds of local authority, because it might weaken and endanger the bonds of national union. One of the most interesting things is the division between him and Holmes in specific instances, where White was, if one may use colloquial, inaccurate terms, for "centralization" and Holmes was for "states' rights."

White had "read" law. He did not have the advantage that you and I have had, of systematic training in the law in a university law school. He was educated by the Jesuits—another very important part of his life, because for him logic and logical analysis played a very important, sometimes an excessive role. Very early he was put on the Supreme Court of Louisiana, but he was there only two years because he was then legislated out of office, or rather the court to which he belonged was. So that he had had only two years of relatively unimportant judicial experience. During those two years he never had a case of the kind which most frequently came to the Supreme Court after he became a member of it. After his brief state judicial career, White practiced law and in 1891 was sent to the Senate of the United States, on the great issue of whether there should or shouldn't be a state lottery. That's a profound question, isn't it? Anyhow, it took him to the Senate of the United States, where he began to play an important part. He was an effective speaker, a man of cultivation, and much respected.

Then comes another one of those incidents which lead me to caution the young in this room not to fix their ambition on becoming the chief justice or even an associate justice of the Supreme Court of the United States. Mr. Justice Blatchford of New York died in 1893 and there were reasons why the natural thing was to pick a New Yorker for his place. This was in the second administration of Cleveland, after he had come back following Harrison's intervening presidency. But the New York politicians had got into an awful row with Cleveland, and the Democratic party in New York was split wide open. The leader of the anti-Cleveland forces, David B. Hill, was in the Senate of the United States. Mr. Cleveland, who was himself a lawyer of very considerable parts and knew the bar, first sent in the name of William B. Hornblower, a leading member of the New York bar. Senator Hill, exercising a historic prerogative of senators, said, "I oppose this nomination." (If a senator from the norminee's state is opposed to him and speaks the traditional words, the nomination fails. This works on the theory of "you scratch my back today and I'll scratch yours tomorrow.") So Mr. Hornblower's name fell by the wayside.

President Cleveland then sent in a second name, Wheeler H. Peckham of New York, another one of the really topnotch lawyers of his day. There was nothing against him except that he was a Cleveland man, but that was enough for David B. Hill. He again rose, swirled the toga about him, and said that he was very sorry but that Mr. Peckham, an otherwise estimable man, is "personally obnoxious." And so Mr. Peckham's name was withdrawn. Cleveland was put to it, and he did what presidents have done before and since. He drew on that powerful force, the club feeling of the Senate. And he said, "I'll fix you. I'll name a senator to the Supreme Court." (They never reject senators for anything, almost.) So he named Senator White of Louisiana, and within fifteen minutes Senator White was confirmed.

That's how White came on the Supreme Court in 1894. He sat for sixteen years as an associate, a very significant member of the Court, until he was made chief justice at the age of sixty-five. He had been a judge for sixteen years, but it's important to remember again that when he was made a judge he had only this rather unimportant, not very relevant, not quite two years on the Louisiana Supreme Court. He remained chief justice from 1910 to 1921.

An important thing in the work of a chief justice which distinguishes him from other members of the Court is that he is the presiding officer, and has guidance of the business of the Court in his charge. It is not what he says in his opinions that is more important than what his brethren say, but what he advises on the mechanics of doing the job—should we give a lawyer extra time, should we hear this case now or later, should we grant a rehearing if the Court is divided? These are things that pertain to the way that the business should be done, things that cannot properly be managed without knowledge of the nature of the business, or, since you deal with eight other human beings, without knowledge of the ways of the other justices.

It is thus very important that, number one, the chief justice should have had some familiarity with the business of the Court before he gets there, and, number two, that he start off on the right foot in his relations with his colleagues, whom he finds there. Of course, influence, in the sense of respect and deference, can be acquired in the course of time, but it makes a lot of difference if the start is a good one. White, when he came to be chief justice in 1910, dealt with men with whom he'd been a judge for periods varying in length from sixteen to a few years. But, as sometimes happens, there soon was a wholesale change in the Court. While a number of the associates remained—McKenna and Holmes and Day—a new lot came on in the other places. A very able lot they were too.

I ought to say something here about the differences in the nature of the business that has come to the Court in different periods. When Fuller assumed office in 1888, the Court dealt a great deal with problems arising from the vast industrialization which the Civil War had set into motion. It was also during Fuller's time that the war with Spain and the acquisition of territory led to new controversies. These events were reflected in the business of the Court—because the Court is a good mirror, of which historians for some reason have little availed themselves, of the struggles of dominant forces outside the Court. Sooner or later the conflicts in the economic and social world result in litigation before the Court. De Tocqueville, in 1832, when he wrote his great book, had the discernment to see what later writers have so often not seen, that by the very nature of our Constitution practically every political question eventually, with us, turns into a judicial question. The question may become somewhat mutilated in the process, but come before the Court it will.

One sometimes reads about the Supreme Court and wonders whether anyone ever studies history any longer. One would suppose that dissenting opinions were a recent discovery. In fact, I am sometimes told that they are an invention brought down by a Harvard professor. Well, the men on Fuller's Court divided drastically and fiercely on the issues of their time. In the Insular Cases, they wrote no fewer than two hundred pages of opinions, which were illuminatingly summarized by that great philosopher, Mr. Dooley, when he said that so far as he could make out, "the Supreme Court decided that the Constitoosh'n follows the flag on Mondays, Wednesdays, and Fridays."

Beginning about in the 'seventies, the states, not yet the Federal Government but the states, began to regulate business. And there came before the Court a series of questions as to the power of the states, in view of the Civil War Amendments. With the Interstate Commerce Act of 1887, we enter upon an era where the Federal Government intervenes. It is the era we are still in, in which I suppose the statistically predominant issues concern the relations between government and business, broadly speaking. During Fuller's period, on the whole, the outlook of the Court was very— what shall I say—inhospitable toward control of business. Restrictions upon the free activities of business came into Court, on the whole, under a serious handicap.

By the time White came to be chief justice the Federal Government had gone in for regulation more and more. Hughes was on the Court, with his great experience, as governor of New York, in regulating business. During White's tenure, Brandeis came on the Court, without any previous judicial experience, but with, I suppose, unparalleled experience in the domain of practical economics, with an understanding of the relations of business to society. Yet, though White came to the chief justiceship with full knowledge of the Court's business and with a strong hold on his colleagues, if anybody thought that merely because of that there would be unanimity of opinion and a want of differences, he was bound to be mistaken. Indeed, during White's tenure the divisions became more frequent and not fewer. But he was master of his job. There was something very impressive about him, both in appearance and otherwise. He was also a great personality.

He was a master of speech, though sometimes too abundant speech. I should suppose, on the whole, his opinions are models of how not to write a legal opinion. He made three words grow, usually, when there was room for only one.

The Court became more and more divided in opinion during his period, not because of him, but because the issues became more contentious, the occasions for making broad decisions were fewer, and cases came more and more to be recognized, as Holmes early pointed out and for fifty years continued to point out, as presenting questions of degree.

White was chief justice for only ten years. When he died an astonishing thing happened, unique in the history of this country and not likely to recur, at least as far as one can look ahead—an ex-president of the United States became the chief justice of the United States. That was, of course, William H. Taft.

Now, his case may contradict what I said about not fixing your ambition on a particular job, because William H. Taft, from the time he came to manhood, wanted to become a member of the Supreme Court. His great ambition in life was to be a justice of the Supreme Court, and he finally not only attained it, but with, as it were, a dividend. He became chief justice of the United States. Yet, if I were you, I wouldn't draw too heavily on Taft for encouragement, let alone derive assurance from his case. Let me tell you why.

Taft was a brilliant student, as we all know, at Yale College. I think he would have continued to be even if he had gone to the Harvard Law School, as his son did after him. He went out to Cincinnati and had a quick success at the bar, vindicating the promise of his youth. At thirty-two he was solicitor general, having been on a lower court in Ohio before that. Shortly after the present system of Courts of Appeals, then called Circuit Courts of Appeals, was established in 1891, he became a circuit judge, and he was a notable judge, for eight years, from 1892 to 1900, when McKinley sent him to the Philippines as governor general.

While he was out there, vacancies occurred on the Supreme Court of the United States, and his then bosom friend, Theodore Roosevelt, who knew of his ambition, twice offered him a place on the Supreme Court. To the very great honor of his name it is to be recorded that Taft twice refused that which his personal ambition was most eager to have, because he thought he owed it to the Philippine people not to leave—what's the phrase? —"the plow in the furrow." So twice he put behind him the realization of his personal ambition, because duty commanded him otherwise.

Then he became secretary of war, and after that President of the United States. His heart must have twinged more than once as he had opportunity to put five men on the Supreme Court and fill places that he himself coveted. In 1913 Taft ceased to be President and was promoted to be a professor of law. Well, if any man ever put behind him the thought that he would ever be on the Court, it was William H. Taft, when he went up to New Haven to profess law. If you want to be foolish, if you want your life subject to the hazards of such fortuities as those which determined the fate of William H. Taft, then you can follow his example. Who could have foreseen that the course of events would be such that in 1921 Warren Gamaliel Harding would be President of the United States and would ask William H. Taft to be chief justice?

Taft became chief justice at the age of sixty-three, having been, as I have indicated, a notable judge, but having been out of the business of judging and out of touch with the Supreme Court, except for having filled five of its nine places, for twenty years. He himself said, and he was very happy to say, with that generosity of his which politicians would do well to, but do not often, imitate, that whatever he did as chief justice was made possible by his great reliance on him whom he called his "lord chancellor," Mr. Justice Van Devanter.

Mr. Justice Van Devanter is a man who plays an important role in the history of the Court, though you cannot find it adequately reflected in the opinions written by him because he wrote so few. But Van Devanter was a man of great experience. He'd been chief justice of Wyoming. He was then made a United States circuit judge and in 1910 he became a member of the Supreme Court. He had a very clear, lucid mind, the mind, should I say, of a great architect. He was a beautiful draftsman and an inventor of legal techniques who did much to bring about the reforms which were effectively accomplished by Taft as chief justice.

Taft's great place in judicial history, I think, will be as a law reformer. In the characteristic way of this country, various federal judges throughout the country were entirely autonomous, little independent sovereigns. Every judge had his own little principality. He was the boss within his district, and his district was his only concern. A judge was a judge where he was, and although he may have had very little business, he couldn't be used in regions where the docket was congested. This, as you know, was changed, and the change has been highly beneficial.

An even more important reform for which Taft was effectively responsible was the legislation authorizing the Supreme Court to be master in its own household, which means that the business which comes to the Supreme Court is the business which the Supreme Court allows to come to it. Very few cases can come up without getting its prior permission. So that cases which never should take the time, energy, and thought of the ultimate tribunal in the land are allowed to rest, if they come from the federal courts, after those courts have had two go's at them, or, if the cases come from the state courts, after they have received the hierarchal adjudication provided by the state. No longer is it true, as it was before the legislation, that a case would come to the Supreme Court automatically after it had gone through, let us say, four other courts, as though having an endless litigation were one of the God-given rights of the American citizen.

So Chief Justice Taft has a place in history, in my judgment, next to Oliver Ellsworth, who originally devised the judicial system. Chief Justice Taft adapted it to the needs of a country that had grown from three million to a hundred and twenty million.

Taft was, of course, very genial. He did not have to learn to be genial. It is better to learn to be genial than not to be genial at all, but Taft was instinctively genial, with great warmth, and a capacity to inspire feelings of camaraderie about him. When he came to the chief justiceship in 1921, the papers had been full, as the papers are from time to time nowadays, of talk about the great divisions on the Court. Laymen are constantly troubled, even as are lawyers, especially when they lose a case, about divisions on the Court. But why should anyone expect nine men, presumably there because of their special capabilities, all to have the same thoughts and views? One would suppose that nine men are put there because you want variety of thought. No one expects such harmony and identity of views among physicists, let alone among professors of sociology or history. Why should they expect nine people to know how to apply in unison and in concord such delightfully vague phrases or concepts as "due process of law," phrases, as a great judge once said, of "calculated ambiguity"? To be sure, there can be no difference of opinion on the proposition that twelve is twelve; and it is clear, therefore, that a jury must have twelve members under the federal system. But when it comes to things like, when does a state encroach upon the right of Congress to regulate commerce, or what kind of limitations may you put upon people who want to speak at Hyde Park, or in Union Square, or on the Lawn of the University of Virginia, that's a different story.

When Taft became chief justice there had been this succession of great divisions on the Court—serious divisions on very serious matters. And every once in a while there were five-to-four decisions. Just as the newspapers do not print, "Mr. and Mrs. Jones have been happily married for fifteen years this day," but would print somewhere in the paper that Mr. and Mrs. Jones are getting a divorce, so the newspapers do not often publicize the cases in which the Court is unanimous. I can assure you that there are a great many such—most of them, in fact. What captures the headlines are the divisions: "The Supreme Court divides on minimum wages. The Supreme Court divides on child labor. The Supreme Court divides on this and that."

The appointment of Taft gave rise to the hope that all this would end. "He's such a charming man, don't you know?" I like to recall a newspaper editorial printed when Mr. Taft was appointed chief justice in June 1921. The present New York *Herald Tribune,* the then New York *Tribune,* commented, as did every paper in the country, on what a delightful man William H. Taft was, how charming, how everybody liked him, and now there would be no more five-to-four opinions. I thought the *Tribune* put it best: "Mr. Taft has such tact and good humor, and has so unconquerable a spirit of fair play, that he is greatly beloved of his fellow citizens. These gifts and this character may not be the first ones sought for in a chief justice, but even the most eminent judges are none the worse for having them. With Justice Taft as a moderator"—now listen to this—"it is probable that not a few asperities that mar the harmony of the celestial chamber, the consulting room, not a few of those asperities will be softened and that not quite so often in the future will the court divide five and four."

I really think that's very funny. The assumption of this serious editorial writer that Taft, C.J., would just smile and then Holmes would say, "Aye, aye, sir," or Justice Van Devanter would say, "For ten years I've been disagreeing with Holmes, but now that you've smiled at both of us, why we just love each other." I suggest a subject for a paper by one of you students. I have never done it, but my impression is strong that a count would show more five-to-four decisions during Taft's time than during White's time, or certainly just as many. Life was very pleasant with Taft as chief justice, but judicial conflicts existed because the problems before the Court evoked them. As for asperities during the period between '21 and '30, when Taft left—I think the conference was just as lively a place. I was not there, but the sparks even carried outside of the conference room to singe the pages of the United States Reports.

Of course Taft knew the men on the Court well, and he found there two whom he had appointed. That did not prevent those two from disagreeing with him, I can assure you. One of the strongest and most memorable of the dissenting opinions against Taft was written by a man whom he had appointed. What judge would be worth his salt if it made any difference to him that the President who appointed him, whether he was on or off the Court, disagreed with him? What judge worth his salt would have his convictions influenced by whether the chief justice is a charming man and a delightful raconteur, or not? That isn't the nature of the enterprise.

In 1930 Taft became ill and retired. He always had the love and affection of his colleagues. He and Brandeis, when Taft was President, crossed swords very fiercely indeed; Brandeis was counsel in the famous Pinchot-Ballinger attack on the administration. But they became fast friends on the Court. One of the things that laymen, even lawyers, do not always understand is indicated by the question you hear so often: "Does a man become any different when he puts on a gown?" I say, "If he is any good, he does."

Taft was followed, of course, by Hughes. Now the last thing that Hughes ever expected to be after he left the Court in 1916 to run for the presidency (I have ventured to say in print that I believe this was the one act of his life which he regretted)—he later became secretary of state, then became a member of the World Court, and finally returned to the bar to, I suppose, as vast a practice as that of any man at the bar in our time, or at any time in the history of this country—the last thing Hughes expected to become was chief justice. He was, to Hoover's great surprise, subjected to severe attack when his name was sent in. He finally was confirmed, though it was a nip and tuck business. He took his seat at the center of the Court, with a mastery, I suspect, unparalleled in the history of the Court, a mastery that derived from his experience, as diversified, intense, and extensive, as any man ever brought to a seat on the Court, combined with a very powerful and acute mind that could mobilize these vast resources in the conduct of the business of the Court. There must be in this room lawyers who came before the Court when Chief Justice Hughes presided. To see him preside was like witnessing Toscanini lead an orchestra.

Aside from the power to assign the writing of opinions, which is his by custom, and of which I shall speak, a chief justice has no authority that any other member of the Court has not. That really is an institution in which every man is his own sovereign. The chief justice is *primus inter pares.* Somebody has to preside at a sitting of nine people, and he presides in court and at conference. But Chief Justice Hughes radiated authority, not through any other quality than the intrinsic moral power that was his. He was master of the business. He could disembowel a brief and a record. He had an extraordinary memory and vast experience in the conduct of litigation, and of course he had been on the Court six years, from 1910 to 1916. And he had intimate and warm relations with some of the men he found on the Court. He was a great admirer of that greatest intellect, in my judgment, who ever sat on the Court, Mr. Justice Holmes. He was an old friend at the bar of Mr. Justice Brandeis. He had been one year in the cabinet with Stone. So he not only felt at home in the courtroom, he felt at home with his colleagues.

I have often used a word which for me best expresses the atmosphere that Hughes generated; it was taut. Everything was taut. He infected and affected counsel that way. Everybody was better because of Hughes, the leader of the orchestra. That was true, too, of Cardozo, when he was chief judge of the New York Court of Appeals. One is told that the same men were somehow or other better when he was chief judge than they were the next day after he had ceased to be chief judge. That is a common experience in life. One man is able to bring things out of you that are there, if they are evoked, if they are sufficiently stimulated and directed. Chief Justice Hughes had that very great quality.

Chief Justice Stone is the antithesis, in the fate that was allotted to him, of Marshall and Taney and Fuller. If you're chief justice for only five years, as Stone was, even though you come to the chief justiceship after having been an associate, the opportunities to realize on the moral opportunities that place gives you are necessarily very limited. Time plays a very important part. Stone came to the head of the Court in 1941. He had been an associate justice since 1925. Before that he had been a professor of law and dean of a law school, an extensive practitioner in New York, and then attorney general of the United States. He was familiar with the business of the Court. He was a very different personality from Hughes. Hughes was dynamic and efficient. That's a bad word to apply to Hughes, because it implies regimentation. It implies something disagreeable, at least to me. I don't like a man to be too efficient. He's likely to be not human enough. But that wasn't true of Hughes. He simply was effective—not efficient, but effective. Stone was much more easygoing. The conference was more leisurely. The atmosphere was less taut, both in the courtroom and the conference room. It has been said that there wasn't free and easy talk in Hughes's day in the conference room. Nothing could be further from the truth. There was less wasteful talk. There was less talk that was repetitious, or indeed foolish. You just didn't talk unless you were dead sure of your ground, because that gimlet mind of his was there ahead of you.

Stone was an "easy boss," as it were. Boss is the worst word to use with reference to a chief justice of the United States, because that's precisely what he is not. Anybody who tried it would not try it long. There is one function, however, that the chief justice has by virtue of being chief justice, other than being the administrator, presiding in open court, presiding at conference and there opening the discussion on each case. That other function is, I believe, the most important of all that pertains to the office of chief justice. I know not how it is in the Supreme Court of Appeals of Virginia. The method of designating the member of the court who writes the opinion for the court varies in the various state courts. In New York, for instance, it goes by rotation. That's a practice very common in this country. Even when it goes that way, a great man can make a dent on the accidental system by which cases come to him. They used to say in New York, until they knew better, "Why is it that Cardozo always gets the interesting cases?" The answer was that no matter what case he got, he made it interesting; he didn't "get" it—it came to him in automatic order. I believe it is a fact, though it is so strange a fact that I shall not identify the state, but I am assured on dependable authority that in the Supreme Court of at least one of our states, and not the least populous of states, they shake dice to determine who should write an opinion. Having it go in order lacks, for my taste at least, that aleatory aspect that dice have.

From Marshall's time in the Supreme Court the chief justice has designated the member of the Court who writes the opinion of the Court. As most of you know, we hear argument five days a week and on Saturday there is a conference. After everybody has had his say, beginning with the chief justice and following in order of seniority—and everybody can say whatever he wants to say—there is a formal vote. In order that the junior should not be influenced, everybody having already expressed his view, the formal voting begins with the junior. (How careful we are not to coerce anybody!) After conference, in cases in which the chief justice is with the majority, as he is in most instances, he designates the member of the Court who is to write the opinion. If he is in the minority, then the next senior justice of those in the majority does the assigning. So that in most of the cases the chief justice decides who is to speak for the Court. As for dissents and concurrences—that's for each member to choose for himself.

You can see the important function that rests with the chief justice in determining who should be the spokesman of the Court in expressing the decision reached. The manner in which a case is stated, the grounds on which a decision is rested—one ground rather than another, or one ground rather than two grounds—how much is said and how it is said, what kind of phrasing will give least trouble in the future in a system of law in which as far as possible you are to decide the concrete issue and not embarrass the future too much—all these things matter a great deal. The deployment of his judicial force by the chief justice is his single most influential function. Some do it with ease. Some do it with great anguish. Some do it with great wisdom. Some have done it with less than great wisdom.

No chief justice, I believe, equaled Chief Justice Hughes in the skill and the wisdom and the disinterestedness with which he made his assignments. Some cases are more interesting than others, and it is the prerogative of the chief justice not only to be kindly and fair and generous in the distribution of cases, but also to appear to be so. The task calls for qualities of tact, understanding, and skill in the effective utilization of the particular qualities that are available. Should one man become a specialist in a subject? Or is it important not to place too much reliance on one man because he's a great authority in the field? Should you pick the man who will write the opinion in the narrowest possible way? Or should you take the chance of putting a few seeds in the earth for future flowering? Those are all very difficult, delicate, and responsible questions.

I must conclude this discursive narrative—this almost absurd attempt, in a short talk, to give you some sense of five men who have been at the head of a Court on which ultimately rests the maintenance of the equilibrium between central authority and the constituent states, between the authority of government, whether state or national, and the liberties of the individual.

As I said earlier, when you deal with such few instances, you do not have a statistical basis for generalization. If I wanted to be a little playful, I might say I leave generalizations to political scientists who sometimes think that the crude details are not worthy of high philosophical attention. I hope I have indicated enough, however, to disclose that in view of the functions of the Supreme Court what you want in a justice is not a specialist in this or that field, not necessarily a man who has had prior experience on the bench, not necessarily a man who has been broadened by high office, as was the case with Hughes, rather than broadened by the depth and range of his reading and his thinking, as in the case of Mr. Justice Holmes.

What is essential for the discharge of functions that are almost too much, I think, for any nine mortal men, but have to be discharged by nine fallible creatures, is that you get men who bring to their task, first and foremost, humility and an understanding of the range of the problems and of their own inadequacy in dealing with them, disinterestedness, and allegiance to nothing except the effort, amid tangled words and limited insights, to find the path through precedent, through policy, through history, to the best judgment that fallible creatures can reach in that most difficult of all tasks: the achievement of justice between man and man, between man and state, through reason called law.

Trouble with the Volstead Act*

JOHN C. KNOX

Elsewhere in this volume judges are talked about; here a judge tells part of his own story. John C. Knox was born in Pennsylvania in 1881, educated at Waynesburg and the University of Pennsylvania, and admitted to the bar in 1904. For eight years he was with the legal department of the Title Guarantee and Trust Company. From 1913 to 1918 he was an assistant United States attorney for the Southern District of New York. Since 1918 he has been Chief Judge of the United States District Court of New York. Recipient of honorary degrees and awards, Judge Knox has written A Judge Comes of Age, *from which what follows is taken;* Order in the Court, *and numerous articles.*

The episode which appears below is preceded by an analysis of the phenomenon of national prohibition, a brief history of laws on liquor, and a description of the Volstead Era. As Judge Knox takes up the tale, courts have crowded dockets, and enforcement is breaking down.

I personally, was in favor of giving prohibition a trial, but as a judge that had no effect on me. My decisions were—to the best of my ability—based upon the law and the evidence. It was the same with all the judges that I knew. We heard such cases and fined and sentenced such offenders until we were sick of them. On one day I heard twenty-one cases in an hour and ten minutes—sentenced nineteen defendants—and was forced to delay my opinions on two. Is it any wonder that I constantly hoped that the *next* person to come before me would be a mail robber or a counterfeiter—anything but another bootlegger in that endless, endless list?

Of all the thousands of such cases that I handled only a few are worth telling about now. One—the account of the rum runner *Javary*—was the first important prohibition case that came to me, and was the first rum-running case to be tried in New York.

In November, 1920, Daniel Docherty purchased the S.S. *Javary* in Baltimore. Early in December the ship sailed with a cargo of sugar and flour consigned to Europe. Also on board were 250 drums of 180-proof alcohol which was being shipped under a government permit to Constantinople.

* From A Judge Comes of Age, by John C. Knox, copyright, 1940, by Charles Scribner's Sons. Reprinted by permission of the publisher.

Leaving Baltimore, the *Javary* put into New York on December 4, ostensibly to obtain fuel oil for the voyage. At first no suspicion was aroused, but a guard on the pier finally reported that he had been offered a bribe of $1,000. Agents were sent aboard in order to inspect the seals placed on the alcohol shipment. They were found intact, but nearly 4,000 gallons of the alcohol had nevertheless disappeared. By means of a syphon, the alcohol had been piped to some "fuel oil barrels" on the pier.

Docherty, the captain and part owner, was indicted on three counts under the Volstead Act and one under the criminal code, and the case came before me. Palmer Canfield, Assistant U.S. Attorney, prosecuted the case, and William J. Fallon, of some of whose activities I shall later have occasion to tell, appeared for the defense.

The prosecution was able. Nevertheless, even that early in the attempted enforcement of the Volstead Act the newspapers commented on what they took to be "hesitation" on the part of the jury to convict under the prohibition law. It is true that in this case the jury held Docherty not guilty on the three counts under the Volstead Act. He was convicted only of the remaining charge, and I sentenced him to the penitentiary for a year and a day. Nevertheless, it seemed to me that jurors, even when they were personally opposed to the prohibition law, were inclined to bring in verdicts based upon the evidence. I know that many juries whose members objected to the law brought in verdicts of guilty when the evidence was strong and well presented. There seemed to be a wide understanding among them that repeal should be advocated by other methods than those of nullification.

It was in 1922 that the first "big" bootlegger came before me. Anthony Cassese was a tobacco merchant in a small town on Long Island. Such a business, it would seem, could hardly be sufficiently profitable to permit its owner to own and operate a seagoing yacht, yet Cassese had one.

At Bayville, Long Island, upon the completion of a voyage to the Bahamas, this yacht was found to contain 12,000 bottles of rye whiskey—about $60,000 worth at bootleg prices. Other evidence connecting Cassese with bootlegging included two drafts totaling $90,000. Obviously Cassese's bootlegging had, in a little over two years, grown to large proportions.

Every member of the jury favored the modification of the Volstead Act, yet they brought in a verdict of guilty in less than half an hour. The result was that Cassese went to Atlanta for two years and paid a fine of $10,000.

A case enormously more important and greatly more interesting than those dealing with bootleggers and rum runners dealt with the restriction that had been placed on physicians in prescribing liquor for their patients.

In asking for the injunction Doctor Lambert declared that there were many patients whose treatment demanded a more or less constant use of stimulants. The law permitted only one pint in ten days for each patient, and limited each medical practioner to one hundred such prescriptions for three months. Joseph S. Auerbach, of the firm of Davies, Auerbach and

Cornell, represented Doctor Lambert, and assistant U.S. Attorney John Holley Clark appeared for the government.

The plaintiff contended that, in effect, the law made Congress practitioners of medicine in that, by limiting the prescription of liquor, it presumed to determine just how much a sufferer from any disease might require.

It was on this point that I based my decision.

"The Eighteenth Amendment," I wrote, "was designed to bring about prohibition of intoxicating liquor 'for beverage purposes' and was not, I think, intended to end the use of liquor for purposes regarded by those who proposed the amendment, and by many of the States that ratified it, as justifiable and proper."

I pointed out, too, that the use of alcohol in sacramental wines, in hospitals, and in the arts and sciences was sanctioned by Congress in enacting the Volstead Act. I quoted from a report of the Senate Judiciary Committee in which, discussing the amendment prior to its submission to the states, it was expressly stated that "alcohol would still be manufactured, distributed and sold under restrictions . . . and its use as a medicine and in the arts would not be interfered with."

I ended my opinion as follows:

"I have reached the conclusion that the limitations of the Volstead Act and its amendments, which make it lawful to prescribe but one pint of intoxicating liquor for internal and medicinal use of a person, who if he is to be properly treated, requires the administration of a greater quantity, are void.

"An injunction *pendente lite* may issue against the defendants."

The reaction to this decision was extraordinary. Scores of editorials were written—cartoons were drawn—jokes were sprung—humorous verse appeared. Will Rogers, in his then highly popular column, had this to say:

"According to the Volstead law as passed by Congress, no patient is allowed to get sick over a pint's worth every ten days. So along comes this judge and says 'Congress is no doctor' (They are all patients). How do they know how sick a man can get? Why for a pint every ten days a man would really not be sick at all; he would just be indisposed. . . ."

For the most part, the reaction was favorable, but opinion was not unanimous. Andrew W. Mellon, who as Secretary of the Treasury played an important part in the enforcement of the law, promptly set about liberalizing the rules. Prohibition Enforcement Commissioner Haynes, on the other hand, favored enforcing the law as it stood. One headline in *The New York World* read "Judge Knox's Liquor Ruling Splits Capital."

Discussion of the subject grew heated enough, and the Department of Justice decided to appeal. First I was reversed by the Circuit Court of Appeals, and after that decision the case was taken to the Supreme Court. Months passed before the ultimate decision was announced. When the news came, the reversal by the Circuit Court of Appeals was upheld on the ground that limitation of the amount of liquor which could be prescribed for medicinal purposes was a provision adopted to promote the purpose of the Eighteenth Amendment.

Still, it was a five to four decision, and Justice Sutherland read a dissenting opinion, in which he was joined by Justices McReynolds, Butler and Stone.

As time passed, bootlegging became more and more a brutalizing activity. So great were the rewards, and so low were many of those engaged, that torture, mayhem and murder came to play an ever increasing part. Bribery, too, was rampant. Police protection was common. No other law ever bred a greater series of crimes or greater hordes of criminals. . . .

In court . . . an occasional case humorously interrupted the monotony of greed and villainy. On one occasion I had grown even more than usually tired of the endless repetition of petty bootlegging stories with the essential details of which I was already so discouragingly familiar. All morning I had been sentencing men to jail for the maintenance of illicit stills and for the possession of untaxed alcohol. I wished for a change of scene. It would have been a relief if the next defendant should have proved to be almost any kind of a scoundrel if only alcohol could be eliminated.

The court clerk, picking up the next indictment, turned toward a colored man.

"William Atkins," droned the clerk, "how do you plead in this indictment that charges you with maintaining an unregistered still, guilty or not guilty?"

"Not guilty, suh, with an explanation," replied the Negro.

Here, at least, was a slight change.

"Well," I said, "go ahead. What is the explanation?"

"Why, yo' Honor," he began. "You see it was this way. This heah mornin' it was awful cold, an' I wasn't workin', so I thought I'd go over t' see my friend Tom Battle. He's got steam heat, an' I aint.

"He takes me in the kitchen, where he got two rockin' chairs, an' he gives me a cigarette. 'N' then I sees a funny-lookin' contraption on the stove.

"'Tom,' I says, 'what's that?'

"'That's a still,' he says. 'I's cookin' a little alcohol. How'd you like a drink?'

"An' he gives me one, an' after while he gives me a couple more. An' it was nice an' warm in the kitchen and I goes t' sleep. An' I didn't wake up 'till these yere gov'ment men is poundin' on the door, an' Tom he's gone. An' here I is. That's all, yo' Honor."

"Well," I told him, "if that's all there is to the story you are guilty of no offense against the government. You should enter a plea of 'not guilty' and go to trial."

"'Deed, yo' Honor," he objected. "I ain't got no lawyer, an' I don't think I wants a trial."

I told him that I would assign a lawyer.

"Thanks, yo' Honor. Thank yuh," he replied. "But I think I'd rather take my chances with yo' Honor."

"But," I told him, "upon your statement I can't sentence you. You'll have to go to trial."

"No, no, yo' Honor," he insisted, "I don't want to put you to no trouble, but *you* take my case, yo' Honor."

I grew a bit peremptory, and told him he'd have to make up his mind whether he was guilty or not guilty.

He shook his head.

"That's turbil hard question to answer, yo' Honor," he told me. "Turbil hard. I don't know which answer will do me the most good."

The spectators laughed and I did, too. Then I leaned over the bench toward him.

"Come, now, Atkins," I told him. "We're wasting time. Please tell me the truth. Are you guilty or not guilty?"

His brow wrinkled and he shook his head.

"I's guilty, yo' Honor," he admitted.

Many of those who came into contact with bootleggers and rum runners were contaminated quickly enough, but it was interesting to me to see how very few of the lawyers who represented them ever came under their influence or failed to conduct themselves on any but a high plane. From time to time some of New York's best lawyers represented bootleggers before me. George Gordon Battle, for instance, represented Anthony Cassese, and a number of younger lawyers, some of whom had previously been in the U.S. Attorney's office, had such clients. John M. Cashin, now Corporation Counsel of Kingston, N.Y., was one. M. Michael Edelstein, who is now in Congress, was another. Edward J. McDonald, Sanford H. Cohen, and many more had such clients from time to time yet retained their sanity and conducted themselves as proper lawyers should.

Here and there, of course, some member of the bar was overwhelmed by the "easy money," but such individuals were few.

Nor could I bring myself to overlook the fact that many a weak character got into the bootlegging game more by accident or force of circumstances than by design. One Negro, for instance, from Hell's Kitchen which, to say the least, is one of New York's less favored districts, was brought in for running a still.

He and his wife and children were new to New York, and were living in abject poverty. He was an unfortunately inefficient fellow, who could not get work or hold a job amid the competition of New York. Faced with starvation, it may be that he had done almost the only thing that he *could* do.

"Where are you from?" I asked.

"South Ca'lina," he replied, dejectedly.

"How long have you been here?"

" 'Bout a yeah."

"Have you had a hard time?"

"Pretty hahd, yes, suh."

"Have you any relatives down South?"

"Yes, suh. There's mah aunt."

"Where does she live?"

" 'Bout six miles from Beaufort."

"Has she any property?"

"Yes, suh. She got fo'ty acres."

"Cotton?"

"Yes, suh."

"The cotton bolls are opening about now, aren't they?"

"Yes, suh. They'll be pickin' pretty soon."

"Who helps your aunt?"

"She got a boy 'bout fifteen. They does all th' work."

"How would she like it if you went down and helped her?"

The man's head lifted suddenly and he looked me in the eye for the first time.

"My God, Judge," he cried. "Are you goin' t' give me a break?"

His wife was in the courtroom and I had her called to the bench.

"We's poor, yo' Honor," she told me. "But we kin eat down yonder. Cain't always do that up here."

So I "sentenced" him.

"I've arranged with the Probation Officer," I told him, "to get you tickets on the bus. But when you get to South Carolina you are to report to the Probation Officer there."

"Yes, suh, yo' Honor."

"And you are never to come back to New York," I told him. "Do you understand?"

"Honest t' God, Judge," he told me seriously. "If ever I sees New York even on a road map, I's just goin' t' overlook it."

So constant were the newspaper accounts of these trials during the era of prohibition, and so rare are the reports now, that it may come as a surprise to learn that six years after the repeal of the Prohibition Amendment, the U.S. Attorney's office for the Southern District of New York obtained the largest indictment against a ring of bootleggers ever filed up to that time in the United States. It took nine months to investigate the case. It took six weeks to try it. The case was a record breaker in many ways, perhaps the most important being that it was the first time any bootleg ring indictment in this district had named as defendants not only the bootleggers, but also the distillers, distributors, truckmen, retailers, large customers, and Federal and local police grafters. All these were accused in the powerful Pelligrino-Lapadura alcohol ring which was credited with depriving the state and federal governments of huge sums in taxes during the period of its existence.

Altogether there were 106 defendants, so it can readily be seen that the story cannot be told in any detail here. So detailed, too, was the evidence that had been obtained by the U.S. Attorney's office that fifty of these men entered pleas of guilty and thirty-four more were convicted. The fines alone amounted to $41,450 which, I have been told, sets an all-time record for collections in alcohol cases.

The case had in it just about all the color and drama that the most lurid fictioneer would require for a bootleg-G-man thriller, even down to a vicious assault just outside the courtroom, upon one man who had turned State's evidence. Yet to me, the high spot in the whole sordid story of strong-armed men, conspiracy, bribery and crime was the evidence given by as rotund, cherubic, soft-voiced, and lisping a Negro as ever appeared in a courtroom.

Realizing that the evidence against him was entirely overwhelming, this person had entered a plea of guilty and was testifying against his erstwhile associates.

Upon direct examination, and in response to the questions of the prosecutor, he had named names, given dates, identified defendants, and explained circumstances in the most deadly and effective manner. In fact, so complete and so convincing was his testimony that he became the star of the proceedings.

Finally, when all this devastating information had been spread upon the record, Mahlon Dickerson, an exceedingly able prosecutor, turned him over to the lawyer for the defense.

Immediately the attorney was on his feet. Hoping, apparently, to frighten the witness he assumed a menacing manner and shouted his questions in a stentorian voice.

"You admit, don't you," he roared, "that you are guilty of the offense charged against you?"

The Negro's manner did not change in the slightest. He replied in the gentlest rustle of a lisp.

"Yes, suh."

Already the contrast was becoming humorous, and the lawyer tried still harder to discredit the witness.

"For what," he shouted, "were you arrested the first time?"

The witness still answered gently.

"Possession of burglar's tools."

"And what did you get for that?" demanded the lawyer.

The lisp became more noticeable.

"Suspended sentence."

There were a few controlled smiles in the courtroom now, and the lawyer tried even harder.

"For what were you arrested the second time?" he yelled.

The witness almost smiled.

"Liquor," he replied gently.

"What did you get for that?" shouted the lawyer.

"Sixty days," came the slow lisp.

Far from satisfied, the lawyer tried again.

"For what were you arrested the third time?" he shouted.

"Liquor," came the soft response.

"And what did you get for that?" roared the lawyer.

Apparently undisturbed, the Negro looked up.

"Why suh," he replied in a voice so soft as hardly to reach the bench, "that theah is *this* time, an' I ain't been sentenced yet."

At this a juror laughed openly and several others followed. Some of them smiled and nodded to each other. But the attorney, certain now that he had as yet failed to create the impression for which he had hoped, decided to make one more effort. It seemed to me that I saw certain signs of desperation. The lawyer pointed dramatically at the Negro.

"For what else have you been arrested?" he demanded.

"Well, suh," came the soft reply. "Theah's nothin' Ah kin recollect."

"Do you mean that?" shouted the lawyer.

"Yes, suh. Ah means whatevah Ah says, suh."

With a solemn manner and a deep voice the lawyer offered another question.

"Do you mean to tell this Court and jury that you were not arrested for rape?"

The witness's face lighted up.

"Oh, yes, suh," he smiled. "Ah clean forgot 'bout dat. It jes' slipped mah mind."

"And what did you get for that?" shrieked the lawyer.

I listened intently for the answer, and so, I am sure, did every juror. Yet the Negro's manner did not change an iota, and his voice, if anything, grew still softer.

"Married," he replied.

The jury laughed. The courtroom roared. I laughed too. In that whole court, only the lawyer and some of his clients failed to see the joke.

Later, policemen, Internal Revenue Agents, Italians, Russians, Hebrews and Negroes were convicted—more than thirty of them. Yet of all the witnesses whose evidence led to that result, the lisping Negro from Harlem certainly led all the rest.

The Future of Wisdom in America*

LEARNED HAND

Many lawyers and judges are well read; some go farther: they write. Such a man is Judge Learned Hand, whose collected essays under the title Spirit of Liberty *appeared in 1952. Judge Hand was born in Albany in 1872, educated at Harvard, and called to the bar in New York in 1897. He turned from private practice to become, from 1909 to 1924, United States District Judge for the Southern District, New York, and finally Judge in the Second Circuit Court in New York (from 1924 to his retirement in 1951), where he wrote his celebrated opinion maintaining the conviction of eleven prominent Communists. His personality and ability made him for many years the people's candidate for the Supreme Court.*

The following eloquent appeal for more knowledge of the humanities in high places and stout attack on the fears of the day is based on an address made by Judge Hand to the Board of Regents of the State of New York.

M ost parts of the Constitution are specific enough to be treated like other legal commands; when we have to decide their meaning, we can proceed just as in the case of a dispute over the meaning of a statute; we look to their history and their setting with confidence that these will disclose their purpose. And that also applies to a large part of the amendments themselves. For instance, no general cultural background is needed to reach a right opinion as to whether a statute has infringed the provision that the accused must be tried in the district where the crime was committed, or that he must be "confronted" by "the witnesses against him."

But the situation is quite different when we are dealing with the broad clauses on which the conduct of a free society must in the end depend. What is "freedom of speech and of the press"; what is the "establishment of religion and the free exercise thereof"; what are "unreasonable searches," "due process of law," and "equal protection of the law"? All these are left wholly undefined and cannot be effectively determined without some acquaintance with what men in the past have thought and felt to be their most precious interests. Indeed, these fundamental canons are not jural concepts at all, in the ordinary sense; and in application they turn out to be no more

* This essay is reprinted by permission of Judge Learned Hand and the *Saturday Review*.

than admonitions of moderation, as appears from the varying and contradictory interpretations that the judges themselves find it necessary to put upon them. Nor can we leave to courts the responsibility of construing and so of enforcing them, for the powers of courts are too limited to reach the more controversial questions that arise under them.

For, as you know, courts will not intervene—or at least they constantly avow that they should not—unless the action challenged infringes the Constitution beyond any fair dispute. While there are any plausible arguments in support of a measure, they must abstain; and so it results that in much the larger part of such controversies it is the voters, speaking through their delegates, who have the final word and the final responsibility; and that in the end it is they, and they alone, who can and will preserve our liberties, if preserved they are to be. For their guidance there are no *vade mecums*, no handbooks, no manuals; they must depend upon such enlightenment as they can muster from within, and upon their conscience, so far as they have one. That enlightenment and that conscience they may indeed find in divine revelation; but when they do, they tap sources that I am not qualified to discuss; not any better qualified than I am to discuss what doctrines are inherent in the nature of man in society. I know of none of either sort, nor can I find direction from those who profess to know. It is because I am shorn of such resort that, to me at any rate, there appears to be no escape in each situation from balancing the conflicting interests at stake with as detached a temper as we can achieve.

A constitution, a statute, a regulation, a rule—in short, a "law" of any kind —is at once a prophecy and a choice. It is a prophecy, because it attempts to forecast what will be its effects; whom it will benefit and in what ways; on whom its impact will prove a burden; how much friction and discontent will arise from the adjustments that conformity to it will require; how completely it can be enforced; what enforcement will cost; how far it will interfere with other projects or existing activities; and, in general, the whole manifold of its indirect consequences. A thoroughgoing and dependable knowledge of these is obviously impossible. For example, although we can anticipate with some degree of assurance who will pay a steeply graded income tax and in what amounts, there is no way to tell what its indirect effects will be: what activities of the taxpayers in the higher brackets it will depress; if they do not work so hard, in what way they will occupy their newly acquired leisure; how any new activities they may substitute will affect others; whether this will be offset by a loss of the mellowed maturity and the wisdom of those who withdraw. Such prophecies infest law of every sort, the more deeply as it is far reaching; and it is an illusion to suppose that there are formulas or statistics that will help in making them. They can rest upon no more than enlightened guesses; but these are likely to be successful as they are made by those whose horizons have been widened, and whose outlook has been clarified, by knowledge of what men have striven to do, and how far their hopes and fears have been realized. There is no substitute for an open mind, enriched by reading and the arts.

So much for what I have called the element of prophecy; refractory as it is, at least it depends only upon facts, however inaccessible. There remains the much more difficult element of choice. In such inquiries, as I have said, I see no escape from a calculus of, and balance between, the group interests —that is, the desires and values—whose conflict the measure under consideration is an attempt to adjust. But desires and values are not quantitatively measureable, for they seldom have any common constituents, and without these they cannot be objectively compared. On the other hand, an individual has the necessary means in his own case, for, although his personal desires and values are absolute, irreducible, and undeducible, and have just that authority which he feels them to have, he has as authoritative a competence to compare them and to prefer one to another as he has to appraise them separately. Thus, although such preferences are themselves as final as the desires and values, it would be easy to choose between the desires and values of conflicting social groups, if we could safely impute to them our own preferences.

But by what right can we do so; and, if we cannot, what other means of vicarious choice have we? I submit that we have none except in so far as we can imaginatively project ourselves into the position of the groups between which we must choose. Surely I need not dilate upon how hard it is to do that. Even in our own affairs how often have we tried to anticipate how we shall feel on a future occasion, only to be surprised by the unexpected difference when it comes to pass. And if it is hard to foreshadow our own feelings, how much harder is it to do so for others. It is not enough to be personally detached, although that is of course a condition; we must also acquire a capacity for an informed sympathy with, and understanding of, the desires and the values of others; and that, I submit, only those have any chance of attaining whose experience is supplemented by some acquaintance, the wider the better, with what others have thought and felt in circumstances as near as possible to those of the groups in question.

I dare hope that it may now begin to be clearer why I am arguing that an education which includes the "humanities" is essential to political wisdom. By "humanities" I especially mean history; but close beside history and of almost, if not quite, equal importance are letters, poetry, philosophy, the plastic arts, and music. Most of the issues that mankind sets out to settle, it never does settle. They are not solved, because, as I have just tried to say, they are incapable of solution properly speaking, being concerned with incommensurables. At any rate, even if that be not always true, the opposing parties seldom do agree upon a solution; and the dispute fades into the past unsolved, though perhaps it may be renewed as history and fought over again. It disappears because it is replaced by some compromise that, although not wholly acceptable to either side, offers a tolerable substitute for victory; and he who would find the substitute needs an endowment as rich as possible in experience, an experience which makes the heart generous and provides his mind with an understanding of the hearts of others.

The great moderates of history were more often than not men of that sort, steeped like Montaigne and Erasmus in knowledge of the past. Let me quote from one of these, our own Franklin. After long, and at times bitter, controversy the final draft of the Constitution was accepted on Saturday, September 12, and was sent to be engrossed over the week end. Nevertheless, there was still doubt about what might happen on Monday when the delegates were to sign. On Sunday Franklin wrote out a statement which Wilson read for him the next day. It is too long to quote in extenso, but I cannot forbear a sentence or two, so appropriate is it to what I am trying to say: "I agree to this Constitution with all its faults, if they are such, because I think a general Government necessary for us and there is no form of Government but what may be a blessing to the people if well administered, and believe further that this is likely to be well administered for a course of years, and can only end in Despotism, as other forms have done before it, when the people shall have become so corrupted as to need despotic Government, being incapable of any other. I doubt too whether any other convention we can obtain may be able to make a better constitution. For when you assemble a number of men to have the advantage of their joint wisdom, you inevitably assemble with those men all their prejudices, their passions, their errors of opinion, their local interests, and their selfish views. From such an Assembly can a perfect production be expected? . . . Thus I consent, Sir, to this Constitution because I expect no better, and because I am not sure that it is not the best."

Out of such a temper alone can come any political success which will not leave behind rancor and vindictiveness that is likely so deeply to infect its benefits as to make victory not worth while, and it is a temper best bred in those who have at least what I like to call a bowing acquaintance with the "humanities." For these are fitted to admonish us how tentative and provisional are our attainments, intellectual and moral; and how often the deepest convictions of one generation are the rejects of the next. That does not indeed deny the possibility that, as time goes on, we shall accumulate some body of valid conclusions; but it does mean that these we can achieve only by accumulation; that wisdom is to be gained only as we stand upon the shoulders of those who have gone before. Just as in science we cannot advance except as we take over what we inherit, so in statecraft no generation can safely start at scratch. The subject matter of science is recorded observation of the external world; the subject matter of statecraft is the

soul of man, and of that too there are records—the records of which I refer
to here. The imagination can be purged and the judgment ripened only by
an awareness of the slow, hesitant, wayward course of human life, its failures, its successes, but its indomitable will to endure.

I cannot but think that we of this generation are politically in especial
need of such education. Our nation is embarked upon a venture, as yet
unproved; we have set our hopes upon a community in which men shall be
given unchecked control of their own lives. That community is in peril; it is
invaded from within, it is threatened from without; it faces a test which it
may fail to pass. The choice is ours whether, when we hear the pipes of Pan,
we shall stampede like a frightened flock, forgetting all those professions
on which we have claimed to rest our polity.

God knows there is risk in refusing to act till the facts are all in; but is
there not greater risk in abandoning the conditions of all rational inquiry?
Risk for risk, for myself I had rather take my chance that some traitors will
escape detection than spread abroad a spirit of general suspicion and distrust, which accepts rumor and gossip in place of undismayed and unintimi-
dated inquiry. I believe that that community is already in process of dissolution where each man begins to eye his neighbor as a possible enemy,
where nonconformity with the accepted creed, political as well as religious,
is a mark of disaffection; where denunciation, without specification or back-
ing, takes the place of evidence; where orthodoxy chokes freedom of dissent;
where faith in the eventual supremacy of reason has become so timid that
we dare not enter our convictions in the open lists to win or lose. Such
fears as these are a solvent which can eat out the cement that binds the
stones together; they may in the end subject us to a despotism as evil as
any that we dread; and they can be allayed only in so far as we refuse to
proceed on suspicion, and trust one another until we have tangible ground
for misgiving.

The mutual confidence on which all else depends can be maintained only
by an open mind and a brave reliance upon free discussion. I do not say
that these will suffice; who knows but we may be on a slope which leads
down to aboriginal savagery. But of this I am sure: if we are to escape,
we must not yield a foot upon demanding a fair field, and an honest race,
to all ideas. "Blame not before thou hast examined; understand first and
then rebuke. Answer not before thou hast heard; interrupt not in the midst
of speech." Those words were written nearly 2000 years ago; they came out
of an experience already long, and refined in the fires of passion and conflict; they are the product of a wisdom bought by ages of bitter trial; and
by that wisdom alone shall we be saved, we, who boast ourselves to be the
apostles of a faith in the eventual triumph of wisdom. Listen also to these
as ancient words that tell of the excellence of wisdom. "There is in her a
spirit quick of understanding, holy, alone in kind, manifold, subtil, freely
moving, clear in utterance, unpolluted, distinct, unharmed, loving what is

good, keen, unhindered, beneficent, loving toward man, steadfast, sure, free from care, all-powerful, all-surveying, and penetrating through all spirits that are quick of understanding, pure, most subtil. . . . And if a man longeth even for much experience, she knoweth the things of old, and divineth the things to come; she understandeth subtilties of speeches and interpretations of dark sayings; she forseeth signs and wonders, and the issues of seasons and times. I determined therefore to take her unto me to live with me, knowing that she is one who would give me good thoughts for counsel, and encourage me in cares and griefs. . . . For she knoweth all things and hath understanding thereof; and in my doings she shall guide me in the ways of soberness, and she shall guard me in her glory. And so shall my works be acceptable, and I shall judge the people righteously, and shall be worthy of my Father's throne."

Law and Literature*

BENJAMIN N. CARDOZO

Judge Benjamin N. Cardozo, like Judge Hand, has long been cited as a personal illustration of the happy relation between law and literature. The essay which follows lays down rules for judicial style and classifies by historical example the various styles of the past, from magisterial to tonsorial. Cardozo (1870–1938) was born in New York, educated at Columbia, and admitted to the bar in 1891. His career led to the New York Supreme Court, 1914–1928, the Court of Appeals and, in 1932, the Supreme Court of the United States, where he made a reputation for intellectual honesty and liberalism. He sometimes suggests Holmes in his rejection of tradition, and sometimes the great English judges by his interest in moral values and in literary style.

I am told at times by friends that a judicial opinion has no business to be literature. The idol must be ugly, or he may be taken for a common man. The deliverance that is to be accepted without demur or hesitation must have a certain high austerity which frowns at winning graces. I fancy that not a little of this criticism is founded in misconception of the true significance of literature, or, more accurately perhaps, of literary style. To some a clearer insight has been given. There are those who have perceived that the highest measure of condensation, of short and sharp and imperative directness, a directness that speaks the voice of some external and supreme authority, is consistent, none the less, with supreme literary excellence. A dictum of Henri Beyle's, recalled not long ago by Mr. Strachey, will point my meaning. The French novelist used to say that "there was only one example of the perfect style, and that was the Code Napoléon; for there alone everything was subordinated to the exact and complete expression of what was to be said." The poor man succumbed to its charm to such an extent that he was in the habit of reading a few paragraphs every morning before breakfast. I do not seek to substitute this regimen for the daily exercise in calisthenics. Some of us prefer our literature like our food in less concentrated tablets. I do no more than suggest that the morsel hastily gulped down may have a savor all its own for the discriminating palate.

* From *Law and Literature* by Benjamin N. Cardozo, copyright, 1931, by Harcourt, Brace and Company, Inc. Reprinted by permission of the publisher.

But I over-emphasize and exaggerate if I seem to paint the picture of any active opposition that is more than sporadic and exceptional to so amiable a weakness as a love of art and letters. A commoner attitude with lawyers is one, not of active opposition, but of amused or cynical indifference. We are merely wasting our time, so many will inform us, if we bother about form when only substance is important. I suppose this might be true if any one could tell us where substance ends and form begins. Philosophers have been trying for some thousands of years to draw the distinction between substance and mere appearance in the world of matter. I doubt whether they succeed better when they attempt a like distinction in the world of thought. Form is not something added to substance as a mere protuberant adornment. The two are fused into a unity. Not long ago I ran across a paragraph in the letters of Henry James in which he blurts out his impatience of these attempts to divide the indivisible. He is writing to Hugh Walpole, now a novelist of assured position, but then comparatively unknown. "Don't let any one persuade you—there are plenty of ignorant and fatuous duffers to try to do it—that strenuous selection and comparison are not the very essence of art, and that Form *is* not substance to that degree that there is absolutely no substance without it. Form alone *takes,* and holds and preserves substance, saves it from the welter of helpless verbiage that we swim in as in a sea of tasteless tepid pudding." This is my own faith. The argument strongly put is not the same as the argument put feebly any more than the "tasteless tepid pudding" is the same as the pudding served to us in triumph with all the glory of the lambent flame. The strength that is born of form and the feebleness that is born of the lack of form are in truth qualities of the substance. They are the tokens of the thing's identity. They make it what it is.

Up to this point at least, I have little fear of opposition. We shall, most of us, be agreed, I think, not merely that style is not an evil in the Sahara of a judicial opinion, but even that it is a positive good, if only it is the right style. *There* is the disquieting condition which checks the forward movement of triumphal demonstration. What is to be deemed the right style, or the right styles if there are more than one of them? Do the examples of the great masters reveal some uniformity of method for the instruction of the tyro? If uniformity is not discoverable, may there not at least be types or standards? If types or standards do not exist, shall we not find stimulus and interest in the coruscations of genius, however vagrant or irregular? If at times there is neither stimulus nor interest, may there not in lieu of these be the awful warning of example?

I suppose there can be little doubt that in matters of literary style the sovereign virtue for the judge is clearness. Judge Veeder in his interesting and scholarly essay, "A Century of Judicature," quotes the comment of Brougham upon the opinions of Lord Stowell: "If ever the praise of being luminous could be bestowed upon human compositions, it was upon his judgments." How shall his successors in the same or other courts attain that standard or approach it? There is an accuracy that defeats itself by the over-emphasis of details. I often say that one must permit oneself, and that quite advisedly and deliberately, a certain margin of misstatement. Of course, one must take heed that the margin is not exceeded, just as the physician must be cautious in administering the poisonous ingredient which magnified will kill, but in tiny quantities will cure. On the other hand, the sentence may be so overloaded with all its possible qualifications that it will tumble down of its own weight. "To philosophize," says Holmes in one of his opinions—I am quoting him from uncertain and perhaps inaccurate recollection—"to philosophize is to generalize, but to generalize is to omit." The picture cannot be painted if the significant and the insignificant are given equal prominence. One must know how to select. All these generalities are as easy as they are obvious, but, alas! the application is an ordeal to try the souls of men. Write an opinion, and read it a few years later when it is dissected in the briefs of counsel. You will learn for the first time the limitations of the power of speech, or, if not those of speech in general, at all events your own. All sorts of gaps and obstacles and impediments will obtrude themselves before your gaze, as pitilessly manifest as the hazards on a golf course. Sometimes you will know that the fault is truly yours, in which event you can only smite your breast, and pray for deliverance thereafter. Sometimes you will feel that the fault is with counsel who have stupidly misread the obvious, in which event, though you rail against the bar and the imperfect medium of speech, you will be solaced, even in your chagrin, by a sense of injured innocence. Sometimes, though rarely, you will believe that the misreading is less stupid than malicious, in which event you will be wise to keep your feelings to yourself. One marvels sometimes at the ingenuity with which texts the most remote are made to serve the ends of argument or parable. But clearness, though the sovereign quality, is not the only one to be pursued, and even if it were, may be gained through many avenues of approach. The opinion will need persuasive force, or the impressive virtue of sincerity and fire, or the mnemonic power of alliteration and antithesis, or the terseness and tang of the proverb and the maxim. Neglect the help of these allies, and it may never win its way. With traps and obstacles and hazards confronting us on every hand, only blindness or indifference will fail to turn in all humility, for guidance or for warning, to the study of examples.

Classification must be provisional, for forms run into one another. As I search the archives of my memory, I seem to discern six types or methods which divide themselves from one another with measurable distinctness. There is the type magisterial or imperative; the type laconic or sententious; the type conversational or homely; the type refined or artificial, smelling of the lamp, verging at times upon preciosity or euphuism; the type demonstrative or persuasive; and finally the type tonsorial or agglutinative, so called from the shears and the pastepot which are its implements and emblem.

I place first in order, for it is first in dignity and power, the type magisterial or imperative. It eschews ornament. It is meager in illustration and analogy. If it argues, it does so with the downward rush and overwhelming conviction of the syllogism, seldom with tentative gropings towards the inductive apprehension of a truth imperfectly discerned. We hear the voice of the law speaking by its consecrated ministers with the calmness and assurance that are born of a sense of mastery and power. Thus Marshall seemed to judge, and a hush falls upon us even now as we listen to his words. Those organ tones of his were meant to fill cathedrals or the most exalted of tribunals. The judicial department, he tells us, "has no will in any case. . . . Judicial power is never exercised for the purpose of giving effect to the will of the judge; always for the purpose of giving effect to the will of the legislature; or in other words, to the will of the law." The thrill is irresistible. We feel the mystery and the awe of inspired revelation. His greatest judgments are framed upon this plane of exaltation and aloofness. The movement from premise to conclusion is put before the observer as something more impersonal than the working of the individual mind. It is the inevitable progress of an inexorable force. Professor Corwin in an interesting volume, *John Marshall and the Constitution*, shows how even his contemporaries, the bitterest critics of his aggrandizement of federal power, were touched by this illusion. "All wrong, all wrong," lamented John Randolph of Roanoke, "but no man in the United States can tell why or wherein." I have reread a few of the most famous of his judgments: Marbury *vs.* Madison; Gibbons *vs.* Ogden; McCulloch *vs.* Maryland; they are all in the grand style.

Listen to the voice of the magistrate in Marbury *vs.* Madison: "The distinction between a government with limited and unlimited powers is abolished if those limits do not confine the persons on which they are imposed, and if acts prohibited and acts allowed are of equal obligation. It is a proposition too plain to be contested: that the Constitution controls any legislative act repugnant to it; or that the legislature may alter the Constitution by an ordinary act. Between these alternatives there is no middle ground. . . . If two laws conflict with each other, the courts must decide on the operation of each. So if a law be in opposition to the Constitution; if both the law and the Constitution apply to a particular case, so that the court must either decide that case conformably to the law, disregarding the Constitution, or conformably to the Constitution, disregarding the law, the court must determine which of these conflicting rules governs the case. This is of the very essence of judicial duty." Nothing is here of doubt; nothing of apology; no blurred edges or uncertain lines. "There is no middle ground." The choice that is made is "of the very essence of judicial duty." The voice has pealed forth. Let the wicked heed it and obey.

One will find this same suggestion of sure and calm conviction in some of the judgments of Lord Mansfield. The slave Somerset captured on the coast of Africa, is sold in bondage in Virginia, and brought to England by his master. The case comes before Mansfield on the return to the writ of habeas corpus: "The state of slavery is of such a nature that it is incapable of being introduced on any reasons, moral or political, but only positive law, which preserved its force long after the reasons, occasions, and time itself from whence it was created, are erased from memory. It is so odious that nothing can be suffered to support it, but positive law. . . . I care not for the supposed *dicta* of judges, however eminent, if they be contrary to all principle. The *dicta* cited were probably misunderstood, and at all events they are to be disregarded. Villainage, when it did exist in this country, differed in many particulars from West India slavery. The lord never could have thrown his villain, whether *regardant* or *in gross*, into chains, sent him to the West Indies, and sold him there to work in a mine or in a cane field. At any rate villainage has ceased in England, and it cannot be revived. The air of England has long been too pure for a slave, and every man is free who breathes it. Every man who comes into England is entitled to the protection of English law, whatever oppression he may heretofore have suffered, and whatever may be the color of his skin. '*Quamvis ille niger, quamvis tu candidus esses.*' Let the negro be discharged."

It is thus men speak when they are conscious of their power. One does not need to justify oneself if one is the mouthpiece of divinity. The style will fit the mood.

I have said that in dignity and power there is no method that can be matched with the method which I have characterized as magisterial or imperative. A changing philosophy of law has tended, none the less, to the use of other methods more conciliatory and modest. The development of law is conceived of, more and more, as a process of adaptation and adjustment. The pronouncements of its ministers are timid and tentative approximations, to be judged through their workings, by some pragmatic test of truth. I find in a dissenting opinion by Mr. Justice Brandeis a striking statement of this attitude of mind. Arguing for the restriction of a rule which had proved itself unworkable, he says: "Such limitations of principles previously announced and such express disapproval of *dicta* are often unnecessary. It is an unavoidable incident of the search by courts of last resort for the true rule. The process of inclusion and exclusion, so often applied in developing a rule, cannot end with its first enunciation. The rule as announced must be deemed tentative. For the many and varying facts to which it will be applied cannot be foreseen. Modification implies growth. It is the life of the law."

One cannot face the law in this spirit of cautious seeking without showing the changing point of view in a changing style and form. Universals will be handled more charily under the dominance of such a philosophy than in days when the law of nature supplied us with data that were supposed to be eternal and unyielding. Yet there are times even now when the magisterial method is utilized by men who know that they are masters of their calling. It is still utilized in fields where some established principle is to be applied to new facts or where the area of its extension or restriction is fairly obvious or narrow. But alas! even then it is the masters, and no others, who feel sure enough of themselves to omit the intermediate steps and stages, and leap to the conclusion. Most of us are so uncertain of our strength, so beset with doubts and difficulties, that we feel oppressed with the need of justifying every holding by analogies and precedents and an exposure of the reasons. The masters are content to say, "The elect will understand, there is no need to write for others." Perhaps there are opinions by Mr. Justice Holmes in which this mood can be discerned. The sluggard unable to keep pace with the swiftness of his thought will say that he is hard to follow. If that is so, it is only for the reason that he is walking with a giant's stride. But giants, after all, are not met at every turn, and for most of us, even if we are not pygmies, the gait of ordinary men is the safer manner of advance. We grope and feel our way. What we hand down in our judgments is an hypothesis. It is no longer a divine command.

I pass to other types which run into each other by imperceptible gradations, the laconic or sententious and the conversational or homely. There has been no stage of our legal history in which these methods have been neglected. The Year Books are full of wise saws and homely illustrations, the epigram, the quip, the jest. Perhaps this is but a phase of that use of the maxim or the proverb which is characteristic of legal systems in early stages of development. Dean Pound in a recent paper has traced the growth and function of the maxim with all the resources of his learning. If the maxim has declined in prevalence and importance, now that the truths of the law have become too complex to be forced within a sentence, there has been no abatement of recourse to the laconic or sententious phrase, to drive home and imbed what might otherwise be lost or scattered. Who will resist Lord Nottingham's adjuration: "Pray let us so resolve cases here, that they may stand with the reason of mankind when they are debated abroad"? Is there any armor proof against a thrust like the dictum of Lord Bowen's: "The state of a man's mind is as much a fact as the state of his digestion"? Next door to the epigram is the homely illustration which makes its way and sinks deep by its appeal to everyday experience. In the wielding of these weapons, the English judges have been masters. The precept may be doubtful in the beginning. How impossible to fight against it when the judge brings it down to earth and makes it walk the ground, the brother of some dictate of decency or of prudence which we have followed all our lives. Perhaps the kinship is not so close or apparent as it is figured. Who of us will have the hardihood to doubt the reality of the tie when it is so blandly assumed to be obvious to all? The common denominator silences and satisfies. The rule that is rooted in identities or analogies of customary belief and practice is felt and rightly felt to be rooted in reality. We glide into acquiescence when negation seems to question our kinship with the crowd. Something must be set down also to the sense of fellowship awakened when judges talk in ways that seem to make us partners in the deliberative process. "I entirely agree with my right honorable and learned friend upon the woolsack." We seem to be let into the mysteries of the conference, the sacrosanct "arcana," to quote Professor Powell's phrase, to which "the uninitiated are not admitted." Given such an atmosphere, with point and pungency thrown into it, the product makes its way into every crack and crevice of our being.

I limit my illustrations, though many are available. Take this by Lord Bramwell: "It does not follow that if a man dies in a fit in a railway carriage, there is a *prima facie* case for his widow and children, nor that if he has a glass in his pocket and sits on it and hurts himself, there is something which calls for an answer or explanation from the company." Take this by Lord Blackburn: "If with intent to lead the plaintiff to act upon it, they put forth a statement which they know may bear two meanings, one of which is false to their knowledge, and thereby the plaintiff, putting that meaning upon it, is misled, I do not think they can escape by saying he ought to have put the other. If they palter with him, in a double sense, it may be that they lie like truth, but I think they lie, and it is a fraud." One could cite other examples without number. What a cobweb of fine-spun casuistry is dissipated in a breath by the simple statement of Lord Esher in *Ex parte* Simonds, that the court will not suffer its own officer "to do a shabby thing." If the word shabby had been left out, and unworthy or dishonorable substituted, I suppose the sense would have been much the same. But what a drop in emotional value would have followed. As it is, we feel the tingle of the hot blood of resentment mounting to our cheeks. For quotable good things, for pregnant aphorisms, for touchstones of ready application, the opinions of the English judges are a mine of instruction and a treasury of joy.

Such qualities on the whole are rarer close at home, yet we have one judge even now who can vie with the best of his English brethren, past as well as present, in the art of packing within a sentence the phosphorescence of a page. If I begin to quote from the opinions of Mr. Justice Holmes, I hardly know where I shall end, yet fealty to a master makes me reluctant to hold back. The sheaf will be a tiny one, made up haphazard, the barest sample of the riches which the gleaner may gather where he will. Some hint of the epigrammatic quality of his style may be found in this: "The Fourteenth Amendment, itself a historical product, did not destroy history for the States and substitute mechanical compartments of law all exactly alike." In this: "We are in danger of forgetting that a strong public desire to improve the public condition is not enough to warrant achieving the desire by a shorter cut than the constitutional way of paying for the change." In this: "Legal obligations that exist but cannot be enforced are ghosts that are seen in the law but that are elusive to the grasp." And finally in this, words of solemn dissent, their impressiveness heightened by the knowledge that the cause has been already lost: "Persecution for the expression of opinions seems to me perfectly logical. If you have no doubt of your premises or your power and want a certain result with all your heart you naturally express your wishes in law and sweep away all opposition. To allow opposition by speech seems to indicate that you think the speech impotent, as when a man says that he has squared the circle, or that you do not care whole-heartedly for the result, or that you doubt either your power or your premises. But when men have realized that time has upset many fighting faiths, they may come to believe even more than they believe the very foundations of their own conduct that the ultimate good desired is better reached by free trade in ideas—that the best test of truth is the power of the thought to get itself accepted in the competition of the market, and that truth is the only ground upon which their wishes safely can be carried out. That at any rate is the theory of our Constitution. It is an experiment, as all life is an experiment. Every year if not every day we have to wager our salvation upon some prophecy based upon imperfect knowledge. While that experiment is part of our system I think that we should be eternally vigilant against attempts to check the expression of opinions that we loathe and believe to be fraught with death, unless they so imminently threaten immediate interference with the lawful and pressing purposes of the law that an immediate check is required to save the country."

There is another type or method which I have spoken of as the refined or artificial, smelling a little of the lamp. With its merits it has its dangers, for unless well kept in hand, it verges at times upon preciosity and euphuism. Held in due restraint, it lends itself admirably to cases where there is need of delicate precision. I find no better organon where the subject matter of discussion is the construction of a will with all the filigree of tentacles, the shades and nuances of differences, the slender and fragile tracery that must be preserved unmutilated and distinct. Judge Finch of the Court of Appeals of New York was an adept in the writing of opinions which carried with them this suggestion of precision and refinement. Occasionally, it shades into a faint and gentle sarcasm which is sometimes the refuge of the spokesman of a minority expressing his dissent. As an illustration, let me quote from the dissenting opinion in an election controversy which provoked in its day no little warmth of difference. The majority had held that despite the provision of the Constitution making each house of the legislature the judge of the elections, returns, and qualifications of its own members, the courts would refuse affirmative aid to a claimant for such an office if it found him ineligible in its own view of the law. Judge Finch protested against this holding. "And so," he said, "I deny the asserted doctrine of 'Invocation'; of a right to do evil that good may come; of excusable judicial usurpation; and if the doctrine has anywhere got its dangerous and destructive hold upon our law, which I do not believe, it should be resolutely shaken off. But let us not deceive ourselves. The excess of jurisdiction is not even excusable, for it has neither occasion nor necessity." A moment later, he has his fears that he has been betrayed into excessive warmth. His closing words are those of apology and deference: "If what I have said does not convince the majority of the court, nothing that I can say will do so. I have tried faithfully, and, I hope, with proper respect, for certainly I have not meant to be wanting in that, to point out the mistake which, it seems to me, they are about to make. Theirs, however, must be both the responsibility and its consequences."

Such a method has its charm and its attraction, though one feels at times the yearning for another more robust and virile. It is here that I pass into the type which I have characterized as demonstrative or persuasive. It is not unlike the magisterial or imperative, yet it differs in a certain amplitude of development, a freer use of the resources of illustration and analogy and history and precedent, in brief, a tone more suggestive of the scientific seeker for the truth and less reminiscent of the priestess on the tripod. One might cite many judges who have used this method with distinction. I think the work of Charles Andrews, for many years a judge and then the Chief Judge of the New York Court of Appeals, is a shining illustration. I can best describe the quality of his opinions in the words of a memorial written upon his death: "The majesty of his personal appearance," it was said, "is reflected in the majesty of his judicial style, the steady and stately march of his opinions from established premises to inevitable conclusions." Such a method, well pursued, has a sanity and a clarity that make it an admirable medium for the declaration of considered judgments. The form is no mere epidermis. It is the very bone and tissue.

My summary of styles may leave a cheerless impression of the solemn and the ponderous. Flashes of humor are not unknown, yet the form of opinion which aims at humor from beginning to end is a perilous adventure, which can be justified only by success, and even then is likely to find its critics almost as many as its eulogists. The story is told by Bernard Shaw of a man who wished to consult the writings of the great naturalist Buffon, and who startled the clerks in the bookstore by the pompous and solemn query, "Have you the books of the celebrated Buffoon?" One of the difficulties about the humorous opinion is exposure to the risk of passing from the class of Buffons where we all like to dwell and entering the class of the celebrated Buffoons. The transition at times is distressingly swift, and when once one has entered the new class, it is difficult, if not indeed impossible, to climb over the fences and back into the old. None the less, there are subjects which only the most resolute have been able to discuss without yielding to the temptation of making profert of their sense of humor. A dog or a cat, or a horse if it is the occasion of a horse trade, has been the signal for unexpected outbursts of mirth and occasionally of pathos from judges slowly stirred to emotion by the cinema of life.

Judge Allen's opinion on the "code duello" among dogs, was on the whole a fine success, but it has been responsible for the writing of some others that were not. There is an opinion by Baron Bramwell which deals with the propensities of pigs. A fence was defective, and the pigs straying did mischief to a trolley car. The decision was that the barrier should have been sufficient to protect the adjoining owner against the incursions, not of all pigs, but of pigs of "average vigour and obstinacy." "Nor do we lay down," said the learned Baron, "that there must be a fence so close and strong that no pig could push through it, or so high that no horse or bullock could leap it. One could scarcely tell the limits of such a requirement, for the strength of swine is such that they would break through almost any fence, if there were a sufficient inducement on the other side. But the company are bound to put up such a fence that a pig not of a peculiarly wandering disposition, nor under any excessive temptation, will not get through it." Perhaps the humor of this ruling was more unwitting than designed. Some may agree with Sir Frederick Pollock that the decision is "almost a caricature of the general idea of the 'reasonable man.' " In all this I would not convey the thought that an opinion is the worst for being lightened by a smile. I am merely preaching caution. Other flights and digressions I find yet more doubtful than the humorous. In days not far remote, judges were not unwilling to embellish their deliverances with quotations from the poets. I shall observe towards such a practice the tone of decent civility that is due to those departed.

I have had in mind in this excursus a humor that was conscious and intended. Perhaps I should have classed the opinion that is humorous or playful as an independent type, but I have preferred to treat it incidentally since I am not aware that any judge has employed it consistently or except on rare occasions. Humor also that is unconscious and unintended may be dug out of the reports if we take the trouble to extract it. I once gathered together for my own edification and amusement some gems that I had unearthed from the opinions of one of our local courts in days when it had an appellate branch of its own and handed down opinions which were faithfully reported. Unluckily, I have lost my memorandum, but a few of the items are still vivid in my mind. The question to be determined was the extent of the amendment of a pleading to be permitted upon the trial. The decisive principle was thus expounded: "The bed that litigants make and lie in up to the trial, should not be then vacated by them. They should continue to lie therein until the jury render their verdict." I understand that the modern Practice Acts have swept this principle away, and that the suitor, who seems to his adversary to be innocently somnolent, may now jump out of bed at the last moment and prove to be very much awake. This is the new doctrine, but where will you find a more vivid statement of the doctrine of an elder day which decried surprise and haste, and was satisfied that justice herself should have the privilege of a nap? I recall, too, a charge to a jury, never reported, but surely fit to be preserved. "In this case," said the trial judge, "I believe that Mr. A (the counsel for the plaintiff) knows as much law as Mr. B (the counsel for the defendant), and I believe that Mr. B knows as much law as Mr. A, but I believe that I in my judicial capacity know as much law as both of them together." Whereupon he forgot to tell the jury anything else, but said they were to consider of their verdict and decide the case in accordance with the rules he had laid down. Well, his charge was sparse, but it enunciated an important truth. Our whole judicial system is built upon some such assumption as the learned judge put forward a trifle crassly and obscurely. This is the great convention, the great fiction, which makes trial in court a fair substitute for trial by battle or by casting lots. The philosopher will find philosophy if he has an eye for it even in a "crowner's" court.

I must not forget my final type of judicial style, the tonsorial or agglutinative. I will not expatiate upon its horrors. They are known but too well. The dreary succession of quotations closes with a brief paragraph expressing a firm conviction that judgment for plaintiff or for defendant, as the case may be, follows as an inevitable conclusion. The writer having delivered himself of this expression of a perfect faith, commits the product of his hand to the files of the court and the judgment of the ages with all the pride of authorship. I am happy to be able to report that this type is slowly but steadily disappearing. As contrasted with its arid wastes, I prefer the sunny, though rather cramped and narrow, pinnacle of a type once much in vogue: "We have carefully examined the record and find no error therein; *therefore* the judgment must be affirmed with costs." How nice a sense of proportion, of the relation between cause and effect, is involved in the use of the illative conjunction "therefore," with its suggestion that other minds less sensitively attuned might have drawn a different conclusion from the same indisputable premises.

I have touched lightly, almost not at all, upon something more important than mere felicities or turn of phrase. Above and beyond all these are what we may term the architectonics of opinions. The groupings of fact and argument and illustration so as to produce a cumulative and mass effect; these, after all, are the things that count above all others. I should despair, however, of any successful analysis of problems at once so large and so difficult within the limits of this paper. One needs a larger easel if one is to follow such a map. Often clarity is gained by a brief and almost sententious statement at the outset of the problem to be attacked. Then may come a fuller statement of the facts, rigidly pared down, however, in almost every case, to those that are truly essential as opposed to those that are decorative and adventitious. If these are presented with due proportion and selection, our conclusion ought to follow so naturally and inevitably as almost to prove itself. Whether it succeeds in doing this or not is something about which the readers of the opinion are not always in accord. To gain a proper breadth of view, one should consult counsel for the vanquished as well as counsel for the victor.

The thought of the vanquished brings me to the opinion that voices a dissent. The protests and the warnings of minorities overborne in the fight have their interest and significance for the student, not only of law itself, but of the literary forms through which law reaches its expression. Comparatively speaking at least, the dissenter is irresponsible. The spokesman of the court is cautious, timid, fearful of the vivid word, the heightened phrase. He dreams of an unworthy brood of scions, the spawn of careless *dicta,* disowned by the *ratio decidendi,* to which all legitimate offspring must be able to trace their lineage. The result is to cramp and paralyze. One fears to say anything when the peril of misunderstanding puts a warning finger to the lips. Not so, however, the dissenter. He has laid aside the rôle of the hierophant, which he will be only too glad to resume when the chances of war make him again the spokesman of the majority. For the moment, he is the gladiator making a last stand against the lions. The poor man must be forgiven a freedom of expression, tinged at rare moments with a touch of bitterness, which magnanimity as well as caution would reject for one triumphant.

A French judge, M. Ransson, a member of the Tribunal of the Seine, wrote some twenty years ago an essay on the art of judging, in which he depicts the feelings of a judge of the first instance when a judgment is reversed. I suppose the state of mind of one reversed is akin in quality to the state of mind of one dissenting, though perhaps differing in degree. "A true magistrate," says M. Ransson, "guided solely by his duty and his conscience, his learning and his reason, hears philosophically and without bitterness that his judgment has not been sustained; he knows that the higher court is there to this end, and that better informed beyond doubt, it has believed itself bound to modify his decision. Ought we even to condemn him, if having done his best, he maintains in his inmost soul the impression that perhaps and in spite of everything he was right? *Victrix causa deis placuit, sed victa Catoni.*" Cato had a fine soul, but history does not record that he feared to speak his mind, and judges when in the minority are tempted to imitate his candor. We need not be surprised, therefore, to find in dissent a certain looseness of texture and depth of color rarely found in the *per curiam.* Sometimes, as I have said, there is just a suspicion of acerbity, but this, after all, is rare. More truly characteristic of dissent is a dignity, an elevation, of mood and thought and phrase. Deep conviction and warm feeling are saying their last say with knowledge that the cause is lost. The voice of the majority may be that of force triumphant, content with the plaudits of the hour, and recking little of the morrow. The dissenter speaks to the future, and his voice is pitched to a key that will carry through the years. Read some of the great dissents, the opinion, for example, of Judge Curtis in Dred Scott *vs.* Sandford, and feel after the cooling time of the better part of a century the glow and fire of a faith that was content to bide its hour. The prophet and the martyr do not see the hooting throng. Their eyes are fixed on the eternities.

I shall be traveling away from my subject if I leave the writing of opinions and turn to arguments at the bar. A word of digression may be pardoned, however, for the two subjects are allied. One is called upon often to make answer to the question, what sort of argument is most effective in an appellate court? Shall it be long or short, terse or discursive? Shall it assume that the judges know the rudiments of law, or shall it attempt in a brief hour to supply the defects in their early training? Shall it state the law or the facts? Shall it take up the authorities and analyze them, or shall it content itself with conclusions and leave analysis for the study? There is, of course, no formula that will fit all situations in appellate courts or elsewhere. If, however, I had to prepare a list of "Don'ts" for the guidance of the novice, I think I would say that only in the rarest instances is it wise to take up one decision after another for the purpose of dissection. Such autopsies have their value at times, but they are wearisome and gruesome scenes. In my list of Don'ts, I would add, don't state the minutiae of the evidence. The judges won't follow you, and if they followed, would forget. Don't attempt to supplement the defects of early training. Your auditors are hardened sinners, not easily redeemed. Above all, don't be long-winded. I have in mind a lawyer, now lifted to the bench, who argued the appeals for one of the civil subdivisions of the State. His arguments lasted about a quarter of an hour. He told us his point and sat down. The audience in the rear of the court room might not applaud, but the audience in front did— at least in spirit—and since the latter audience has the votes, it is best to make your play for them. If you faithfully observe these cautions, let not your spirits droop too low when the decision is adverse, even though there be the added gall and wormwood of a failure of the court to crown your brilliant effort with the dignity of an opinion. Many a gallant argument has met the same unworthy fate.

Young men as they approach admission to the bar must sometimes say to themselves that the great problems have been solved, that the great battles of the forum have been fought, that the great opportunities are ended. There are moods in which for a moment I say the same thing to myself. If I do, the calendar of the following day is as likely as not to bring the exposure of the error. It is a false and cramping notion that cases are made great solely or chiefly by reason of something intrinsic in themselves. They are great by what we make of them. McCulloch *vs.* Maryland—to choose almost at random—is one of the famous cases of our history. I wonder, would it not be forgotten, and even perhaps its doctrine overruled, if Marshall had not put upon it the imprint of his genius. "Not one of his great opinions," says Professor Corwin, speaking of Marshall's work, "but might easily have been decided on comparatively narrow grounds in precisely the same way in which he decided it on broad, general principles, but with the probable result that it would never again have been heard of outside the law courts." So, too, the smaller issues await the transfiguring touch. "To a genuine accountant," says Charles Lamb, "the difference of proceeds is as nothing. The fractional farthing is as dear to his heart as the thousands which stand before it. He is the true actor, who, whether his part be a prince or a peasant, must act it with like authority." That is the spirit in which judge or advocate is to look upon his task. He is expounding a science, or a body of truth which he seeks to assimilate to a science, but in the process of exposition he is practicing an art. The Muses look at him a bit impatiently and wearily at times. He has done a good deal to alienate them, and sometimes they refuse to listen, and are seen to stop their ears. They have a strange capacity, however, for the discernment of strains of harmony and beauty, no matter how diffused and scattered through the ether. So at times when work is finely done, one sees their faces change, and they take the worker by the hand. They know that by the lever of art the subject the most lowly can be lifted to the heights. Small, indeed, is the company dwelling in those upper spaces, but the few are also the elect.

Old Judge and Young Lawyer*

JAMES GOULD COZZENS

This section on judges opened on a note of fact; it ends on a note of fiction, which has, however, all the authority of fact. James Gould Cozzens' novel The Just and the Unjust *(1942) has been recommended by the Harvard reading list for law students as the finest modern legal novel. Cozzens was born in 1903, educated at Kent School and Harvard; he is the author of* S.S. San Pedro, Guard of Honor *(Pulitzer Prize, 1948), and the recent* By Love Possessed, *which describes two days in the life of a lawyer, his first novel in nine years.*

The passage which follows is the ending of The Just and the Unjust. *Although a novel is ordinarily hard, if not impossible, to anthologize, this excerpt is an entity, and the reader need not know what has come before. The judge's valedictory is warm with emotion and full of wisdom and dignity.*

Abner drove his car into the old stables. The cement floor on which he halted had been laid down more than twenty years ago when Judge Coates decided—an unusual step at the time—to keep two cars. To make room, some disused horse stalls were ripped out, and it was discovered then that the old floor was rotten. When the new cement floor was finished and the workmen gone for the day, Abner put his initials in the still-soft surface with a stick; and for good measure, impressed his bare footprints beside them; and for still better measure, impressed also the bare footprints of Caesar, an Airedale dog they then had.

Time had not obliterated those marks. By the glare of the headlights against the back wall, Abner could still see them, just to the left of the door of what had been the harness room. He remembered all that perfectly; taking off the sneaker he wore; and the cement cool and moist against the sole of his foot; and Caesar, years dead and forgotten, alive and struggling in consternation as Abner pressed down his paw. The exact object, if Abner had any beyond showing interest in a material that could be soft today, yet hard as stone tomorrow, was not clear—perhaps just this; that some day, years after, he might notice the marks and think with satisfaction that he had made them. Snapping off the headlights, Abner got out. He noticed and thought, just as the boy perhaps planned.

Closing the doors, he stood a moment in the broad moonlight looking at the big dark mound of the house. These things, he thought, remained—only for a while, of course; but longer, at any rate, than a man did. His grandfather built the house, and for him it had been new and desirable; a showplace, with its great ornamented bargeboards, its cavernous arched verandas and round shingled tower, in the Childerstown of dirt streets and gas lights in the 'eighties. The Judge, the Old Judge, would not have been surprised—what sentient man could be?—to find that the new became old; and the desirable, undesirable; and the house, once so fine-looking, grotesque. As an exercise in reason this was not hard; but how hard to grasp it, to know that the real today, the seen and felt today, and everything around you, and you, yourself as you stood thinking, would dissolve and pale to a figment of mind, existing, like the future you tried to think of, only in thought!

While Abner stood, the old courthouse clock struck twelve (his grandfather would have noticed that the new courthouse clock carried clearly out here). The faint deep bongs rose over the tree tops and the sleeping hill. Surprised to find that it was so late, Abner walked down the brick path.

Under the moonlit roof of the kitchen wing, in the shadow of the shining slates, a voice said suddenly, "Who's that?"

Starting, Abner looked up. In the window of the bedroom where Lucius and Honey slept, the shape of a head a little darker than the darkness, and the shoulders of a dull white pajama coat, showed. Abner said, "All right, Lucius. Who do you think it is?"

"Mr. Abner? I hear that car. Then, nobody comes down. It might be burglars."

"It's all right. Sorry if I woke you up."

"You didn't wake me, Mr. Abner. I keep an eye on things around here. Judge laid up and you out, somebody's got to. You finish that trial?"

"Yes."

"I guess it's curtains for those gangsters?"

"They'll get twenty years in jail, I think."

There was a silence.

"They not going to electrocute them? They kill that man, and they not going to electrocute them?"

"The jury didn't seem to think they did kill him," Abner said.

"Oh!" said Lucius. "Well, I surely thought it was the chair for them! Well, I guess I'll tell Honey. She thought it was."

"All right," Abner said. "Good night."

"Good night."

There was no light in the lower hall, but a dim glow fell on the head of the stairs, showing that the door of his father's room was open. Abner turned the night latch, found the first step with a practiced foot, and went up quickly and steadily on tiptoe. He was expecting his father to call; but when no call came, he stepped faster, with a tremor of alarm, and stood in the bedroom door. His father rested propped up on pillows, his eyes closed, the paralyzed side of his big face hanging with forlorn helplessness. He breathed roughly, but calm and even; and Abner saw that he was only asleep.

Judge Coates stirred. His face worked a moment, his eyes opened. He brought up his good hand and laid the back of it against his paralyzed cheek, as though to cover while he brought it under what control he could, a spectacle that he knew was distressing. "Well, son," he said with difficulty. "Must have drowsed off! Late?"

"Just struck twelve, sir."

"Jury trouble?"

"And plenty of it," Abner said. "Do you want to go to sleep?"

"No, I don't! Sit down! Sit down!" His voice gained clearness as the muscles limbered. "Tell me about it. Verdict in? Smoke a cigarette." He got one from between the piled books on the table. "Sit down," he said. "Light it myself when I get ready."

"Second degree murder," Abner said, sitting down. "Judge Irwin read the jury a lecture."

"Against the evidence?"

"As square as anything could be. Vredenburgh was fit to be tied."

"Harry make a good speech?"

"That's about the size of it," Abner said. "And plain contrariness. I think Marty may have taken it a little too much for granted—"

Abner broke off. The criticism had been just and judicious when he first formulated it to himself, sitting in chagrin at the Commonwealth's table. There was no disloyalty in the silent recognition of a mistake when Marty made one; and no complacency in noting, warned by the mistake, logical ways to avoid it. When he let himself voice the criticism to someone else, there was a little of both: disloyalty in criticizing when his only object must be the trifling but infamous one of trying to dissociate himself from the failure of an enterprise in which he had shared; complacency, for when he pointed out a mistake, he left it plain that it was not one he himself would have committed. "I mean," he said, "Marty had the case cold. There couldn't be two answers to the facts. He more or less left it at that. Kinsolving, an F.B.I. witness we had, who may be a liar but he is certainly no fool, told me afterward that he thought the jury was jibbing at executing two men for something they argued a third man had really done."

Judge Coates said, "A jury has its uses. That's one of them. It's like a—" he paused. "It's like a cylinder head gasket. Between two things that don't

give any, you have to have something that does give a little, something to
seal the law to the facts. There isn't any known way to legislate with an
allowance for right feeling."

"Well, Vredenburgh told Harry this Court wasn't enforcing the Sixth
Commandment."

"From the bench?"

"Oh, no. Afterward, in the Attorneys Room. I guess he thought the jury
had given a little more than it needed to. He said he was disgusted with it."

"He won't feel that way tomorrow. Tom's got better sense than that. In
his time, he's had trouble with his temper."

"What was that?"

"It was long ago," Judge Coates said. "When he was district attorney,
he used to go off the handle now and then. He got over it. It isn't a matter
of any interest now. Juries didn't always find what he thought they ought
to in those days, either. Justice is an inexact science. As a matter of fact, a
judge is so greatly in a jury's debt, he shouldn't begrudge them the little
things they help themselves to."

"I don't follow," Abner said.

"The ancient conflict between liberty and authority. The jury protects the
Court. It's a question how long any system of courts could last in a free
country if judges found the verdicts. It doesn't matter how wise and experienced the judges may be. Resentment would build up every time the find-
ings didn't go with current notions or prejudices. Pretty soon half the community would want to lynch the judge. There's no focal point with a jury;
the jury is the public itself. That's why a jury can say when a judge couldn't,
'I don't care what the law is, that isn't right and I won't do it.' It's the
greatest prerogative of free men. They have to have a way of saying that
and making it stand. They may be wrong, they may refuse to do the things
they ought to do; but freedom just to be wise and good isn't any freedom.
We pay a price for lay participation in the law; but it's a necessary expense."

"You mean," said Abner, "that in order to show he's free, a man shouldn't
obey the laws."

"A free man always has been and always will be the one to decide what
he'd better do," Judge Coates said. "Entrapment is perfectly legal. The law
lets you arrange an opportunity for a suspected thief to steal so that you
can catch him. I don't think right feeling can ever stoop to it. Compound-
ing a felony is an indictable offense; but a man feels, just the same, that he
has a right to forgive those who injure him, and no talk about his duty to
society will change that feeling. In a case of larceny, it may be no defense
in law that the party from whom the goods were stolen, himself stole them;
but the feeling of the average man does in part defend it by saying it
served him right to lose what didn't belong to him. It is held that drunken-
ness does not aggravate a common law offense any more than it excuses it."

He shook his head. "Depending on the circumstances, it may do either.

Most people would feel that committing perjury drunk was not so bad as committing it cold sober; while committing an involuntary manslaughter drunk would be worse than committing it sober. Well, I'm rambling on. I don't know what makes old men like to talk so much. Maybe they're just talking to themselves, trying to find out what they think. I saw the *Examiner* about the Field thing. That's another case mixed up with what people feel. Judging by Maynard's editorial, I don't know that it makes for justice."

"What it made for," Abner said, "was the Board giving Rawle a vote of confidence tonight. Maynard was pretty sore about it."

Judge Coates reached over and took a cigarette lighter from the table. By pressing the top, he made a flame snap up and lit the cigarette.

"Where did you get that?" Abner said.

"Present. Matter of fact, if I have to smoke, I ought to use matches. I was getting pretty handy with them. Mosher is enthusiastic about these wretched little accomplishments. Yes. Cousin Mary gave it to me. She came in this morning."

"What did she want?"

"That's right; she did," Judge Coates said. "She'd heard about the school board business, and she was worried about what was going to happen to Bonnie. I think she thought I might be able to take a hand in it. Of course, there was nothing I could do."

"So you told her not to worry; if Rawle was kicked out and Bonnie lost her job, you'd get her another."

"In substance, yes. When Cousin Mary worries, it shakes the house. You have to stop that at any cost. She has a hard time, really."

"Well," said Abner, "I don't know whether it will make it any easier; but her daughter and I are getting married. Bonnie gave me some supper down there; and we thought we would. I suppose I ought to ask if you mind if we live here awhile."

"When are you going to get married?"

"Some time this month, probably. There are so many forms and certificates and things, you can't say when." He paused. "Don't you like the idea? Last night you were saying I was so damn phlegmatic I hadn't sense enough to get married."

"That was an unfortunate choice of words," Judge Coates said. "I didn't realize you were going to take it so hard. Yes. I like the idea." His face contorted a little, and Abner was stunned to see tears appear in the corner of his eyes. "Are you all right, sir?" he said, starting up.

"Sit down!" said Judge Coates. He plucked at a pile of tissues on the table until he got hold of one. He daubed at his eyes. "You can't tell what I mean by what I do," he said hoarsely. "It would be a favor to me if you wouldn't give things I can't help quite so much attention. Damnation, I'm a sick man!" He dropped the crumpled tissue.

"Well, I didn't mean to upset you," Abner said in distress.

"Phlegmatic wasn't the word; it was obtuse," Judge Coates said. "What did I say that for? I don't mean it. You'd think I wanted to make you mad. I don't want to make anyone mad. I'm not fit to stand up to it. You least of all—"

He brought the cigarette up shakily, cocked it between his lips, and took a puff. "There, that's over," he said. "It just hit me a certain way. If I had to explain it I would only make it sillier. Foolish question, do I mind if you live here. I might ask you, do you mind if you live here. I'll have another stroke and die pretty soon; or if I don't, I'll be a driveling idiot. Don't know whether you want to be in the same house with it. I wouldn't."

Abner said, "I don't think that follows at all. Jesse Gearhart told me his father had a stroke and practically got over it."

"Well," said Judge Coates, "that's true; Mike did. I suppose I might. Just don't want to be such a fool as to count on it. When did Jesse tell you about his father?"

"The other day."

"Oh. I wondered." He crushed out the cigarette awkwardly. "You're probably well out of that. I never liked politics myself. I don't mean I thought I was too good for it. Or if I did, it was when I was very young. Men act through self-interest; and if they do things you wouldn't do, you'd better not assume it's because you have a nobler character. There are noble and disinterested actions done every day; but I think most of them are impulsive. I don't think there's any such thing as a deliberate noble action. Deliberation always has half an eye on how it will look; it wants something, if only admiration, for what it does. Did you ever see a law suit which aimed at disinterested justice?" He took another tissue and wiped his mouth. "Senator Perkins used to say that when a man said he was seeking justice, what he meant, if he was plaintiff, was that he aimed to do someone dirt and the Court ought to help him; and if he was the defendant, that he already had done someone dirt, and the Court ought to protect him."

"That's about it, I guess," Abner said. "I had to get in those Blessington will papers this morning. It's certainly doing the Blessington sisters dirt. Well, I got them in. Intelligent self-interest. I guess what I thought to myself was that I couldn't afford to turn down any business. I don't know."

Judge Coates said heavily, "Woe unto you also, ye lawyers! For ye lade men with burdens grievous to be borne, and ye yourselves touch not the burdens with one of your fingers. Yes. We're vulnerable. A lawyer can't very well do to others as he would be done by. Not in the line of business. I don't know whether you're asking my advice. It's the same conflict we were speaking of before—well, I was speaking of before. You don't get much chance to speak, do you?" He worked himself up a little higher on his pillows.

"Here's your Blessington situation. It's provided by law, primarily by statute, that one of a man's rights which the courts shall protect him in, is the disposal of his property after his death according to his intentions expressed in an attested will. It is a very important right. It is part and parcel of human freedom and dignity. Just as the jury must be free to find against the evidence, we have to hold that a man must be free, if he has the legal capacity to make a will, to make an unequal, unjust, and unreasonable will.

"True, we can't let him make it against public policy. Expediency will set bounds to his freedom. You cannot define exactly and forever what the right bounds of expediency may be; but you can say what they must not be. The intention to realize is not the intention of the Court, nor the intention of Abner Coates, Counselor at Law. In ethics and morals their intentions may be demonstrably better and wiser and fairer than the testator's intention. You've been saying, in effect, that you'd like to devise a better and juster disposal of Blessington's goods. You have no right to do it. The Court has no more right. The point for you is not whether you personally think the will just and good, but whether you can dispassionately and disinterestedly submit to the Court reasons in law and equity that bear out what you feel to be the testator's intention to leave the money to the clients you represent."

Judge Coates coughed, holding up his good hand so that Abner would not interrupt him. "Sorry," he said, gasping. "Now, if you don't feel and believe that such was the testator's intention, you should have nothing to do with it. In your case, I think it is obvious that the testator's intention, or his contingent intention, was that Enoch's college should get the money. If that was his intention, and if it is not an illegal intention, it ought to be realized. Granted that Blessington intended an injustice (and remember, that is an opinion; you and most other people may hold it, but it remains an opinion), would you say to me that the law ought to betray its great first principle and pay off one injustice (a matter of opinion) with another injustice (a matter of indisputable fact)? I think not."

"I think not, too," Abner said. "It isn't what the law should do; it's what I should do." He repressed a yawn. The long day had tired him, not physically in a way to make him sleepy, but in the protracted drain of nervous energy. He could not seem to whip his mind up to the heavy labor of manipulating abstractions. He said, "I'd like to do what was right. Who wouldn't? Maybe that's only one of those deliberate noble actions you don't think much of. It has something to do with how things look, what people think of me." He paused. "Jesse told me your Senator Perkins said you wouldn't worry so much about what people were thinking of you if you remembered that most of the time they weren't. I'm not so good on comebacks. It took me until now to see what was wrong with that."

In spite of himself, Abner did yawn. "What's he mean? Does he mean that most of the time there's nobody looking, so you can do what you want? I don't give a damn whether anybody is looking or not. I'm looking. I care whether I look like a louse. Certainly I care what people think of me. They may only do it for ten seconds once in ten years, but I still care."

Judge Coates said, "Well, we all have our pride. It does a good deal to make us fit for human company. But I don't know how far the world at large, or Jesse in particular, is in duty bound to minister to yours. You made your decision. Don't go on arguing it over."

"Well," said Abner, "today I guess I unmade it. Jesse asked me again, and I told him I'd run."

"You did?" Judge Coates said. "Why did you do that?"

"Because it was what I really wanted to do," Abner said somewhat defiantly. "At least, I suppose that's why."

"Well, that's a good enough reason," Judge Coates said. "Why do you think it isn't?"

"I don't know that I do think it isn't," Abner said. His mind in desperation refused him its services. "I'd like to think there was more to it than just my own advantage. I wish I weren't so sure of that part of it. If it cost me something instead of paying me something—"

"It seems to me it costs you a good deal," Judge Coates said. "For the last few weeks you've been running yourself ragged on this case, this Howell-Basso thing. What do you get out of it? It puts you on edge, all right; I can tell you that."

"I get my salary out of it," Abner said. "Why shouldn't I run myself ragged? It's my job."

"Then just go on doing it, and don't worry. You take care of your job and other things will take care of themselves."

"I don't remember that things ever did. Things don't look as if they would. You can see them cooking up another war for us in Europe; and when they do, I guess all bets are off."

"Don't be cynical," Judge Coates said. "A cynic is just a man who found out when he was about ten that there wasn't any Santa Claus, and he's still upset. Yes, there'll be more war; and soon, I don't doubt. There always has been. There'll be deaths and disappointments and failures. When they come, you meet them. Nobody promises you a good time or an easy time. I don't know who it was who said when we think of the past we regret and when we think of the future we fear. And with reason. But no bets are off. There is the present to think of, and as long as you live there always will be. In the present, every day is a miracle. The world gets up in the morning and is fed and goes to work, and in the evening it comes home and is fed again and perhaps has a little amusement and goes to sleep. To make that possible, so much has to be done by so many people that, on the face of it, it is impossible. Well, every day we do it; and every day, come hell, come high water, we're going to have to go on doing it as well as we can."

"So it seems," said Abner.

"Yes, so it seems," said Judge Coates, "and so it is, and so it will be! And that's where you come in. That's all we want of you."

Abner said, "What do you want of me?"

"We just want you to do the impossible," Judge Coates said.

Section III

THE COURTROOM

Trial of Sir Walter Ralegh (Part I)*

CATHERINE DRINKER BOWEN

The recent life of Sir Edward Coke by Catherine Drinker Bowen (see page 26) is a vivid re-creation of a man and his times. We follow Coke as Attorney General, Speaker, and Chief Justice, and see him compose the Petition of Right. Important men—Bacon, Ralegh, Essex—move through the pages against the glitter and the squalor, the plotting and the gallantry, the rawness and the splendor which make Renaissance England a fascinating study in dualism.

The following selection covers the trial of Sir Walter Ralegh, who was to evade the block for twelve years after this apparently final conviction. Coke has gone through Cambridge and the Inner Temple, married and fought with Lady Hatton, sent Essex to his doom, and been knighted. Ahead of him are the Gunpowder Plot, Bonham's Case, Peacham's Case, the Over-bury murder, dismissal, the Tower—and also the Reports *and the* Institutes *of the Laws of England.*

> 'Twas a dark kind of treason, and the veil is still upon it.
> RUSHWORTH, *Historical Collections* (1659)

> I thinke Sir Walter's hearte is well fixed in every honest thinge. He seemeth wondrously fitted, both by art and nature, to serve the state. In good troth I pitie him and doubte the dice be fairly thrown, if his life be the losing stake.
> SIR JOHN HARINGTON (*written October, 1603, between Ralegh's arrest and trial*)

O n the seventeenth of November, 1603, Ralegh was taken down the hill for trial. When he came with his guard to the Bishop's palace, the old stone hall was crowded. People sat in the minstrels' gallery, leaned against the stone pillars until their legs must have ached. Some of them had been there since dawn; many had waited all night in the street before the

* From *The Lion and the Throne*, by Catherine Drinker Bowen, by permission of Little, Brown & Co. and Hamish Hamilton, Ltd., London, publishers of the British edition.

doors. Lady Arabella Stuart—*Arbella,* everyone called her—sat with the old
Earl of Nottingham. Before the day was out she would have her say; the
indictment was full of her name. Poor Arbella—forever the center of plots
she had not conceived! One look at her seemed enough to turn men's
ambitions elsewhere. Lord Cobham had said that once he saw Arbella he
"resolved never to hazard his estate for her." Yet she was herself to die a
prisoner in the Tower. Here in the Bishop's palace, Cobham lay imprisoned
beneath the courtroom or in some turret chamber. And Cobham was
Ralegh's only accuser, the single witness on whom the prosecution must
build its case.

A Special Commission of Oyer and Terminer had been appointed for the
trial; it included seven laymen and four judges: Popham (Chief Justice of
King's Bench), Justice Anderson of Common Pleas and the puisne judges,
Gawdy and Warburton. The laymen were Mountjoy (Lord Deputy of
Ireland), who had said he would flee England rather than come under
the file of Coke's tongue; Sir William Waad (Clerk of the Privy Council),
a zealous and unscrupulous trapper of recusants who had escorted Ralegh
in the coach from London; the Earl of Suffolk, who had fought with Ralegh
at Cadiz; Sir John Stanhope of the King's household. And lastly, to the
eternal shame of the King, who had approved his appointment, sat Sir
Walter's greatest enemy, the man that had poisoned James's mind against
him: Lord Henry Howard, who four times changed his religion and in
whom the truth did not dwell.

The jury of twelve knights had been brought down from Middlesex
County. Such a panel was considered harsh and somewhat biased; King
James himself remarked that he would not wish to be tried by a Middlesex
jury. There was rumor that Sir Edward Darcy, Ralegh's friend and neighbor, had been named and removed overnight from the panel. But there is
no proof that the jury was packed, though the mere fact of Lord Henry
Howard's presence as commissioner is suspicious. Ralegh declined to challenge a single juror. He "thought them all honest and Christian men and
knew his own innocency." He had however one request. His memory was
never good, sickness in prison had weakened him. Might he answer questions severally, as they came up, rather than all at once? Coke objected,
as he had with Essex. The King's evidence, "ought not to be broken or
dismembered, whereby it might lose much of its grace and vigor."

The judges conceded the point to Ralegh. Yet Coke's remark concerning
the King's evidence came as no surprise in Winchester Hall. A threat to the
sovereign was a threat to every English subject, dangerous moreover to a
Protestant Reformation which even yet was not secure. The King's evidence
(not the prisoner's) must serve as focal point. To bring out this evidence
was the business of the Attorney General. Unfortunately for Ralegh, his
four judges considered it their business too, as did the seven lay commissioners who sat upon the dais with the judges. The majority of these men

already knew the evidence by heart. Since the moment of Ralegh's arrest (and likely a month before) they had been searching it out, fitting part to part until confession matched confession. In Essex's case such "preparation" had been easy; hundreds saw his armed passage through London. With Ralegh the evidence was slim. Moreover, the court considered that it had here a knight far cleverer than Essex, one who by common parlance was an easy liar; in Coke's own words, "the father of wiles."

Ralegh's judges plainly were part of the prosecution, determined from the start to prove the prisoner guilty. Yet there could have been no question of collusion; Popham, old Judge Anderson, Gawdy, Warburton were neither venal nor corrupt. On the contrary, they were men of high character who sat to do their duty. And judicial duty, in the year 1603 (and for two centuries after) meant bringing forward every damaging fact of character and circumstance which could be gathered in the King's favor—hearsay evidence, gossip at third hand, the confession of confederates. In treason cases smoke was hot as fire and bare suspicion tantamount to the act overt. Those keeping company with traitors were *ipso facto* guilty; any evidence could pass. Yet Coke, Chief Justice Popham, Robert Cecil, who sat with the commissioners, took pride in the English legal tradition, pride even in their system of trial at common law. Was not such trial by accusation rather than inquisition, as in France and Spain? Was it not, by general agreement, speedy, open, viewed by any citizen who cared to come? Above all, was not the accused permitted to speak in his own defense, holding, if he wished, a day-long altercation with judges, commissioners, Attorney General? "Sir Walter Ralegh," wrote Cecil to a Privy Councilor before the trial, "yet persists in denial of the main treason. Few men can conceive it comes from a clear heart. Always, he shall be left to the law, which is the right all men are born unto."

Cecil believed what he said. Moreover he was to be the only man in Winchester courtroom who stood out for Sir Walter in the matter of his legal rights and privileges.

Ralegh's indictment, read aloud by the Clerk, was short: Sir Walter had conspired to "kill the King, raise a rebellion with intent to change religion and subvert the government." The overt acts charged were listening to Spanish bribes, conferring with Lord Cobham concerning Arabella Stuart's claim, together with promises, plans, statements and conspiracies to that end.

Serjeant Heale opened for the Crown. He was brief, his speech is remembered only for a startlingly facetious peroration where he remarked that as for the Lady Arabella, upon his conscience she had no more title to the Crown than he had himself, "which, before God," he finished, "I utterly renounce." Even Ralegh smiled. It was the last time he would smile that day.

Coke followed and spoke at length. Foul treasons had been unearthed, though no torture was employed to find them, and no "rigorous usage." (The prosecution invariably took care to make this claim in treason trials and the audience took care to disbelieve it.) "This great and honorable assembly," Coke said, "doth look to hear this day what before hath been carried on the rack of scattering reports. . . ."

There was no telling who might be listening, hidden in some dark gallery. Arthur's Hall, up the hill, had a pipe in the wall behind the judges' dais, leading to a little chamber where kings had anciently sat concealed, their ear to all that passed. People knew about it, knew also that James was visiting at a nearby country house. Those who had witnessed Essex's trial recalled the sudden appearance of Cecil from the parted arras. . . .

Two conspiracies had been discovered, Coke reminded the jury; the *Bye Plot* and the *Main*, they were called. The Bye was the Priests' Plot, hatched by Watson and Clarke; the Main was Ralegh's conspiracy. As Coke continued, it became plain he was describing, not Ralegh's plot at all, but the Bye, a business far more flagrant and more foolish. Ralegh broke in, addressing the jury: "I pray you, Gentlemen, remember that I am not charged with the *Bye*, which was the treason of the priests."

No, Coke said; Sir Walter was not so charged. Yet all these treasons, "like Sampson's foxes, were joined together at the tails, though their heads were severed." Coke went on to describe and define the law of treason, and was proceeding reasonably enough until, after a sugary panegyric on the character of James, he suddenly turned on Ralegh and demanded, "To whom, Sir Walter, did you bear malice? To the royal children?"

It was the first of Coke's attacks, unexpected, startling, brought on perhaps by Ralegh's quick positive denial of Coke's charge, perhaps by the realization that here was a prisoner equipped to defend himself with skill and passion. "Mr. Attorney," Ralegh answered, "I pray you, to whom or to what end speak you all this? I protest I do not understand what a word of this means, except it be to tell me news. What is the treason of Markham and the priests to me?"

COKE: I will then come close to you; I will prove you to be the most notorious traitor that ever came to the bar! You are indeed upon the Main, but you have followed them of the Bye in imitation; I will charge you with the words.

RALEGH: Your words cannot condemn me; my innocency is my defense. I pray you go to your proofs. Prove against me any one thing of the many that you have broken, and I will confess all the indictment, and that I am the most horrible traitor that ever lived, and worthy to be crucified with a thousand torments.

COKE: Nay, I will prove all. Thou art a monster! Thou hast an English face but a Spanish heart. . . . I look to have good words from you, and purpose not to give you worse than the matter press me unto. But if you provoke me, I will not spare you and I have warrant for it. . . . You would have stirred England and Scotland both. You incited the Lord Cobham. . . .

Cobham, rich, discontented and apparently somewhat of a fool, had been one of the "diabolical triplicity" which, according to Lord Henry Howard, met at Durham House to conspire the King's death and set Arbella in his place. Cobham planned to cross the Channel and obtain money for the support of Arbella's title—a bargain which included promise of a "toleration of the Popish religion in England." All this, said Coke, Lord Cobham had confessed: dealing with Aremberg, the Spanish agent; Aremberg's offer of 600,000 crowns. Ralegh, Coke urged, pretended the money was merely a Spanish offer "to forward the peace." Yet if the Spanish King had in mind such an offer, would he have chosen a recipient like Cobham, who was "neither politician nor swordsman?" No! It required a Ralegh to carry through these plans. "Such," said Coke, "was Sir Walter's secrecy and Machiavellian policy that he would confer with none but Cobham, 'because,' saith he, 'one witness can never condemn me.' It will be stood upon Sir Walter Ralegh today," Coke continued, "that we have but one witness. But I will show your Lordships that it is not necessary to have two witnesses."

On this point, so crucial to Ralegh, Coke was securely within the law. It was true that during the reign of Edward VI (1547–1552), statutes had been enacted, declaring for two witnesses. But on the accession of Mary Tudor, these statutes were repealed (1553), and since then, one witness was held sufficient in cases of felony tried under the common law. This was the legal view as known to every barrister who had argued in Westminster Hall. Nevertheless, the country at large clung stubbornly to the old two-witness rule. The Bible declared for it, and was not Holy Scripture corroborative of the common law?

Coke, in this first long offensive, did not stop upon the point. It would come up again and could more properly be dealt with by the judges. "In our case in hand," Coke proceeded, "we have more than two witnesses. For when a man, in his accusation of another, shall by the same accusation also condemn himself and make himself liable to the same punishment, this is by our law more forcible than many witnesses, equal to the inquest of twelve men. For *the law presumes that a man will not accuse himself in order to accuse another.*"

Coke turned now to the jury and repeated the charge of setting up Arbella as "titular queen." On Ralegh's interrupting, Coke retorted angrily that he did not wonder to see Sir Walter "moved." "Nay," Ralegh replied, "you fall out with yourself. I have said nothing to you. I am in no case to be angry."

As the reporter's bare account moves forward, it is hard to see why

Ralegh's calm interpolations were to Coke so palpably infuriating. Was it something in Sir Walter's manner, the old easy arrogance, impossible of description, which for thirty years had earned a host of enemies? Whatever it was, it caused Coke to lose control again and again, spitting out words shameful, unworthy, never to be forgotten. After Ralegh's quiet rebuke, Coke reverted once again to the Bye plot, of which the prosecution well knew that Sir Walter was innocent, yet which, as the tale unfolded, seemed to implicate the prisoner by the very telling. As Coke talked, his anger mounted. "And now," he informed the jury, "you shall see the most horrible practices that ever came out of the bottomless pit of the lowest hell. . . ."

There followed the recitation of an involved, fantastic maneuver of Cobham's, turning on a forged letter "placed in a Spanish Bible," an answer forged and falsely dated.

RALEGH: What is that to me? Here is no treason of mine done. If my Lord Cobham be a traitor, what is that to me?

COKE: All that he did was by thy instigation, thou viper: For I *thou* thee, thou traitor! I will prove thee the rankest traitor in all England.

RALEGH: No no, Mr. Attorney, I am no traitor! Whether I live or die, I shall stand as true a subject as any the King hath. You may call me a traitor at your pleasure, yet it becomes not a man of quality and virtue to do so. But I take comfort in it, it is all you can do, for I do not yet hear that you charge me with any treason.

CHIEF JUSTICE POPHAM: Sir Walter Ralegh, Mr. Attorney speaks out of zeal of his duty for the service of the King, and you for your life. Be patient on both sides.

Coke now ordered the Clerk to read Cobham's confession from the Tower, dated July twentieth. It was almost a repetition of the formal indictment, but more impressive, coming direct from Cobham: "Confesseth: that he had conference with the Count Aremberg about procuring 500 or 600,000 crowns, and a passport to go into Spain to deal with the King, and to return by Jersey. And that nothing should be done until he had spoken with Sir Walter Ralegh for distribution of the money to them which were discontented in England. Being shown a note under Ralegh's hand [Cobham], when he had perused the same, brake forth, saying, 'O traitor! O villain! I will now tell you all the truth!' And then said that he had never entered into these courses but by Ralegh's instigation, and that he [Ralegh] would never let him alone."

Coke directed the Clerk to repeat the last words—"Sir Walter would never let Cobham alone." As for the "note under Ralegh's hand," so disturbing to Cobham, it was to prove one of the deadliest facts toward Ralegh's conviction. Written in July, before Sir Walter's imprisonment, it

was addressed to Cecil. Coke explained the occasion. At Windsor, when
Ralegh first was questioned by the Privy Council, he had said he knew of
no plots between Cobham and the Spanish agent. But later the same afternoon, Sir Walter, riding home to London, remembered an incident of early
spring, after Cobham had spent an evening at Durham House. Cobham
had left by the water gate, and Ralegh, looking out a turret window, saw
the barge turn upstream, glide past Cobham's own stairs and stop at the
house of La Rensi, a Spanish agent. As soon as Sir Walter returned from
Windsor, he wrote out the story and sent it to Cecil.

To the jury, this action of Ralegh's was positively damning. Why should
Sir Walter, this early in the game, have taken it on himself gratuitously to
inform against his friends, unless as a guilty man he hoped by such betrayal
to save his own skin? Cobham, when first arrested, had sworn to Ralegh's
innocence of all plots and "conversations." Only when shown this letter,
had Cobham broken down and accused Ralegh of treason.

Sir Walter, in rebuttal, asked to see Cobham's confession. While it was
being carried to him, he addressed the court: "Gentlemen of the Jury, this
is absolutely all the evidence that can be brought against me. This is that
which must either condemn me or give me life, which must free me or send
my wife and children to beg their bread about the streets. This is that which
must prove whether I am a notorious traitor or a true subject to the
King. . . ." Having read Cobham's confession, Sir Walter answered at once
concerning his own July letter to Cecil. Yes, he had written it. But it revealed
to Cecil nothing new. Long since, in the late Queen's time, said Ralegh, it
was known that Cobham had dealings with agents from the Low Countries.
Even Cecil's father, Lord Burghley, had been aware of it. Cobham, glimpsing
this letter in the Tower, had jumped, added Ralegh, to wild unwarranted
conclusions. Were not Lord Cobham's bitter railings well known? The
man's passions, indeed, had "such violence," said Ralegh, "that his best
friends could never temper them."

The note was never produced in court. Apparently, it had vanished, or at
least it made no part of the bundle of depositions at Coke's disposal. Chief
Justice Popham now intervened. He himself had been in Cobham's Tower
cell when Cobham saw this letter. The Lords of Council had brought it at
the exact moment when Cobham was signing his first statement of innocence. (Actually, Cobham had balked at signing. Subscription was like
taking an oath. And noblemen, Cobham protested, were not required to
swear to documents, their bare word being considered sufficient.) At
Popham's insistence however, Cobham took up a pen—and as he wrote
his name the Lords walked in the door, bearing Ralegh's note "of betrayal."
Cobham looked at it and burst into fury, calling out upon Sir Walter as a
wretch and a traitor. "Hath he used me thus? Nay then, I will tell you all!"
Cobham's face as he said it (testified Popham) was the face of a man
speaking truth; his face and all his actions.

The testimony of a Chief Justice is not easy to disregard. Clearly, Popham believed in Cobham's word, which meant he disbelieved in Ralegh's. And upon this point—which man spoke truth, Ralegh or Cobham—the trial hung, and Ralegh's life. To the jury in Winchester courtroom, Ralegh's word was if anything less reliable than Cobham's. Both were liars, opportunists. Sir Walter by all reports was much the cleverer and stronger. Did it not follow he was also the more guilty?

It was now Ralegh's turn to speak in full. He had two lines to pursue: (1) show that Cobham's word was not to be trusted; (2) convince the jury that his own circumstances made the alleged plots ridiculous, his past history being incompatible with such ill-timed and evil machinations. He began with the second argument, and what he said covers three printed pages; it is instinct with poetry and dignity, and, throughout, magnificently reasonable. By nature his voice was low; in Parliament men had complained they could not hear him when he spoke. Why, he asked now, if he desired to plot with Spain, would he have chosen this time of all times, when England was strengthened by a union with Scotland, the Irish rebels quieted, the Low Countries at peace with England, Denmark's friendship assured by the royal marriage—and on the English throne, "instead of a Lady whom time had surprised, we had now an active King, a lawful successor to the Crown who was able to attend to his own business?"

Elizabeth, the old Queen! *A Lady whom time had surprised.* No man had said it half so well. The phrase would be repeated, would become famous. "I was not such a madman," Ralegh was saying, "as to make myself in this time a Robin Hood, a Wat Tyler, a Kett, or a Jack Cade. I knew also the state of Spain well, his weakness and poorness and humbleness at this time. I knew that he was discouraged and dishonoured. I knew that six times we had repulsed his forces, thrice in Ireland, thrice at sea, and once at Cadiz on his own coast. Thrice had I served against him myself at sea, wherein for my country's sake I expended of my own properties, four thousand pound. I knew that where beforetime he was wont to have forty great sails at the least in his ports, now he hath not past six or seven; and for sending to his Indies he was driven to hire strange vessels—a thing contrary to the institutions of his proud ancestors, who straitly forbad, in case of any necessity, that the Kings of Spain should make their case known to strangers. I knew . . ."

It was a saga, as Ralegh told it; it was the story of England's glory unrolling. Men who had forgotten Drake, forgotten Hawkins, remembered them now and for one quick moment remembered also the days before '88, when England, a small and feeble island, had lived in terror of the Spaniard. Ralegh had never lost his broad Devon accent. It was impressive, here in the courtroom; it breathed of the sailor, not the courtier.

"What pawn had we to give the King of Spain?" Ralegh went on, passionately. "What did we offer him?" He turned to Coke. "And to show I was not *Spanish,* as you term me, I had written at this time a Treatise to the King's Majesty of the present state of Spain, and reasons against the peace. . . ."

The jury listened. ("Never," wrote a spectator, "any man spoke so well in times past nor would do in the world to come.") Yet as Ralegh left his own history and came to Cobham's dubious character—his second argument —what he said seemed less convincing. Sir Walter acknowledged an intimacy with Cobham, an "inwardness," he called it. But their frequent meetings had been concerned only with private business; Cobham had wished advice about his estate. Moreover, Ralegh argued, if he himself desired a treasonable confederate, why would he have chosen Cobham, one of the richest noblemen of England? Discontented earls, such as Bothwell and Westmoreland, were easily available—"men of better understanding than Cobham, ready to beg their bread."

Poverty or riches, the condition of a man's estate, played a large part in treason trials. Rich men seldom make revolutions. As had been said of the Essex affair, "Poverty soonest plungeth the English into rebellion." Essex's final act of violence had come when the Queen took away his monopoly of sweet wines and he felt himself nearing destitution. Ralegh finished speaking, and Cobham's second Examination was read by the Clerk: When he had been about to return from Spain with the 600,000 crowns, Cobham had feared to stop at Jersey and confer according to plan. At Jersey he would have been wholly in Ralegh's power, and Ralegh "might well have delivered him and all the money to the King."

Was Ralegh, then, doubly nefarious, mistrusted even by his accomplices, ready to play his cards both ways and betray his own confederate for credit with the King? Even if Cobham lied, these plots and counterplots were shocking, disturbing. They could not be all invention. . . . Had Cobham, Sir Walter asked quickly, put his signature to this second statement in the Tower? No, Coke replied. A declaration given in the presence of Privy Councilors needed no subscription to be valid.

RALEGH: Surely, Mr. Attorney, you would not allow a bare scroll to have credit with a jury?

COKE: Sir Walter, you say the Lord Cobham's accusing you was upon heat and passion. This is manifestly otherwise; for after that the Lord Cobham had twice called for the letter and twice paused a good while upon it and saw that his dealing with Count Aremberg was made known, then he thought himself discovered and after said, 'O wretch and traitor, Ralegh!' As to improbability, is it probable that my Lord Cobham would turn the weapon against his own bosom and overthrow himself in estate, in honour and in all his fortunes, out of malice to accuse you? . . . If he feared that you would betray him, there must of necessity be a trust between you. No man can betray another but he that is trusted, to my understanding. . . . You seek to wash away all that is said, by affirming the evidence against you to be but a bare accusation, without circumstances or reason to confirm it. That I will fully satisfy. For as my Lord Cobham's confession stands upon many circumstances, and concerns many others, I will, by other means, prove every circumstance thereof to be true.

RALEGH: But, my Lords, I claim to have my accuser brought here face to face to speak. And though I know not how to make my best defence by law, yet since I was a prisoner, I have learned that by the law and statutes of this realm in case of treason, a man ought to be convicted by the testimony of two witnesses if they be living. I will not take it upon me to defend the matter upon the statute *25th Edward III,* though that requires an overt act. . . .

Ralegh referred, of course, to the great statute of 1351, upon which, for six hundred years, subsequent statutes were based and which defined treason as "compassing or imagining the king's death, levying war against the king, and adhering to the king's enemies." Not the killing of a king but the compassing or imagining his death—*intent to kill him:* this was treason. For centuries therefore the question was to arise: Whether mere words, when plainly evident of intent to kill the king (or to subvert the state), could be construed as an overt act? In times of national emergency, courts invariably have so construed them. In times of peace and national security, the overt act takes narrower construction, and courts require deeds as well as words before they will convict of treason. On this vital question, Coke as Chief Justice was himself to alter, on occasion, his own interpretation, giving, under Stuart kings, far greater latitude to the accused than he gave to Ralegh or even to Essex—and not only in the matter of the act overt but the rule concerning two witnesses.

Sir Walter went on to cite the statutes of Edward VI (1547, 1548) concerning two witnesses. "Mr. Attorney," he said, "if you proceed to condemn me by bare inference, without an oath, without a subscription, without witnesses, upon a paper accusation, you try me by the Spanish inquisition. If my accuser were dead or abroad, it were something. But he liveth and is in this very house!"

Ralegh turned to the Commissioners. "Consider, my Lords, it is no rare case for a man to be falsely accused, aye, and falsely condemned, too! And my Lords the Judges—remember, I beseech you, what one of yourselves said in times past. I mean Fortescue, a reverend Chief Justice of this kingdom, touching the remorse of his conscience for proceeding upon such slender proof. 'So long as he lived [he said] he should never purge his conscience of that deed.' And my Lords, remember too the story of Susannah; she was falsely accused. . . . I may be told that the statutes I before named be repealed, for I know the diversity of religion in the Princes of those days caused many changes. Yet the equity and reason of those laws remains. They are still kept to illustrate how the common law was then taken and ought to be expounded. By the Law of God therefore, the life of man is of such price and value that no person, whatever his offence is, ought to die unless he be condemned on the testimony of two or three witnesses."

It was a long speech and there was more, referring not only to Deuteronomy but to St. Paul. How the judges were to receive it would presently be seen, but to the audience it was supremely effectual. Ralegh, in calling on the Law of God, appealed not alone to religious faith but to the national conception of LAW as apart from *the laws*—a distinction sharp in English minds: *the laws* were made by men and could be found in statute book or in judicial maxim and decision. LAW was deeper, higher, derived from God. LAW antedated *the laws* and would exist if every man-made statute were expunged. It was a native conception, part of the common inheritance. Sir Walter had presented the law as plain citizens knew it in their minds and held it in their hearts, no matter what construction had been put upon it by legalists now or in Queen Mary Tudor's time.

"If then," Ralegh finished, "by the statute law, by the civil law and by God's word it be required that there be two witnesses at the least, bear with me if I desire one. Prove me guilty of these things by one witness only, and I will confess the indictment. If I have done these things I deserve not to live, whether they be treasons by the law or no. Why then, I beseech you, my Lords, let Cobham be sent for! Let him be charged upon his soul, upon his allegiance to the King. And if he then maintain his accusation to my face, I will confess myself guilty."

Trial of Sir Walter Ralegh
(Part II)

> Sir Walter answered with that temper, wit, learning, courage and judgment, that, save it went with the hazard of his life, it was the happiest day he ever spent. And so well he shifted all advantages that were taken against him, that were not *fama malum gravius quam res*, and an ill name, half-hanged in the opinion of all men, he had been acquitted.
>
> CARLETON TO CHAMBERLAIN, *Nov. 27, 1603*

It was now midday, the trial was half over. Through high windows, light drifted down; on stone floors the rushes were pulled around chilly feet. Ralegh had argued brilliantly from the statutes but his judges were quick with refutation. The laws quoted did not apply, later statutes had repealed them. "I marvel, Sir Walter," Judge Warburton said, "that you being of such experience and wit, should stand on this point; for many horse-stealers should escape if they may not be condemned without witnesses. By law, a man may be condemned upon presumption and circumstances, without any witness to the main fact. As, if the King (whom God defend!) should be slain in his chamber, and one is shown to come forth of the chamber with his sword drawn and bloody, were not this evidence both in law and opinion without further inquisition?"

RALEGH: Yet by your favour, my Lord, the trial of fact at the common law is by jury and witnesses.

POPHAM: No! The trial at the common law is by *examination*. If three conspire a treason and they all confess it, here is never a witness, and yet they may all be condemned of treason.

RALEGH: I know not, my Lord, how you conceive the law; but if you affirm it, it must be a law to all posterity.

POPHAM: Nay, we do not conceive the law. We know the law.

RALEGH: Notwithstanding, my Lords, let me have thus much for my life. For though the law may be as your Lordships have stated it, yet is it a strict and rigorous interpretation of the law. Now the King of England at his coronation swears to observe the equity and not the rigour of the law. And if ever we had a just and good King, it is his Majesty; and such doth he wish his ministers and judges to be. Though, therefore, by the rigour and severity of the law, this may be sufficient evidence, without producing the witness, yet your Lordships, as Ministers of the King, are bound to administer the law in equity.

POPHAM: Equity must proceed from the King. You can only have justice from us.

Popham was confident in what he said. To him as to every lawyer in the hall, Sir Walter's trial had proceeded according to law. Should the King, after Ralegh's condemnation, pardon him, it would be done by virtue of his Majesty's prerogative. That was what Ralegh implied by "equity," and to the judges it was confusion deliberately created. The spectators reacted otherwise; to them these fancy distinctions meant nothing. Sir Walter had shown himself not only eloquent but reasonable; he seemed to know more law than the judges. Many in the hall had sat at Essex's trial, an occasion when the Attorney General made much of overt acts, stating that conviction in England was by the act overt, never on bare words alone. Yet where here was an overt act? The jury waited.

To Coke, Ralegh's arguments were mere casuistry. Laymen who talked law were irritating and Sir Walter, in this respect, was worse than Essex. Ralegh had lived in rooms at the Temple when Coke was a student; yet it did not follow Sir Walter had studied the law. These swordsmen and sailors who skimmed the cream of knowledge—these swashbuckling poetical lords and Queen's favorites with their persuasive tongues—spouted law as the devil quotes Scripture.

"The Crown," Coke said, "shall never stand one year on the head of the King if a traitor may not be condemned by circumstances. . . . *Scientia sceleris est mera ignorantia* [the wisdom of a scoundrel is pure ignorance]. You, Sir Walter, have read the letter of the law but understand it not."

It was the old contention, the old debate between lawyers and laymen: Which shall prevail, law or justice? To Ralegh's audience the words were not synonymous. Yet in the centuries-old calendar of criminal courts, no crime had been more difficult to construe than treason. Sir Walter's judges could cite a whole array of recent statutes, passed to strengthen Queen Elizabeth's position and to give to the Crown all advantage in the struggle against Spain, France, Rome, and against such domestic extremists as cherished ambition to alter the government and religion of England. When statutes, being new, were doubtful of application, the Crown was always favored, not the suspect. Sir Walter's judges saw no reason to take a new position.

Ralegh's own words were now produced, as taken down in the Tower on August thirteenth: "He confesseth the Lord Cobham offered him 10,000 crowns of the [Spanish] money for furthering the peace between England and Spain, and that he should have it within three days; but said, 'When I see the money I will make you an answer,' for [Ralegh] thought it one of [Cobham's] idle conceits and therefore made no account thereof."

To the jury, this was a serious acknowledgment: Ralegh had actually listened to an offer from Spain. That he had not accepted the money— had never even seen it—they promptly forgot. Men who listened to bribes were tainted men, dangerous, vulnerable. . . . Ralegh's "confession" (which in truth confessed nothing) upset this jury of Middlesex knights who knew little of the tangled politics of faction, the bargains by which courtiers lived and moved and the shifting of loyalties with each wind that blew from Europe. (Cecil himself was later to accept a pension from Spain.) Ralegh saw that he had lost ground and urged again that Cobham be produced in court. "Were the case but for a small copyhold, you would have witnesses or good proof to lead the jury to the verdict. And I am here for my life!" Once more the Chief Justice refused: "Sir Walter, you plead hard for yourself, but the laws plead as hard for the King." Cecil interposed. Might he hear the opinion of all the Judges on this point?

The judges all answered that in respect it might be a mean to cover many treasons and might be prejudicial to the King, therefore by law it was not sufferable.

As the afternoon wore on, spectators showed themselves restless; the temper of the hall was seen to alter. ("Sir Walter behaved himself so worthily, so wisely, so temperately, that in half a day the mind of all the company was changed from the extremest hate to the greatest pity.") Ralegh had employed no histrionics but bore himself with simplicity, abusing no one beyond his own accuser, Cobham, and keeping his argument to the law and the state of the realm. Coke, on the other hand, digressed into any field that seemed fruitful. One of the indicted priests, Watson, had quoted in the Tower words spoken by some nobleman (unnamed), suggesting annihilation of James and his family. Coke let the words roll from his tongue, managing, during the recital, to repeat them three times: "Now let us destroy the King and all his cubs, not leaving one!"

RALEGH: O barbarous! Do you bring the words of these hellish spiders against me? If they, like unnatural villains, used those words, shall I be charged with them?

COKE: Thou art thyself a spider of hell, for thou dost confess the King to be a most sweet and gracious Prince, yet thou hast conspired against him.

The matter of a treasonable book was next. In Ralegh's library a manuscript had been found, written by a lawyer in the 1580's to justify Queen Elizabeth's proceedings against Mary Queen of Scots. By inference it argued against James's title to the English crown. Ralegh acknowledged possession but said he had borrowed the book years ago from Lord Treasurer Burghley. "I marvel," Ralegh said, "that it should now be urged as a matter so treasonable in me to have such books, when it is well known there comes out nothing in these times but I have it and might as freely have it as another. And as my Lord Cecil hath said of his library, I think a man might find in my house all the libels that have been made against the late Queen."

COKE: You were no Councillor of State, Sir Walter, and I hope never shall be.

CECIL: Sir Walter Ralegh was truly no *sworn* Councillor of State. Yet he hath been often called to consultations.

Coke now produced, with something of a flourish, his only oral witness of the trial, an English sailor, a pilot named Dyer, who put his hand on the Bible and testified that last July, in Lisbon, he had heard "a Portugal gentleman say that King James would never be crowned, for Don Cobham and Don Ralegh would cut his throat first."

Nobody was impressed; such a fellow could palpably be bought for a few pounds. The sailor retreated. Ralegh spoke contemptuously: "This is the saying of some wild Jesuit or beggarly priest. But what proof is it against me?"

COKE: It must perforce arise out of some preceding intelligence and shows that your treason had wings.

Again it was the old tactic of the treason trial, wherein the prosecution quotes damaging statements made by anybody at all, and then, by hinting association, or merely by constant repetition of the words, hypnotizes a jury into laying on the prisoner the initial responsibility for what was said. Robert Cecil, at this point, rose to remark that two innocent names had been implicated. Count Aremberg, the Ambassador, should not be blamed for "what others said to him or presumed of him, but of how far he consented or approved." (Ralegh, hearing this, must truly have despaired; he was himself being tried on nothing beyond "what others said to him or presumed.") Among the auditory, Cecil went on, was a noble lady whose name should be cleared, seeing the indictment charged a plot to set her on the throne. All eyes turned to the box where sat Arbella with the Earl of Nottingham. The old Earl rose. "The Lady," he said, "doth here protest upon her salvation that she never dealt in any of these things."

That, apparently, disposed of Arbella, a lady habitually dragged into public notice and then summarily dismissed. Coke, however, had reserved his two best points of evidence. He now produced the first one: a confession by Cobham, under date of October 13, saying that Ralegh had sent a letter to the Tower, bidding Cobham not to be dismayed because "one witness could not condemn him." If they both kept silence, both were safe. The man who carried it was Kemys, a soldier and sea captain who had accompanied Ralegh to Guiana in 1595.

RALEGH: I deny the writing of any such letter! For Kemys, I never sent him on any such message. This poor man hath been a close prisoner these eighteen weeks and hath been threatened with the rack to make him confess, but I dare stand upon it he will not say it now.

Instant clamor broke among the commissioners; the lords all spoke at once. There had been no torturing of any prisoner. The King had given order that "no rigor should be used."

RALEGH: Was not the keeper of the rack sent for and he threatened with it?

SIR WILLIAM WAAD, from the commissioners' bench: When Mr. Solicitor [Fleming] and myself examined Kemys, we told him he deserved the rack but did not threaten him with it.

COMMISSIONERS: That was more than we knew.

The matter was dropped, but not until Kemys's own confession had been read, wherein he swore he had delivered the letter to Cobham. This time it was Ralegh's word against his own servant, a man known to be both faithful and brave. To the jury it looked as if Mr. Attorney had trapped Sir Walter into a lie. For the last time, Ralegh begged to have Cobham brought into court. "It is you, then, Mr. Attorney, that should press his testimony, and I ought to fear his producing, if all that be true which you have alleged." Cecil supported Sir Walter. Could not the proceedings be delayed while the judges sent to ascertain the King's pleasure in this matter?

But the judges resolved that the proceedings must go on and receive an end. . . . Whereupon Sir Walter Ralegh addressed himself to the Jury and used a speech to this effect. . . .

What Sir Walter said now included little of law or logic. It was a simple, eloquent appeal: "You, Gentlemen of the jury: for all that is said to the contrary, you see my only accuser is the Lord Cobham, who with tears hath lamented his false accusing me, and repented of it as if it had been an horrible murder. I will not expect anything of you but what reason, religion and conscience ask for every man. . . . Remember what St. Augustine saith, 'So judge as if you were about to be judged yourselves, for in the end there is but one Judge and one Tribunal for all men.' . . . Now if you yourselves would like to be hazarded in your lives, disabled in your posterities—your lands, goods and all you have confiscated—your wives, children and servants left crying to the world; if you should be content all this should befall you upon a trial by suspicions and presumptions—upon an accusation not subscribed by your accuser, without the open testimony of a single witness— then so judge me as you would yourselves be judged!"

Serjeant Phillips, ordered by Popham to sum up for the Crown, repeated the charges briefly, adding that Cobham had confessed to all of them. "Now the question is," Phillips said, "whether Sir Walter Ralegh be guilty as inciting or procuring the Lord Cobham to this treason. If the Lord Cobham say truth, Sir Walter Ralegh is guilty. If Sir Walter Ralegh say true, then he is free; so which of them says true is the whole question. Sir Walter Ralegh hath no proof for his acquittal, though he hath as much wit as man can have. But he uses only his bare denial. But the denial of a criminal is not sufficient to clear him, neither is the evidence on oath of a defendant in his own cause allowed to clear him in any Court of law or equity, much less therefore in matters of treason."

Now the business, [wrote the reporter] seemed to be at an end. Then said Sir Walter Ralegh, "Mr. Attorney, have you done?"

COKE: Yes, if you have no more to say.
RALEGH: If you have done, then I have somewhat more to say.
COKE: Nay, I will have the last word for the King.
RALEGH: Nay, I will have the last word for my life.

COKE: Go to, I will lay thee upon thy back for the confidentest traitor that ever came to the bar!

CECIL: Be not so impatient, good Mr. Attorney. Give him leave to speak.

COKE: I am the King's sworn servant and must speak. If I may not be patiently heard, you discourage the King's Counsel and encourage traitors.

Was it now the spectators hissed? (A spectator, writing afterward, said the auditory hissed at Coke, not specifying the moment.)

Mr. Attorney, [says the reporter] sat down in a chafe and would speak no more until the Commissioners urged and entreated him. After much ado, he went on and made a long repetition of the evidence for the direction of the jury. And at the repeating of some things, Sir Walter Ralegh interrupted him and said he did him wrong.

It was here that Coke lost all control, speaking words which are held forever to his shame. Nor were they phrases a man can whisper. Coke stood directly in front of Ralegh. Sir Edward was a big man and, at fifty-two, still in the prime of strength and vigor; his full dark robes made him seem even larger. Long afterward, it was said he shook his fist at Ralegh, though no eyewitness mentioned it. Nevertheless, Coke's voice must have filled the hall: "Thou art the most vile and execrable traitor," he shouted, "that ever lived!"

RALEGH: You speak indiscreetly, uncivilly and barbarously.

COKE: Thou art an odious fellow! Thy name is hateful to all the realm of England for thy pride.

RALEGH: It will go near to prove a measuring cast between you and me, Mr. Attorney.

COKE: Well, I will now lay you open for the greatest traitor that ever was. This, my Lords, is he that hath set forth so gloriously his services against the Spaniard, and hath ever so detested him! This is he that hath written a book against the peace [with Spain]. I will make it appear to the world that there never lived a viler viper on the face of the earth than thou! I will show you wholly Spanish, and that you offered yourself a pensioner to Spain for intelligence. Then let all that have heard you this day judge what you are, and what a traitor's heart you bear, whatever you pretended.

During this terrible exchange, Coke carried in his hand a scroll. It was his final evidence, a surprise card he had withheld, a last damning word against Ralegh, given by Cobham only yesterday from his prison cell. Coke's first words would indicate he held the paper up so all could view it. "See, my Lords, what it hath pleased God to work in the heart of my Lord Cobham, even since his coming hither to Winchester! He could not sleep quietly till he had revealed the truth to the Lords, and therefore voluntarily wrote the whole matter to them, but yesterday. And to discover you, Ralegh, and all your Machiavelian tricks, hear what the Lord Cobham hath written under his own hand, which I will read with a loud voice, though I be not able to speak this s'ennight after."

Turning to the audience, Coke began to read Cobham's words, "commenting," says the reporter, "as he went along":

"Sir Walter Ralegh, four nights before my coming from the Tower, caused a letter, inclosed in an apple, to be thrown in at my chamber window, desiring me to set down under my hand and send to him an acknowledgment that I had wronged him, and renouncing what I had formerly accused him of. His first letter I made no answer to; the next day he wrote me another, praying me, for God's sake, if I pitied him, his wife and children, that I would answer him in the points he set down, informing me that the Judges had met at Mr. Attorney's house, and putting me in hope that the proceedings against me would be stayed. Upon this I wrote him a letter as he desired. I since have thought how he went about only to clear himself by betraying me. Whereupon I have resolved to set down the truth, and under my hand to retract what he cunningly got from me, craving humble pardon of his Majesty and your Lordships for my double dealing. . . ."

"The truth"—as Cobham saw it in this last retraction—was Ralegh's bargain with Aremberg for a flat yearly pension of 1500 pounds in return for spying service, "to tell and advertise what was intended by England against Spain, the Low Countries or the Indies." To the jury this was new and shocking. Bribes had been mentioned, but nothing so damning as a continuous, yearly payment. As instance—Cobham wrote further—Sir Walter, returning one night from the palace at Greenwich, revealed "what was agreed upon betwixt the King and the Low Countrymen, that I should impart it to Count Aremberg. . . . And Sir Walter in his last letter advised me not to be overtaken by confessing to any preacher as the Earl of Essex had. . . ."

Here Coke broke off his reading, and turning to Ralegh, spoke in passion: "O damnable atheist! He counsels not to confess to preachers, as the Earl of Essex did! That noble Earl died indeed for his offence, but he died the child of God, and God honored him at his death. Thou, Ralegh, wast by when he died. *Et lupus et turpes instant morientibus ursae!*"

Wolves and bears press close upon the dying. The Latin, rolling out, was like a curse; it was anathema, incantation, and, considering Coke's own part in Essex's trial, was least excusable. This was not law but rabble-rousing. It was the stones and mire hurled once more at Ralegh. Whatever the jury thought of it, they could not disregard the new evidence—a letter written at Winchester not twenty-four hours past. Tomorrow or next day, Cobham himself would stand trial in this very hall. Impossible that a man with death so close upon him would lie thus to the Lords. What had he to gain thereby? Was any favor, Popham inquired of the commissioners, "promised or offered" to Cobham for the writing of this letter? No, Cecil replied; to his knowledge there was none. "I dare say not," Ralegh interposed drily. "But my Lord Cobham received a letter from his wife that there was no way to save his life but to accuse me."

This, to the jury, was beside the point. "The Lord Cobham's confession," wrote the reporter, "seemed to give great satisfaction and cleared all the former evidence, which stood very doubtful." Coke's triumph was plain. For him, the trial was over. The withholding of this evidence until the end had been wise, he could tell himself—especially in dealing with a man of Ralegh's skill. Now it was too late for denial. No trick of Sir Walter's, no appeal of eloquence could counteract this final accusation of his enemy. Ralegh, said the reporter, stood "much amazed."

"Now, Ralegh," Coke said, "if thou hast the grace, humble thyself to the King and confess thy treasons."

But Coke (though for the last time) underestimated his adversary. Sir Walter too had reserved a surprise.

By-and-by, [wrote the reporter] Sir Walter Ralegh seemed to gather his spirits again, and said: "I pray you hear me a word. You have heard tale of a strange man. . . . Before my Lord Cobham's coming from the Tower, I was advised by some of my friends to get a confession from him. Therefore I wrote to him thus, 'You or I must go to trial. If I first, then your accusation is the only evidence against me!' Therefore it was not ill of me to beg of him to say the truth. But his first letter was not to my contenting. I wrote a second, and then he wrote me a very good letter."

Ralegh thrust a hand in his breast and produced a folded small sheet. "It is true," he said, "I got a poor fellow in the Tower to cast up an apple with the letter in it, at Lord Cobham's window; which I am loath to mention lest Mr. Lieutenant of the Tower might be blamed, though I protest Sir George Harvey is not to blame for what passed. No keeper in the world could so provide but it might happen. But I sent him his letter again, because I heard it was likely now he should be first tried. But the Lord Cobham sent me the letter a second time, saying it was not unfit I should have such a letter."

Ralegh held up the paper. "And here you may see it, and I pray you read it."

The Clerk came forward to take the note. The jury watched. In the history of trials, had evidence ever been so given and retracted, so sworn and forsworn? No matter what this new note of Cobham's might say, Ralegh, in producing it, confessed what he had earlier denied—communication with Cobham in the Tower. "But what say you," Popham interposed, "to the pension of 1500 pounds a year?"

He could not deny it, Ralegh replied, though it was never his purpose to accept it. "It was my fault I did conceal it, and this fault of concealing, I acknowledge. But for attempting or conspiring any treason against the King or the State, I still deny it to the death and it can never be proved against me."

"I perceive," Popham said gravely, "you are not so clear a man as you have protested all this while, for you should have discovered this matter to the King."

The Clerk, during this exchange, stood waiting, Cobham's letter in his hand. "Hear now, I pray you," Ralegh said, "what Cobham hath written to me."

Mr. Attorney would not have this letter read, saying that it was unfairly obtained from Lord Cobham. And upon Lord Cecil's advising to hear it, he said, "My Lord Cecil, mar not a good cause!"

CECIL: Mr. Attorney, you are more peremptory than honest. You must not come here to show me what to do.

RALEGH: I pray my Lord Cecil particularly to read the letter, as he knoweth my Lord Cobham's hand.

Then was read the letter of the Lord Cobham to Sir Walter Ralegh, to this effect: "Now that the arraignment draws near, not knowing which should be first, I or you, to clear my conscience, satisfy the world with truth and free myself from the cry of blood, I protest upon my soul and before God and his angels, I never had conference with you in any treason, nor was ever moved by you to the things I heretofore accused you of. And for any thing I know, you are as innocent and as clear from any treasons against the King as is any subject living. Therefore I wash my hands and pronounce with Daniel, *Purus sum a sanguine hujus.* And so God deal with me and have mercy on my soul, as this is true!"

It was impressive; this was a day when men did not lightly call upon God's name. Ralegh followed it quickly. "My Masters of the Jury," he said, "this is a confession made under oath, and the deepest protestations a Christian man can make." Yet the jury was weary with these retractations and denials of retractations; they came too late. Cobham's confession of yesterday, as read aloud by Coke, invalidated this earlier statement, eloquent though it had been. Too much lay counter to it—notes tied to apples, servants bearing secret letters, connivance and what looked like deliberate falsehood in court. "The acknowledging," wrote the reporter, "of this 1500 pounds a year pension made the rest of the Lord Cobham's accusation the better credited. . . ." Chief Justice Popham addressed Ralegh direct. "In my conscience I am persuaded that Cobham accused you truly. I observed his manner of speaking. I protest before the living God I am persuaded he spoke nothing but the truth."

The prosecution rested its case. Coke's three points had been stated, embellished, gone over until twelve knights of Middlesex knew them by heart:

(1) Ralegh's July letter to Cecil, informing of Cobham's midnight visit to La Rensi; (2) Ralegh's letter to Cobham in the Tower, reminding Cobham that two witnesses were necessary for conviction and urging that as long as Cobham kept silence, they both were safe; (3) Cobham's confession of November 16, given from his cell in Winchester. The first two points were hearsay, the letters never seen by the jury, never produced in court. Yet testimony which the judges accepted, the jury accepted also. As for Point 2, the fact that Ralegh denied the writing of such a letter seemed only to enhance his guilt; Kemys had confessed to delivery of it. That Cobham had three times retracted his testimony proved only that he was, like all traitors, untrustworthy and should be destroyed. The Attorney General had trapped Sir Walter into a lie concerning communication with Cobham in the Tower. And though Magna Carta said that no man should be forced to testify against himself, in the jury's mind Coke's harsh questioning was no derogation of this law. On the contrary, the prisoner had been given every opportunity to reply and clear himself of guilt.

The day was done, the light was gone. Winchester gates were shut and barred. On its hillside the ancient Hall of Arthur loomed in shadow; lanterns swung behind the tall grilled gates that led to the cells and dungeon far below. . . .

The Jury were willed to go together; who departed and stayed not a quarter of an hour, when they returned, bringing in their verdict, GUILTY OF TREASON.

Ralegh was led to the bar. Chief Justice Popham stood up, bare-headed. In his hand he held the black cap that signified a death sentence. "Sir Walter Ralegh," he said, "I am sorry to see this fallen upon you this day. You have always been taken for a wise man. And I cannot but marvel to see that a man of your wit, as this day you have approved it, could be entangled with so many treasons. I grieve to find that a man of your quality would have sold yourself for a spy to the enemy of your country for 1500 pounds a year. This covetousness is like a canker, that eats the iron place where it lives. . . ."

There was more; to Ralegh it must have been well nigh unendurable. "O God!" he had written to his wife from the Tower, "I cannot live to think how I am derided, the scorns I shall receive, the cruel words of lawyers, the infamous taunts and despites, to be made a wonder and a spectacle! O death, destroy the memory of these and lay me up in dark forgetfulness!"

Of all these cruel taunts, Popham's solemn pronouncement was the worst. Coke had raved but Ralegh could answer him. Now, for Ralegh, denial and affirmation were forever blocked. What the Chief Justice said, the world (or so thought Ralegh) would take as truth. "It now comes to my mind," Popham continued, "why you may not have your accuser brought face to face: for such an one is easily brought to retract when he seeth there is no hope of his own life. . . . It now only remaineth to pronounce the judgment, which I would to God you had not to receive this day of me. I never saw the like trial, and I hope I shall never see the like again."

Raising both hands with the deliberation of an aged man, Popham set the black cap on his head. "Sir Walter Ralegh," he said, "since you have been found guilty of these horrible treasons, the judgment of this court is, That you shall be had from hence to the place whence you came, there to remain until the day of execution. And from thence you shall be drawn upon a hurdle through the open streets to the place of execution, there to be hanged and cut down alive, and your body shall be opened, your heart and bowels plucked out, and your privy members cut off and thrown into the fire before your eyes. Then your head to be stricken off from your body, and your body shall be divided into four quarters, to be disposed of at the King's pleasure.

"And God have mercy upon your soul."

The Devil and Daniel Webster*

STEPHEN VINCENT BENÉT

*There has never been another trial like that of Jabez Stone before Justice
Hathorne with the Devil and Daniel Webster as opposing counsel. This is
a tall story with local color and Faustian overtones, a modern classic which
has been filmed, televised, and turned into an opera. Even in fantasy there
is verisimilitude when an artist like Stephen Vincent Benét is at work. The
result in this case is a masterpiece which will be read with pleasure by
lawyers always. Benét (1898–1943) was educated at Yale and the Sorbonne.
From the age of seventeen, he published a steady stream of stories, novels,
and poems, winning the Pulitzer Prize for poetry in 1929 for* John Brown's
Body. *Benét's tenderness comes out beautifully in the short story of adoles-
cence "Too Early Spring"; his Orwellian gift of prophecy is seen in the
story "By the Waters of Babylon" and the poetic "Manhattan Nightmares I
and III."*

It's a story they tell in the border country, where Massachusetts joins
Vermont and New Hampshire.

Yes, Dan'l Webster's dead—or, at least, they buried him. But every
time there's a thunderstorm around Marshfield, they say you can hear his
rolling voice in the hollows of the sky. And they say that if you go to his
grave and speak loud and clear, "Dan'l Webster—Dan'l Webster!" the
ground'll begin to shiver and the trees begin to shake. And after a while
you'll hear a deep voice saying, "Neighbor, how stands the Union?" Then
you better answer the Union stands as she stood, rock-bottomed and cop-
per-sheathed, one and indivisible, or he's liable to rear right out of the
ground. At least, that's what I was told when I was a youngster.

You see, for a while, he was the biggest man in the country. He never
got to be President, but he was the biggest man. There were thousands that
trusted in him right next to God Almighty, and they told stories about him
that were like the stories of patriarchs and such. They said, when he stood
up to speak, stars and stripes came right out in the sky, and once he spoke
against a river and made it sink into the ground. They said, when he
walked the woods with his fishing rod, Killall, the trout would jump out

* From *Selected Works of Stephen Vincent Benét*, Rinehart & Company, Inc. Copyright, 1936, by Stephen Vincent Benét.

330

of the streams right into his pockets, for they knew it was no use putting up a fight against him; and, when he argued a case, he could turn on the harps of the blessed and the shaking of the earth underground. That was the kind of man he was, and his big farm up at Marshfield was suitable to him. The chickens he raised were all white meat down to the drumsticks, the cows were tended like children, and the big ram called Goliath had horns with a curl like a morning-glory vine and could butt through an iron door. But Dan'l wasn't one of your gentlemen farmers; he knew all the ways of the land, and he'd be up by candlelight to see that the chores got done. A man with a mouth like a mastiff, a brow like a mountain and eyes like burning anthracite—that was Dan'l Webster in his prime. And the biggest case he argued never got written down in the books, for he argued it against the devil, nip and tuck and no holds barred. And this is the way I used to hear it told.

There was a man named Jabez Stone, lived at Cross Corners, New Hampshire. He wasn't a bad man to start with, but he was an unlucky man. If he planted corn, he got borers; if he planted potatoes, he got blight. He had good-enough land, but it didn't prosper him; he had a decent wife and children, but the more children he had, the less there was to feed them. If stones cropped up in his neighbor's field, boulders boiled up in his; if he had a horse with the spavins, he'd trade it for one with the staggers and give something extra. There's some folks bound to be like that, apparently. But one day Jabez Stone got sick of the whole business.

He'd been plowing that morning and he'd just broke the plowshare on a rock that he could have sworn hadn't been there yesterday. And as he stood looking at the plowshare, the off horse began to cough—that ropy kind of cough that means sickness and horse doctors. There were two children down with the measles, his wife was ailing, and he had a whitlow on his thumb. It was about the last straw for Jabez Stone. "I vow," he said, and he looked around him kind of desperate—"I vow it's enough to make a man want to sell his soul to the devil! And I would, too, for two cents!"

Then he felt a kind of queerness come over him at having said what he'd said; though, naturally, being a New Hampshireman, he wouldn't take it back. But, all the same, when it got to be evening and, as far as he could see, no notice had been taken, he felt relieved in his mind, for he was a religious man. But notice is always taken, sooner or later, just like the Good Book says. And, sure enough, next day, about suppertime, a soft-spoken, dark-dressed stranger drove up in a handsome buggy and asked for Jabez Stone.

Well, Jabez told his family it was a lawyer, come to see him about a legacy. But he knew who it was.

He didn't like the looks of the stranger, nor the way he smiled with his teeth. They were white teeth, and plentiful—some say they were filed to a point, but I wouldn't vouch for that. And he didn't like it when the dog took one look at the stranger and ran away howling, with his tail between his legs. But having passed his word, more or less, he stuck to it, and they went out behind the barn and made their bargain. Jabez Stone had to prick his finger to sign, and the stranger lent him a silver pin. The wound healed clean, but it left a little white scar.

After that, all of a sudden, things began to pick up and prosper for Jabez Stone. His cows got fat and his horses sleek, his crops were the envy of the neighborhood, and lightning might strike all over the valley, but it wouldn't strike his barn. Pretty soon, he was one of the prosperous people of the county; they asked him to stand for selectman, and he stood for it; there began to be talk of running him for state senate. All in all, you might say the Stone family was as happy and contented as cats in a dairy. And so they were, except for Jabez Stone.

He'd been contented enough, the first few years. It's a great thing when bad luck turns; it drives most other things out of your head. True, every now and then, especially in rainy weather, the little white scar on his finger would give him a twinge. And once a year, punctual as clockwork, the stranger with the handsome buggy would come driving by. But the sixth year, the stranger lighted, and, after that, his peace was over for Jabez Stone.

The stranger came up through the lower field, switching his boots with a cane—they were handsome black boots, but Jabez Stone never liked the look of them, particularly the toes. And, after he'd passed the time of day, he said, "Well, Mr. Stone, you're a hummer! It's a very pretty property you've got here, Mr. Stone."

"Well, some might favor it and others might not," said Jabez Stone, for he was a New Hampshireman.

"Oh, no need to decry your industry!" said the stranger, very easy, showing his teeth in a smile. "After all, we know what's been done, and it's been according to contract and specifications. So when—ahem—the mortgage falls due next year, you shouldn't have any regrets."

"Speaking of that mortgage, mister," said Jabez Stone, and he looked around for help to the earth and the sky, "I'm beginning to have one or two doubts about it."

"Doubts?" said the stranger, not quite so pleasantly.

"Why, yes," said Jabez Stone. "This being the U. S. A. and me always having been a religious man." He cleared his throat and got bolder. "Yes, sir," he said, "I'm beginning to have considerable doubts as to that mortgage holding in court."

"There's courts and courts," said the stranger, clicking his teeth. "Still, we might as well have a look at the original document." And he hauled out a big black pocketbook, full of papers. "Sherwin, Slater, Stevens, Stone," he muttered. "I, Jabez Stone, for a term of seven years—Oh, it's quite in order, I think."

But Jabez Stone wasn't listening, for he saw something else flutter out of the black pocketbook. It was something that looked like a moth, but it wasn't a moth. And as Jabez Stone stared at it, it seemed to speak to him in a small sort of piping voice, terrible small and thin, but terrible human. "Neighbor Stone!" it squeaked. "Neighbor Stone! Help me! For God's sake, help me!"

But before Jabez Stone could stir his hand or foot, the stranger whipped out a big bandanna handkerchief, caught the creature in it, just like a butterfly, and started tying up the ends of the bandanna.

"Sorry for the interruption," he said. "As I was saying—"

But Jabez Stone was shaking all over like a scared horse.

"That's Miser Stevens' voice!" he said, in a croak. "And you've got him in your handkerchief!"

The stranger looked a little embarrassed.

"Yes, I really should have transferred him to the collecting box," he said with a simper, "but there were some rather unusual specimens there and I didn't want them crowded. Well, well, these little contretemps will occur."

"I don't know what you mean by contertan," said Jabez Stone, "but that was Miser Stevens' voice! And he ain't dead! You can't tell me he is! He was just as spry and mean as a woodchuck, Tuesday!"

"In the midst of life—" said the stranger, kind of pious. "Listen!" Then a bell began to toll in the valley and Jabez Stone listened, with the sweat running down his face. For he knew it was tolled for Miser Stevens and that he was dead.

"These long-standing accounts," said the stranger with a sigh; "one really hates to close them. But business is business."

He still had the bandanna in his hand, and Jabez Stone felt sick as he saw the cloth struggle and flutter.

"Are they all as small as that?" he asked hoarsely.

"Small?" said the stranger. "Oh, I see what you mean. Why, they vary." He measured Jabez Stone with his eyes, and his teeth showed. "Don't worry, Mr. Stone," he said. "You'll go with a very good grade. I wouldn't trust you outside the collecting box. Now, a man like Dan'l Webster, of course—well, we'd have to build a special box for him, and even at that, I imagine the wing spread would astonish you. But, in your case, as I was saying—"

"Put that handkerchief away!" said Jabez Stone, and he began to beg and to pray. But the best he could get at the end was a three years' extension, with conditions.

But till you make a bargain like that, you've got no idea of how fast four years can run. By the last months of those years, Jabez Stone's known all over the state and there's talk of running him for governor—and it's dust and ashes in his mouth. For every day, when he gets up, he thinks, "There's one more night gone," and every night when he lies down, he thinks of the black pocketbook and the soul of Miser Stevens, and it makes him sick at heart. Till, finally, he can't bear it any longer, and, in the last days of the last year, he hitches up his horse and drives off to seek Dan'l Webster. For Dan'l was born in New Hampshire, only a few miles from Cross Corners, and it's well known that he has a particular soft spot for old neighbors.

It was early in the morning when he got to Marshfield, but Dan'l was up already, talking Latin to the farm hands and wrestling with the ram, Goliath, and trying out a new trotter and working up speeches to make against John C. Calhoun. But when he heard a New Hampshireman had come to see him, he dropped everything else he was doing for that was Dan'l's way. He gave Jabez Stone a breakfast that five men couldn't eat, went into the living history of every man and woman in Cross Corners, and finally asked him how he could serve him.

Jabez Stone allowed that it was a kind of mortgage case.

"Well, I haven't pleaded a mortgage case in a long time, and I don't generally plead now, except before the Supreme Court," said Dan'l, "but if I can, I'll help you."

"Then I've got hope for the first time in ten years," said Jabez Stone, and told him the details.

Dan'l walked up and down as he listened, hands behind his back, now and then asking a question, now and then plunging his eyes at the floor, as if they'd bore through it like gimlets. When Jabez Stone had finished, Dan'l puffed out his checks and blew. Then he turned to Jabez Stone and a smile broke over his face like the sunrise over Monadnock.

"You've certainly given yourself the devil's own row to hoe, Neighbor Stone," he said, "but I'll take your case."

"You'll take it?" said Jabez Stone, hardly daring to believe.

"Yes," said Dan'l Webster. "I've got about seventy-five other things to do and the Missouri Compromise to straighten out, but I'll take your case. For if two New Hampshiremen aren't a match for the devil, we might as well give the country back to the Indians."

Then he shook Jabez Stone by the hand and said, "Did you come down here in a hurry?"

"Well, I admit I made time," said Jabez Stone.

"You'll go back faster," said Dan'l Webster, and he told 'em to hitch up Constitution and Constellation to the carriage. They were matched grays with one white forefoot, and they stepped like greased lightning.

Well, I won't describe how excited and pleased the whole Stone family was to have the great Dan'l Webster for a guest, when they finally got there. Jabez Stone had lost his hat on the way, blown off when they overtook a wind, but he didn't take much account of that. But after supper he sent the family off to bed, for he had most particular business with Mr. Webster. Mrs. Stone wanted them to sit in the front parlor, but Dan'l Webster knew front parlors and said he preferred the kitchen. So it was there they sat, waiting for the stranger, with a jug on the table between them and a bright

fire on the hearth—the stranger being scheduled to show up on the stroke
of midnight, according to specifications.

Well, most men wouldn't have asked for better company than Dan'l
Webster and a jug. But with every tick of the clock Jabez Stone got sadder
and sadder. His eyes roved round, and though he sampled the jug you
could see he couldn't taste it. Finally, on the stroke of 11:30 he reached
over and grabbed Dan'l Webster by the arm.

"Mr. Webster, Mr. Webster!" he said, and his voice was shaking with
fear and a desperate courage. "For God's sake, Mr. Webster, harness your
horses and get away from this place while you can!"

"You've brought me a long way, neighbor, to tell me you don't like my
company," said Dan'l Webster, quite peaceable, pulling at the jug.

"Miserable wretch that I am!" groaned Jabez Stone. "I've brought you a
devilish way, and now I see my folly. Let him take me if he wills. I don't
hanker after it, I must say, but I can stand it. But you're the Union's stay
and New Hampshire's pride! He mustn't get you, Mr. Webster! He mustn't
get you!"

Dan'l Webster looked at the distracted man, all gray and shaking in the
firelight, and laid a hand on his shoulder.

"I'm obliged to you, Neighbor Stone," he said gently. "It's kindly thought
of. But there's a jug on the table and a case in hand. And I never left a
jug or a case half finished in my life."

And just at that moment there was a sharp rap on the door.

"Ah," said Dan'l Webster, very coolly, "I thought your clock was a trifle
slow, Neighbor Stone." He stepped to the door and opened it. "Come in!"
he said.

The stranger came in—very dark and tall he looked in the firelight. He
was carrying a box under his arm—a black, japanned box with little air
holes in the lid. At the sight of the box, Jabez Stone gave a low cry and
shrank into a corner of the room.

"Mr. Webster, I presume," said the stranger, very polite, but with his eyes
glowing like a fox's deep in the woods.

"Attorney of record for Jabez Stone," said Dan'l Webster, but his eyes
were glowing too. "Might I ask your name?"

"I've gone by a good many," said the stranger carelessly. "Perhaps Scratch
will do for the evening. I'm often called that in these regions."

Then he sat down at the table and poured himself a drink from the jug.
The liquor was cold in the jug, but it came steaming into the glass.

"And now," said the stranger, smiling and showing his teeth, "I shall call
upon you, as a law-abiding citizen, to assist me in taking possession of
my property."

Well, with that the argument began—and it went hot and heavy. At first,
Jabez Stone had a flicker of hope, but when he saw Dan'l Webster being
forced back at point after point, he just scrunched in his corner, with his

eyes on that japanned box. For there wasn't any doubt as to the deed or the signature—that was the worst of it. Dan'l Webster twisted and turned and thumped his fist on the table, but he couldn't get away from that. He offered to compromise the case; the stranger wouldn't hear of it. He pointed out the property had increased in value, and state senators ought to be worth more; the stranger stuck to the letter of the law. He was a great lawyer, Dan'l Webster, but we know who's the King of Lawyers, as the Good Book tells us, and it seemed as if, for the first time, Dan'l Webster had met his match.

Finally, the stranger yawned a little. "Your spirited efforts on behalf of your client do you credit, Mr. Webster," he said, "but if you have no more arguments to adduce, I'm rather pressed for time"—and Jabez Stone shuddered.

Dan'l Webster's brow looked dark as a thundercloud.

"Pressed or not, you shall not have this man!" he thundered. "Mr. Stone is an American citizen, and no American citizen may be forced into the service of a foreign prince. We fought England for that in '12 and we'll fight all hell for it again!"

"Foreign?" said the stranger. "And who calls me a foreigner?"

"Well, I never yet heard of the dev—of your claiming American citizenship," said Dan'l Webster with surprise.

"And who with a better right?" said the stranger, with one of his terrible smiles. "When the first wrong was done to the first Indian, I was there. When the first slaver put out for the Congo, I stood on her deck. Am I not in your books and stories and beliefs, from the first settlements on? Am I not spoken of, still, in every church in New England? 'Tis true the North claims me for a Southerner and the South for a Northerner, but I am neither, I am merely an honest American like yourself—and of the best descent—for, to tell the truth, Mr. Webster, though I don't like to boast of it, my name is older in this country than yours."

"Aha!" said Dan'l Webster, with the veins standing out in his forehead. "Then I stand on the Constitution! I demand a trial for my client!"

"The case is hardly one for an ordinary court," said the stranger, his eyes flickering. "And, indeed, the lateness of the hour—"

"Let it be any court you choose, so it is an American judge and an American jury!" said Dan'l Webster in his pride. "Let it be the quick or the dead; I'll abide the issue!"

"You have said it," said the stranger, and pointed his finger at the door. And with that, and all of a sudden, there was a rushing of wind outside and a noise of footsteps. They came, clear and distinct, through the night. And yet, they were not like the footsteps of living men.

"In God's name, who comes so late?" cried Jabez Stone, in an ague of fear.

"The jury Mr. Webster demands," said the stranger, sipping at his boiling glass. "You must pardon the rough appearance of one or two; they will have come a long way."

And with that the fire burned blue and the door blew open and twelve men entered, one by one.

If Jabez Stone had been sick with terror before, he was blind with terror now. For there was Walter Butler, the loyalist, who spread fire and horror through the Mohawk Valley in the times of the Revolution; and there was Simon Girty, the renegade, who saw white men burned at the stake and whooped with the Indians to see them burn. His eyes were green, like a catamount's, and the stains on his hunting shirt did not come from the blood of the deer. King Philip was there, wild and proud as he had been in life, with the great gash in his head that gave him his death wound, and cruel Governor Dale, who broke men on the wheel. There was Morton of Merry Mount, who so vexed the Plymouth Colony, with his flushed, loose, handsome face and his hate of the godly. There was Teach, the bloody pirate, with his black beard curling on his breast. The Reverend John Smeet, with his strangler's hands and his Geneva gown, walked as daintily as he had to the gallows. The red print of the rope was still around his neck, but he carried a perfumed handkerchief in one hand. One and all, they came into the room with the fires of hell still upon them, and the stranger named their names and their deeds as they came, till the tale of twelve was told. Yet the stranger had told the truth—they had all played a part in America.

"Are you satisfied with the jury, Mr. Webster?" said the stranger mockingly, when they had taken their places.

The sweat stood upon Dan'l Webster's brow, but his voice was clear.

"Quite satisfied," he said. "Though I miss General Arnold from the company."

"Benedict Arnold is engaged upon other business," said the stranger, with a glower. "Ah, you asked for a justice, I believe."

He pointed his finger once more, and a tall man, soberly clad in Puritan garb, with the burning gaze of the fanatic, stalked into the room and took his judge's place.

"Justice Hathorne is a jurist of experience," said the stranger. "He presided at certain witch trials once held in Salem. There were others who repented of the business later, but not he."

"Repent of such notable wonders and undertakings?" said the stern old justice. "Nay, hang them—hang them all!" And he muttered to himself in a way that struck ice into the soul of Jabez Stone.

Then the trial began, and, as you might expect, it didn't look anyways good for the defense. And Jabez Stone didn't make much of a witness in his own behalf. He took one look at Simon Girty and screeched, and they had to put him back in his corner in a kind of swoon.

It didn't halt the trial, though; the trial went on, as trials do. Dan'l

Webster had faced some hard juries and hanging judges in his time, but this was the hardest he'd ever faced, and he knew it. They sat there with a kind of glitter in their eyes, and the stranger's smooth voice went on and on. Every time he'd raise an objection, it'd be "Objection sustained," but whenever Dan'l objected, it'd be "Objection denied." Well, you couldn't expect fair play from a fellow like this Mr. Scratch.

It got to Dan'l in the end, and he began to heat, like iron in the forge. When he got up to speak he was going to flay that stranger with every trick known to the law, and the judge and jury too. He didn't care if it was contempt of court or what would happen to him for it. He didn't care any more what happened to Jabez Stone. He just got madder and madder, thinking of what he'd say. And yet, curiously enough, the more he thought about it, the less he was able to arrange his speech in his mind.

Till, finally, it was time for him to get up on his feet, and he did so, all ready to bust out with lightnings and denunciations. But before he started he looked over the judge and jury for a moment, such being his custom. And he noticed the glitter in their eyes was twice as strong as before, and they all leaned forward. Like hounds just before they get the fox, they looked, and the blue mist of evil in the room thickened as he watched them. Then he saw what he'd been about to do, and he wiped his forehead, as a man might who's just escaped falling into a pit in the dark.

For it was him they'd come for, not only Jabez Stone. He read it in the glitter of their eyes and in the way the stranger hid his mouth with one hand. And if he fought them with their own weapons, he'd fall into their power; he knew that, though he couldn't have told you how. It was his own anger and horror that burned in their eyes; and he'd have to wipe that out or the case was lost. He stood there for a moment, his black eyes burning like anthracite. And then he began to speak.

He started off in a low voice, though you could hear every word. They say he could call on the harps of the blessed when he chose. And this was just as simple and easy as a man could talk. But he didn't start out by condemning or reviling. He was talking about the things that make a country a country, and a man a man.

And he began with the simple things that everybody's known and felt— the freshness of a fine morning when you're young, and the taste of food when you're hungry, and the new day that's every day when you're a child. He took them up and he turned them in his hands. They were good things for any man. But without freedom, they sickened. And when he talked of those enslaved, and the sorrows of slavery, his voice got like a big bell. He talked of the early days of America and the men who had made those days. It wasn't a spread-eagle speech, but he made you see it. He admitted all the wrong that had ever been done. But he showed how, out of the wrong and the right, the suffering and the starvations, something new had come. And everybody had played a part in it, even the traitors.

Then he turned to Jabez Stone and showed him as he was—an ordinary man who'd had hard luck and wanted to change it. And, because he'd wanted to change it, now he was going to be punished for all eternity. And yet there was good in Jabez Stone, and he showed that good. He was hard and mean, in some ways, but he was a man. There was sadness in being a man, but it was a proud thing too. And he showed what the pride of it was till you couldn't help feeling it. Yes, even in hell, if a man was a man, you'd know it. And he wasn't pleading for any one person any more, though his voice rang like an organ. He was telling the story and the failures and the endless journey of mankind. They got tricked and trapped and bamboozled, but it was a great journey. And no demon that was ever foaled could know the inwardness of it—it took a man to do that.

The fire began to die on the hearth and the wind before morning to blow. The light was getting gray in the room when Dan'l Webster finished. And his words came back at the end to New Hampshire ground, and the one spot of land that each man loves and clings to. He painted a picture of that, and to each one of that jury he spoke of things long forgotten. For his voice could search the heart, and that was his gift and his strength. And to one, his voice was like the forest and its secrecy, and to another like the sea and the storms of the sea; and one heard the cry of his lost nation in it, and another saw a little harmless scene he hadn't remembered for years. But each saw something. And when Dan'l Webster finished he didn't know whether or not he'd saved Jabez Stone. But he knew he'd done a miracle. For the glitter was gone from the eyes of judge and jury, and, for the moment, they were men again, and knew they were men.

"The defense rests," said Dan'l Webster, and stood there like a mountain. His ears were still ringing with his speech, and he didn't hear anything else till he heard Judge Hathorne say, "The jury will retire to consider its verdict."

Walter Butler rose in his place and his face had a dark, gay pride on it.

"The jury has considered its verdict," he said, and looked the stranger full in the eye. "We find for the defendant, Jabez Stone."

With that, the smile left the stranger's face, but Walter Butler did not flinch.

"Perhaps 'tis not strictly in accordance with the evidence," he said, "but even the damned may salute the eloquence of Mr. Webster."

With that, the long crow of a rooster split the gray morning sky, and judge and jury were gone from the room like a puff of smoke and as if they had never been there. The stranger turned to Dan'l Webster, smiling wryly.

"Major Butler was always a bold man," he said. "I had not thought him quite so bold. Nevertheless, my congratulations, as between two gentlemen."

"I'll have that paper first, if you please," said Dan'l Webster, and he took it and tore it into four pieces. It was queerly warm to the touch. "And now," he said, "I'll have you!" and his hand come down like a bear trap on the stranger's arm. For he knew that once you bested anybody like Mr. Scratch in fair fight, his power on you was gone. And he could see that Mr. Scratch knew it too.

The stranger twisted and wriggled, but he couldn't get out of that grip. "Come, come, Mr. Webster," he said, smiling palely. "This sort of thing is ridic—ouch!—is ridiculous. If you're worried about the costs of the case, naturally, I'd be glad to pay—"

"And so you shall!" said Dan'l Webster, shaking him till his teeth rattled. "For you'll sit right down at that table and draw up a document, promising never to bother Jabez Stone nor his heirs or assigns nor any other New Hampshireman till doomsday! For any hades we want to raise in this state, we can raise ourselves, without assistance from strangers."

"Ouch!" said the stranger. "Ouch! Well, they never did run very big to the barrel, but—ouch!—I agree!"

So he sat down and drew up the document. But Dan'l Webster kept his hand on his coat collar all the time.

"And, now, may I go?" said the stranger, quite humble, when Dan'l had seen the document was in proper and legal form.

"Go?" said Dan'l, giving him another shake. "I'm still trying to figure out what I'll do with you. For you've settled the costs of the case, but you haven't settled with me. I think I'll take you back to Marshfield," he said, kind of reflective. "I've got a ram there named Goliath that can butt through an iron door. I'd kind of like to turn you loose in his field and see what he'd do."

Well, with that the stranger began to beg and to plead. And he begged and he pled so humble that finally Dan'l, who was naturally kind-hearted, agreed to let him go. The stranger seemed terrible grateful for that and said, just to show they were friends, he'd tell Dan'l's fortune before leaving. So Dan'l agreed to that, though he didn't take much stock in fortune-tellers ordinarily. But, naturally, the stranger was a little different.

Well, he pried and he peered at the lines in Dan'l's hands. And he told him one thing and another that was quite remarkable. But they were all in the past.

"Yes, all that's true, and it happened," said Dan'l Webster. "But what's to come in the future?"

The stranger grinned, kind of happily, and shook his head.

"The future's not as you think it," he said. "It's dark. You have a great ambition, Mr. Webster."

"I have," said Dan'l firmly, for everybody knew he wanted to be President.

"It seems almost within your grasp," said the stranger, "but you will not attain it. Lesser men will be made President and you will be passed over."

"And, if I am, I'll still be Daniel Webster," said Dan'l. "Say on."

"You have two strong sons," said the stranger, shaking his head. "You look to found a line. But each will die in war and neither reach greatness."

"Live or die, they are still my sons," said Dan'l Webster. "Say on."

"You have made great speeches," said the stranger. "You will make more."

"Ah," said Dan'l Webster.

"But the last great speech you will make will turn many of your own against you," said the stranger. "They will call you Ichabod; they will call you by other names. Even in New England, some will say you have turned your coat and sold your country, and their voices will be loud against you till you die."

"So it is an honest speech, it does not matter what men say," said Dan'l Webster. Then he looked at the stranger and their glances locked.

"One question," he said. "I have fought for the Union all my life. Will I see that fight won against those who would tear it apart?"

"Not while you live," said the stranger, grimly, "but it will be won. And after you are dead, there are thousands who will fight for your cause, because of words that you spoke."

"Why, then, you long-barreled, slab-sided, lantern-jawed, fortune-telling note shaver!" said Dan'l Webster, with a great roar of laughter, "be off with you to your own place before I put my mark on you! For, by the thirteen original colonies, I'd go to the Pit itself to save the Union!"

And with that he drew back his foot for a kick that would have stunned a horse. It was only the tip of his shoe that caught the stranger, but he went flying out of the door with his collecting box under his arm.

"And now," said Dan'l Webster, seeing Jabez Stone beginning to rouse from his swoon, "let's see what's left in the jug, for it's dry work talking all night. I hope there's pie for breakfast, Neighbor Stone."

But they say that whenever the devil comes near Marshfield, even now, he gives it a wide berth. And he hasn't been seen in the state of New Hampshire from that day to this. I'm not talking about Massachusetts or Vermont.

Bardell v. Pickwick*

CHARLES DICKENS

In London, in June of 1836, Greville, the great diarist, noted that "the town has been full of Lord Melbourne's trial." This was a suit brought by the Hon. George Chapple Norton against the Prime Minister, Lord Melbourne, accusing him of adultery with his wife the beautiful Caroline Norton. The shorthand reporter for The Morning Chronicle, *a young man named Charles Dickens, attended the trial at Westminster, which was notable only for the flimsy evidence of some discharged servants and the obvious innocence of the letters exchanged between the lord and lady. (The jury delivered their verdict in favor of the Prime Minister without leaving the court.) Some weeks before, Charles Dickens had begun to write his first great popular success,* The Pickwick Papers, *and undoubtedly some of the funniest lines in* Bardell v. Pickwick *were suggested by the Norton-Melbourne proceedings. There may have been other sources. Edmund Wilson names* Jorrocks *by William Surtees, but the result, as in every work of art, is a transformation, not a borrowing.*

Those critics who assert, and not without reason, that The Pickwick Papers *is Dickens' masterpiece may also claim that* Bardell v. Pickwick *is the brightest example of its author's comic exuberance. It has this advantage over certain other masterpieces of the past, that it is just as amusing now as when it was written more than a century ago.*

"I wonder what the foreman of the jury, whoever he'll be, has got for breakfast," said Mr. Snodgrass, by way of keeping up a conversation on the eventful morning of the fourteenth of February.

"Ah!" said Perker, "I hope he's got a good one."

"Why so?" inquired Mr. Pickwick.

"Highly important; very important, my dear sir," replied Perker. "A good, contented, well-breakfasted juryman, is a capital thing to get hold of. Discontented or hungry jurymen, my dear sir, always find for the plaintiff."

"Bless my heart," said Mr. Pickwick, looking very blank; "what do they do that for?"

"Why, I don't know," replied the little man, coolly; "saves time, I suppose. If it's near dinner-time, the foreman takes out his watch when the jury

* From *The Pickwick Papers.*

has retired, and says, 'Dear me, gentlemen, ten minutes to five, I declare!
I dine at five, gentlemen.' 'So do I,' says everybody else, except two men
who ought to have dined at three, and seem more than half disposed to
stand out in consequence. The foreman smiles, and puts up his watch:—
'Well, gentlemen, what do we say, plaintiff or defendant, gentlemen? I
rather think, so far as I am concerned, gentlemen,—I say, I rather think,—
but don't let that influence you—I *rather* think the plaintiff's the man.'
Upon this, two or three other men are sure to say that they think so too—as
of course they do; and then they get on very unanimously and comfortably.
Ten minutes past nine!" said the little man, looking at his watch. "Time we
were off, my dear sir; breach of promise trial—court is generally full in
such cases. You had better ring for a coach, my dear sir, or we shall be
rather late."

Mr. Pickwick immediately rang the bell; and a coach having been pro-
cured, the four Pickwickians and Mr. Perker ensconced themselves therein,
and drove to Guildhall; Sam Weller, Mr. Lowten, and the blue bag, followed
in a cab.

"Lowten," said Perker, when they reached the outer hall of the court,
"put Mr. Pickwick's friends in the students' box; Mr. Pickwick himself had
better sit by me. This way, my dear sir, this way." Taking Mr. Pickwick
by the coatsleeve, the little man led him to the low seat just beneath the
desks of the King's Counsel, which is constructed for the convenience of
attorneys, who from that spot can whisper into the ear of the leading
counsel in the case, any instructions that may be necessary during the progress of the trial. The occupants of this seat are invisible to the great body of
spectators, inasmuch as they sit on a much lower level than either the
barristers or the audience, whose seats are raised above the floor. Of course
they have their backs to both, and their faces towards the judge.

"That's the witness-box, I suppose?" said Mr. Pickwick, pointing to a kind
of pulpit, with a brass rail, on his left hand.

"That's the witness-box, my dear sir," replied Perker, disinterring a quantity of papers from the blue bag, which Lowten had just deposited at
his feet.

"And that," said Mr. Pickwick, pointing to a couple of enclosed seats
on his right, "that's where the jurymen sit, is it not?"

"The identical place, my dear sir," replied Perker, tapping the lid of
his snuff-box.

Mr. Pickwick stood up in a state of great agitation, and took a glance at
the court. There were already a pretty large sprinkling of spectators in
the gallery, and a numerous muster of gentlemen in wigs, in the barristers'
seats: who presented, as a body, all that pleasing and extensive variety of
nose and whisker for which the bar of England is so justly celebrated. Such
of the gentlemen as had a brief to carry, carried it in as conspicuous a
manner as possible, and occasionally scratched their noses therewith, to

impress the fact more strongly on the observation of the spectators. Other gentlemen, who had no briefs to show, carried under their arms goodly octavos, with a red label behind, and that underdone-pie-crust-coloured cover, which is technically known as "law calf." Others, who had neither briefs nor books, thrust their hands into their pocket, and looked as wise as they conveniently could; others, again, moved here and there with great restlessness and earnestness of manner, content to awaken thereby the admiration and astonishment of the uninitiated strangers. The whole, to the great wonderment of Mr. Pickwick, were divided into little groups, who were chatting and discussing the news of the day in the most unfeeling manner possible,—just as if no trial at all were coming on.

A bow from Mr. Phunky, as he entered, and took his seat behind the row appropriated to the King's Counsel, attracted Mr. Pickwick's attention; and he had scarcely returned it, when Mr. Serjeant Snubbin appeared, followed by Mr. Mallard, who half hid the Serjeant behind a large crimson bag, which he placed on his table, and, after shaking hands with Perker, withdrew. Then there entered two or three more Serjeants; and among them, one with a fat body and a red face, who nodded in a friendly manner to Mr. Serjeant Snubbin, and said it was a fine morning.

"Who's that red-faced man, who said it was a fine morning, and nodded to our counsel?" whispered Mr. Pickwick.

"Mr. Serjeant Buzfuz," replied Perker. "He's opposed to us; he leads on the other side. That gentleman behind him is Mr. Skimpin, his junior."

Mr. Pickwick was on the point of inquiring, with great abhorrence of the man's cold-blooded villainy, how Mr. Serjeant Buzfuz, who was counsel for the opposite party, dared to presume to tell Mr. Serjeant Snubbin, who was counsel for him, that it was a fine morning, when he was interrupted by a general rising of the barristers, and a loud cry of "Silence!" from the officers of the court. Looking round, he found that this was caused by the entrance of the judge.

Mr. Justice Stareleigh (who sat in the absence of the Chief Justice, occasioned by indisposition), was a most particularly short man, and so fat, that he seemed all face and waistcoat. He rolled in, upon two little turned legs, and having bobbed gravely to the bar, who bobbed gravely to him, put his little legs underneath his table, and his three-cornered hat upon it; and when Mr. Justice Stareleigh had done this, all you could see of him was two queer little eyes, one broad pink face, and somewhere about half of a big and very comical-looking wig.

The judge had no sooner taken his seat, than the officer on the floor of the court called out "Silence!" in a commanding tone, upon which another officer in the gallery cried "Silence!" in an angry manner, whereupon three or four more ushers shouted "Silence!" in a voice of indignant remonstrance. This being done, a gentleman in black, who sat below the judge, proceeded to call over the names of the jury; and after a great deal of bawling, it was discovered that only ten special jurymen were present. Upon this, Mr. Serjeant Buzfuz prayed a *tales;* the gentleman in black then proceeded to press into the special jury, two of the common jurymen; and a greengrocer and a chemist were caught directly.

"Answer to your names, gentlemen, that you may be sworn," said the gentleman in black. "Richard Upwitch."

"Here," said the green-grocer.

"Thomas Groffin."

"Here," said the chemist.

"Take the book, gentlemen. You shall well and truly try—"

"I beg this court's pardon," said the chemist, who was a tall, thin, yellow-visaged man, "but I hope this court will excuse my attendance."

"On what grounds, sir?" said Mr. Justice Stareleigh.

"I have no assistant, my Lord," said the chemist.

"I can't help that, sir," replied Mr. Justice Stareleigh. "You should hire one."

"I can't afford it, my Lord," rejoined the chemist.

"Then you ought to be able to afford it, sir," said the judge, reddening; for Justice Stareleigh's temper bordered on the irritable, and brooked not contradiction.

"I know I *ought* to do, if I got on as well as I deserved, but I don't, my Lord," answered the chemist.

"Swear the gentleman," said the judge, peremptorily.

The officer had got no further than the "You shall well and truly try," when he was again interrupted by the chemist.

"I am to be sworn, my Lord, am I?" said the chemist.

"Certainly, sir," replied the testy little judge.

"Very well, my Lord," replied the chemist, in a resigned manner. "Then there'll be murder before this trial's over; that's all. Swear me, if you please, sir;" and sworn the chemist was, before the judge could find words to utter.

"I merely wanted to observe, my Lord," said the chemist, taking his seat with great deliberation, "that I've left nobody but an errand-boy in my shop. He is a very nice boy, my Lord, but he is not acquainted with drugs; and I know that the prevailing impression on his mind is, that Epsom salts means oxalic acid; and syrup of senna, laudanum. That's all, my Lord." With this, the tall chemist composed himself into a comfortable attitude, and, assuming a pleasant expression of countenance, appeared to have prepared himself for the worst.

Mr. Pickwick was regarding the chemist with feelings of the deepest horror, when a slight sensation was perceptible in the body of the court; and immediately afterwards Mrs. Bardell, supported by Mrs. Cluppins, was led in, and placed in a drooping state, at the other end of the seat on which Mr. Pickwick sat. An extra sized umbrella was then handed in by Mr.

Dodson, and a pair of pattens by Mr. Fogg, each of whom had prepared
a most sympathising and melancholy face for the occasion. Mrs. Sanders
then appeared, leading in Master Bardell. At sight of her child, Mrs. Bardell
started; suddenly recollecting herself, she kissed him in a frantic manner;
then relapsing into a state of hysterical imbecility, the good lady requested
to be informed where she was. In reply to this, Mrs. Cluppins and Mrs.
Sanders turned their heads away and wept, while Messrs. Dodson and Fogg
intreated the plaintiff to compose herself. Serjeant Buzfuz rubbed his eyes
very hard with a large white handkerchief, and gave an appealing look
towards the jury, while the judge was visibly affected, and several of the
beholders tried to cough down their emotions.

"Very good notion, that, indeed," whispered Perker to Mr. Pickwick.
"Capital fellows those Dodson and Fogg; excellent ideas of effect, my
dear sir, excellent."

As Perker spoke, Mrs. Bardell began to recover by slow degrees, while
Mrs. Cluppins, after a careful survey of Master Bardell's buttons and the
button-holes to which they severally belonged, placed him on the floor
of the court in front of his mother,—a commanding position in which he
could not fail to awaken the full commiseration and sympathy of both judge
and jury. This was not done without considerable opposition, and many
tears, on the part of the young gentleman himself, who had certain inward
misgivings that the placing him within the full glare of the judge's eye was
only a formal prelude to his being immediately ordered away for instant
execution, or for transportation beyond the seas, during the whole term of
his natural life, at the very least.

"Bardell and Pickwick," cried the gentleman in black, calling on the case,
which stood first on the list.

"I am for the plaintiff, my Lord," said Mr. Serjeant Buzfuz.

"Who is with you, brother Buzfuz?" said the judge. Mr. Skimpin bowed,
to intimate that he was.

"I appear for the defendant, my Lord," said Mr. Serjeant Snubbin.

"Anybody with you, brother Snubbin?" inquired the court.

"Mr. Phunky, my Lord," replied Serjeant Snubbin.

"Serjeant Buzfuz and Mr. Skimpin for the plaintiff," said the judge, writing down the names in his note-book, and reading as he wrote; "for the
defendant, Serjeant Snubbin and Mr. Monkey."

"Beg your Lordship's pardon, Phunky."

"Oh, very good," said the judge; "I never had the pleasure of hearing
the gentleman's name before." Here Mr. Phunky bowed and smiled, and
the judge bowed and smiled too, and then Mr. Phunky, blushing into the
very whites of his eyes, tried to look as if he didn't know that everybody
was gazing at him: a thing which no man ever succeeded in doing yet, or
in all reasonable probability, ever will.

"Go on," said the judge.

The ushers again called silence, and Mr. Skimpin proceeded to "open the case"; and the case appeared to have very little inside it when he had opened it, for he kept such particulars as he knew, completely to himself, and sat down, after a lapse of three minutes, leaving the jury in precisely the same advanced stage of wisdom as they were in before.

Serjeant Buzfuz then rose with all the majesty and dignity which the grave nature of the proceedings demanded, and having whispered to Dodson, and conferred briefly with Fogg, pulled his gown over his shoulders, settled his wig, and addressed the jury.

Serjeant Buzfuz began by saying, that never, in the whole course of his professional experience—never, from the very first moment of his applying himself to the study and practice of the law—had he approached a case with feelings of such deep emotion, or with such a heavy sense of the responsibility imposed upon him—a responsibility, he would say, which he could never have supported, were he not buoyed up and sustained by a conviction so strong, that it amounted to positive certainty that the cause of truth and justice, or, in other words, the cause of his much-injured and most oppressed client, must prevail with the high-minded and intelligent dozen of men whom he now saw in that box before him.

Counsel usually began in this way, because it puts the jury on the very best terms with themselves, and makes them think what sharp fellows they must be. A visible effect was produced immediately; several jurymen beginning to take voluminous notes with the utmost eagerness.

"You have heard from my learned friend, gentlemen," continued Serjeant Buzfuz, well knowing that, from the learned friend alluded to, the gentlemen of the jury had heard just nothing at all—"you have heard from my learned friend, gentlemen, that this is an action for a breach of promise of marriage, in which the damages are laid at £1,500. But you have not heard from my learned friend, inasmuch as it did not come within my learned friend's province to tell you, what are the facts and circumstances of the case. Those facts and circumstances, gentlemen, you shall hear detailed by me, and proved by the unimpeachable female whom I will place in that box before you."

Here Mr. Serjeant Buzfuz, with a tremendous emphasis on the word "box," smote his table with a mighty sound, and glanced at Dodson and Fogg, who nodded admiration of the serjeant, and indignant defiance of the defendant.

"The plaintiff, gentlemen," continued Serjeant Buzfuz, in a soft and melancholy voice, "the plaintiff is a widow; yes, gentlemen, a widow. The late Mr. Bardell, after enjoying, for many years, the esteem and confidence of his sovereign, as one of the guardians of his royal revenues, glided almost imperceptibly from the world, to seek elsewhere for that repose and peace which a custom-house can never afford."

At this pathetic description of the decease of Mr. Bardell, who had been knocked on the head with a quart-pot in a public-house cellar, the learned serjeant's voice faltered, and he proceeded with emotion:

"Some time before his death, he had stamped his likeness upon a little boy. With this little boy, the only pledge of her departed exciseman, Mrs. Bardell shrunk from the world, and courted the retirement and tranquillity of Goswell Street; and here she placed in her front parlour-window a written placard, bearing this inscription—'Apartments furnished for a single gentleman. Inquire within.'" Here Serjeant Buzfuz paused, while several gentlemen of the jury took a note of the document.

"There is no date to that, is there, sir?" inquired a juror.

"There is no date, gentlemen," replied Serjeant Buzfuz; "but I am instructed to say that it was put in the plaintiff's parlour-window just this time three years. I intreat the attention of the jury to the wording of this document. 'Apartments furnished for a single gentleman'! Mrs. Bardell's opinions of the opposite sex, gentlemen, were derived from a long contemplation of the inestimable qualities of her lost husband. She had no fear, she had no distress, she had no suspicion, all was confidence and reliance. 'Mr. Bardell,' said the widow; 'Mr. Bardell was a man of honour, Mr. Bardell was a man of his word, Mr. Bardell was no deceiver, Mr. Bardell was once a single gentleman himself; *to* single gentlemen I look for protection, for assistance, for comfort, and for consolation; *in* single gentlemen I shall perpetually see something to remind me of what Mr. Bardell was, when he first won my young and untried affections; to a single gentleman, then, shall my lodgings be let.' Actuated by this beautiful and touching impulse (among the best impulses of our imperfect nature, gentlemen), the lonely and desolate widow dried her tears, furnished her first floor, caught the innocent boy to her maternal bosom, and put the bill up in her parlour-window. Did it remain there long? No. The serpent was on the watch, the train was laid, the mine was preparing, the sapper and miner was at work. Before the bill had been in the parlour-window three days—three days—gentlemen—a Being, erect upon two legs, and bearing all the outward semblance of a man, and not of a monster, knocked at the door of Mrs. Bardell's house. He inquired within; he took the lodgings; and on the very next day he entered into possession of them. This man was Pickwick—Pickwick, the defendant."

Serjeant Buzfuz, who had proceeded with such volubility that his face was perfectly crimson, here paused for breath. The silence awoke Mr. Justice Stareleigh, who immediately wrote down something with a pen without any ink in it, and looked unusually profound, to impress the jury with the belief that he always thought most deeply with his eyes shut. Serjeant Buzfuz proceeded.

"Of this man Pickwick I will say little; the subject presents but few attractions; and I, gentlemen, am not the man, nor are you, gentlemen, the men, to delight in the contemplation of revolting heartlessness, and of systematic villainy."

Here Mr. Pickwick, who had been writhing in silence for some time, gave a violent start, as if some vague idea of assaulting Serjeant Buzfuz, in the august presence of justice and law, suggested itself to his mind. An admonitory gesture from Perker restained him, and he listened to the learned gentleman's continuation with a look of indignation, which contrasted forcibly with the admiring faces of Mrs. Cluppins and Mrs. Sanders.

"I say systematic villainy, gentlemen," said Serjeant Buzfuz, looking through Mr. Pickwick, and talking *at* him; "and when I say systematic villainy, let me tell the defendant Pickwick, if he be in court, as I am informed he is, that it would have been more decent in him, more becoming, in better judgment, and in better taste, if he had stopped away. Let me tell him, gentlemen, that any gestures of dissent or disapprobation in which he may indulge in this court will not go down with you; that you will know how to value and how to appreciate them; and let me tell him further, as my lord will tell you, gentlemen, that a counsel, in the discharge of his duty to his client, is neither to be intimidated, nor bullied, nor put down; and that any attempt to do either the one or the other, or the first, or the last, will recoil on the head of the attempter, be he plaintiff or be he defendant, be his name Pickwick, or Noakes, or Stoakes, or Stiles, or Brown, or Thompson."

This little divergence from the subject in hand, had of course, the intended effect of turning all eyes to Mr. Pickwick. Serjeant Buzfuz, having partially recovered from the state of moral elevation into which he had lashed himself, resumed:

"I shall show you, gentlemen, that for two years Pickwick continued to reside constantly, and without interruption or intermission, at Mrs. Bardell's house. I shall show you that Mrs. Bardell, during the whole of that time waited on him, attended to his comforts, cooked his meals, looked out his linen for the washerwoman when it went abroad, darned, aired, and prepared it for wear, when it came home, and, in short, enjoyed his fullest trust and confidence. I shall show you that, on many occasions, he gave halfpence, and on some occasions even sixpences, to her little boy; and I shall prove to you, by a witness whose testimony it will be impossible for my learned friend to weaken or controvert, that on one occasion he patted the boy on the head, and, after inquiring whether he had won any *alley tors* or *commoneys* lately (both of which I understand to be a particular species of marbles much prized by the youth of this town), made use of this remarkable expression: 'How should you like to have another father?' I shall prove to you, gentlemen, that about a year ago, Pickwick suddenly began to absent himself from home, during long intervals, as if with the intention of gradually breaking off from my client; but I shall show you also, that his resolution was not at that time sufficiently strong, or that his better feelings conquered, if better feelings he has, or that the charms and accomplishments of my client prevailed against his unmanly intentions; by proving to you, that on one occasion, when he returned from the country, he distinctly and in terms, offered her marriage: previously however, taking special care that there should be no witness to their solemn contract; and I am in a situation to prove to you, on the testimony of three of his own friends,—most unwilling witnesses, gentlemen—most unwilling witnesses—that on that morning he was discovered by them holding the plaintiff in his arms, and soothing her agitation by his caresses and endearments."

A visible impression was produced upon the auditors by this part of the learned serjeant's address. Drawing forth two very small scraps of paper, he proceeded:

"And now, gentlemen, but one word more. Two letters have passed between these parties, letters which are admitted to be in the handwriting of the defendant, and which speak volumes indeed. These letters, too, bespeak the character of the man. They are not open, fervent, eloquent epistles, breathing nothing but the language of affectionate attachment. They are covert, sly, underhanded communications, but, fortunately, far more conclusive than if couched in the most glowing language and the most poetic imagery—letters that must be viewed with a cautious and suspicious eye—letters that were evidently intended at the time, by Pickwick, to mislead and delude any third parties into whose hands they might fall. Let me read the first:—'Garraway's, twelve o'clock. Dear Mrs. B.—Chops and Tomato sauce. Yours, PICKWICK.' Gentlemen, what does this mean? Chops and Tomato sauce! Yours, Pickwick! Chops! Gracious heavens! and Tomato sauce! Gentlemen, is the happiness of a sensitive and confiding female to be trifled away, by such shallow artifices as these? The next has no date whatever, which in itself is suspicious. 'Dear Mrs. B., I shall not be at home till to-morrow. Slow coach.' And then follows this very remarkable expression. 'Don't trouble yourself about the warming-pan.' The warming-pan! Why, gentlemen, who *does* trouble himself about a warming-pan? When was the peace of mind of man or woman broken or disturbed by a warming-pan, which is in itself a harmless, a useful, and I will add, gentlemen, a comforting article of domestic furniture? Why is Mrs. Bardell so earnestly entreated not to agitate herself about this warming-pan, unless (as is no doubt the case) it is a mere cover for hidden fire—a mere substitute for some endearing word or promise, agreeably to a preconcerted system of correspondence, artfully contrived by Pickwick with a view to his contemplated desertion, and which I am not in a condition to explain? And what does this allusion to the slow coach mean? For aught I know, it may be a reference to Pickwick himself, who has most unquestionably been a criminally slow coach during the whole of this transaction, but whose speed will now be very unexpectedly accelerated, and whose wheels, gentlemen, as he will find to his cost, will very soon be greased by you!"

Mr. Serjeant Buzfuz paused in his place, to see whether the jury smiled at his joke: but as nobody took it but the greengrocer, whose sensitiveness on the subject was very probably occasioned by his having subjected a chaise-cart to the process in question on that identical morning, the learned serjeant considered it advisable to undergo a slight relapse into the dismals before he concluded.

"But enough of this, gentlemen," said Mr. Serjeant Buzfuz, "it is difficult to smile with an aching heart; it is ill jesting when our deepest sympathies are awakened. My client's hopes and prospects are ruined, and it is no figure of speech to say that her occupation is gone indeed. The bill is down —but there is no tenant. Eligible single gentlemen pass and repass—but there is no invitation for them to inquire within or without. All is gloom and silence in the house; even the voice of the child is hushed; his infant sports are disregarded when his mother weeps; his 'alley tors' and his 'com-moneys' are alike neglected; he forgets the long familiar cry of 'knuckle down,' and at tip-cheese, or odd and even, his hand is out. But Pickwick, gentlemen, Pickwick, the ruthless destroyer of this domestic oasis in the desert of Goswell Street—Pickwick, who has choked up the well, and thrown ashes on the sward—Pickwick, who comes before you to-day with his heart-less Tomato sauce and warming-pans—Pickwick still rears his head with unblushing effrontery, and gazes without a sigh on the ruin he has made. Damages, gentlemen—heavy damages—is the only punishment with which you can visit him; the only recompense you can award to my client. And for those damages she now appeals to an enlightened, a high-minded, a right-feeling, a conscientious, a dispassionate, a sympathising, a contem-plative jury of her civilised countrymen." With this beautiful peroration, Mr. Serjeant Buzfuz sat down, and Mr. Justice Stareleigh woke up.

"Call Elizabeth Cluppins," said Serjeant Buzfuz, rising a minute after-wards, with renewed vigour.

The nearest usher called for Elizabeth Tuppins; another one, at a little distance off, demanded Elizabeth Jupkins; and a third rushed in a breath-less state into King Street, and screamed for Elizabeth Muffins till he was hoarse.

Meanwhile Mrs. Cluppins, with the combined assistance of Mrs. Bardell, Mrs. Sanders, Mr. Dodson, and Mr. Fogg, was hoisted into the witness-box; and when she was safely perched on the top step, Mrs. Bardell stood on the bottom one, with the pocket-handkerchief and pattens in one hand, and a glass bottle that might hold about a quarter of a pint of smelling salts in the other, ready for any emergency. Mrs. Sanders, whose eyes were in-tently fixed on the judge's face, planted herself close by, with the large umbrella: keeping her right thumb pressed on the spring with an earnest countenance, as if she were fully prepared to put it up at a moment's notice.

"Mrs. Cluppins," said Serjeant Buzfuz, "pray compose yourself, ma'am." Of course, directly Mrs. Cluppins was desired to compose herself she sobbed with increased vehemence, and gave divers alarming manifestations of an approaching fainting fit, or, as she afterwards said, of her feelings being too many for her.

"Do you recollect, Mrs. Cluppins?" said Serjeant Buzfuz, after a few unimportant questions, "do you recollect being in Mrs. Bardell's back one pair of stairs, on one particular morning in July last, when she was dusting Pickwick's apartment?"

"Yes, my Lord and Jury, I do," replied Mrs. Cluppins.

"Mr. Pickwick's sitting-room was the first-floor front I believe?"

"Yes, it were, sir," replied Mrs. Cluppins.

"What were you doing in the back room, ma'am?" inquired the little judge.

"My Lord and Jury," said Mrs. Cluppins, with interesting agitation, "I will not deceive you."

"You had better not, ma'am," said the little judge.

"I was there," resumed Mrs. Cluppins, "unbeknown to Mrs. Bardell; I had been out with a little basket, gentlemen, to buy three pound of red kidney purtaties, which was three pound tuppence ha'penny, when I see Mrs. Bardell's street door on the jar."

"On the what?" exclaimed the little judge.

"Partly open, my Lord," said Serjeant Snubbin.

"She *said* on the jar," said the little judge, with a cunning look.

"It's all the same, my Lord," said Serjeant Snubbin. The little judge looked doubtful, and said he'd make a note of it. Mrs. Cluppins then resumed:

"I walked in, gentlemen, just to say good mornin', and went, in a permiscuous manner, up-stairs, and into the back room. Gentlemen, there was the sound of voices in the front room, and—"

"And you listened, I believe, Mrs. Cluppins?" said Serjeant Buzfuz.

"Beggin' your pardon, sir," replied Mrs. Cluppins, in a majestic manner, "I would scorn the haction. The voices was very loud, sir, and forced themselves upon my ear."

"Well, Mrs. Cluppins, you were not listening, but you heard the voices. Was one of those voices, Pickwick's?"

"Yes, it were, sir."

And Mrs. Cluppins, after distinctly stating that Mr. Pickwick addressed himself to Mrs. Bardell, repeated, by slow degrees, and by dint of many questions, the conversation with which our readers are already acquainted.

The jury looked suspicious, and Mr. Serjeant Buzfuz smiled and sat down. They looked positively awful when Serjeant Snubbin intimated that he should not cross-examine the witness, for Mr. Pickwick wished it to be distinctly stated that it was due to her to say, that her account was in substance correct.

Mrs. Cluppins having once broken the ice, thought it a favourable opportunity for entering into a short dissertation on her own domestic affairs; so, she straightway proceeded to inform the court that she was the mother of eight children at that present speaking, and that she entertained confident expectations of presenting Mr. Cluppins with a ninth, somewhere about that day six months. At this interesting point, the little judge interposed most irascibly; and the effect of the interposition was, that both the worthy lady and Mrs. Sanders were politely taken out of court, under the escort of Mr. Jackson, without further parley.

"Nathaniel Winkle!" said Mr. Skimpin.

"Here!" replied a feeble voice. Mr. Winkle entered the witness-box, and having been duly sworn, bowed to the judge with considerable deference.

"Don't look at me, sir," said the judge, sharply, in acknowledgment of the salute; "look at the jury."

Mr. Winkle obeyed the mandate, and looked at the place where he thought it most probable the jury might be; for seeing anything in his then state of intellectual complication was wholly out of the question.

Mr. Winkle was then examined by Mr. Skimpin, who, being a promising young man of two or three and forty, was of course anxious to confuse a witness who was notoriously predisposed in favour of the other side, as much as he could.

"Now, sir," said Mr. Skimpin, "have the goodness to let his Lordship and the jury know what your name is, will you?" and Mr. Skimpin inclined his head on one side to listen with great sharpness to the answer, and glanced at the jury meanwhile, as if to imply that he rather expected Mr. Winkle's natural taste for perjury would induce him to give some name which did not belong to him.

"Winkle," replied the witness.

"What's your Christian name, sir?" angrily inquired the little judge.

"Nathaniel, sir."

"Daniel,—any other name?"

"Nathaniel, sir—my Lord, I mean."

"Nathaniel Daniel, or Daniel Nathaniel?"

"No, my Lord, only Nathaniel; not Daniel at all."

"What did you tell me it was Daniel for, then, sir?" inquired the judge.

"I didn't, my Lord," replied Mr. Winkle.

"You did, sir," replied the judge, with a severe frown. "How could I have got Daniel on my notes, unless you told me so, sir?"

This argument was, of course, unanswerable.

"Mr. Winkle has rather a short memory, my Lord," interposed Mr. Skimpin, with another glance at the jury. "We shall find means to refresh it before we have quite done with him, I daresay."

"You had better be careful, sir," said the little judge, with a sinister look at the witness.

Poor Mr. Winkle bowed, and endeavoured to feign an easiness of manner,

which, in his then state of confusion, gave him rather the air of a disconcerted pickpocket.

"Now, Mr. Winkle," said Mr. Skimpin, "attend to me, if you please, sir;
and let me recommend you, for your own sake, to bear in mind his Lordship's injunction to be careful. I believe you are a particular friend of
Pickwick, the defendant, are you not?"

"I have known Mr. Pickwick now, as well as I recollect at this moment,
nearly—"

"Pray, Mr. Winkle, do not evade the question. Are you, or are you not,
a particular friend of the defendant's?"

"I was just about to say, that—"

"Will you, or will you not, answer my question, sir?"

"If you don't answer the question you'll be committed, sir," interposed
the little judge, looking over his note-book.

"Come, sir," said Mr. Skimpin, "yes or no, if you please."

"Yes, I am," replied Mr. Winkle.

"Yes, you are. And why couldn't you say that at once, sir? Perhaps you
know the plaintiff, too? Eh, Mr. Winkle?"

"I don't know her; I've seen her."

"Oh, you don't know her, but you've seen her? Now, have the goodness
to tell the gentlemen of the jury what you mean by *that*, Mr. Winkle."

"I mean that I am not intimate with her, but I have seen her when I
went to call on Mr. Pickwick in Goswell Street."

"How often have you seen her, sir?"

"How often?"

"Yes, Mr. Winkle, how often? I'll repeat the question for you a dozen
times, if you require it, sir." And the learned gentleman, with a firm and
steady frown, placed his hands on his hips, and smiled suspiciously at the
jury.

On this question there arose the edifying brow-beating, customary on
such points. First of all, Mr. Winkle said it was quite impossible for him to
say how many times he had seen Mrs. Bardell. Then he was asked if he
had seen her twenty times, to which he replied, "Certainly,—more than
that." Then he was asked whether he hadn't seen her a hundred times—
whether he couldn't swear that he had seen her more than fifty times—
whether he didn't know that he had seen her at least seventy-five times—
and so forth; the satisfactory confusion which was arrived at, at last, being,
that he had better take care of himself, and mind what he was about. The
witness having been by these means reduced to the requisite ebb of nervous
perplexity, the examination was continued as follows:

"Pray, Mr. Winkle, do you remember calling on the defendant Pickwick
at these apartments in the plaintiff's house in Goswell Street, on one particular morning, in the month of July last?"

"Yes, I do."

"Were you accompanied on that occasion by a friend of the name of Tupman, and another of the name of Snodgrass?"

"Yes, I was."

"Are they here?"

"Yes, they are," replied Mr. Winkle, looking very earnestly towards the spot where his friends were stationed.

"Pray attend to me, Mr. Winkle, and never mind your friends," said Mr. Skimpin, with another expressive look at the jury. "They must tell their stories without any previous consultation with you, if none has yet taken place (another look at the jury). Now, sir, tell the gentlemen of the jury what you saw on entering the defendant's room, on this particular morning. Come; out with it, sir; we must have it, sooner or later."

"The defendant, Mr. Pickwick, was holding the plaintiff in his arms, with his hands clasping her waist," replied Mr. Winkle with natural hesitation, "and the plaintiff appeared to have fainted away."

"Did you hear the defendant say anything?"

"I heard him call Mrs. Bardell a good creature, and I heard him ask her to compose herself, for what a situation it was, if anybody should come, or words to that effect."

"Now, Mr. Winkle, I have only one more question to ask you, and I beg you to bear in mind his Lordship's caution. Will you undertake to swear that Pickwick, the defendant, did not say on the occasion in question, 'My dear Mrs. Bardell, you're a good creature; compose yourself to this situation, for to this situation you must come,' or words to *that* effect?"

"I—I didn't understand him so, certainly," said Mr. Winkle, astounded at this ingenious dove-tailing of the few words he had heard, "I was on the staircase, and couldn't hear distinctly; the impression on my mind is—"

"The gentlemen of the jury want none of the impressions on your mind, Mr. Winkle, which I fear would be of little service to honest, straightforward men," interposed Mr. Skimpin. "You were on the staircase, and didn't distinctly hear; but you will not swear that Pickwick did not make use of the expressions I have quoted? Do I understand that?"

"No, I will not," replied Mr. Winkle; and down sat Mr. Skimpin with a triumphant countenance.

Mr. Pickwick's case had not gone off in so particularly happy a manner, up to this point, that it could very well afford to have any additional suspicion cast upon it. But as it could afford to be placed in a rather better light, if possible, Mr. Phunky rose for the purpose of getting something important out of Mr. Winkle in cross-examination. Whether he did get anything important out of him, will immediately appear.

"I believe, Mr. Winkle," said Mr. Phunky, "that Mr. Pickwick is not a young man?"

"Oh, no," replied Mr. Winkle, "old enough to be my father."

"You have told my learned friend that you have known Mr. Pickwick a long time. Had you ever any reason to suppose or believe that he was about to be married?"

"Oh no; certainly not;" replied Mr. Winkle with so much eagerness, that Mr. Phunky ought to have got him out of the box with all possible dispatch. Lawyers hold that there are two kinds of particularly bad witnesses: a reluctant witness, and a too-willing witness; it was Mr. Winkle's fate to figure in both characters.

"I will even go further than this, Mr. Winkle," continued Mr. Phunky in a most smooth and complacent manner. "Did you ever see anything in Mr. Pickwick's manner and conduct towards the opposite sex, to induce you to believe that he ever contemplated matrimony of late years, in any case?"

"Oh no; certainly not," replied Mr. Winkle.

"Has his behaviour, when females have been in the case, always been that of a man, who, having attained a pretty advanced period of life, content with his own occupations and amusements, treats them only as a father might his daughters?"

"Not the least doubt of it," replied Mr. Winkle, in the fulness of his heart. "That is—yes—oh yes—certainly."

"You have never known anything in his behaviour towards Mrs. Bardell, or any other female, in the least degree suspicious?" said Mr. Phunky, preparing to sit down; for Serjeant Snubbin was winking at him.

"N–n–no," replied Mr. Winkle, "except on one trifling occasion, which, I have no doubt, might be easily explained."

Now, if the unfortunate Mr. Phunky had sat down when Serjeant Snubbin winked at him, or if Serjeant Buzfuz had stopped this irregular cross-examination at the outset (which he knew better than to do; observing Mr. Winkle's anxiety, and well knowing it would, in all probability, lead to something serviceable to him), this unfortunate admission would not have been elicited. The moment the words fell from Mr. Winkle's lips, Mr. Phunky sat down, and Serjeant Snubbin rather hastily told him he might leave the box, which Mr. Winkle prepared to do with great readiness, when Serjeant Buzfuz stopped him.

"Stay, Mr. Winkle, stay!" said Serjeant Buzfuz, "will your lordship have the goodness to ask him, what this one instance of suspicious behaviour towards females on the part of this gentleman, who is old enough to be his father, was?"

"You hear what the learned counsel says, sir," observed the judge, turning to the miserable and agonised Mr. Winkle. "Describe the occasion to which you refer."

"My Lord," said Mr. Winkle, trembling with anxiety, "I—I'd rather not."

"Perhaps so," said the little judge; "but you must."

Amid the profound silence of the whole court, Mr. Winkle faltered out, that the trifling circumstance of suspicion was Mr. Pickwick's being found in a lady's sleeping apartment at midnight; which had terminated, he believed, in the breaking off of the projected marriage of the lady in question, and had led, he knew, to the whole party being forcibly carried before George Nupkins, Esq., magistrate and justice of the peace, for the borough of Ipswich!

"You may leave the box, sir," said Serjeant Snubbin. Mr. Winkle *did* leave the box, and rushed with delirious haste to the George and Vulture, where he was discovered some hours after, by the waiter, groaning in a hollow and dismal manner, with his head buried beneath the sofa cushions.

Tracy Tupman, and Augustus Snodgrass, were severally called into the box; both corroborated the testimony of their unhappy friend; and each was driven to the verge of desperation by excessive badgering.

Susannah Sanders was then called, and examined by Serjeant Buzfuz, and cross-examined by Serjeant Snubbin. Had always said and believed that Pickwick would marry Mrs. Bardell; knew that Mrs. Bardell's being engaged to Pickwick was the current topic of conversation in the neighbourhood, after the fainting in July; had been told it herself by Mrs. Mudberry which kept a mangle, and Mrs. Bunkin which clear-starched, but did not see either Mrs. Mudberry or Mrs. Bunkin in court. Had heard Pickwick ask the little boy how he should like to have another father. Did not know that Mrs. Bardell was at that time keeping company with the baker, but did know that the baker was then a single man and is now married. Couldn't swear that Mrs. Bardell was not very fond of the baker, but should think that the baker was not very fond of Mrs. Bardell, or he wouldn't have married somebody else. Thought Mrs. Bardell fainted away on the morning in July, because Pickwick asked her to name the day; knew that she (witness) fainted away stone dead when Mr. Sanders asked *her* to name the day, and believed that everybody as called herself a lady would do the same, under similar circumstances. Heard Pickwick ask the boy the question about the marbles, but upon her oath did not know the difference between an alley tor and a commoney.

By the COURT.—During the period of her keeping company with Mr. Sanders, had received love letters, like other ladies. In the course of their correspondence Mr. Sanders had often called her a "duck," but never "chops," nor yet "tomato sauce." He was particularly fond of ducks. Perhaps if he had been as fond of chops and tomato sauce, he might have called her that, as a term of affection.

Serjeant Buzfuz now rose with more importance than he had yet exhibited, if that were possible, and vociferated: "Call Samuel Weller."

It was quite unnecessary to call Samuel Weller; for Samuel Weller stepped briskly into the box the instant his name was pronounced; and placing his hat on the floor, and his arms on the rail, took a bird's-eye view of the bar, and a comprehensive survey of the bench, with a remarkably cheerful and lively aspect.

"What's your name, sir?" inquired the judge.

"Sam Weller, my Lord," replied that gentleman.

"Do you spell it with a 'V' or a 'W'?" inquired the judge.

"That depends upon the taste and fancy of the speller, my Lord," replied Sam; "I never had occasion to spell it more than once or twice in my life, but I spells it with a 'V.'"

Here a voice in the gallery exclaimed aloud, "Quite right too, Samivel, quite right. Put it down a we, my Lord, put it down a we."

"Who is that, who dares to address the court?" said the little judge, looking up. "Usher."

"Yes, my Lord."

"Bring that person here instantly."

"Yes, my Lord."

But as the usher didn't find the person, he didn't bring him; and, after a great commotion, all the people who had got up to look for the culprit, sat down again. The little judge turned to the witness as soon as his indignation would allow him to speak, and said,

"Do you know who that was, sir?"

"I rayther suspect it was my father, my Lord," replied Sam.

"Do you see him here now?" said the judge.

"No, I don't, my Lord," replied Sam, staring right up into the lantern in the roof of the court.

"If you could have pointed him out, I would have committed him instantly," said the judge.

Sam bowed his acknowledgments and turned, with unimpaired cheerfulness of countenance, towards Serjeant Buzfuz.

"Now, Mr. Weller," said Serjeant Buzfuz.

"Now, sir," replied Sam.

"I believe you are in the service of Mr. Pickwick, the defendant in this case. Speak up, if you please, Mr. Weller."

"I mean to speak up, sir," replied Sam; "I am in the service o' that 'ere gen'l'man, and a wery good service it is."

"Little to do, and plenty to get, I suppose?" said Serjeant Buzfuz, with jocularity.

"Oh, quite enough to get, sir, as the soldier said ven they ordered him three hundred and fifty lashes," replied Sam.

"You must not tell us what the soldier, or any other man, said, sir," interposed the judge; "it's not evidence."

"Wery good, my Lord," replied Sam.

"Do you recollect anything particular happening on the morning when you were first engaged by the defendant; eh, Mr. Weller?" said Serjeant Buzfuz.

"Yes, I do, sir," replied Sam.

"Have the goodness to tell the jury what it was."

"I had a reg'lar new fit out o' clothes that mornin', gen'l'men of the jury," said Sam, "and that was a wery partickler and uncommon circumstance vith me in those days."

Hereupon there was a general laugh; and the little judge, looking with an angry countenance over his desk, said, "You had better be careful, sir."

"So Mr. Pickwick said at the time, my Lord," replied Sam; "and I was wery careful o' that 'ere suit o' clothes; wery careful indeed, my Lord."

The judge looked sternly at Sam for full two minutes, but Sam's features were so perfectly calm and serene that the judge said nothing, and motioned Serjeant Buzfuz to proceed.

"Do you mean to tell me, Mr. Weller," said Serjeant Buzfuz, folding his arms emphatically, and turning half-round to the jury, as if in mute assurance that he would bother the witness yet: "Do you mean to tell me, Mr. Weller, that you saw nothing of this fainting on the part of the plaintiff in the arms of the defendant, which you have heard described by the witnesses?"

"Certainly not," replied Sam. "I was in the passage 'till they called me up, and then the old lady was not there."

"Now, attend, Mr. Weller," said Serjeant Buzfuz, dipping a large pen into the inkstand before him, for the purpose of frightening Sam with a show of taking down his answer. "You were in the passage, and yet saw nothing of what was going forward. Have you a pair of eyes, Mr. Weller?"

"Yes, I have a pair of eyes," replied Sam, "and that's just it. If they wos a pair o' patent double million magnifyin' gas microscopes of hextra power, p'raps I might be able to see through a flight o' stairs and a deal door; but bein' only eyes, you see, my wision's limited."

At this answer, which was delivered without the slightest appearance of irritation, and with the most complete simplicity and equanimity of manner, the spectators tittered, the little judge smiled, and Serjeant Buzfuz looked particularly foolish. After a short consultation with Dodson and Fogg, the learned Serjeant again turned towards Sam, and said, with a painful effort to conceal his vexation, "Now, Mr. Weller, I'll ask you a question on another point, if you please."

"If you please, sir," rejoined Sam, with the utmost good-humour.

"Do you remember going up to Mrs. Bardell's house, one night in November last?"

"Oh yes, very well."

"Oh, you *do* remember that, Mr. Weller," said Serjeant Buzfuz, recovering his spirits; "I thought we should get at something at last."

"I rayther thought that, too, sir," replied Sam; and at this the spectators tittered again.

"Well; I suppose you went up to have a little talk about this trial—eh, Mr. Weller?" said Serjeant Buzfuz, looking knowingly at the jury.

"I went up to pay the rent; but we *did* get a talkin' about the trial," replied Sam.

"Oh, you did get a talking about the trial," said Serjeant Buzfuz, brightening up with the anticipation of some important discovery. "Now what passed about the trial; will you have the goodness to tell us, Mr. Weller?"

"Vith all the pleasure in life, sir," replied Sam. "Arter a few unimportant obserwations from the two wirtuous females as has been examined here, to-day, the ladies gets into a very great state o' admiration at the honourable conduct of Mr. Dodson and Fogg—them two gen'l'men as is settin' near you now." This, of course, drew general attention to Dodson and Fogg, who looked as virtuous as possible.

"The attorneys for the plaintiff," said Mr. Serjeant Buzfuz. "Well! They spoke in high praise of the honourable conduct of Messrs. Dodson and Fogg, the attorneys for the plaintiff, did they?"

"Yes," said Sam, "they said what a wery gen'rous thing it was o' them to have taken up the case on spec, and to charge nothing at all for costs, unless they got 'em out of Mr. Pickwick."

At this very unexpected reply, the spectators tittered again, and Dodson and Fogg, turning very red, leant over to Serjeant Buzfuz, and in a hurried manner whispered something in his ear.

"You are quite right," said Serjeant Buzfuz aloud, with affected composure. "It's perfectly useless, my lord, attempting to get at any evidence through the impenetrable stupidity of this witness. I will not trouble the court by asking him any more questions. Stand down, sir."

"Would any other gen'l'man like to ask me anythin'?" inquired Sam, taking up his hat, and looking round most deliberately.

"Not I, Mr. Weller, thank you," said Serjeant Snubbin, laughing.

"You may go down, sir," said Serjeant Buzfuz, waving his hand impatiently. Sam went down accordingly, after doing Messrs. Dodson and Fogg's case as much harm as he conveniently could, and saying just as little respecting Mr. Pickwick as might be, which was precisely the object he had had in view all along.

"I have no objection to admit, my Lord," said Serjeant Snubbin, "if it will save the examination of another witness, that Mr. Pickwick has retired from business, and is a gentleman of considerable independent property."

"Very well," said Serjeant Buzfuz, putting in the two letters to be read. "Then that's my case, my Lord."

Serjeant Snubbin then addressed the jury on behalf of the defendant; and a very long and a very emphatic address he delivered, in which he bestowed the highest possible eulogiums on the conduct and character of Mr. Pickwick; but inasmuch as our readers are far better able to form a correct estimate of that gentleman's merits and deserts, than Serjeant Snubbin could possibly be, we do not feel called upon to enter at any length into the learned gentleman's observations. He attempted to show that the letters which had been exhibited, merely related to Mr. Pickwick's dinner, or to the preparations for receiving him in his apartments on his return from some country excursion. It is sufficient to add in general terms, that he did the best he could for Mr. Pickwick; and the best, as everybody knows, on the infallible authority of the old adage, could do no more.

Mr. Justice Stareleigh summed up, in the old-established and most approved form. He read as much of his notes to the jury as he could decipher on so short a notice, and made running comments on the evidence as he went along. If Mrs. Bardell were right, it was perfectly clear that Mr. Pickwick was wrong, and if they thought the evidence of Mrs. Cluppins worthy of credence they would believe it, and, if they didn't, why, they wouldn't. If they were satisfied that a breach of promise of marriage had been committed, they would find for the plaintiff with such damages as they thought proper; and if, on the other hand, it appears to them that no promise of marriage had ever been given, they would find for the defendant with no damages at all. The jury then retired to their private room to talk the matter over, and the judge retired to *his* private room, to refresh himself with a mutton chop and a glass of sherry.

An anxious quarter of an hour elapsed; the jury came back; the judge was fetched in. Mr. Pickwick put on his spectacles, and gazed at the foreman with an agitated countenance and a quickly beating heart.

"Gentlemen," said the individual in black, "are you all agreed upon your verdict?"

"We are," replied the foreman.

"Do you find for the plaintiff, gentlemen, or for the defendant?"

"For the plaintiff."

"With what damages, gentlemen?"

"Seven hundred and fifty pounds."

Mr. Pickwick took off his spectacles, carefully wiped the glasses, folded them into their case, and put them in his pocket; then having drawn on his gloves with great nicety; and stared at the foreman all the while, he mechanically followed Mr. Perker and the blue bag out of court.

They stopped in a side room while Perker paid the court fees; and here, Mr. Pickwick was joined by his friends. Here, too, he encountered Messrs. Dodson and Fogg, rubbing their hands with every token of outward satisfaction.

"Well, gentlemen," said Mr. Pickwick.

"Well, sir," said Dodson: for self and partner.

"You imagine you'll get your costs, don't you, gentlemen?" said Mr. Pickwick.

Fogg said they thought it rather probable. Dodson smiled, and said they'd try.

"You may try, and try, and try again, Messrs. Dodson and Fogg," said Mr. Pickwick vehemently, "but not one farthing of costs or damages do you ever get from me, if I spend the rest of my existence in a debtor's prison."

"Ha, ha!" laughed Dodson. "You'll think better of that, before next term, Mr. Pickwick."

"He, he, he! We'll soon see about that, Mr. Pickwick," grinned Fogg.

Speechless with indignation, Mr. Pickwick allowed himself to be led by his solicitor and friends to the door, and there assisted into a hackney-coach, which had been fetched for the purpose, by the ever watchful Sam Weller.

Sam had put up the steps, and was preparing to jump upon the box, when he felt himself gently touched on the shoulder; and looking round, his father stood before him. The old gentleman's countenance wore a mournful expression, as he shook his head gravely, and said, in warning accents:

"I know'd what 'ud come o' this here mode 'o doin' bisness. Oh Sammy, Sammy, vy worn't there a alleybi!"

Bleak House *and the Procedure of the Court of Chancery**

WILLIAM S. HOLDSWORTH

A good deal has been written on Dickens' knowledge of the law. The selection below by William S. Holdsworth (Kt., O.M., K.C., D.C.L.) is typical. The author, a graduate of Oxford with distinction in history and law, never practiced, but lectured, taught, and wrote in both areas. His seventy-three years (1871–1944) saw him produce a monumental History of English Law *and win the honor of being named Vinerian Professor of Law at Oxford and Bencher of Lincoln's Inn. For further information see the* Law Quarterly Review *for April, 1944, which contains several entries on his life, personality, and service.*

If it be true that the Lord Chancellor described in the third chapter of *Bleak House* is Lord Lyndhurst, the time at which the action of the story takes place must be taken to be in or about 1827, when he was made Chancellor in succession to Lord Eldon. That was the very worst period of the Court of Chancery. The report of the first Chancery Commission, which had been published in the preceding year, had revealed a monstrous state of affairs, and as yet the Legislature had not begun the long task of applying a remedy. Obviously, in considering the contribution which *Bleak House* makes to the history of the Court of Chancery, we must keep this date in mind; and we must distinguish between this date, and the date when the story was written. The story appeared in parts between March, 1852, and September, 1853—at a time when considerable reforms had already been made, and on the eve of a very much larger instalment of reform.

The attention of Dickens had been directed to the Court of Chancery by the fact that in 1844 he had, as we have seen, been the plaintiff in five Chancery actions to restrain breaches of copyright. He had been victorious; but he had failed to recover the costs from the defendants; and the small glimpse which he had had of the working of the court, seems to have had an effect on his mind similar to the effect which it had on the mind of Bentham. Two years later he was advised to take further proceedings for

* From *Charles Dickens as Legal Historian*, by W. S. Holdsworth; copyright, 1928, by Yale University Press. Reprinted by permission of the publisher.

other piracies. He wrote, "My feeling is the feeling common, I suppose, to three-fourths of the reflecting part of the community in our happiest of all possible countries, and that is, that it is better to suffer a great wrong than to have recourse to the much greater wrong of the law. I shall not easily forget the expense and anxiety, and horrible injustice of the *Carol* case, wherein, in asserting the plainest right on earth, I was really treated as if I were the robber, instead of the robbed. I know of nothing that *could* come, even of a successful action, which would be worth the mental trouble and disturbance it would cost."

In 1850 he wrote an article in *Household Words* on "The Martyrs of Chancery," which dealt with the hopeless lot of persons committed for contempt of court, who were forgotten, and left to die in prison. Sir Edward Sugden (the future Lord St. Leonards) had no difficulty in showing that that particular abuse was then a thing of the past. Dickens was mistaken when he alleged in 1850 that this was at that date an existing abuse. But, assuming that the action of the story of *Bleak House* takes place in 1827, I do not think that it can be alleged that his statements of fact in that book are erroneous. He says in his Preface that "everything set forth in these pages concerning the Court of Chancery is substantially true and within the truth." That is not wholly true if he meant, as I think he did, to refer to the date when the book was written—though much of it was then still true. It would have been wholly true if he had meant to refer to the date of the action of the story. In fact, I am sure that it would be possible to produce an edition of *Bleak House,* in which all Dickens's statements could be verified by the statements of the witnesses who gave evidence before the Chancery Commission, which reported in 1826.

Let us look at the thing to be examined. The following extract from my history summarizes what the Chancery Commissioners of 1850 found to be then the course of the procedure of the court:

The plaintiff began his suit by addressing a bill to the chancellor, praying process against the defendant to compel him to appear and put in an answer. The bill asked for relief, and required the defendant to make discovery, i.e. to give on oath an answer to the matters stated and the interrogatories contained in the bill. The bill was then engrossed on parchment and filed with the proper officer of the court. A subpœna then issued, requiring the defendant to appear and answer. This subpœna contained no intimation of the object of the suit. The defendant must then appear and get an office copy of the bill. Having obtained this copy, the defendant must decide whether he would demur or plead or answer. He might demur, either on the substantial ground that no case had been made out for the interference of the court, or by reason of a technical objection to the form of the bill. A plea was generally a statement of matters not appearing on the face of the bill, which showed a reason why the suit should be either barred or delayed. The answer, which was generally given on oath, both answered the plaintiff's interrogatories contained in the bill and set out other facts essential to the defendant's defence. Unless the defendant lived within twenty miles of London, a special commission issued to take the answer. This involved office fees, charges by the London solicitor who took it out, and fees to the Commissioners for swearing. There were frequent applications to a master for more time to answer, and appeals from his decision to the court. Omission to put in an answer in the proper time was punished by attachment; and, if the defendant was attached, all applications for time must be made to the court. After a sufficient answer was filed, a motion was made by the plaintiff for the production of documents in the defendant's possession. This order was also the occasion of considerable expense. It often happened that the answer of the defendant made it necessary for the plaintiff to amend his bill, in order either to traverse the facts stated in the answer, or to introduce new facts. Further answers were then called for; and the case could then either be heard on these answers, or the plaintiff could put in a formal replication denying the answers. The pleadings being thus at an end, the next step was to lay them before counsel to advise on the evidence, and to prepare interrogatories for the examination of witnesses. On these interrogatories the witnesses were examined in private, none of the parties or their agents being present. As the interrogatories were framed by counsel without knowing what witnesses would be forthcoming, or what answers they would give, it was necessary to frame questions to meet many possible contingencies. It is obvious that in these circumstances, no effective cross-examination was possible, so that it was seldom resorted to. It was necessary to issue a special commission to take the evidence of witnesses in the country—a process which was at once expensive and slow. When all the evidence had been taken it was published; and the parties could get copies on payment of fees. The case was then ripe for hearing; but it could be delayed by motions to suppress depositions, or to issue another commission to take further evidence. When the case was set down for hearing, there were often further delays, by reason of objections taken on account of the misjoinder of a party, or non-joinder of necessary parties, or the death of a party, or the emerging of new facts. This was the occasion of bills of revivor or supplement, which often meant that the same tedious course of procedure must be started anew. Even if all these defects were cured, it was often still not possible for the court to pronounce a final judgment unless it was a judgment dismissing the bill. It was often necessary to send the case to a master to take accounts or to make inquiries. Again, if at the hearing a question of law arose, a special case might be sent to a court of law, or the court might require a plaintiff to test his legal right by bringing an action at law. Moreover, if on the depositions the court could not come to a clear conclusion as to the facts, it might direct that an issue should be tried by a jury in a court of common law. Even if final judgment were at length given, many more delays could be interposed by a petition for rehearing or an appeal.

The physical fog amidst which *Bleak House* opens, which is so aptly made to typify the moral fog which enveloped the procedure of the Court of Chancery, is I think the finest piece of descriptive writing in the whole of Dickens's works. This moral fog had been produced by a variety of causes, operating through centuries; and its density had made the court the most crying abuse of an age in which there were many abuses. Let us glace rapidly at some of its causes. They can, I think, be grouped under four heads.

In the first place, the officers of the court were wholly inadequate to cope with its business. In its main outlines the official machinery was mediæval. No doubt it had been added to from time to time; but it had been added to piecemeal by the process of allowing the original officials to employ deputies. The original officials gathered in the fees which grew as the business of the court expanded; and the work was done by underpaid deputies. In the second place, even if its official machinery had been adequate, its practice had become so technical, and its procedure had become so slow, that the length of time taken to decide even uncontested cases amounted to a denial of justice. This was due to the fact that, for centuries, there had been no adequate supervision either of the officials, or of the procedural rules of the court. . . . In the third place, even if the orders of the Chancellors had been carried out, there were still left a large crop of survivals of older rules of practice, which increased the delay and expense—survivals which it was impossible to get rid of, because officials had a vested interest in their maintenance. I will give two examples out of many. (i) At one time the parties had been represented by the clerks of the court. Later they employed their own solicitors. But the fees to the clerks of the court remained. (ii) To conserve the profits of the officials of the court, the parties were made to purchase from them office copies of documents which, in the eighteenth century, were wholly useless. Fourthly and lastly, the court had bound itself by the rigid rule that, if it acted at all, it must assume entire control. It would not, for instance, decide a single doubtful point connected with the administration of an estate, without administering the whole estate. All the weary procedure must be gone through; and, if as was likely, new parties were born there was a lengthy procedure to add the necessary parties. Gibbon's comment on the condition of Roman law in the time of Justinian applies exactly to the procedure of the Court of Chancery in 1827—it was "a mysterious science and a profitable trade," and, "the innate perplexity of the study was involved in tenfold darkness by the private industry of the practitioners."

The result was the case of *Jarndyce* v. *Jarndyce*—the greatest Chancery suit, as Mr. Kenge explained, ever known. If we remember that, when, between 1824 and 1826, the court was put on its trial before the first Chancery Commission, witnesses were found to defend all parts of its procedure, we can see that the views as to that case, attributed to Mr. Kenge, were by no means outrageous.

"Not heard of Jarndyce—the greatest of Chancery suits known? Not of Jarndyce and Jarndyce—the—a—in itself a monument of Chancery practice. In which (I would say) every difficulty, every contingency, every masterly fiction, every form of procedure known in that court, is represented over and over again? It is a cause that could not exist, out of this free and great country. I should say that the aggregate of costs in Jarndyce and Jarndyce amounts at the present hour to from *six-ty* to *seven-ty thousand pounds!*" said Mr. Kenge, leaning back in his chair.

On the other hand the view of the ordinary suitor is well represented by John Jarndyce:

"A certain Jarndyce, in an evil hour, made a great fortune, and made a great Will. In the question how the trusts under that Will are to be administered, the fortune left by the Will is squandered away; the legatees under the Will are reduced to such a miserable condition that they would be sufficiently punished, if they had committed an enormous crime in having money left them; and the Will itself is made a dead letter. All through the deplorable cause, everything that everybody in it, except one man, knows already, is referred to that only one man who don't know it, to find out—all through the deplorable cause, everybody must have copies, over and over again, of everything that has accumulated about it in the way of cartloads of papers (or must pay for them without having them, which is the usual course, for nobody wants them); and must go down the middle and up again, through such an infernal country-dance of costs and fees and nonsense and corruption, as was never dreamed of in the wildest visions of a Witch's Sabbath. Equity sends questions to Law, Law sends questions back to Equity; Law finds it can't do this, Equity finds it can't do that; neither can so much as say it can't do anything, without this solicitor instructing and this counsel appearing for A, and that solicitor instructing and that counsel appearing for B; and so on through the whole alphabet, like the history of the Apple Pie. And thus, through years and years, and lives and lives, everything goes on, constantly beginning over and over again, and nothing ever ends. And we can't get out of the suit on any terms, for we are made parties to it, and *must be* parties to it, whether we like it or not."

The manner in which Dickens makes this great Chancery suit the centre of the story; the manner in which he makes it affect nearly all the characters, from Jo the crossing sweeper to Lady Honoria Dedlock; the manner in which all the abuses of the procedure of the court are naturally introduced into the story—unite to make *Bleak House* the greatest triumph of his art.

Let us now consider a little more in detail some of the abuses of the procedure of the court which are especially illustrated by *Bleak House*. I shall take (1) the Bill; (2) the mode of taking evidence; (3) the Masters and the Six Clerks; (4) the procedure in court; (5) the attempt to do complete justice and its effects; (6) process.

The filing of the Bill was the first step in the case. It contained the plaintiff's statement of his case. It is not particularly described by Dickens; but it is graphically and accurately described by Lord Bowen. "A bill was a marvellous document, which stated the plaintiff's case at full length, and three times over. There was first the part in which the story was circumstantially set forth. Then came the part which charged its truth against the defendant—or, in other words, which set it forth all over again in an aggrieved tone. Lastly came the interrogatory part, which converted the original allegations into a chain of subtly penned interrogatories addressed to the defendant." In the course of the many years that a suit in equity might last, there occurred deaths, births, and marriages. That meant that new bills must be filed to bring the new parties before the court. As Lord Bowen says, "Whenever any death occurred, bills of review or supplemental suits became necessary to reconstitute the charmed circle of the litigants which had been broken. . . . It was satirically declared that a suit to which fifty defendants were necessary parties . . . could never hope to end at all, since the yearly average of deaths in England was one in fifty, and a death, as a rule, threw over the plaintiff's bill for at least a year." Dickens has picturesquely described this state of things:

Innumerable children have been born into the cause; innumerable young people have married into it; innumerable old people have died out of it. Scores of persons have deliriously found themselves made parties in Jarndyce and Jarndyce, without knowing how or why; whole families have inherited legendary hatreds with the suit. The little plaintiff or defendant, who was promised a new rocking-horse when Jarndyce and Jarndyce should be settled, has grown up, possessed himself of a real horse, and trotted away into the other world. Fair wards of court have faded into mothers and grandmothers; a long procession of Chancellors has come in and gone out; the legion of bills in the suit have been transformed into mere bills of mortality; there are not three Jarndyces left upon the earth perhaps, since old Tom Jarndyce in despair blew his brains out at a coffee-house in Chancery Lane.

I shall summarize what I have said at greater length in my history, as to the mode of taking evidence.

The first step was to prepare the interrogatories. These were prepared by the plaintiff's and defendant's counsel. As counsel could not tell what the answers of the witnesses would be, they were necessarily lengthy and minute; and for the same reason the number of the witnesses was often multiplied unnecessarily. Then the commissioners must be appointed. These commissioners and their clerks then repaired to an inn at the place where the examination was to take place. There they lived at the expense of the parties during the whole time that the examination took place. Each commissioner was paid at the rate of two guineas a day, and each clerk at the rate of fifteen shillings, in addition to his expenses at the inn. There was also two guineas a day to each of the solicitors, and the expenses of the witnesses. At the examination the witnesses were examined "without the presence of the solicitor, or any one representing the parties, or any one acquainted with the circumstances of the case, to see that all the information wanted was drawn forth." The interrogatories were always expressed in very technical language, so that often the witnesses did not understand their meaning. The evidence given was put into the third person, and the phrasing was generally that of the commissioners; so that there was every chance that, in the course of this transposition, its effect would be materially altered. At the close of the examination of each witness, his depositions were engrossed and signed by him. When all the witnesses had been examined—a process which often took many months—the depositions were sealed up and sent to the court; and thus, as Bentham pointed out, the person who took the evidence had nothing to do with the work of applying it to its proper use. It is obvious that, under these circumstances, cross-examination was useless if not dangerous.

After the depositions were all returned to the court an order of the court was got for their publication. This might be delayed by a motion to enlarge the time allowed for publication, if it appeared that further evidence was needed. Further delays might be caused by a motion, before publication, to suppress depositions. Generally no further evidence could be taken after publication, as it was supposed that if this was allowed it would lead to subornation of perjury; but, even after publication, leave might be given on special motion to take a fresh examination as to the credit of a particular witness.

The slowness of this system is obvious. It is equally obvious that it was both costly and inefficient. Unnecessary numbers of witnesses were examined at great expense; and their testimony was often the reverse of satisfactory, because they did not understand the questions put to them. Two concrete illustrations will suffice to illustrate these two defects. Mr. Lowe, in his evidence to the Chancery Commission, cited a case in which, though there was absolutely no dispute, the cost of examining wholly unnecessary witnesses to prove a will was £100. Mr. Vizard, another witness, said, "I had received a written statement from a witness living in the county of Devon, as to information he could give; I had other means of ascertaining that the information he sent to me was correct; I, in consequence, brought him to town to be examined at a very considerable expense; he went before the examiner and was examined; and when the depositions came to be published, I found the information which he had given directly opposite to that I had expected; upon which I sent him a copy of his letter to me, and a copy of the evidence he had given, and asked him to account for the difference; the explanation I received was that he had wholly mistaken the question as it was put to him."

This mode of taking evidence was so futile that it was necessary to invent some method of getting the facts before the court. Two methods had been invented—one by the court, and the other by the parties, which really extracted evidence, but which added to the length and expense of a suit in equity.

The method invented by the court was the device of settling a disputed question of fact by sending an issue to be tried by a court of common law.

At the end of the eighteenth century, the practice was constantly resorted to by the chancellor. "So sensible," wrote Blackstone, "is the court of the deficiency of trial by written depositions, that it will not bind the parties thereby, but usually directs the matter to be tried by a jury; especially such important facts as the validity of a will, or whether A is heir-at-law to B. . . . But as no jury can be summoned to attend this court, the fact is usually directed to be tried at the bar of the court of king's bench or at the assizes, upon a *feigned issue*. For, (in order to bring it there, and have the point in dispute, and that only, put in issue) an action is feigned to be brought, wherein the pretended plaintiff declares that he laid a wager of £5 with the defendant, that A was the heir-at-law to B; and then avers that he is so; and brings his action for the £5. The defendant allows the wager, but avers that A is not the heir to B; and thereupon that issue is joined, which is directed out of Chancery to be tried; and thus the verdict of the jurors at law determines the fact in the court of equity."

The method invented by the parties was explained by Mr. Lowe in his evidence to the Chancery Commission of 1826. He was asked, "Do you avoid going before the examiner whenever you can?" He replied, "Certainly; and that is one of the reasons that I amend my bills. I get from the defendant by answers all the facts." And, in answer to another question he said, "it frequently happens that it is absolutely necessary to scrape the defendant's conscience by continuing to amend the bill: I have amended a bill against one of the first merchants in the city of London three times, in one of the plainest cases that ever was; for that I was very much abused; at last he could not evade the questions put to him, and paid my client the thousand pounds in dispute." It would appear from Bentham that this was generally considered to be a very much more efficient mode of extracting evidence than the regular mode of examining witnesses before an examiner or commissioners.

In the course of a suit it was generally necessary to refer very various matters to the masters of the court. It was in the masters' offices that some of the worst delays took place, and the greatest expense was incurred.

The procedure before the masters was almost inconceivably dilatory. For every attendance at a master's office a warrant must be taken out, and a fee paid. It was the custom, on leaving the papers to be copied, to take out a warrant for attendance. But, if the papers to be copied were long, the solicitor knew that they could not be ready in time, and so the custom sprang up of never attending till the second, third, or even the fourth warrant. Each attendance was only for an hour; and though, if all the parties were friendly, two or three successive hours might be arranged, this was seldom possible owing to the engagements of the master. If the parties were not friendly the hour would never be exceeded; and the business might be infinitely protracted by failure to attend or to attend punctually. For it would seem that the master's powers to deal with defaulters were very slight.

In particular, they had for a long time no power to proceed in the absence of the parties; and, when they got that power, they did not use it; so that if two out of three solicitors attended and the third did not, nothing could be done, though the client was obliged to pay the fees of the two who had attended.

This procedure took its rise at a time when the master and his clerks were paid by fees for each piece of work done. Every warrant, every copy, every report, carried its fee. This led to the abuse of compelling the suitor to take office copies, which permeated the whole system of Chancery procedure. It is true that this mode of remunerating the masters had ceased in 1833; but the system was still in force when *Bleak House* was written; and the Act of 1833 had done little to remedy the abuse. All that it had effected was to transfer the fees to a fee fund, so that the old procedure and the old fees still remained. It was for this reason that it was to the interest of the master to lengthen his report, and to adhere to a needlessly complicated method of taking accounts. And this, in its turn, led to many opportunities for motions to the court excepting to the master's report. It was proved in 1826 that the expense incurred in the master's offices amounted to nearly half the expenses of the whole suit.

The Six Clerks were originally supposed to act as the attorneys of the parties. During the eighteenth century this duty devolved upon their deputies the Sixty Clerks; and, at the end of the eighteenth century the parties employed their own solicitors. But traces of the old system survived in the fees paid by the suitors. Every suitor was obliged to appoint a clerk in court, who was supposed to act as his solicitor in court, to advise his private solicitor, and from whom copies of the pleadings must be obtained. Though the fees paid to these clerks in court amounted to an insignificant sum, compared with the vast sums which were spent in the masters' offices, they all added to the expense; and they obviously tended to increase the delay of a suit. One solicitor told the Chancery Commissioners that he paid them annually about £200 a year out of the money of his clients; and many witnesses agreed that they were wholly useless. That these witnesses were right can be seen from the fact that it was quite a usual occurrence for the same clerk in court to act for adverse parties; and from Mr. Lowe's statement in his evidence to the Chancery Commission, that a "Mr. Shaddick was a good clerk in court even when he was a lunatic." Indeed as he pointed out he had reason to regret the lunatic, "His successor has, since his declared lunacy, got my bills from the office, and has doubled the charges for attendance. It is shameful the way they get money from us and the suitors for ideal attendances."

Dickens knew something of these facts when he wrote, "From the master, upon whose impaling files reams of dusty warrants in Jarndyce and Jarndyce have grimly writhed into many shapes; down to the copying-clerk in the Six Clerks' Office, who has copied his tens of thousands of Chanceryfolio-pages under that eternal heading; no man's nature has been made better by it. In trickery, evasion, procrastination, spoliation, botheration, under false pretences of all sorts, there are influences which can never come to good."

A case came many times before the court; for at all stages motions might be made for many purposes. Maddock, in his book on the Chancery, gives a list of thirteen motions which might be made by a plaintiff after the bill was filed and before answer, and a list of fourteen motions which might be made after demurrer, plea or answer. And any number of counsel could be briefed at the hearing of these motions. Dickens has given us two graphic pictures of a scene in court at the hearing of these motions:

Thus, in the midst of the mud and at the heart of the fog, sits the Lord High Chancellor in his High Court of Chancery.

"Mr. Tangle," says the Lord High Chancellor, latterly something restless under the eloquence of that learned gentleman.

"Mlud," says Mr. Tangle. Mr. Tangle knows more of Jarndyce and Jarndyce than anybody. He is famous for it—supposed never to have read anything else since he left school.

"Have you nearly concluded your argument?"

"Mlud, no—variety of points—feel it my duty tsubmit—ludship," is the reply that slides out of Mr. Tangle.

"Several members of the bar are still to be heard, I believe?" says the Chancellor, with a slight smile.

Eighteen of Mr. Tangle's learned friends, each armed with a little summary of eighteen hundred sheets, bob up like eighteen hammers in a pianoforte, make eighteen bows, and drop into their eighteen places of obscurity.

"We will proceed with the hearing on Wednesday fortnight," says the Chancellor. For the question at issue is only a question of costs, a mere bud on the forest tree of the parent suit, and really will come to a settlement one of these days.

The Lord Chancellor threw down a bundle of papers from his desk to the gentlemen below him, and somebody said, "*Jarndyce and Jarndyce.*" Upon this there was a buzz, and a laugh, and a general withdrawal of the bystanders, and a bringing in of great heaps, and piles, and bags and bags full of papers.

I think it came on "for further directions,"—about some bill of costs, to the best of my understanding, which was confused enough. But I counted twenty-three gentlemen in wigs, who said they were "in it"; and none of them appeared to understand it much better than I. They chatted about it with the Lord Chancellor, and contradicted and explained among themselves, and some of them said it was this way, and some of them said it was that way, and some of them jocosely proposed to read huge volumes of affidavits, and there was more buzzing and laughing, and everybody concerned was in a state of idle entertainment, and nothing could be made of it by anybody. After an hour or so of this, and a good many speeches being begun and cut short, it was "referred back for the present," as Mr. Kenge said, and the papers were bundled up again, before the clerks had finished bringing them in.

Finally it should be noticed that all these causes of delay were aggravated, at the period at which the scene of the story is laid, by the fact that the judicial staff of the court was so inadequate that much time elapsed between the time when the case was ready for hearing, and the time when it was actually heard. Since a case came before the court many times at different stages, this waiting time increased enormously the existing delays. In fact the time consumed in merely waiting to be heard amounted almost to a denial of justice. C. P. Cooper writing in 1828 said, "Two briefs in causes on Further Directions set down before the Vice-Chancellor are at this moment on my table. The real and personal estates in both cases are considerable, and neither the legatees nor residuary legatees have yet received any part of their bequests. In one suit the bill was filed rather more, and in the other rather less than twenty years since, and, during more than half that time, the causes have, in different stages, been waiting their turn to be heard."

Of the attempt to do complete justice and its effects I have already said something. The court refused to act at all unless it took charge of the whole matter. In the simplest case, it might be a mere question of the construction of a sentence in a will, it administered the whole estate, and compelled the parties (however friendly they might be) to go through all the forms of a hostile suit. Dickens has dealt with this aspect of the Chancery procedure in the tale which Gridley, the man from Shropshire, tells to John Jarndyce:

"Mr. Jarndyce," he said, "consider my case. As true as there is a Heaven above us, this is my case. I am one of two brothers. My father (a farmer) made a will, and left his farm and stock, and so forth, to my mother, for her life. After my mother's death, all was to come to me, except a legacy of three hundred pounds that I was then to pay my brother. My mother died. My brother, some time afterwards, claimed his legacy. I, and some of my relations, said that he had had a part of it already, in board and lodging, and some other things. Now mind! That was the question, and nothing else. No one disputed the will; no one disputed anything but whether part of that three hundred pounds had been already paid or not. To settle that question, my brother filing a bill, I was obliged to go into this accursed Chancery; I was forced there, because the law forced me, and would let me go nowhere else. Seventeen people were made defendants to that simple suit! It first came on, after two years. It was then stopped for another two years, while the Master (may his head rot off!) inquired whether I was my father's son—about which there was no dispute at all with any mortal creature. He then found out that there were not defendants enough—remember, there were only seventeen as yet!—but that we must have another who had been left out; and must begin all over again. The costs at that time—before the thing was begun!—were three times the legacy. My brother would have given up the legacy, and joyful, to escape more costs. My whole estate, left to me in that will of my father's, has gone in costs. The suit, still undecided, has fallen into rack, and ruin, and despair, with everything else—and here I stand, this day!"

"My whole estate, left to me in that will of my father's, has gone in costs." That was the inevitable end of many Chancery suits. Mr. Bickersteth, in his evidence before the Chancery Commission said, "Cases have occurred within my own knowledge in which the whole property sought to be administered in Chancery has proved insufficient to pay the costs of the suit; and in which the last question discussed in the cause has been how the deficient fund was to be apportioned among the different solicitors in part payment of their respective bills." This was what happened in *Jarndyce* v. *Jarndyce*. It is no doubt true that the discovery of a missing will could not have put a summary end to the case; for, as Sir F. Pollock has said, "Every tyro in equity practice knows that the only immediate effect must have been to add one or more parties to the suit." But I do not think that Dickens suggests this. It is clear that the suit had ended, before the effect of the missing will was considered, because the whole estate had been absorbed in costs; and this does represent what must have been a not uncommon occurrence. Here is Dickens's account of the matter:

"Is this Will considered a genuine document, sir?" said Allan; "will you tell us that?"

"Most certainly, if I could," said Mr. Kenge; "but we have not gone into that, we have not gone into that."

"We have not gone into that," repeated Mr. Vholes, as if his low inward voice were an echo.

"You are to reflect, Mr. Woodcourt, that this has been a great cause, that this has been a protracted cause, that this has been a complex cause. Jarndyce and Jarndyce has been termed, not inaptly, a Monument of Chancery practice."

"And Patience has sat upon it a long time," said Allan.

"Very well indeed, sir," returned Mr. Kenge, with a certain condescending laugh he had. "Very well! You are further to reflect, Mr. Woodcourt," becoming dignified almost to severity, "that on the numerous difficulties, contingencies, masterly fictions, and forms of procedure in this great cause, there has been expended study, ability, eloquence, knowledge, intellect, Mr. Woodcourt, high intellect. For many years, the—a—I would say the flower of the Bar, and the—a—I would presume to add, the matured autumnal fruits of the Woolsack—have been lavished upon Jarndyce and Jarndyce. If the public have the benefit, and if the country have the adornment, of this great Grasp, it must be paid for in money or money's worth, sir."

"Mr. Kenge," said Allan, appearing enlightened all in a moment. "Excuse me, our time presses. Do I understand that the whole estate is found to have been absorbed in costs?"

"Hem! I believe so," returned Mr. Kenge. "Mr. Vholes, what do *you* say?"

"I believe so," said Mr. Vholes.

"And that thus the suit lapses and melts away?"

"Probably," returned Mr. Kenge. "Mr. Vholes?"

"Probably," said Mr. Vholes.

Enormous were the delays of the process used to get an unwilling defendant before the court, to enforce an answer, and to enforce obedience to a decree. But the worst consequence of the last named process was this: if the defendant had no estate, or not sufficient estate, he could be imprisoned, and, as Mr. Bickersteth pointed out to the Chancery Commission, he might remain in gaol for the rest of his life. This was what most stirred Dickens's wrath—as witness his account of the sad case of the cobbler in the Fleet prison, who had been the executor of a will, contested first in the ecclesiastical courts, and then in the court of Chancery:

"Well," said the cobbler, "he left five thousand pounds behind him."

"And wery gen-teel in him so to do," said Sam.

"One of which," continued the cobbler, "he left to me, 'cause I'd married his relations, you see."

"Wery good," murmured Sam.

"And being surrounded by a great number of nieces and nevys, as was always a quarrelling and fighting among themselves for the property, he makes me his executor, and leaves the rest to me: in trust, to divide it among 'em as the will provided."

"Wot do you mean by leavin' it on trust?" inquired Sam, waking up a little. "If it ain't ready money, where's the use on it?"

"It's a law term, that's all," said the cobbler.

"I don't think that," said Sam, shaking his head. "There's wery little trust at that shop. Hows'ever, go on."

"Well," said the cobbler: "when I was going to take out a probate of the will, the nieces and nevys, who was desperately disappointed at not getting all the money, enters a caveat against it."

"What's that?" inquired Sam.

"A legal instrument, which is as much as to say, it's no go," replied the cobbler.

"I see," said Sam, "a sort of brother-in-law o' the have-his-carcase. Well."

"But," continued the cobbler, "finding that they couldn't agree among themselves, and consequently couldn't get up a case against the will, they withdrew the caveat, and I paid all the legacies. I'd hardly done it, when one nevy brings an action to set the will aside. The case comes on, some months afterwards, afore a deaf old gentleman, in a back room somewhere down by Paul's Churchyard; and arter four counsels had taken a day a-piece to bother him regularly, he takes a week or two to consider, and read the evidence in six vollums, and then gives his judgment that how the testator was not quite right in his head, and I must pay all the money back again, and all the costs. I appealed; the case come on before three or four very sleepy gentlemen, who had heard it all before in the other court, where they're lawyers without work; the only difference being, that, there, they're called doctors, and in the other place delegates, if you understand that, and they very dutifully confirmed the decision of the old gentleman below. After that, we went into Chancery, where we are still, and where I shall always be. My lawyers have had all my thousand pound long ago; and what between the estate, as they call it, and the costs, I'm here for ten thousand, and shall stop here, till I die, mending shoes. Some gentlemen have talked of bringing it afore parliament, and I dare say would have done it, only they hadn't time to come to me, and I hadn't power to go to them, and they got tired of my long letters, and dropped the business. And this is God's truth, without one word of suppression or exaggeration, as fifty people, both in this place and out of it, very well know."

It was the contrast between the smug complacency and respectability of the court, and the ruin which it brought upon all persons and things which it got within its grasp, which inspired Dickens's pen.

To see everything going on so smoothly, and to think of the roughness of the suitors' lives and deaths; to see all that full dress and ceremony, and to think of the waste, and want, and beggared misery it represented; to consider that, while the sickness of hope deferred was raging in so many hearts, this polite show went calmly on from day to day, and year to year, in such good order and composure; to behold the Lord Chancellor, and the whole array of practitioners under him, looking at one another and at the spectators, as if nobody had ever heard that all over England the name in which they were assembled was a bitter jest: was held in universal horror, contempt, and indignation: was known for something so flagrant and bad, that little short of a miracle could bring any good out of it to any one.

It was this lesson which Dickens drove into the minds of his readers by his description of the tragic death of Tom Jarndyce, of the life of poor half-crazed Miss Flite, of the effect produced on the character of Richard Carstone by his growing interest in the fatal suit.

As I have already pointed out, some reforms had been made when *Bleak House* was written. But, as the Chancery Commission of 1850 proved, much remained to be done. In fact, at the very time when *Bleak House* began to appear (March, 1852), things were going badly in the Court of Chancery. Mr. Atlay says: "The existence in its full integrity of the historical office of Lord Chancellor was never in greater peril. The prolonged illness of Lord Cottenham and the habits of procrastination which he developed during his later days had once more piled up the arrears in Chancery. The issuing of new Orders, the increase in the judicial staff, even the abolition of the Six Clerks' Office, had been powerless to cope with the evil. Never had the public mind been more inflamed; a competent observer declared that the most popular measure which could be introduced into the House of Commons would be one for the abolition *sans phrase* of the Court of Chancery."

But relief was at hand. The result of the Chancery Commission of 1850 was the Chancery Procedure Acts of 1852. They reformed both the pleading of the court, and its system of procedure. The form of the Bill was changed. It was to consist of a concise narrative of material facts divided into numbered paragraphs, and it was not to contain interrogatories. The masters, and the cumbrous machinery of the masters' offices, were abolished. Their duties were handed over to the judges sitting in Chambers, and to their chief clerks. Certain powers, formerly belonging only to the common law courts, were given to the Court of Chancery, and *vice versa,* so that the Court of Chancery could no longer hang up a suit by sending a case for the consideration of the common law courts. The changes made by these acts in equity procedure, and by the contemporary Common Law Procedure Acts in common law procedure, paved the way to the fusion of jurisdiction effected by the Judicature Act in 1875, and to the formation of the modern code of procedure contained in the rules of the Supreme Court. Of these reforms I shall have something more to say after I have examined, in the next lecture, the procedure of the common law.

Phineas Finn Awaits Trial
or
Chaffanbrass on the Law*

ANTHONY TROLLOPE

Perhaps it was the frankness of his Autobiography, perhaps the inevitable decline that any writer suffers after his death—at any rate it was not until the early 1920's that the solid merits of Anthony Trollope as a novelist were rediscovered. Regarding this Sir Edward Marsh tells a delightful story.

"Barrie (Sir J. M. Barrie) told me of a night in a strange bedroom when he had needed something to read himself to sleep with, but found on the bookshelf nothing by any known author except a Trollope, whose title Is He Popenjoy? seemed so inane and repellent that he could hardly bring himself to open it. However, there was nothing for it: he began to read— and sat up into the small hours." This formidable undercurrent of enthusiasm and the writings of Michael Sadleir and Lord David Cecil have contributed to the present reestablishment of Trollope's high reputation.

The scene that follows is extracted from Phineas Redux, one of the Parliamentary novels which are just as good in their own way as the Barchester stories. Here Mr. Chaffanbrass, the old criminal barrister, has something to say, equally with Charles P. Curtis (see p. 2), which sums up as well as it has ever been said the duties and ideals of the courtroom lawyer.

As to the actual situation in the novel into which the reader of this anthology is plunged, let it be said that Phineas Finn is a young member of Parliament accused of murder, and the circumstantial evidence which has led to his arrest has been supplied by Lord Fawn, a minor member of the Government and a friend of Phineas. The vital piece of evidence is a grey overcoat which the murderer wore when the murder was committed. Madame Goesler is a lady of wealth, in love with our hero, who has supplied the funds for his defense. Let it be said too that in the course of the story Mr. Finn, being innocent, is acquitted.

There was a scene in the private room of Mr. Wickerby, the attorney in Hatton Garden, which was very distressing indeed to the feelings of Lord Fawn, and which induced his lordship to think that he was being

* From *Phineas Redux*.

treated without that respect which was due to him as a peer and a member of the Government. There were present at this scene Mr. Chaffanbrass, the old barrister, Mr. Wickerby himself, Mr. Wickerby's confidential clerk, Lord Fawn, Lord Fawn's solicitor,—that same Mr. Camperdown whom we saw in the last chapter calling upon Lady Eustace,—and a policeman. Lord Fawn had been invited to attend, with many protestations of regret as to the trouble thus imposed upon him, because the very important nature of the evidence about to be given by him at the forthcoming trial seemed to render it expedient that some questions should be asked. This was on Tuesday, the 22nd June, and the trial was to be commenced on the following Thursday. And there was present in the room, very conspicuously, an old heavy grey greatcoat, as to which Mr. Wickerby had instructed Mr. Chaffanbrass that evidence was forthcoming, if needed, to prove that that coat was lying on the night of the murder in a downstairs room in the house in which Yosef Mealyus was then lodging. The reader will remember the history of the coat. Instigated by Madame Goesler, who was still absent from England, Mr. Wickerby had traced the coat, and had purchased the coat, and was in a position to prove that this very coat was the coat which Mr. Meager had brought home with him to Northumberland Street on that day. But Mr. Wickerby was of opinion that the coat had better not be used. "It does not go far enough," said Mr. Wickerby. "It don't go very far, certainly," said Mr. Chaffanbrass. "And if you try to show that another man has done it, and he hasn't," said Mr. Wickerby, "it always tells against you with a jury." To this Mr. Chaffanbrass made no reply, preferring to form his own opinion, and to keep it to himself when formed. But in obedience to his instructions, Lord Fawn was asked to attend at Mr. Wickerby's chambers, in the cause of truth, and the coat was brought out on the occasion. "Was that the sort of coat the man wore, my lord?" said Mr. Chaffanbrass, as Mr. Wickerby held up the coat to view. Lord Fawn walked round and round the coat, and looked at it very carefully before he would vouchsafe a reply. "You see it is a grey coat," said Mr. Chaffanbrass, not speaking at all in the tone which Mr. Wickerby's note had induced Lord Fawn to expect.

"It is grey," said Lord Fawn.

"Perhaps it's not the same shade of grey, Lord Fawn. You see, my lord, we are most anxious not to impute guilt where guilt doesn't lie. You are a witness for the Crown, and, of course, you will tell the Crown lawyers all that passes here. Were it possible, we would make this little preliminary inquiry in their presence;—but we can hardly do that. Mr. Finn's coat was a very much smaller coat."

"I should think it was," said his lordship, who did not like being questioned about coats.

"You don't think the coat the man wore when you saw him was a big coat like that? You think he wore a little coat?"

"He wore a grey coat," said Lord Fawn.

"This is grey;—a coat shouldn't be greyer than that."

"I don't think Lord Fawn should be asked any more questions on the matter till he gives his evidence in court," said Mr. Camperdown..

"A man's life depends on it, Mr. Camperdown," said the barrister. "It isn't a matter of cross-examination. If I bring that coat into court I must make a charge against another man by the very act of doing so. And I will not do so unless I believe that other man to be guilty. It's an inquiry I can't postpone till we are before the jury. It isn't that I want to trump up a case against another man for the sake of extricating my client on a false issue. Lord Fawn doesn't want to hang Mr. Finn if Mr. Finn be not guilty."

"God forbid!" said his lordship.

"Mr. Finn couldn't have worn that coat, or a coat at all like it."

"What is it you do want to learn, Mr. Chaffanbrass?" asked Mr. Camperdown.

"Just put on the coat, Mr. Scruby." Then at the order of the barrister, Mr. Scruby, the attorney's clerk, did put on Mr. Meager's old greatcoat, and walked about the room in it. "Walk quick," said Mr. Chaffanbrass;— and the clerk did "walk quick." He was a stout, thick-set little man, nearly half a foot shorter than Phineas Finn. "Is that at all like the figure?" asked Mr. Chaffanbrass.

"I think it is like the figure," said Lord Fawn.

"And like the coat?"

"It's the same colour as the coat."

"You wouldn't swear it was not the coat?"

"I am not on my oath at all, Mr. Chaffanbrass."

"No, my lord;—but to me your word is as good as your oath. If you think it possible that was the coat—"

"I don't think anything about it at all. When Mr. Scruby hurries down the room in that way he looks as the man looked when he was hurrying under the lamppost. I am not disposed to say any more at present."

"It's a matter of regret to me that Lord Fawn should have come here at all," said Mr. Camperdown, who had been summoned to meet his client at the chambers, but had come with him.

"I suppose his lordship wishes us to know all that he knew, seeing that it's a question of hanging the right man or the wrong one. I never heard such trash in my life. Take it off, Mr. Scruby, and let the policeman keep it. I understand Lord Fawn to say that the man's figure was about the same as yours. My client, I believe, stands about twelve inches taller. Thank you, my lord;—we shall get at the truth at last, I don't doubt." It was afterwards said that Mr. Chaffanbrass's conduct had been very improper in enticing Lord Fawn to Mr. Wickerby's chambers; but Mr. Chaffanbrass never cared what any one said. "I don't know that we can make much of it," he said, when he and Mr. Wickerby were alone, "but it may be as well to bring it into court. It would prove nothing against the Jew even if that fellow,"—he meant Lord Fawn,—"could be made to swear that the coat worn was exactly similar to this. I am thinking now about the height."

"I don't doubt but you'll get him off."

"Well;—I may do so. They ought not to hang any man on such evidence as there is against him, even though there were no moral doubt of his guilt. There is nothing really to connect Mr. Phineas Finn with the murder,— nothing tangible. But there is no saying now-a-days what a jury will do. Juries depend a great deal more on the judge than they used to do. If I were on trial for my life, I don't think I'd have counsel at all."

"No one could defend you as well as yourself, Mr. Chaffanbrass."

"I didn't mean that. No;—I shouldn't defend myself. I should say to the judge, 'My lord, I don't doubt the jury will do just as you tell them, and you'll form your own opinion quite independent of the arguments.'"

"You'd be hung, Mr. Chaffanbrass."

"No; I don't know that I should," said Mr. Chaffanbrass slowly. "I don't think I could affront a judge of the present day into hanging me. They've too much of what I call thick-skinned honesty for that. It's the temper of the time to resent nothing,—to be mealy-mouthed and mealy-hearted. Jury-men are afraid of having their own opinion, and almost always shirk a verdict when they can."

"But we do get verdicts."

"Yes; the judges give them. And they are mealy-mouthed verdicts, tend-ing to equalise crime and innocence, and to make men think that after all it may be a question whether fraud is violence, which, after all, is manly, and to feel that we cannot afford to hate dishonesty. It was a bad day for the commercial world, Mr. Wickerby, when forgery ceased to be capital."

"It was a horrid thing to hang a man for writing another man's name to a receipt for thirty shillings."

"We didn't do it, but the fact that the law held certain frauds to be hanging matters, operated on the minds of men in regard to all fraud. What with the joint-stock working of companies, and the confusion between directors who know nothing and managers who know everything, and the dislike of juries to tread upon people's corns, you can't punish dishonest trading. Caveat emptor is the only motto going, and the worst proverb that ever came from dishonest stony-hearted Rome. With such a matter as that to guide us, no man dare trust his brother. Caveat lex,—and let the man who cheats cheat at his peril."

"You'd give the law a great deal to do."

"Much less than at present. What does your Caveat emptor come to? That every seller tries to pick the eyes out of the head of the purchaser. Sooner or later the law must interfere, and Caveat emptor falls to the ground. I bought a horse the other day; my daughter wanted something to look pretty, and like an old ass as I am I gave a hundred and fifty pounds for the brute. When he came home he wasn't worth a feed of corn."

"You had a warranty, I suppose?"

"No, indeed! Did you ever hear of such an old fool?"

"I should have thought any dealer would have taken him back for the sake of his character."

"Any dealer would; but—I bought him of a gentleman."

"Mr. Chaffanbrass!"

"I ought to have known better, oughtn't I? Caveat emptor."

"It was just giving away your money, you know."

"A great deal worse than that. I could have given the—gentleman—a hundred and fifty pounds, and not have minded it much. I ought to have had the horse killed, and gone to a dealer for another. Instead of that,—I went to an attorney."

"Oh, Mr. Chaffanbrass;—the idea of your going to an attorney."

"I did then. I never had so much honest truth told me in my life."

"By an attorney!"

"He said that he did think I'd been born long enough to have known better than that! I pleaded on my own behalf that the gentleman said the horse was all right. 'Gentleman!' exclaimed my friend. 'You go to a gentleman for a horse; you buy a horse from a gentleman without a warranty; and then you come to me! Didn't you ever hear of Caveat emptor, Mr. Chaffanbrass? What can I do for you?' That's what my friend, the attorney, said to me."

"And what came of it, Mr. Chaffanbrass? Arbitration, I should say?"

"Just that;—with the horse eating his head off every meal at ever so much per week,—till at last I fairly gave in from sheer vexation. So the—gentleman—got my money, and I added something to my stock of experience. Of course, that's only my story, and it may be that the gentleman could tell it another way. But I say that if my story be right, the doctrine of Caveat emptor does not encourage trade. I don't know how we got to all this from Mr. Finn. I'm to see him tomorrow."

"Yes;—he is very anxious to speak to you."

"What's the use of it, Wickerby? I hate seeing a client. What comes of it?"

"Of course he wants to tell his own story."

"But I don't want to hear his own story. What good will his own story do me? He'll tell me either one of two things. He'll swear he didn't murder the man—"

"That's what he'll say."

"Which can have no effect upon me one way or the other; or else he'll say that he did,—which would cripple me altogether."

"He won't say that, Mr. Chaffanbrass."

"There's no knowing what they'll say. A man will go on swearing by his God that he is innocent, till at last, in a moment of emotion, he breaks down, and out comes the truth. In such a case as this I do not in the least want to know the truth about the murder."

"This is what the public wants to know."

"Because the public is ignorant. The public should not wish to know anything of the kind. What we should all wish to get at is the truth of the evidence about the murder. The man is to be hung not because he committed the murder,—as to which no positive knowledge is attainable; but because he has been proved to have committed the murder,—as to which proof, though it be enough for hanging, there must always be attached some shadow of doubt. We were delighted to hang Palmer,—but we don't know that he killed Cook. A learned man who knew more about it than we can know seemed to think that he didn't. Now the last man to give us any useful insight into the evidence is the prisoner himself. In nineteen cases out of twenty a man tried for murder in this country committed the murder for which he is tried."

"There really seems to be a doubt in this case."

"I dare say. If there be only nineteen guilty out of twenty, there must be one innocent; and why not Mr. Phineas Finn? But, if it be so, he, burning with the sense of injustice, thinks that everybody should see it as he sees it. He is to be tried, because on investigation, everybody sees it just in a different light. In such case he is unfortunate, but he can't assist me in liberating him from his misfortune. He sees what is patent and clear to him,—that he walked home that night without meddling with any one. But I can't see that, or make others see it, because he sees it."

"His manner of telling you may do something."

"If it do, Mr. Wickerby, it is because I am unfit for my business. If he have the gift of protesting well, I am to think him innocent; and, therefore, to think him guilty, if he be unprovided with such eloquence! I will neither believe or disbelieve anything that a client says to me,—unless he confess his guilt, in which case my services can be but of little avail. Of course I shall see him, as he asks it. We had better meet then,—say at half-past ten." Whereupon Mr. Wickerby wrote to the governor of the prison begging that Phineas Finn might be informed of the visit.

Phineas had now been in gaol between six and seven weeks, and the very fact of his incarceration had nearly broken his spirits. Two of his sisters, who had come from Ireland to be near him, saw him every day, and his two friends, Mr. Low and Lord Chiltern, were very frequently with him; Lady Laura Kennedy had not come to him again; but he heard from her frequently through Barrington Erle. Lord Chiltern rarely spoke of his sister,—alluding to her merely in connection with her father and her late husband. Presents still came to him from various quarters,—as to which he hardly knew whence they came. But the Duchess and Lady Chiltern and Lady Laura all catered for him,—while Mrs. Bunce looked after his wardrobe, and saw that he was not cut down to prison allowance of clean shirts

and socks. But the only friend whom he recognised as such was the friend
who would freely declare a conviction of his innocence. They allowed him
books and pens and paper, and even cards, if he chose to play at patience
with them or build castles. The paper and pens he could use because he
could write about himself. From day to day he composed a diary in which
he was never tired of expatiating on the terrible injustice of his position.
But he could not read. He found it to be impossible to fix his attention
on matters outside himself. He assured himself from hour to hour that it
was not death he feared,—not even death from the hangman's hand. It was
the condemnation of those who had known him that was so terrible to
him;—the feeling that they with whom he had aspired to work and live,
the leading men and women of his day, ministers of the Government and
their wives, statesmen and their daughters, peers and members of the
House in which he himself had sat;—that these should think that before all
he had been a base adventurer unworthy of their society! That was the
sorrow that broke him down, and drew him to confess that his whole life
had been a failure.

Mr. Low had advised him not to see Mr. Chaffanbrass;—but he had persisted in declaring that there were instructions which no one but himself could give to the counsellor whose duty it would be to defend him at
the trial. Mr. Chaffanbrass came at the hour fixed, and with him came
Mr. Wickerby. The old barrister bowed courteously as he entered the
prison room, and the attorney introduced the two gentlemen with more
than all the courtesy of the outer world. "I am sorry to see you here, Mr.
Finn," said the barrister.

"It's a bad lodging, Mr. Chaffanbrass, but the term will soon be over.
I am thinking a good deal more of my next abode."

"It has to be thought of, certainly," said the barrister. "Let us hope that
it may be all that you would wish it to be. My services shall not be wanting
to make it so."

"We are doing all we can, Mr. Finn," said Mr. Wickerby.

"Mr. Chaffanbrass," said Phineas, "there is one special thing that I want
you to do." The old man, having his own idea as to what was coming,
laid one of his hands over the other, bowed his head and looked meek.
"I want you to make men believe that I am innocent of this crime."

This was better than Mr. Chaffanbrass expected. "I trust that we may
succeed in making twelve men believe it," said he.

"Comparatively I do not care a straw for the twelve men. It is not to
them especially that I am anxious that you should address yourself—"

"But that will be my bounden duty, Mr. Finn."

"I can well believe, sir, that though I have myself been bred a lawyer,
I may not altogether understand the nature of an advocate's duty to his
client. But I would wish something more to be done than what you
intimate."

"The duty of an advocate defending a prisoner is to get a verdict of acquittal if he can, and to use his own discretion in making the attempt."

"But I want something more to be attempted, even if in the struggle something less be achieved. I have known men to be so acquitted that every man in court believed them to be guilty."

"No doubt;—and such men have probably owed much to their advocates."

"It is not such a debt that I wish to owe. I know my own innocence."

"Mr. Chaffanbrass takes that for granted," said Mr. Wickerby.

"To me it is a matter of astonishment that any human being should believe me to have committed this murder. I am lost in surprise when I remember that I am here simply because I walked home from my club with a loaded stick in my pocket. The magistrate, I suppose, thought me guilty."

"He did not think about it, Mr. Finn. He went by the evidence;—the quarrel, your position in the streets at the time, the colour of the coat you wore and that of the coat worn by the man whom Lord Fawn saw in the street; the doctor's evidence as to the blows by which the man was killed; and the nature of the weapon which you carried. He put these things together, and they were enough to entitle the public to demand that a jury should decide. He didn't say you were guilty. He only said that the circumstances were sufficient to justify a trial."

"If he thought me innocent he would not have sent me here."

"Yes, he would;—if the evidence required that he should do so."

"We will not argue about that, Mr. Chaffanbrass."

"Certainly not, Mr. Finn."

"Here I am, and to-morrow I shall be tried for my life. My life will be nothing to me unless it can be made clear to all the world that I am innocent. I would be sooner hung for this,—with the certainty at my heart that all England on the next day would ring with the assurance of my innocence, than be acquitted and afterwards be looked upon as a murderer." Phineas, when he was thus speaking, had stepped out into the middle of the room, and stood with his head thrown back, and his right hand forward. Mr. Chaffanbrass, who was himself an ugly, dirty old man, who had always piqued himself on being indifferent to appearance, found himself struck by the beauty and grace of the man whom he now saw for the first time. And he was struck, too, by his client's eloquence, though he had expressly declared to the attorney that it was his duty to be superior to any such influence. "Oh, Mr. Chaffanbrass, for the love of Heaven, let there be no quibbling."

"We never quibble, I hope, Mr. Finn."

"No subterfuges, no escaping by a side wind, no advantage taken of little forms, no objection taken to this and that as though delay would avail us anything."

"Character will go a great way, we hope."

"It should go for nothing. Though no one would speak a word for me, still am I innocent. Of course the truth will be known some day."

"I am not so sure of that, Mr. Finn."

"It will certainly be known some day. That it should not be known as yet is my misfortune. But in defending me I would have you hurl defiance at my accusers. I had the stick in my pocket,—having heretofore been concerned with ruffians in the street. I did quarrel with the man, having been insulted by him at the club. The coat which I wore was such as they say. But does that make a murderer of me?"

"Somebody did the deed, and that somebody could probably say all that you say."

"No, sir;—he, when he is known, will be found to have been skulking in the streets; he will have thrown away his weapon; he will have been secret in his movements; he will have hidden his face, and have been a murderer in more than the deed. When they came to me in the morning did it seem to them that I was a murderer? Has my life been like that? They who have really known me cannot believe that I have been guilty. They who have not known me, and do believe, will live to learn their error."

He then sat down and listened patiently while the old lawyer described to him the nature of the case,—wherein lay his danger, and wherein what hope there was of safety. There was no evidence against him other than circumstantial evidence, and both judges and jury were wont to be unwilling to accept such, when uncorroborated, as sufficient in cases of life and death. Unfortunately, in this case the circumstantial evidence was very strong against him. But, on the other hand, his character, as to which men of great mark would speak with enthusiasm, would be made to stand very high. "I would not have it made to stand higher than it is," said Phineas. As to the opinion of the world afterwards, Mr. Chaffanbrass went on to say, of that he must take his chance. But surely he himself might fight better for it living than any friend could do for him after his death. "You must believe me in this, Mr. Finn, that a verdict of acquittal from the jury is the one object that we must have before us."

"The one object that I shall have before me is the verdict of the public," said Phineas. "I am treated with so much injustice in being thought a murderer that they can hardly add anything to it by hanging me."

When Mr. Chaffanbrass left the prison he walked back with Mr. Wickerby to the attorney's chambers in Hatton Garden, and he lingered for a while on the Viaduct expressing his opinion of his client. "He's not a bad fellow, Wickerby."

"A very good sort of fellow, Mr. Chaffanbrass."

"I never did,—and I never will,—express an opinion of my own as to the guilt or innocence of a client till after the trial is over. But I have sometimes felt as though I would give the blood out of my veins to save a man. I never felt in that way more strongly than I do now."

"It'll make me very unhappy, I know, if it goes against him," said Mr. Wickerby.

"People think that the special branch of the profession into which I have chanced to fall is a very low one,—and I do not know whether, if the world were before me again, I would allow myself to drift into an exclusive practice in criminal courts."

"Yours has been a very useful life, Mr. Chaffanbrass."

"But I often feel," continued the barrister, paying no attention to the attorney's last remark, "that my work touches the heart more nearly than does that of gentlemen who have to deal with matters of property and of high social claims. People think I am savage,—savage to witnesses."

"You can frighten a witness, Mr. Chaffanbrass."

"It's just a trick of the trade that you learn, as a girl learns the notes of her piano. There's nothing in it. You forgot it all the next hour. But when a man has been hung whom you have striven to save, you do remember that. Good morning, Mr. Wickerby. I'll be there a little before ten. Perhaps you may have to speak to me."

Madame Luneau's Case*

GUY DE MAUPASSANT

(Translated by Ernest Boyd)

"Oh, spirit of Maupassant, come to my aid! This must be a triumph of robust and vivid concision." So prayed Henry James in 1888 as he embarked on one of his shorter stories. Later, looking back, James was to speak of Maupassant differently and was to describe the group of writers whom he had known in Paris as a young man (including Flaubert and Maupassant) as "corrupt." The tale which follows—vivid, robust, compact, as it is—is not corrupt, but it is written with a total cynicism that is astonishing even today.

The fat Justice of the Peace, with one eye closed and the other half-open, is listening with evident displeasure to the plaintiffs. Once in a while he gives a sort of grunt that foretells his opinion, and in a thin voice resembling that of a child, he interrupts them to ask questions. He has just rendered judgment in the case of Monsieur Joly against Monsieur Petitpas, the contestants having come to court on account of the boundary line of a field which had been accidentally displaced by Monsieur Petitpas's farm-hand, while the latter was plowing.

Now he calls the case of Hippolyte Lacour, vestryman and ironmonger, against Madame Céleste Cesarine Luneau, widow of Anthime Isidore Luneau.

Hippolyte Lacour is forty-five years old; he is tall and gaunt, with a clean-shaven face like a priest, long hair, and he speaks in a slow, singsong voice.

Madame Luneau appears to be about forty years of age. She is built like a prize-fighter, and her narrow and clinging dress is stretched tightly over her portly form. Her enormous hips hold up her overflowing bosom in front, while in the back they support the great rolls of flesh that cover her shoulders. Her face, with strongly-cut features, rests on a short, fat neck, and her strong voice is pitched at a key that makes the windows and the

* From *The Sisters Rondoli and Other Stories*, in *The Collected Novels and Short Stories of Guy de Maupassant*, translated by Ernest Boyd, copyright, 1923, by Alfred A. Knopf, Inc., renewal copyright, 1951, by Alfred A. Knopf, Inc. Reprinted by permission of Alfred A. Knopf, Inc.

eardrums of her auditors vibrate. She is about to become a mother and her huge form protrudes like a mountain.

The witnesses for the defense are waiting to be called.

The judge begins: Hippolyte Lacour, state your complaint.

The plaintiff speaks: Your Honour, it will be nine months on Saint-Michael's day since the defendant came to me one evening, after I had rung the Angelus, and began an explanation relating to her barrenness.

The Justice of the Peace: Kindly be more explicit.

Hippolyte: Very well, your Honour. Well, she wanted to have a child and desired my participation. I didn't raise any objection, and she promised to give me one hundred francs. The thing was cut and dried, and now she refuses to acknowledge my claim, which I renew before your Honour.

The Justice: I don't understand in the least. You say that she wanted a child! What kind of child? Did she wish to adopt one?

Hippolyte: No, your Honour, she wanted a new one.

The Justice: What do you mean by a new one?

Hippolyte: I mean a newborn child, one that we were to beget as if we were man and wife.

The Justice: You astonish me. To what end did she make this abnormal proposition?

Hippolyte: Your Honour, at first I could not make out her reasons, and was taken a little aback. But as I don't do anything without thoroughly investigating beforehand, I called on her to explain matters to me, which she did. You see, her husband, Anthime Isidore, whom you knew as well as you know me, had died the week before, and his money reverted to his family. This greatly displeased her on account of the loss it meant, so she went to a lawyer who told her all about what might happen if a child should be born to her after ten months. I mean by this that if she gave birth to a child inside of the ten months following the death of Anthime Isidore, her offspring would be considered legitimate and would entitle her to the inheritance. She made up her mind at once to run the risk, and came to me after church, as I have already had the honour of telling you, seeing that I am the father of eight living children, the oldest of whom is a grocer in Caen, department of Calvados, and legitimately married to Victoire-Elisabeth Rabou—

The Justice: These details are superfluous. Go back to the subject.

Hippolyte: I am getting there, your Honour. So she said to me: "If you succeed, I'll give you one hundred francs as soon as I get the doctor's report." Well, your Honour, I made ready to give entire satisfaction, and after eight weeks or so I learned with pleasure that I had succeeded. But when I asked her for the hundred francs she refused to pay me. I renewed my demands several times, never getting so much as a pin. She even called me a liar and a weakling, a libel which can be destroyed by glancing at her.

The Justice: Defendant, what have you to say?

Madame Luneau: Your Honour, I say that this man is a liar.

The Justice: How can you prove this assertion?

Madame Luneau (red in the face, choking and stammering): How can I prove it? What proofs have I? I haven't a single real proof that the child isn't his. But, your Honour, it isn't his, I swear it on the head of my dead husband.

The Justice: Well, whose is it, then?

Madame Luneau (stammering with rage): How do I know? How do—do I know? Everybody's, I suppose. Here are my witnesses, your Honour, they're all here, the six of them. Now make them testify, make them testify. They'll tell—

The Justice: Collect yourself, Madame Luneau, collect yourself and reply calmly to my questions. What reasons have you to doubt that this man is the father of the child you are carrying?

Madame Luneau: What reasons? I have a hundred to one. A hundred? No, two hundred, five hundred, ten thousand, a million and more reasons to believe he isn't. After the proposal I made to him, with the promise of one hundred francs, didn't I learn that he wasn't the father of his own children, your Honour, not the father of one of 'em?

Hippolyte (calmly): That's a lie.

Madame Luneau (exasperated): A lie! A lie, is it? I think his wife has been around with everybody around here. Call my witnesses, your Honour, and make them testify!

Hippolyte (calmly): It's a lie.

Madame Luneau: It's a lie, is it? How about the red-haired ones, then? I suppose they're yours, too?

The Justice: Kindly refrain from personal attacks, or I shall be obliged to call you to order.

Madame Luneau: Well, your Honour, I had my doubts about him, and said I to myself, two precautions are better than one, so I explained my position to Césaire Lepic, the witness who is present. Says he to me, "At your disposal, Madame Luneau," and he lent me his assistance in case Hippolyte's should turn out to be unreliable. But as soon as the other witnesses heard that I wanted to make sure against any disappointment, I could have had more than a hundred, your Honour, if I had wanted them. That tall one over there, Lucas Chandelier, swore at the time that I oughtn't to give Hippolyte Lacour a cent, for he hadn't done more than the rest of them who had obliged me for nothing.

Hippolyte: What did you promise for? I expected the money, your Honour. No mistake with me—a promise given, a promise kept.

Madame Luneau (beside herself): One hundred francs! One hundred francs! One hundred francs for that, you liar! The others there didn't ask a red cent! Look at 'em, all six of them! Make them testify, your Honour, they'll tell you. (To Hippolyte) Look at 'em, you liar! They're as good as you. They're only six, but I could have had one, two, three, five hundred of 'em for nothing, too, you robber!

Hippolyte: Well, even if you'd had a hundred thousand—

Madame Luneau: I could, if I'd wanted them.

Hippolyte: I did my duty, so it doesn't change our agreement.

Madame Luneau (slapping her protuberant form with both hands): Then prove that it's you that did it, prove it, you robber! I defy you to prove it!

Hippolyte (calmly): Maybe I didn't do any more than anybody else. But you promised me a hundred francs for it. What did you ask the others for, afterwards? You had no right to. I could have done it alone.

Madame Luneau: It is not true, robber! Call my witnesses, your Honour; they'll answer, for certain.

The Justice calls the witnesses in behalf of the defense. Six individuals appear, blushing, awkward looking, with their arms swinging at their sides.

The Justice: Lucas Chandelier, have you any reason to suppose that you are the father of the child Madame Luneau is carrying?

Lucas Chandelier: Yes, sir.

The Justice: Célestin-Pierre Sidoine, have you any reason to suppose that you are the father of the child Madame Luneau is carrying?

Célestin-Pierre Sidoine: Yes, sir.

The four other witnesses testified to the same effect.

The Justice, after having thought for awhile, pronounced judgment: Whereas the plaintiff has reasons to believe himself the father of the child which Madame Luneau desired, Lucas Chandelier, Célestin-Pierre Sidoine, and others, have similar, if not conclusive reasons to lay claim to the child.

But whereas Mme. Luneau had previously asked the assistance of Hippolyte Lacour for a duly stated consideration of one hundred francs:

And whereas one may not question the absolute good faith of Hippolyte Lacour, though it is questionable whether he had a perfect right to enter into such an agreement, seeing that the plaintiff is married, and compelled by the law to remain faithful to his lawful spouse: Whereas, farther, etc., etc.

Therefore the Court condemns Madame Luneau to pay an indemnity of twenty-five francs to Hippolyte Lacour for loss of time and seduction.

The Baccarat Case*

AN OFFICER CROSS-EXAMINED

EDWARD WILFRID FORDHAM

"There were during the period of the nineties, two scandals accompanied by trials in the law courts, both of which produced an immense sensation and a din of public hooting." Thus the rounded Edwardian periods of E. F. Benson.† *These two scandals in the opinion of some observers were the first cracks in the enamelled façade of the British Empire: certainly the savage comment they invoked in the newspapers of Europe and particularly in France and Germany revealed the isolation and hatred by which England was surrounded. The first of these scandals was the Tranby Croft affair in 1891, commonly known as "The Baccarat Case." The presence of Edward VII, then Prince of Wales, as a member of the house party accounted for the heated public interest. The observant reader will note, in following the cross-examination, that one of the guests, Mr. Reuben Sassoon, seems to have acted as banker for the Prince of Wales. The company he kept, at least as much as the fact that he gambled, accounted for the wave of indignation against the Prince. All was forgiven the heir to the throne when in 1896 his horse "Persimmon" won the Derby. At the end of the trial Sir William Gordon-Cumming walked out of the court a ruined man.*

T he Baccarat Case was an action for slander in which Sir William Gordon-Cumming, Bart., was plaintiff, and the defendants were Mrs. Arthur Wilson, Mr. Arthur Stanley Wilson, Mr. C. Lycett Green, and Mr. Berkeley Levett.

The action was the ultimate result of an allegation that Sir William, the plaintiff, had cheated at cards. He had been one of a house-party at Tranby Croft, the home of Mr. and Mrs. Arthur Wilson, in September 1890. An illustrious member of the house-party was the Prince of Wales of that day, and this largely accounted for the extraordinary public interest shown in the case.

The cheating alleged was that, while playing baccarat on two evenings,

* From E. W. Fordham, *Notable Cross-Examinations.* Reprinted by permission of The Macmillan Company and Constable & Co., Ltd.

† "As We Were" published by Longmans, Green and Co., copyright 1930 by E. F. Benson.

September 8th and 9th, Sir William had so manipulated his counters, representing stakes of £5 and £10 each, as to secure winnings to which he was not legitimately entitled. On the evening of September 10th, Lord Coventry, who was a fellow-guest, informed Sir William that this allegation had been made against him by certain of the players. Sir William at once categorically denied the charge, and this denial he repeated later to the Prince of Wales in the presence of Lord Coventry and another guest, General Owen Williams. Ultimately, and after much discussion, Sir William consented to sign, and did sign, a document in these terms: *"In consideration of the promise made by the gentlemen whose names are subscribed to preserve silence with reference to an accusation which has been made with regard to my conduct at baccarat on the nights of Monday and Tuesday, the 8th and 9th of September 1890, at Tranby Croft, I will, on my part, solemnly undertake never to play cards again as long as I live."*

Despite the promise of silence contained in this document, which no doubt was honourably kept by the signatories, it was inevitable, having regard to the number and composition of the house-party, that the alleged facts should leak out: and leak out they did. The result was that Sir William's position both in the Army and in Society became intolerable, and he was, in effect, forced to bring an action for slander against his accusers.

In this action it is Sir Charles Russell's cross-examination with regard to the signed document, and the implication of its signature by the plaintiff, with which we shall here be concerned. The evidence of those who believed they saw Sir William fraudulently manipulating his counters, and his evidence denying that he had done anything of the sort, are of course fully set out in the record of the trial; but that side of the case, interesting though it is, is of less psychological interest than is the question as to what is the true deduction to be drawn from the fact that so remarkable a document was signed by Sir William Gordon-Cumming.

The action was tried by the Lord Chief Justice (Lord Coleridge). The leading counsel were: for the plaintiff, the Solicitor-General (Sir Edward Clarke, Q.C.); for the defendants, Sir Charles Russell, Q.C., and Mr. H. H. Asquith, Q.C. The hearing began on Monday, June 1st, and ended on Tuesday, June 9th, 1891, when the jury found for the defendants, and judgment was given accordingly.

· · · · ·

FROM THE CROSS-EXAMINATION OF SIR WILLIAM GORDON-CUMMING
BY SIR CHARLES RUSSELL, Q.C.

(Sir Charles Russell, cross-examining, is dealing with Sir William's reasons for signing the document in which he undertakes never to play cards again.)

After the signing of the document, did you say you proposed to go to the races the next day, and did General Owen Williams say to you, "Certainly you cannot; you must leave the first thing in the morning"? —He suggested that I should leave the house as soon as possible, and I did leave first thing.

Now I put one question which I ask you anxiously to consider. Do you suggest, as has been suggested by learned counsel today, that Lord Coventry and General Owen Williams advised you to sign that paper, and asked you to leave the house believing you to be an innocent man? Did they so believe you?—I am totally unable to say.

And as you stand there now, are you unable to say?—I am perfectly unable to say. I have had no conversation with either of them since, except on one occasion, and they never expressed any opinion as to my innocence or guilt.

So you are quite unable to say whether, in advising you, they were advising you as an old friend whom they believed to be innocent?—I had a communication from them, the gist of which was, to the best of my recollection, that there was no possibility of believing other than my guilt from the fact of there being five to one against me. I received that letter two days after leaving Tranby Croft.

Then the suggestion made on your behalf that these gentlemen could not possibly believe you guilty was not yours?—I do not understand.

(Sir Edward Clarke here intervened, saying that he had made the statement in opening the case.)

Your first interview in which anything was communicated to you as to this serious charge was before dinner on the evening of Wednesday, the 11th?—On Wednesday.

It was on this occasion you expressed a desire to have an interview with the Prince?—It was.

That interview you had in the presence of himself, Lord Coventry, and General Owen Williams, after dinner. At what hour?—I should say about half-past ten or eleven.

Then you retired, and the last and final interview was when Lord Coventry and General Owen Williams gave you the paper which you signed? —Yes.

All that would be about half-past eleven?—Yes.

Did you think that in signing that paper you were doing a dishonouring act or not?—I felt I was doing a foolish one.

Did you think it was a dishonouring act?—At the time I had no thought, but I have thought since that it was.

Since the case of Lord de Ros, a good many years ago now, have you ever heard of a gentleman and a man of honour signing a paper in which he pledges himself not to play cards as a consideration for silence on an accusation of cheating?—No, I have not.

You read the paper?—Yes.

More than once?—No.

You discussed it?—Yes, I discussed it.

You pointed out to Lord Coventry and General Williams that it was virtually an admission of guilt?—I said it was virtually an admission, and they agreed that it would be.

There was no name appended to it at the time it was put before you?—No.

The other signatures to it were not there?—No.

Sir William Gordon-Cumming, why did you, as an innocent man, sign that paper?—Because it was put to me by these two friends of mine, on whom I placed implicit reliance, that I had no chance of clearing myself; that however often I reiterated my innocence, I had no chance of proving it against five witnesses. I was told a horrible scandal would follow, in which my name, my regiment and everything would suffer, unless I signed that paper.

You were told that the scandal would be all over the place?—Yes.

The horrible scandal would be that you, an officer in the Guards, had been accused by five witnesses of cheating at cards?—Probably the word scandal was used by General Williams—a scandal to which the name of the Prince of Wales and of other persons would be attached.

How?—It would not be desirable that the name of the Prince of Wales should be associated with a game of baccarat with an officer who had been accused of cheating by his hosts, or by the people of the house in which the Prince of Wales was staying.

I think you told me that it was an innocent game?—It was a scandal for a man in my position.

And to avoid that scandal you signed that paper?—Yes, to avoid the scandal I signed that paper, and I have never ceased to regret that I did so.

Now I ask you again, do you not know that, rightly or wrongly, these friends of yours were advising you as they thought best in your interests as a guilty man?—I was not aware on what grounds they gave their advice.

Do you think they were honestly advising you?—I think that nothing could have been worse than the advice they gave me, and nothing could have been more unwise than my following it.

I was not asking you whether the advice was good or bad. Did you not know—did you not believe that it was the advice of men who were advising you in your interest and in the belief that you were guilty?—No; I do not think they believed it at the time.

You did within twenty-four hours?—That is a different thing. I had signed the paper in twenty-four hours.

Were you not warned by General Williams that you were not to meet the Prince of Wales?—No; it was by letter—not warned, but requested.

(There followed a legal argument as to the admissibility of a letter. The cross-examination then continued.)

Before I read this letter, am I right in saying that you signed the promise on the advice of Lord Coventry and General Williams and on their advice alone?—Yes.

No one else advised you?—No.

You do not suggest that the Prince of Wales did?—I did not see the Prince after the one interview.

I now read two letters—the first from you to General Williams: *"Thursday September 11th.—Dear Owen,—I hope you will take an opportunity of telling the Prince of Wales how entirely I was guided in my action yesterday by his advice and yours and Coventry's."* Why did you speak of the advice of His Royal Highness?—Because I believed that the document was submitted to the Prince of Wales before being sent to me.

"While utterly and entirely denying the truth of the allegations brought against me, I thoroughly see now, for my own sake as well as that of others, it is essential to avoid an open row and the scandal arising therefrom. It is difficult for anyone, however innocent he may know himself to be, and however unstained his character may be, to come well out of an accusation brought by numbers against one alone, and I shrink, therefore, from doing as perhaps I ought, and court a full and thorough investigation. What a cruel blow it is to me to know that any men, even if almost strangers to me, should tell me that I have deliberately cheated them at cards, or to feel that men like His Royal Highness and Coventry, against whom never a word has been said, and who have been called upon to advise me on such a charge, possibly believe, from the fact of my signing that paper, that I am in any way unfitted to associate with you and men like you. Of course my word is passed as regards cards; but it was quite unnecessary, for I should never, under any circumstances, have touched them again. As regards the money I won on the week, I feel it impossible for me to take it. I believe it was mainly won from the Prince, but Sassoon need know nothing as to whether I received it or not. His Royal Highness will doubtless insist upon paying it, but I should wish it to be disposed of in any way in which he may think fit either to a hospital or for a charity. I intend to fulfil my engagements in Scotland and elsewhere as if this had not occurred though with a very sore heart. This I owe to myself. Again thanking you and Coventry, I am yours sincerely,
                                                    W. GORDON-CUMMING."

You wrote that letter just read and left it to be given to General Owen Williams on the morning of your departure?—I did.

This is the answer: *"Tranby Croft. September 11th, 1890: Dear Cumming, —I have shown the letter I received from you this morning to the Prince of Wales and Lord Coventry.—(Signed) O.W."* Then followed this memorandum, signed by the Prince, by Lord Coventry and by General Williams: *"We have no desire to be unnecessarily hard upon you, but you must clearly understand that in the face of the overwhelming evidence against you it is useless to attempt to deny the accusation. So long as you comply with the conditions you have signed, silence will be strictly maintained as far as we are concerned. In this we have dealt with you as old friends and in your interest, but we must plainly tell you that we consider we have acted quite as leniently as we possibly could under the painful circumstances of the case. As a matter of course, you will receive a cheque from Mr. Sassoon for the money owing you, in which proceeding we all agree, and it will then rest with you to dispose of it as you think fit."* Have you disposed of it?—The money is in my possession.

As a fact the cheque has been paid into the bank?—But the money is in my possession.

(After adjournment.)

I put to you (yesterday) Sir William Gordon-Cumming, the letter of September 11th—the day on which you left Tranby Croft—signed by the Prince of Wales, Lord Coventry and General Williams. Did you get another note from General Williams, and is this your letter acknowledging it?—It is in my handwriting.

The letter is as follows:—*"Harriet Street, Lowndes Square—Dear Owen,— Your letter received to-day. I had hoped that you, at all events, would have seen your way to give me the benefit of any doubt in the matter, but it seems this is not to be. This secret is in the hands of far too many to remain one long, and I have little before me to make life worth having. I suppose that in the meantime I must try and live as of old.— Yours always the same,*

WILLIAM GORDON-CUMMING."

Now the letter that you had already received, Sir William Gordon-Cumming, and which I read yesterday, stated two things—that it was useless for you to attempt to deny the accusation and that they had dealt with you as old friends and in your own interest, concluding, *"We must plainly tell you that we have acted as leniently as we could."* Had you any doubt after the receipt of those communications that they believed you guilty, or that they were acting, so far as they could, to shield

you?—I did believe that Lord Coventry and General Williams thought
me guilty.

And the Prince?—And the Prince.

And that they had acted as they did, wisely or unwisely, in your interest,
and to shield you as far as they could?—And in their own.

In your interest and in their own?—Yes.

What interest had General Williams of his own to shield?—Neither General Williams nor Lord Coventry, as I said yesterday, wished their
names to be connected with any scandal, such as would have ensued
in connection with this case.

But as far as General Williams was concerned, what would be the scandal
except his being, or having been, the friend of a man accused of
cheating at cards?—I do not say that General Williams was not actuated
by friendly motives towards me.

What interest had Lord Coventry to shield?—I really cannot say.

Upon the occasion of the interview with the Prince of Wales, was one
word said as to your signing the memorandum?—The memorandum
had not come up then. No question of that kind had been entered into.

Kindly answer "Yes" or "No." Is your answer "No"?—Repeat your question please.

At the interview with the Prince of Wales, at which Lord Coventry and
General Williams were present, was one word suggested as to your
signing any undertaking?—No.

The interest of the Prince of Wales, as I understood you to suggest yesterday, was in not liking to have his name mixed up with a scandal of
that kind?—Precisely.

The scandal being that a man of position, as my learned friend has
properly said, and a distinguished person, had been accused by five
witnesses of cheating?—Certainly.

Now, at all events, we have got to a time when, if you had ever thought
it, you could no longer entertain the respect of these men whose friendship you had enjoyed. You had reached that point?—I beg your pardon.

When you received these letters, you had reached the point of knowing
that you no longer retained the respect, as an honourable man, of these
men whose friendship and esteem you valued?—If I had been guilty of
the offence, yes.

Of course you knew—though it was perhaps a comparatively unimportant
matter—that you were regarded by these five persons as having been
guilty of dishonourable conduct?—Apparently, as they accused me of
being so.

Why did you not, even then, take steps to assert your innocence and to
vindicate yourself by bringing yourself face to face with your accusers?
—Because I considered that, having taken that very fatal and foolish

step of signing the document, it would be impossible to succeed, as many people would think me guilty, whether I was or not.

Does that mean that you regarded signing the document, and believed that it would be regarded by others, as an admission of your guilt?—No.

Let me remind you, Sir William Gordon-Cumming, that you have said that the document was put before you and that you then said—in your own language—that it would be regarded as a virtual admission of your guilt, and that you were told by Lord Coventry——Excuse me, Sir Charles; I think I said that it would be considered by some as an admission of guilt.

I do not think you said "considered by some." However, you said that it was tantamount to an admission of guilt, and that you were told by Lord Coventry and by General Williams that it was so?—They assented to my statement that it was so.

Then what has altered the position of things from 18th September, except the fact that somehow or other this very melancholy story has become public property?—After signing the paper and committing the act of gross folly, as I characterised it yesterday, and after a reflection of four-and-twenty hours, I saw the mistake I had made. But on the assurance by letter from General Williams that by no possibility could it come out, except to the persons immediately concerned, I lived for some time in a fool's paradise, hoping and believing that that would be the case.

Then, although in the eyes of these once-valued and esteemed friends, you were a dishonoured man, you were content to remain so if secrecy were continued?—It does not follow that because these five people believed me guilty I was guilty. I knew perfectly well that I was not.

Pray attend to my question?—I have answered your question.

I assure you you have not, Sir William Gordon-Cumming. Although you knew—rightly or wrongly—that in the eyes of these gentlemen, whose respect and esteem you valued, you were a dishonoured man you were content to remain so?—I was not content to remain so.

Attend, attend! You were content to remain so, so long as secrecy was maintained?—I had no alternative.

Then I ask you again the question to which I have not yet got an answer. What has since taken place which has altered the position as it was when those letters arrived in September, except the fact that this story has become public property?—The mere fact of its becoming public property was quite sufficient for me.

Was that the only reason?—Are you asking me my reasons for taking these proceedings?

I am asking the question which I have put to you. I will now repeat it for the third or fourth time, and I hope you will kindly attend. You have told me that when you received those letters in September, you then became aware of the fact that you were regarded—rightly or wrongly—by these esteemed friends as a dishonoured man, and you have said in effect that you were content not to take proceedings provided the secrecy was maintained—

Sir Edward Clarke: Those are not the words of the witness.

Sir Charles Russell: In effect.

Sir Edward Clarke: When my learned friend says "in effect" I know what he means.

Sir Charles Russell continued: My question is, what is the altered condition of things except the breach of the secrecy and the story becoming public property?—The thing had become such public property that I thought the matter would be at once taken up by my Clubs, by my regiment, and by my friends.

That is your answer, and that is the answer I expected you to have given long ago. Did you get a letter from General Williams on September 13th?—I cannot recollect how many letters I got from General Williams. I think I did get another letter.

And did you answer his letter on 15th September?—If I received a letter from General Williams I probably answered it. The letter produced is my letter.

I will take it from you not producing General Williams' letter that you have not got it?—I can recollect what was in it now that I have seen my answer to it. I have not got the letter, but I recollect it very well.

What did you do with it?—Burned it.

You are entitled to say what was in the letter, if you like?—It was a very friendly letter, expressing extreme regret at what had occurred, saying that he was glad he was there to suppress a horrible scandal, and saying that the matter would remain a secret, and that not another word would be said about it. That is as nearly as I can recollect.

And this is your answer, dated September 15th, Monday: "*My dear Owen,—Thanks for your letter of the 13th. You can well understand how deeply I feel the great kindness and friendship you have shown me in the matter. I have taken your advice about . . . —Yours ever very truly, William Gordon-Cumming.*—Will you kindly say what is the last word in that letter, Sir Charles?

"*Thanks for your letter of 13th. You can well understand how deeply I feel the great kindness and friendship you have shown me in the matter. I have taken your advice about Mar.*"—Precisely.

Was that advice that you were not to meet the Prince of Wales at Mar?—It was.

I think you told us yesterday that you have not met the Prince since?—I have not.

You know also that, in order that there should be as far as possible no suspicion raised, Lord Coventry and General Owen Williams have, if they have met you casually at the clubs, recognised you in the ordinary way?—Certainly.

But you have never met either of them in Society since?—In the clubs and on the race-course. Nowhere else, except once at General Williams's house.

That is this very year?—Yes.

I am coming to that. At the interview with Lord Coventry and the Prince of Wales and General Owen Williams you disclaimed the intention of taking the money which you had won on September 8th and 9th?—No; I never suggested it.

Not at the interview?—I did not.

Here is the cheque for the money you received. I think it was paid into your bankers?—Precisely.

Into your general account?—Into my general account.

Then when you said you had this £228 still, you meant that you had that balance at your banker's still?—Yes.

You paid it into the bank and then drew your cheques in the ordinary way?—Precisely.

I do not think you even acknowledged the receipt of the cheque?—Receiving it and paying it in would constitute a receipt.

True, in law; I quite agree. The end of September passes, the whole of October, the whole of November, and up to the month of December, you had done nothing?—In what way?

In any way towards your vindication, or your reinstatement in the good opinion of your friends?—I had done nothing of any sort or kind.

And did you, then, at the end of December—on December 27th—receive an anonymous telegram from Paris?—A letter.

Have you got it?—Yes.

It is in French, but I will read it, translating as I go. It is dated "Paris" and it says—"*They are beginning to talk much here of what passed at Newmarket this summer and of your sad adventure. If you come to Paris or to Monte Carlo, be very reserved and do not touch a card. They have talked too much about it*" and the signature is "*Someone who pities you*"?—Precisely.

I may just ask you, in passing, is the place from which this was written 4 Place de la Concorde?—Yes.

Is that a club that you belong to?—Yes, it is.

Upon receiving this anonymous letter, did you at once send it to General Owen Williams?—I did.

.   .   .   .   .

As recounted above, the jury found for the defendants.

It is only fair to the memory of Sir William Gordon-Cumming to add that in Sir Edward Clarke's opinion the verdict was wrong. "I believe," he wrote, "that Sir William Gordon-Cumming was innocent of the offence charged against him."

The Trial of Oscar Wilde*

H. MONTGOMERY HYDE

The second great English scandal of the nineties was the trial of Oscar Wilde on charges of homosexuality, as a result of an action brought by Wilde against the Marquis of Queensberry. The extract which follows is from the cross-examination on the afternoon of the second day when Wilde, who up to that point had toyed with the great cross-examiner Sir Edward Carson, made his one fatal slip. "Carson is the one and only counsel I have come across who really is formidable to a man with brains. He is even clever enough not to mind being made to look like a fool." † The reader will note, especially if he reads the full report of the trial, how time and again during the cross-examination Wilde scored brilliantly off his opponent, and how like a terrier Carson returned to the attack until, as the afternoon shadows were lengthening in the Old Bailey, Wilde with a contemptuous wave of his hand let down his guard. It was to mean little to Wilde then, that after his death the nature of his fall and the tragedy of his end were to be the pillars of his fame.

First Trial. Second Day—Thursday, 4th April, 1895

Evidence for the Prosecution (concluded)

O scar Wilde, *cross-examination continued*—You told me yesterday that you were intimate with Taylor?—I do not call him an intimate friend. He was a friend of mine. It was he who arranged the meeting of myself with Wood about the letters at his residence, 13 Little College Street. I have known Taylor since the early part of October, 1892. He used to come to my house, to my chambers, and to the Savoy. I have been several times to his house, some seven or eight times, perhaps.

You used to go to tea parties there—afternoon tea parties?—Yes.

How many rooms did he occupy?—He had the upper part of the house—two stories. He had a bedroom, a sitting room, a bathroom and a kitchen. I think he did not keep a servant.

---

* From *The Trials of Oscar Wilde*, edited by H. Montgomery Hyde, M.P., *Notable British Trials Series* (Hodge, London, 1948). Quoted by permission.

† Lord Alfred Douglas: The Autobiography of Lord Alfred Douglas, London: Martin Secker, 1929.

Did he use to do his own cooking?—I don't know. I don't think he did anything wrong.

I have not suggested that he did?—Well, cooking is an art.

Another art? Did he always open the door to you?—No; sometimes he did; sometimes his friends did.

Did his rooms strike you as being peculiar?—No, except that he displayed more taste than usual.

There was rather elaborate furniture in the room, was there not?—The rooms were furnished in good taste.

Is it true that he never admitted daylight into them?—Really, I don't know what you mean.

Well, was there always candle or gas light there?—No.

Did you ever see the rooms lighted otherwise than by gas or candles whether by day or night?—Yes, certainly.

Did you ever see the curtains drawn back in the sitting-room?—When I went to see Taylor, it was generally in the winter about five o'clock—tea-time—but I am under the impression of having seen him earlier in the day when it was daylight.

Are you prepared to say that you ever saw the curtains otherwise than drawn across?—Yes, I think so.

It would not be true, then, to say that he always had a double lot of curtains drawn across the windows, and the room, day or night, artificially lighted?—I don't think so.

Can you declare specifically that any daylight was ever admitted into the room?—Well, I can't say as to that.

Who was there when you went in the daylight?—I think Mr. Taylor only.

Can you recall any specific time at which you saw daylight enter that room?—Yes; it was a Monday in March. Nobody else was there. In the winter the curtains would naturally be drawn.

Were the rooms strongly perfumed?—Yes, I have known him to burn perfumes. I would not say the rooms were always perfumed. I am in the habit of burning perfumes in my own rooms.

Did you ever meet Wood there?—I saw Wood there only on one occasion when I met him at tea.

Did you ever meet a man named Sidney Mavor there?—Yes.

How old was he?—About twenty-five or twenty-six.

Is he your friend still?—Yes.

When did you see him last?—I have not seen him for about a year, when he dined with me.

Where is he now?—I have not the slightest idea where he is. Last Sunday I asked Mr. Taylor to go down to see Mr. Mavor's mother and tell him I wanted to see him. I was told that Mavor was away. I was not told where he had gone.

Were you told that Mavor had disappeared within the last week?—No.

Have you found him since?—I don't know what you mean by "found him." Mr. Mavor has not called upon me, though I wish to see him.

Did you know that Taylor had a lady's costume—a lady's fancy dress— in his rooms?—No.

Did you ever see him with one on?—No. I was never told that he had such dresses. He is a man of great taste and intelligence, and I know he was brought up at a good English school.

Is he a literary man?—I have never seen any created work of his.

Did you discuss literature with him?—He used to listen. He was a very artistic, pleasant fellow.

Was he an artist?—Not in the sense of creating anything. He was extremely intellectual and clever, and I liked him very much.

Are you in the habit of constantly communicating with him by telegraph? —No. I have telegraphed to him. He was a friend of mine.

Did you get him to arrange dinners at which you could meet young men? —No.

But you have dined with young men?—Often. Ten or a dozen times, perhaps, at Kettner's, the Solferino, and the Florence.

Always in a private room?—Generally, not always; but I prefer a private room.

Did you send him this telegram—"Alfred Taylor, 13 Little College Street, S.W. Could you call at six o'clock, Savoy?—Oscar"?—Yes.

What did you want him for?—I wanted him because I had received an anonymous letter saying that Alfred Wood was going to blackmail me in respect of certain letters stolen from Lord Alfred Douglas.

Again, you wired from Goring: "Cannot manage the dinner to-morrow. Am so sorry. Oscar"?—Yes.

Did you send this telegram to Taylor: "Obliged to see Tree at five o'clock, so don't come to Savoy. Let me know at once about Fred. Oscar"?—I do not recollect it.

Who was Fred?—A young man to whom I was introduced by the gentleman whose name was written down yesterday. His other name was Atkins.

What was it you wanted to know?—I cannot remember.

Were you very familiar with him?—I liked him. I never had any trouble about him.

Did Atkins call you "Oscar"?—Yes. I called him "Fred," because I always call by their Christian names people whom I like. People I dislike I call something else.

Now, did you know that Taylor was being watched by the police?—No, I never heard that.

Did you know that Taylor and Parker were arrested in a raid upon a house in Fitzroy Square last year?—Yes.

Did you know Parker?—Yes. I don't think I ever saw him at Mr. Taylor's rooms in Little College Street, but I have seen him at Chapel Street, to which he removed.

Now, did you not know that Taylor was notorious for introducing young men to older men?—I never heard that in my life. He has introduced young men to me.

How many has he introduced to you?—Do you mean of those mentioned in this case?

No; young men with whom you afterwards became intimate?—About five.

They were young men whom you would call by their Christian names?—Yes.

Were these young men all about twenty?—Yes; twenty or twenty-two. I like the society of young men.

What was their occupation?—I do not know if these particular young men had occupations.

Have you given money to them?—Yes. I think to all five—money or presents.

Did they give you anything?—Me? Me? No!

Among these five did Taylor introduce you to Charles Parker?—Yes.

Did you become friendly with him?—Yes, he was one with whom I became friendly.

Did you know that Parker was a gentleman's servant out of employment?—No.

But if he were, you would still have become friendly with him?—Yes. I would become friendly with any human being I liked.

How old was he?—Really, I do not keep a census.

Never mind about a census. Tell me how old he was?—I should say he was about twenty. He was young, and that was one of his attractions.

Was he a literary character?—Oh, no.

Was he intellectual? Was he an educated man?—Culture was not his strong point. He was not an artist. Education depends on what one's standard is.

Where is he now?—I haven't the slightest idea. I have lost sight of him.

How much money did you give Parker?—During the time I have known him I should think £4 or £5.

Why? For what reason?—Because he was poor, and I liked him. What better reason could I have?

Did you ask what his previous occupation was?—I never inquire about people's pasts.

Nor their future?—Oh, that is problematical.

Sir EDWARD CLARKE—There is no use in arguing about that.

Cross-examination continued—Where did you first meet him?—At Kettner's. I was introduced by Mr. Taylor.

Did you become friendly with Parker's brother?—Yes. They were my guests, and as such I became friendly with them.

On the very first occasion that you saw them?—Yes. It was Taylor's birthday, and I asked him to dinner, telling him to bring any of his friends.

Did you know that one Parker was a gentleman's valet, and the other a groom?—I did not know it, but if I had I should not have cared. I didn't care twopence what they were. I liked them. I have a passion to civilize the community.

What enjoyment was it to you to entertain grooms and coachmen?—The pleasure to me was being with those who are young, bright, happy, careless, and free. I do not like the sensible and I do not like the old.

Taylor accepted your invitation by bringing a valet and a groom to dine with you?—That is your account, not mine.

Were they persons of that class?—I am surprised at your description of them. They did not seem to have the manners of that class. They seemed to me pleasant and nice. They spoke of a father at Datchet as a person of wealth—well, not of wealth but of some fortune. Charlie Parker told me that he was desirous to go on the stage.

Did you call him "Charlie"?—Yes.

What did you have for dinner?—Well, really I forget the menu.

Was it a good dinner?—Kettner's is not so gorgeous as some restaurants, but it was Kettner at his best.

With the best of Kettner's wines?—Yes, certainly.

All for the valet and the groom?—No; for my friends; for Mr. Taylor, whose birthday it was.

You did the honours to the valet and the groom?—I entertained Taylor and his two guests.

In a private room, of course?—Yes, certainly.

Did you give them an intellectual treat?—They seemed deeply impressed.

During the dinner did you become more intimate with Charles than the other?—I liked him better.

Did Charles Parker call you "Oscar"?—Yes. I like to be called "Oscar" or "Mr. Wilde."

You had wine?—Of course.

Was there plenty of champagne?—Well, I did not press wine upon them.

You did not stint them?—What gentleman would stint his guests?

What gentleman would stint the valet and the groom? [Witness and his counsel protested against this remark.]

Now, after dinner, did you say, referring to Charles Parker, in the presence of Taylor and William Parker, the brother, "This is the boy for me"?—Certainly not.

And did you ask Charles, "Will you come with me"?—No. After dinner I went back to the Savoy Hotel, but I did not take Charles Parker with me.

Did you not drive him to the Savoy?—No, he did not come to the Savoy at all.

Did any of these men who visited you at the Savoy have whiskies and sodas and iced champagne?—I can't say what they had.

Do you drink champagne yourself?—Yes; iced champagne is a favourite drink of mine—strongly against my doctor's orders.

Never mind your doctor's orders, sir?—I never do. About a week later Charles Parker and Taylor dined with me at Kettner's again. The second dinner at Kettner's was arranged by myself. I first gave Parker money in December, 1893. I did not ask Taylor what these young men friends of his were. Sufficient for me that they were friends of his. Charlie Parker wished to go on the stage. What his brother's ambition was I never knew. Taylor did not tell me that he had met them in the St. James's Rooms. I had rooms at St. James's Place. Taylor wrote to me saying Charlie Parker was in town, and I replied asking him to come to tea. We had tea on the terrace. Parker came to tea five or six times there.

What was he doing there?—Visiting me. I liked his society. Sometimes he came with Taylor, sometimes alone. I gave him a Christmas present—a silver cigarette case, not a gold chain ring. I also gave him £3 or £4, as he was hard up, and asked me if I could let him have the money. I don't think he was ever in my bedroom, unless I was putting on my coat to go out or something of that sort.

Did improprieties take place there?—None whatever.

When he came to tea what was he doing all the time?—What was he doing? Why, having his tea, smoking cigarettes, and, I hope, enjoying himself.

What was there in common between this young man and yourself? What attraction had he for you?—I delight in the society of people much younger than myself. I like those who may be called idle and careless. I recognize no social distinctions at all of any kind; and to me youth, the mere fact of youth, is so wonderful that I would sooner talk to a young man for half-an-hour than be—well, cross-examined in Court.

Do I understand that even a young boy you might pick up in the street would be a pleasing companion?—I would talk to a street arab, with pleasure.

You would talk to a street arab?—If he would talk to me. Yes, with pleasure.

And take him into your rooms?—Be it so. I remember that Charles Parker lived at 7 Camera Square in Chelsea. I did not get him clothes. He has lunched with me at the Café Royal and at St. James's Place. I never went to see him at Camera Square. It is a very different thing his coming to tea with me and my going to see him. It would not have been interesting for him to see me, while it was interesting for me to see him. I remember that

Charles Parker was present at a dinner which I gave at the Solferino Restaurant. There was no one else present, and we dined in the public room.

Did you write him any beautiful letters?—I don't think I have ever written any letters to him.

Have you any letters of his?—Only one.

[Counsel read the following letter from Parker]: "Am I to have the pleasure of dining with you this evening? If so, kindly reply by messenger or wire to the above address. I trust you can, and we can spend a pleasant evening." The letter is signed "Yours faithfully."

Sir EDWARD CLARKE—I should like to see the handwriting.

Mr. CARSON—We will see all about that. Parker himself will be here, which is better.

Cross-examination continued—In March or April of last year did you go one night to visit Parker at 50 Park Walk, about half-past twelve at night? —No.

Is Park Walk about ten minutes' walk from Tite Street?—I don't know. I never walk.

I suppose when you pay visits you always take a cab?—Always.

And if you visited, you would leave the cab outside?—If it were a good cab.

When did you see Charles Parker last?—I don't think I have seen him since February of last year.

Did you ever hear what became of him?—I heard that he had gone into the army—enlisted as a private.

You saw in the papers of the arrest of Taylor and Parker?—Yes; I read that they were arrested.

You know that they were charged with felonious practices?—I knew nothing of the charges.

That when they were arrested they were in company with several men in women's clothing?—I read of it in the newspapers that two men, in women's clothes, music-hall artistes, drove up to the house and were arrested outside.

Did you not think it a somewhat serious thing that Mr. Taylor, your great friend, and Charles Parker, another great friend, should have been arrested in a police raid?—I was very much distressed at the time, and wrote to him, but the magistrates took a different view of the case, because they dismissed the charge. It made no difference to my friendship for him.

Was this same Taylor lunching with you on Tuesday last?—Not lunching. He came to my house to see me.

When did you first meet Fred Atkins?—In October, 1892. He told me he was connected with a firm of bookmakers. He was about nineteen or twenty. I was introduced to him in the rooms of a gentleman in Margaret Street, off Regent Street. I did not know him through making bets. I did not ask him to dinner on the first day I met him. I met him at a dinner given by another gentleman whose rooms I met him in first. I was friendly with Atkins on that occasion. I called him "Fred" and he called me "Oscar." He was in employment, but apologized and said he neglected his business.

Did he seem to you an idle fellow?—Well, yes. But he was ambitious to go on the music-hall stage. We did not discuss literature. I would not have allowed him to. The art of the music-hall was as far as he got.

Did you ask him to go to Paris with you?—I must explain. One Sunday I saw him and the gentleman, who has been mentioned, lunching at the Café Royal. I was going to Paris on my own account in reference to the publication of a book. This other gentleman was also going to Paris about a position on Dalziel's Agency. It was suggested that we should all go together, as he had promised to take Atkins. It was arranged that we should go on a Monday, but subsequently the gentleman found that he could not go until Tuesday or Wednesday. Then, as Atkins seemed very much disappointed, the gentleman asked me if I would take Fred over. I said, "With the greatest pleasure," and I took him.

How long had you known Atkins then?—About a fortnight. We went by the Club train. I paid for his ticket, but the money was refunded to me afterwards by the gentleman. I did not suggest to Atkins that he should go as my secretary—ridiculous, it's childish to ask such a thing. I took him to the same rooms I occupied in the hotel—29 Boulevard des Capucines. I engaged three bedrooms, having one in reserve. They all three opened on to each other. I never asked Fred to copy some manuscript for me. I took him to lunch at the Café Julien. He was practically my guest, as representing the gentleman I have mentioned.

After lunch did you suggest that Atkins should have his hair curled?—He suggested it himself, and I said it would be very unbecoming, and I told him it was a silly thing to do, an absurd thing. I should have been very angry if he had had his hair curled.

Well, did he get his hair curled at Pascal's, the hairdresser, under the Grand Hotel?—I think not.

You dined with him?—Yes.

Gave him an excellent dinner?—I never had anything else. I do everything excellently.

Did you give him plenty of wine at dinner?—As I have said before, any one who dines at my table is not stinted in wine. If you mean, did I ply him with wine, I say "No!" It's monstrous, and I won't have it.

I have not suggested it.—But you have suggested it before.

After dinner did you give him a sovereign to go to the Moulin Rouge?—Yes. I went that night, I think, to a French theatre, and when I got back to the hotel Atkins had gone to bed.

[The witness here denied any impropriety with Atkins in Paris, and added that it would be an infamous lie for anyone to say so.]

Did the gentleman referred to arrive next day?—He came on the Wednesday, and we all three returned together. I gave Fred a cigarette case. I found him a pleasant, good-humoured companion, but I did not see much of him after I got to Paris, as I had business to look after. Shortly after getting back to London I was ill in bed, and I wrote to the gentleman to ask Atkins to call upon me at Tite Street. I don't think he came by himself.

Did you ask him to promise that he would say nothing about going to Paris?—No. I thought it was the great event of his life, as it was. I knew before going to Paris that Atkins was living in Pimlico. I have written several letters to Atkins this year, one enclosing him tickets for my play at the theatre. I went to Atkins's rooms to tea in February, 1894. On that occasion there was one other gentleman there—an actor. It was at Osnaburgh Street.

How old was he?—About twenty.

Did you give Atkins any money?—Yes; £3 15s. to buy his first song for the music-hall stage. He told me that the poets who wrote for the music-hall never took less. I had the pleasure of meeting one of the poets.

Did you consider Atkins respectable?—Respectable? Yes. I thought him pleasant and young. He was good-natured, and was going on to the music-hall stage. I heard him sing. He was interesting.

Was he alone when he came to you at St. James's Place?—No; I think he was accompanied by the young actor. I will swear that Atkins was not alone in the room with me.

Did any improprieties ever take place between you and Atkins?—None whatever.

You knew a man named Ernest Scarfe?—Yes. He was introduced to me by Taylor. He is a young man of about twenty, of no occupation. He had been in Australia at the gold-diggings.

Did you know he was a valet and is a valet still?—No. I have never met him in Society, though he has been in my society, which is more important.

How did Taylor introduce this man Scarfe?—Well, Taylor told me he knew a young man who, on board ship going out to Australia, had met Lord Douglas of Hawick. He had introduced him to Lord Alfred Douglas at a skating rink. I asked Scarfe to dine with myself and Taylor at Kettner's. I did not afterwards take him back to my rooms at St. James's. I have never embraced, kissed or caressed him.

Why did you ask him to dinner?—Because I am so good-natured. It is a good action to ask to dinner those beneath one in social station.

Did you ever give Scarfe any money?—Never.

Did you give him any presents?—Yes, a cigarette case. It cost £4. It is my custom to present cigarette cases. I last saw Scarfe in February when he dined with me at the Avondale Hotel.

When did you first know Sidney Mavor?—In September, 1892. He was introduced to me by the same gentleman who introduced Atkins.

Do you know where that gentleman is now?—No. I have not heard of him for eighteen months or two years. I never gave Mavor any money, nor did I give money to Taylor to hand to Mavor. I don't think I even gave him a cigarette case, but it may be true that on 3rd October I ordered Thornhill's in Bond Street to send him one of the value of £4 11s. 6d.

Did you tell them to send it?—Well, if it is there, perhaps I did.

But you had known him only a month?—Quite long enough to get to feel an interest in him.

Why did you give him a cigarette case when you had known him only a month?—I give what presents I like to anybody I like. Mavor stayed with me one night at an hotel in Albemarle Street in October, 1892. I asked him to stay with me for companionship, pleasure, amusement. I like to have people staying with me. I took two bedrooms, one for Mavor and one for myself. He never stayed with me another night. On the occasion referred to I was passing through London and I wanted his society, as he was a smart, pleasant young fellow.

And did you find pleasure in his society that night?—Yes, in the evening and at breakfast. It amused and pleased him that I should ask him to be my guest at a very nice, charming hotel.

WITNESS (on being shown a photograph of Mavor)—Ah, taken at a period earlier than that at which I knew him. (Counsel held up a cigarette case.) No, really, I could not. I have given so many I could not recognize it.

Cross-examination continued—Do you know Walter Grainger?—Yes.

How old is he?—He was about sixteen when I knew him. He was a servant at a certain house in High Street, Oxford, where Lord Alfred Douglas had rooms. I have stayed there several times. Grainger waited at table. I never dined with him. If it is one's duty to serve, it is one's duty to serve; and if it is one's pleasure to dine, it is one's pleasure to dine.

Did you ever kiss him?—Oh, dear no. He was a peculiarly plain boy. He was, unfortunately, extremely ugly. I pitied him for it.

Was that the reason why you did not kiss him?—Oh, Mr. Carson, you are pertinently insolent.

Did you say that in support of your statement that you never kissed him? —No. It is a childish question.

Did you ever put that forward as a reason why you never kissed the boy?—Not at all.

Why, sir, did you mention that this boy was extremely ugly?—For this reason. If I were asked why I did not kiss a door-mat, I should say because

I do not like to kiss door-mats. I do not know why I mentioned that he was ugly, except that I was stung by the insolent question you put to me and the way you have insulted me throughout this hearing. Am I to be cross-examined because I do not like it?

Why did you mention his ugliness?—It is ridiculous to imagine that any such thing could have occurred under any circumstances.

Then why did you mention his ugliness, I ask you?—Perhaps you insulted me by an insulting question.

Was that a reason why you should say the boy was ugly?—

[Here the witness began several answers almost inarticulately, and none of them he finished. His efforts to collect his ideas were not aided by Mr. Carson's sharp staccato repetition: "Why? Why? Why did you add that?" At last the witness answered]: You sting me and insult me and try to un-nerve me; and at times one says things flippantly when one ought to speak more seriously. I admit it.

Then you said it flippantly?—Oh, yes, it was a flippant answer.

Cross-examination continued—No indecencies ever took place between myself and Grainger. I went down in June, 1893, to stay at a cottage at Goring. I brought over Grainger as under-butler. He had asked me to get him a situation. I never on any occasion asked him to come into my bed-room. I don't know where the butler I had then is now.

Did you know a masseur at the Savoy named Antonio Migge?—Yes. He used occasionally to massage me in the morning. I stayed at the Savoy in March, 1893, but never on that occasion brought boys into my bedroom there.

Did you ever bring boys into your rooms at the hotel in Paris?—Never.

Or into your sitting-room?—What do you mean by boys?

Boys of eighteen or twenty?—Oh, yes; many called to see me.

Did any of them come late at night—twelve or one o'clock—and stay till four in the morning?—Certainly not.

Is it not true that there has been a scandal at the Savoy Hotel?—None whatever.

[An incident that was said to have occurred at the Savoy Hotel was put to the witness and absolutely denied. "It never occurred," he declared, "never, never." Other questions were put to him containing criminal sug-gestions, only to be denied strenuously and absolutely with gestures of dis-dain and disgust.]

The day but one after your return to London did you give Atkins a silver cigarette case?—I gave him one in Paris.

You say he called on you at Tite Street shortly afterwards?—Yes, he came with a gentleman I know. I thought it was very kind of Atkins to come. It is not everybody in the world who is grateful.

You paid for his lunch in Paris?—Certainly, I paid for his lunch.

He had not the means to pay himself?—Certainly not—not for the kind of lunch I like.

When you lunched with Wood at the Florence, before his departure for America, did you have champagne?—Not champagne; I never drink in the middle of the day.

Where did you first meet Charles Parker?—At Kettner's.

Who introduced you?—Mr. Taylor.

Where is Parker now?—I don't know.

You never asked him his age?—I think it vulgar to ask people their age. He may have been sixteen or forty-five. Don't ask me. What is the use of cross-examining me on what I don't know.

Was the money that you gave him given to him all at once?—Yes, all at once.

And you gave him a silver cigarette case?—Yes.

What did he do when he came to tea with you?—You ask me what a youth would do?

What was Parker doing there?—Nothing.

Did you ever have a servant called "Ginger"?—Oh, no.

Did you ever know a man named Preston who was mixed up in the Cleveland Street scandal?—I never heard of him.

You gave Alphonse Conway a walking-stick, didn't you?—Yes.

It was a handsome stick for a boy of that class?—I did not think myself that it was a beautiful stick.

You still deny that you made Atkins have his hair curled in Paris?—I told him that it would be silly; and I still think I was right in my opinion.

How did Taylor come to bring Scarfe to you?—Shall I tell you? He brought him to my rooms at St. James's Place—

The honour was quite unexpected?—It was no shock, but I did not expect him. It was early in the afternoon. I made an appointment for them to dine with me on another day. I forget whether it was in a public or a private room.

What was Scarfe?—He was then employed as a clerk in St. Paul's Churchyard.

Only one question more. Would you know the waiter at the hotel in the Boulevard des Capucines in Paris?—Yes. I think I would.

Re-examined by Sir EDWARD CLARKE (Counsel handed witness several letters written by the defendant)—Was it from these letters that you first learned that Lord Queensberry objected to your acquaintance with his son, Lord Alfred Douglas?—Yes.

Carter's Hotel,
Albemarle Street, W.1.,
Sunday, 1st April, 1894.

Alfred,—It is extremely painful for me to have to write to you in the strain I must; but please understand that I decline to receive any answers from you in writing in return. After your recent hysterical impertinent ones I refuse to be annoyed with such, and I decline to read any more letters. If you have anything to say, do come here and say it in person. Firstly, am I to understand that, having left Oxford as you did, with discredit to yourself, the reasons of which were fully explained to me by your tutor, you now intend to loaf and loll about and do nothing? All the time you were wasting at Oxford I was put off with an assurance that you were eventually to go into the Civil Service or to the Foreign Office, and then I was put off with an assurance that you were going to the Bar. It appears to me that you intend to do nothing. I utterly decline, however, to just supply you with sufficient funds to enable you to loaf about. You are preparing a wretched future for yourself, and it would be most cruel and wrong for me to encourage you in this. Secondly, I come to the more painful part of this letter—your intimacy with this man Wilde. It must either cease or I will disown you and stop all money supplies. I am not going to try and analyse this intimacy, and I make no charge; but to my mind to pose as a thing is as bad as to be it. With my own eyes I saw you both in the most loathsome and disgusting relationship as expressed by your manner and expression. Never in my experience have I seen such a sight as that in your horrible features. No wonder people are talking as they are. Also I now hear on good authority, but this may be false, that his wife is petitioning to divorce him for sodomy and other crimes. Is this true, or do you not know of it? If I thought the actual thing was true, and it became public property, I should be quite justified in shooting him at sight. These Christian English cowards and men, as they call themselves, want waking up. Your disgusted so-called father,

QUEENSBERRY.

Re-examination continued—Is there any foundation for the statement that your wife was petitioning for a divorce?—Not the slightest.

[Sir EDWARD CLARKE began to read the second letter to Lord Alfred Douglas.]

3rd April, 1894.

You impertinent young jackanapes. I request that you will not send such messages to me by telegraph.

Mr. CARSON (interrupting)—Read the telegram from Lord Alfred Douglas to his father.

[Sir EDWARD CLARKE read the telegram, which was handed in.]

2nd April, 1894.
To Queensberry, Carter's Hotel, Albemarle Street.
What a funny little man you are.   ALFRED DOUGLAS.

[Sir EDWARD CLARKE continued his reading of the second letter.]

If you send me any more such telegrams, or come with any impertinence, I will give you the thrashing you deserve. Your only excuse is that you must be crazy. I hear from a man at Oxford that you were thought crazy there, and that accounts for a good deal that has happened. If I catch you again with that man I will make a public scandal in a way you little dream of; it is already a suppressed one. I prefer an open one, and at any rate I shall not be blamed for allowing such a state of things to go on. Unless this acquaintance ceases I shall carry out my threat and stop all supplies, and if you are not going to make any attempt to do something I shall certainly cut you down to a mere pittance, so you know what to expect.

[Sir EDWARD CLARKE then read the following letters. The first was addressed to Mr. Alfred Montgomery, father of Lord Queensberry's first wife, from whom he had been divorced. The second letter was to Lord Alfred Douglas.]

Skindles Hotel,
Maidenhead, 6th July, 1894.

Sir,

I have changed my mind, and as I am not at all well, having been very much upset by what has happened the last ten days, I do not see why I should come dancing attendance upon you. Your daughter is the person who is supporting my son to defy me. She won't write, but she is now telegraphing on the subject to me. Last night, after hearing from you, I received a very quibbling, prevaricating message from her, saying the boy denied having been at the Savoy for the last year; but why send the telegram unless he could deny that he had been there with Oscar Wilde at all? As a matter of fact he did, and there has been a stinking scandal. I am told they were warned off, but the proprietor would not admit this. This hideous scandal has been going on for years. Your daughter must be mad by the way she is behaving. She evidently wants to make out that I want to make out a case against my son. It is nothing of the kind. I have made out a case against Oscar Wilde and I have to his face accused him of it. If I was quite certain of the thing I would shoot the fellow on sight, but I can only accuse him of posing. It now lies in the hands of the two whether they will further defy me. Your daughter appears now to be encouraging them, although she can hardly intend this. I don't believe Wilde will now dare defy me. He plainly showed the white feather the other day when I tackled him—damned cur and coward of the Rosebery type. As for the so-called son of mine, he is no son of mine, and I will have nothing to do with him. He may starve as far as I am concerned after his behaviour to me. His mother may support him, but she shan't do that here in London with this awful scandal going on. But your daughter's conduct is outrageous, and I am now fully convinced that the Rosebery-Gladstone-Royal insult that came to me through my other son, that she worked that—I thought it was you. I saw Drumlanrig here on the river, which much upset me. It shall be known some day by all that Rosebery not only insulted me by lying to the Queen, which makes her as bad as him and Gladstone, but also has made a lifelong quarrel between my son and I.

Scotland, 21st August, 1894.

I have received your post-card, which I presume is from you, but as the writing is utterly unreadable to me, have been unable to make out hardly one sentence. My object of receiving no written communication from you is therefore kept intact. All future cards will go into the fire unread. I presume these are the "hyerogliphics" (sic) of the O.W. posing-club, of which you have the reputation of being such a shining light. I congratulate you on your autography; it is beautiful, and should help you to get a living. I don't know what at, but, say crossing-sweeping. My friend I am staying with has made out some of your letter, and wished to read it to me, but I declined to hear a word. However, according to his advice I shall keep it as a specimen, and also as a protection in case I ever feel tempted to give you the thrashing you really deserve. You reptile. You are no son of mine and I never thought you were.

QUEENSBERRY.

The Seddon Case*

EDWARD MARJORIBANKS

Following Sir Edward Carson, though certainly not his equal, the most famous English criminal lawyer of his day was Sir Edward Marshall Hall. In the words of Edward Marjoribanks, his biographer, "He was the last of his kind: his mantle has fallen on no successor." Marshall Hall's examination of Sir William Willcox in defence of the poisoner Seddon is a masterpiece of ingenious scientific reasoning and that it failed detracts nothing from the attempt. The extract which follows will be of additional interest to the lawyer for the cross-examination by another great trial lawyer Sir Rufus Isaacs, then Attorney General. The quiet opening question and the prisoner's reply sent Seddon to the gallows.

Edward Marjoribanks was marked for a brilliant career. Born in 1900, educated at Eton and Oxford, where he was President of the Union, he was admitted to the bar in 1924 and became a Member of Parliament in 1929. The author of For the Defence *and the first volume of a life of Sir Edward Carson, he died by his own hand in 1932.*

Very different from the amiable little Dr. Crippen was the insurance agent, Frederick Henry Seddon. None of the circumstances which explained and extenuated Crippen's conduct appeared in the latter's case, nor was there any such gentleness or unselfishness in his character to excite pity or sympathy.

One day, a very young solicitor in north London, aged twenty-two, whose name had only just appeared on the roll, had a piece of luck; a new client called on Mr. T. W. Saint of Islington. The new client was a superintendent of the London and Manchester Industrial Assurance Company, and lived in the same street. He had in his hand a summons to attend and give evidence at an inquest. It was all very awkward; an "old girl" who had been his lodger had suddenly died in his house a month or two ago; her body had been exhumed, and it appeared that poison had been found in her remains. Would Mr. Saint represent him at the inquest? Mr. Saint, very young himself, had recently briefed a very young counsel, Mr. Gervais Rentoul, in a country case. Although the fee was only one guinea, Rentoul had taken a great deal of trouble, and Saint rewarded him with the brief for the Seddons at the inquest. During the progress of the inquest, Seddon and his wife were arrested, and Rentoul represented them both throughout the police court proceedings. They were committed to trial for murder, and the case became, not only the great sensation of the time, but deeply interesting as a scientific enquiry. Obviously a leader had to be briefed. "Whom shall we have?" asked Walter Saint. "You can have any leader you like."

"Oh, if that's the case," said his young counsel reverently, "I think we ought to have Marshall Hall."

For Marshall had now reached a unique position at the Bar: as a defender of prisoners on the capital charge, it was now recognised that he was second to none, and his name had acquired a high prestige. In this case, at any rate, no better choice could have been made. For he had a knowledge of scientific medicine unequalled by any other member of the Bar; it was a store of knowledge upon which he had had, as yet, no occasion to draw in a capital case.

So Marshall Hall was briefed in his first great poison defence through the choice of a very "white-wigged" admirer, who, in turn, had won this golden opportunity by doing a young solicitor a favour. It was decided better to leave Marshall Hall, in effect, to lead for the defence for both prisoners, though Mrs. Seddon was nominally defended separately by Rentoul. Marshall Hall had as juniors Mr. R. Dunstan and Mr. Wellesley Orr. On its scientific side, Marshall was enthralled, but after reading the papers he became very unhappy and depressed about the personal aspect of the case. "This is the blackest case I've ever been in," he observed at the first consultation.

This pessimism and lack of faith in his client at the very outset was almost unique in the history of the great defender. He would have to conduct this case without that passionate personal belief in his man's innocence which had carried him through so many of his trials. But this did not affect his devotion to the great task before him. He returned all other work, and could think of nothing but the Seddon case. In the many anxious consultations, he repeated again and again, "Remember, two people's lives depend upon us." He said to Saint, "If ever you want to see me, come—night or day, I shall be at home to see you." He went into training like an athlete for a race and a student for a fellowship examination, going to bed early and saturating his mind with works on the scientific questions involved in the case.

If Seddon was guilty, the case was certainly an exceedingly black one. For there was no great overmastering passion, no sudden, mad impulse, no long, harrowing tragedy, no bitter provocation to excuse this sordid crime, if crime there had been. Mere greed of gold had driven the man to it. The accused was now forty years old, and had for twenty years served his insurance company with efficiency and credit, rising from the very lowest rung to his present post of trust and responsibility. He was a hard taskmaster, disliked by his subordinates, but his credit stood high with his employers. He had married a North-Country woman, who had borne him five children; he had been an eloquent lay preacher; and was quite a light in the Masonic world. Owing to great thrift, he had a little money put away: his income amounted to about £400 a year. Some of his savings had been invested in a house at 63 Tollington Park, in which, not being able to find a tenant, he decided to reside himself, using the basement as his office and the top floor as a separate flat for lodgers. So far, nothing was known against Mr. Seddon, except, perhaps, an excessive devotion to money-making, and much to his credit. In his little world he was no doubt regarded as a pillar of society and a coming man.

In response to his advertisement during July 1910, a middle-aged spinster of forty-eight years, named Eliza Barrow, came to lodge on his top floor; she brought with her a little boy named Ernest Grant, whom she had practically adopted, and a married couple, a Mr. and Mrs. Hook, who were related to him. Miss Barrow was devoted to the little boy, and the Hooks were to be allowed to live rent-free in her rooms. Very soon a quarrel occurred between Miss Barrow and the Hooks, and Seddon gave them notice on Miss Barrow's behalf.

Miss Barrow was now left alone at the Seddons' with the little boy. She became very depressed and worried: at the best of times she was an extraordinary woman of quarrelsome and offensive habits. She had stayed, immediately before her arrival at the Seddons', with some cousins of her own called Vonderahe, and, when residing there, she had been known to spit in her hostess's face. Her chief characteristics were slovenliness, parsimony, and love of gold. She was a real miser: she loved to keep bank-notes and golden coins in her possession, and hoarded hundreds of pounds in this way. Her chief interest in life was her little inherited fortune of about £3,000 capital value; but what little natural affection was left in her she gave to little Ernest Grant. Her money was invested in India Stock, and in the lease of a public house. The India Stock had lately depreciated considerably, and the Liberal policy of licensing and taxation threatened her public house. Seddon discovered that these worries were preying upon the old maid's mind, and she soon found him a very plausible and efficient man of business, as indeed he was. Seddon, as an insurance monger, considered that Miss Barrow's life was not a good one to insure; but, conversely, an excellent one on which to grant an annuity; and, after she had lived with him for twelve months, he persuaded her to make over her entire fortune to him in return for an annuity of £150 a year or thereabouts. Miss Barrow, as her relatives said, was a "hard nut to crack," and no doubt considered that she had made a good bargain, as she thus obtained about

£30 more a year from Seddon than she could have wrung from an insurance company or the Post Office. Seddon paid her the annuity punctually until September 1911, usually in gold, but the poor lady had further financial worries. The Birkbeck Bank trouble caused her acute anxiety; perhaps she talked the matter over with Seddon. At any rate, in company with Mrs. Seddon, she went to the London and Finsbury Savings Bank, and drew out £216 of her savings in gold, and took it home. After her death, Seddon said that he had raised objections to her storing so much gold in his house, and that Miss Barrow had replied, "I know what to do with it."

On September 1st, Miss Barrow was taken ill, and Dr. Sworn, the Seddons' family physician, found her to be suffering from acute diarrhœa and sickness. As the next few days went by, Miss Barrow became worse, and admittedly certain chemical fly-papers, soaked in water, were used in her sickroom to destroy the flies that buzzed in extraordinary numbers round the bed of the invalid, attracted by the pungent odour of the sickroom. Her selfishness and eccentricity were shown by the fact that she insisted on the little boy, Ernest, sleeping in the same bed with her during her illness. She was a troublesome patient, and refused to take her medicine. A new one was prescribed, which Seddon on one occasion induced her to take. Mrs. Seddon nursed her attentively, and Miss Barrow told the doctor that she would far rather be looked after by the Seddons than go to hospital; but, though she "dictated" a will to Seddon, which she signed, leaving her personal effects (all she now had to leave) to Ernest Grant and his little sister, with Seddon as executor, the Seddons did not take her illness very seriously; for, on September 13th, Seddon's sister and his niece came to stay in the house, and he himself went to the Marlborough Theatre. He came back late with a story that he had been cheated of sixpence by the box-office clerk. This was very typical of the man. At about 11.30, the little boy said that "Chickie," by which name he knew Miss Barrow, wanted Mrs. Seddon. The wretched woman had crawled out of bed, and was sitting on the floor in agony. "I am dying," she said. During the night the little boy was sent to a separate room, and Mrs. Seddon sat by the lodger's bed, while Seddon sat on the landing outside, reading a paper, smoking a pipe, and occasionally fetching himself a drink from downstairs. At 6.30, Miss Barrow began to breathe heavily and died. Seddon, as executor, immediately began to search for her money; but, according to his own account, he found only £4 10s. 0d. in her cash-box, and £5 10s. 0d. hidden in a drawer. In the morning, Seddon advised Dr. Sworn of her death, and, without a visit, the latter gave him a certificate that Miss Barrow had died of epidemic diarrhœa. Seddon paid a visit to the undertakers, and, although in Miss Barrow's papers was a document showing that she had a right to be buried in a family vault at Kensal Green, he arranged for her to be buried for an inclusive fee of £4 in a common grave. Indeed, he accepted a commission of 12s. 6d. from the undertaker for introducing the business. Meanwhile, Ernest had been packed off to Southend, and no relatives of Miss Barrow received any notifications from Seddon, although the Vonderahes, her first cousins, lived, to Seddon's knowledge, in the near neighbourhood. Seddon afterwards claimed to have written to them, and certainly kept a "carbon" copy of such a letter. The corpse was removed from the house that day; Mrs. Seddon ordered a wreath of her own design, and kissed the poor dead woman's face. Seddon took round to a jeweller's a watch which Miss Barrow had "presented" to Mrs. Seddon, to have the name of her mother removed from it. Moreover, he attended to his business on the day of Miss Barrow's death, and was seen by two of his subordinate canvassers to be counting out quantities of gold. He took a bag of gold, and said to one of them, as a joke, "Smith, here's your wages." However, the strain of Miss Barrow's death and of overwork had told on him, and, at the end of September, Seddon and his family joined Ernest Grant at Southend for a fortnight's holiday.

Meanwhile, the Vonderahes had begun to talk, and, when they discovered in a personal interview that all their cousin's money had been made over to Seddon in return for an annuity, they drew the most unfavourable conclusions. The body was exhumed, and Sir William Willcox found, on a careful scientific analysis, that the corpse contained two and a half grains of arsenic. An inquest was held, and Seddon was required to give evidence. It was then that he consulted Mr. Saint, and told him that the "old girl" must have drunk some of the water in which the fly-papers had been soaked. "Oh," said Mr. Saint, "you can't buy poisonous things like that, can you, at an ordinary chemist's?" (In fact, each fly-paper contained enough arsenic at least to kill one person.) "Can't you?" said Seddon. "You can get them at any chemist's"; and Mrs. Seddon sent her little daughter, Maggie, round to the shop of a Mr. Price to prove it. When she gave her name, the chemist refused to supply her. Meanwhile, she had been closely watched by the police, who knew that another chemist in the neighbourhood, Mr. Walter Thorley, had supplied a packet of these papers to a fair-haired girl on August 26th. Thorley was taken to the police station and identified Margaret Seddon as the girl who had made the August purchase. Seddon had been arrested on December 4th, and on his arrest he had made a very curious statement which did not at all help him. "Absurd," he said. "What a terrible charge, wilful murder! It is the first of our family that have ever been accused of such a crime. Are you going to arrest my wife as well? Have they found arsenic in the body?"

The trial came on at the Old Bailey on March 4th, 1912. In accordance with the custom in poison trials at the Old Bailey, the Attorney-General himself came down to lead for the Crown. The holder of that office was now Marshall's old friend Sir Rufus Isaacs. With him were Muir, Rowlatt (soon to be a judge), and Travers Humphreys, surely as strong a combination as has ever appeared at the Old Bailey. The Crown had indeed brought down their heavy guns against the two wretched people in the dock, and in truth they had not miscalculated. Seddon himself was a man of great ability, and all the Attorney-General's powers of penetrating enquiry were needed to break down his facile fencing. After his exhaustive and masterly opening, Marshall whispered to a colleague, "They're all out for a conviction, aren't they?"

This trial, the longest capital case in which Marshall was ever engaged, lasted for ten days, and was remarkable for two great forensic duels, in which the combatants were well matched. Until the trial was over there were no very dramatic incidents such as characterised the Yarmouth or the Camden Town cases; it was a hard, dogged fight—question and answer, argument for argument, day after day.

The first great duel was a scientific one. The theory of the prosecution, supported by the expert evidence of Sir William Willcox, was that Miss Barrow had died of "acute" arsenical poisoning, that is, a fatal dose administered within twenty-four hours of death; and that the only people who had the opportunity of administering such a dose were the Seddons. For this contention evidence of motive was obviously relevant. The defence was twofold: negative and positive. The negative defence, which had great cogency, was that the prosecution rested entirely on indirect evidence; the second, that Miss Barrow had died of epidemic diarrhœa, as the doctor had certified, perhaps aggravated by "chronic" arsenical poisoning, or arsenic taken for a long period of time before death. The defence also kept in the background, as a possibility, the alternative theory of suicide.

Now, if Marshall Hall could prove that Miss Barrow died, not of acute, but of chronic arsenical poisoning, Seddon was as good as saved, as it was admitted that such taking of arsenic over a prolonged period might reasonably aggravate the effects of a violent attack of epidemic diarrhœa. The evidence by which the prosecution stood or fell on this point was that of Sir William Willcox, the Home Office analyst. Now, calculation of the total quantity of arsenic found in the body was based upon the results of scientific experiment, which had never before been brought forward as evidence in a court of law. Whereas in two component parts of the body, viz. the liver and the intestines, it was practicable to *weigh* the arsenic found in the body, it was not practicable to weigh that found in the other more widely distributed parts. In the liver and the intestines, by a process of weighing, .63, or well over half, of a grain of arsenic was found. Indeed, a quarter of the weight of the whole liver was accounted for by the arsenic present in it. Now, two grains of arsenic make a fatal dose, and it was therefore necessary to make further researches to bring home the case against the prisoner. Arsenic is a poison which very rapidly spreads throughout the whole body, and it necessarily follows, to any mind conversant with medicine, that, if so much arsenic was present in the liver and the intestines, it was present elsewhere. But it was not practicable to ascertain, by weighing, a substance so widely distributed, and Sir William had recourse to Marsh's test, a chemical experiment by which arsenic is extracted from a minute specimen of a part of the body in the form of a gas, and deposited on the surface of a tube, technically called a "mirror." For instance, from a minute part of the stomach a minute proportion of arsenic is found. The minute portion of arsenic is multiplied proportionately to the total weight of the stomach as compared with the minute part of the stomach analysed by Marsh's test. In this way the total amount of arsenic found in the whole stomach is ascertained. Thus all the main component parts of the body, stomach, bone, muscle, etc., were analysed in this way, and the total arsenic found in the whole body, by weighing in the case of the liver and the intestines, and by Marsh's test as regards the rest, was 2.01 grains. Tiny quantities were found in the skin, the nails, and the hair, but these were not counted. Now 2.01 grains was enough for a fatal dose, but arsenic being a poison which is very quickly expelled from the system, Dr. Willcox estimated that at least 5 grains of arsenic had been administered to Miss Barrow, within a short time before her death, to leave 2.01 grains therein after death.

This experiment was no doubt sound, and even conservative, in its solution; but it is one thing for a scientist to prove to his own satisfaction that, for obvious scientific reasons and by an elaborate scientific experiment, 5 grains must have been administered to the dead woman shortly before death, and another thing to convince a sensible British jury as to the truth of this theory, when only .63 of a grain, or less than a third of a fatal dose, had been found in the body by the only rational and intelligible method, that of weighing. None knew this better than Marshall Hall, and he attacked the whole experiment. He first made Sir William admit that any initial error made in the experiment itself would be multiplied hundreds, or, in the case of some parts of the body, thousands of times in the calculation which followed it. Having established this, he made an excellent point: the muscle, one of the largest component parts of the body, two fifths of the whole in Willcox's calculation, contains a greater proportion of water than any of the other parts. But the corpse of Miss Barrow, in the ordinary process of decay, had shrunk from ten stone odd, her weight when alive, to something round about four stone at the time of exhumation. Now water is the first substance in a corpse to evaporate; therefore the weight of the muscle, being so largely composed of water, would decrease much more quickly than the other parts. But Willcox had used as his basis of calculation that the muscle was two-fifths of the weight of the whole body, and this would be true for only a short time after death, owing to the rapid evaporation of water. The vital question was then put.

"And I am sure it was an oversight—I mean—I may be wrong—but in making this calculation you have made no allowance whatever for the loss of water?"—"No, I have not."

Marshall had thus established a great deal: he had successfully assailed the scientific experiment in an important particular, and Englishmen always appreciate the spectacle of science confounded on its own ground. Much had already been achieved when he passed to a simpler point, a stronger one and more easily comprehended.

Among the abundant literature which he had been perusing for the purposes of this case was the report of the Royal Commission on Arsenic, convened at the beginning of the century as a result of a widespread epidemic of arsenical poisoning arising from beer-drinking. Now Marshall Hall had in the forefront of his mind every detail of the conclusions of this commission; Sir William Willcox, on the other hand, had them stored in the back of his memory, but had not read the report for some time. From a wide examination of cases the commission had reported this: that arsenic does not penetrate even into the "proximal" hair (that is, hair nearest the scalp) unless taken by the person affected some weeks before, and does not penetrate to the "distal" hair (the hair away from the roots) unless the person affected has taken arsenic at a considerably distant period—months, perhaps years, ago. For the arsenic remains in the hair as it grows; and, the hair growing about five or six inches a year, it is possible to compute how long ago the arsenic was taken by the distance it is away from the scalp in the case of a woman with long hair. Now, Sir William Willcox had examined a portion of Miss Barrow's hair of about twelve inches in length. Very innocently, Marshall asked him first about the proximal, then about the distal, ends of the hair.

"In the proximal end of the hair you found one-eightieth of a milligram?" —"Yes."

"What did you find in the distal end of the hair?"—"One three-thousandth —about a quarter as much," replied Sir William, with a smile at being asked about so small a quantity.

But the questions were not innocent: if arsenic was found in the ends of the hair, as Marshall went on to prove slowly, question by question, then Miss Barrow must have taken arsenic weeks ago, months ago, even years ago, before she ever went to live with the Seddons; and, if this was so, the defence had as good as won, as the jury, with Willcox's admissions in their ears, would certainly prefer the theory of the defence, that the poor lady had died of epidemic diarrhœa, aggravated by chronic arsenical poisoning, rather than the theory of the prosecution that she had died of acute arsenical poisoning, administered by the Seddons. When everything was prepared, Marshall obtained these answers from Dr. Willcox, which were indeed a triumph for his painstaking advocacy.

"Is the finding of the arsenic in the hair corroborative of acute arsenical poisoning, or of chronic arsenic-taking?"—"If arsenic is found in the hair it indicates that probably the arsenic had been taken for some period."

"I am sure you will give me a fair answer. Apart from all other symptoms, or any other questions, if you only find arsenic in the hair, you would take that as being a symptom of a prolonged course of arsenic?"—"Of a course of arsenic over some period."

"And the minimum period would be something about three months?"—"I think that."

"In the proximal portion, but . . . you would not expect to find it in the distal ends in three months, would you?"—"Not in large amounts."

"Not in the amount you have got here . . . ? This minute quantity in the distal end might possibly mean some arsenic might have been taken, perhaps a year or more ago. . . . A year ago or more?"—"More than a year ago."

Here, I think, Marshall Hall should have sat down. If he had, Seddon might well have gone free, and Marshall, by sheer scholarship and skill in using it, would have achieved a marvellous forensic triumph. "I had not got that part of the report in my mind," Sir William told me. "He very nearly tied me up. I don't think I've ever been so nearly trapped as I was then—it was extraordinarily clever of him." But, unfortunately—or, rather, fortunately for the ends of justice—Marshall went on driving the point home so that the jury could not possibly mistake the importance of the admissions, and all this time his learned and brilliant antagonist was thinking hard. "He is quite right," thought Willcox; "if the arsenic got into the hair through the system—but I am certain that the woman died of *acute* arsenical poisoning, which would be surprising if she was a confirmed taker of arsenic. Could the arsenic have got into the hair by any other means?"

Before Marshall had finished giving the famous analyst a lesson in analysis, Willcox had thought of the true explanation. Miss Barrow's long hair had become contaminated by the blood-stained fluid which was dispersed all over the coffin, and in this way had become tainted with arsenic. Before he left the box he made a discreet suggestion that this was the true explanation. Marshall poured scorn on this as an afterthought, as indeed it was. "Did you not wash the hair with all care, before making the experiment?" he asked.

That was late on the Thursday afternoon. The case now literally hung by a hair. Willcox quietly went home and thought more about the matter. Then he paid a visit to his hospital, and begged a long length of hair from one of his fair patients. This lovely strand of hair was then soaked in the blood-stained fluid from Miss Barrow's coffin, in which the latter's hair had been found matted at her exhumation. The experiment was then entrusted to another medical man, Dr. Webster; the hair was washed just as Miss Barrow's had been, and it was found to contain arsenic just as Miss Barrow's had done. On the following Tuesday, Sir William was re-called to give evidence as to this experiment. The experiment was a simple one with a successful result, which any juryman could appreciate, and the effect of Marshall's brilliant cross-examination was gone.

The other duel in the trial—and it was a real duel—was that fought be-tween the Attorney-General and the male prisoner. Seddon was an exceed-ingly vain man, with a great belief in his own abilities. When he heard that the Attorney-General himself, the great Sir Rufus Isaacs, was coming down to prosecute him, far from being alarmed, he was delighted, and from that moment made up his mind that he would cross swords with him. Marshall Hall from the date of his first interview with Seddon had been strongly opposed to calling him as a witness. "If the evidence does not con-vict this man," he said, "his conceit will." He told Mr. Saint that he must on no account prevent Seddon from going into the witness box, but that he must warn him in the clearest way of the dangers. Just before the case for the prosecution had closed, he himself went over to the dock, and gave Seddon a final warning. But the prisoner was determined. He had heard Rufus Isaacs' masterly opening, and thought that he, Seddon, could easily defeat him. He was, in fact, longing for the fray. So, after Marshall Hall had called two witnesses to prove that Seddon was in the habit of keeping large sums in gold in his house, Seddon went into the box on the afternoon of the fifth day of the trial. For over two hours on that day he was exam-ined by Marshall Hall, and made a clear and admirable witness. Finally, late in the morning, he stated, "I never purchased arsenic in my life, in any shape or form. I never administered arsenic. I never advised, directed, or instructed the administration of arsenic, that I swear."

The Attorney-General rose to cross-examine. The first two questions could not have been more skilful, and dramatic in their effect, spoken as they were in a cool, courteous tone.

"Miss Barrow lived with you from the 26th of July, 1910, till the morning of the 14th of September, 1911?"—"Yes."

"Did you like her?"—"Did I like her?" echoed the prisoner.

"Yes, that is the question." Seddon now hesitated, for the only time in the whole of his ordeal, obviously unprepared for this searching question. The question put him in a dilemma: if he said "Yes," he would be patently a hypocrite; the dreadful meanness of his conduct after her death, culminat-ing in the pauper's funeral which he gave her, would tell even more heavily against him than otherwise. If he said "No," he would be strongly prejudiced at the outset. After some hesitation he gave the best answer possible under the circumstances.

"She was not a woman that you could be in love with, but I deeply sympathised with her."

"During the time she was living with you at your house did you advise her on her financial affairs?"—"Certainly I advised her."

Then the Attorney-General went through the details of Miss Barrow's little fortune, and made the prisoner admit them.

"She came to you, then, with India Three and a half per cent. Stock bringing in one pound a week, the leasehold property bringing in one hundred and twenty pounds a year, and over two hundred pounds in the Finsbury Savings Bank; that is right?"—"Yes."

"She remained in your house from that date, 26th of July, 1910, till the 14th of September, 1911, when you examined all that there was to see of the property that was left?"—"Yes."

"On the 14th of September, 1911, when she died, was all the property that was found of hers a sum of ten pounds in gold, and furniture, jewellery, and other belongings to the value of sixteen pounds, fourteen shillings, and sixpence?"—"According to the inventory taken by Mr. Gregory, a reputed auctioneer and appraiser, it was sixteen pounds odd." The skill and effect of these questions needs no comment.

For the rest of the sixth day, and for the greater part of the seventh day, Seddon stood in the box under the patient, relentless, but increasingly intense light of the Attorney-General's enquiries, all the more deadly because of the unfailing courtesy of that beautiful voice. At a dinner of his community that celebrated his return from India, I heard an admirable compliment paid to Lord Reading. Sir Herbert Samuel had compared him to Rufus Curtius, a great proconsul of the Emperor Tiberius. "I am glad," said Lord Merrivale in a later speech, "that even in those days there was a Rufus—courteous." And courteous he certainly was even to the wretch Seddon, even in his fiercest questions. He always addressed his prisoner as "Mr. Seddon."

Seddon had a very quick and agile mind: at first his clever parries and retorts were very effective. He had an explanation and a reason for everything. But gradually his very cleverness and his inhuman coolness began to disgust the jury. His performance in the witness box makes a strange contrast to that of Robert Wood. Wood, innocent, made a bad, futile witness, and did not seem to understand the points made against him. Seddon, guilty, made an excellent witness, and missed nothing. Yet Wood, by his very incompetence in the box, made an impression of innocence on the jury: Seddon, with all his surprising competence, by his skilful quips and retorts, gave all his hearers a secret conviction of his guilt. Only towards the end did he break out and lose his composure. When he was asked as to the counting of the gold on the day of Miss Barrow's death, he showed his first sign of anger.

"The prosecution are suggesting that I am dealing with the deceased woman's gold. That I should bring it down from the top of the house to the bottom, into the office in the presence of my assistants, and count it up—is it feasible? . . . I am not a degenerate. That would make it out that I was a greedy, inhuman monster. . . . The suggestion is scandalous."

Seddon did himself more good by this angry outburst than by all his cool cleverness, but he ruined its effect by adding with a sarcastic smile, "I would have all day to count the money."

He again became very indignant when Mr. Attorney came to the statement made by him on his arrest, when he was alleged to have said, "Are you going to arrest my wife too?" He said the explanation of this was that the officer had first said, "You will see your wife at the station." "That," he said, "I swear before God, is the words that took place, and I have been waiting the opportunity to get into this box for to relate the true words that were spoken on this occasion."

"All the statements," commented the Attorney-General quietly, "that you are making are statements before God."

Little by little, Sir Rufus gained ground, and for all his cleverness the soul of Seddon was laid bare before the Court, if soul it could be called; for its god was gold, and his mean, calculating character, which obviously cared for nothing but Seddon and his worldly possessions, aroused the contempt and loathing of almost everybody in court. Here was a man who would do anything for gain. "Never," said an onlooker, "have I seen a soul stripped so naked as that."

Mrs. Seddon went into the box and was faced by the same ordeal. It was she who had taken Miss Barrow's bank-notes to be cashed, and had endorsed them with a false name and address. She explained lamely that she had never cashed notes before, and that she did not like to give her own name.

"Did you think it quite an ordinary thing to write your name at the back, or rather to write a false name at the back, when you were asked for your name?"—"No, it never struck me. . . . I never thought there was any harm in it whatever."

She was a harassed woman who had once been pretty: now she was aged beyond her thirty-four years by being Seddon's drudge for so long. She was obviously deeply moved and broken by the tragedy of her position. Even in her examination she broke down when she was asked about Miss Barrow's death scene. She was, nevertheless, able to describe it in detail till she reached the stage where her husband had "lifted up her eyelid and said—" At this point she began to sob helplessly. "I cannot say it. . . . I don't like to say it."

"Never mind," said her young counsel, "say it low."

"He said," she whispered, " 'Good God, she's dead.' "

She was one of those people who have a nervous habit of smiling. She was asked about the last dreadful night, when Miss Barrow had called out, "I'm dying," and she had taken no steps to fetch a doctor.

"Did you tell your husband about it when he came in?"—

"Yes, I did," answered Mrs. Seddon, and with tragic inappropriateness she gave one of her nervous smiles.

"Did you smile at it?" asked the Attorney-General sternly.—"Well, I have a usual way of smiling at almost everything, I think. I cannot help it. It is my way. No matter how serious anything was, I think I would smile. I cannot help it."

When she crept back to the dock, poor, miserable, forlorn woman, she had created an impression on the jury—which foreshadowed an acquittal— as a woman who had been used and broken by the cruel, cold, mean man her husband, and who counted for nothing in his life but as a tool and a household drudge. Quite unobtrusively the truth, for all her loyalty through-out the trial, slipped out. "He never used to take any notice when I said anything to him; he always had other things to think of. . . . I did not tell my husband everything I done: he never told me everything."

When Sir William Willcox had been recalled towards the end of the eighth day and gave the result of his experiment, the atmosphere in court had turned strongly against Seddon. The one great scientific attack on the evidence against him had been defeated. There was only one link in the chain of circumstances which was still open to a real doubt, and it was a very material one. Mr. Filson Young inclines to the view that the Crown did not, at any rate without Seddon's own evidence, make out its case against him. But it is difficult to see how, save for one weak link in the chain of circumstances alleged, short of producing a witness who had actually seen him administer the poison, they could have proved more. There was overwhelming evidence of motive, overwhelming evidence of opportunity; further, there was overwhelming evidence as to the prisoner's furtive attempts, after Miss Barrow's death, to prevent suspicion falling upon himself; furthermore, the dead woman was proved to have died of acute arsenical poisoning, and enough arsenic to poison several people had admittedly been purchased by the Seddons. The weak link in the chain was one of identification. Thorley, the chemist who ultimately had identi-fied Maggie Seddon as the girl who had bought a packet of arsenic fly-papers on August 26th, did not come till late upon the scene. Maggie Seddon was a friend of his daughter's, and had called several times to see her at the side door of the shop. He had seen her on one of these private visits, but did not know her name, and it was only after he had seen Maggie Seddon's photograph in the newspapers in connection with the case that he was asked to come down to the police station to identify, among twenty women and girls, the girl who had bought the arsenic papers from him on August 26th. He at once identified Maggie Seddon, but she and another among the twenty were the only girls with their hair down. Marshall Hall was confident throughout that Thorley was an honest but a mistaken witness, and this weakness in the identification of Maggie was a real point for the defence. The matter was made worse by the fact that the police had cross-examined poor little Maggie Seddon before she gave evidence in any court, and had asked her difficult questions which she had answered inaccurately. She was asked, when the police knew perfectly well that she had done so on December 6th, whether she went to a chemist's "to purchase fly-papers." She answered "No," but her explanation for this was that she misunderstood the question, and thought that the police were asking whether she had ever gone and actually purchased fly-papers. At all events, the girl's slip was used to discredit her evidence at the trial by the Attorney-General, and Marshall Hall was able to comment on the un-English and inquisitorial method by which the police had approached the daughter of the prisoner at the very outset, not in the interest of truth, but in order to discredit whatever she might say on behalf of her father.

Eight days of this trial had punished Marshall cruelly: he had felt the responsibility of *two* human lives on his shoulders, one of whom, the woman, he was sure was innocent; for this paramount reason he kept an iron grip on his self-control, and, knowing his own weakness, studiously avoided any kind of friction with the Bench. The Chattell case had made him, in the end, a much finer advocate. Undoubtedly his was the commanding personality in that great court, even with the Attorney-General there against him. In no way did Marshall Hall show an inferiority, throughout this memorable trial, to the leader of the Bar. Those who consider that Marshall Hall was a superficial man, who won his fame and victories by an overbearing, masterful personality and flamboyant rhetoric, would do well to study his cross-examination of Sir William Willcox, which was a profound, scholarly, and patient effort, and an intellectual achievement of which any man could be proud. Indeed, it showed an academic knowledge which could only have been derived from days and nights of careful research, and which, at one point at any rate, gave him the advantage over a man whose life's business it was to pursue this special and intricate branch of science.

When Marshall Hall rose to address the jury on the ninth day he looked tired and haggard, and, as a witness has told me, years older than at the beginning of the trial. The strain had been so great that he expressed the hope that this would be the last capital case of his career. "Gentlemen," he said at the commencement, "nobody can attempt to deny that this is one of the most interesting cases that probably have ever been tried in this building or in the building of which it is the successor." At great length, and with exhaustive detail, he repeated his arguments as to the scientific evidence, and referred with contempt to Sir William Willcox's "further experiments," made simply because his primary evidence was "self-destructive." He went carefully into Miss Barrow's financial resources, Seddon's agreement to give her an annuity, and proved that Seddon benefited by her death only to the extent of £1 8s. 0d. a week. "People," he said, "do not commit murders for one pound ten shillings a week." He maintained that, if the prisoners were guilty, they had shown a refinement of cruelty that was incredible. He asked the jury to think, if the Seddons were guilty, of their cold-blooded patience in sitting near her to watch her die, tortured by an agonizing poison, even administering palliatives to prolong her agony in order to simulate a natural death. One would search the annals of Italian poisoners in vain to find a parallel. During this passage, Mrs. Seddon broke down completely, put her face in her hands, and sobbed hysterically. Marshall put forward finally as the theory of the defence "that in some way or other some portion of the arsenic, not sufficient to cause her death, but sufficient in the state in which she was to aggravate the symptoms from which she was suffering—some portion, by some means or other, got into this unfortunate woman's stomach, and so into her body."

Then came his peroration; once more he repeated, almost word for word and gesture for gesture, the scales of Justice simile, which had been so effective in the Lawrence trial; but more effective still was his last argument of all, a reference to the scientific evidence upon which the Crown sought to hang these two people.

"Gentlemen," he said, "the great scientists who have been here have told us much of the marvels of science and of the deductions that can be made from science. But there is one thing all scientists have never been able to find, never yet been able to discover, with all their research, and with all their study, and this is, how to replace the little vital spark we call life. Upon your verdict here depends, so far as I am concerned, the life of this man. If your verdict is against him, that vital spark will be extinguished, and no science known to the world can ever replace it."

Marshall Hall had pleaded for a little over four hours. In that space of time he had spoken with his usual rapidity: altogether, something above thirty-seven thousand words, thus averaging nine thousand two hundred and fifty words an hour. The Attorney-General, who followed with the final speech, spoke for about the same time, and spoke nearly twenty-nine thousand words. Thus Marshall Hall packed into each hour nearly two thousand words more than his antagonist. When he sat down, Richard Muir scribbled a note and sent it to him. "MY DEAR MARSHALL,—A truly great speech—of many good things I have heard you do, quite the best. Yours always, R. D. MUIR."

The Attorney-General's speech was masterly; speaking in an even, courteous voice, he missed no single point against the prisoners. Marshall had said, "People do not commit murders for one pound ten shillings a week." Rufus Isaacs showed that this was precisely what this man Seddon might do, and every circumstance seemed to prove that he did. To show how much thought and care had been spent on this speech, one point of detail serves. Little Ernest Grant went to the same school as the Vonderahes' little boys. Seddon said he sent a letter to the Vonderahes to announce Miss Barrow's death; the Crown's contention was that Seddon never sent such a letter, and that he did everything to keep the news of Miss Barrow's death from them. Rufus Isaacs then brought forward the seemingly insignificant fact that the Seddons had not let Ernest Grant go to school on the morning of Miss Barrow's death, but had sent him down to Southend. Had he gone to school, he might have met the little Vonderahes and told them something.

Rufus Isaacs continued hour after hour, piling up his terrible indictment against both prisoners. The speech was really almost as deadly against Mrs. Seddon as against her husband. At the very end, Mr. Attorney gave a slight hint that there was a distinction between the two cases. "Supposing you come to the conclusion that you have no reasonable doubt with regard to the male prisoner, but that you have some doubt—you are not quite satisfied beyond all reasonable doubt—that the woman is guilty, then it would be your duty to acquit her."

After this last speech, came Mr. Justice Bucknill's summing-up. After the ten days' trial it was expected that he would sum up for the best part of a day: actually he spoke something above two hours. Many were disappointed that he did not give the jury the benefit of a more exhaustive analysis of the evidence. As to the scientific controversy, he said, "I should not be surprised if you said that you are satisfied beyond reasonable doubt that this lady died of acute arsenical poisoning as distinct from chronic. . . ." He gave a clear hint to the jury to acquit the woman, but his directions as regards Seddon excited much comment at the time. After referring to his mean character and to the fact that he did not send for a doctor when the woman was in such agony, he said, "Do not be too much prejudiced." These words implied that there must be some prejudice, and of course prejudice in general is wrong. But Marshall Hall had himself denounced Seddon's meanness in the strongest language, and the judge's language was moderate and sensible: he could have used these circumstances in a far more deadly fashion against the prisoner, had he so chosen, and have remained strictly within the proper limits.

The jury retired at 3.58, and returned into court exactly an hour later. They found Seddon guilty. His face flushed, but otherwise he maintained his composure. Immediately afterwards they pronounced his wife not guilty. Seddon went across, embraced her, and kissed her on the lips. So silent was the court that every one present must have heard the sound of that tragic gesture of farewell. Immediately afterwards she was taken away to be discharged. Much of the prejudice that had gathered round the prisoner was dissipated by this one incident. Many were moved to tears by it. Then the formal question was asked, by the officer of the court, to which very seldom is an answer given by the prisoner, at any rate in capital cases, where no words of his can affect his sentence. "Frederick Henry Seddon, you stand convicted of wilful murder. Have you anything to say for yourself why the Court should not give you judgment of death according to law?"

Then a surprising thing happened. "I have, sir," replied the prisoner. He cleared his throat, took out some notes, and made a calm and admirable little speech in his own defence. He declared his innocence of the murder and denied any knowledge of it. Finally, knowing the judge to be a zealous Freemason, he made it clear to the judge that they belonged to the same brotherhood, whose members bind themselves solemnly to help each other through life, and especially in extremity. "I declare," he concluded, "before the Great Architect of the Universe, I am not guilty, my lord."

This appeal utterly unnerved the judge. His clerk arranged the black square of cloth upon his head, which seemed to overshadow and darken his whole face. The chaplain was summoned, and the usher called out, "Oyez! Oyez! Oyez! My lords the King's justices do strictly charge and command all persons to keep silence while sentence of death is passing upon the prisoner at the bar, upon pain of imprisonment. God save the King!"

But no words came from the judge: in a silence that could be felt there were only two sounds to be heard—the ticking of the court clock and the loud sobs of the judge about to speak the words of condemnation. It seemed a long time before he could pull himself together, yet it could not have been more than a minute in all. Then, in a voice broken with emotion, the judge admonished the prisoner for his barbarous crime. "It is not for me to harrow your feelings," he said.

"It does not affect me," said the prisoner; "I have a clear conscience."

"Try to make peace with your Maker," the judge continued.

"I am at peace," said the prisoner.

"You and I know we both belong to the same brotherhood, and it is all the more painful to me to have to say what I am saying. But our brotherhood does not encourage crime; on the contrary, it condemns it. I pray you again to make your peace with the Great Architect of the Universe. Mercy—pray for it, ask for it. . . . And now I have to pass sentence. The sentence of the Court is that you be taken from hence to a lawful prison, and from thence to a place of execution, and that you be there hanged by the neck until you are dead; and that your body be buried within the precincts of the prison in which you shall have been confined after your conviction; and may the Lord have mercy on your soul."

The great battle had been both won and lost; it needed the most athletic advocacy to conduct the defence of both prisoners without prejudicing either of them, and for this reason, perhaps, Marshall Hall's oration for the

Seddons was the most artistic of all his speeches. The Attorney-General sent him a glowing tribute. He wrote on March 15th:

"MY DEAR MARSHALL,—Quite frankly, and sincerely, not as A.-G., but an old friend, do let me say how much I admired your defence and whole conduct of the Seddons' case. Your five minutes' outburst for Mrs. Seddon made a most powerful impression; and, in my view, did much—if not the most—for her acquittal. His case was a terribly difficult one—the chain was as complete as circumstantial evidence can make it—and you had a very hard task, when it was so plain to all that the man had such a covetous nature, and was such a shrewd, cunning fellow. But I didn't mean to discuss the case. I wanted to say again what I had said in your absence, in my speech, that it was a really magnificent forensic effort, and the whole defence was conducted by you in accordance with the highest traditions of our profession. I know you won't think it impertinent for me to write this to you. It is meant, and will be understood by you, as the expression of an opponent, who loves to see work well and nobly done—and of a friend who has always received such generous (over-generous, I think) recognition from you.

"I am so glad I went away before the verdict was given. I hope your wife is better. Please remember me to her.

"Yours ever,
"RUFUS D. ISAACS."

For his own part, Marshall Hall had expected the verdict to be as it was. He regarded the appeal as hopeless, but for two days he argued for Seddon in the Court of Criminal Appeal. Although this court had been founded in 1908, this was the first appeal of importance which Marshall Hall had argued. He hated appearing in any court of appeal, but he argued this case splendidly, the chief argument being that there was not sufficient evidence to go to a jury. He was unsuccessful, but one observation in the course of the argument by Mr. Justice Darling is interesting as showing how far the interpretation of the Criminal Evidence Act had changed in the course of years. "No one," said the learned judge, "who is well acquainted with criminal administration is ignorant of the fact that, to-day, prisoners are practically bound to go into the box, and that in the great majority of cases they say what is not true."

If this judicial dictum was well founded, Marshall Hall himself was largely responsible for the change in the practice. At the beginning of the century, counsel were very cautious in advising their clients whether to make use of the "privilege" conferred by the Act. But his great triumphs in the Wood and the Lawrence cases, in which he had put the prisoners in the witness box, had made a great effect. In the latter case the judge had expressly said that the prisoner would probably have been found guilty if he had not given evidence. From this time many more prisoners went into the box, and to-day it is a bolder thing to keep a prisoner out of the box than to put him into it.

After Seddon's appeal had failed, the public conscience began to grow uneasy: it was widely known that Seddon had been convicted on scientific evidence, and, with the usual British distrust and dislike of science, over 300,000 people signed the petition for his reprieve. But the Home Secretary did not reprieve him, and Seddon was executed on April 18th, 1912. When he knew all was over, he seemed quite unmoved. "This is nothing to me," he said, in his last interview with his solicitor, and went on to discuss the sale of his property. He could not be made to talk of anything else. When he heard how little his goods had fetched at the auction, he said, "That's finished," and he was really upset when he heard that his motor-car, of which he had been inordinately proud, had gone for a smaller price than he had paid for it. He would not talk of his wife or family, or their prospects. Perhaps this was from indifference, or perhaps from some more human reason he found himself unable to do so. Who shall say? "There is no question of my confessing," he said. "If you hear it, do not believe it." He wrote to the same effect to his wife and family, expressing his absolute innocence and his trust in Jesus Christ. So he died, an obstinate, conceited, hypocritical, cold-blooded, avaricious man. In him all the common virtues of the Anglo-Saxon were distorted into vices: he had but one real virtue, and this was courage; yet, if he had not had that one great temptation, the arrival of a helpless, well-to-do old maid to lodge in his house, he might to-day be a pillar of Islington municipal life, a director of an insurance company, hated as a hard taskmaster by his subordinates, but high in the favours of his board. His best epitaph, and one of which he would have been proud, was one given to him by Marshall Hall: "The ablest man I ever defended on the capital charge."

After his death a new sensation brought back his tragedy to the public mind. A few months afterwards his wife married again, and suffered much persecution. Two articles appeared over her signature in the *Weekly Dispatch* in which she admitted that she had seen Seddon give Miss Barrow arsenic, and that he had threatened to kill her, his wife, with a revolver if she gave him away. She had stood by him at the trial for the sake of her children. She described in some detail her miserable life with Seddon, and begged the public not to regard her as a murderess. Much public outcry arose at this "confession," which of course, if true, would have exposed her to a prosecution for perjury. Soon afterwards, by the instrumentality of *John Bull*, she was asked to sign a recantation of her confession: she did so. She said that it was false, and that her evidence at the trial was the whole truth. She was obviously a woman easily influenced. Later, she went out, with her husband, to Australia to try and make a new life for herself.

Incidentally, she was able to do this only through the generosity of the young solicitor who had defended her. Only one comment needs to be made as to her "confession" in the *Weekly Dispatch*. Seddon *had* a revolver. One of his legal advisers went to view his house before his arrest: there was a picture in the worst of taste hanging on his dining-room wall, depicting a husband shooting his wife's lover. "There," said Seddon, gratuitously calling attention to the print, and throwing down a revolver on the table, "that's the sort of man I am—only I would have shot them both."

The Manner of Cross-Examination*

FRANCIS L. WELLMAN

For a note on Francis L. Wellman see page 86.

It needs but the simple statement of the nature of cross-examination to demonstrate its indispensable character in all trials of questions of fact. No cause reaches the stage of litigation unless there are two sides to it. If the witnesses on one side deny or qualify the statements made by those on the other, which side is telling the truth? Not necessarily which side is offering perjured testimony,—there is far less intentional perjury in the courts than the inexperienced would believe. But which side is honestly mistaken,—for, on the other hand, evidence itself is far less trustworthy than the public usually realizes. The opinions of which side are warped by prejudice or blinded by ignorance? Which side has had the power or opportunity of correct observation? How shall we tell, how make it apparent to a jury of disinterested men who are to decide between the litigants? Obviously, by the means of cross-examination.

If all witnesses had the honesty and intelligence to come forward and scrupulously follow the letter as well as the spirit of the oath, "to tell the truth, the whole truth, and nothing but the truth," and if all advocates on either side had the necessary experience, combined with honesty and intelligence, and were similarly sworn to *develop* the whole truth and nothing but the truth, of course there would be no occasion for cross-examination, and the occupation of the cross-examiner would be gone. But as yet no substitute has ever been found for cross-examination as a means of separating truth from falsehood, and of reducing exaggerated statements to their true dimensions.

The system is as old as the history of nations. Indeed, to this day, the account given by Plato of Socrates's cross-examination of his accuser, Miletus, while defending himself against the capital charge of corrupting the youth of Athens, may be quoted as a masterpiece in the art of cross-questioning.

Cross-examination is generally considered to be the most difficult branch of the multifarious duties of the advocate. Success in the art, as some one has said, comes more often to the happy possessor of a genius for it. Great lawyers have often failed lamentably in it, while marvellous success has crowned the efforts of those who might otherwise have been regarded as of a mediocre grade in the profession. Yet personal experience and the emulation of others, trained in the art, are the surest means of obtaining proficiency in this all-important prerequisite of a competent trial lawyer.

It requires the greatest ingenuity; a habit of logical thought; clearness of perception in general; infinite patience and self-control; power to read men's minds intuitively, to judge of their characters by their faces, to appreciate their motives; ability to act with force and precision; a masterful knowledge of the subject-matter itself; an extreme caution; and, above all, the *instinct to discover the weak point* in the witness under examination. One has to deal with a prodigious variety of witnesses testifying under an infinite number of differing circumstances. It involves all shades and complexions of human morals, human passions, and human intelligence. It is a mental duel between counsel and witness.

In discussing the methods to employ when cross-examining a witness, let us imagine ourselves at work in the trial of a cause, and at the close of the direct examination of a witness called by our adversary. The first inquiries would naturally be: Has the witness testified to anything that is material against us? Has his testimony injured our side of the case? Has he made an impression with the jury against us? Is it necessary for us to cross-examine him at all?

Before dismissing a witness, however, the possibility of being able to elicit some new facts in our own favor should be taken into consideration. If the witness is apparently truthful and candid, this can be readily done by asking plain, straightforward questions. If, however, there is any reason to doubt the willingness of the witness to help develop the truth, it may be necessary to proceed with more caution, and possibly put the witness in a position where it will appear to the jury that he could tell a good deal if he wanted to, and then leave him. The jury will thus draw the inference that, had he spoken, it would have been in our favor.

But suppose the witness has testified to material facts against us, and it becomes necessary to break the force of his testimony, or else abandon all hope of a jury verdict. How shall we begin? How shall we tell whether the witness has made an honest mistake, or has committed perjury? The methods to be used in his cross-examination in the two alternatives would naturally be quite different. There is a marked distinction between discrediting the *testimony* and discrediting the *witness*. It is largely a matter of instinct on the part of the trained examiner. Some people call it the language of the eye, or the tone of the voice, or the countenance of the witness, or his "manner of testifying," or all combined, that betrays the wilful perjurer. It is difficult to say exactly what it is, excepting that constant practice seems to enable a trial lawyer to form a fairly accurate judgment on this point. A skilful cross-examiner seldom takes his eye from an important witness while he is being examined by his adversary. Every expression of his face, especially his mouth, even every movement of his hands, his manner of expressing himself, his whole bearing—all help the examiner to arrive at an accurate estimate of his integrity.

Let us assume, then, that we have been correct in our judgment of this particular witness, and that he is trying to describe honestly the occurrences to which he has testified, but has fallen into a serious mistake, through ignorance, blunder, or what not, which must be exposed to the minds of the jury. How shall we go about it? This brings us at once to the first important factor in our discussion, the *manner* of the cross-examiner.

It is absurd to suppose that any witness who has sworn, positively to a certain set of facts, even if he has inadvertently stretched the truth, is going to be readily induced by a lawyer to alter them and acknowledge his mistake. People as a rule do not reflect upon their meagre opportunities for observing facts, and rarely suspect the frailty of their own powers of observation. They come to court, when summoned as witnesses, prepared to tell what they think they know; and in the beginning they resent an attack upon their story as they would one upon their integrity.

If the cross-examiner allows the witness to suspect, from his manner toward him at the start, that he distrusts his integrity, he will straighten himself in the witness chair and mentally defy him at once. If, on the other hand, the counsel's manner is courteous and conciliatory, the witness will soon lose the fear all witnesses have of the cross-examiner, and can almost imperceptibly be induced to enter into a discussion of his testimony in a fair-minded spirit, which, if the cross-examiner is clever, will soon disclose the weak points in the testimony. The sympathies of the jury are invariably on the side of the witness, and they are quick to resent any discourtesy toward him. They are willing to admit his *mistakes,* if you can make them apparent, but are slow to believe him *guilty of perjury.* Alas, how often this is lost sight of in our daily court experiences! One is constantly brought face to face with lawyers who act as if they thought that every one who testifies against their side of the case is committing wilful perjury. No wonder they accomplish so little with their *cross*-examination! By their shouting, browbeating style they often confuse the wits of the witness, it is true; but they fail to discredit him with the jury. On the contrary, they elicit sympathy for the witness they are attacking, and little realize that their "vigorous cross-examination," at the end of which they sit down with evident self-satisfaction, has only served to close effectually the mind of at least one fair-minded juryman against their side of the case, and as likely as not it has brought to light some important fact favorable to the other side which had been overlooked in the examination-in-chief.

There is a story told of Reverdy Johnson, who once, in the trial of a case, twitted a brother lawyer with feebleness of memory, and received the prompt retort, "Yes, Mr. Johnson; but you will please remember that, unlike the lion in the play, I have something more to do than *roar*."

The only lawyer I ever heard employ this roaring method successfully was Benjamin F. Butler. With him politeness, or even humanity, was out of the question. And it has been said of him that "concealment and equivocation were scarcely possible to a witness under the operation of his methods." But Butler had a wonderful personality. He was aggressive and even pugnacious, but picturesque withal; witnesses were afraid of him. Butler was popular with the masses; he usually had the numerous "hangers-on" in the court room on his side of the case from the start, and each little point he would make with a witness met with their ready and audible approval. This greatly increased the embarrassment of the witness and gave Butler a decided advantage. It must be remembered also that Butler had a contempt for scruple which would hardly stand him in good stead at the present time. Once he was cross-questioning a witness in his characteristic manner. The judge interrupted to remind him that the witness was a Harvard professor. "I know it, your Honor," replied Butler; "we hanged one of them the other day."

On the other hand, it has been said of Rufus Choate, whose art and graceful qualities of mind certainly entitle him to the foremost rank among American advocates, that in the cross-examination of witnesses, "He never aroused opposition on the part of the witness by attacking him, but disarmed him by the quiet and courteous manner in which he pursued his examination. He was quite sure, before giving up, to expose the weak parts of his testimony or the bias, if any, which detracted from the confidence to be given it." (One of Choate's *bon mots* was that "a lawyer's vacation consisted of the space between the question put to a witness and his answer.")

Judah P. Benjamin, "the eminent lawyer of two continents," used to cross-examine with his eyes. "No witness could look into Benjamin's black, piercing eyes and maintain a lie."

Among the English barristers, Sir James Scarlett, Lord Abinger, had the reputation, as a cross-examiner, of having outstripped all advocates who, up to that time, had appeared at the British Bar. "The gentlemanly ease, the polished courtesy, and the Christian urbanity and affection, with which he proceeded to the task, did infinite mischief to the testimony of witnesses who were striving to deceive, or upon whom he found it expedient to fasten a suspicion."

Even so experienced an advocate as Sir James, however, sometimes loses his self-control in Court, and meets with the usual result.

At a trial between certain music publishing houses, as to an alleged piracy of a popular song, Tom Cooke, a well-known actor and musician, was subpoenaed as an expert witness by one of the parties. On his cross-examination by Sir James Scarlett, that learned gentleman rather flippantly questioned him in this wise:—

"Sir, you say that the two melodies are the same but different. Now, what do you mean by that?"

To this Cooke promptly answered, "I said that the notes in the two copies are alike, but with a different accent, the one being in a common time and the other is six-eighth time; and consequently the position of the accent of the notes was different."

Sir James. "What is a musical accent?"

Cooke. "My terms are nine guineas a quarter, sir." [A laugh.]

Sir James (rather ruffled). "Never mind your terms here; I ask you, what is a musical accent? Can you *see* it?"

Cooke. "No, Sir James."

Sir James. "Can you *feel* it?"

Cooke. "A *musician* can." [Great laughter.]

Sir James (very angry). "Now, pray, sir, don't beat about the bush, but explain to his Lordship, and the jury, who are expected to know nothing about music, the meaning of what you call accent."

Cooke. "Accent in music is a certain stress laid upon a particular *note* in the same manner as you would lay a stress upon a given word for the purpose of being better understood. Thus, if I were to say, 'You are an *ass*,' the accent rests on 'ass'; but if I were to say, '*You* are an ass,' it rests on *you*, Sir James."

Reiterated shouts of laughter by the whole court, in which the bench itself joined, followed this repartee.

A good advocate should be a good actor. The most cautious cross-examiner will often elicit a damaging answer. Now is the time for the greatest self-control. If you show by your face how the answer hurt, you may lose your case by that one point alone. How often one sees the cross-examiner fairly staggered by such an answer. He pauses, perhaps blushes, and after he has allowed the answer to have its full effect, finally regains his self-possession, but seldom his control of the witness. With the really experienced trial lawyer, such answers, instead of appearing to surprise or disconcert him, will seem to come as a matter of course, and will fall perfectly flat. He will proceed with the next question as if nothing had happened, or else perhaps give the witness an incredulous smile, as if to say, "Who do you suppose would believe that for a minute?"

An anecdote apropos of this point is told of Rufus Choate. "A witness for his antagonist let fall, with no particular emphasis, a statement of a most important fact from which he saw that inferences greatly damaging to his client's case might be drawn if skilfully used. He suffered the witness to go through his statement and then, as if he saw in it something of great value to himself, requested him to repeat it carefully that he might take it down correctly. He as carefully avoided cross-examining the witness, and in his argument made not the least allusion to his testimony. When the opposing counsel, in his close, came to that part of his case in his argument, he was so impressed with the idea that Mr. Choate had discovered that there was something in that testimony which made in his favor, although he could not see how, that he contented himself with merely remarking that though Mr. Choate had seemed to think that the testimony bore in favor of his client, it seemed to him that it went to sustain the opposite side and then went on with the other parts of his case."

It is the love of combat which every man possesses that fastens the attention of the jury upon the progress of the trial. The counsel who has a pleasant personality; who speaks with apparent frankness; who appears to be an earnest searcher after truth; who is courteous to those who testify against him; who avoids delaying constantly the progress of the trial by innumerable objections and exceptions to perhaps incompetent but harmless evidence; who seems to know what he is about and sits down when he has accomplished it, exhibiting a spirit of fair play on all occasions—he it is who creates an atmosphere in favor of the side which he represents, a powerful though subconscious influence with the jury in arriving at their verdict. Even if, owing to the weight of testimony, the verdict is against him, yet the amount will be far less than the client has schooled himself to expect.

On the other hand, the lawyer who wearies the court and the jury with endless and pointless cross-examinations; who is constantly losing his temper and showing his teeth to the witnesses; who wears a sour, anxious expression; who possesses a monotonous, rasping, penetrating voice; who presents a slovenly, unkempt personal appearance; who is prone to take unfair advantage of witness or counsel, and seems determined to win at all hazards—soon prejudices a jury against himself and the client he represents, entirely irrespective of the sworn testimony in the case.

The evidence often *seems* to be going all one way, when in reality it is not so at all. The cleverness of the cross-examiner has a great deal to do with this; he can often create an atmosphere which will obscure much evidence that would otherwise tell against him. This is part of the "generalship of a case" in its progress to the argument, which is of such vast consequence.

There is eloquence to be displayed in the examination of witnesses as well as on the argument. "There is *matter* in *manner*." I do not mean to advocate that exaggerated manner one often meets with, which divides the attention of your hearers between yourself and your question, which often diverts the attention of the jury from the point you are trying to make and centres it upon your own idiosyncrasies of manner and speech. As the man who was somewhat deaf, and could not get near enough to Henry Clay in one of his finest efforts, exclaimed, "I didn't hear a word he said, but, great Jehovah, didn't he make the motions!" The very intonations of voice and the expression of face of the cross-examiner can be made to produce a marked effect upon the jury, enabling them to appreciate fully a point they might otherwise lose altogether.

"Once, when cross-examining a witness by the name of Sampson, who was sued for libel as editor of the *Referee*, Russell asked the witness a question which he did not answer. 'Did you hear my question?' said Russell in a low voice. 'I did,' said Sampson. 'Did you understand it?' asked Russell, in a still lower voice. 'I did,' said Sampson. 'Then,' said Russell, raising his voice to its highest pitch, and looking as if he would spring from his place and seize the witness by the throat, 'why have you not answered it? Tell the jury why you have not answered it.' A thrill of excitement ran through the court room. Sampson was overwhelmed, and he never pulled himself together again."

Speak distinctly yourself, and compel your witness to do so. Bring out your points so clearly that men of the most ordinary intelligence can understand them. Keep your audience, the jury, always interested and on the alert. Remember it is the minds of the jury you are addressing, even though your question is put to the witness. Suit the modulations of your voice to the subject under discussion. Rufus Choate's voice would seem to take hold of the witness, to exercise a certain sway over him, and to silence the court room into a hush. He allowed his rich voice to exhibit, in the examination of witnesses, much of its variety and all of its resonance. The contrast between his tone in examining and that of the counsel who followed him was very marked.

"Mr. Choate's appeal to the jury began long before his final argument; it began when he first took his seat before them and looked into their eyes. He generally contrived to get his seat as near them as convenient, if possible having his table close to the Bar, in front of their seats, and separated from them only by a narrow space for passage. There he sat, calm, contemplative; in the midst of occasional noise and confusion solemnly unruffled; always making some little headway either with the jury, the court, or the witness; never doing a single thing which could by possibility lose him favor, ever doing some little thing to win it; smiling benignantly upon the counsel when a good thing was said; smiling sympathizingly upon the jury when any juryman laughed or made an inquiry; wooing them all the time with his magnetic glances as a lover might woo his mistress; seeming to preside over the whole scene with an air of easy superiority; exercising from the very first moment an indefinable sway and influence upon the minds of all before and around him. His manner to the jury was that of a *friend*, a friend solicitous to help them through their tedious investigation; never that of an expert combatant, intent on victory, and looking upon them as only instruments for its attainment."

The genial, courteous attitude of the late John B. Stanchfield toward everyone he came in contact with in the trial of his cases was one of the secrets of his success. Shortly before he died he told me of his experiences in Washington when he was retained by some of the leaders of the Washington Bar to conduct, with them, the defence of the president of the Riggs Bank. Immediately upon his arrival in Washington, Mr. Stanchfield was summoned to a meeting of all the lawyers in the case and was told that he had been selected to assume the burden of the trial. He was warned, however, that the feeling against the bank official was so intense, and the bias of the judge who was to preside at the trial was so marked that there was little hope of a successful defense, unless Mr. Stanchfield could so irritate the trial judge that he would not only display his prejudice to the jury and thus arouse their sympathy, but also make erroneous rulings that might upset the verdict upon appeal. It was apparent to Mr. Stanchfield that he had been called from New York to undertake a task none of the local attorneys was willing to assume. He promptly refused to depart from his usual method or conduct the trial upon any such lines as were laid down by the Washington lawyers. He would try the case in his own way or not at all.

Throughout the trial Mr. Stanchfield's attitude toward the court was one of extreme courtesy and respect. At the end of a week the issue had narrowed down practically to the single question of *reasonable doubt*. Was the defendant guilty "beyond all reasonable doubt?"—otherwise he should be acquitted. Mr. Stanchfield devoted practically his entire summing up to the jury to this question. He cited authorities and explained with great minuteness all the intricacies of this perplexing rule of law—to such good effect that when the judge came to charge the jury, he complimented the courteous gentleman from New York upon the clearness and accuracy with which he had stated the law to the jury and ended by saying he could think of nothing he could add to or subtract from Mr. Stanchfield's statement. The result was a prompt acquittal. When the jury had rendered their verdict, the judge invited Mr. Stanchfield into his private chambers and then remarked: "Mr. Stanchfield, when I heard that you had been called from New York to try this case before me, I could almost see you arriving in the city and almost hear the instructions that were given you as to how to conduct yourself during the trial. I just want to say this one thing to you: *it pays to be a gentleman.*"

The Cross-Examination of
Mrs. Reginald Vanderbilt*

FRANCIS L. WELLMAN

For a note on Francis L. Wellman see page 86.

"THE CROSS-EXAMINATION OF MRS. REGINALD VANDERBILT BY HERBERT C. SMYTH,
IN THE CELEBRATED HABEAS CORPUS PROCEEDING BROUGHT BY MRS. VANDERBILT
AGAINST MRS. HARRY PAYNE WHITNEY, TO RECOVER THE CUSTODY OF HER CHILD."

S eldom in recent years has any case been tried in the civil branch of our
local courts that occasioned so much publicity, discussion, criticism
and even notoriety as the suit brought by Mrs. Gloria Vanderbilt, through
habeas corpus proceedings, to recover the possession of her eleven-year-old
daughter who she claimed had been technically kidnaped by her paternal
aunt, Mrs. Harry Payne Whitney, with whom the child had been living at
her Long Island country estate for about two years before the inception
of this suit.

During the first few days of the trial the court room was packed to the
doors, and hundreds of a sensation-loving public were daily refused admission. Then out of a clear sky an ill-advised question put to one of the servant
witnesses in cross-examination by Mrs. Vanderbilt's counsel—apparently for-
getful of the precept about "where angels fear to tread"—provoked such a
scandalous answer that the presiding justice thereafter peremptorily excluded every one from the court room excepting counsel and interested
parties and their witnesses and proceeded to conduct the subsequent four
weeks of the trial, as it were, *in camera.* Not even the newspaper reporters
were allowed to be present, and the parties to this litigation, as well as
their attorneys and such witnesses as were present from time to time, were
not only put on their honor not to disclose anything that transpired in the
court room, but were threatened with contempt proceedings in case the
court order was not strictly obeyed.

Mr. Nathan Burkan brought the proceeding on behalf of Mrs. Vanderbilt, and Mr. Herbert C. Smyth acted as trial counsel for Mrs. Whitney and personally conducted the proceedings throughout the litigation.

The presumption in favor of a mother's right to the possession and custody of her own daughter is so powerful that, in order to succeed, it was incumbent upon Mrs. Whitney and her lawyer to produce indisputable evidence of the mother's inexcusable neglect of her child during the nine years which followed the death of the father, Mr. Reginald Vanderbilt.

Many witnesses were called *pro* and *con*, but the task of convincing the Court, out of the mouth of the mother herself, that Mrs. Vanderbilt had forfeited the right to the custody of her child, rested on the shoulders of Mr. Smyth, fortified as he was with the all-powerful weapon of cross-examination.

It had been testified by witnesses that the mother, a young and beautiful woman, had paid scant attention to her child's welfare for many years preceding the trial. She had herself traveled most of the time, sometimes taking her young daughter along with her, from New York to London—Paris—Biarritz—Cannes—as suited her fancy, so that the child was never allowed to remain in any one place long enough to form the friendship or enjoy the companionship of other children. It had also been claimed she had neglected the child to such a degree that she had lost her daughter's affection; so much so that the daughter had threatened that if she were compelled to go back to her mother now that she was in Mrs. Whitney's care, she would throw herself out of the window. The child was submitted to a long examination by the Judge himself in his private chambers, but nothing could shake her in this dread of her mother and determination to end her own life if she had to resume her experiences of the past.

At this stage the trial had literally become the talk of the town. It was the prevailing topic of discussion at nearly every social gathering—dinner parties, clubs, and, it may almost be said, in every household, even the humblest. Prince Hohenlohe, Lady Furness, Mrs. Vanderbilt's twin sister, and her brother had all hastily taken passage from abroad to be present at the trial and to testify in Mrs. Vanderbilt's behalf. Other names of people prominent in London society had been brought into the testimony, Mrs. Vanderbilt herself being widely known socially throughout the principal cities of Europe, so that the trial had come to assume an international aspect.

The popular sympathy was naturally all in favor of the mother who was trying to regain possession of her child, but the more conservative judgment waited to hear what the mother had to say in her own behalf.

When Mrs. Vanderbilt took the stand as her own last witness, she assumed the attitude of an hysterical, much abused young mother. She was frequently unable to continue her story coherently, to a degree that prompted the court to order a succession of short recesses so that the witness might regain her self-possession, and the court attendants were called upon to administer to her wants on frequent occasions. I am told that at the end of Mrs. Vanderbilt's direct examination everybody in the court room, perhaps with the exception of the opposing lawyers, felt that the lady had been inexcusably abused.

Possibly once in the career of every prominent attorney who has lived his life, so to speak, in a court room, there arises a situation such as confronted Mr. Smyth at this stage of the litigation. There was no jury, no audience, no public, no daily newspapers to win over to his side. His one task was to unmask the witness's habits during her widowhood, and to exhibit her to the presiding Judge as a young, pleasure-loving woman—a mother who always made her undoubted affection for her offspring subservient to her own enjoyment of her youth, freedom to travel and opportunity to enjoy the attentions and allurements that foreigners are wont to shower upon any beautiful American woman who will entertain them at her sumptuous apartments in Paris and elsewhere, attended as she was by a retinue of servants and all the luxuries that go with such surroundings.

This could only be done by a patient, lengthy, painstaking, persistent cross-examination, and few know how to conduct that kind of examination better than does Mr. Smyth.

At this stage of the case the odds were undoubtedly in favor of the mother. True, her maid and her child's governess had given very damaging testimony against her; and even her own mother had corroborated much of their evidence. But the statements of discharged domestic servants are never regarded as very convincing evidence, while the surprising conduct of Mrs. Vanderbilt's mother in voluntarily testifying against her—however estimable a woman Mrs. Morgan might be—was bound to detract from the weight given to whatever she might say.

Altogether, the success or failure of this cross-examination might very well prove to be the turning point in the case. Mr. Smyth knew he had some valuable material with which to confront the witness, but could it be used with sufficient telling effect to counteract the favorable impression she had made during her direct testimony?

The cross-examination occupied three days, so that it would be impossible to include here more than a few excerpts from it. In any event the measure of Mr. Smyth's success is best evidenced by the court decision overwhelmingly in his client's favor.

His first unusual move was to take a position at such a point in the court room that the witness would be obliged to look at him across the bench, thereby allowing the Judge to observe every expression of her face which accompanied her spoken words. Few lawyers would have thought to avail themselves of this advantage.

Throughout his examination Mr. Smyth treated the witness with the utmost courtesy, even deference at times, and never confronted her with her obvious contradictions, as would have been done were there a jury present. Instead, he left it to the sagacity of the ever alert, attentive Judge to form his own opinion whether the witness was frank and willing to tell the whole story, or prone to suppress or distort important portions of it.

The cross-examination had proceeded only a few minutes before the weeping mother began to exhibit a fighting mood. Her tears promptly disappeared, and she was ever on the alert, many times with caustic comments and replies which proved, at least to Mr. Smyth, that it was obviously stage play which she had indulged in during her direct examination and had now suddenly forgotten.

The object of the cross-examination, as has already been said, was to lead the witness throughout the history of her life during the preceding nine years, and thereby to demonstrate by his questions and her answers how little attention she had paid to her daughter while she was consorting with people who could have no sympathy with the child's welfare, and further to demonstrate, if he could, the thoughtless if not flagrant neglect of the mother, right up to the time when she was suddenly faced with the horrible possibility of losing all claim to the custody of her only child—and incidentally, the allowance of $4,000 a month paid out of the child's property.

There had been much evidence previously sworn to regarding the intimate relations existing between Mrs. Vanderbilt and Prince Hohenlohe. But any adverse effect of this testimony was largely mitigated by the undisputed fact that the couple were for two years engaged to be married. The marriage had been abandoned because, as the mother said, she wished to have her child brought up in America rather than abroad, and also for the reason that neither of them had sufficient means of their own outside of the allowance for the support of the daughter. And that allowance might possibly be revoked or much reduced if the daughter took up her permanent residence outside of the United States.

However, there was still another suggestion of impropriety introduced by Mrs. Whitney's witnesses in relation to an intimacy between Mrs. Vanderbilt and a married man named Blumenthal, who enjoyed the nickname of "Blumie." Mrs. Vanderbilt had insisted that her acquaintance with Mr. Blumenthal was purely casual and, in this one connection, Mr. Smyth apparently could not resist the temptation to lead his witness into a trap, in order to demonstrate her lack of sincerity as a witness. This maneuver, judging from the wording of his opinion, evidently made a profound impression on the Court. Mr. Smyth had in his possession what he considered an important telegram which he had succeeded in quietly marking for identification during Mrs. Vanderbilt's direct examination, reserving the right to disclose its contents and to use it at the psychological moment.

It appeared that shortly before one of the mother's numerous trips to Europe, Mrs. Whitney had sent her a telegram suggesting that they meet on a certain day for luncheon at Mrs. Whitney's home, when they could discuss the welfare of the child for the coming winter. It was the reply, signed "Blumie," that Mr. Smyth used with an effect that only a dyed-in-the-wool cross-examiner knows how to achieve. He first casually asked Mrs. Vanderbilt if she had any acquaintance by the name of "Blumie," to which she replied with an emphatic *"no."* She was asked about the invitation to lunch with Mrs. Whitney, which she remembered but could not recall whether she had telephoned or telegraphed her acquiescence. Here was the opportunity Mr. Smyth had been waiting for. He very quietly confronted her with the telltale telegram which he proceeded to read aloud: *"We are very happy to see you Thursday noon, love—Blumie."*

This message produced a stunning effect upon her and she began to flounder about in an effort to find any plausible explanation. First she rather helplessly insisted it must have been a mistake of some kind, but when pressed further she had to admit that the telegram bearing the initials "A. H."—those of the Ambassador Hotel—must have come from that hotel, where Mr. Blumenthal lived and also had an office. She still insisted, however, that it must have been sent by mistake as she could not imagine how "love—Blumie" could have been signed to a telegram sent by her. She tried to argue that the mistake must have been made by Mr. Blumenthal's secretary, but as the telegram showed that it had been sent after secretarial hours, the most natural inference that could be drawn from the occurrence was that she was at least on that occasion definitely in Mr. Blumenthal's apartment and under circumstances which, for whatever reason, precluded both of them from realizing their embarrassing error.

Mr. Smyth backed up this incident by drawing Mrs. Vanderbilt's attention to the fact that she had sailed without her child on the *Europa*, but in company with this same Mr. Blumenthal. She first expressed doubt that he was on board but thought "possibly he was." She was then shown the printed passenger list which did not disclose either his or her name—a fact that elicited a triumphant smile from her. But later, when confronted with photographs that were taken of her and Mr. Blumenthal just before the sailing of the ship and were published in the New York newspapers the following day, the smile suddenly vanished.

Mr. Smyth. "I now show you the list headed 'No Publicity' and ask if you find your name as well as Mr. Blumenthal's on *that* list."

A. "I do, and I also find Mr. Rockefeller's."

Q. "He had nothing to do with you, had he?"

A. "Neither had Mr. Blumenthal."

Q. "Are you sure about that?"

A. "I am quite sure about it."

Q. "You have never seen Mr. Rockefeller, have you?"

A. "I don't know him."

Q. "So there is no reason you can think of to put him in the same category with yourself, excepting as one other passenger who might wish to conceal his sailing date?"

(No answer.)

Q. "Let us see. You notice there are only five names under the heading of 'No Publicity'?"

A. "I suppose all these gentlemen sailed with me."

Q. "No indeed. It appears here that the only single man is Mr. Blumenthal. Look at it. He was not even single, but he was there without his wife."

A. "I am sure I don't know what that means."

Q. "How far away from his stateroom was yours?"

A. "I can't remember that. It must have been—I don't know whether it was on the same side, or not."

Q. "You see that your number is 94?"

A. "I can't remember the number. You must show me a plan of the boat."

Q. "I have got it here for you (handing to witness); you were both on the same deck, were you not?"

A. "Yes, I believe we were."

Q. "You believe you were?"

A. "Yes."

Q. "Didn't you have cocktails in your room when Mr. Blumenthal came in there?"

A. "No. I didn't have a suite and Mr. Blumenthal was not in my stateroom."

Q. "You are sure about that?"

A. "I am quite sure of it."

Q. "What deck were you on?"

A. "I do not remember."

Q. "It is marked here somewhere. You know ship plans pretty well, do you not?"

A. "Yes."

Q. "You know that those that are colored blue mean the very good ones and the large rooms?"

A. "Suites."

Q. "Now, you were in 94?"

A. "Show me the plan, please."

Q. "I will show it to you. I want to find it so that you will not have to look at too much. This is on Deck A. Those are the quarters which you had (indicating)."

A. "Yes, the white. It is not a suite."

Q. "True enough. Now, look at Mr. Blumenthal's."

A. "I suppose it is the marked one."

Q. "138. You see that?"

A. "138, yes."

Q. "You see this little stateroom that is right back of Mr. Blumenthal's (indicating)?"

A. "Yes."

Q. "That was your maid's room, was it not?"

A. "It was."

Q. "How did it happen that your maid had a stateroom right adjoining and connecting with Mr. Blumenthal's?"

A. "That is purely an accident, Mr. Smyth."

Q. "I see."

A. "You don't think for one single moment—I know the insinuation you are trying to make—considering my friendship with Mr. Blumenthal that I would park my maid in the cabin next door so that she could listen to everything that went on?"

Q. "No, but it did give access to Mr. Blumenthal's room?"

A. "You mean to insinuate that I went through my maid's room into Mr. Blumenthal's room. Really you are Machiavellian in thinking things up."

Q. "Mr. Blumenthal had 138. That was a suite?"

A. "Yes, it was."

Q. "And part of the suite was your maid's room?"

A. "My maid had a room. I don't know whose suite it was. I understood it was next to Mr. Blumenthal's drawing room."

Q. "Were you ever in Mr. Blumenthal's drawing room?"

A. "I was."

After some other questions which showed the witness that the cross-examiner knew more of the facts than she originally had thought, she admitted that she and Mr. Blumenthal with some other passengers dined together every night the vessel was at sea. Although she had tried to say that Mr. Blumenthal's being on the vessel was quite a coincidence, she admitted the authenticity of the photographs, and finally in relation to purchasing her transportation the following was brought out:

Q. "When you got the transportation on the *Europa,* from what agent did you get it?"

A. "Well, that is a long story."

Q. "I can shorten it for you. It was Mr. Benjamin, was it not?"

A. "Yes, it was Mr. Benjamin."

Q. "Mr. Benjamin is the agent from whom Mr. Blumenthal got his transportation?"

A. "Yes, I introduced him."

The trial justice showed plainly the impression this Blumenthal episode was making upon him, and in his written opinion he criticized Mrs. Vanderbilt for subjecting herself to the notoriety that must necessarily follow the disclosure of her friendship with a married man, especially one so well known to New York's "night life."

The trial was unique in many other respects, not the least of which was that Mrs. Vanderbilt's mother had steeled herself to take the witness stand against her, in spite of the fact that she had for years been living on her daughter's bounty. Mrs. Morgan even produced many letters which she had received from her grandchild expressing distrust and fear of her mother.

Mrs. Vanderbilt's father had died a year or so before this trial, but during her cross-examination she was obliged to admit that she had received a letter from him enclosing a petition which he intended to use in the Surrogate's Court in this city, severely criticizing his daughter's conduct and her extravagant mode of living in her luxurious Paris apartment.

Mr. Smyth's sole effort was to create a situation which would entirely justify his client, Mrs. Whitney, in her claim that the child's best welfare depended upon her being allowed to remain in Mrs. Whitney's custody and to live a healthful, outdoor, childish existence at her country estate on Long Island, where she could also have proper medical care and schooling. To this end he pressed Mrs. Vanderbilt to give him some motive for her mother and father taking the attitude that they did against her, other than a conviction that it was for the best interests of the child. And he especially demanded some explanation as to what had caused her father to assume the position he had taken in his attempt to lay the whole matter before the New York Surrogate who had awarded the $48,000 yearly allowance to Mrs. Vanderbilt as custodian of her child. Mrs. Vanderbilt's only explanation was that her mother was motivated by money and hinted that Mrs. Whitney was probably back of the whole thing.

Mr. Smyth. "Let me read you a paragraph from this document which you say your father sent you with the information that he was proposing to use it in the Surrogate's Court. Please try to concentrate your attention on this:

(Reading) "That in the City of Paris the said Gloria M. Vanderbilt has maintained a large apartment consisting of fifteen to sixteen rooms, has had from twelve to fifteen servants and has been living in the most extravagant and most luxurious manner and has been entertaining her friends, many of bad reputation, and improperly and irregularly spending almost all the moneys which had been dispensed and directed by this Court to be used for the maintenance, education and support of the above-named infant." [1]

Q. "Of course, you don't agree with that, do you?"

---

[1] This paper was not admitted in evidence as proof of the truth of its statements—the father not being a witness—but the Court allowed it to be used as contradicting Mrs. Vanderbilt's assertion in her direct testimony that her father was fully aware of and approved the life she lived abroad and her care of her daughter.

A. "Well, as the infant was living with me in all this luxury that my father writes about in that document, I really cannot see how she did not benefit by it. You say fifteen servants for fifteen rooms—one servant for every room—lavish entertainment and so on, I should say my child would benefit by that." (It is the French custom to have most of a large staff of servants live at their own homes.)

Q. "How did your child benefit by this lavish entertainment?"

A. "She may have entertained herself and her friends."

Q. "At four years of age?"

A. "She had little friends come in. You know Mrs. Whitney has children."

Q. "The remark you made a moment ago was that your child benefited by this lavish entertainment, was that right?"

A. "No, I said by that whole paragraph that you read just now."

Q. "How could the child possibly benefit?"

A. "She might have given parties. No, I might have given them for her."

Q. "You didn't keep her up late at night, did you?"

A. "I didn't say at night."

Q. "Your entertainments were usually at night?"

A. "Were they? Luncheon, is that an entertainment at night? Tea, is that at night?"

Q. "Didn't you have dinner parties?"

A. "I had dinner parties."

Q. "Was the child there?"

A. "No."

Q. "Well, did the child benefit by that?"

A. "She might have from the friends I made for her."

Q. "This four-year-old child?"

A. "Yes."

Q. "Are you sincere about that?"

A. "Yes."

Q. "Were you then creating friendships for the benefit of your child which she could benefit by when she grew up?"

A. "When she went to Paris, yes."

Q. "Were any of them titled people in Europe?"

A. "Some were people living in Paris, there were French, there were some English, there were some Scotch, some German, some Swiss. Maybe Italians. I don't know."

Q. "Did you expect that that was going to be for the benefit of your child later on in life?"

A. "Why certainly, why not?"

Q. "How much of your allowance did you spend in entertaining Prince Hohenlohe?"

A. "That is an insulting question. I did not entertain Prince Hohenlohe.

I gave dinner parties, but it was not for the Prince especially, although he may have been there with others."

Mr. Smyth. "I read further from the document which you admit your father sent to you:

(Reading) "That during the time that the aforesaid infant was living in Biarritz in a château or villa at that place her mother indulged in the same extravagance and consorted with and brought to said infant's home persons of evil repute and bad moral character and both in Paris and Biarritz failed to extend the care, kindness and solicitude to the above named infant which motherly instincts and duty should prompt."

Q. "Now you read that, didn't you?"

A. "Yes, I did, but my father later retracted it."

Q. "I thought you said a little while ago that your father fully approved of the way you brought up your child and your mode of living in Paris."

A. "Well, I can only repeat that my father retracted, in my presence and in my sister's presence, the statements made in that document and, in any event, I am sure it was done upon the instigation of my mother, and I will add that Mrs. Whitney knew all about this document because I told her about it and I told her that my mother, Mrs. Morgan, was trying to take my child away from me. I told her that in July, 1934. Yes, I told Mrs. Whitney that and I can look her straight in the face when I say it now. One of the last words my father said was that his only regret in life was this document, and my sister was present at the time."

Q. "What was the occasion for your having this conversation with Mrs. Whitney?"

A. "Well, I just thought I could speak to her. I trusted Mrs. Whitney, but I misplaced my trust and that is all I can say. I told Mrs. Whitney that my father, through the instigation of my mother, had written me a document, but that I had seen my father many times after that document was written. I was at the head of his bed when he died and that document was never mentioned once." (This contradicts her previous statements about her father's dying words.)

Q. "Did you tell Mrs. Whitney that your father had retracted it?"

A. "I do not remember. I believe I must have."

Q. "You knew that your mother was very fond of her grandchild, your daughter, did you not?"

A. "I would say my mother is unnaturally fond of that child."

Q. "What do you mean by that?"

A. "I think she is hysterically fond of that child. I think she exaggerates things."

Q. "Can you imagine any motive that your mother could have for saying anything against you except the welfare of the child?"

A. "Yes, I can."

Q. "I am willing you should state it. What motive can your mother have?"

A. "I am sorry to say that the only motive that my mother can have is money."

Q. "Why should money come into this as the motive on the part of your mother to take sides against you?"

A. "You better ask Mrs. Whitney that."

Q. "Is that your only answer?"

A. "It is a very hard thing for me to say, but I must say it, even though it is against my mother, since you are forcing me to say this. She wants the guardianship of the child so she can have the $48,000 a year allowance."

Q. "Then you think that Mrs. Morgan's motive in trying to take the child away from you is so that she can have the expenditure of $4,000 a month, is that right?"

A. "Yes, that is right."

Q. "Do you really mean that?"

A. "I certainly do. My mother is money-mad."

Mrs. Whitney was shown to be a woman of very considerable wealth who, in addition to her own three children, had eight grandchildren for whom she had provided separate, private homes surrounding her country place. At the very end of the cross-examination the following colloquy occurred:

Mr. Smyth. "Let me ask you this question and it is an important one. You know that Mrs. Whitney is the grandmother of eight grandchildren, do you not?"

A. "Yes, I do."

Q. "You know also that she has undertaken the care of a large family ever since her own three children were born?"

A. "No, I don't know that. What do you mean that she has undertaken the care of a large family?"

Q. "Well, she has, hasn't she?"

A. "What large family?"

Q. "Three children and eight grandchildren. Isn't that a pretty good sized family nowadays?"

A. "Does she bring them all up? Don't they live with their own mothers?"

Q. "You know, don't you, that Mrs. Whitney in the country, close to her own house, has erected three private houses for her three children in addition to her central home down there where her eight grandchildren are being raised? Don't you know that?"

A. "No, I don't. I have never been in that house and I don't know a thing about them."

Q. "You know she has eight grandchildren, don't you?"

A. "I suppose she has if you say so."

Q. "Don't you know that she is interested in the welfare of all these children?"

A. "I don't know. What is she doing, conducting an orphan asylum? Don't their own mothers look after their own children?"

Q. "You are not listening to my question."

A. "I cannot answer such a stupid question."

Q. "You don't know what my question is going to be."

A. "I have answered what you said so far."

Q. "Now, bearing in mind the multiple responsibilities that Mrs. Whitney has outside her own family circle, her own private art museum on West 10th Street, her own activities as a sculptress, and in view of all these activities can you now or will you now tell this court any motive that Mrs. Whitney can have in her effort to keep the custody of her brother's child, excepting to care for its welfare?"

A. "That is very difficult for me to answer."

Q. "I should say so."

A. "But wait a minute. I want to say this. That if Mrs. Whitney insists upon bringing up her eight grandchildren and my child as well, she can only have a mania for rearing children."

Q. "Then your response is this—that as to your mother you think she is money-mad and as to Mrs. Whitney that she has an obsession to bring up children, is that it?"

A. "No, it is not right, it is what you say."

Q. "Haven't you said it?"

A. "No, I see no reason why Mrs. Whitney should want to bring up my child. I cannot give any reason because I do not know what her motives are. I do not pretend to be behind that brain of hers."

Q. "You know about Mrs. Whitney's philanthropies, don't you?"

A. "Yes."

Q. "Can you imagine how any philanthropic woman can be actuated by any ulterior motive to have the custody of her brother's child excepting the welfare of that child?"

A. "There is a certain little child here in New York that needs Mrs. Whitney's looking after more than mine does."

Q. "Are you trying now to bring something else into this picture that we do not know about?"

A. "You are opening many doors to me to say many things."

Q. "You can open any door and at your risk say anything you choose, but I am *now* asking you this question—can you imagine what motive Mrs. Whitney has to take care of her brother's child excepting the welfare of that child, unless you charge her, as you apparently do, with having a mania for bringing up children?"

A. "No, Mrs. Whitney has told me herself repeatedly and as she has testified on the witness stand, she has never seen me drunk or unladylike, that her mother liked me and respected me, and I really do not see why Mrs. Whitney wants my child.

"It is still a mystery to me. I can only say that if my child, after spending two years with Mrs. Whitney, is in a state of mind where she shrinks at the thought of me, then it is high time that the child should be taken away from Mrs. Whitney."

The Reputation of the Dead*

JOSEPH DEAN

It must not be assumed, because of the verdict rendered in the trial that follows, any more than in any other verdict, that justice and truth have triumphed. Even during his lifetime certain whispers attached themselves to the name of Viscount Gladstone. Queen Victoria, who it must be said was never friendly toward him or his ministry, suspected him of immoral behavior with common women. When he heard this from Lord Stanmore, Gladstone remarked, "If the Queen thinks that of me, she is quite right to treat me as she does." But the reader will note that this is not a denial, although the words may imply a denial. Certain it is that he was in the habit of walking back from the House of Commons late at night to talk with the prostitutes who spotted the pavements. Whether this was from curiosity, compassion, or other motives will now never be known.

The interesting thing to the lawyer about the cross-examination which follows is that Norman Birkett, the prosecutor, concentrates far less on the truth or falsehood of the statements about Gladstone's private life than on the character of Captain Peter Wright, the defendant. He was able, in a cross-examination which lasted three days, to make the defendant "both offensive and ridiculous." Norman Birkett is now the Right Honorable Lord Justice Birkett, Lord Justice of Appeal since 1950.

A Captain Peter Wright, old Harrovian and Balliol man and during the 1914–18 War secretary and interpreter on the Supreme War Council, had published a book of essays. One chapter of this book contained a thumb-nail sketch of the Conservative statesman, Lord Salisbury. "To high literary powers he joined an acute scientific intellect," wrote Peter Wright. "His fastidious spirit was still further repelled by Liberalism, either in its members who worshipped God and Mammon with equal zeal, assigning to Mammon the inward service and leaving God to content Himself with the outward professions, or in its leader, Gladstone, who founded the great tradition since observed by many of his followers and successors with such pious fidelity, in public to speak the language of the highest and strictest principle, and in private to pursue and possess every sort of woman."

* The selection from Joseph Dean, *Hatred, Ridicule, or Contempt,* copyright by Joseph Dean, 1953, is used with permission.

In a review of Peter Wright's book in *The Nation* the question was asked how a reputable publishing house could allow such a gross statement about Mr. Gladstone to appear. Peter Wright replied: "I referred to Gladstone's pursuit of women in his own level of life, and I had the best of reasons for so doing. Lord Milner, who was a young and active politician forty-five years ago, told me that Mr. Gladstone was governed by his seraglio."

By this time Lord Gladstone and his brother had seen the book, and they wrote the following letter:

Mr. Peter Wright,

Your garbage about Mr. Gladstone in "Portraits and Criticisms" has come to our knowledge. You are a liar. Because you slander a dead man, you are a coward. Because you think the public will accept invention from such as you, you are a fool.

GLADSTONE.

I associate myself with this letter.

H. N. GLADSTONE.

Lord Gladstone (unknown at the time to Peter Wright) sent copies of this letter to *The Nation* and to Peter Wright's publishers. Peter Wright himself sent a copy to the *Daily Mail*, together with his reply:

My Lord,—I am in receipt of your lordship's outburst dated July 22nd.

I attributed to Mr. Gladstone the character of a hypocrite in matters of sex. I have evidence of his conduct as good as any that exists about events in the past. I wrote what I did write on the authority of the late Lord Milner. (Again he quoted Lord Milner's expression.) This foible had considerable political effects. One affair turned Mr. Gladstone from being a friend of Turkey and an enemy of Russia, as he was in the 'fifties, into being a friend of Russia and an enemy of Turkey, as he was in the 'eighties.

Mr. Gladstone's hypocritical character (which in no way detracts from his merits as a public financier) is the common, though it may not be the official, reputation of him that has descended to us. It was crystallized in Labouchère's famous epigram, "that Gladstone might be caught playing cards with a fifth ace up his sleeve: but he would only explain that God had put it there." This contemporary reputation is strikingly confirmed by the circumstances of the Parnell case as we now know them. Gladstone not only connived at Parnell's illicit relations with Mrs. O'Shea: but utilised them for his own political purposes. Parnell's sin was Gladstone's opportunity. As soon as the misconduct was made known and public in divorce proceedings, Gladstone was foremost in denouncing its immorality.

This hypocrisy in the case of another is more heinous than any hypocrisy in the case of himself. Strong temptations might excuse his own departure from his own avowed principles: no such excuse can be found in the case of another. Knowing he could commit the greater offence I do not find it difficult to believe he could commit the lesser.

These various considerations prompted the remarks about Mr. Gladstone at which you take offence. Thus based, my views are unshaken even by the impact of your Lordship's controversial language, which, if I may say so without impoliteness, must rather have been acquired by practice in your Lordship's pantry than by the exercise of your Lordship's talents for debate in the House of Lords.

PETER E. WRIGHT.

The Bath Club, Dover Street, W.

Lord Gladstone now carried his offensive into the Bath Club, on whose notepaper Peter Wright's letters had been written. He sent two letters to the Secretary:

Dear Wilson Taylor,

Mr. Peter Wright appears to be a member of the Bath Club. In a book he made a foul charge against my father. He elaborated this in a letter to The Nation. . . . *He wrote on Bath Club notepaper.*

My brother and I wrote and told him that he was a liar and a coward, the law, in the case of a dead man, giving no remedy.

In a letter published this morning by the Daily Mail *he amplified his slander and his lies, not daring apparently to face us in Court. Again he writes on Bath Club notepaper. It seems to me that this is a matter for the Committee.*

Sincerely yours,

GLADSTONE.

I have this moment received a letter from Messrs. E. Nash and Grayson, Mr. Peter Wright's publishers, to say that when they accepted the work it did not contain the passage to which we take exception. Otherwise "we should have declined to publish them."

It appears they were put into a proof and when it went back to the printer the publisher did not observe them.

This shows the sort of man he is. I can tell you more about him—he is a foul fellow.

My dear Wilson Taylor,

Many thanks for your letter. Of course, I do not wish to take part personally in any discussion or action of the committee with reference to P. W. I wrote to you because I was so indignant that the fellow was sheltering in my old Club, which, for my brother, myself and my wife becomes uninhabitable so long as it is polluted by his presence.

As an "officer" in His Majesty's Army, he has accepted the description of a liar and a coward. By his baseless attacks on my father he has wantonly and deliberately insulted the fellow members of his club.

As a result of these letters Peter Wright was illegally expelled from the Bath Club—illegally because the Committee did not give him a hearing before reaching their decision—and for this wrong he obtained an injunction and £125 damages against the Club. The first of these two letters he made the subject of a libel action against Lord Gladstone. The action came on before Mr. Justice Avory and a special jury in January and February, 1927. Boyd Merriman, K.C. (now Lord Merriman), appeared for Peter Wright and Lord Gladstone was represented by Norman Birkett, K.C. (now Lord Justice Birkett).

The debunking of the Grand Old Man had shocked the country's memories, and the five days of the trial naturally attracted tremendous interest. It was really a prolonged scrutiny of Peter Wright's integrity as an author. In the witness-box he was obliged to disclose the full extent of his historical research. This was not, he declared, mere gossip, but let the reader judge for himself, as did the jury at the trial.

Peter Wright said that, while he was still at Harrow, he was told by Mr. James Haslam that Lily Langtry had been Gladstone's mistress, and in support of this charge he now produced a cartoon by Phil May headed, "We visit Mrs. Langtry," from a book called *Parson and Painter: Their Wanderings and Excursions among Men and Women,* by the Rev. Joseph Slapkins. This devastating piece of artistic evidence showed a man who closely resembled Mr. Gladstone, standing at a Stage Door and holding a bunch of Mr. Disraeli's favourite primroses.

Then Dr. Greatorex, a physician with a West End practice, had told Peter Wright of complaints by his women patients that Gladstone had tried to make their acquaintance in the street. Moreover as an Oxford undergraduate Peter Wright had heard from Walter Morison of Gladstone's relations with Olga Novikoff.

"Who," asked counsel, "was Olga Novikoff?" Peter Wright replied: "She was a very lovely Russian who was sent over by the Tsarist Government in the 'seventies for the special purpose of fascinating Mr. Gladstone, and she thoroughly succeeded." Lord Malmesbury had told him, Peter Wright explained, that the detectives who guarded Gladstone during the Fenian troubles complained that they were kept till the early hours outside Olga Novikoff's house, and yet were expected to be at early Divine Service.

But this was by no means all. A friend in Paris had told Peter Wright that a French actress called Brassine had had an intrigue with Gladstone, and Charlie Thomson, a well-known amateur steeplechaser, had mentioned that Mr. Gladstone had once tried to make advances to a lady whom he had left for a moment outside a shop.

There was Laura Bell, "the most famous courtesan of the nineteenth century," whose name had been connected with an orator and statesman "who was all things to all men and most things to most women." Even Lord Granville, Gladstone's own Foreign Secretary, had said, "I have known five of Queen Victoria's Prime Ministers, all of whom have committed adultery." An inference was also read into contrasting passages in Morley's life of Gladstone and Morgan's life of Morley concerning Gladstone's knowledge of the relations between Parnell and Mrs. O'Shea.

The whole thing was clinched, Peter Wright felt, by what Lord Milner had told him. "After Lord Milner had used that phrase," Wright said, "I remember asking him about Mr. Gladstone's relations with Olga Novikoff. Lord Milner said nothing, but fell into his ordinary reserve." Here the Judge put a question:

"Were any other words used except 'being governed by his seraglio'?"—I cannot remember."

"In connection with what matter," Merriman asked, "did Lord Milner use the phrase?"—"The change of relations between England and Turkey."

Apart from these reports from highly varied sources, Peter Wright relied in one instance upon the evidence of his own eyes, perhaps the most deadly piece of direct evidence with which a party has ever destroyed his own case.

"About fourteen years ago," he said, "I saw at Eastbourne a man named Cecil Gladstone whose resemblance to the statesman was unmistakable. I was told he was an illegitimate son, but I cannot identify my informant."

"Of what kind was the resemblance?" his counsel asked.—"Facial. I should say that he was a larger and inferior edition of Mr. Gladstone."

"Was he inferior in point of intellect?" asked Avory.—"He had not the distinguished air of the statesman."

This was the sum of Peter Wright's inside information. It was Norman Birkett's task to show, if he could, that the witness had been dishonestly indifferent to the truth or falsity of his charge against Gladstone. In a cross-examination which persisted into three days, he was able, not only to go far towards this objective, but also to make the forty-six-year-old Captain appear—by comparison with the Gladstone brothers, who were both in their seventies—both offensive and ridiculous.

"Do you regard yourself," was Birkett's first question, "as a serious journalist?"—"I try not to be dull."

"Does that mean that all serious people are bores?" snapped the Judge, and Birkett changed the adjective. "Do you regard yourself as a responsible journalist?"—"Certainly. The newspapers treat me as one, and I conclude that I am one. I speak the truth."

"Do you agree that the charge you make is about as horrible a charge as can be made?"—"No, because it has been made against innumerable great men."

"Is it a charge that Mr. Gladstone was a gross sensualist?"—"Yes, I think
    that that describes him."
"Is not a charge that a man is a gross sensualist one of the most horrible
    charges that can be made against him?"—"No, because it has been
    made against innumerable great men."
"Is it not a charge which reflects on all the women who honoured Glad-
    stone with their friendship?"—"No, certainly not. He might behave
    very well at Carlton Gardens, but not elsewhere."
"Do you agree that it is a very grave charge of hypocrisy?"—"Oh, yes.
    That is what this charge is. It is much more a charge of hypocrisy than
    one of immorality."
"His religion, you intended to say, was a mockery?"—"No, Gladstone
    was not like ordinary people."
"Does it not mean that he was the rankest kind of hypocrite?"—"Yes, but,
    being a wonderful sort of man, he was a wonderful sort of hypocrite."
"Does it not follow from that that his professed religion was a simple
    mockery?"—"No, because he was such an actor and he threw himself
    so entirely into the part that he became it." One could not say, the
    Captain added, that Mr. Gladstone disbelieved what he said, and yet
    he acted in a way which was a complete contradiction of what he
    had said.
Birkett read the passage in Lord Rosebery's panegyric on Gladstone
which referred to Mrs. Gladstone as having "for sixty years shared all the
sorrows and all the joys of Mr. Gladstone's life, received his confidence,
shared his triumphs, and cheered him in his defeats."
"Is this charge of yours that Mr. Gladstone was faithless to that wife of
    sixty years?"—"Yes, of course it is. Men who are very fond of their
    wives are often faithless to them."
"Do you regard immorality in a man as an ordinary thing?"—"No. I re-
    gard it as culpable."
"But not horrible?"—"No." The Captain agreed, however, that his charge,
    if made falsely, was a foul charge, though a person who made it
    falsely was not necessarily a "foul fellow." That, he said, was Lord
    Gladstone's bad English; "foul fellow" meant a dissolute person.
"If a person made a foul charge against you or your dead father what
    would you call him in your beautiful English?"—"I should call him
    intemperate." But Peter Wright admitted that a man who made a
    false charge without evidence, or without caring whether it was true
    or not, would be a liar.
Birkett continued to lay the foundations of his attack.
"Do you agree that a great degree of care is required in writing about
    the living when you are making serious charges?"—"Care to speak the
    truth? Yes, certainly."
"Do you agree that in the case of the dead who cannot speak for them-

selves a greater degree of care is required?"—"I think that the same degree of care is required for both."

"When a writer makes a serious charge against a dead man, would you regard that as a responsible task?"—"A serious writer ought to regard all he writes as a responsible task."

"A responsible journalist would regard it as his duty to verify the facts before making a serious charge against anybody?"—"Not if he thought that he knew them: otherwise he could never write anything."

"He might proceed upon information given to him without verifying a single thing if he had formed a decided opinion?"—"In this case my charge against Gladstone is one primarily of hypocrisy. If a man has formed that opinion, and the reason is there, why should he go through some process of verification? It would paralyse him."

The debonair self-assurance of some of these replies had made its impression on the Court. Birkett then began to investigate Peter Wright's sources. With regard to Lord Milner's phrase about Gladstone's "seraglio," Peter Wright alluded to T. P. O'Connor's obituary notice of Lord Milner for confirmation that Milner had used the expression. But what T. P. O'Connor wrote, referring to Milner as a young man, was this: "If Gladstone were mentioned—Gladstone was then in the zenith of the blind worship which he received from so many millions of his fellow citizens—the tall young scholar, straight apparently from the college hall, would answer with a laugh that you could not tell what Gladstone was going to do till you knew what the seraglio had decided: it was by this disrespectful word, said with a laugh, that the daring and sceptical youngster spoke of the devoted wife and daughter who looked after the domestic comforts of the great liberal leader."

But when this passage was read to him, Peter Wright remained unconvinced. "In the mouth of a man like Lord Milner, who was a great literary artist even when he was a young man," he said, " 'seraglio' could not mean wife and daughter." Even when he had read, at Birkett's request, a passage from the *Life of Dr. Johnson,* in which Boswell says, "We surely cannot but admire the benevolent exertions of this great and good man. . . . He has sometimes suffered me to talk jocularly of his group of females and call them his 'seraglio' "—even then Peter Wright was sure that, while Boswell might jest, Lord Milner would not.

"A literary artist might use the word jocularly?"—"Yes, but Lord Milner was not a jester, although he was sometimes ironical and sarcastic. At the end of his life he had not the wonderful style he had as a young man, but he spoke very precise English."

Birkett turned his attention to the little matter of Gladstone's putative bastard observed by Peter Wright in Eastbourne.

"Did you make any enquires [*sic*] about Cecil Gladstone?" he asked.—

"I did not deliberately make enquiries. I should never write anything if I did."

"You believed what you heard and acted upon it?"—"I did."

Counsel handed up to the witness a birth and a marriage certificate, each stating that Cecil Gladstone was the son of William Gladstone, general merchant. Peter Wright now fell into the trap which Birkett set for him.

"So those two documents would appear to show the birth of Cecil Gladstone?" he was asked. "Yes, to William Gladstone."

"You want to emphasise the 'William' to the jury?"—"Yes: they both have the same Christian name and surname."

"You mean that William Ewart Gladstone was also a William?"—"Yes."

"The certificates would appear to show that Cecil Gladstone was the son of William Gladstone, a merchant?"—"A general merchant, yes, a very large category of people."

"Do you think that a Prime Minister is covered by that description?"— "I don't know that it does not. You are trying to show that Cecil Gladstone cannot be the son of the statesman, but I am not certain whether your proof is quite conclusive."

Cecil Gladstone's death certificate was next produced.

"Is the widow alive?"—"I don't know."

"Do you know whether she lives in Eastbourne now?"—"I do not."

"You have never made an enquiry about it?"—"No: I was only showing the process of thought by which I arrived at my conclusion."

"About what you were told by people whom you do not remember?"— "Whom I do not identify."

"Your words yesterday were 'Persons I cannot remember,'" snapped Mr. Justice Avory, and Birkett went remorselessly on:

"You never from that day made any enquiry?"—"Certainly not."

"Do these documents influence your judgment at all?"—"They don't seem to be quite so very conclusive on your side, because, if Gladstone had an illegitimate son, this is rather the way in which he would deal with it. It does not seem completely to refute my view."

"In your view these documents are forgeries reeking with false information?"—"They might be."

"Given by a Prime Minister of this country?"—"If he had an illegitimate son; but he was not Prime Minister at the time."

"You think the certificates are full of false information?"—"Yes, by a Cabinet Minister who did not dare speak the truth."

Birkett now held up *Lodge's Peerage*, wherein it was disclosed that Cecil Gladstone's father William was Gladstone's first cousin, a fact which might not unnaturally account for the facial likeness. Wright was obliged to withdraw his accusation. Then came the inevitable question:

"Don't you think that you should be more careful before you make suggestions?"

Birkett, having made the killing as painful and protracted as possible, then held a *post mortem* on the incident. "When you saw the birth certificate, did it not seem to you that it was not usual for an illegitimate son to be registered in the name of his father?"—"It did not: but if a child were the illegitimate son of a statesman it would not be registered in his name."

"When I asked you whether a Cabinet Minister would be likely to be guilty of forgery and lying, your suggestion still was that Gladstone might have had something to do with it?"—"No, you were trying to suggest that because a man was a Cabinet Minister he could not speak an untruth, and I thought that that was a forensic trick."

"You now agree that the information on which you acted was quite unreliable?"—"Yes, but I thought I was right at the time."

Birkett next disposed of the French actress, Brassine, in a few short questions—all of which he then put into one omnibus question: "Apart from the fact that a man, now dead, told you as a lad of twenty that an actress twenty years before had an intrigue in London with Gladstone when he was seventy-two, you made no further enquiries?"—"No: why should I?"

After some further questions, Birkett said,

"Lord Milner is dead, Haslam is dead, Dr. Greatorex is dead; Morison is dead, Novikoff is dead, Laura Bell is dead, Sir Francis Burnand is dead, Labouchère is dead, and Lord Morley is dead?"—"Yes: and Gladstone was born six years before the battle of Waterloo."

"It is difficult when people are dead to get at the exact facts?"—"Nearly every character in history is dead; I don't know whether you have observed that, Mr. Birkett."

"Where is Charlie Thomson? Is he alive?"—"I don't know."

"Mrs. Langtry is alive, is she not?"—"Yes, she lives on the Riviera."

"Did you think that the charge you made might cause her grievous pain?" —"Yes, I am afraid it would; it is most annoying to think that I might cause grief to a living person. I am very sorry about it; more than I can say."

"Did you ever speak to Mrs. Langtry in your life?"—"No. I have seen her, of course."

On the next morning of the trial Birkett read a telegram which had been sent to him personally from Monte Carlo: "Strongly repudiate slanderous accusations by Peter Wright. Lily Langtry." Peter Wright's counsel allowed this message to be put in as evidence, a gesture which was tantamount to dropping this charge also.

But Peter Wright would not yet admit defeat. When Birkett, turning to

Madame Novikoff, said that he had all her correspondence with Gladstone in Court, and asked Peter Wright:

"Are you prepared to accept that in not one of those letters is there the faintest hint of impropriety?"—the reply was, "I should be perfectly certain of it where Gladstone was concerned."

"May I take it that had you known every word of the correspondence between Madame Novikoff and Mr. Gladstone it would not have made any difference to what you said?"—"No, because the very charge I made was one of hypocrisy."

"Do you know that physically she was most unattractive?"—"I certainly do not. I always heard the very opposite." (Later Merriman countered this suggestion by producing two photographs. The Judge said, "Can I take judicial notice of when a woman is seductive?" to which Merriman replied, "Your Lordship can take judicial notice of whether Mr. Birkett's question was well founded.")

Lord Gladstone had actually known Madame Novikoff and would be able to tell the Court about her, but Peter Wright dismissed his evidence in advance by calling him "the arch-humbug." And even if Lord Gladstone swore that his father knew nothing of the relationship between Parnell and Mrs. O'Shea, it would only be "a typical instance of Gladstonian humbug."

When the time came for Laura Bell to be discussed, Birkett produced another certificate—her marriage to Mr. Thistlethwaite, and asked, "Did you know that she had lived with her husband till his death?"—"He shot himself, poor chap," was the answer.

"Did you know that at the inquest his death was stated to be accidental?" —"No, but it makes no difference to my opinion."

"Did you know she was a very religious woman when she met Gladstone?"—"She combined preaching with being a courtesan, which was one of the most remarkable things about her," the witness responded, adding that Gladstone had taught her the preaching.

Gradually Birkett wore his agile opponent down. He attacked his motives.

"The offending sentence about Lord Gladstone is not essential to your article on Lord Robert Cecil and the League of Nations?"—"Digression is one of the arts of essay writing. This is an essay, not an affidavit."

"It appears to be as unreliable," growled the Judge.

"Do you think it would be a cowardly thing to slander the dead?"—"All history, as someone has said, is a register of crimes and follies, and so nearly all history is a slander of dead men. All history cannot be abolished for the benefit of Mr. Gladstone."

"That," said the Judge, "is not an answer to the question. Is your answer No?"

The answer was that it was not cowardly if the slanderer was writing as a historian.

"You do not suggest that you were writing this essay in the role of a
historian?" Birkett asked, and he had really returned to his first question of all.

But the cross-examination was not over. It was suggested that Wright
was a coward, not only for slandering the dead, but also because of his
reluctance to bring this action. This he denied. Every libel must be "published," and before any action for damages can be brought, the libeller
must publish it to some one other than the libellee. Peter Wright's explanation was that he did not know Lord Gladstone's first letter had been published to a third party until after he had published it himself by sending
it to the *Daily Mail* together with his reply—a step which naturally deprived
him of any right to claim damages for it in a libel action. Some doubt was
thrown on the genuineness of this explanation by a sentence which he had
written in a letter to Lord Gladstone—"Weak and dull as my poor weapon
of controversy is . . . I disdain to lift its point against so unworthy a
descendant of so mighty a sire." This matter, however, was perhaps an unworthy one to be raised against the Plaintiff. For when Lord Gladstone repeated his charges in his letter to the Bath Club and in the course of time
Peter Wright issued his writ, Lord Gladstone pleaded, not only that his
charges were true, but also, whether they were true or not, that they were
published "on a privileged occasion" and therefore not actionable except
upon proof of malice.

  Lord Gladstone, however, when giving his evidence, said that this defence was put in without his instructions. When asked whether he
  wished to stand by it (a question which Avory ruled out of order)
  he declared, "I wish that the case should be decided in its broad public
  aspect—to determine whether Captain Wright was justified in what he
  said and whether I was justified in using the words which I did in
  denouncing it."
  "Proceedings might have been taken on the first letter," the Judge muttered, "when no question of privilege would have arisen."
  "Does your Lordship seriously suggest that?" asked Merriman.
  "I never suggest anything in a Court of Law unless I suggest seriously,"
  was Avory's testy answer. And Merriman was left to say, "Your Lordship has given an answer which the witness should have given. I cannot cross-examine your Lordship, and so I will leave it."
  Birkett now drew Peter Wright's attention to Gladstone's work for the
  rescue of women from the streets as a possible explanation of the many
  rumours which had been circulated. In 1848 Gladstone had been one
  of the founders of the Church Penitentiary Association for the Rec-
  lamation of Fallen Women, and had contributed throughout his life
  to this and similar charities. "If," asked Birkett, "a man spends his

time sincerely employed in the work of reclaiming fallen women, so that he speaks to them in the street and visits them in their homes, do you think that that is liable to misconception?"—"There is," Wright replied, "a genuine difficulty in the way of my answering that, and I cannot do so."

Peter Wright felt very strongly about the terms of Lord Gladstone's letter to the Club. "Lord Gladstone first made a charge of mendacity and then one of cowardice," he exclaimed. "Then he thought that that was not quite hot enough to get me expelled from the Club, so he added a charge of trickery, and thinking that that was not strong enough he called me a foul fellow."

Birkett: "Did you think that he would write with indignation?"—"Yes, but when one writes with indignation one should take care to write the exact truth."

"When you are writing, with or without indignation, about a charge which defames the memory of a great man you should write with great care?"—"Not when you write a book with a paltry circulation of 500 copies. A single sentence in an obscure and unsuccessful book would not have the serious result of a letter sent for the purpose of getting a man expelled from a Club."

"Did you," asked Mr. Justice Avory, "expect your book to be obscure and unsuccessful?"—"I did not expect it to have any great success," was Peter Wright's answer. "I spoke of Gladstone as a historical figure, as I would have done of Wellington or Napoleon." He had no intention, he said, of hurting Gladstone's family.

"Does this mean," the Judge asked, "that you now regret and are sorry for having written this?"—"My Lord, I—"

"Do give me a direct answer to that question. You say that if you had had an opportunity you would have expressed regret. Are you sorry that you wrote it?"—"Yes, my Lord: but it is difficult to express it if Lord Gladstone does not retract the abusive language which he used. I do not regret it because it is untrue, but because it caused pain to his family. I would still express regret if they would retract the statement that I am a liar, a coward, and a fool. I regret that I hurt their feelings."

"Do you think it is any satisfaction to say to a person: I regret that I said what I did, but it is true?"—"I would say that I did not want to hurt their feelings."

"I hope," Merriman intervened, "your Lordship will ask the same question of the defendant."

Birkett continued to press Wright on this point, until the witness became annoyed and finally said, emphasising each word by striking the front of the witness-box: "I regret most emphatically hurting the feelings of

Lord Gladstone and his family, and if they had given me anything of a chance I would have said so. I would say it now."

"Don't," said the Judge, "knock the furniture about."

When Peter Wright left the witness-box after ten-and-a-half hours under fire he had already lost the battle. The thing then turned into a rout. Birkett opened the defence with a scathing attack on the plaintiff, and then put the defendant into the witness-box. As Lord Gladstone had been from 1880 a Member both of the House of Commons and of the Government, and had lived with his father until his death in 1898, he was able to speak with personal knowledge of events and personalities which were known to Peter Wright only by hearsay. Lord Gladstone denied every charge absolutely.

There was no doubt that Mr. Justice Avory had taken an unfavourable view of the plaintiff from early in his examination. His questions were all, so to speak, one way.

To Lord Gladstone, however, he was nothing but helpful. Speaking of Labouchère's epigram, Lord Gladstone said, "It was a gibe, and to some extent a very very clever gibe."

Mr. Justice Avory: "Was he a jester?"—"Oh, very much so."

Merriman: "Sometimes the truth is spoken in jest and sometimes it is clothed in jest."

Mr. Justice Avory: "Is not Labouchère famous for having said during a debate in the House of Commons on a proposed new railway in the Lake District, that, in his opinion, no landscape was complete without a railway train in the distance?"

Merriman read to Lord Gladstone an article in *Vanity Fair* which hinted at an intrigue between Gladstone and Madame Novikoff, an article of which no notice had been taken, and asked:

"Had not Mr. Gladstone the plainest cause to sue *Vanity Fair* for saying that his public conduct was influenced by his immoral relations with Madame Novikoff?" But the Judge nullified the question by observing: "If that action were tried before me I should have to consider whether the words were capable of any such meaning. The whole article is directed to the suggestion that Mr. Gladstone was improperly negotiating with a Russian agent" (and not carrying on a clandestine love affair). Merriman pressed the matter, and the Judge put in the question which normally would have had to wait for re-examination: "So far as you know, did your father ever see that article?"

When Lord Gladstone was asked what evidence he had for supposing that the Gladstone-Novikoff correspondence was complete, the Judge interrupted, "How can he answer that question?" But he could: anyone looking through the pile, he said, could see there were no gaps. What was more, as his father's private secretary he had opened all his correspondence without restrictions.

But with or without the hostility of the Judge counsel for Peter Wright had virtually nothing to go on. Apart from the article in *Vanity Fair* and Mrs. O'Shea's assertion that Gladstone was always aware of her relations with Parnell, the most that was established by the cross-examination of Lord Gladstone was that on a number of occasions his father had been called a hypocrite—a charge which few Prime Ministers escape.

Lord Gladstone was supported by his brother, and after their evidence no one wished to dispute their honourable intentions. "We were the only sons living, and as soon as we had gone there would be nobody with our knowledge of the facts. It was our duty to force him into a Court of Law so that we might have justice done to our father."

Lord Phillimore, Lord Malmesbury, Lady Gwendoline Cecil and Mr. T. P. O'Connor also gave evidence. The latter, who had been a Member of the House since 1880, and was an intimate friend of Parnell's, threw light on that interesting period of Irish politics. In his opinion Gladstone neither knew nor thought of the Parnell-O'Shea liaison. Of the relations between Mr. and Mrs. Gladstone he said, that "the extraordinary solicitude with which Mrs. Gladstone watched the comings and goings of her husband was notorious, and there was evidence of it every day in the House of Commons and the Lobby. There was a special corner of the Speaker's Gallery where she was to be seen as inevitably as was Mr. Gladstone in the House whenever he had a great speech to make. Very often she was in the inner lobby waiting to take him home, and she would muffle him up if the weather were bad."

Peter Wright's publisher was called. He swore that he had no knowledge of the offending passage, which was inserted in the galley proofs. Merriman read to him some passages in other books which he had recently published. First of all there was an authoress who called herself, "A woman of no importance" who had written:

"We have lately heard a good deal about Lord Beaconsfield's love affairs, but not much of Gladstone's. This is not fair, for he had quite a pretty taste in women—why should he have been less human than the rest of the world . . . ? I could tell some very illuminating stories if so inclined, but will only say that I have seen him indulging in little tender transports of love and rapture. I once accidentally surprised him kissing, quite a harmless little affair, but it impressed itself upon my memory, for she was pretty, soft and round, while he looked like a hungry hawk, with fierce eyes and beak pecking at her. He was a wonderful man, and in his old age distinctly amorous."

Then there was a book called *The Fall of Tsardom*, wherein it was written of Madame Novikoff: "She is well known and had many friends. . . .

There was a time when Madame X was a greater power for Tsardom than she is to-day. . . . At the height of her fame she cast her spell successfully over no less a person than William Ewart Gladstone . . . but now her influence has waned and Tsardom has cast her off, but she is still with us."

The Judge objected to the reading of "this tosh," but he gave Norman Birkett in re-examination permission to read another passage from this book—so that the jury might know the kind of book it was. The words which Birkett read to an amused Court were these:

"In the half-lighted shades and the perfume-laden atmosphere, as her victim reclined at ease with his feet on the mantelpiece, she carefully displays her well-rounded arms and snowy neck, and whispers about that Bill in Congress as if her soul lay in its rejection."

The last witness for the defence was a surprise. Birkett called Mr. Charlie Thomson, the steeplechaser who had told Peter Wright the story of Gladstone's attempt to pick up a lady in the street. He had indeed told Peter Wright the story, and Peter Wright had asked him to send it in a letter to the Committee of the Bath Club, but on consideration he had written to Peter Wright, refusing to have anything more to do with it, partly because he thought it unfair to the memory of Gladstone, partly because the lady in question was of doubtful character and what she said might be open to suspicion. The case was complete.

At long last the time had come for "final speeches" and summing up. The issues and the state of the evidence were by now very clear. But Avory's summing up was needlessly partial: he took the bad as well as the good points against the plaintiff. On the issue of malice, for instance, which only arose if the jury rejected Lord Gladstone's defence of justification, he as good as directed a verdict for the defendant. "The mere fact that language was intemperate would not, in the absence of evidence that it was not used bona fide, be evidence of malice. If the defendant was actuated by righteous indignation or a desire to do his duty he would be protected even if his language was violent or excessively strong. They must bear that in mind in deciding whether the defendant was actuated by malice, i.e., a desire to do something other than that which it was his duty to do—namely, refute this calumny and vindicate his father's name." How this end could be furthered by an attempt to expel Peter Wright from his club the Judge did not explain. On the main question of justification it was perhaps unnecessary, in view of what had been demonstrated in the witness-box, for the Judge to emphasise his own opinion. But he stigmatised Peter Wright's case with one of his favourite alliterations: "If history is to be made of the tittle-tattle of the Upper Tooting tea-tables, you will no doubt consider whether it would not be better that history should not be made at all."

"Is not the man who slanders the dead a coward?" Avory continued. "Is not a man who makes a foul charge a 'foul fellow'? The plaintiff has chosen to put upon that expression an extravagant meaning—that he is a person

of dissolute and vicious life—but the primary meaning of 'foul' is 'unclean,'
and a secondary meaning is that a foul fellow is one who uses scurrilous
or abusive language or one who indulges in foul play. Shakespeare, whom
the plaintiff would no doubt deem to be no less eminent than himself, wrote:

> 'Is't not enough thou hast suborned these women
> To accuse this worthy man, but, in foul mouth
> And in the witness of his proper ear, to call him villain?' "

The jury were out for two-and-a-half hours. At 7.15 P.M. the Court re-
assembled, and Avory said:

"I understand that you are agreed that the gist of the defendant's letter
of July 27th is true?" To which the foreman answered, "That is so, my Lord."

"Then," said the Judge, "you need not trouble about the other matter
(the question of malice)—that was only an alternative. This is a verdict for
the defendant."

The verdict was greeted with loud applause. When this had been suppressed, the foreman of the jury announced: "We are of unanimous opinion
that the evidence which has been placed before us has completely vindicated
the high moral character of the late Mr. W. E. Gladstone."

Norman Birkett thanked the jury for these words, and as the Court rose
a throng of friends and admirers pressed round Lord and Lady Gladstone
and Mr. H. N. Gladstone and congratulated them on their family victory.
The idol of the English Liberal tradition remained unfallen.

Section IV

THE LAW

On the Law*

MONTAIGNE

There is more to law than the lawyer, the judge, and the courtroom—more than the law or a law, as a matter of fact, for there is the theory of law and the relation of law and justice. Many writers and philosophers have spoken on the principles of law. One of the ablest was Michel de Montaigne (1533–1592), the father of the essay, typical man of the Renaissance. His essays are the flowers of a lifetime of study, of observation, of thought, of travel. The topics range from cannibalism to the education of children. Although Montaigne was a skeptic—his motto was Que sçay-je? (What do I know?)—he could be mellow, even sentimental and idealistic; thus, though he influenced Bacon, the men were not spiritually akin.

Although the Florio translation remains a favorite for its color and contemporaneity, the modern Trechmann version is given here lest the Elizabethan idiom of the former trouble the reader and because the latter is more accurate. Montaigne's remarks are taken from the essay "Of Experience."

There is no more natural desire than the desire for knowledge. We try all ways that may lead us to it. When reason fails we resort to experience:

> By various proofs Experience art has made,
> Example pointing out the way; (MANILIUS.)

which is a more ineffectual and less worthy means. But the truth is so great a thing that we should despise no means that may lead us to it. Reason has so many shapes that we know not which to lay hold of: experience has no fewer. The inference we try to draw from the likeness of events is uncertain, because they are always unlike.

No quality is so universal, in the appearance of things, as diversity and variety. To express the highest degree of similarity, both the Greeks and Latins, as well as ourselves, use eggs as an example. Yet there have been men, and notably one at Delphi, who could distinguish marks of difference in different eggs so well that he never mistook one for another. And

* From *The Essays of Montaigne*, translated by E. J. Trechmann, Oxford University Press. Used by permission of the publishers.

although he had a great number of hens he was able to tell which of them laid a particular egg.

Dissimilarity intrudes of itself into our works; no skill can attain similarity. Neither Perrozet nor any other can smoothe and whiten the backs of his cards so carefully that no gamester can distinguish between them on merely seeing them slipping through another's hands. Resemblance does not make things so much alike as difference makes them unlike. Nature has obliged herself to make nothing other that was not unlike.

Therefore I do not much like the opinion of the man who thought that to multiply the laws was to curb the authority of the judges, by cutting up their meat for them. He did not realize that there was as much liberty and latitude in interpreting the laws as in the making of them. And they fool themselves who think they can lessen and put a stop to our disputes by referring us to the actual words of the Bible, since our mind finds the field no less spacious for controverting another's meaning than for urging its own. As if we showed less animosity and tartness in commenting than in inventing!

We see how much he was mistaken. For in France we have more laws than all the rest of the world together, and more than necessary to rule all the worlds of Epicurus. *As formerly we suffered from crimes, so now we suffer from the laws* (Tacitus). And yet we have left so much to the opinions and decisions of our judges that there has never been such complete liberty and licence.

What have our legislators gained by selecting a hundred thousand particular cases and actions, and applying to them a hundred thousand laws? This number is quite out of proportion to the infinite variety of human actions. By multiplying our invented cases we shall never arrive at the number and variety of possible cases. Add to them a hundred times as many more, and yet no future case will ever be found so to tally with, so exactly to fit and match another of the many thousands of selected and registered cases, that there will not remain some circumstance and diversity that will require a separate consideration and decision.

There is little relation between our actions, which are perpetually changing, and fixed and unchangeable laws. The most desirable laws are those which are most rare, most simple and general; and I still believe it would be better to have none at all, than to have them in such numbers as we have.

The laws that Nature gives us are always happier than those we give ourselves. Witness the Golden Age as depicted by the poets, and the condition in which we see those nations to be living which have no other laws.

Here we have a people who have no judges, but call upon the first traveller who passes through their mountains to decide their quarrels for them. And these others elect one from among themselves, on market-days, to settle all their suits on the spot.

Where would be the danger if the wisest should thus settle ours, according to the circumstances and at sight, without being tied to precedents and issues? To every foot its shoe.

When King Ferdinand sent colonists to the Indies he wisely provided that they should take with them no men learned in the law, for fear lest law-suits might breed in that new world, since it is a branch of learning that of its nature generates altercations and divisions; deciding, with Plato, that "lawyers and doctors are a bad provision for a country."

Why is it that our common language, so easy for all other uses, becomes obscure and unintelligible in wills and contracts, and that this language that can express itself so clearly, whatever it may say or write, here finds no way of declaring its meaning that does not involve doubt and contradiction? Unless it be that the princes of that art, applying themselves with a particular attention to picking out solemn words and contriving artful formulas, have so carefully weighed each syllable and so accurately analysed every kind of combination that we see them trammelled and embroiled in the endless number of figures and such minute partitions that they cease to fall within any rule and prescription, and to convey any definite meaning. *Whatever is beaten into powder becomes confused* (Seneca).

Have you ever seen a boy attempting to divide a quantity of quicksilver into a certain number of parts? The more he works and squeezes it, and tries to bring it under control the more does he provoke the freedom of that noble metal; it escapes his ingenuity, and keeps dispersing into small particles beyond all reckoning. So it is here; for by subdividing those subtleties they teach men to increase their doubts; they put us into a way of magnifying and diversifying the difficulties; they lengthen them out and disperse them. By scattering questions abroad and cutting them up they make the world to fructify and abound in uncertainties and quarrels; as the earth is made more fertile the more deeply it is dug up and crumbled. *It is learning that creates difficulties* (Quintilian).

We are perplexed by Ulpian; we are still perplexed by Bartolus and Baldus. We should blot out all traces of these innumerable differences of opinion, instead of using them to show off our learning and swelling the heads of posterity with them. I know not what to say to it, but experience tells us that so many interpretations disperse the truth and destroy it.

Aristotle wrote to be understood; since he was expressing his own ideas, if he did not succeed, still less will another succeed who is not so clever as Aristotle. We open the matter, and spread it out by diluting it; of one subject we make a thousand, and by multiplying and subdividing fall again into the infinity of atoms of Epicurus.

Never did two men judge alike on the same matter; it is impossible to find two opinions exactly agreeing, not only in different persons, but in the same person at different times. I commonly find matter for doubt in a thing of which the commentator has disdained to take notice. I am most apt to trip on smooth ground, like certain horses that I know, that more often stumble on a level road.

Who would not say that glosses increase doubt and ignorance, since there is no book about which the world busies itself, whether of human or divine origin, of which the difficulties evaporate by interpretation? The hundredth commentator hands it on to his successor, more knotty and slippery than the first had found it. When did we ever agree that "this book has been sufficiently commented upon, that there is henceforth nothing more to be said about it?"

This is best seen in law-practice. We attribute legal authority to an endless number of doctors, an endless number of judgements and as many interpretations. And yet do we see any end to the need of interpreting? Do we see any progress and advance towards peace? Do we need fewer lawyers and judges than when this great body of law was yet in its first infancy? On the contrary, we darken and bury the understanding; we discover it only hidden behind so many hedges and barriers.

Men do not realize the natural infirmity of their mind; it does nothing but ferret and hunt around, incessantly wheeling about, contriving, involving itself in its own work, like a silkworm, and there suffocating. *A mouse in a barrel of pitch* (Latin proverb).

It thinks it sees in the distance something like a glimmer of light and imaginary truth; but, while it is hastening thither, its path is crossed by so many difficulties, so many obstacles and so many new quests, that it goes off the track and becomes dazed. Not much unlike the dogs in Aesop's fable who, discovering something resembling a dead body floating on the sea, and unable to come near it, set to work to drink up the water and lay the passage dry, and choke themselves. . . .

Since the ethical laws, which are concerned with the individual duties of every man in himself, are so difficult to establish, as we see them to be, it is no wonder if those which govern so many individuals are more so. Consider the form of this justice which rules us; it is a true testimony of human feebleness, so full is it of errors and contradictions. What we regard as partiality and severity in justice—and we find so much of them, that I doubt whether impartiality is as often met with—are sickly parts and unjust members of the very body and essence of justice.

Some countrymen recently informed me in great haste that they had just left, in a wood that belongs to me, a man with a hundred wounds, still breathing, who entreated them for pity's sake to give him water and help him to rise. They said they did not dare to go near him, and ran away for fear the officers of justice might catch them there, and (as happens with those who are found near a murdered person) they should be made accountable for that mischance, which would be their undoing, since they had neither the ability nor the money to defend their innocence. What could I say to them? It is certain that that act of humanity would have brought them into trouble.

How many innocent people we have known to be punished, I mean without the fault of the judges; and how many are there that we have not known of! This happened in my time: Certain men are condemned to death for murder; the sentence, if not pronounced, is at least decided and fixed. At that point the judges are informed, by the officers of an inferior court near by, that they hold several men in custody who openly confess to that murder, and are able to throw a light on the whole business that admits of no doubt. And yet they deliberate whether they shall interrupt and defer the execution of the sentence passed upon the first accused. They consider the novelty of the case, and its consequence for suspending judgements; that the sentence is juridically passed, and the judges have no reason to repent of it. To sum up, those poor devils are sacrificed to the forms of justice.

Philip, or some other, dealt with a like dilemma in this way: He had pronounced judgement on a man and condemned him to pay a heavy fine to another. The true facts of the case having come to light some time after, it was found that he had condemned him wrongfully. On the one side was the right of the cause, on the other the right of judicial forms. He in some sort satisfied both by allowing the sentence to stand, and making up the loss to the condemned out of his own purse.

But he had to do with a retrievable miscarriage; my men were irretrievably hanged. How many condemnations I have witnessed more criminal than the crime!

All this brings to my mind these ancient theses: That he must needs do wrong in detail who would do right wholesale, and injustice in little things if he would achieve justice in great;

That human justice is formed after the model of medicine, according to which all that is profitable is also right and honest;

That, as the Stoics hold, Nature herself, in most of her works, goes against justice;

That, as the Cyrenaics contend, there is nothing just of itself; that customs and laws make justice;

That, according to the Theodorians, the wise man is right to commit theft, sacrilege, every kind of lechery, if he knows it to be profitable to him.

There is no remedy. I agree with Alcibiades, and will never, if I can help it, place myself in the power of a man who can dispose of my head, when my honour and life depend on the skill and activity of a solicitor more than on my innocence. I would risk a kind of justice that would take account of my good actions as well as my bad; that would give me as much cause to hope as to fear. To be indemnified is not sufficient coin for a man who does better than not to go wrong. Our justice offers us only one of her hands, and that is the left. Let him be who he may, he comes off with loss.

In China, a kingdom whose governments and arts, having had no contact with or knowledge of ours, offer examples that surpass ours in many excellent features; from whose history I learn how much wider and more diverse the world is than either the ancients or we moderns have been able to conceive, the officers deputed by the ruler to inspect the condition of the provinces, whilst punishing those who are guilty of corruption in administering their office, also reward, from pure liberality, those whose conduct has been more than ordinarily honourable, and more so than mere duty required. These men come forward not only to answer for their conduct but to gain; not to be simply paid but to receive a present.

No judge has yet, thank God, spoken to me as a judge in any cause whatsoever, whether my own or another's, whether criminal or civil. No prison has ever received me, not even as a visitor. Imagination makes even the outside of a jail odious to me. I am so hungry for freedom that if any one were to forbid me access to some corner of the Indies I should feel my life to be a little more constrained. And as long as I can find earth and air free and open elsewhere, I will never lurk in a place where I must hide.

Good heavens, how I should chafe if I were reduced to the condition of so many people I know of, riveted to a district of this kingdom, deprived of the right to enter the chief towns and courts and to make use of the public roads, for having quarrelled with our laws! If those laws I observe were to threaten only the tip of my little finger I should immediately go in search of others, wherever they may be. All the little caution I possess, in these Civil wars in which we are engaged, is exercised to prevent their curtailing my freedom of coming and going.

Now the laws maintain their credit not because they are just but because they are laws. That is the mystic foundation of their authority, and they have no other. And that is, indeed, their advantage. They are often made by fools; more often by men who, in their hatred of equality, are wanting in equity; but always by men, vain and unsteadfast authors. Nothing is so clumsily and widely, nor so ordinarily, faulty as the laws. Whoever obeys them because they are just does not obey them for the reason for which they should rightly be obeyed.

Our French laws, by their irregularity and formlessness, rather lend a helping hand to the confusion and corruption that we see in their administration and execution. Their authority is so confused and inconsistent that in some sort it excuses both disobedience and mistakes in their interpretation, administration and observance. Whatever then may be the fruit of experience, that which we derive from foreign examples will make us little wiser if we profit so little from that which we have of ourselves, which is more familiar to us, and certainly sufficient to tell us what we need.

I study myself more than any other subject; that is my Metaphysics, that is my Physics;

> With how much skill this mighty world is ruled;
> Whence comes the rising moon, and where she sets;
> How 'tis she joins her horns, and every month
> Comes to the full; where winds surmount the sea;
> What regions Eurus seizes with his blast;
> Why waters turn to clouds; if ever a day
> Will come, when all these earthly towers
> Are overthrown: let them inquire whose minds
> Are moved to know the secrets of the world.
>   (PROPERTIUS and LUCAN.)

In this universe of things I allow myself to be ignorantly and carelessly guided by the general law of the world. I shall know it well enough when I feel it. My learning cannot make it alter its course. It will not modify itself for my sake. It is folly to expect it, and greater folly to be disturbed about it, since it is necessarily the same for all of us. The goodness and capability of our Pilot must relieve us fully and absolutely from all anxiety about steering. . . .

Unjust Laws*

HENRY DAVID THOREAU

Among the iconoclasts who have thought about crime and punishment and about unjust laws was Henry David Thoreau (1817–1862), author of Walden. *He stands out as an individualist, particularly today in an age of conformity. While many might not wish to live in a shanty, take odd jobs, and watch birds, some could learn about inner strength from rereading Thoreau. "Of Civil Disobedience" is an example of his magazine writing. It is based on an incident involving his refusal to pay poll tax to a government which allowed slavery.*

The practical reason why, when the power is once in the hands of the people, a majority are permitted, and for a long period continue, to rule is not because they are most likely to be in the right, nor because this seems fairest to the minority, but because they are physically the strongest. But a government in which the majority rule in all cases cannot be based on justice, even as far as men understand it. Can there not be a government in which majorities do not virtually decide right and wrong, but conscience? —in which majorities decide only those questions to which the rule of expediency is applicable? Must the citizen ever for a moment, or in the least degree, resign his conscience to the legislator? Why has every man a conscience, then? I think that we should be men first, and subjects afterward. It is not desirable to cultivate a respect for the law, so much as for the right. The only obligation which I have a right to assume is to do at any time what I think right. It is truly enough said, that a corporation has no conscience; but a corporation of conscientious men is a corporation *with* a conscience. Law never made men a whit more just; and, by means of their respect for it, even the well-disposed are daily made the agents of injustice. A common and natural result of an undue respect for law is, that you may see a file of soldiers, colonel, captain, corporal, privates, powder-monkeys, and all, marching in admirable order over hill and dale to the wars, against their wills, ay, against their common sense and conscience, which makes it very steep marching indeed, and produces a palpitation of the heart. They have no doubt that it is a damnable business in which they are concerned; they are all peaceably inclined. Now, what are they? Men at all? or small movable forts and magazines, at the service of some unscrupulous man in power? Visit the Navy-Yard, and behold a marine, such a man as an

* From *On the Duty of Civil Disobedience.*

American government can make, or such as it can make a man with its black arts,—a mere shadow and reminiscence of humanity, a man laid out alive and standing, and already, as one may say, buried under arms with funeral accompaniments, though it may be,—

"Not a drum was heard, not a funeral note,
  As his corse to the rampart we hurried;
Not a soldier discharged his farewell shot
  O'er the grave where our hero we buried."

The mass of men serve the state thus, not as men mainly, but as machines, with their bodies. They are the standing army, and the militia, jailers, constables, posse comitatus, etc. In most cases there is no free exercise whatever of the judgment or of the moral sense; but they put themselves on a level with wood and earth and stones; and wooden men can perhaps be manufactured that will serve the purpose as well. Such command no more respect than men of straw or a lump of dirt. They have the same sort of worth only as horses and dogs. Yet such as these even are commonly esteemed good citizens. Others—as most legislators, politicians, lawyers, ministers, and office-holders—serve the state chiefly with their heads; and, as they rarely make any moral distinctions, they are as likely to serve the devil, without *intending* it, as God. A very few,—as heroes, patriots, martyrs, reformers in the great sense, and *men*—serve the state with their consciences also, and so necessarily resist it for the most part; and they are commonly treated as enemies by it. A wise man will only be useful as a man, and will not submit to be "clay," and "stop a hole to keep the wind away," but leave that office to his dust at least:—

"I am too high-born to be propertied,
To be a secondary at control,
Or useful serving-man and instrument
To any sovereign state throughout the world."

He who gives himself entirely to his fellow-men appears to them useless and selfish; but he who gives himself partially to them is pronounced a benefactor and philanthropist.

How does it become a man to behave toward this American government to-day? I answer, that he cannot without disgrace be associated with it. I cannot for an instant recognize that political organization as *my* government which is the *slave's* government also.

All men recognize the right of revolution; that is, the right to refuse allegiance to, and to resist, the government, when its tyranny or its inefficiency are great and unendurable. But almost all say that such is not the case now. But such was the case, they think, in the Revolution of '75. If one were to tell me that this was a bad government because it taxed certain foreign commodities brought to its ports, it is most probable that I should not make an ado about it, for I can do without them. All machines have their friction; and possibly this does enough good to counterbalance the evil. At any rate, it is a great evil to make a stir about it. But when the friction comes to have its machine, and oppression and robbery are organized, I say, let us not have such a machine any longer. In other words, when a sixth of the population of a nation which has undertaken to be the refuge of liberty are slaves, and a whole country is unjustly overrun and conquered by a foreign army, and subjected to military law, I think that it is not too soon for honest men to rebel and revolutionize. What makes this duty the more urgent is the fact that the country so overrun is not our own, but ours is the invading army.

Paley, a common authority with many on moral questions, in his chapter on the "Duty of Submission to Civil Government," resolves all civil obligation into expediency; and he proceeds to say, "that so long as the interest of the whole society requires it, that is, so long as the established government cannot be resisted or changed without public inconvenience, it is the will of God that the established government be obeyed, and no longer. . . . This principle being admitted, the justice of every particular case of resistance is reduced to a computation of the quantity of the danger and grievance on the one side, and of the probability and expense of redressing it on the other." Of this, he says, every man shall judge for himself. But Paley appears never to have contemplated those cases to which the rule of expediency does not apply, in which a people, as well as an individual, must do justice, cost what it may. If I have unjustly wrested a plank from a drowning man, I must restore it to him though I drown myself. This, according to Paley, would be inconvenient. But he that would save his life, in such a case, shall lose it. This people must cease to hold slaves, and to make war on Mexico, though it cost them their existence as a people.

In their practice, nations agree with Paley; but does any one think that Massachusetts does exactly what is right at the present crisis?

> *"A drab of state, a cloth-o'-silver slut,*
> *To have her train borne up, and her soul trail in the dirt."*

Practically speaking, the opponents to a reform in Massachusetts are not a hundred thousand politicians at the South, but a hundred thousand merchants and farmers here, who are more interested in commerce and agriculture than they are in humanity, and are not prepared to do justice to the slave and to Mexico, *cost what it may.* I quarrel not with far-off foes, but with those who, near at home, coöperate with, and do the bidding of, those far away, and without whom the latter would be harmless. We are accustomed to say, that the mass of men are unprepared; but improvement is slow, because the few are not materially wiser or better than the many. It is not so important that many should be as good as you, as that there be some absolute goodness somewhere; for that will leaven the whole lump.

There are thousands who are *in opinion* opposed to slavery and to the war, who yet in effect do nothing to put an end to them; who, esteeming themselves children of Washington and Franklin, sit down with their hands in their pockets, and say that they know not what to do, and do nothing; who even postpone the question of freedom to the question of free-trade, and quietly read the prices-current along with the latest advices from Mexico, after dinner, and, it may be, fall asleep over them both. What is the price-current of an honest man and patriot to-day? They hesitate, and they regret, and sometimes they petition; but they do nothing in earnest and with effect. They will wait, well disposed, for others to remedy the evil, that they may no longer have it to regret. At most, they give only a cheap vote, and a feeble countenance and God-speed, to the right, as it goes by them. There are nine hundred and ninety-nine patrons of virtue to one virtuous man. But it is easier to deal with the real possessor of a thing than with the temporary guardian of it.

All voting is a sort of gaming, like checkers or backgammon, with a slight moral tinge to it, a playing with right and wrong, with moral questions; and betting naturally accompanies it. The character of the voters is not staked. I cast my vote, perchance, as I think right; but I am not vitally concerned that that right should prevail. I am willing to leave it to the majority. Its obligation, therefore, never exceeds that of expediency. Even voting *for the right* is *doing* nothing for it. It is only expressing to men feebly your desire that it should prevail. A wise man will not leave the right to the mercy of chance, nor wish it to prevail through the power of the majority. There is but little virtue in the action of masses of men. When the majority shall at length vote for the abolition of slavery, it will be because they are indifferent to slavery, or because there is but little slavery left to be abolished by their vote. *They* will then be the only slaves. Only *his* vote can hasten the abolition of slavery who asserts his own freedom by his vote.

I hear of a convention to be held at Baltimore, or elsewhere, for the selection of a candidate for the Presidency, made up chiefly of editors, and men who are politicians by profession; but I think, what is it to any independent, intelligent, and respectable man what decision they may come to. Shall we not have the advantage of his wisdom and honesty, nevertheless? Can we not count upon some independent votes? Are there not many individuals in the country who do not attend conventions? But no: I find that the respectable man, so called, has immediately drifted from his position, and despairs of his country, when his country has more reason to despair of him. He forthwith adopts one of the candidates thus selected as the only *available* one, thus proving that he is himself *available* for any purposes of the demagogue. His vote is of no more worth than that of any unprincipled foreigner or hireling native, who may have been bought. O for a man who is a *man*, and, as my neighbor says, has a bone in his back which you cannot pass your hand through! Our statistics are at fault: the population has been returned too large. How many *men* are there to a square thousand miles in this country? Hardly one. Does not America offer any inducement for men to settle here? The American has dwindled into an Odd Fellow,— one who may be known by the development of his organ of gregariousness, and a manifest lack of intellect and cheerful self-reliance; whose first and chief concern, on coming into the world, is to see that the Almshouses are in good repair; and, before yet he has lawfully donned the virile garb, to collect a fund for the support of the widows and orphans that may be; who, in short, ventures to live only by the aid of the Mutual Insurance company, which has promised to bury him decently.

It is not a man's duty, as a matter of course, to devote himself to the eradication of any, even the most enormous wrong; he may still properly have other concerns to engage him; but it is his duty, at least, to wash his hands of it, and, if he gives it no thought longer, not to give it practically his support. If I devote myself to other pursuits and contemplations, I must first see, at least, that I do not pursue them sitting upon another man's shoulders. I must get off him first, that he may pursue his contemplations too. See what gross inconsistency is tolerated. I have heard some of my townsmen say, "I should like to have them order me out to help put down an insurrection of the slaves, or to march to Mexico,—see if I would go"; and yet these very men have each, directly by their allegiance, and so indirectly, at least, by their money, furnished a substitute. The soldier is applauded who refuses to serve in an unjust war by those who do not refuse to sustain the unjust government which makes the war; is applauded by those whose own act and authority he disregards and sets at nought; as if the State were penitent to that degree that it hired one to scourge it while it sinned, but not to that degree that it left off sinning for a moment. Thus, under the name of Order and Civil Government, we are all made at last to pay homage to and support our own meanness. After the first blush of sin, comes its indifference; and from immoral it becomes, as it were, *un*moral, and not quite unnecessary to that life which we have made.

The broadest and most prevalent error requires the most disinterested virtue to sustain it. The slight reproach to which the virtue of patriotism is commonly liable, the noble are most likely to incur. Those who, while they disapprove of the character and measures of a government, yield to it their allegiance and support are undoubtedly its most conscientious supporters, and so frequently the most serious obstacles to reform. Some are petitioning the State to dissolve the Union, to disregard the requisitions of the President. Why do they not dissolve it themselves,—the union between themselves and the State,—and refuse to pay their quota into its treasury? Do not they stand in the same relation to the State, that the State does to the Union? And have not the same reasons prevented the State from resisting the Union, which have prevented them from resisting the State?

How can a man be satisfied to entertain an opinion merely, and enjoy *it*?

Is there any enjoyment in it, if his opinion is that he is aggrieved? If you are cheated out of a single dollar by your neighbor, you do not rest satisfied with knowing that you are cheated, or with saying that you are cheated, or even with petitioning him to pay you your due; but you take effectual steps at once to obtain the full amount, and see that you are never cheated again. Action from principle, the perception and the performance of right, changes things and relations; it is essentially revolutionary, and does not consist wholly with anything which was. It not only divides states and churches, it divides families; ay, it divides the *individual*, separating the diabolical in him from the divine.

Unjust laws exist: shall we be content to obey them, or shall we endeavor to amend them, and obey them until we have succeeded, or shall we transgress them at once? Men generally, under such a government as this, think that they ought to wait until they have persuaded the majority to alter them. They think that, if they should resist, the remedy would be worse than the evil. But it is the fault of the government itself that the remedy *is* worse than the evil. *It* makes it worse. Why is it not more apt to anticipate and provide for reform? Why does it not cherish its wise minority? Why does it cry and resist before it is hurt? Why does it not encourage its citizens to be on the alert to point out its faults, and *do* better than it would have them? Why does it always crucify Christ, and excommunicate Copernicus and Luther, and pronounce Washington and Franklin rebels?

One would think, that a deliberate and practical denial of its authority was the only offense never contemplated by government; else, why has it not assigned its definite, its suitable and proportionate penalty? If a man who has no property refuses but once to earn nine shillings for the State, he is put in prison for a period unlimited by any law that I know, and determined only by the discretion of those who placed him there; but if he should steal ninety times nine shillings from the state, he is soon permitted to go at large again.

If the injustice is part of the necessary friction of the machine of government, let it go, let it go: perchance it will wear smooth,—certainly the machine will wear out. If the injustice has a spring, or a pulley, or a rope, or a crank, exclusively for itself, then perhaps you may consider whether the remedy will not be worse than the evil; but if it is of such a nature that it requires you to be the agent of injustice to another, then, I say, break the law. Let your life be a counter friction to stop the machine. What I have to do is to see, at any rate, that I do not lend myself to the wrong which I condemn.

As for adopting the ways which the State has provided for remedying the evil, I know not of such ways. They take too much time, and a man's life will be gone. I have other affairs to attend to. I came into this world, not chiefly to make this a good place to live in, but to live in it, be it good or bad. A man has not everything to do, but something; and because he cannot do *everything*, it is not necessary that he should do *something* wrong. It is not my business to be petitioning the Governor or the Legislature any more than it is theirs to petition me; and if they should not hear my petition, what should I do then? But in this case the State has provided no way: its very Constitution is the evil. This may seem to be harsh and stubborn and unconciliatory; but it is to treat with the utmost kindness and consideration the only spirit that can appreciate or deserves it. So is all change for the better, like birth and death, which convulse the body.

I do not hesitate to say, that those who call themselves Abolitionists should at once effectually withdraw their support, both in person and property, from the government of Massachusetts, and not wait till they constitute a majority of one, before they suffer the right to prevail through them. I think that it is enough if they have God on their side, without waiting for that other one. Moreover, any man more right than his neighbors constitutes a majority of one already.

I meet this American government, or its representative, the State government, directly, and face to face, once a year—no more—in the person of its tax-gatherer; this is the only mode in which a man situated as I am necessarily meets it; and it then says distinctly, Recognize me; and the simplest, the most effectual, and, in the present posture of affairs, the indispensablest mode of treating with it on this head, of expressing your little satisfaction with and love for it, is to deny it then. My civil neighbor, the tax-gatherer, is the very man I have to deal with,—for it is, after all, with men and not with parchment that I quarrel,—and he has voluntarily chosen to be an agent of the government. How shall he ever know well what he is and does as an officer of the government, or as a man, until he is obliged to consider whether he shall treat me, his neighbor, for whom he has respect, as a neighbor and well-disposed man, or as a maniac and disturber of the peace, and see if he can get over this obstruction to his neighborliness without a ruder and more impetuous thought or speech corresponding with his action. I know this well, that if one thousand, if one hundred, if ten men whom I could name,—if ten *honest* men only,—ay, if *one* HONEST man, in this State of Massachusetts, *ceasing to hold slaves,* were actually to withdraw from this copartnership, and be locked up in the county jail therefor, it would be the abolition of slavery in America. For it matters not how small the beginning may seem to be: what is once well done is done forever. But we love better to talk about it: that we say is our mission. Reform keeps many scores of newspapers in its service, but not one man. If my esteemed neighbor, the State's ambassador, who will devote his days to the settlement of the question of human rights in the Council Chamber, instead of being threatened with the prisons of Carolina, were to sit down the prisoner of Massachusetts, that State which is so anxious to foist the sin of slavery upon her sister,—though at present she can discover only an act of inhospitality to be the ground of a quarrel with her,—the Legislature would not wholly waive the subject the following winter.

Under a government which imprisons any unjustly, the true place for a just man is also a prison. The proper place to-day, the only place which Massachusetts has provided for her freer and less desponding spirits, is in her prisons, to be put out and locked out of the State by her own act, as they have already put themselves out by their principles. It is there that the fugitive slave, and the Mexican prisoner on parole, and the Indian come to plead the wrongs of his race should find them; on that separate, but more free and honorable ground, where the State places those who are not *with* her but *against* her,—the only house in a slave State in which a free man can abide with honor. If any think that their influence would be lost there, and their voices no longer afflict the ear of the State, that they would not be as an enemy within its walls, they do not know by how much truth is stronger than error, nor how much more eloquently and effectively he can combat injustice who has experienced a little in his own person. Cast your whole vote, not a strip of paper merely, but your whole influence. A minority is powerless while it conforms to the majority; it is not even a minority then; but it is irresistible when it clogs by its whole weight. If the alternative is to keep all just men in prison, or give up war and slavery, the State will not hesitate which to choose. If a thousand men were not to pay their tax-bills this year, that would not be a violent and bloody measure, as it would be to pay them, and enable the State to commit violence and shed innocent blood. This is, in fact, the definition of a peaceable revolution if any such is possible. If the tax-gatherer, or any other public officer, asks me, as one has done, "But what shall I do?" my answer is, "If you really wish to do anything, resign your office." When the subject has refused allegiance, and the officer has resigned his office, then the revolution is accomplished. But even suppose blood should flow. Is there not a sort of blood shed when the conscience is wounded? Through this wound a man's real manhood and immortality flow out, and he bleeds to an everlasting death. I see this blood flowing now.

I have contemplated the imprisonment of the offender, rather than the seizure of his goods,—though both will serve the same purpose,—because they who assert the purest right, and consequently are most dangerous to a corrupt State, commonly have not spent much time in accumulating property. To such the State renders comparatively small service, and a slight tax is wont to appear exorbitant, particularly if they are obliged to earn it by special labor with their hands. If there were one who lived wholly without the use of money, the State itself would hesitate to demand it of him. But the rich man—not to make any invidious comparison—is always sold to the institution which makes him rich. Absolutely speaking, the more money, the less virtue; for money comes between a man and his objects, and obtains them for him; and it was certainly no great virtue to obtain it. It puts to rest many questions which he would otherwise be taxed to answer; while the only new question which it puts is the hard but superfluous one, how to spend it. Thus his moral ground is taken from under his feet. The opportunities of living are diminished in proportion as what are called the "means" are increased. The best thing a man can do for his culture when he is rich is to endeavour to carry out those schemes which he entertained when he was poor. Christ answered the Herodians according to their condition. "Show me the tribute-money," said he;—and one took a penny out of his pocket;—If you use money which has the image of Cæsar on it, and which he has made current and valuable, that is, *if you are men of the State,* and gladly enjoy the advantages of Cæsar's government, then pay him back some of his own when he demands it; "Render therefore to Cæsar that which is Cæsar's, and to God those things which are God's,"—leaving them no wiser than before as to which was which; for they did not wish to know.

When I converse with the freest of my neighbors, I perceive that, whatever they may say about the magnitude and seriousness of the question, and their regard for the public tranquillity, the long and the short of the matter is, that they cannot spare the protection of the existing government, and they dread the consequences to their property and families of disobedience to it. For my own part, I should not like to think that I ever rely on the protection of the State. But, if I deny the authority of the State when it presents its tax-bill, it will soon take and waste all my property, and so harass me and my children without end. This is hard. This makes it impossible for a man to live honestly, and at the same time comfortably, in outward respects. It will not be worth the while to accumulate property; that would be sure to go again. You must hire or squat somewhere, and raise but a small crop, and eat that soon. You must live within yourself, and depend upon yourself always tucked up and ready for a start, and not have many affairs. A man may grow rich in Turkey even, if he will be in all respects a good subject of the Turkish government. Confucius said: "If a state is governed by the principles of reason, poverty and misery are subjects of shame; if a state is not governed by the principles of reason, riches and honors are the subjects of shame." No: until I want the protection of Massachusetts to be extended to me in some distant Southern port, where my liberty is endangered, or until I am bent solely on building up an estate at home by peaceful enterprise, I can afford to refuse allegiance to Massachusetts, and her right to my property and life. It costs me less in every sense to incur the penalty of disobedience to the State than it would to obey. I should feel as if I were worth less in that case.

Some years ago, the State met me in behalf of the Church, and commanded me to pay a certain sum toward the support of a clergyman whose preaching my father attended, but never I myself. "Pay," it said, "or be locked up in the jail." I declined to pay. But, unfortunately, another man saw fit to pay it. I did not see why the schoolmaster should be taxed to support the priest, and not the priest the schoolmaster; for I was not the State's schoolmaster, but I supported myself by voluntary subscription. I did not see why the lyceum should not present its tax-bill, and have the State to back its demand, as well as the Church. However, at the request of the selectmen, I condescended to make some such statement as this in writing:—"Know all men by these presents, that I, Henry Thoreau, do not wish to be regarded as a member of any incorporated society which I have not joined." This I gave to the town clerk; and he has it. The State, having thus learned that I did not wish to be regarded as a member of that church, has never made a like demand on me since; though it said that it must adhere to its original presumption that time. If I had known how to name them, I should then have signed off in detail from all the societies which I never signed on to; but I did not know where to find a complete list.

I have paid no poll-tax for six years. I was put into a jail once on this account, for one night; and, as I stood considering the walls of solid stone, two or three feet thick, the door of wood and iron, a foot thick, and the iron grating which strained the light, I could not help being struck with the foolishness of that institution which treated me as if I were mere flesh and blood and bones, to be locked up. I wondered that it should have concluded at length that this was the best use it could put me to, and had never thought to avail itself of my services in some way. I saw that, if there was a wall of stone between me and my townsmen, there was a still more difficult one to climb or break through before they could get to be as free as I was. I did not for a moment feel confined, and the walls seemed a great waste of stone and mortar. I felt as if I alone of all my townsmen had paid my tax. They plainly did not know how to treat me, but behaved like persons who are underbred. In every threat and in every compliment there was a blunder; for they thought that my chief desire was to stand the other side of that stone wall. I could not but smile to see how industriously they locked the door on my meditations, which followed them out again without let or hindrance, and *they* were really all that was dangerous. As they could not reach me, they had resolved to punish my body; just as boys, if they cannot come at some person against whom they have a spite, will abuse his dog. I saw that the State was half-witted, that it was timid as a lone woman with her silver spoons, and that it did not know its friends from its foes, and I lost all my remaining respect for it, and pitied it.

Thus the State never intentionally confronts a man's sense, intellectual or moral, but only his body, his senses. It is not armed with superior wit or honesty, but with superior physical strength. I was not born to be forced. I will breathe after my own fashion. Let us see who is the strongest. What force has a multitude? They only can force me who obey a higher law than I. They force me to become like themselves. I do not hear of *men* being *forced* to live this way or that by masses of men. What sort of life were that to live? When I meet a government which says to me, "Your money or your life," why should I be in haste to give it my money? It may be in a great strait, and not know what to do: I cannot help that. It must help itself; do as I do. It is not worth the while to snivel about it. I am not responsible for the successful working of the machinery of society. I am not the son of the engineer. I perceive that, when an acorn and a chestnut fall side by side, the one does not remain inert to make way for the other, but both obey their own laws, and spring and grow and flourish as best they can, till one, perchance, overshadows and destroys the other. If a plant cannot live according to its nature, it dies; and so a man.

The Profession of the Law*

OLIVER WENDELL HOLMES

For a note on Holmes, see page 26. "The Profession of the Law" came at the end of a talk at Harvard in 1886.

And now, perhaps, I ought to have done. But I know that some spirit of fire will feel that his main question has not been answered. He will ask, What is all this to my soul? You do not bid me sell my birth-right for a mess of pottage; what have you said to show that I can reach my own spiritual possibilities through such a door as this? How can the laborious study of a dry and technical system, the greedy watch for clients and practice of shopkeepers' arts, the mannerless conflicts over often sordid interests, make out a life? Gentlemen, I admit at once that these questions are not futile, that they may prove unanswerable, that they have often seemed to me unanswerable. And yet I believe there is an answer. They are the same questions that meet you in any form of practical life. If a man has the soul of Sancho Panza, the world to him will be Sancho Panza's world; but if he has the soul of an idealist, he will make—I do not say find—his world ideal. Of course, the law is not the place for the artist or the poet. The law is the calling of thinkers. But to those who believe with me that not the least godlike of man's activities is the large survey of causes, that to know is not less than to feel, I say—and I say no longer with any doubt—that a man may live greatly in the law as well as elsewhere; that there as well as elsewhere his thought may find its unity in an infinite perspective; that there as well as elsewhere he may wreak himself upon life, may drink the bitter cup of heroism, may wear his heart out after the unattainable. All that life offers any man from which to start his thinking or his striving is a fact. And if this universe is one universe, if it is so far thinkable that you can pass in reason from one part of it to another, it does not matter very much what that fact is. For every fact leads to every other by the path of the air. Only men do not yet see how, always. And your business as thinkers is to make plainer the way from some thing to the whole of things; to show the rational connection between your fact and the frame of the universe. If your subject is law, the roads are plain to anthropology, the science of man, to political economy, the theory of legislation, ethics, and thus by several

* Reprinted by permission of Little, Brown & Company, publishers.

494

paths to your final view of life. It would be equally true of any subject. The only difference is in the ease of seeing the way. To be master of any branch of knowledge, you must master those which lie next to it; and thus to know anything you must know all.

Perhaps I speak too much the language of intellectual ambition. I cannot but think that the scope for intellectual, as for physical adventure, is narrowing. I look for a future in which the ideal will be content and dignified acceptance of life, rather than aspiration and the passion for achievement. I see already that surveys and railroads have set limits to our intellectual wildernesses,—that the lion and the bison are disappearing from them, as from Africa and the no longer boundless West. But that undelightful day which I anticipate has not yet come. The human race has not changed, I imagine, so much between my generation and yours but that you still have the barbaric thirst for conquest, and there is still something left to conquer. There are fields still open for occupation in the law, and there are roads from them that will lead you where you will.

But do not think I am pointing you to flowery paths and beds of roses,— to a place where brilliant results attend your work, which shall be at once easy and new. No result is easy which is worth having. Your education begins when what is called your education is over,—when you no longer are stringing together the pregnant thoughts, the "jewels five words long," which great men have given their lives to cut from the raw material for results which you do not see, cannot predict, and which may be long in coming,—when you take the fact which life offers you for your appointed task. No man has earned the right to intellectual ambition until he has learned to lay his course by a star which he has never seen,—to dig by the divining rod for springs which he may never reach. In saying this, I point to that which will make your study heroic. For I say to you in all sadness of conviction, that to think great thoughts you must be heroes as well as idealists. Only when you have worked alone,—when you have felt around you a black gulf of solitude more isolating than that which surrounds the dying man, and in hope and in despair have trusted to your own unshaken will,—then only will you have achieved. Thus only can you gain the secret isolated joy of the thinker, who knows that, a hundred years after he is dead and forgotten, men who never heard of him will be moving to the measure of his thoughts,—the subtle rapture of a postponed power, which the world knows not because it has no external trappings, but which to his prophetic vision is more real than that which commands an army. And if this joy should not be yours, still it is only thus that you can know that you have done what it lay in you to do,—can say that you have lived, and be ready for the end.

The Path of the Law[*]

OLIVER WENDELL HOLMES

"The Path of the Law" was a talk given in 1897. For a note on Holmes, see page 26.

When we study law we are not studying a mystery but a well known profession. We are studying what we shall want in order to appear before judges, or to advise people in such a way as to keep them out of court. The reason why it is a profession, why people will pay lawyers to argue for them or to advise them, is that in societies like ours the command of the public force is intrusted to the judges in certain cases, and the whole power of the state will be put forth, if necessary, to carry out their judgments and decrees. People want to know under what circumstances and how far they will run the risk of coming against what is so much stronger than themselves, and hence it becomes a business to find out when this danger is to be feared. The object of our study, then, is prediction, the prediction of the incidence of the public force through the instrumentality of the courts.

The means of the study are a body of reports, of treatises, and of statutes, in this country and in England, extending back for six hundred years, and now increasing annually by hundreds. In these sibylline leaves are gathered the scattered prophecies of the past upon the cases in which the axe will fall. These are what properly have been called the oracles of the law. For the most important and pretty nearly the whole meaning of every new effort of legal thought is to make these prophecies more precise, and to generalize them into a thoroughly connected system. The process is one, from a lawyer's statement of a case, eliminating as it does all the dramatic elements with which his client's story has clothed it, and retaining only the facts of legal import, up to the final analyses and abstract universals of theoretic jurisprudence. The reason why a lawyer does not mention that his client wore a white hat when he made a contract, while Mrs. Quickly would be sure to dwell upon it along with the parcel gilt goblet and the sea-coal fire, is that he foresees that the public force will act in the same way whatever his client had upon his head. It is to make the prophecies easier to be remembered and to be understood that the teachings of the decisions of the past are put into general propositions and gathered into

[*] Reprinted by permission of *Harvard Law Review*.

496

text-books, or that statutes are passed in a general form. The primary rights and duties with which jurisprudence busies itself again are nothing but prophecies. One of the many evil effects of the confusion between legal and moral ideas, about which I shall have something to say in a moment, is that theory is apt to get the cart before the horse, and to consider the right or the duty as something existing apart from and independent of the consequences of its breach, to which certain sanctions are added afterward. But, as I shall try to show, a legal duty so called is nothing but a prediction that if a man does or omits certain things he will be made to suffer in this or that way by judgment of the court;—and so of a legal right.

The number of our predictions when generalized and reduced to a system is not unmanageably large. They present themselves as a finite body of dogma which may be mastered within a reasonable time. It is a great mistake to be frightened by the ever increasing number of reports. The reports of a given jurisdiction in the course of a generation take up pretty much the whole body of the law, and restate it from the present point of view. We could reconstruct the corpus from them if all that went before were burned. The use of the earlier reports is mainly historical, a use about which I shall have something to say before I have finished.

I wish, if I can, to lay down some first principles for the study of this body of dogma or systematized prediction which we call the law, for men who want to use it as the instrument of their business to enable them to prophesy in their turn, and, as bearing upon the study, I wish to point out an ideal which as yet our law has not attained.

The first thing for a business-like understanding of the matter is to understand its limits, and therefore I think it desirable at once to point out and dispel a confusion between morality and law, which sometimes rises to the height of conscious theory, and more often and indeed constantly is making trouble in detail without reaching the point of consciousness. You can see very plainly that a bad man has as much reason as a good one for wishing to avoid an encounter with the public force, and therefore you can see the practical importance of the distinction between morality and law. A man who cares nothing for an ethical rule which is believed and practised by his neighbors is likely nevertheless to care a good deal to avoid being made to pay money, and will want to keep out of jail if he can.

I take it for granted that no hearer of mine will misrepresent what I have to say as the language of cynicism. The law is the witness and external deposit of our moral life. Its history is the history of the moral development of the race. The practice of it, in spite of popular jests, tends to make good citizens and good men. When I emphasize the difference between law and morals I do so with reference to a single end, that of learning and understanding the law. For that purpose you must definitely master its specific marks, and it is for that that I ask you for the moment to imagine yourselves indifferent to other and greater things.

I do not say that there is not a wider point of view from which the distinction between law and morals becomes of secondary or no importance, as all mathematical distinctions vanish in presence of the infinite. But I do say that that distinction is of the first importance for the object which we are here to consider, a right study and mastery of the law as a business with well understood limits, a body of dogma enclosed within definite lines. I have just shown the practical reason for saying so. If you want to know the law and nothing else, you must look at it as a bad man, who cares only for the material consequences which such knowledge enables him to predict, not as a good one, who finds his reasons for conduct, whether inside the law or outside of it, in the vaguer sanctions of conscience. The theoretical importance of the distinction is no less, if you would reason on your subject aright. The law is full of phraseology drawn from morals, and by the mere force of language continually invites us to pass from one domain to the other without perceiving it, as we are sure to do unless we have the boundary constantly before our minds. The law talks about rights, and duties, and malice, and intent, and negligence, and so forth, and nothing is easier, or, I may say, more common in legal reasoning, than to take these words in their moral sense, at some stage of the argument, and so to drop into fallacy. For instance, when we speak of the rights of man in a moral sense, we mean to mark the limits of interference with individual freedom which we think are prescribed by conscience, or by our ideal, however reached. Yet it is certain that many laws have been enforced in the past, and it is likely that some are enforced now, which are condemned by the most enlightened opinion of the time, or which at all events pass the limit of interference as many consciences would draw it. Manifestly, therefore, nothing but confusion of thought can result from assuming that the rights of man in a moral sense are equally rights in the sense of the Constitution and the law. No doubt simple and extreme cases can be put of imaginable laws which the statute-making power would not dare to enact, even in the absence of written constitutional prohibitions, because the community would rise in rebellion and fight, and this gives some plausibility to the proposition that the law, if not a part of morality, is limited by it. But this limit of power is not coextensive with any system of morals. For the most part it falls far within the lines of any such system, and in some cases may extend beyond them, for reasons drawn from the habits of a particular people at a particular time. I once heard the late Professor Agassiz say that a German population would rise if you added two cents to the price of a glass of beer. A statute in such a case would be empty words, not because it was wrong, but because it could not be enforced. No one will deny that wrong statutes can be and are enforced, and we should not all agree as to which were the wrong ones.

The confusion with which I am dealing besets confessedly legal conceptions. Take the fundamental question, What constitutes the law? You will find some text writers telling you that it is something different from what is decided by the courts of Massachusetts, or England, that it is a system of reason, that it is a deduction from principles of ethics or admitted axioms or what not, which may or may not coincide with the decisions. But if we take the view of our friend the bad man we shall find that he does not care two straws for the axioms or deductions, but that he does want to know what the Massachusetts or English courts are likely to do in fact. I am much of this kind. The prophecies of what the courts will do in fact, and nothing more pretentious, are what I mean by the law.

Take again a notion which as popularly understood is the widest conception which the law contains;—the notion of legal duty, to which already I have referred. We fill the word with all the content which we draw from morals. But what does it mean to a bad man? Mainly, and in the first place, a prophecy that if he does certain things he will be subjected to disagreeable consequences by way of imprisonment or compulsory payment of money. But from his point of view, what is the difference between being fined and being taxed a certain sum for doing a certain thing? That his point of view is the test of legal principles is shown by the many discussions which have arisen in the courts on the very question whether a given statutory liability is a penalty or a tax. On the answer to this question depends the decision whether conduct is legally wrong or right, and also whether a man is under compulsion or free. Leaving the criminal law on one side, what is the difference between the liability under the mill acts or statutes authorizing a taking by eminent domain and the liability for what we call a wrongful conversion of property where restoration is out of the question? In both cases the party taking another man's property has to pay its fair value as assessed by a jury, and no more. What significance is there in calling one taking right and another wrong from the point of view of the law? It does not matter, so far as the given consequence, the compulsory payment, is concerned, whether the act to which it is attached is described in terms of praise or in terms of blame, or whether the law purports to prohibit it or to allow it. If it matters at all, still speaking from the bad man's point of view, it must be because in one case and not in the other some further disadvantages, or at least some further consequences, are attached to the act by the law. The only other disadvantages thus attached to it which I ever have been able to think of are to be found in two somewhat insignificant legal doctrines, both of which might be abolished without much disturbance. One is, that a contract to do a prohibited act is unlawful, and the other, that, if one of two or more joint wrongdoers has to pay all the damages, he cannot recover contribution from his fellows. And that I believe is all. You see how the vague circumference of the notion of duty shrinks and at the same time grows more precise when we wash it with cynical acid and expel everything except the object of our study, the operations of the law.

Nowhere is the confusion between legal and moral ideas more manifest than in the law of contract. Among other things, here again the so-called primary rights and duties are invested with a mystic significance beyond what can be assigned and explained. The duty to keep a contract at common law means a prediction that you must pay damages if you do not keep it,—and nothing else. If you commit a tort, you are liable to pay a compensatory sum. If you commit a contract, you are liable to pay a compensatory sum unless the promised event comes to pass, and that is all the difference. But such a mode of looking at the matter stinks in the nostrils of those who think it advantageous to get as much ethics into the law as they can. It was good enough for Lord Coke, however, and here, as in many other cases, I am content to abide with him. In Bromage *v.* Genning, a prohibition was sought in the King's Bench against a suit in the marches of Wales for the specific performance of a covenant to grant a lease, and Coke said that it would subvert the intention of the covenantor, since he intends it to be at his election either to lose the damages or to make the lease. Sergeant Harris for the plaintiff confessed that he moved the matter against his conscience, and a prohibition was granted. This goes further than we should go now, but it shows what I venture to say has been the common law point of view from the beginning, although Mr. Harriman, in his very able little book upon Contracts has been misled, as I humbly think, to a different conclusion.

I have spoken only of the common law, because there are some cases in which a logical justification can be found for speaking of civil liabilities as imposing duties in an intelligible sense. These are the relatively few in which equity will grant an injunction, and will enforce it by putting the defendant in prison or otherwise punishing him unless he complies with the order of the court. But I hardly think it advisable to shape general theory from the exception, and I think it would be better to cease troubling ourselves about primary rights and sanctions altogether, than to describe our prophecies concerning the liabilities, commonly imposed by the law in those inappropriate terms.

I mentioned, as other examples of the use by the law of words drawn from morals, malice, intent, and negligence. It is enough to take malice as it is used in the law of civil liability for wrongs,—what we lawyers call the law of torts,—to show you that it means something different in law from what it means in morals, and also to show how the difference has been obscured by giving to principles which have little or nothing to do with each other the same name. Three hundred years ago a parson preached a sermon and told a story out of Fox's Book of Martyrs of a man who had assisted at the torture of one of the saints, and afterward died, suffering compensatory inward torment. It happened that Fox was wrong. The man was alive and chanced to hear the sermons, and thereupon he sued the parson. Chief Justice Wray instructed the jury that the defendant was not liable, because the story was told innocently, without malice. He took malice in the moral sense, as importing a malevolent motive. But nowadays no one doubts that a man may be liable without any malevolent motive at all, for false statements, manifestly calculated to inflict temporal damage. In stating the case in pleading, we still should call the defendant's conduct malicious; but, in my opinion at least, the word means nothing about motives, or even about the defendant's attitude toward the future, but only signifies that the tendency of his conduct under the known circumstances was very plainly to cause the plaintiff temporal harm.

In the law of contract the use of moral phraseology has led to equal confusion, as I have shown in part already, but only in part. Morals deal with the actual internal state of the individual's mind, what he actually intends. From the time of the Romans down to now, this mode of dealing has affected the language of the law as to contract, and the language used has reacted upon the thought. We talk about a contract as a meeting of the minds of the parties, and thence it is inferred in various cases that there is no contract because their minds have not met; that is, because they have intended different things or because one party has not known of the assent of the other. Yet nothing is more certain than that parties may be bound by a contract to things which neither of them intended, and when one does not know of the other's assent. Suppose a contract is executed in due form and in writing to deliver a lecture, mentioning no time. One of the parties thinks that the promise will be construed to them at once, within a week. The other thinks that it means when he is ready. The court says that it means within a reasonable time. The parties are bound by the contract as it is interpreted by the court, yet neither of them meant what the court declares that they have said. In my opinion no one will understand the true theory of contract or be able even to discuss some fundamental questions intelligently until he has understood that all contracts are formal, that the making of a contract depends not on the agreement of two minds in one intention, but on the agreement of two sets of external signs,—not on the parties' having *meant* the same thing but on their having *said* the same thing. Furthermore, as the signs may be addressed to one sense or another,—to sight or to hearing—on the nature of the sign will depend the moment when the contract is made. If the sign is tangible, for instance, a letter, the contract is made when the letter of acceptance is delivered. If it is necessary that the minds of the parties meet, there will be no contract until the acceptance can be read,—none, for example, if the acceptance be snatched from the hand of the offerer by a third person.

This is not the time to work out a theory in detail, or to answer many obvious doubts and questions which are suggested by these general views. I know of none which are not easy to answer, but what I am trying to do now is only by a series of hints to throw some light on the narrow path

of legal doctrine, and upon two pitfalls which, as it seems to me, lie perilously near to it. Of the first of these I have said enough. I hope that my
illustrations have shown the danger, both to speculation and to practice, of
confounding morality with law, and the trap which legal language lays for
us on that side of our way. For my own part, I often doubt whether it would
not be a gain if every word of moral significance could be banished from
the law altogether, and other words adopted which should convey legal
ideas uncolored by anything outside the law. We should lose the fossil
records of a good deal of history and the majesty got from ethical associations, but by ridding ourselves of an unnecessary confusion we should gain
very much in the clearness of our thought.

So much for the limits of the law. The next thing which I wish to consider is what are the forces which determine its content and its growth.
You may assume, with Hobbes and Bentham and Austin, that all law
emanates from the sovereign, even when the first human beings to enun-
ciate it are the judges, or you may think that law is the voice of the
Zeitgeist, or what you like. It is all one to my present purpose. Even if
every decision required the sanction of an emperor with despotic power
and a whimsical turn of mind, we should be interested none the less, still
with a view to prediction, in discovering some order, some rational explanation, and some principle of growth for the rules which he laid down.
In every system there are such explanations and principles to be found. It
is with regard to them that a second fallacy comes in, which I think it
important to expose.

The fallacy to which I refer is the notion that the only force at work in
the development of the law is logic. In the broadest sense, indeed, that
notion would be true. The postulate on which we think about the universe
is that there is a fixed quantitative relation between every phenomenon
and its antecedents and consequents. If there is such a thing as a phenomenon without these fixed quantitative relations, it is a miracle. It is outside
the law of cause and effect, and as such transcends our power of thought,
or at least is something to or from which we cannot reason. The condition
of our thinking about the universe is that it is capable of being thought
about rationally, or, in other words, that every part of it is effect and cause
in the same sense in which those parts are with which we are most familiar.
So in the broadest sense it is true that the law is a logical development, like
everything else. The danger of which I speak is not the admission that the
principles governing other phenomena also govern the law, but the notion
that a given system, ours, for instance, can be worked out like mathematics
from some general axioms of conduct. This is the natural error of the
schools, but it is not confined to them. I once heard a very eminent judge
say that he never let a decision go until he was absolutely sure that it was
right. So judicial dissent often is blamed, as if it meant simply that one

side or the other were not doing their sums right, and, if they would take more trouble, agreement inevitably would come.

This mode of thinking is entirely natural. The training of lawyers is a training in logic. The processes of analogy, discrimination, and deduction are those in which they are most at home. The language of judicial decision is mainly the language of logic. And the logical method and form flatter that longing for certainty and for repose which is in every human mind. But certainty generally is illusion, and repose is not the destiny of man. Behind the logical form lies a judgment as to the relative worth and importance of competing legislative grounds, often an inarticulate and unconscious judgment, it is true, and yet the very root and nerve of the whole proceeding. You can give any conclusion a logical form. You always can imply a condition in a contract. But why do you imply? It is because of some belief as to the practice of the community or of a class, or because of some opinion as to policy, or, in short, because of some attitude of yours upon a matter not capable of founding exact logical conclusions. Such matters really are battle grounds where the means do not exist for determinations that shall be good for all time, and where the decision can do no more than embody the preference of a given body in a given time and place. We do not realize how large a part of our law is open to reconsideration upon a slight change in the habit of the public mind. No concrete proposition is self-evident, no matter how ready we may be to accept it, not even Mr. Herbert Spencer's. Every man has a right to do what he wills, provided he interferes not with a like right on the part of his neighbors.

Why is a false and injurious statement privileged, if it is made honestly in giving information about a servant? It is because it has been thought more important that information should be given freely, than that a man should be protected from what under other circumstances would be an actionable wrong. Why is a man at liberty to set up a business which he knows will ruin his neighbor? It is because the public good is supposed to be best subserved by free competition. Obviously such judgments of relative importance may vary in different times and places. Why does a judge instruct a jury that an employer is not liable to an employee for an injury received in the course of his employment unless he is negligent, and why do the jury generally find for the plaintiff if the case is allowed to go to them? It is because the traditional policy of our law is to confine liability to cases where a prudent man might have foreseen the injury, or at least the danger, while the inclination of a very large part of the community is to make certain classes of persons insure the safety of those with whom they deal. Since the last words were written, I have seen the requirement of such insurance put forth as part of the programme of one of the best known labor organizations. There is a concealed, half conscious battle on the question of legislative policy, and if any one thinks that it can be

settled deductively, or once for all, I only can say that I think he is
theoretically wrong, and that I am certain that his conclusion will not be
accepted in practice *semper ubique et ab omnibus.*

Indeed, I think that even now our theory upon this matter is open to
reconsideration, although I am not prepared to say how I should decide
if a reconsideration were proposed. Our law of torts comes from the old
days of isolated, ungeneralized wrongs, assaults, slanders, and the like,
where the damages might be taken to lie where they fell by legal judgment.
But the torts with which our courts are kept busy today are mainly the
incidents of certain well known businesses. They are injuries to person or
property by railroads, factories, and the like. The liability for them is estimated, and sooner or later goes into the price paid by the public. The
public really pays the damages, and the question of liability, if pressed far
enough, is really the question how far it is desirable that the public should
insure the safety of those whose work it uses. It might be said that in such
cases the chance of a jury finding for the defendant is merely a chance,
once in a while rather arbitrarily interrupting the regular course of recovery,
most likely in the case of an unusually conspicuous plaintiff, and therefore
better done away with. On the other hand, the economic value even of a
life to the community can be estimated, and no recovery, it may be said,
ought to go beyond that amount. It is conceivable that some day in certain
cases we may find ourselves imitating, on a higher plane, the tariff for life
and limb which we see in the Leges Barbarorum.

I think that the judges themselves have failed adequately to recognize
their duty of weighing considerations of social advantage. The duty is inevitable, and the result of the often proclaimed judicial aversion to deal
with such considerations is simply to leave the very ground and foundation
of judgments inarticulate, and often unconscious, as I have said. When socialism first began to be talked about, the comfortable classes of the community were a good deal frightened. I suspect that this fear has influenced
judicial action both here and in England, yet it is certain that it is not a
conscious factor in the decisions to which I refer. I think that something
similar has led people who no longer hope to control the legislatures to look
to the courts as expounders of the Constitutions, and that in some courts
now principles have been discovered outside the bodies of those instruments,
which may be generalized into acceptance of the economic doctrines which
prevailed about fifty years ago, and a wholesale prohibition of what a
tribunal of lawyers does not think about right. I cannot but believe that if
the training of lawyers led them habitually to consider more definitely
and explicitly the social advantage on which the rule they lay down must
be justified, they sometimes would hesitate where now they are confident,
and see that really they were taking sides upon debatable and often burning
questions.

So much for the fallacy of logical form. Now let us consider the present condition of the law as a subject for study, and the ideal toward which it tends. We still are far from the point of view which I desire to see reached. No one has reached it or can reach it as yet. We are only at the beginning of a philosophical reaction, and of a reconsideration of the worth of doctrines which for the most part still are taken for granted without any deliberate, conscious, and systematic questioning of their grounds. The development of our law has gone on for nearly a thousand years, like the development of a plant, each generation taking the inevitable next step, mind, like matter, simply obeying a law of spontaneous growth. It is perfectly natural and right that it should have been so. Imitation is a necessity of human nature, as has been illustrated by a remarkable French writer, M. Tarde, in an admirable book, *Les Lois de l'Imitation.* Most of the things we do, we do for no better reason than that our fathers have done them or that our neighbors do them, and the same is true of a larger part than we suspect of what we think. The reason is a good one, because our short life gives us no time for a better, but it is not the best. It does not follow, because we all are compelled to take on faith at second hand most of the rules on which we base our action and our thought, that each of us may not try to set some corner of his world in the order of reason, or that all of us collectively should not aspire to carry reason as far as it will go throughout the whole domain. In regard to the law, it is true, no doubt, that an evolutionist will hesitate to affirm universal validity for his social ideals, or for the principles which he thinks should be embodied in legislation. He is content if he can prove them best for here and now. He may be ready to admit that he knows nothing about an absolute best in the cosmos, and even that he knows next to nothing about a permanent best for men. Still it is true that a body of law is more rational and more civilized when every rule it contains is referred articulately and definitely to an end which it subserves, and when the grounds for desiring that end are stated or are ready to be stated in words.

At present, in very many cities, if we want to know why a rule of law has taken its particular shape, and more or less if we want to know why it exists at all, we go to tradition. We follow it into the Year Books, and perhaps beyond them to the customs of the Salian Franks, and somewhere in the past, in the German forests, in the needs of Norman kings, in the assumptions of a dominant class, in the absence of generalized ideas, we find out the practical motive for what now best is justified by the mere fact of its acceptance and that men are accustomed to it. The rational study of law is still to a large extent the study of history. History must be a part of the study, because without it we cannot know the precise scope of rules which it is our business to know. It is a part of the rational study, because it is the first step toward a deliberate reconsideration of the worth of those rules. When you get the dragon out of his cave on to the plain and in the daylight, you can count his teeth and claws, and see just what is his

strength. But to get him out is only the first step. The next is either to kill
him, or to tame him and make him a useful animal. For the rational study
of the law the black-letter man may be the man of the present, but the man
of the future is the man of statistics and the master of economics. It is
revolting to have no better reason for a rule of law than that so it was laid
down in the time of Henry IV. It is still more revolting if the grounds upon
which it was laid down have vanished long since, and the rule simply
persists from blind imitation of the past. I am thinking of the technical
rule as to trespass *ab initio,* as it is called, which I attempted to explain in
a recent Massachusetts case.

Let me take an illustration, which can be stated in a few words, to show
how the social end which is aimed at by a rule of law is obscured and
only partially attained in consequence of the fact that the rule owes its
form to a gradual historical development, instead of being reshaped as a
whole, with conscious articulate reference to the end in view. We think it
desirable to prevent one man's property being misappropriated by another,
and so we make larceny a crime. The evil is the same whether the mis-
appropriation is made by a man into whose hands the owner has put the
property, or by one who wrongfully takes it away. But primitive law in its
weakness did not get much beyond an effort to prevent violence, and very
naturally made a wrongful taking, a trespass, part of its definition of the
crime. In modern times the judges enlarged the definition a little by holding that, if the wrong-doer gets possession by a trick or device, the crime
is committed. This really was giving up the requirement of a trespass, and
it would have been more logical, as well as truer to the present object of
the law, to abandon the requirement altogether. That, however, would have
seemed too bold, and was left to statute. Statutes were passed making embezzlement a crime. But the force of tradition caused the crime of embezzlement to be regarded as so far distinct from larceny that to this day, in
some jurisdictions at least, a slip corner is kept open for thieves to contend,
if indicted for larceny, that they should have been indicted for embezzlement, and if indicted for embezzlement, that they should have been indicted for larceny, and to escape on that ground.

Far more fundamental questions still await a better answer than that we
do as our fathers have done. What have we better than a blind guess to
show that the criminal law in its present form does more good than harm?
I do not stop to refer to the effect which it has had in degrading prisoners
and in plunging them further into crime, or to the question whether fine and
imprisonment do not fall more heavily on a criminal's wife and children
than on himself. I have in mind more far-reaching questions. Does punishment deter? Do we deal with criminals on proper principles? A modern
school of Continental criminalists plumes itself on the formula, first suggested, it is said, by Gall, that we must consider the criminal rather than
the crime. The formula does not carry us very far, but the inquiries which

have been started look toward an answer of my questions based on science for the first time. If the typical criminal is a degenerate, bound to swindle or to murder by as deep seated an organic necessity as that which makes the rattlesnake bite, it is idle to talk of deterring him by the classical method of imprisonment. He must be got rid of; he cannot be improved, or frightened out of his structural reaction. If, on the other hand, crime, like normal human conduct, is mainly a matter of imitation, punishment fairly may be expected to help to keep it out of fashion. The study of criminals has been thought by some well known men of science to sustain the former hypothesis. The statistics of the relative increase of crime in crowded places like large cities, where example has the greatest chance to work, and in less populated parts, where the contagion spreads more slowly, have been used with great force in favor of the latter view. But there is weighty authority for the belief that, however this may be, "not the nature of the crime, but the dangerousness of the criminal, constitutes the only reasonable legal criterion to guide the inevitable social reaction against the criminal."

The impediments to rational generalization, which I illustrated from the law of mercy, are shown in the other branches of the law, as well as in that of crime. Take the law of tort or civil liability for damages apart from contract and the like. Is there any general theory of such liability, or are the cases in which it exists simply to be enumerated, and to be explained each on its special ground, as is easy to believe from the fact that the right of action for certain well known classes of wrongs like trespass or slander has its special history for each class? I think that there is a general theory to be discovered, although resting in tendency rather than established and accepted. I think that the law regards the infliction of temporal damage by a responsible person as actionable, if under the circumstances known to him the danger of his act is manifest according to common experience, or according to his own experience if it is more than common, except in cases where upon special grounds of policy the law refuses to protect the plaintiff or grants a privilege to the defendant. I think that commonly malice, intent, and negligence mean only that the danger was manifest to a greater or less degree, under the circumstances known to the actor, although in some cases of privilege malice may mean an actual malevolent motive, and such a motive may take away a permission knowingly to inflict harm, which otherwise would be granted on this or that ground of dominant public good. But when I stated my view to a very eminent English judge the other day, he said: "You are discussing what the law ought to be; as the law is, you must show a right. A man is not liable for negligence unless he is subject to a duty." If our difference was more than a difference in words, or with regard to the proportion between the exceptions and the rule, then, in his opinion, liability for an act cannot be referred to the manifest tendency of the act to cause temporal damage in general as a sufficient explanation, but must be referred to the special nature of the damage, or must be derived from some special circumstances outside of the tendency of the act, for which no generalized explanation exists. I think that such a view is wrong, but it is familiar, and I dare say generally is accepted in England.

Everywhere the basis of principle is tradition, to such an extent that we even are in danger of making the role of history more important than it is. The other day Professor Ames wrote a learned article to show, among other things, that the common law did not recognize the defense of fraud in actions upon specialties, and the moral might seem to be that the personal character of that defence is due to its equitable origin. But if, as I have said, all contracts are formal, the difference is not merely historical, but theoretic, between defects of form which prevent a contract from being made, and mistaken motives which manifestly could not be considered in any system that we should call rational except against one who was privy to those motives. It is not confined to specialties, but is of universal application. I ought to add that I do not suppose that Mr. Ames would disagree with what I suggest.

However, if we consider the law of contract, we find it full of history. The distinctions between debt, covenant, and assumpsit are merely historical. The classification of certain obligations to pay money, imposed by the law irrespective of any bargain as quasi contracts, is merely historical. The doctrine of consideration is merely historical. The effect given to a seal is to be explained by history alone.—Consideration is a mere form. Is it a useful form? If so, why should it not be required in all contracts? A seal is a mere form, and is vanishing in the scroll and in enactments that a consideration must be given, seal or no seal.—Why should any merely historical distinction be allowed to affect the rights and obligations of business men?

Since I wrote this discourse I have come on a very good example of the way in which tradition not only overrides rational policy, but overrides it after first having been misunderstood and having been given a new and broader scope than it had when it had a meaning. It is the settled law of England that a material alteration of a written contract by a party avoids it as against him. The doctrine is contrary to the general tendency of the law. We do not tell a jury that if a man ever has lied in one particular he is to be presumed to lie in all. Even if a man has tried to defraud, it seems no sufficient reason for preventing him from proving the truth. Objections of like nature in general go to the weight, not to the admissibility, of evidence. Moreover, this rule is irrespective of fraud, and is not confined to evidence. It is not merely that you cannot use the writing, but that the contract is at an end. What does this mean? The existence of a written contract depends on the fact that the offerer and offeree have interchanged their written expressions, not on the continued existence of those expressions. But in the case of a bond the primitive notion was different. The contract was inseparable from the parchment. If a stranger destroyed it, or tore off the seal, or altered it, the obligee could not recover, however free from fault, because the defendant's contract, that is, the actual tangible bond which he had sealed, could not be produced in the form in which it bound him. About a hundred years ago Lord Kenyon undertook to use his reason on this tradition, as he sometimes did to the detriment of the law, and, not understanding it, said he could see no reason why what was true of a bond should not be true of other contracts. His decision happened to be right, as it concerned a promissory note, where again the common law regarded the contract as inseparable from the paper on which it was written, but the reasoning was general, and soon was extended to other written contracts, and various absurd and unreal grounds of policy were invented to account for the enlarged rule.

I trust that no one will understand me to be speaking with disrespect of the law, because I criticise it so freely. I venerate the law, and especially our system of law, as one of the vastest products of the human mind. No one knows better than I do the countless number of great intellects that have spent themselves in making some addition or improvement, the greatest of which is trifling when compared with the mighty whole. It has the final title to respect that it exists, that it is not a Hegelian dream, but a part of the lives of men. But one may criticise even what one reveres. Law is the business to which my life is devoted, and I should show less than devotion if I did not do what in me lies to improve it, and, when I perceive what seems to me the ideal of its future, if I hesitated to point it out and to press toward it with all my heart.

Perhaps I have said enough to show the part which the study of history necessarily plays in the intelligent study of the law as it is today. In the teaching of this school and at Cambridge it is in no danger of being undervalued. Mr. Bigelow here and Mr. Ames and Mr. Thayer there have made important contributions which will not be forgotten, and in England the recent history of early English law by Sir Frederick Pollock and Mr. Maitland has lent the subject an almost deceptive charm. We must beware of the pitfall of antiquarianism, and must remember that for our purposes our only interest in the past is for the light it throws upon the present. I look forward to a time when the part played by history in the explanation of dogma shall be very small, and instead of ingenious research we shall spend our energy on a study of the ends sought to be attained and the reasons for desiring them. As a step toward that ideal it seems to me that every lawyer ought to seek an understanding of economics. The present divorce between the schools of political economy and law seems to me an evidence of how much progress in philosophical study still remains to be made. In the present state of political economy, indeed, we come again upon history on a larger scale, but there we are called on to consider and weigh the ends of legislation, the means of attaining them, and the cost. We learn that for everything we have to give up something else, and we are taught to set the advantage we gain against the other advantage we lose, and to know what we are doing when we elect.

There is another study which sometimes is undervalued by the practical minded, for which I wish to say a good word, although I think a good deal of pretty poor stuff goes under that name. I mean the study of what is called jurisprudence. Jurisprudence, as I look at it, is simply law in its most generalized part. Every effort to reduce a case to a rule is an effort of jurisprudence, although the name as used in English is confined to the broadest rules and most fundamental conceptions. One mark of a great lawyer is that he sees the application of the broadest rules. There is a story of a Vermont justice of the peace before whom a suit was brought by one farmer against another for breaking a churn. The justice took time to consider, and then said that he had looked through the statutes and could find nothing about churns, and gave judgment for the defendant. The same state of mind is shown in all our common digests and textbooks. Applications of rudimentary rules of contract or tort are tucked away under the head of Railroads or Telegraphs or go to swell treatises on historical subdivisions, such as Shipping or Equity, or are gathered under an arbitrary title which is thought likely to appeal to the practical mind, such as Mercantile Law. If a man goes into law it pays to be a master of it, and to be a master of it means to look straight through all the dramatic incidents and to discern the true basis of prophecy. Therefore, it is well to have an accurate notion of what you mean by law, by a right, by a duty, by malice, intent, and negligence, by ownership, by possession, and so forth. I have in my mind cases in which the highest courts seem to me to have floundered because they had no clear ideas on some of these themes. I have illustrated their importance already. If a further illustration is wished, it may be found by reading the Appendix to Sir James Stephen's *Criminal Law* on the subject of possession, and then turning to Pollock and Wright's enlightened book. Sir James Stephen is not the only writer whose attempts to analyze legal ideas have been confused by striving for a useless quintessence of all systems, instead of an accurate anatomy of one. The trouble with Austin was that he did not know enough English law. But still it is a practical advantage to master Austin, and his predecessors, Hobbes and Bentham, and his worthy successors, Holland and Pollock. Sir Frederick Pollock's recent little book is touched with the felicity which marks all his works, and is wholly free from the perverting influence of Roman models.

The advice of the elders to young men is very apt to be as unreal as a list of the hundred best books. At least in my day I had my share of such counsels, and high among the unrealities I place the recommendation to study the Roman law. I assume that such advice means more than collecting a few Latin maxims with which to ornament the discourse,—the purpose for which Lord Coke recommended Bracton. If that is all that is wanted, the title *De Regulis Juris Antiqui* can be read in an hour. I assume that, if it is well to study the Roman law, it is well to study it as a working system. That means mastering a set of technicalities more difficult and less understood than our own, and studying another course of history by which even more than our own the Roman law must be explained. If any one doubts me, let him read Keller's *Der Romische Civil Process und die Actionen,* a treatise on the praetor's edict, Muirhead's most interesting *Historical Introduction to the Private Law of Rome* and, to give him the best chance possible, Sohm's admirable Institutes. No. The way to gain a liberal view of your subject is not to read something else, but to get to the bottom of the subject itself. The means of doing that are, in the first place, to follow the existing body of dogma into its highest generalizations by the help of jurisprudence; next, to discover from history how it has come to be what it is; and, finally, so far as you can, to consider the ends which the several rules seek to accomplish, the reasons why those ends are desired, what is given up to gain them, and whether they are worth the price.

We have too little theory in the law rather than too much, especially on this final branch of study. When I was speaking of history, I mentioned larceny as an example to show how the law suffered from not having embodied in a clear form a rule which will accomplish its manifest purpose. In that case the trouble was due to the survival of forms coming from a time when a more limited purpose was entertained. Let me now give an example to show the practical importance, for the decision of actual cases, of understanding the reasons of the law, by taking an example from rules which, so far as I know, never have been explained or theorized about in any adequate way. I refer to statutes of limitation and the law of prescription. The end of such rules is obvious, but what is the justification for depriving a man of his rights, a pure evil as far as it goes, in consequence of the lapse of time? Sometimes the loss of evidence is referred to, but that is a secondary matter. Sometimes the desirability of peace, but why is peace more desirable after twenty years than before? It is increasingly likely to come without the aid of legislation. Sometimes it is said that, if a man neglects to enforce his rights, he cannot complain if, after a while, the law follows his example. Now if this is all that can be said about it, you probably will decide a case I am going to put, for the plaintiff; if you take the view which I shall suggest, you possibly will decide it for the defendant. A man is sued for trespass upon land, and justifies under a right of way. He proves that he has used the way openly and adversely for twenty years, but it turns out that the plaintiff had granted a license to a person whom he reasonably supposed to be the defendant's agent, although not so in fact, and therefore had assumed that the use of the way was permissive, in which case no right would be gained. Has the defendant gained a right or not? If his gaining it stands on the fault and neglect of the landowner in the ordinary sense, as seems commonly to be supposed, there has been no such neglect, and the right of way has not been acquired. But if I were the defendant's counsel, I should suggest that the foundation of the acquisition of rights by lapse of time is to be looked for in the position of the person who gains them, not in that of the loser. Sir Henry Maine has made it fashionable to connect the archaic notion of property with prescription. But the connection is further back than the first recorded history. It is in the nature of man's mind. A thing which you have enjoyed and used as your own for a long time, whether property or an opinion, takes root in your being and cannot be torn away without your resenting the act and trying to defend yourself, however you came by it. The law can ask no better justification than the deepest instincts of man. It is only by way of reply to the suggestion that you are disappointing the former owner, that you refer to his neglect having allowed the gradual dissociation between himself and what he claims, and the gradual association of it with another. If he knows that another is doing acts which on their face show that he is on the way toward establishing such an association, I should argue that in justice to that other he was bound at his peril to find out whether the other was acting under his permission, to see that he was warned, and, if necessary, stopped.

I have been speaking about the study of the law, and I have said next to nothing of what commonly is talked about in that connection,—text-books and the case system, and all the machinery with which a student comes most immediately in contact. Nor shall I say anything about them. Theory is my subject, not practical details. The modes of teaching have been improved since my time, no doubt, but ability and industry will master the raw material with any mode. Theory is the most important part of the dogma of the law, as the architect is the most important man who takes part in the building of a house. The most important improvements of the last twenty-five years are improvements in theory. It is not to be feared as unpractical, for, to the competent, it simply means going to the bottom of the subject. For the incompetent, it sometimes is true, as has been said, that an interest in general ideas means an absence of particular knowledge. I remember in army days reading of a youth who, being examined for the lowest grade and being asked a question about squadron drill, answered that he never had considered the evolutions of less than ten thousand men. But the weak and foolish must be left to their folly. The danger is that the able and practical minded should look with indifference or distrust upon ideas the connection of which with their business is remote. I heard a story, the other day, of a man who had a valet to whom he paid high wages, subject to deduction for faults. One of his deductions was, "For lack of imagination, five dollars." The lack is not confined to valets. The object of ambition, power, generally presents itself nowadays in the form of money alone. Money is the most immediate form, and is a proper object of desire. "The fortune," said Rachel, "is the measure of the intelligence." That is a good text to waken people out of a fool's paradise. But, as Hegel says, "It is in the end not the appetite, but the opinion, which has to be satisfied." To an imagination of any scope the most far-reaching form of power is not money, it is the command of ideas. If you want great examples read Mr. Leslie Stephen's *History of English Thought in the Eighteenth Century,* and see how a hundred years after his death the abstract speculations of Descartes had become a practical force controlling the conduct of men. Read the works of the great German jurists, and see how much more the world is governed to-day by Kant than by Bonaparte. We cannot all be Descartes or Kant, but we all want happiness. And happiness, I am sure from having known many successful men, cannot be won simply by being counsel for great corporations and having an income of fifty thousand dollars. An intellect great enough to win the prize needs other food beside success. The remoter and more general aspects of the law are those which give it universal interest. It is through them that you not only become a great master in your calling, but connect your subject with the universe and catch an echo of the infinite, a glimpse of its unfathomable process, a hint of the universal law.

The Case of the Speluncean Explorers *

IN THE SUPREME COURT OF NEWGARTH, 4300

LON L. FULLER

One way of "bringing into a common focus certain divergent philosophies of law and government" is to write a piece of fiction with the impact of fact. "The Case of the Speluncean Explorers" is dated 4300, and the issue is murder and cannibalism.

Professor Lon L. Fuller has been Carter Professor of General Jurisprudence in the Harvard Law School since 1948. He was born in 1902 and educated at California and Stanford. His Massachusetts law practice has been with Ropes, Gray, Best, Coolidge, and Rugg of Boston. He is also the author of The Law in Quest of Itself.

The defendants, having been indicted for the crime of murder, were convicted and sentenced to be hanged by the Court of General In-stances of the County of Stowfield. They bring a petition of error before this Court. The facts sufficiently appear in the opinion of the Chief Justice.

TRUEPENNY, C. J. The four defendants are members of the Speluncean Society, an organization of amateurs interested in the exploration of caves. Early in May of 4299 they, in the company of Roger Whetmore, then also a member of the Society, penetrated into the interior of a limestone cavern of the type found in the Central Plateau of this Commonwealth. While they were in a position remote from the entrance to the cave, a landslide occurred. Heavy boulders fell in such a manner as to block completely the only known opening to the cave. When the men discovered their predicament they settled themselves near the obstructed entrance to wait until a rescue party should remove the detritus that prevented them from leaving their underground prison. On the failure of Whetmore and the defendants to return to their homes, the Secretary of the Society was notified by their families. It appears that the explorers had left indications at the headquarters of the Society concerning the location of the cave they proposed to visit. A rescue party was promptly dispatched to the spot.

The task of rescue proved one of overwhelming difficulty. It was necessary to supplement the forces of the original party by repeated increments of men and machines, which had to be conveyed at great expense to the remote and isolated region in which the cave was located. A huge temporary camp of workmen, engineers, geologists, and other experts was established. The work of removing the obstruction was several times frustrated by fresh landslides. In one of these, ten of the workmen engaged in clearing the entrance were killed. The treasury of the Speluncean Society was soon exhausted in the rescue effort, and the sum of eight hundred thousand frelars, raised partly by popular subscription and partly by legislative grant, was expended before the imprisoned men were rescued. Success was finally achieved on the thirty-second day after the men entered the cave.

Since it was known that the explorers had carried with them only scant provisions, and since it was also known that there was no animal or vegetable matter within the cave on which they might subsist, anxiety was early felt that they might meet death by starvation before access to them could be obtained. On the twentieth day of their imprisonment it was learned for the first time that they had taken with them into the cave a portable wireless machine capable of both sending and receiving messages. A similar machine was promptly installed in the rescue camp and oral communication established with the unfortunate men within the mountain. They asked to be informed how long a time would be required to release them. The engineers in charge of the project answered that at least ten days would be required even if no new landslides occurred. The explorers then asked if any physicians were present, and were placed in communication with a committee of medical experts. The imprisoned men described their condition and the rations they had taken with them, and asked for a medical opinion whether they would be likely to live without food for ten days longer. The chairman of the committee of physicians told them that there was little possibility of this. The wireless machine within the cave then remained silent for eight hours. When communication was re-established the men asked to speak again with the physicians. The chairman of the physicians' committee was placed before the apparatus, and Whetmore, speaking on behalf of himself and the defendants, asked whether they would be able to survive for ten days longer if they consumed the flesh of one of their number. The physicians' chairman reluctantly answered this question in the affirmative. Whetmore asked whether it would be advisable for them to cast lots to determine which of them should be eaten. None of the physicians present was willing to answer the question. Whetmore then asked if there were among the party a judge or other official of the government who would answer this question. None of those attached to the rescue camp was willing to assume the role of advisor in this matter. He then asked if any minister or priest would answer their question, and none was found who would do so. Thereafter no further messages were received from within the cave, and it was assumed (erroneously, it later appeared) that the electric batteries of the explorers' wireless machine had become exhausted. When the imprisoned men were finally released it was learned that on the twenty-third day after their entrance into the cave Whetmore had been killed and eaten by his companions.

From the testimony of the defendants, which was accepted by the jury, it appears that it was Whetmore who first proposed that they might find the nutriment without which survival was impossible in the flesh of one of their own number. It was also Whetmore who first proposed the use of some method of casting lots, calling the attention of the defendants to a pair of dice he happened to have with him. The defendants were at first reluctant to adopt so desperate a procedure, but after the conversations by wireless related above, they finally agreed on the plan proposed by Whetmore. After much discussion of the mathematical problems involved, agreement was finally reached on a method of determining the issue by the use of the dice.

Before the dice were cast, however, Whetmore declared that he withdrew from the arrangement, as he had decided on reflection to wait for another week before embracing an expedient so frightful and odious. The others charged him with a breach of faith and proceeded to cast the dice. When it came Whetmore's turn, the dice were cast for him by one of the defendants, and he was asked to declare any objection he might have to the fairness of the throw. He stated that he had no such objections. The throw went against him, and he was then put to death and eaten by his companions.

After the rescue of the defendants, and after they had completed a stay in a hospital where they underwent a course of treatment for malnutrition and shock, they were indicted for the murder of Roger Whetmore. At the trial, after the testimony had been concluded, the foreman of the jury (a lawyer by profession) inquired of the court whether the jury might not find a special verdict, leaving it to the court to say whether on the facts as found the defendants were guilty. After some discussion, both the Prosecutor and counsel for the defendants indicated their acceptance of this procedure, and it was adopted by the court. In a lengthy special verdict the jury found the facts as I have related them above, and found further that if on these facts the defendants were guilty of the crime charged against them, then they found the defendants guilty. On the basis of this verdict, the trial judge ruled that the defendants were guilty of murdering Roger Whetmore. The judge then sentenced them to be hanged, the law of our Commonwealth permitting him no discretion with respect to the penalty to be imposed. After the release of the jury, its members joined in a communication to the Chief Executive asking that the sentence be commuted to an imprisonment of six months. The trial judge addressed a similar communication to the Chief Executive. As yet no action with respect to these pleas has been taken, as the Chief Executive is apparently awaiting our disposition of this petition of error.

It seems to me that in dealing with this extraordinary case the jury and the trial judge followed a course that was not only fair and wise, but the only course that was open to them under the law. The language of our statute is well known: "Whoever shall willfully take the life of another shall be punished by death." N. C. S. A. (N. s.) § 12-A. This statute permits of no exception applicable to this case, however our sympathies may incline us to make allowance for the tragic situation in which these men found themselves.

In a case like this the principle of executive clemency seems admirably suited to mitigate the rigors of the law, and I propose to my colleagues that we follow the example of the jury and the trial judge by joining in the communications they have addressed to the Chief Executive. There is every reason to believe that these requests for clemency will be heeded, coming as they do from those who have studied the case and had an opportunity to become thoroughly acquainted with all its circumstances. It is highly improbable that the Chief Executive would deny these requests unless he were himself to hold hearings at least as extensive as those involved in the trial below, which lasted for three months. The holding of such hearings (which would virtually amount to a retrial of the case) would scarcely be compatible with the function of the Executive as it is usually conceived. I think we may therefore assume that some form of clemency will be extended to these defendants. If this is done, then justice will be accomplished without impairing either the letter or spirit of our statutes and without offering any encouragement for the disregard of law.

FOSTER, J. I am shocked that the Chief Justice, in an effort to escape the embarrassments of this tragic case, should have adopted, and should have proposed to his colleagues, an expedient at once so sordid and so obvious. I believe something more is on trial in this case than the fate of these unfortunate explorers; that is the law of our Commonwealth. If this Court declares that under our law these men have committed a crime, then our law is itself convicted in the tribunal of common sense, no matter what happens to the individuals involved in this petition of error. For us to assert that the law we uphold and expound compels us to a conclusion we are ashamed of, and from which we can only escape by appealing to a dispensation resting within the personal whim of the Executive, seems to me to amount to an admission that the law of this Commonwealth no longer pretends to incorporate justice.

For myself, I do not believe that our law compels the monstrous conclusion that these men are murderers. I believe, on the contrary, that it declares them to be innocent of any crime. I rest this conclusion on two independent grounds, either of which is of itself sufficient to justify the acquittal of these defendants.

The first of these grounds rests on a premise that may arouse opposition until it has been examined candidly. I take the view that the enacted or positive law of this Commonwealth, including all of its statutes and precedents, is inapplicable to this case, and that the case is governed instead by what ancient writers in Europe and America called "the law of nature."

This conclusion rests on the proposition that our positive law is predicated on the possibility of men's coexistence in society. When a situation arises in which the coexistence of men becomes impossible, then a condition that underlies all of our precedents and statutes has ceased to exist. When that condition disappears, then it is my opinion that the force of our positive law disappears with it. We are not accustomed to applying the maxim *cessante ratione legis, cessat et ipsa lex* to the whole of our enacted law, but I believe that this is a case where the maxim should be so applied.

The proposition that all positive law is based on the possibility of men's coexistence has a strange sound, not because the truth it contains is strange, but simply because it is a truth so obvious and pervasive that we seldom have occasion to give words to it. Like the air we breathe, it so pervades our environment that we forget that it exists until we are suddenly deprived of it. Whatever particular objects may be sought by the various branches of our law, it is apparent on reflection that all of them are directed toward facilitating and improving men's coexistence and regulating with fairness and equity the relations of their life in common. When the assumption that men may live together loses its truth, as it obviously did in this extraordinary situation where life only became possible by the taking of life, then the basic premises underlying our whole legal order have lost their meaning and force.

Had the tragic events of this case taken place a mile beyond the territorial limits of our Commonwealth, no one would pretend that our law was applicable to them. We recognize that jurisdiction rests on a territorial basis. The grounds of this principle are by no means obvious and are seldom examined. I take it that this principle is supported by an assumption that it is feasible to impose a single legal order upon a group of men only if they live together within the confines of a given area of the earth's surface. The premise that men shall coexist in a group underlies, then, the territorial principle, as it does all of law. Now I contend that a case may be removed morally from the force of a legal order, as well as geographically. If we look to the purposes of law and government, and to the premises underlying our positive law, these men when they made their fateful decision were as remote from our legal order as if they had been a thousand miles beyond our boundaries. Even in a physical sense, their underground prison was separated from our courts and writ-servers by a solid curtain of rock that could be removed only after the most extraordinary expenditures of time and effort.

I conclude, therefore, that at the time Roger Whetmore's life was ended by these defendants, they were, to use the quaint language of nineteenth-century writers, not in a "state of civil society" but in a "state of nature." This has the consequence that the law applicable to them is not the enacted and established law of this Commonwealth, but the law derived from those principles that were appropriate to their condition. I have no hesitancy in saying that under those principles they were guiltless of any crime.

What these men did was done in pursuance of an agreement accepted by all of them and first proposed by Whetmore himself. Since it was apparent that their extraordinary predicament made inapplicable the usual principles that regulate men's relations with one another, it was necessary for them to draw, as it were, a new charter of government appropriate to the situation in which they found themselves.

It has from antiquity been recognized that the most basic principle of law or government is to be found in the notion of contract or agreement. Ancient thinkers, especially during the period from 1600 to 1900, used to base government itself on a supposed original social compact. Skeptics pointed out that this theory contradicted the known facts of history, and that there was no scientific evidence to support the notion that any government was ever founded in the manner supposed by the theory. Moralists replied that, if the compact was a fiction from a historical point of view, the notion of compact or agreement furnished the only ethical justification on which the powers of government, which include that of taking life, could be rested. The powers of government can only be justified morally on the ground that these are powers that reasonable men would agree upon and accept if they were faced with the necessity of constructing anew some order to make their life in common possible.

Fortunately, our Commonwealth is not bothered by the perplexities that beset the ancients. We know as a matter of historical truth that our government was founded upon a contract or free accord of men. The archeological proof is conclusive that in the first period following the Great Spiral the survivors of that holocaust voluntarily came together and drew up a charter of government. Sophistical writers have raised questions as to the power of those remote contractors to bind future generations, but the fact remains that our government traces itself back in an unbroken line to that original charter.

If, therefore, our hangmen have the power to end men's lives, if our sheriffs have the power to put delinquent tenants in the street, if our police have the power to incarcerate the inebriated reveler, these powers find their moral justification in that original compact of our forefathers. If we can find no higher source for our legal order, what higher source should we expect these starving unfortunates to find for the order they adopted for themselves?

I believe that the line of argument I have just expounded permits of no rational answer. I realize that it will probably be received with a certain discomfort by many who read this opinion, who will be inclined to suspect that some hidden sophistry must underlie a demonstration that leads to so many unfamiliar conclusions. The source of this discomfort is, however, easy to identify. The usual conditions of human existence incline us to think of human life as an absolute value, not to be sacrificed under any circumstances. There is much that is fictitious about this conception even when it is applied to the ordinary relations of society. We have an illustration of this truth in the very case before us. Ten workmen were killed in the process of removing the rocks from the opening to the cave. Did not the engineers and government officials who directed the rescue effort know that the operations they were undertaking were dangerous and involved a serious risk to the lives of the workmen executing them? If it was proper that these ten lives should be sacrificed to save the lives of five imprisoned explorers, why then are we told it was wrong for these explorers to carry out an arrangement which would save four lives at the cost of one?

Every highway, every tunnel, every building we project involves a risk to human life. Taking these projects in the aggregate, we can calculate with some precision how many deaths the construction of them will require; statisticians can tell you the average cost in human lives of a thousand miles of a four-lane concrete highway. Yet we deliberately and knowingly incur and pay this cost on the assumption that the values obtained for those who survive outweigh the loss. If these things can be said of a society functioning above ground in a normal and ordinary manner, what shall we say of the supposed absolute value of a human life in the desperate situation in which these defendants and their companion Whetmore found themselves?

This concludes the exposition of the first ground of my decision. My second ground proceeds by rejecting hypothetically all the premises on which I have so far proceeded. I concede for purposes of argument that I am wrong in saying that the situation of these men removed them from the effect of our positive law, and I assume that the Consolidated Statutes have the power to penetrate five hundred feet of rock and to impose themselves upon these starving men huddled in their underground prison.

Now it is, of course, perfectly clear that these men did an act that violates the literal wording of the statute which declares that he who "shall willfully take the life of another" is a murderer. But one of the most ancient bits of legal wisdom is the saying that a man may break the letter of the law without breaking the law itself. Every proposition of positive law, whether contained in a statute or a judicial precedent, is to be interpreted reasonably, in the light of its evident purpose. This is a truth so elementary that it is hardly necessary to expatiate on it. Illustrations of its application are numberless and are to be found in every branch of the law. In *Commonwealth v. Staymore* the defendant was convicted under a statute making it a crime to leave one's car parked in certain areas for a period longer than two hours. The defendant had attempted to remove his car, but was prevented from doing so because the streets were obstructed by a political demonstration in which he took no part and which he had no reason to anticipate. His conviction was set aside by this Court, although his case fell squarely within the wording of the statute. Again, in *Fehler v. Neegas* there was before this Court for construction a statute in which the word "not" had plainly been transposed from its intended position in the final and most crucial section of the act. This transposition was contained in all the successive drafts of the act, where it was apparently overlooked by the draftsmen and sponsors of the legislation. No one was able to prove how the error came about, yet it was apparent that, taking account of the contents of the statute as a whole, an error had been made, since a literal reading of the final clause rendered it inconsistent with everything that had gone before and with the object of the enactment as stated in its preamble. This Court refused to accept a literal interpretation of the statute, and in effect rectified its language by reading the word "not" into the place where it was evidently intended to go.

The statute before us for interpretation has never been applied literally. Centuries ago it was established that a killing in self-defense is excused. There is nothing in the wording of the statute that suggests this exception. Various attempts have been made to reconcile the legal treatment of self-defense with the words of the statute, but in my opinion these are all merely ingenious sophistries. The truth is that the exception in favor of self-defense cannot be reconciled with the *words* of the statute, but only with its *purpose*.

The true reconciliation of the excuse of self-defense with the statute making it a crime to kill another is to be found in the following line of reasoning. One of the principal objects underlying any criminal legislation is that of deterring men from crime. Now it is apparent that if it were declared to be the law that a killing in self-defense is murder such a rule could not operate in a deterrent manner. A man whose life is threatened will repel his aggressor, whatever the law may say. Looking therefore to the broad purposes of criminal legislation, we may safely declare that this statute was not intended to apply to cases of self-defense.

When the rationale of the excuse of self-defense is thus explained, it becomes apparent that precisely the same reasoning is applicable to the case at bar. If in the future any group of men ever find themselves in the tragic predicament of these defendants, we may be sure that their decision whether to live or die will not be controlled by the contents of our criminal code. Accordingly, if we read this statute intelligently it is apparent that it does not apply to this case. The withdrawal of this situation from the effect of the statute is justified by precisely the same considerations that were applied by our predecessors in office centuries ago to the case of self-defense.

There are those who raise the cry of judicial usurpation whenever a court, after analyzing the purpose of a statute, gives to its words a meaning that is not at once apparent to the casual reader who has not studied the statute closely or examined the objectives it seeks to attain. Let me say emphatically that I accept without reservation the proposition that this Court is bound by the statutes of our Commonwealth and that it exercises its powers in subservience to the duly expressed will of the Chamber of Representatives. The line of reasoning I have applied above raises no question of fidelity to enacted law, though it may possibly raise a question of the distinction between intelligent and unintelligent fidelity. No superior wants a servant who lacks the capacity to read between the lines. The stupidest housemaid knows that when she is told "to peel the soup and skim the potatoes" her mistress does not mean what she says. She also knows that when her master tells her to "drop everything and come running" he has overlooked the possibility that she is at the moment in the act of rescuing the baby from the rain barrel. Surely we have a right to expect the same modicum of intelligence from the judiciary. The correction of obvious legislative errors or oversights is not to supplant the legislative will, but to make that will effective.

I therefore conclude that on any aspect under which this case may be viewed these defendants are innocent of the crime of murdering Roger Whetmore, and that the conviction should be set aside.

TATTING, J. In the discharge of my duties as a justice of this Court, I am usually able to dissociate the emotional and intellectual sides of my reactions, and to decide the case before me entirely on the basis of the latter. In passing on this tragic case I find that my usual resources fail me. On the emotional side I find myself torn between sympathy for these men and a feeling of abhorrence and disgust at the monstrous act they committed. I had hoped that I would be able to put these contradictory emotions to one side as irrelevant, and to decide the case on the basis of a convincing and logical demonstration of the result demanded by our law. Unfortunately, this deliverance has not been vouchsafed me.

As I analyze the opinion just rendered by my brother Foster, I find that it is shot through with contradictions and fallacies. Let us begin with his first proposition: these men were not subject to our law because they were not in a "state of civil society" but in a "state of nature." I am not clear why this is so, whether it is because of the thickness of the rock that imprisoned them, or because they were hungry, or because they had set up a "new charter of government" by which the usual rules of law were to be supplanted by a throw of the dice. Other difficulties intrude themselves. If these men passed from the jurisdiction of our law to that of "the law of nature," at what moment did this occur? Was it when the entrance to the cave was blocked, or when the threat of starvation reached a certain undefined degree of intensity, or when the agreement for the throwing of the dice was made? These uncertainties in the doctrine proposed by my brother are capable of producing real difficulties. Suppose, for example, one of these men had had his twenty-first birthday while he was imprisoned within the mountain. On what date would we have to consider that he had attained his majority—when he reached the age of twenty-one, at which time he was, by hypothesis, removed from the effects of our law, or only when he was released from the cave and became again subject to what my brother calls our "positive law"? These difficulties may seem fanciful, yet they only serve to reveal the fanciful nature of the doctrine that is capable of giving rise to them.

But it is not necessary to explore these niceties further to demonstrate the absurdity of my brother's position. Mr. Justice Foster and I are the appointed judges of a court of the Commonwealth of Newgarth, sworn and empowered to administer the laws of that Commonwealth. By what authority do we resolve ourselves into a Court of Nature? If these men were indeed under the law of nature, whence comes our authority to expound and apply that law? Certainly *we* are not in a state of nature.

Let us look at the contents of this code of nature that my brother proposes we adopt as our own and apply to this case. What a topsy-turvy and odious code it is! It is a code in which the law of contracts is more fundamental than the law of murder. It is a code under which a man may make a valid agreement empowering his fellows to eat his own body. Under the provisions of this code, furthermore, such an agreement once made is irrevocable, and if one of the parties attempts to withdraw, the others may take the law into their own hands and enforce the contract by violence—for though my brother passes over in convenient silence the effect of Whetmore's withdrawal, this is the necessary implication of his argument.

The principles my brother expounds contain other implications that cannot be tolerated. He argues that when the defendants set upon Whetmore and killed him (we know not how, perhaps by pounding him with stones) they were only exercising the rights conferred upon them by their bargain. Suppose, however, that Whetmore had had concealed upon his person a revolver, and that when he saw the defendants about to slaughter him he had shot them to death in order to save his own life. My brother's reasoning applied to these facts would make Whetmore out to be a murderer, since the excuse of self-defense would have to be denied to him. If his assailants were acting rightfully in seeking to bring about his death, then of course he could no more plead the excuse that he was defending his own life than could a condemned prisoner who struck down the executioner lawfully attempting to place the noose about his neck.

All of these considerations make it impossible for me to accept the first part of my brother's argument. I can neither accept his notion that these men were under a code of nature which this Court was bound to apply to them, nor can I accept the odious and perverted rules that he would read into that code. I come now to the second part of my brother's opinion, in which he seeks to show that the defendants did not violate the provisions of N. C. S. A. (N. S.) § 12-A. Here the way, instead of being clear, becomes for me misty and ambiguous, though my brother seems unaware of the difficulties that inhere in his demonstrations.

The gist of my brother's argument may be stated in the following terms: No statute, whatever its language, should be applied in a way that contradicts its purpose. One of the purposes of any criminal statute is to deter. The application of the statute making it a crime to kill another to the peculiar facts of this case would contradict this purpose, for it is impossible to believe that the contents of the criminal code could operate in a deterrent manner on men faced with the alternative of life or death. The reasoning by which this exception is read into the statute is, my brother observes, the same as that which is applied in order to provide the excuse of self-defense.

On the face of things this demonstration seems very convincing indeed. My brother's interpretation of the rationale of the excuse of self-defense is in fact supported by a decision of this court, *Commonwealth v. Parry,* a precedent I happened to encounter in my research on this case. Though *Commonwealth v. Parry* seems generally to have been overlooked in the texts and subsequent decisions, it supports unambiguously the interpretation my brother has put upon the excuse of self-defense.

Now let me outline briefly, however, the perplexities that assail me when I examine my brother's demonstration more closely. It is true that a statute should be applied in the light of its purpose, and that *one* of the purposes of criminal legislation is recognized to be deterrence. The difficulty is that other purposes are also ascribed to the law of crimes. It has been said that one of its objects is to provide an orderly outlet for the instinctive human demand for retribution. *Commonwealth v. Scape.* It has also been said that its object is the rehabilitation of the wrongdoer. *Commonwealth v. Make-over.* Other theories have been propounded. Assuming that we must interpret a statute in the light of its purpose, what are we to do when it has many purposes or when its purposes are disputed?

A similar difficulty is presented by the fact that although there is authority for my brother's interpretation of the excuse of self-defense, there is other authority which assigns to that excuse a different rationale. Indeed, until I happened on *Commonwealth v. Parry* I had never heard of the explanation given by my brother. The taught doctrine of our law schools, memorized by generations of law students, runs in the following terms: The statute concerning murder requires a "willful" act. The man who acts to repel an aggressive threat to his own life does not act "willfully," but in response to an impulse deeply ingrained in human nature. I suspect that there is hardly a lawyer in this Commonwealth who is not familiar with this line of reasoning, especially since the point is a great favorite of the bar examiners.

Now the familiar explanation for the excuse of self-defense just expounded obviously cannot be applied by analogy to the facts of this case. These men acted not only "willfully" but with great deliberation and after hours of discussing what they should do. Again we encounter a forked path, with one line of reasoning leading us in one direction and another in a direction that is exactly the opposite. This perplexity is in this case compounded, as it were, for we have to set off one explanation, incorporated in a virtually unknown precedent of this Court, against another explanation, which forms a part of the taught legal tradition of our law schools, but which, so far as I know, has never been adopted in any judicial decision.

I recognize the relevance of the precedents cited by my brother concerning the displaced "not" and the defendant who parked overtime. But what are we to do with one of the landmarks of our jurisprudence, which again my brother passes over in silence? This is *Commonwealth v. Valjean.* Though the case is somewhat obscurely reported, it appears that the defendant was indicted for the larceny of a loaf of bread, and offered as a defense that he was in a condition approaching starvation. The court refused to accept this defense. If hunger cannot justify the theft of wholesome and natural food, how can it justify the killing and eating of a man? Again, if we look at the thing in terms of deterrence, is it likely that a man will starve to death to avoid a jail sentence for the theft of a loaf of bread? My brother's demonstrations would compel us to overrule *Commonwealth v. Valjean,* and many other precedents that have been built on that case.

Again, I have difficulty in saying that no deterrent effect whatever could be attributed to a decision that these men were guilty of murder. The stigma of the word "murderer" is such that it is quite likely, I believe, that if these men had known that their act was deemed by the law to be murder they would have waited for a few days at least before carrying out their plan. During that time some unexpected relief might have come. I realize that this observation only reduces the distinction to a matter of degree, and does not destroy it altogether. It is certainly true that the element of deterrence would be less in this case than is normally involved in the application of the criminal law.

There is still a further difficulty in my brother Foster's proposal to read an exception into the statute to favor this case, though again a difficulty not even intimated in his opinion. What shall be the scope of this exception? Here the men cast lots and the victim was himself originally a party to the agreement. What would we have to decide if Whetmore had refused from the beginning to participate in the plan? Would a majority be permitted to overrule him? Or, suppose that no plan were adopted at all and the others simply conspired to bring about Whetmore's death, justifying

LON L. FULLER

their act by saying that he was in the weakest condition. Or again, that a plan of selection was followed but one based on a different justification than the one adopted here, as if the others were atheists and insisted that Whetmore should die because he was the only one who believed in an after-life. These illustrations could be multiplied, but enough have been suggested to reveal what a quagmire of hidden difficulties my brother's reasoning contains.

Of course I realize on reflection that I may be concerning myself with a problem that will never arise, since it is unlikely that any group of men will ever again be brought to commit the dread act that was involved here. Yet, on still further reflection, even if we are certain that no similar case will arise again, do not the illustrations I have given show the lack of any coherent and rational principle in the rule my brother proposes? Should not the soundness of a principle be tested by the conclusions it entails, without reference to the accidents of later litigational history? Still, if this is so, why is it that we of this Court so often discuss the question whether we are likely to have later occasion to apply a principle urged for the solution of the case before us? Is this a situation where a line of reasoning not originally proper has become sanctioned by precedent, so that we are permitted to apply it and may even be under an obligation to do so?

The more I examine this case and think about it, the more deeply I become involved. My mind becomes entangled in the meshes of the very nets I throw out for my own rescue. I find that almost every consideration that bears on the decision of the case is counterbalanced by an opposing consideration leading in the opposite direction. My brother Foster has not furnished to me, nor can I discover for myself, any formula capable of resolving the equivocations that beset me on all sides.

I have given this case the best thought of which I am capable. I have scarcely slept since it was argued before us. When I feel myself inclined to accept the view of my brother Foster, I am repelled by a feeling that his arguments are intellectually unsound and approach mere rationalization. On the other hand, when I incline toward upholding the conviction, I am struck by the absurdity of directing that these men be put to death when their lives have been saved at the cost of the lives of ten heroic workmen. It is to me a matter of regret that the Prosecutor saw fit to ask for an indictment for murder. If we had a provision in our statutes making it a crime to eat human flesh, that would have been a more appropriate charge. If no other charge suited to the facts of this case could be brought against the defendants, it would have been wiser, I think, not to have indicted them at all. Unfortunately, however, the men have been indicted and tried, and we have therefore been drawn into this unfortunate affair.

Since I have been wholly unable to resolve the doubts that beset me about the law of this case, I am with regret announcing a step that is, I believe, unprecedented in the history of this tribunal. I declare my withdrawal from the decision of this case.

KEEN, J. I should like to begin by setting to one side two questions which are not before this Court.

The first of these is whether executive clemency should be extended to these defendants if the conviction is affirmed. Under our system of government, that is a question for the Chief Executive, not for us. I therefore disapprove of that passage in the opinion of the Chief Justice in which he in effect gives instructions to the Chief Executive as to what he should do in this case and suggests that some impropriety will attach if these instructions are not heeded. This is a confusion of governmental functions—a confusion of which the judiciary should be the last to be guilty. I wish to state that if I were the Chief Executive I would go farther in the direction of clemency than the pleas addressed to him propose. I would pardon these men altogether, since I believe that they have already suffered enough to pay for any offense they may have committed. I want it to be understood that this remark is made in my capacity as a private citizen who by the accident of his office happens to have acquired an intimate acquaintance with the facts of this case. In the discharge of my duties as judge, it is neither my function to address directions to the Chief Executive, nor to take into account what he may or may not do, in reaching my own decision, which must be controlled entirely by the law of this Commonwealth.

The second question that I wish to put to one side is that of deciding whether what these men did was "right" or "wrong," "wicked" or "good." That is also a question that is irrelevant to the discharge of my office as a judge sworn to apply, not my conceptions of morality, but the law of the land. In putting this question to one side I think I can also safely dismiss without comment the first and more poetic portion of my brother Foster's opinion. The element of fantasy contained in the arguments developed there has been sufficiently revealed in my brother Tatting's somewhat solemn attempt to take those arguments seriously.

The sole question before us for decision is whether these defendants did, within the meaning of N. C. S. A. (N. S.) § 12-A, willfully take the life of Roger Whetmore. The exact language of the statute is as follows: "Whoever shall willfully take the life of another shall be punished by death." Now I should suppose that any candid observer, content to extract from these words their natural meaning, would concede at once that these defendants did "willfully take the life" of Roger Whetmore.

Whence arise all the difficulties of the case, then, and the necessity for so many pages of discussion about what ought to be so obvious? The difficulties, in whatever tortured form they may present themselves, all trace back to a single source, and that is a failure to distinguish the legal from the moral aspects of this case. To put it bluntly, my brothers do not like the fact that the written law requires the conviction of these defendants. Neither do I, but unlike my brothers I respect the obligations of an office that requires me to put my personal predilections out of my mind when I come to interpret and apply the law of this Commonwealth.

Now, of course, my brother Foster does not admit that he is actuated by a personal dislike of the written law. Instead he develops a familiar line of argument according to which the court may disregard the express language of a statute when something not contained in the statute itself, called its "purpose," can be employed to justify the result the court considers proper. Because this is an old issue between myself and my colleague, I should like, before discussing his particular application of the argument to the facts of this case, to say something about the historical background of this issue and its implications for law and government generally.

There was a time in this Commonwealth when judges did in fact legislate very freely, and all of us know that during that period some of our statutes were rather thoroughly made over by the judiciary. That was a time when the accepted principles of political science did not designate with any certainty the rank and function of the various arms of the state. We all know the tragic issue of that uncertainty in the brief civil war that arose out of the conflict between the judiciary, on the one hand, and the executive and the legislature, on the other. There is no need to recount here the factors that contributed to that unseemly struggle for power, though they included the unrepresentative character of the Chamber, resulting from a division of the country into election districts that no longer accorded with the actual distribution of the population, and the forceful personality and wide popular following of the then Chief Justice. It is enough to observe that those days are behind us, and that in place of the uncertainty that then reigned we now have a clear-cut principle, which is the supremacy of the legislative branch of our government. From that principle flows the obligation of the judiciary to enforce faithfully the written law, and to interpret that law in accordance with its plain meaning without reference to our personal desires or our individual conceptions of justice. I am not concerned with the question whether the principle that forbids the judicial revision of statutes is right or wrong, desirable or undesirable; I observe merely that this principle has become a tacit premise underlying the whole of the legal and governmental order I am sworn to administer.

Yet though the principle of the supremacy of the legislature has been accepted in theory for centuries, such is the tenacity of professional tradition and the force of fixed habits of thought that many of the judiciary have still not accommodated themselves to the restricted role which the new order imposes on them. My brother Foster is one of that group; his way of dealing with statutes is exactly that of a judge living in the 3900's.

We are all familiar with the process by which the judicial reform of disfavored legislative enactments is accomplished. Anyone who has followed the written opinions of Mr. Justice Foster will have had an opportunity to see it at work in every branch of the law. I am personally so familiar with the process that in the event of my brother's incapacity I am sure I could write a satisfactory opinion for him without any prompting whatever, beyond being informed whether he liked the effect of the terms of the statute as applied to the case before him.

The process of judicial reform requires three steps. The first of these is to divine some single "purpose" which the statute serves. This is done although not one statute in a hundred has any such single purpose, and although the objectives of nearly every statute are differently interpreted by the different classes of its sponsors. The second step is to discover that a mythical being called "the legislator," in the pursuit of this imagined "purpose," overlooked something or left some gap or imperfection in his work. Then comes the final and most refreshing part of the task, which is, of course, to fill in the blank thus created. *Quod erat faciendum.*

My brother Foster's penchant for finding holes in statutes reminds one of the story told by an ancient author about the man who ate a pair of shoes. Asked how he liked them, he replied that the part he liked best was the holes. That is the way my brother feels about statutes; the more holes they have in them the better he likes them. In short, he doesn't like statutes.

One could not wish for a better case to illustrate the specious nature of this gap-filling process than the one before us. My brother thinks he knows exactly what was sought when men made murder a crime, and that was something he calls "deterrence." My brother Tatting has already shown how much is passed over in that interpretation. But I think the trouble goes deeper. I doubt very much whether our statute making murder a crime really has a "purpose" in any ordinary sense of the term. Primarily, such a statute reflects a deeply-felt human conviction that murder is wrong and that something should be done to the man who commits it. If we were forced to be more articulate about the matter, we would probably take refuge in the more sophisticated theories of the criminologists, which, of course, were certainly not in the minds of those who drafted our statute. We might also observe that men will do their own work more effectively and live happier lives if they are protected against the threat of violent assault. Bearing in mind that the victims of murders are often unpleasant people, we might add some suggestion that the matter of disposing of undesirables is not a function suited to private enterprise, but should be a state monopoly. All of which reminds me of the attorney who once argued before us that a statute licensing physicians was a good thing because it would lead to lower life insurance rates by lifting the level of general health. There is such a thing as overexplaining the obvious.

If we do not know the purpose of § 12-A, how can we possibly say there is a "gap" in it? How can we know what its draftsmen thought about the question of killing men in order to eat them? My brother Tatting has revealed an understandable, though perhaps slightly exaggerated revulsion to cannibalism. How do we know that his remote ancestors did not feel the same revulsion to an even higher degree? Anthropologists say that the dread felt for a forbidden act may be increased by the fact that the conditions of a tribe's life create special temptations toward it, as incest is most severely condemned among those whose village relations make it most likely to occur. Certainly the period following the Great Spiral was one that had implicit in it temptations to anthropophagy. Perhaps it was for that very reason that our ancestors expressed their prohibition in so broad and unqualified a form. All of this is conjecture, of course, but it remains abundantly clear that neither I nor my brother Foster knows what the "purpose" of § 12-A is.

Considerations similar to those I have just outlined are also applicable to the exception in favor of self-defense, which plays so large a role in the reasoning of my brothers Foster and Tatting. It is of course true that in *Commonwealth v. Parry* an obiter dictum justified this exception on the assumption that the purpose of criminal legislation is to deter. It may well also be true that generations of law students have been taught that the true explanation of the exception lies in the fact that a man who acts in self-defense does not act "willfully," and that the same students have passed their bar examinations by repeating what their professors told them. These last observations I could dismiss, of course, as irrelevant for the simple reason that professors and bar examiners have not as yet any commission to make our laws for us. But again the real trouble lies deeper. As in dealing with the statute, so in dealing with the exception, the question is not the conjectural *purpose* of the rule, but its *scope*. Now the scope of the exception in favor of self-defense as it has been applied by this Court is plain: it applies to cases of resisting an aggressive threat to the party's own life. It is therefore too clear for argument that this case does not fall within the scope of the exception, since it is plain that Whetmore made no threat against the lives of these defendants.

The essential shabbiness of my brother Foster's attempt to cloak his remaking of the written law with an air of legitimacy comes tragically to the surface in my brother Tatting's opinion. In that opinion Justice Tatting struggles manfully to combine his colleague's loose moralisms with his own sense of fidelity to the written law. The issue of this struggle could only be that which occurred, a complete default in the discharge of the judicial function. You simply cannot apply a statute as it is written and remake it to meet your own wishes at the same time.

Now I know that the line of reasoning I have developed in this opinion will not be acceptable to those who look only to the immediate effects of a decision and ignore the long-run implications of an assumption by the judiciary of a power of dispensation. A hard decision is never a popular decision. Judges have been celebrated in literature for their sly prowess in devising some quibble by which a litigant could be deprived of his rights where the public thought it was wrong for him to assert those rights. But I believe that judicial dispensation does more harm in the long run than hard decisions. Hard cases may even have a certain moral value by bringing home to the people their own responsibilities toward the law that is ultimately their creation, and by reminding them that there is no principle of personal grace that can relieve the mistakes of their representatives.

Indeed, I will go farther and say that not only are the principles I have been expounding those which are soundest for our present conditions, but that we would have inherited a better legal system from our forefathers if those principles had been observed from the beginning. For example, with respect to the excuse of self-defense, if our courts had stood steadfast on the language of the statute the result would undoubtedly have been a legislative revision of it. Such a revision would have drawn on the assistance of natural philosophers and psychologists, and the resulting regulation of the matter would have had an understandable and rational basis, instead of the hodge-podge of verbalisms and metaphysical distinctions that have emerged from the judicial and professorial treatment.

These concluding remarks are, of course, beyond any duties that I have to discharge with relation to this case, but I include them here because I feel deeply that my colleagues are insufficiently aware of the dangers implicit in the conceptions of the judicial office advocated by my brother Foster.

I conclude that the conviction should be affirmed.

HANDY, J. I have listened with amazement to the tortured ratiocinations to which this simple case has given rise. I never cease to wonder at my colleagues' ability to throw an obscuring curtain of legalism about every issue presented to them for decision. We have heard this afternoon learned disquisitions on the distinction between positive law and the law of nature, the language of the statute and the purpose of the statute, judicial functions and executive functions, judicial legislation and legislative legislation. My only disappointment was that someone did not raise the question of the legal nature of the bargain struck in the cave—whether it was unilateral or bilateral, and whether Whetmore could not be considered as having revoked an offer prior to action taken thereunder.

What have all these things to do with the case? The problem before us is what we, as officers of the government, ought to do with these defendants. That is a question of practical wisdom, to be exercised in a context, not of abstract theory, but of human realities. When the case is approached in this light, it becomes, I think, one of the easiest to decide that has ever been argued before this Court.

Before stating my own conclusions about the merits of the case, I should

like to discuss briefly some of the more fundamental issues involved—issues
on which my colleagues and I have been divided ever since I have been on
the bench.

I have never been able to make my brothers see that government is a
human affair, and that men are ruled, not by words on paper or by abstract
theories, but by other men. They are ruled well when their rulers understand the feelings and conceptions of the masses. They are ruled badly
when that understanding is lacking.

Of all branches of the government, the judiciary is the most likely to
lose its contact with the common man. The reasons for this are, of course,
fairly obvious. Where the masses react to a situation in terms of a few
salient features, we pick into little pieces every situation presented to us.
Lawyers are hired by both sides to analyze and dissect. Judges and attorneys
vie with one another to see who can discover the greatest number of difficulties and distinctions in a single set of facts. Each side tries to find cases,
real or imagined, that will embarrass the demonstrations of the other side.
To escape this embarrassment, still further distinctions are invented and
imported into the situation. When a set of facts has been subjected to this
kind of treatment for a sufficient time, all the life and juice have gone out
of it and we have left a handful of dust.

Now I realize that wherever you have rules and abstract principles lawyers are going to be able to make distinctions. To some extent the sort of
thing I have been describing is a necessary evil attaching to any formal
regulation of human affairs. But I think that the area which really stands
in need of such regulation is greatly overestimated. There are, of course,
a few fundamental rules of the game that must be accepted if the game is
to go on at all. I would include among these the rules relating to the
conduct of elections, the appointment of public officials, and the term during which an office is held. Here some restraint on discretion and dispensation, some adherence to form, some scruple for what does and what does
not fall within the rule, is, I concede, essential. Perhaps the area of basic
principle should be expanded to include certain other rules, such as those
designed to preserve the free civilmoign system.

But outside of these fields I believe that all government officials, including judges, will do their jobs best if they treat forms and abstract concepts
as instruments. We should take as our model, I think, the good administrator, who accommodates procedures and principles to the case at hand,
selecting from among the available forms those most suited to reach the
proper result.

The most obvious advantage of this method of government is that it permits us to go about our daily tasks with efficiency and common sense. My
adherence to this philosophy has, however, deeper roots. I believe that it
is only with the insight this philosophy gives that we can preserve the

flexibility essential if we are to keep our actions in reasonable accord with the sentiments of those subject to our rule. More governments have been wrecked, and more human misery caused, by the lack of this accord between ruler and ruled than by any other factor that can be discerned in history. Once drive a sufficient wedge between the mass of people and those who direct their legal, political, and economic life, and our society is ruined. Then neither Foster's law of nature nor Keen's fidelity to written law will avail us anything.

Now when these conceptions are applied to the case before us, its decision becomes, as I have said, perfectly easy. In order to demonstrate this I shall have to introduce certain realities that my brothers in their coy decorum have seen fit to pass over in silence, although they are just as acutely aware of them as I am.

The first of these is that this case has aroused an enormous public interest, both here and abroad. Almost every newspaper and magazine has carried articles about it; columnists have shared with their readers confidential information as to the next governmental move; hundreds of letters-to-the-editor have been printed. One of the great newspaper chains made a poll of public opinion on the question, "What do you think the Supreme Court should do with the Speluncean explorers?" About ninety per cent expressed a belief that the defendants should be pardoned or let off with a kind of token punishment. It is perfectly clear, then, how the public feels about the case. We could have known this without the poll, of course, on the basis of common sense, or even by observing that on this Court there are apparently four-and-a-half men, or ninety per cent, who share the common opinion.

This makes it obvious, not only what we should do, but what we must do if we are to preserve between ourselves and public opinion a reasonable and decent accord. Declaring these men innocent need not involve us in any undignified quibble or trick. No principle of statutory construction is required that is not consistent with the past practices of this Court. Certainly no layman would think that in letting these men off we had stretched the statute any more than our ancestors did when they created the excuse of self-defense. If a more detailed demonstration of the method of reconciling our decision with the statute is required, I should be content to rest on the arguments developed in the second and less visionary part of my brother Foster's opinion.

Now I know that my brothers will be horrified by my suggestion that this Court should take account of public opinion. They will tell you that public opinion is emotional and capricious, that it is based on half-truths and listens to witnesses who are not subject to cross-examination. They will tell you that the law surrounds the trial of a case like this with elaborate safeguards, designed to insure that the truth will be known and that every rational consideration bearing on the issues of the case has been taken into account. They will warn you that all of these safeguards go for naught if a mass opinion formed outside this framework is allowed to have any influence on our decision.

But let us look candidly at some of the realities of the administration of our criminal law. When a man is accused of crime, there are, speaking generally, four ways in which he may escape punishment. One of these is a determination by a judge that under the applicable law he has committed no crime. This is, of course, a determination that takes place in a rather formal and abstract atmosphere. But look at the other three ways in which he may escape punishment. These are: (1) a decision by the Prosecutor not to ask for an indictment; (2) an acquittal by the jury; (3) a pardon or commutation of sentence by the executive. Can anyone pretend that these decisions are held within a rigid and formal framework of rules that prevents factual error, excludes emotional and personal factors, and guarantees that all the forms of the law will be observed?

In the case of the jury we do, to be sure, attempt to cabin their deliberations within the area of the legally relevant, but there is no need to deceive ourselves into believing that this attempt is really successful. In the normal course of events the case now before us would have gone on all of its issues directly to the jury. Had this occurred we can be confident that there would have been an acquittal or at least a division that would have prevented a conviction. If the jury had been instructed that the men's hunger and their agreement were no defense to the charge of murder, their verdict would in all likelihood have ignored this instruction and would have involved a good deal more twisting of the letter of the law than any that is likely to tempt us. Of course the only reason that didn't occur in this case was the fortuitous circumstance that the foreman of the jury happened to be a lawyer. His learning enabled him to devise a form of words that would allow the jury to dodge its usual responsibilities.

My brother Tatting expresses annoyance that the Prosecutor did not, in effect, decide the case for him by not asking for an indictment. Strict as he is himself in complying with the demands of legal theory, he is quite content to have the fate of these men decided out of court by the Prosecutor on the basis of common sense. The Chief Justice, on the other hand, wants the application of common sense postponed to the very end, though like Tatting, he wants no personal part in it.

This brings me to the concluding portion of my remarks, which has to do with executive clemency. Before discussing that topic directly, I want to make a related observation about the poll of public opinion. As I have said, ninety per cent of the people wanted the Supreme Court to let the men off entirely or with a more or less nominal punishment. The ten per cent constituted a very oddly assorted group, with the most curious and divergent opinions. One of our university experts has made a study of this group and has found that its members fall into certain patterns. A substantial portion of them are subscribers to "crank" newspapers of limited circulation that gave their readers a distorted version of the facts of the case. Some thought that "Speluncean" means "cannibal" and that anthropophagy is a tenet of the Society. But the point I want to make, however, is this: although almost every conceivable variety and shade of opinion was represented in this group, there was, so far as I know, not one of them, nor a single member of the majority of ninety per cent, who said, "I think it would be a fine thing to have the courts sentence these men to be hanged, and then to have another branch of the government come along and pardon them." Yet this is a solution that has more or less dominated our discussions and which our Chief Justice proposes as a way by which we can avoid doing an injustice and at the same time preserve respect for law. He can be assured that if he is preserving anybody's morale, it is his own, and not the public's, which knows nothing of his distinctions. I mention this matter because I wish to emphasize once more the danger that we may get lost in the patterns of our own thought and forget that these patterns often cast not the slightest shadow on the outside world.

I come now to the most crucial fact in this case, a fact known to all of us on this Court, though one that my brothers have seen fit to keep under the cover of their judicial robes. This is the frightening likelihood that if the issue is left to him, the Chief Executive will refuse to pardon these men or commute their sentence. As we all know, our Chief Executive is a man now well advanced in years, of very stiff notions. Public clamor usually operates on him with the reverse of the effect intended. As I have told my brothers, it happens that my wife's niece is an intimate friend of his secretary. I have learned in this indirect, but, I think, wholly reliable way, that he is firmly determined not to commute the sentence if these men are found to have violated the law.

No one regrets more than I the necessity for relying in so important a matter on information that could be characterized as gossip. If I had my way this would not happen, for I would adopt the sensible course of sitting down with the Executive, going over the case with him, finding out what his views are, and perhaps working out with him a common program for handling the situation. But of course my brothers would never hear of such a thing.

Their scruple about acquiring accurate information directly does not prevent them from being very perturbed about what they have learned indirectly. Their acquaintance with the facts I have just related explains why the Chief Justice, ordinarily a model of decorum, saw fit in his opinion to flap his judicial robes in the faces of the Executive and threaten him with excommunication if he failed to commute the sentence. It explains, I suspect, my brother Foster's feat of levitation by which a whole library of law books was lifted from the shoulders of these defendants. It explains also why even my legalistic brother Keen emulated Pooh-Bah in the ancient comedy by stepping to the other side of the stage to address a few remarks to the Executive "in my capacity as a private citizen." (I may remark, incidentally, that the advice of Private Citizen Keen will appear in the reports of this court printed at taxpayers' expense.)

I must confess that as I grow older I become more and more perplexed at men's refusal to apply their common sense to problems of law and government, and this truly tragic case has deepened my sense of discouragement and dismay. I only wish that I could convince my brothers of the wisdom of the principles I have applied to the judicial office since I first assumed it. As a matter of fact, by a kind of sad rounding of the circle, I encountered issues like those involved here in the very first case I tried as Judge of the Court of General Instances in Fanleigh County.

A religious sect had unfrocked a minister who, they said, had gone over to the views and practices of a rival sect. The minister circulated a handbill making charges against the authorities who had expelled him. Certain lay members of the church announced a public meeting at which they proposed to explain the position of the church. The minister attended this meeting. Some said he slipped in unobserved in a disguise; his own testimony was that he had walked in openly as a member of the public. At any rate, when the speeches began he interrupted with certain questions about the affairs of the church and made some statements in defense of his own views. He was set upon by members of the audience and given a pretty thorough pommeling, receiving among other injuries a broken jaw. He brought a suit for damages against the association that sponsored the meeting and against ten named individuals who he alleged were his assailants.

When we came to the trial, the case at first seemed very complicated to me. The attorneys raised a host of legal issues. There were nice questions on the admissibility of evidence, and, in connection with the suit against the association, some difficult problems turning on the question whether the minister was a trespasser or a licensee. As a novice on the bench I was eager to apply my law school learning and I began studying these questions closely, reading all the authorities and preparing well-documented rulings. As I studied the case I became more and more involved in its legal intricacies and I began to get into a state approaching that of my brother Tatting in this case. Suddenly, however, it dawned on me that all these perplexing issues really had nothing to do with the case, and I began examining it in the light of common sense. The case at once gained a new perspective, and I saw that the only thing for me to do was to direct a verdict for the defendants for lack of evidence.

I was led to this conclusion by the following considerations. The melee in which the plaintiff was injured had been a very confused affair, with some people trying to get to the center of the disturbance, while others were trying to get away from it; some striking at the plaintiff, while others were apparently trying to protect him. It would have taken weeks to find out the truth of the matter. I decided that nobody's broken jaw was worth that much to the Commonwealth. (The minister's injuries, incidentally, had meanwhile healed without disfigurement and without any impairment of normal faculties.) Furthermore, I felt very strongly that the plaintiff had to a large extent brought the thing on himself. He knew how inflamed passions were about the affair, and could easily have found another forum for the expression of his views. My decision was widely approved by the press and public opinion, neither of which could tolerate the views and practices that the expelled minister was attempting to defend.

Now, thirty years later, thanks to an ambitious Prosecutor and a legalistic jury foreman, I am faced with a case that raises issues which are at bottom much like those involved in that case. The world does not seem to change much, except that this time it is not a question of a judgment for five or six hundred frelars, but of the life or death of four men who have already suffered more torment and humiliation than most of us would endure in a thousand years. I conclude that the defendants are innocent of the crime charged, and that the conviction and sentence should be set aside.

TATTING, J. I have been asked by the Chief Justice whether, after listening to the two opinions just rendered, I desire to re-examine the position previously taken by me. I wish to state that after hearing these opinions I am greatly strengthened in my conviction that I ought not to participate in the decision of this case.

The Supreme Court being evenly divided, the conviction and sentence of the Court of General Instances is *affirmed*. It is ordered that the execution of the sentence shall occur at 6 A.M., Friday, April 2, 4300, at which time the Public Executioner is directed to proceed with all convenient dispatch to hang each of the defendants by the neck until he is dead.

POSTSCRIPT

Now that the court has spoken its judgment, the reader puzzled by the choice of date may wish to be reminded that the centuries which separate us from the year 4300 are roughly equal to those that have passed since the Age of Pericles. There is probably no need to observe that the *Speluncean Case* itself is intended neither as a work of satire nor as a prediction in any ordinary sense of the term. As for the judges who make up Chief Justice Truepenny's court, they are, of course, as mythical as the facts and precedents with which they deal. The reader who refuses to accept this view, and who seeks to trace out contemporary resemblances where none is intended or contemplated, should be warned that he is engaged in a frolic of his own, which may possibly lead him to miss whatever modest truths are contained in the opinions delivered by the Supreme Court of Newgarth. The case was constructed for the sole purpose of bringing into a common focus certain divergent philosophies of law and government. These philosophies presented men with live questions of choice in the days of Plato and Aristotle. Perhaps they will continue to do so when our era has had its say about them. If there is any element of prediction in the case, it does not go beyond a suggestion that the questions involved are among the permanent problems of the human race.

The Criminal Law *

H. L. MENCKEN

H. L. Mencken (1880–1956) came of German-American stock. He was for years connected with the Baltimore Sun, *the* Smart Set *(from which the next piece is taken), and the early* American Mercury *(1924–1933). Writing with a pungent vocabulary which included erudite or slangy expressions, depending on the need, he had a wide following in the 1920's because of his attacks on sham and goody-goodies; then there was a lull, and he was supposed to be dated, but with* The American Language *he acquired new public stature. Three volumes of memoirs won old and new followers. People remembered the days of Mencken and Nathan, and recalled how the former had pushed ahead writers like Dreiser and Lewis.*

H. L. M. had a sting. He may or may not have been in the same league with Swift, Voltaire, and Shaw, but he played the same game. (He called a whole series of volumes Prejudices.) *Right or wrong, he made people think. In the following he takes a characteristic swing at the weakness of some of our laws.*

The science of penology, in these days, is chiefly in the hands of sentimentalists, and in consequence it shows all the signs of glycosuria. The idea seems to be to turn the dungeons and bullpens of the law into laboratories of the uplift, so that the man who goes in a burglar will come out a Y.M.C.A. secretary. To this end all harsh handling of the felon is frowned upon, and on the slightest showing of renascent piety in him he is delivered from his cage, almost with apologies.

At the bottom of this softness, of course, there is a sound instinct, and that is the instinct of revolt against cruel and excessive punishments. We inherited such a system of punishments from the English Common Law; in the Bill of Rights there is the first evidence of a rebellion against them. But our current error lies in the fact that softness has not stopped with disposing of the punishments that were barbarous and excessive; it has also sorely limited and conditioned the punishments that were reasonable and fitting; and so the problem of dealing effectively with crime remains a puzzle, and crime itself continues to flourish.

* Reprinted from *A Mencken Chrestomathy*, by H. L. Mencken, copyright, 1922, 1949, by Alfred A. Knopf, Inc., with the permission of Alfred A. Knopf, Inc.

When I say crime, of course, I mean the thing in its conventional sense. In the abstract it scarcely has any existence. Practically all so-called crimes are justifiable on occasion, and nine-tenths of them, to certain kinds of men, are unavoidable on occasion. It is a platitude that you will find quite as many intelligent and honest men in the average prison as you will find in the average club, and when it comes to courage, enterprise and determination— in brief, to the special virtues which mark the superior man—you will probably find a great many more. But society, in order to protect the weak and botched against the bold and original, has had to proclaim certain human acts, under certain circumstances, as too dangerous to be permitted, and hence as what we call criminal. Most of us aspire to the majority of those acts in secret, and some of us commit them surreptitiously, but the man who performs them in such a manner that the fact becomes notorious is a menace to the security of the rest of us, and we go through the solemn hocus-pocus of seizing him and trying him, and pump up indignation over his rascality, and finally visit upon him the thing called punishment.

The trouble with this so-called punishment, in a great many cases, is that it is hypocritical and dishonest at bottom, and thus at constant war with abstract justice and common sense. What we find practically is a crowd of poltroons in the jury box venting their envious hatred of enterprise and daring upon a man who, at worst, is at least as decent as they are; and a scoundrel on the bench lording it over a scoundrel in the dock because the latter is less clever than he is. In the old days this ill nature took the form of floggings, mutilations and damnations. In our own days, with an evil conscience gnawing the gizzard of the world, it takes the shape of formalities which tend to grow more and more ineffective, sentimental and meaningless. In particular, it takes the shape of a grotesquely circumscribed répertoire of penalties, so that the business of fitting the punishment to the crime becomes more and more difficult, even to the stray judge with intelligence. In a few rare cases he may condemn a prisoner to death; in all other cases he has a Hobson's choice between a mulcting in damages which seldom punishes at all, and a deprivation of liberty which usually punishes inappropriately, and often too much. The medieval judge had an almost unlimited series of choices; if no habitual punishment suited his purposes, he could devise a new one to fit the case. But the modern judge must forever oscillate absurdly between fine and imprisonment—in other words, between allowing one prisoner to pay a bribe for his liberty, and taking away the liberty of another prisoner because he hasn't got the bribe.

It is a deep consciousness of this absurdity which lies at the bottom of all the fantastic experiments of modern penology, and of many of the extravagances which we witness on the bench. It seemed ridiculous, perhaps, for Judge Kenesaw Mountain Landis, LL.B., to fine the Standard Oil Company $29,240,000, but in its essence it was an honest effort to bring an offender to something approaching scientifically exact justice. It seems (and may be) sugarishly sentimental for uplifters to transform prisons into moving-picture parlors, but underneath it there is the sound doctrine that locking up a man in a cell is, for most crimes, too harsh, and that its effect on the man is precisely the opposite of the one intended, for it makes him a more determined antagonist of so stupid and cruel a society than ever he was before. What we need is a thorough overhauling of our punishments—an overhauling looking to their rescue from formalism and imbecility. They must be made more fluent, more intelligible, more various. We must get rid of the mawkish and false humanity which shrinks from simple and forthright penalties, and restore the true humanity which makes the criminal stop doing what he is doing, and yet halts before it has made a hopeless wreck of him. If revenge is admitted (and I suppose it always will be), it must be admitted openly and unblushingly, and not swathed in that dishonest concealment which now seeks to make it appear as something else.

In medieval law, as I have hinted, there are suggestions that should engage the penological reformer of tomorrow. The medieval mind was unburdened by transcendental theories as to the nature and causes of crime. It was realistic in habit, and disdained to seek behind the palpable fact for hidden portents and significances. In particular, it disdained to conceal its workings beneath gossamers of fabulous purpose. It thus defined its crimes simply and clearly, and punished them frankly. For the runaway clodhopper the obvious punishment was hamstringing, and, being obvious, it was executed without further ado. For the perjurer, the removal of his offending tongue. For the scoundrel who bit in clinches, extraction of the incisors. For the rowdy housewife and husband-baiter, prolonged immersion in a horse-pond—that is, enforced and painful silence. For the habitual thief, branding of the forehead with a large and warning T. For the shortweight grocer, three hours in the pillory, that his victims might pay him up with his own eggs and mark him well for future avoidance.

A judge, in those naïve and far-off days, had to be a fellow of resource and ingenuity, a man capable of quick and accurate reasoning. His public expected him, not merely to punish crime, but to punish it in some germane and felicitous fashion. If he could get a touch of humor into his sentence, so much the better, for the common people, then as now, remembered a jocosity much longer than they remembered a syllogism. In any event he had to maintain some intelligible connection between the offense and the penalty, that its lesson might be plain. If, finding the application of capsicum plasters to the pantaloons an efficient punishment for napping catchpolls, he next day prescribed it for a pirate, a witch, or a well-poisoner, then he was himself laughed at as a jackass, and perhaps even cashiered. In brief, he had to keep his wits about him if he would go on wallowing in the ermine. The law presumed him to be a man of sagacity, of ingenuity, of resource; and if, by any stupidity, he showed that he wasn't, its wrath consumed him.

The judge of today needs no such virtues. He is not the agent and exponent of justice, but its mere lackey. A great body of intricate law and precedent protects the felon against his effort to ferret out and determine the crime, and another great body of law protects the felon against his effort to fit the punishment to it. Consider, for example, the difficulties confronting him when he faces a very familiar task: the sentencing of a convicted pickpocket. Two or three considerations must inevitably flit through his darkened mind in this situation. One is that picking pockets requires a very high degree of manual skill—that it is an avocation as difficult technically as dentistry or playing the piano. Another, following upon the first, is that it is almost always pursued professionally—that, generally speaking, the pickpocket always devotes his whole time to it. A third is that, having thus entered the profession deliberately, and mastered its excessive difficulties, and taken over its known risks, he is firmly set in it, and cannot be shaken out by any process which leaves his actual expertness undamaged.

In other words, the pickpocket is a deliberate, habitual and incurable criminal, and neither chaining him by the leg nor forcing him to view moral moving-picture shows will ever cure him. To be bagged now and then, to make occasional sojourns in prison—all that, to him, is mere professional risk. When, by some mischance, he is taken and jailed, he lays the business to the fortunes of war, as a surgeon does when a patient dies on the table or a lawyer when a client is caught. As soon as he has paid his debt to the law he resumes the practise of his profession. If anything, a term in prison heartens and emboldens him, for he commonly debits it, not to the acts preceding it, but to the acts to follow it. In brief, he regards it as a sort of fee or license, paid to the community for the privilege of extracting wallets. No one ever heard of a reformed pickpocket; he exists only in the dreams of sentimental penologists. He may give up the business when his eyes give out, or his fingers get too stiff, but so long as he can snatch a pocketbook and get away he will keep on at it. And yet, so absurd is our law that we try to cure him by making him stop temporarily—by locking him up for two or three years, or maybe for only six months. As well try to cure a poet by forbidding him, for six months, to get drunk.

But what better offers? Something enormously better. The simple device, in brief, of condemning the detected pickpocket to lose the third phalange of the index finger of his right hand—a quick, safe, wholly painless operation, almost as easy as having a boil lanced. And yet quite as certain in its effects as life imprisonment. The pickpocket is not appreciably mutilated. The loss of that one phalange does not show itself. He is fit for almost any honest work that can be imagined. But he can no more pick a pocket, with the chief of his highly trained tools gone, than a fiddler, in like case, could play a cadenza. All of his special capacity for crime is gone, and with it his special temptation is gone, too. At every other variety of felony he is as much an amateur and blunderer as the judge on the bench.

I present only this one concrete example of what might be accomplished if we could rid our criminal laws of falsehood and sentimentality, and restore them to sense. The mind of every reflective judge must be full of simple, just and effective punishments that he would inflict if he could—punishments enormously more apt and efficient than the fine which penalizes too little and the imprisonment which penalizes arbitrarily, unintelligibly and usually too much. Why jail embezzlers? Why not put them to work as slaves of their victims, and make them work out what they have stolen? Why jail wife-beaters? Why not try to discourage them with a few strokes of the bastinado? Why jail grafters in office? Why not simply seize their stealings, strip them bare, and then forbid them the city, state and country?

Many old punishments deserve revival: ducking, whipping, transportation, branding, forfeiture of goods. They are simpler and cheaper than those we have; it is obvious that they would work better. In the South Seas we have scores of almost uninhabited islands. Why not ship our felons out there and let them learn discipline by preying on one another? Or send them to Arkansas to butcher the politicians and clergy? It is not only a way to get rid of them, and of the heavy expense of keeping them; it is a way to civilize Arkansas and the South Seas. Criminals are like the rest of us. Given the right kind of chance, they show their sound metal. Australia was settled by them, so were Maryland, and part of Virginia. Who notices it, or even remembers it, today?

In the forfeiture of goods there are the same great possibilities. This punishment would be the best of all weapons against stock-waterers, trade-restrainers, war-profiteers and other such powerful recalcitrants. Personally, I am in favor of these scoundrels, but if they are criminals by law, then let us deal with them in a way that will dispose of them. The fine of $29,240,000, even if collected, would not have hurt John D. Rockefeller. But a decree of forfeiture, taking over all his goods and making invalid any contract made with him or any security owned by him, would have converted him into a penniless Baptist colporteur overnight, and so brought down the price of gasoline.

Every day, by extra-legal means, our judges try to reach out for these new and more effective penalties. The punishment provided by law for one of the commonest of police court offenses—the stupid yielding to amorous suggestion called seduction—is a complex and unworkable combination of fine by instalments and threat of imprisonment. No sane judge ever inflicts it. What he does is to make the victim marry the party of the first part. The device is just and sensible, and it works. The victim is appropriately penalized for his numskullery, and the damage that society might have suffered from it is obliterated.

This is what we need in punishments—first, a reasonable fitness and justice, and secondly, a removal of the damage or menace to social order and security. Our present system fails in both departments. It is arbitrary, unintelligent and alternately too cruel and too soft; and it wholly fails to make crime difficult and unattractive.

The Growth of Substantive Law *

ARTHUR T. VANDERBILT

*Nearing the end of a large volume, we may take stock of the historical scene
—lawyer, judge, courtroom, law. Naturally, no short piece can give the
whole story, but the following lecture by Arthur T. Vanderbilt suggests
the whole. Many of the people and ideas in the foregoing pages are drawn
together with fine control and perspective.*

*This is what one might expect of the author. Judge Vanderbilt (1888–
1957), Chief Justice of the Supreme Court of New Jersey from 1948 on, was
educated at Wesleyan and Columbia Law; he held honorary degrees from
twenty-six universities. He was admitted to the bar in 1913, was a professor
of law at New York University from 1914 to 1948, was President of the
American Bar Association, and had his name on many lectureships, committees, commissions, and trusteeships. Perhaps his supreme accolade was
his title of "lawyer's lawyer." Vanderbilt was the author of many books, including* Men and Measures in the Law, *from which the following excerpt
is taken.*

I n this lecture I shall comment on the growth of substantive law, reserving the more difficult matters of procedural law and the improvement
of the administration of justice for subsequent discussion.

In viewing the broad sweep of Anglo-American legal history over the
centuries it is surprising to note how much of the growth of the law re-
volves around individuals. Some of these individuals who are pre-eminent
in the history of the law have been kings or presidents, some judges, some
writers, some both judges and writers. In the group of kings and presidents
among the outstanding figures are Edward I, often called the English Justinian, Theodore Roosevelt, Woodrow Wilson, and Franklin D. Roosevelt.
Among judges we must list Coke, Mansfield, and Stowell in England, along
with the giants of equity, Bacon, Nottingham, Hardwicke, and Eldon, and in
this country Marshall, Kent, and Story. Coke's claim to fame is based on
his services as a judge, as a writer of legal classics, but above all as a
courageous parliamentary leader. Stowell shares with Mansfield the credit
for developing a new body of substantive law, prize law, but Mansfield's

domain was far broader. The development of a body of prize law, moreover, was inevitable in Stowell's time, but Mansfield's contributions in the main involved a deliberate choice on his part as to whether large bodies of law such as the law merchant and quasi-contracts should be incorporated in the common law. Equity was molded not by one man but by several, the chief being Bacon, Nottingham, Hardwicke, and Eldon in England, Kent and Story in America. No judge has ever equaled Marshall in his contributions to the field of public law. With both Kent and Story reputation as jurist is merged in pre-eminence as writer. Among English law writers Glanvil and Bracton, Littleton and Fortescue, Coke and Bentham stand out. Blackstone, in respect to influence, belongs to America as much as to England. In this country Kent and Story were the leaders among the writers who made law, but as surely as Story is entitled to be called the father of conflict of laws should Dillon be given credit for the law of municipal corporations and Keener for quasi-contracts. Nor is the list closed; what renowned executives, great jurists, and distinguished writers have done in earlier ages and often in the grand manner still remains to be repeated on innumerable fronts and in each state by their modern successors.

Not all of the great achievements in the law, however, may be traced to individuals. Much has been accomplished by small groups of men working together. The barons at Runnymede forcing Magna Carta on a hostile king, and the Founding Fathers in Independence Hall drafting the Federal Constitution, are outstanding examples of group accomplishments.

The first thing that strikes one studying the broad course of the growth of our substantive law is the important place of legislation. At no time was this more true than in the reign of Edward I. Sir Matthew Hale, equally distinguished as a judge and as a law writer (1609–76), credits Edward with "the very scheme, mould and model of the common law," and describes his influence on English jurisprudence in these significant words:

Yet the Laws did never in any one Age receive so great and sudden an advancement, nay, I think I may safely say, all the Ages since his Time have not done so much in reference to the orderly settling and establishing of the distributive Justice of this Kingdom, as he did within a short Compass of the Thirty five years of his Reign, especially about the first Thirteen Years thereof.

Lest it be thought that I am returning to the Dark Ages for an example of the influence of a single man, let me quote the concluding paragraph of Pollock and Maitland's *The History of English Law before the Time of Edward I,* on his present-day significance for all of us:

It was the critical moment in English legal history and therefore in the innermost history of our land and our race. It was the moment when old custom was brought into contact with new science. Much in our national life and character depended on the result of that contact. It was a perilous moment. There was the danger of an unintelligent "reception" of misunderstood and alien institutions. There was the danger of a premature and formless equity. On the other hand, there was the danger of a stubborn *Nolumus*, a refusal to learn from foreigners and from the classical past. If that had not been avoided, the crash would have come in the sixteenth century and Englishmen would have been forced to receive without criticism what they once despised. Again, we have stood at the parting of the ways of the two most vigorous systems of law that the modern world has seen, the French and the English. Not about what may seem the weightier matters of jurisprudence do these sisters quarrel, but about "mere matters of procedure," as some would call them, the one adopting the canonical inquest of witnesses, the other retaining, developing, transmuting the old *enquete du pays*. But the fate of two national laws lies here. Which country made the wiser choice no Frenchman and no Englishman can impartially say: no one should be judge in his own cause. But of this there can be no doubt, that it was for the good of the whole world that one race stood apart from its neighbours, turned away its eyes at an early time from the fascinating pages of the *Corpus Iuris*, and, more Roman than the Romanists, made the grand experiment of a new formulary system. Nor can we part with this age without thinking once more of the permanence of its work. Those few men who were gathered at Westminster round Pateshull and Raleigh and Bracton were penning writs that would run in the name of kingless commonwealths on the other shore of the Atlantic Ocean; they were making right and wrong for us and for our children.

Although a few statutes of the Tudor period are still important, we may move on three centuries before we come to other great legislation that arrests our attention. The Petition of Right, the statutes that establish the control of Parliament over taxation, direct and indirect, the legislation abolishing Star Chamber and other administrative courts, and the Habeas Corpus Act were all passed by Parliaments bitterly opposed to the aggressions of the Stuarts. All of these acts were victories of the common law through Parliament over the absolutistic pretensions of the Stuarts. Foremost among the small group of parliamentary leaders in the early part of this movement was Coke, advocating in the House of Commons the principles he had championed on the bench before he was summarily dismissed as Chief Justice of the Court of King's Bench by James I for refusing to submit to his command not to proceed with the hearing of a case involving the King's prerogative. The triumph of the parliamentary forces was due to his moral courage as much as to his vast knowledge of the law and the justice of his cause. In admiration of his public service we can afford to forget some of his personal meanness. Can there be any doubt that the example set by him and his parliamentary associates was a source of inspiration to the revolutionary patriots of America a century later? These constitutional gains of Englishmen were crowned in the Glorious Revolution of 1688 by the Bill of Rights and the Act of Settlement, which marked, among other things, the achievement of the independence of the judiciary.

We may skip nearly two centuries more before we come to the era of social reform signalized by the passage of the long overdue Reform Act of 1832. This era of unprecedented legislation, rivaled only by that of Edward I, was the result primarily of the changed living conditions brought on by the industrial revolution. It was delayed for nearly half a century through fear that the excesses of the French Revolution might sweep across the English Channel, but the delay at least served the good purpose of making the statutory program more thoroughgoing than it otherwise would have been. Jeremy Bentham died at the advanced age of eighty-four, the day before the Reform Act received the royal assent, but more than any other man he was responsible for it and the ensuing legislative program that transformed the daily life of the English people as well as ancient notions of the sphere of governmental activities. From the anonymous publication in 1776 of his *Fragment of Government*—at first variously attributed to Mansfield, Camden, and Dunning, so excellent were its contents—to the time of his death he strove to induce his countrymen to look at the facts of government realistically and to measure the worth of every political institution by the utilitarian test of the greatest good to the greatest number. So great was his influence that Sir Henry Maine has termed Benthamism the English counterpart of the *jus naturale* of the Roman Law. Bentham was the guiding spirit of his age. His disciples had long known what some other law reformers have not always seemed to grasp—that it is not enough merely to have good ideas; the ideas must be exploited. In bringing the Reform Act into existence they had themselves come into power as the leaders of the new Parliament. Their accession to office gave them new resources. As Sir Cecil Thomas Carr, the distinguished editor of the English *Statutory Rules and Orders* and of the *Revised Statutes*, graphically describes it:

The new Parliament (and its successors), impulsive, rather undisciplined, and very serious, knew that the country expected it to experiment and to risk the impact of State interference upon individual liberties. A series of non-party royal commissions and committees explored social conditions; their disclosures shocked public opinion and revealed the gap in the local administration of those times between efficient government in some places and scandalous neglect in too many others. Parliament, fortified by the reports and recommendations of these exploratory bodies, gave a smooth passage to several controversial Bills which were in no way the product of the government machine. And so Britain got a quick and quiet revolution in the laws of factories, poor relief, municipal corporations, prisons, and presently public health, while striking changes were also being made in civil procedure and summary jurisdiction and mitigation of savage punishments. This reinforcement of the governmental process by a concentration of the intelligence of men of independent mind, not always attached either to Parliament or to political parties, is an object lesson to which our eyes turn in these no less stimulating times.

This vast statutory program ushered in modern administrative law. The success of social reform depended upon uniformity of administration throughout the country, and uniformity of administration in turn necessitated a tremendous increase in the activity of the central government. This increased activity of the central government meant paid professional officials replacing local amateurs. It also required much delegation of legislative power to these professional officials, for Parliament could not be expected to legislate on the intricacies of such a complex legislative program. The delegation of legislative power in turn involved grave questions of what were proper standards of administrative action. Most of all did it lead to the bureaucratic attitude in government. It is not easy to convey the reforming spirit of this new age in a few words, but Carr has hit it off in a brief paragraph describing Bentham's literary secretary, Edwin Chadwick:

He was a great investigator of social conditions, a great writer of bluebooks, and a great sanitary reformer. One modern historian has attributed to him the vices as well as the virtues of the official mind—rigidity, ruthlessness, a certainty that he was right, and a conviction that his opponents represented merely "sinister interests." Another has written of him that, born in 1801 in a Lancashire farmhouse where the children were washed all over every day, he made it his life's object to wash the people of England all over every day by executive order. Let us dwell rather upon his virtues. He was seized when young with what he called the "sanitary idea"—the idea that unhealthy conditions produced disease, and disease produced poverty. When he was not busy with other crusades, such as pensions for teachers, public promenades, physical training for trade unionists, and employers' liability for blameless accidents (our workmen compensation of today), he was devoting himself to every kind of sanitary research and improvement, whether it was housing, sewerage, water supply, prevention of epidemics, disposal of the dead, registration of the causes of death, or the cure of intemperance. At the age of eighty-six, when he wrote a vigorous essay advocating the uses of tricycles by the police, he pointed out that not only would the constables thus have the legs of the criminals but they would also find tricycling a valuable sanitary exercise. When he died in 1890, a post-mortem examination would surely have revealed that word "sanitary" graven upon his heart.

It will not do, however, merely to smile at the reformers. In a single generation they turned the criminal law from what Dr. R. M. Jackson has called "more brutal and savage than that of any civilized country," into a system of law enforcement that has become the envy of all mankind. They did more to alleviate the condition of the poor and the underprivileged than had been accomplished in centuries. They not only awakened the conscience of England; they cast it into statutory mold.

Thus we have had exemplified the three chief instruments of legislative reform: first, the ruler, aided, of course, by experts; second, a small group of legislative leaders; and third, a broad popular movement sparked by the ideas of genius and fanned into flame by ceaseless agitation. In contrast with such epoch-making statutes is ordinary legislation, which has always involved the influence of pressure groups and legislative logrolling. We too often think of logrolling as a vulgar process, a product of our modern materialistic age. To illustrate its persistence even in the most spacious days, let me quote some genteel correspondence between the great Lord Chancellor Hardwicke and Lord Fitzwilliam:

Lord Fitzwilliam presents his compliments to the Lord Chancellor, and will be glad of the disposal of the encumbency of Rawmarsh at the next vacancy.

The Lord Chancellor presents his compliments to Lord Fitzwilliam, and has other views as to the disposal of the benefice of Rawmarsh.

Lord Fitzwilliam presents his compliments to the Lord Chancellor, and will for the future manage for his own benefit his political influence in the West Riding of Yorkshire.

The Lord Chancellor presents his compliments to Lord Fitzwilliam and the benefice of Rawmarsh will be at his disposal at the next vacancy.

This exchange of greetings is matched in thought, if not in felicity of phrasing, by the famous query in a letter addressed by William Jennings Bryan, when Secretary of State, to the Receiver of Customs in San Domingo:

. . . can you let me know what positions you have at your disposal, with which to reward deserving Democrats? . . . You have had enough experience in politics to know how valuable workers are when the campaign is on; and how difficult it is to find rewards for all the deserving.

The era of social reform in England has been a more or less continuous process since 1832, with an especially large wave of legislation from 1906 to World War I. All of these statutes find their source, as Dicey has pointed out in his *Law and Public Opinion in England,* in popular sentiment, which as in the Benthamite period was very largely the result of endless discussion and agitation, but without any single inspiring genius such as Bentham. The socialist government that swept into office following World War II has undertaken further social experiments in a series of nationalization acts covering the Bank of England, the coal industry, civil aviation, communications, electric power, and transportation. It is interesting to observe that over the past three quarters of a century many of the social reforms of England, with more or less regularity, have found their way across the Atlantic. The recent nationalization acts of the present socialist government of England raise the interesting question whether this sequence will still continue. Or does, perchance, the adoption of the Federal Administrative Procedure Act of 1946 mark a turn in the tide of legislative opinion not only as to the conduct of our own bureaucracy, but also with respect to the further acceptance here of English social experiments?

In modern times it is rare, indeed, that an individual has been able to make himself felt in Parliament as the sponsor of private bills. Sir A. P. Herbert is an interesting exception to the general rule. Long a member of the staff of *Punch*, as well as a barrister of the Inner Temple, he published in 1934 *Holy Deadlock*, a legally accurate novel, in which he satirized the divorce law of England. The following year he was elected to the House of Commons to represent Oxford University. He promptly introduced a bill to meet the deficiencies in English divorce law. Ordinarily a private member's bill has very little chance of passage because of the exigencies of the government's legislative program. His wit and his skill at popularizing his cause eventually won the day. His bill was passed as the Matrimonial Laws Act, 1937, but is popularly known as the Herbert Act. Divorce in England and Wales is governed by it.

In the United States social legislation began long before the English Reform Act of 1832. In the period following the American Revolution down to the Civil War important legislative reforms aimed at advancing the rights of the individual. In part this legislative movement was in response to the political philosophy of the seventeenth and eighteenth centuries, which was dominated by the idea of perfecting the individual. In part the new legislation reflected the conditions of frontier life, characterized by simple economic and social conditions. Self-reliance was the predominant virtue, equality of opportunity the grand objective. Fortunately the interest of the individual in acquiring property subserved the social interest of conquering the wilderness. The Bill of Rights of the Federal Constitution, drafted by George Mason of Virginia and ratified in 1791, and the corresponding provisions in the several state constitutions were hardly more fundamental than the disestablishment of churches, which began in Virginia in 1786; the abolition of slavery in the northern states from 1781 to 1804; the legislation providing for the abolition of entail in Virginia in 1776 and of primogeniture in Georgia in 1777; the grant of universal manhood suffrage, beginning in Vermont in 1777; free compulsory public education, instituted in Massachusetts in 1852, though urged long before by Jefferson; and the abolition of the disabilities of married women, starting in New York and Pennsylvania in 1848. These reforms, seeking to equalize and advance the individual as such, reflected in large measure the political ideals of Thomas Jefferson. Only one of them was in any sense socialistic; in free public education for the first time in this country we find the state, through legislation, giving positive aid to the individual rather than merely removing negative obstacles. Even free education was first proposed as a means of advancing the individual; its ultimate effect on society was deemed secondary. In practically all of this legislation the United States was well in advance of England.

The period following the Civil War was marked by a tremendous increase in legislative activity, the importance of which has tended to be underestimated in both the professional and the popular mind by reason of the attention focused throughout this period on the judiciary and particularly the United States Supreme Court. Legislation directed at business, such as the Sherman Act, aimed primarily at preventing monopoly. Railroad legislation, exemplified by the Interstate Commerce Act, sought to eliminate the evils of monopoly. Tariff legislation was offset by labor and immigration legislation. Gradually the original sanctions for the enforcement of legislation by the criminal law came to be superseded, or at least supplemented, by the new methods of administrative regulation. Conservation legislation seeking to put an end to the wasting of natural resources did not gain a foothold until the turn of the century. The "Square Deal" of Theodore Roosevelt forecast the "New Freedom" of Woodrow Wilson with its Federal Reserve System, Federal Trade Commission, and the Clayton Act. The financial crash of 1929 paved the way for the social program of the "New Deal," which was really a continuation of the "Square Deal" and the "New Freedom." The "Square Deal," the "New Freedom," and the "New Deal" were emphatically the work of individual leaders. The hegemony of the executive had arrived. The forces that have produced a large part of our social legislation, however, have been the same as those which led to the English Reform Act of 1832 and the burst of legislation that followed in its train. As John Dewey, the philosopher, has pointedly observed:

> Quite aside, however, from the allegation that "Big Business" plays the tune and pulls the strings to which bosses dance, it is true that parties are not creators of policies to any large extent at the present time. For parties yield in piece-meal accommodation to social currents, irrespective of professed principles. As these lines are written a weekly periodical remarks: "Since the end of the Civil War practically all the more important measures which have been embodied in federal legislation have been reached without a national election which turned upon the issue and which divided the two major parties." Reform of civil service, regulation of railways, popular election of senators, national income tax, suffrage for women, and prohibition are supported to substantiate the statement.

Substitute Theodore Roosevelt, Woodrow Wilson, and Franklin D. Roosevelt for Edward I, the Founding Fathers at Philadelphia for the barons at Runnymede, and Thomas Jefferson, the political philosopher, for Jeremy Bentham, and you have the three chief methods of achieving social reform clearly illustrated in the course of American legislation, along with the inevitable activities of pressure groups and logrolling omnipresent in ordinary legislation.

So much for the manner in which substantive changes in the law have been effected by statute. Even before our national Constitution was adopted, the writers of the *Federalist* papers, though they could not possibly anticipate the plethora of legislation that afflicts us, gave voice to their well-grounded fears:

It will be of little avail to the people, that the laws are made by men of their own choice, if the laws be so voluminous that they cannot be read, or so incoherent that they cannot be understood; if they be repealed or revised before they are promulgated, or undergo such incessant changes, that no man who knows what the law is today, can guess what it will be tomorrow.

For our legislative ills we have only ourselves to blame. When Boswell reported to Dr. Johnson that a friend had told him that any plodding blockhead could excel in the legal profession, the good doctor expostulated: "Why, Sir, in the *formulary* and *statutory* part of law a plodding blockhead may excel; but in the *ingenious* and *rational* part of law a plodding blockhead never can excel." It is this disparaging attitude toward legislation, to which I have already alluded more than once, that is chiefly responsible for the generally low estate of our statute law. Our attitude, of course, has been utterly irrational in view of the enormous importance of legislation over the centuries. All too slowly are we coming to realize that too much care cannot be given to the drafting of legislative bills, both with respect to their content and technical style as well as to the periodic—indeed, the continuous—overhauling of the entire statute book now made in but a few states. The work of drafting a bill or revising a statute or perfecting a code is infinitely more difficult than that of preparing a brief or writing an opinion or even a textbook. All of these activities call for an accurate knowledge of the law and insight into its application. In addition not only must the lawyer laboring in the legislative field have the rare gift of peering into the future, but he must also be peculiarly endowed with the art of precise expression. Nearly all states now have legislative reference bureaus. Some states go beyond mere library service and provide technical research for the legislators in the form of elaborate briefs. Most states also offer their lawmakers bill-drafting facilities, generally as part of their legislative reference bureaus. In spite of all these precautions the legislative product varies from the skillfully wrought bills of the National Conference of Commissioners on Uniform State Laws, one of the most successful of American efforts at co-operation in the law, to the slipshod, litigation-producing draftsmanship of pressure groups, of which some of the state fair-trade acts constitute a horrible example. In 1931 the first fair-trade act was enacted in California; it embodied in one section language that was not only grammatically incorrect but utterly lacking in meaning. This California act, as amended in 1933, was blindly copied verbatim in Iowa, Maryland, New Jersey, New York, Oregon, and Pennsylvania without correction of the error. It was only after litigation arose in some of the blundering states, in which the Illinois statute, which had corrected the error, was contrasted with the offending acts, that amendment necessarily followed. However, the egregious blunder of this paragraph still remains on the statute books in Iowa.

Even if all our legislation were well drawn, the problems of our statute book would still be with us. There remains the perennial need of cutting out the deadwood by repealers and republishing only that which is still living. By this process in England in the 1860's 118 volumes were trimmed to 18. Without periodic revision the mass of our statutes would, indeed, be forbidding. Revision, however, is but a first step in making our statute law available to the profession and the public. Especially in the field of local public law do statutes on various topics tend to grow like mushrooms. Unless all of the statutes on a given subject are occasionally merged into a single statute, they will perforce constitute a labyrinth in those mazes in which even the most skillful lawyer may well become lost. This process of consolidation is a much more difficult task than that of revision. It should be the work of lawyers who are trained in the arts of legislation and in addition thoroughly familiar with the actual operation of the laws in question. A rare example of what can be accomplished in this field is the recent consolidation of the Education Law of New York under the direction of Dr. Frank P. Graves, a competent lawyer who was for nineteen years Commissioner of Education for the State of New York. Some of the finest legislative work of this type was done by able jurists in the period following the American Revolution in adapting to the needs of the new states the laws of England and of the respective colonies. The laws of New York were successively compiled by such persons as Samuel Jones and Richard Varick in 1789, and James Kent and Jacob Radcliff in 1801, and were re-examined and revised from 1825 to 1828 by Benjamin F. Butler, John Duer, John C. Spencer, and Henry Wheaton. William Paterson, Governor and Chancellor of New Jersey, later a justice of the United States Supreme Court, spent eight years, from 1792 to 1800, in preparing a revision of the statutes of England and of New Jersey, which the legislature enacted into law. In Connecticut former Chief Justice Zephaniah Swift was chairman of a legislative committee that published an invaluable revision of the laws of his state in 1820–3.

What is most needed in each state is an agency that would be charged not only with the proper drafting of every bill that is introduced in the legislature, but with the *continuous* revision of the statutes as they appear on the statute books. In several states, notably Wisconsin and Kentucky, such action has been undertaken. There the entire statute book has been overhauled up to a certain date, and the work of revision and consolidation, the pruning of outmoded enactments, the combination of similar statutes, and the correction of stylistic errors, together with topical consolidation, is a continuous task, carried on by a trained body especially charged with these responsibilities. Moreover, the public and the profession are further aided by the provision for the biennial republication of the statutes in these states, thus making available in most useful form the complete statutory law. The result of the continual work of statutory consolidation is best illustrated in Wisconsin, a pioneer in this activity, in which state, during one five-year period, the volume of the statutes increased only by sixteen pages.

Codification goes a step further than consolidation in dealing not only with statutes but with the decisions of the common law with a view to incorporating all of the law of any subject in systematic written form. In its most ambitious aspect it seeks to cover the entire law written and unwritten. As might be expected, Jeremy Bentham was its great advocate. The very words "codify" and "codification" were coined by him. It was he who inspired Edward Livingston to draft his penal code, which was finally completed in 1825, but never enacted into law. Livingston also composed a Code of Civil Procedure regulating Louisiana practice and completed a revision of the Civil Code which became law in that state. The great name in American codification, however, is David Dudley Field. From 1839, when he had been admitted to the bar only eleven years, to his death, in 1894, he not only worked on the drafting of his codes, but agitated for them. His Code of Civil Procedure was adopted in New York in 1848 and rapidly spread westward, finding acceptance in whole or in part in twenty-four states. His Penal Code was adopted in 1881, but his Civil Code was twice rejected by the Assembly, thrice passed by it, twice with the concurrence of the Senate, only to be vetoed each time by the Governor. The battle was bitterly fought between Field and James C. Carter, representing the Association of the Bar of the City of New York. Field almost became the American Justinian. Largely through the influence of his brother, Mr. Justice Stephen J. Field, of the United States Supreme Court, all five of Field's codes, the Codes of Civil and of Criminal Procedure, and the Political, Civil, and Penal Codes, were adopted in California.

Codification in England took a different turn. Macaulay, the historian, labored for years on what ultimately became the Indian Penal Code, replete with definitions and concrete examples. Sir James Stephen, after years of experience in India, came back to England in 1872 fired with the possibility of codification at home, but his draft of a penal code was lost in the House of Commons. Codification in England received a new impetus when Sir Frederick Pollock, influenced by Macaulay and Stephen, made a digest of the law of partnership in 1877, which later became the basis for the partnership Act of 1890. Influenced in turn by Pollock's Digest, in 1878 Sir Mackenzie Chalmers had made a digest of the law of negotiable instruments, which became the Bills of Exchange Act. He also drafted the statutes codifying the law of the sale of goods in 1893 and the law of marine insurance in 1906. With these, codification became almost a dead letter in England. Professor Munroe Smith with his customary clarity has pointed out the parallel between Anglo-American and Roman legal development, showing that codification is most likely to prevail in the field of the organization of government, including the definition of the powers of public officers, both general and local, as well as with respect to the law of crimes and criminal procedure.

A fourth method of improving statutes is of more recent origin. In 1934 Lord Chancellor Sankey appointed a Law Revision Committee made up of members representing every branch of the legal profession "to consider how far, having regard to the statute law and to judicial decisions, such legal maxims and doctrines as the Lord Chancellor may from time to time refer to the committee may require revision in modern conditions." The committee before the war had reported on eight matters that had been referred to it, and seven of their reports were accepted by Parliament. They covered such important matters as contribution between joint tort-feasors, the liability of a husband for the torts of his wife, the maxim that a personal action dies with the person, and the statute of limitations. The Lord Chancellor has also appointed other committees such as the Company Law Reform Committee, most of whose recommendations were embodied in statute in 1947, the Alternative Remedies Committee, whose recommendations for the abolition of the doctrine of common employment have also become law, and a committee to consider the law of libel and slander. There is still another committee on the practice and procedure of the Supreme Court of Judicature. In New York, owing in large part to the influence of Mr. Justice Cardozo's plea for "a ministry of justice," a Law Revision Commission was created in 1934, which has done more work in this field than has been done in all the rest of the states combined, as its annual reports attest.

These perennial problems of the science of legislation give weight to the recent words of Sir Hartley Shawcross, the English Attorney General, that

. . . by the end of the 1914–1918 war it had become very obvious that the necessity for strong government was accompanied by the need of a civil service experienced in the technique both of preparing legislation for submission to parliament, and of administering such legislation when its principles were enacted. . . .

When he speaks of civil service, he, of course, has in mind the English practice whereby examinations govern all appointments up to and including under-secretaries under a competitive system that ensures not only the broadest liberal education but also technical skill. These are matters that have been relatively neglected in this country, particularly at the higher levels, until comparatively recent times, though now progress is being made, noticeably in the selection of hearing commissioners under the Federal Administrative Procedure Act under the aegis of the United States Civil Service Commission. But even superior official personnel will not avail, as I have intimated before, in the face of a general professional distaste for statute law. What is most needed is a rational attitude toward legislation as a mode of lawmaking. This, it would seem, must be sought first of all in the law schools.

As I turn from legislation to the broad field of judicial decisions, I am confronted with an embarrassment of riches. One might select cases illustrating the gradual growth of the law to meet new conditions, such as Judge Cardozo's great decision in MacPherson v. Buick Motor Co., granting redress against a manufacturer to a person injured by latent defects in an article purchased at retail, when the defect might have been discovered if the manufacturer had exercised vigilance. Or one might consider a case like Funk v. United States, where Mr. Justice Sutherland, speaking for the Court, enacted law as truly as any legislature ever does. The background of this case is that Congress, unlike most state legislatures, had failed to abolish the ancient common-law rule that precluded a wife from testifying in behalf of her husband in a criminal proceeding against him, though it had done away with many other common-law disabilities of witnesses. Weary of waiting for Congress to act, the Court proceeded to dispose of this common-law disability saying: "That this court and the other federal courts, in this situation and by right of their own powers, may decline to enforce the ancient rule of the common law under conditions as they now exist we think is not fairly open to doubt."

These two cases illustrate the two fundamental kinds of growth in the common law in modern times, the arch-demons of fiction having long since been slain by Bentham, and equity having in most jurisdictions been fused into the common law. But instead of seeking to study the growth of the law in individual cases, would it not be more profitable to turn our attention to the judge who has made the most extensive contributions to the growth of law and, what is even more to the point, made it largely as a matter of free volition. Stowell, it is true, made the prize law of England, and Marshall set the course for our constitutional law, but they were both confronted with specific cases calling for decisions in their respective fields. Mansfield, by his liberal judicial attitude, encouraged the bringing of cases that led to his development of the action of *indebitatus assumpsit,* the creation of the doctrines of quasi-contract and restitution, and the incorporation of the law merchant into the common law. One cannot imagine any other judge of his time who could or would have done so. Certain it is that there were many judges and lawyers who did not look at all with favor on his importation of equitable principles into the law, but his efforts to avoid legal technicalities and to adapt the law to the needs of the period appealed greatly to the common sense of businessmen. The reception of the law merchant into the common law of England is the work of his peculiar genius, as was his contribution to the improvement of the administration of justice, an aspect of his activities too long neglected by a profession preoccupied with private substantive law, but of which I shall necessarily speak in my next lecture.

Lord Mansfield has fascinated me since the first day I encountered him in my law school course on contracts. I had more or less successfully navigated the course through Offer and Acceptance without having been asked to accept too much that to my youthful mind seemed irrational, but as I traversed the dismal swamp of Consideration, I felt as if I had been left to myself without a map or compass or means of communication with the strange forms around me. When at length I turned the page to Pillans v. Van Mierop, I knew that I was in the presence of a great mind who, fortunately for me, spoke a modern language I could understand. Why shouldn't a promise in writing intended as a business transaction be good, regardless of consideration? It made sense to me, and it accorded with the civil law. A few pages later on I felt almost a personal sense of injury when I discovered in Rann v. Hughes that the House of Lords had overruled Pillans v. Van Mierop, declaring that:

All contracts are, by the laws of England, distinguished into agreements by specialty, and agreements by parol; nor is there any such third class as some of the counsel have endeavored to maintain, as contracts in writing. If they be merely written and not specialties, they are parol, and a consideration must be proved.

Imagine my delight in discovering two years later in the summary to Dean Ames's *Cases on Bills and Notes* his convincing demonstration that beyond the peradventure of a doubt negotiable instruments were and always have been specialties in the English law though not under seal, Chief Baron Skynner and his brethren to the contrary notwithstanding. It is interesting to note that the English Law Revision Committee in one of its reports has sided with Lord Mansfield. When in due season I came to the cases on conditions in contracts in our casebook, Mansfield's opinions in Kingston v. Preston and Boone v. Eyre stood out like beacon lights in the midst of much murky thinking. To study his decisions in Keener's *Cases on Quasi-Contract* was a rare treat, rivaled only by the pleasure of reading by myself his contributions in Wambaugh's *Cases on Insurance*.

I am never quite certain whether I am moved more by his opinions or by the dazzling achievements of the man himself in spite of seemingly insuperable obstacles. William Murray, the later Lord Mansfield, was born in 1705, a younger son of a poor Scotch peer, in a family tainted with the Jacobite heresy. He attended the grammar school at Perth until the age of thirteen, when at the suggestion of his elder brother James, Secretary of State for the Old Pretender, he was entered at Westminster. His career at Westminster and at Christ Church, Oxford, was distinguished. At Oxford he first crossed swords with William Pitt over a prize poem on the death of George I, and the rivalry there begun continued in the House of Lords until the death of the Earl of Chatham. At Lincoln's Inn his self-education marked the man. At a time when instruction at the Inns of Court was a mere form, he schooled himself to master not only the common law, but international law, *Justinian's Institutes,* the *Corpus Juris Feudalis,* the standard works of his native Scotland—Stair and McKenzie—as well as the *Ordinance de la Marine* for the grasp it might give him of the law merchant. In addition, moreover, to studying special pleading under Denison and conveyancing with Booth, to quote Dr. Johnson, "when he first came to town [he] 'drank champagne with the wits.' He was the friend of Pope." This literary giant thought sufficiently of Murray to inscribe odes to him in imitation of Horace, praising his young friend, only to call forth parodies at the hands of the envious. Scotchman, Jacobite, and one of the wits! In that day with what further handicaps for success in his profession could genius burden itself?

Called to the bar in 1730 at the age of twenty-five, he soon made a name for himself as a junior in two appeals from the Court of Sessions of Scotland to the House of Lords. Within eight years he had made his way to the front and was appearing in the leading matters of the day, such as representing the City of Edinburgh in the parliamentary inquiry into the Porteous riots. In the same year he married the amiable Lady Elizabeth Finch, daughter of the Earl of Winchelsea and a descendant of Lord Chancellor Nottingham. Four years later he became Solicitor General, a position that he held for fourteen years—"the longest and most brilliant solicitor generalship recorded in the annals of Westminster Hall," according to the acidulous Lord Campbell—and during all of this period he also served as the resourceful leader of the majority in the House of Commons. In 1754 he succeeded Sir Dudley Ryder as Attorney General. On Ryder's death, two years later, in the last days of the ministry of the Duke of Newcastle, despite the Duke's entreaties that he remain in the House of Commons, he achieved his life's ambition of becoming Chief Justice of England, a position that he filled for thirty-two years with the highest distinction.

Although Murray served many years as a parliamentary leader, his activities as a barrister and his conduct as one of the chief Law officers of the kingdom left little doubt of his primary interest in the law and its administration. This selection as Chief Justice was one of those rare cases where the man, the office, and the times were ideally suited. This is not to say that his life was no longer crowded with conflict or beset with controversy, for reforms of the magnitude that he contemplated were not to be accomplished without violent objections from the adherents of the established order.

His greatest achievement on the substantive side of the law was the reception of the law merchant into the body of the common law. This he was able to accomplish because of his broad knowledge of Continental authorities in this field, based on his studies which began during his student days at Lincoln's Inn. But not content with this learning, he consulted personally with the merchants to ascertain the customs of their business. Furthermore, to aid in the trial of commercial cases he resorted to the ancient device of a special jury of merchants, but with him a special jury became an established institution of his court. Lord Campbell recalls that several of these gentlemen survived when he began to attend Guild Hall as a student and were designated and honored as "Lord Mansfield's jurymen." Lord Mansfield is said not only to have conversed with them freely in court, but to have won their confidence by inviting them to dine with him.

Even so, Mansfield's task was not an easy one. His predecessors, and even Lord Chancellor Hardwicke, were inclined to admit in each case evidence of relevant mercantile customs, with the result that every such case would be merely decisive of the facts presented in it, without enunciating any general rule. On the other hand, if such evidence of customs were excluded, there was the danger that the law might lose touch with prevailing mercantile practice. Mansfield solved the problem by declining to admit evidence of mercantile customs that had already been established as law, applying them as general rules of law, but if a particular custom had not already been established as law, he would allow evidence concerning it and, if reasonable, would accept it as law. The obscure archaic language that abounded in mercantile documents he construed liberally to meet the true intent of the parties, regardless of the actual words, with the result that in the course of time the construction that he put upon these instruments developed a body of law as to their meaning. The principles developed in his court covered the wide range of commercial law, maritime law, and the law of marine insurance, the details of which cannot be traced here. It is not too much to say that it was he who put all of these subjects on a sound footing in English law. To a very large extent the principles of his opinions have been codified in the British Marine Insurance Act of 1906 and only to a slightly less degree have his rulings on negotiable instruments found their way into the English Bills of Exchange Act and the American Uniform Negotiable Instruments Act.

In the field of contract law Mansfield's attempt to harmonize the law of consideration with the Continental law was overruled, as we have seen, but his clear recognition in Kingston v. Preston that terms in a contract might be concurrent as well as dependent or independent served to advance clear thinking in a complicated phase of the law. It was in the field of quasi-contracts that he made his bravest attempt to change the course of English legal history by seeking to give to the action of *indebitatus assumpsit* the effect of a bill in equity. Although he did not succeed in this goal, *indebitatus assumpsit* did come to cover a wide variety of cases where the plaintiff was allowed a recovery on the ground of the unjust enrichment of the defendant. If he did not succeed in making *indebitatus assumpsit* the equivalent of a bill in equity, he at least introduced into the common law the equitable doctrines of estoppel by conduct, the doctrine of stoppage *in transitu,* and the rule that there is no right of stoppage *in transitu* against the assignee of the consignee. Above and beyond matters of specific rules, he definitely broke the ties of the common law with the formalism of the black-letter law dear to Coke; through him the spirit of equity had entered much of the common law.

There were other spheres in which he was quite unsuccessful in reforming the law. In Perrin v. Blake he attempted to reduce the rule in Shelley's Case to a rule of construction. This led to a bitter attack on him by Fearne, the author of the well-known work on *Contingent Remainders*. Fearne charged that Mansfield when a barrister had given an opinion on Shelley's Case exactly contrary to his decision as a judge. Mansfield, of course, did not deign to reply. Suffice it to say that his decision eventually was viewed with favor by Parliament, which vindicated his position by abolishing the rule in Shelley's Case in the Law of Property Act, 1925. As to Fearne, Sir Frederick Pollock tells with obvious delight of Macaulay's lament over Fearne's devotion of a life to the barbarous puzzles of contingent remainders.

Mansfield's most unfortunate experiences were in the field of criminal law, but there he also experienced some of his greatest triumphs. Neither the legislature nor the profession has approved his efforts to limit the power of the jury to return a general verdict in cases of criminal libel, which called forth the savage attacks on him of Junius. When his whole record, however, is reviewed, it may be justly said that no one judge has ever made a greater contribution to our law or done more to raise its moral level. The maxim "Let justice be done though the heavens fall," attributed to him, expresses his aim as a judge. It is what we would expect from the advocate who, when criticized for his moderation in the prosecution of the rebel Scotch lords, could say with dignity:

If I had been counsel for the Crown against Sir Walter Raleigh, and that unfortunate man had been as clearly guilty of high treason as the rebel lords, I would not have made Sir Edward Coke's speech against him to gain all Sir Edward Coke's estate and all his reputation.

No judge in these days may hope to rival Mansfield's contribution to the growth of the law, but every judge and every lawyer may learn much from his skill in adapting the law to the needs of the times. His judicial work is the outstanding example of the results obtainable from the use of the comparative method in the law.

Language, Legal and Literary *

JOHN MASON BROWN

Earlier in this volume we have quoted Justice Cardozo on the literary qualities displayed by English judges in their opinions. It is fitting, therefore, to bring the volume to an end with a selection from an American, not a lawyer by profession, but a distinguished literary figure, whose words are lit by the same happy gift of phrasing and an equal nobility of thought. The following address by John Mason Brown was delivered before the American Law Institute on May 23, 1952.

At this moment I understand more fully than I ever have before what Percy Hammond meant when, writing about some happily forgotten play, he said that in its presence he felt as out of place as an Elk at Oxford. I face you quakingly as a DP, untutored in your language and addressing you in a tongue which to some of you may seem foreign.

In the past you have demonstrated your wisdom by limiting your speakers to lawyers and jurists. I am honored to follow them, humbled by the remembrance of their distinction, and more frightened than it would be manly to admit. Surely, on the damaging evidence of my presence, the American Law Institute has decided to turn this evening into a kind of "Amateur Night." No less surely, if I may use a word which has been occupying the attention of the Supreme Court and the country, the judgment of your president has for once, and once only, been the victim of a "seizure." For I am here as what Justice Cardozo called an "uninitiated interlocutor."

Although I come from a long line of lawyers, certainly my knowledge of the law is anything but professional. It is, I am afraid, largely derived from Portia, Dickens, Galsworthy, Edmund Pearson, William Roughead, and such melodramas as *On Trial, The Thirteenth Chair,* and *The Trial of Mary Dugan.* There is a reason for this which might as well be confessed at once. By employment I am a critic and a writer. I am, in short, what is sometimes identified as a "word-man." But you are "word-men," too. This is one of the things we have in common, regardless of how much the language as we choose to use it may sound as if it had been taken from different dictionaries.

The mention of word-men leads me to Gertrude Stein. She was a word-

* Reprinted by permission of John Mason Brown and the *Saturday Review.*

girl, and a wise one. Although she could write clearly when she wanted to, she sometimes eluded being understood as successfully as if she had been a lawyer. In a recent critical study Donald Sutherland has given an unforgettable account of Miss Stein's death. He tells us, "Just before she died, she asked, 'What is the answer?' No answer came. She laughed and said, 'In that case, what is the question?' Then she died." I know of no better proof of Miss Stein's wisdom, which was part of her originality.

I will not be able to give the answers this evening. But, at least, I know the questions I am trying to find the answers to. My endeavor will be to touch upon the differences and similarities between the language of the law and the language of literature. Yes, and to discuss the means, the goals, and the obligations of good writing in both fields.

With all my heart I wish what I have to say here were as worth saying and said as well as what Catherine Drinker Bowen said in "The Lawyer and the King's English," that brilliant paper she read in Philadelphia in 1951 before the Brandeis Lawyers Society. Mrs. Bowen pointed out that, though "you and I—the lawyer and the writer—do not, actually, belong to the same species, at least we can be classified under one genus . . . *articulate man.*" Lawyers and writers, she added, are "interested in the techniques of utterance, and in what lies behind utterance—*intent*: the motivations of man."

In Mrs. Bowen's fashion I am concerned tonight with the shared articulateness of lawyers and writers, and the different techniques of utterance we so frequently employ. Perhaps Washington, D.C., is not the ideal setting for a discussion of the nuances, the beauties, and the noble possibilities of language. Anyone attempting such a discussion here is bound to resemble a preacher who has strayed into the pulpit of a church of another denomination.

For surely in no free area of the earth are there more men and women crowded together who daily do more damage to language than in the Government bureaus of Washington. So far as the beauties of language are concerned, they form a wrecking crew. Their talent for misusing it, for making it drab, ugly, or deliberately incomprehensible can only be described as genius. Yet, in spite of those responsible for the gibberish of Governmentese, some of the truest eloquence this country or the world has known has been produced by those working for the Government in high and varied stations in this very city.

Among the troubles with Washington from a literary standpoint is that it is a place where a writer does not have to be dead to be a ghost. The scale and absurdity of Washington as a ghost town was indicated by Yale's president, A. Whitney Griswold, when a few months back he spoke to the National Booksellers Association in New York. Mr. Griswold had learned with proper dismay that in Washington a university was about to open a course for ghostwriters, who "will be taught to write in such a way that orators will understand at all times what they are saying." There are more than 150 such writers on the top level in Washington alone, an official of that university declared, and most of them have a hard time adjusting their talents "to fit the mental and oratorical capacities" of the men for whom they are writing.

Speaking words that others have written, having a voice but no style of your own, may be a necessary practice for overworked officials. But one thing it is not—and that is authorship. An author's style is his written voice; his spirit and mind caught in ink. It is as individual, hence unmistakable, as the cadences of Winston Churchill, a government official who, however overworked, has never failed to make himself heard in print. Mr. Churchill must also have had suggestions submitted to him by scores of experts, but what they have suggested he has possessed. And as surely as possession is nine-tenths of the law, possession (in terms of one's own very personal usage of language) is ten-tenths of authorship.

The late Alexander Woollcott was fond of describing himself as an ink-stained wretch. All of us, writers and lawyers alike, are ink-stained in our different ways. "Ink-stained" brings to mind another kind of wretch, one that offers a warning to us all by his ugly, if protective, habits. I am thinking of the squid which releases his homemade ink for the sole purpose of creating obscurity. You, as lawyers and judges, have, of course, never been guilty of such a practice any more than have we, the unbenched and ungowned writers. Clarity is one of our joint aims, at least I assume it often is.

Over a revolving door in the Ritz Hotel in Boston there is a sign printed large which reads, "This door is not an accredited egress." A squid or a bureaucrat could have written that. It is not a sentence which perpetuates the literary tradition of Emerson, Thoreau, or William James. As language, it could be said to represent the deflowering of New England. Unfortunately, there are those who, because they do not like the law and are confused by its terminology, would be willing to mistake such phrasing for standard legal usage.

Let us face the truth. Critics and lawyers have more things in common than their addiction to words. We have detractors, if not enemies; men and women who, oddly enough, do not dote on us and have attacked us with eloquence. Precious little criticism has been as sprightly or vivid as the abuse it has provoked. I could cite a hundred treasured phrases which creative writers have used to castigate reviewers with the understandable scorn that Man-o'-War would have shown had he, in the long and fruitful years of his retirement from the track, been judged by a jury of geldings. Let me content myself with repeating one of my favorites, Maxwell Anderson's dismissal of New York's drama critics as "the Jukes family of journalism."

You who have crossed the bar also have your belittlers. Some of these feel your gift for obfuscation is such that Prince Hal must have had you, rather than Falstaff, in mind when he said, "How now, my sweet creature of bombast?" Burton in *The Anatomy of Melancholy* was another of your depreciators. "Our wrangling lawyers . . . are so litigious and busy here on earth," said he, "that I think they will plead their clients' causes hereafter,— some of them in hell."

I regret to say the picture of the law most securely hung in the minds of many people is scarcely a flattering likeness, if indeed it be a likeness at all. It is—you must remember it—the description in *Bleak House* of Jarndyce and Jarndyce, that "famous scarecrow of a suit," which over the long and dragging years had become so complicated that no living man knew what it meant. What were the symbols Dickens chose for the law and its processes? It pains me to state—fog, and gas, "Fog everywhere, fog up the river . . . fog down the river—gas looming through the fog in divers streets—never can there come fog too thick, never can there come mud and mire too deep" as "some score of members of the High Court of Chancery . . . are mistily engaged in one of the ten thousand stages of an endless cause, tripping one another up on slippery precedents, groping knee-deep in technicalities . . . and making a pretense of equity with serious faces, as players might."

That is the popular conception, or shouldn't I as your guest say misconception, of the law held both by the law's victims and the clients of lawyers, if a distinction from the layman's point of view can be made between the two. Like Shakespeare's reputation and Shaw's, this notion of the law is built, in the phrase GBS used to describe his own fame, "fast and solid . . . on an impregnable basis of dogmatic reiteration"—and, no doubt, some truth.

Dr. Johnson refused to subscribe to such an idea. He came to the defense of your profession. "It is unjust, sir," he rumbled to Boswell, "to censure lawyers for multiplying words when they argue; it is often necessary for them to multiply words." Authors have been guilty of the same indulgence, especially when paid space rates. Then they have been tempted to set down thousands of words they should have been paid to omit.

At this point we are forced back again without choice to a consideration of words, hence to writers and lawyers as word-men. Words are a strange and tantalizing commodity. The mere twenty-six letters in our alphabet are responsible for the limitless variety and the full, fabulous range of our language, call it English or American. Gathered together in dictionaries, these words are available to everyone. They literally pine for suitors. They are like the suffragette of long ago who wanted something badly, and thought it was the vote. They yearn to be possessed. Yet they are used by each individual as differently as those individuals use life itself. They are either wasted or enjoyed, faced drably or approached with zest, accepted as routine or converted into that high adventure which is literature.

Certainly most of what is written or published has no more relation to literature than ordering meals has to do with conversation. The businessman who dictates "Yours of the 15th inst. received and duly noted" is getting off a letter, but he neither seeks nor pretends to be functioning as a man of letters. Although he is employing words, his only interest in them is to transact business. If his answer were phrased in language such as Horace Walpole, Lamb, Shaw, Ellen Terry, or Thomas Wolfe might have used, he would soon be without a job. And rightly so.

In the same way, signs reading "Exit," "No Parking," and "Keep Off the Grass" fulfil their function admirably. They are as eloquent as they are meant to be. Yet, though they warn and inform us, they hardly inspire us. They feed none of the hungers which are among the excuses, the pleasures, and the needs of literature.

All of us sense the distinction between communication on the low level of utility and communication when it is raised to literature. The main Post Office in New York City supplies an illustration of these two extremes. Inside the building are signs for "Stamps," "Letters," "Parcel Post," "Air Mail," etc., and we are grateful for these directions. Outside, however, above the row of columns are curved those great, singing words of Herodotus, "Neither snow, nor rain, nor heat, nor gloom of night stays these couriers from the swift completion of their appointed rounds." Instantly, instead of leading us to a window, these words open windows for us on the challenges of nature, the concept of duty, and the invincibility of the human spirit.

Most of what we read in newspapers, magazines, or books is mere hack work. Most legal writing is drudgery of the same kind. Assuredly, drawing up a contract or a will is not an act of creative authorship. No one doubts the advisability, indeed the necessity, of both wills and contracts. Even so, preparing them must be as tedious as reading them for pleasure is impossible unless, above the dissonances of their English, can be heard the sweet music of the prospects of money. Those dreary parties, "the party of the first part" and "the party of the second part"; those ugly "whereases" and "aforesaids"; those strung-beads of synonyms, such as "give, devise, and bequeath," "rest, residue, and remainder," are not fashioned to delight. Their sole purpose is to make the document water-tight by closing up the chinks.

It is plain libel to assume, as some people do, that lawyers and jurists always employ English as if they were drawing up wills. Lawyers and jurists as writers do face certain dangers unknown to professional authors. They are excused from the necessity of entertaining and interesting their readers, and all too often—let's face the evidence—they take a cruel advantage of this enviable exemption. Nonetheless, some of the best writing that we have has come from the pens of lawyers and especially judges.

Experience itself, if only one has the ability to respond to it and translate it into words, is a better teacher of composition than our colleges know. Those who preside over courtrooms or argue in them cannot escape from life. They may not approach it as novelists, dramatists, journalists, or historians would, but they cannot duck it. This constant confrontation with the actual is what Dr. Johnson had in mind when he said, "Lawyers know life practically. A bookish person should always have them to converse with. Lawyers have what the writer wants."

Although every exposure to living helps, there are professions which, even if followed briefly, seem to make their unique contributions to a writer's training. Painting is one of these. The years were not wasted which William Hazlitt spent as a young man trying to become an artist by painting in the manner of Rembrandt and Titian. When he discovered he could not "engraft Italian art on English nature," he may have flung away his brush and pencil "in disgust and despair," but he never stopped being a painter. He merely exchanged words for colors and used them as if they were pigments. He had learned to see life with a painter's eyes; to develop a sharp awareness of shadows and highlights; above all, to seize upon those details in a man's face, dress, or posture which lay bare his spirit.

Medicine is another profession which can contribute to the writer's growth. Chekhov and Somerset Maugham are proofs of this. "If I am a writer," Chekhov once wrote, "I have to live among people." As a physician, he had done this and in the process learned much from the confessional of pain. Maugham's clinical dispassion can, at least in part, be traced to his years at St. Thomas's Hospital. By his own admission it was there he first became aware that "the normal is what you find but rarely" and that the most amazing contradictions "can all exist in a single person and form a plausible harmony."

Although listening to music with a hearing ear may or may not offer a man professional employment, it, too, can contribute much to the writer. Shaw, in this respect, is the ideal witness. "Do not suppose for one moment that I learned my art from English men of letters," he boasted. "My masters were the masters of a universal language. They were Haydn, Mozart, Beethoven, and Wagner." Among these, count Mozart the chief influence, as anyone must know who, again with a hearing ear, has listened to Shaw's prose. His claim was that *Don Giovanni* had taught him how to write seriously without being dull. "If it were only for the sense of the value of fine workmanship which I gained from it," Shaw added, "I should still esteem that lesson the most important part of my education."

Count law among the professions which may help the writer whether he lives by it or escapes from it. The law's perils from a literary point of view are many and grave. Its advantages, however, can be no less real. Chief among its dangers is that heavy-footed jargon which so many lawyers are persuaded by the pressure of their duties and their deafness or indifference to language to mistake for English. But arguing a case, preparing a brief, or writing a decision offers a superb and muscular exercise in the ordering of facts, the integration of ideas, and the mastery of logic. Surely, Scott and Stevenson were no more hurt as writers by having studied law than Jefferson and Lincoln were harmed as stylists by having practised it.

All great writing is the result of more than a great gift. Yet the gift must be there before the man, however large of spirit or mind, can write greatly. As for the gift itself, there is no explaining it. Like health, physical graces, and a talent for life, it is among the inequalities that no "Deal"—Square, New, or Fair—can correct. If all of us in my profession, for example, could write as well as we would like to, the world would be cluttered with masterpieces. You in your profession face the same disparity between hope and ability. Some of the best justices, I am told, have been among the most maladroit of writers. The judges who have contributed to literature as well as justice belong to an overprivileged breed. They are doubly endowed. They happen to be fine writers in addition to being fine jurists. Perhaps George Orwell found the best expression for this inequality when he said, "All men are born equal, but some are more equal than others."

Although the best writing-judges and the best authors share more than a command of words, they do not write for the same reasons. Since their minds are preoccupied with different concerns and their purposes have little in common, they are bound to employ the language in different ways. The law is as special in the demands it makes upon those who serve it as the drama, poetry, fiction, history, criticism, or journalism.

What, after all, is the law? At its best, at least as laymen see it, isn't it an attempt to methodize the madness of mankind? Isn't it a high-minded endeavor to create group sanity out of individual surrenders to folly, and to regulate personal impulse so that it becomes social order? Doesn't it seek to superimpose a pattern of reason on a world of passion, and to offer a guarantee of continuity by relating the precedent of the past with the dilemmas of the present?

Coleridge, a colossus among literary critics, was wise enough to recognize that you cannot pass an act of uniformity against the poets. As critics of behavior, judges are obligated to pass acts of uniformity in the interest of society. The great judges are concerned with interpretation, the great writers with revelation. Judges are devoted to protection—the protection of human rights, of property, of men against man, the structure of the state, and that beckoning and majestic concept known as justice. Creative writers do not share this absorption. They apply their gifts to human emotions, problems, frailties, or possibilities seen in terms of persons rather than abstractions. Where the great judges' interest is, so to speak, the spine and bony structure of society, the creative writers' interest is the flesh. Jurists do not see people caught in controversies or misfortunes as particular individuals, but as invitations to establish, reaffirm, or advance principles.

The justice writing an opinion carries a burden unknown to the playwright, the poet, or the novelist. It is a burden of public responsibility so heavy that its weight often makes itself felt in his prose. Wisdom is what we want from a judge, not wit; clarity of phrase, before beauty; decision rather than diversion. No wonder judges' opinions, being the awesome

things they are, using language as an instrument of action and capable of
changing the history of a nation, are seldom read as literature. No wonder
the official judicial style has had throughout history a ponderous, Roman
cadence, and has been Corinthian in its ornamentation. No wonder, as
Justice Frankfurter has pointed out, the pens of even gifted judges are
inevitably constrained. "Caution and reticence in writing," said he, "make
for qualifications and circumlocutions that stifle spontaneity, slow the
rhythm of speech, check the play of imagination. . . . Law as literature is
restricted by its responsibility."

Fortunately, this is not always so. The grave demands of the law have
been unable to muffle the writing gifts of such justices as Holmes, Cardozo,
Brandeis or Learned Hand. These men, and there are many others, have
functioned as masters of the language no less than of the law. What we
admire as the high judicial calm—that calm which comes from thinking on
an altitude far above the timberline of the trivial—has been theirs. Yet it
has never chilled them or their writings.

Their speeches, their books, even their opinions, though models of ration-
ality, have always been warmed with emotion. Their pages are heated by
the strong, undeviating passion they feel for what Holmes called "our
mistress, the law," and their proud conviction, again in his phrase, that no
other calling plunges one so deep in the stream of life . . . its passions, its
battles, its despair, and its triumphs, both as witness and actor.

Deep personal emotion can make men eloquent who are not noted for
their eloquence. It did this to Calvin Coolidge when, crushed by the death
of his son Calvin, he inscribed a friend's book with these words, "To my
friend, in recollection of his son and my son, who, by the grace of God,
have the privilege of being boys throughout Eternity."

Moral passion even more than sorrow can fuel the minds and spirits, and
hence the language, of those fired by it. It is moral passion of the finest sort
which has directed the considerations and ignited the prose of the great
judges, including those I have named. Light and heat, Shaw insisted, are
the two vital qualities demanded of literature, adding that he who has
nothing to assert has no style, and can have none. The great judges have
never lacked something to say and, at their best, have said it with light
and heat.

They have loved words. They have relished the adventure which the
quest for the right ones represents. They have known that there are no
such things as wilted words; there are only wilted people who use them.
They have hated verbosity and taken pains, when expressing themselves,
to clear away the thick underbrush and ugly weeds which obstruct most
legal language. They have shared Hazlitt's contempt for the "Occult School"
and Joubert's dislike of "words which have not been able to get currency
in the world and are only calculated to form a special language." English
to them has been a music which they have heard and which, in their writ-

ing, they have made us hear. They have had Churchill's veneration for the structure of a sentence. They have known better than to believe, as someone tried to prove a few years ago, that the ideal sentence is seventeen words long. Part of their wisdom is that they have recognized that a good sentence is as long as it needs to be and no longer, and that a long sentence is more than acceptable if only it seems short.

These judges have belonged to what Mrs. Bowen called a race of "poet lawyers." Only a lawyer who was also a poet could write such a sentence as Holmes's, "Who of us could endure a world, although cut up into five-acre lots and having no man upon it who was not well fed and well housed, without the divine folly of honor, without the senseless passion for knowledge outreaching the flaming bounds of the possible, without ideals the essence of which is that they never can be achieved?"

To turn to Holmes again—and it is hard to turn away from him—only a poet-lawyer could have written, "I was walking homeward on Pennsylvania Avenue near the Treasury, and as I looked beyond Sherman's Statue to the west the sky was aflame with scarlet and crimson from the setting sun. But, like the note of downfall in Wagner's opera, below the sky line there came from little globes the pallid discord of the electric lights. And I thought to myself the Götterdämmerung will end, and from those globes clustered like evil eggs will come the new masters of the sky. It is like the time in which we live. But then I remembered the faith that I partly have expressed, faith in a universe not measured by our fears, a universe that has thought and more than thought inside of it, and as I gazed, after the sunset and above the electric lights there shone the stars."

May I add that only a poet-lawyer could have told us what liberty is in a definition as stirring as Judge Hand's. "What do we mean when we say that first of all we seek liberty? I often wonder whether we do not rest our hopes too much upon constitutions, upon laws and upon courts. These are false hopes; believe me, these are false hopes. Liberty lies in the hearts of men and women; when it dies there, no constitution, no law, no court can save it; no constitution, no law, no court can even do much to help it. While it lies there it needs no constitution, no law, no court to save it."

The great judges, whose business is opinions, dissenting or favorable, have never been opinionated. Being philosophers as well as poets and lawyers, they have searched for truth with open minds. "One learns from time," Holmes observed, "an amiable latitude with regard to beliefs and tastes."

There are some words which Judge Hand has confessed he would like to see written over the portals of every church, every school, every courthouse, and every legislative body in the United States. What are they? They are the words Oliver Cromwell spoke just before the Battle of Dunbar. "I beseech ye in the bowels of Christ think that ye may be mistaken."

Such judges belong, as I have admitted, to an overprivileged breed.

"There is more truth in law than in lawyers, more poetry in justice than in judges," David Loth reminds us in his life of John Marshall. "But once in a while a man mounts the bench with the salt of life, the spice of wisdom, and the sweetness of humor blended in him so subtly yet so successfully that those who are quite unlearned in the law glimpse some of its beauties."

The beauties of the law are not the only ones the great judges have opened up to us. They, like their blood-relations the great word-men in literature, have lighted up the world for us by using language as a beacon. The shadows will always be with us. They are a part of the health of our thinking. They mean that we recognize gradations, that we keep even our certainties open to question, and do not sink into the dangerous oversimplification of believing everything is either black or white. Shadows and darkness, however, are not the same thing. Illumination, the kind of illumination which banishes darkness though it leaves shadows, is among the paramount obligations of literary no less than legal writing. It has never been more needed than now when so many are tempted to lose hope and to surrender to despair.

In *One Man's America*, Alistair Cooke's collection of his broadcasts from this country to England, Mr. Cooke tells a story which illustrates my point. "The time," he says, "was the 19th of May, 1780. The place was Hartford, Connecticut. The day has gone down in New England history as a terrible foretaste of Judgment Day. For at noon the skies turned from blue to gray and by midafternoon had blackened over so densely that, in that religious age, men fell on their knees and begged a final blessing before the end came. The Connecticut House of Representatives was in session. And as some men fell down and others clamored for an immediate adjournment, the Speaker of the House, one Colonel Davenport, came to his feet. He silenced them and said these words: 'The Day of Judgment is either approaching or it is not. If it is not, there is no cause for adjournment. If it is, I choose to be found doing my duty. I wish, therefore, that candles may be brought.'

"Ladies and gentlemen, let candles be brought."

Ladies and gentlemen, let candles be brought indeed.

A List of One Hundred Legal Novels*

JOHN H. WIGMORE

And finally, by natural projection, we go from language, legal and literary, to legal literature, with an article and reading list in the field of legal novels. "There's no such thing as a 'legal novel,'" wrote Arthur Train in Yankee Lawyer; *but this is a technical quibble from a man who wrote many legal novels. We have seen men of law writing well enough to be thought literary men; we have seen literary men writing in a legal background; if there were space, we could branch out into poetry, plays, and other forms of art. Forgive the editor if attention is called to articles in the* Journal of the American Bar Association *for October, 1955, and September, 1957, under his name, which show how far the adventure can go.*

Years ago, Dean Wigmore and others wrote to the general effect that reading the best that has been thought and said will make a better man of the lawyer and a better lawyer of the man. John Henry Wigmore (1863–1943), Harvard-educated, possessor of honorary degrees, teacher in Tokyo, professor and dean at Northwestern for many years, was the author or editor of some two dozen volumes, many on evidence. He received medals and honors from France and Japan. He has been widely quoted, and in the best sense was a dean of the profession. Let the following essay be the best kind of ending, the ending that looks ahead. It appeared originally in 1908 and in its final, revised form in 1922.

1. And what, pray, is a "legal" novel? For there have surely not been many illegal novels. The illegalities in which the great novelists have figured have commonly been not suits for libels committed by them, but gallant struggles (like those of Charles Reade) to protect their copyrights against pirates, or to vindicate themselves (like poor Cooper) against envenomed reviewers.

A "legal" novel, as here meant, will be simply a novel in which a lawyer, most of all, ought to be interested, because the principles or the profession of the law form a main part of the author's theme.

As for any definition or further subdividing of the "legal" novel, it is

* John Henry Wigmore's "A List of One Hundred Legal Novels" is reprinted from the *Illinois Law Review* (Northwestern University School of Law), Volume 17, Number 1, 1922, with special permission.

perhaps unprofitable and certainly difficult, being decidedly open to difference of taste and opinion. Nevertheless, for those who care to pick and choose, there may be noted, in the rough, four kinds:

(A) Novels in which some *trial scene* is described—perhaps including a skilful cross-examination;

(B) Novels in which the *typical traits of a lawyer or judge,* or the *ways of professional life,* are portrayed;

(C) Novels in which the methods of law in the *prosecution and punishment of crime* are delineated; and

(D) Novels in which some *point of law,* affecting the rights or the conduct of the personages, *enters into the plot.*

In the following list these sorts are indicated by the letters A, B, C, D. But let it be understood that such an indication is suggestive only; for the class of a particular novel is often a matter for difference of opinion. Moreover, the list will include only those in which one of these circumstances is a more or less prominent feature.

2. But the list need not try to include *all* such works of fiction—good, bad, or indifferent. Where shall the line be drawn? On the one hand, it must not exclude all but the works of the great masters, from Fielding and Dickens to Stevenson and Howells. Yet it may properly be confined to what may be called literature, i.e., novels in which character is delineated by a writer of whom style may be predicated. A few notable novels, indeed, must be included to which many would not concede these qualities—for example, *Mr. Meeson's Will;* and a few must be excluded, because, though possibly within that definition, they belong to a class whose influence is bad—such as the Raffles stories. It is obvious, too, that the ordinary detective story—even Mr. Julian Hawthorne's and Mrs. Green's—does not fulfill the canons, while Mr. Aldrich's *Stillwater Tragedy,* Sir Conan Doyle's *Sherlock Holmes* [stories], and M. Gaboriau's *Monsieur Lecoq* do cross the line safely.

3. But, after all, what is served by such a list? Does a lawyer go to a novel to learn his law? And would he even recommend the layman to look into works of fiction for forming correct notions of the ways of the law? Do not even the greatest of the "legal" novels portray rather the shortcomings and abuses of justice? And will not their perusal by the layman tend rather to fix in his mind (perhaps already prejudiced) a picture distorted and untrue? And even in the commonplace legal incidents of novels, are there not examples galore of the most impossible and unlegal doings? Does not the judge sometimes, in a novel, dictatorially order the jury to declare a defendant guilty of murder? Or the plaintiff to pay damages when a verdict in a civil case is found for the defendant? Or the sheriff to sell off the debtor's property before action is begun—et alia enormia? In short, why encourage the layman to read a "legal" novel?

Well, let us repeat, we are not making a list for laymen. We have in mind rather the novel in which the lawyer himself is, or ought to be, most interested. And from this point of view we can think of several reasons why such a list is worth the labor. For it is certain that the lawyer must, like other men, for his pastime and mental ease, abandon himself now and then to the thrall of fiction. He will not read *all* the novels—even all the good ones; he will probably not read many. He must select. Let him, then, select those which will mean something to him as a lawyer, will have a special interest for one of that elect profession with all its traditions, its memories, its secrets of the craft. And thus, since he *must* select, he will want to select those which as a lawyer he cannot afford to ignore.

❋   ❋   ❋

4. In the first place, there are certain episodes or types of character in professional life whose descriptions by famous novelists have become classical in literature, such as Sergeant Buzfuz and the action of *Bardell* v. *Pickwick* in the *Pickwick Papers,* the chancery suit in *Bleak House,* Effie Dean's trial in *The Heart of Midlothian.* With these every lawyer must be acquainted. This is not merely because of his general duty as a cultivated man, but because of his special professional duty to be familiar with *those features of his profession which have been taken up into general thought and literature.* What lawyer can go through life unfamiliar with such classical gifts to the world as the character of Advocate Pleydell in *Guy Mannering,* of Attorney Tulkinghorn in *Bleak House,* of Magistrate Popinot in *César Birotteau,* and *A Commission in Lunacy,* of Attorney Godeschal's office in *A Start in Life?* What lawyer can neglect to tread the paths of his professional progenitors' pursuits in *Copperfield* and *Pendennis* and *Redgauntlet* and *The Lesser Bourgeoisie?* Or to be ignorant of the never-fading scenes in *The Scarlet Letter* and *Les Misérables*—the perpetual possession of humanity? Or to know Smith's Leading Cases while unfamiliar with *Pebbles* v. *Planestones* and *Jarndyce* v. *Jarndyce?*

And there are many romances, not yet exalted into classical niches, which claim us in every other respect—the thrilling trial scenes in Hale's *Philip Nolan's Friends,* in Reade's *Griffith Gaunt,* in Harte's *Gabriel Conroy,* in Blackmore's *Lorna Doone,* in Holland's *Sevenoaks,* in Foote's *John Bodewin's Testimony,* in Gray's *Silence of Dean Maitland.* And shall "Pudd'n-head Wilson" be forgot? Scott and Dickens are of course pre-eminently the lawyer's novelists. But no lawyer can fail to believe that certain others wrote their books especially for him (books not classical, nor marked perhaps by any single undying episodes). We are here thinking of the lawyers' careers in Trollope's *Orley Farm,* in Ford's *Peter Stirling* (said to reflect a career like that of ex-President Cleveland), and in Warren's *Ten Thousand a Year* (*the* book for lawyers by a lawyer); the sheriff's life in Alice French's (Octave Thanet) stories, particularly "The Missionary Sheriff"; the lawyers and the law that permeate the books of Mary Murfree ("Charles Craddock," herself the daughter of a lawyer and legal author), of Charles Reade, of Anthony Trollope, of Stanley Weyman. And who cannot want to peruse, woven into romance in Eggleston's *The Graysons,* Abraham Lincoln's oft-told maneuver with the almanac, the tale of a liar exposed, or Jeffreys' brutal trial of Lady Lisle, the friend of the fugitives, in Conan Doyle's *Micah Clarke?*

5. Then, again, there are the *great movements of legal progress* which have been aided or reflected in the novelist's works. It is one thing to know that imprisonment for debt has been abolished; or to con a catalogue of the reforms of the nineteenth century in the *Select Essays in Anglo-American Legal History;* or to read the lives of Eldon, Denman, Brougham, or Field. But it is another, and a necessary thing, to know the spirit of those times— to realize the operation of the old rules now gone—to feel their meaning in human life and to appreciate the bitter conflicts and their lessons for today. This deepest sense of their reality we shall get only in the novels.

Two great figures stand out as leaders—Charles Dickens and Charles Reade. No man can truly apportion the meed of influence between them and the lawyer-legislators—Mackintosh, Romilly, Brougham, Denman, Campbell. But it is certain that the former sunned and watered what the latter sowed and reaped. We must go to *Bleak House* to learn the real meaning of chancery's delays—to *Oliver Twist* to see the actual system of police and petty justice in London—to *Pickwick Papers* to appreciate the technicalities of civil justice. Was jail-reform more aided by Bentham's essays or by Charles Reade's *Never Too Late to Mend?* How soon would the right to imprison sane people in the private lunatic asylums have been abolished if *Hard Cash* had not been written? That great author's life, in fact, was one long knight-errantry against the dragons and giants of the times.

But even when we leave these eminent leaders we find the institutional abuses of contemporary life pictured in novels here and there with a realism which makes them almost appendices to the law books. Henry Kingsley's *Austin Elliott* is said to have inspired a stringent legislation against duelling. Balzac's *César Birotteau* exposes the misery and chicanery of bankruptcy proceedings. Cooper's *Ways of the Hour* tried trial by jury on its merits. Besant's *Chaplain of the Fleet* makes us wonder how the miseries of the old Fleet debtors' prison could have been allowed to exist as long as they did. No man who has not read Besant's *The Orange Girl* can appreciate the terrible significance of the punishment of the pillory. Cooper's *Satanstoe* and *Chainbearer* (and *The Redskins* belongs also to the series) reflect the system of land-tenure in early New York and that "anti-rent" agitation which was so intense a problem in those days that we wonder it could ever have been forgotten. The system of transporting convicts to Botany Bay has been a favorite theme; in the best of these stories, though not ranked among the classics, are John Boyle O'Reilly's *Moondyne,* Rolf Boldrewood's Australian books, and Becke's and Jeffrey's *A First Fleet Family.* Can a lawyer know his profession and its past without knowing these things, and the parts that these many legal institutions have played in the life of the community?

Perhaps here belong, too, many novels which depict a special problem or institution of law, not having in mind its abuses or reforms, but full of instruction and reflection for the lawyer, or notable as classics of romance— *Felix Holt,* for example, with a plot turning on a base fee in land; *Paul Clifford,* with its terrible problem for the judge; *Eugene Aram,* an elaborated transcript of a notable English murder trial.

Here, too, are to be noted the interesting pictures of alien systems of justice—Caine's *The Deemster,* Erckmann-Chatrian's *Polish Jew* (said to be the foundation of Irving's play, *The Bells*), Franzos' Austrian stories, Jókai's Hungarian stories, Crawford's for Italy, Tolstoi's superb *Resurrection,* and, of course, Balzac, Gaboriau, Sue and Dumas for France, and Scott for the ancient modes of trial.

6. And again, there are the *novels which depict history* for us—that is, the scenes in legal annals which general history has made famous. Here, of course, the magic of Scott has done most. The Vehmgericht in *Anne of Geierstein*—the cruel justice of Louis XI in *Quentin Durward*—the ancient trial by battle in *Ivanhoe*—and the trial by ordeal in *The Fair Maid of Perth* —are there not many who will never know (nor need to know) more of these things than are chronicled by the great romancer? And the unspeakable Jeffreys. All the serious rehabilitations of modern historians (including Mr. Zane) will not avail to lighten the picture which the novelists have drawn of his trials; for those have supplied one of the favorite topics—at London, in *Peveril of the Peak* and in *Lorna Doone,* and on the circuit of the Bloody Assizes, in Besant's *For Faith and Freedom* and in Conan Doyle's *Micah Clarke* (this surely must begin to be placed among our classics; it is not too soon). And in *Kidnapped* Stevenson has given us the very pages from Howell's State Trials. *Barnaby Rudge,* too, almost echoes the witnesses in Lord Gordon's trial for the riot, and we may study Lord Mansfield here. Going further afield we live over again the times of the ill-fated Roman Republic in *Rienzi,* and observe the tragic fate of the DeWitts in Dumas' *Black Tulip.* There is in fact hardly an end to the line of boundary where history and law unite in the pages of the novelist.

And who cannot feel that this lore is meant for him as a lawyer? What man can say that he is a member of our profession and not *want* to be familiar with these things? And so, shall there not be a list of "legal" novels?

7. But there is a higher standpoint yet. For the novel—the true work of fiction—is a *catalogue of life's characters.* And the lawyer must know human nature. He must deal understandingly with its types, its motives. These he cannot find—all of them—close around him; life is not long enough, the range is not broad enough for him to learn them by personal experience before he needs to use them. For this learning, then, he must go to fiction, which is the gallery of life's portraits. When Balzac's great design dawned on him, to

form a complete series of characters and motives, he conceived his novels as conveying just such learning. He even enumerated the total number of characters. His task was, he says:

> To paint the three or four thousand salient figures of an epoch—for that is about the number of types presented by the generation of which this human comedy is the contemporary and the exponent. This number of figures, of characters, this multitude of portraits, needed frames. Out of this necessarily grew the classification of my work into Scenes. Under these heads I have classed all those studies of manners and morals which form the general history of Society. . . . If the meaning of my work is understood, my readers will see that I give to the recurring events of daily life (secret or manifest), and to the actions of individuals, with their hidden springs and motives, as much importance as the historian bestows on the public life of a nation.

In this view the work of the novelist is to provide a museum of human characters, traits and motives—just as we might go to a museum of zoölogy to observe an animal which we desired to understand but had never yet seen alive; this was Balzac's idea:

> There have always been, and always will be, social species, just as there are zoological species. If Buffon achieved a great work when he put together in one book the whole scheme of zoology, is there not a work of the same kind to be done for Society? . . . There are as many different men as there are species in zoology. The differences between a soldier, a workman, a merchant, a sailor, a poet, a beggar, a priest, though more difficult to decipher, are at least as marked as those which separate the wolf, the lion, the ass, the crow, the shark, the seal, the lamb and so on.

And so the lawyer, whose highest problems call for a perfect understanding of human character and a skilful use of this knowledge, must ever expect to seek in fiction as in an encyclopedia, that learning which he cannot hope to compass in his own limited experience of the humans whom chance enables him to observe at close range.

This learning has been sought, possessed, and valued by many great advocates. Perhaps they have seldom openly inculcated its value. But we find at hand one singularly direct exposition of this theme, which must here be quoted:

> Read the literature of the lawyers. Read the lives of those great lawyers and judges of England. Read the literature of human nature. The lawyers can gain many points by reading.
>
> To my mind Balzac is the greatest judge of human nature after Shakespeare. I think I learned more of human nature (outside of my own experience) from Balzac than I have from any other author except Shakespeare. I recall especially *Eugénie Grandet*, the history of a miser. I have read that book two or three times, and this is how it profited me afterwards. I was retained in a very serious case of fraud. I studied the party on the other side. I made up my mind that if ever there

was a miser out of the pages of literature, that was the man, and that Grandet was his literary father-in-law. I studied *Eugénie Grandet* again, and then I attacked that opponent. It was an eight years' task. But the image of Grandet helped me to hound that man so that at the end of eight years there was not anything left but his hide. The greatest admirer of the work I did is that man's own lawyer; but he will not give me credit for having any legal acumen. He maintains that I knew all the facts beforehand. Yet the truth of the matter was that I did not; I drew the bill before I had the facts. I merely judged the man's character from what I had read of *Eugénie Grandet*. That experience was to me a life lesson.

Let me allude also to another case, one that nearly broke me down with the mental and physical strain. I had bought every printed trial I could find on that particular subject. I had a year to prepare for the actual trial of the case. There were very eminent lawyers on the other side. I will not mention names, for the parties are living. But I did not receive from all these books as much light as I did from a certain classical novel, one that characterized exactly the plaintiff's object and put that party in the lime-light. With that aid I was able to follow all the ins and outs of his maneuvers, and finally to win the case. It was a work of fiction that guided me to a right solution of that person's character, and a knowledge of his character that was essential to victory.

Still another lesson I now recall which I learned from reading—a lesson I will never forget. It related to a gentleman by the name of Gil Blas. Gil had various and sundry adventures, and among others he was made secretary to the Archbishop of Toledo. The Archbishop said to him one day: "Gil, I look upon you as a very likely young man, I like your intelligence and acumen. Now I am getting old. I have to preach once a month. Make it your duty to let me know when you see any failing signs in my mental powers. I will trust you as a friend to tell me about it." So Gil noted the character of the sermon the next month. Then he heard the ensuing sermon; and he thought the Archbishop showed signs of age and senility. At the third sermon he was more satisfied of this, and the fourth was shockingly significant. He complimented the Archbishop on the first sermon, and spoke fairly of the second, but of the others he did not. The Archbishop asked, "Now, Gil, what is the truth?" Gil said: "Your eminence, your mental powers are failing rapidly." "Gil," responded the Archbishop, "I find that I am mistaken in your acumen. The treasurer will pay you and you will leave the house." I have never forgotten the moral of that story. Such incidents of literature add to your knowledge.

And so the best literature—drama or poetry, philosophy or fiction—must always be an arsenal for the lawyer. This, to be sure, is a larger matter than our "legal" novels; yet it includes the best of them.

*   *   *

8. But there is one more thing worth lingering over, before we come to our list itself, and that is the sources of the information and skill of our "legal" novelists. Where did they learn their legal lore? How could they find and use the materials for their legal scenes and characters?

This, of course, has varied greatly with the individual methods of work. Yet, on the whole, it is possible to distinguish certain general differences. There are, broadly, three groups. There are the novelists who were themselves lawyers, or were trained for the law. There are also a few who learned much of it by personal experience in litigation of their own. And then there are those—the most part—who prepared for the legal episodes by special research.

To the first belong, of course, in prime rank, Fielding, Scott, Balzac and Dickens. A long life in the law, as barristers and as magistrates, gave to Fielding and to Scott the material of the law as a second nature. Balzac was destined and trained for it; only at the last moment could he evade his family's ambitions to chain him for life to the lawyer's desk. Dickens, as an attorney's clerk and a court reporter, had all the direct experience which a lawyer's life gives, and almost all the training which a lawyer was then expected to have. There are, too, among today's contemporaries, notable like instances—Robert Grant, Anthony Hope Hawkins, Frederic J. Stimson; though it is odd that most of these avoid the legal life in their fiction. Arthur Train, however, with the vantage point of a District Attorney's office, may well be deemed our modern Fielding, now that he has broadened his canvas.

In the second group are pre-eminent Cooper and Reade. During the latter half of their lives, it would seem that not a year passed, for either, without a lawsuit pending; and thus they came to observe the lawyer within his native lair. Reade, indeed, did enter at Lincoln's Inn, and was called to the bar; but it does not appear that he studied or worked or ever held a brief, or did more than eat the perfunctory dinners; and his most intense interest in the law was not shown until after he had himself brought a suit to rescue a young friend from an asylum. His law he must have learned mostly from the controversies of reform which he took up and from his own constant lawsuits and the numerous lawyers retained by him. These latter, indeed, he sampled variously and judged freely and dictatorially. Listen to this passage from a letter: "My successes have been hardly won. In this case I had to dismiss Jessel for incapacity, Ballantine for colloquy with defendant's attorney, Teesdale because of his chief clerk's incapacity, and Rickerd's managing clerk." The client who could dismiss Jessel and Ballantine must indeed have been self-confident in his own legal acumen. But Charles Reade, after all, was himself "the people's lawyer," a never-tiring advocate for humanity. Cooper, too, seems to have engaged in his lawsuits largely as a matter of principle—to defend the rights of authors and the liberty of thought. This famous romancer, much misunderstood and disliked in his own generation (first by our alien kin across seas, and then by his own neighbors and community), found himself from 1837 onwards in almost continuous litigation; and it is noticeable that the majority of his novels with legal episodes and characters date in that period. Himself without legal training, he was by nature (like Charles Reade) an uncompromising fighter for his rights—a striking example of the type of man whom Ihering's *Struggle for Rights* delights to honor. He had usually an unpopular cause, and he was an unpopular man; but he accomplished the remarkable feat, which the greatest of lawyers might envy, of succeeding with judge and jury when he argued his own cause. No such record can probably be found in history. It is no wonder that he was entitled to weave into his novels, with every claim of verisimilitude, whatever he pleased of legal episode and character.

In the third group belong, naturally, most of the novelists who have dealt with phases of the law. Not having the lawyer's profession or a plentiful experience of lawsuits as their source of information, they have been obliged to obtain by special study the sources adapted to their immediate purpose. Many, of course, have failed, for lack of thoroughness; and the successes are due (where traceable) to the persistent resolve of accuracy in research —the directness of touch with the material of life. Charles Reade, to be sure, belongs in this group also, for perhaps no great realist of contemporary life (except Balzac) made so systematic a search for materials of life pictures— the objective truth of his character facts. His system of newspaper clippings and scrap-books is well known. His preliminary search of Parliamentary documents and other verified data made him an insuperable opponent in his many controversies over contemporary law and fact. Here is an example of his reply to a sneering reviewer:

Can any man offer a fairer test of a book's veracity than I did? I said, in my preface to *Hard Cash,* that the whole thing rested on a mass of *legal evidence*— bluebooks, pamphlets, newspapers, private letters, diaries of alleged lunatics, reports of tried cases. I offered, in print, to show these, at my own house, to any anonymous writer who might care to profit by my labor—the labor of Hercules. . . . How many, do you suppose, accepted this infallible test of mendacity or veracity in my book? Not one!

But, naturally, the methods differed with the individual. It would be interesting to trace out the methods of the other great delineators of legal episodes. George Eliot's success, in what must have been purely a tour de force, is well known, and has earned approval from no less than Sir Frederick Pollock, in his history of The Land Laws:

The curious kind of estate created by the conveyance in fee simple of a tenant in tail in possession, without the concurrence of the owners of estates preceding his own, is called a *base fee.* Though uncommon, it is not unknown in practice; and it has been used by George Eliot, in *Felix Holt,* with great effect and with perfect correctness, as part of the machinery of the plot; insomuch that conveyancers reading the novel have been known to comment seriously, as if the thing had happened to one of their own clients, that the parties did not take better advice.

But it is Robert Louis Stevenson—that beautiful soul of authorship—who has furnished us perhaps the most interesting instance of conscientious and painstaking preparation of the correct scenery of a legal drama to which the author adds the magic spirit of life and action. No one ever read *Kidnapped* and its sequel, *David Balfour,* with a cool thought as to the construction of its plot, or the historic foundation; but the story was in fact woven out of a recorded trial, used for the purpose. Mrs. Stevenson thus tells of its creation.

I concluded to try and write it myself (i.e., a play called "The Hanging Judge"). As I wanted a trial scene in the Old Bailey, I chose the period of 1700 for my purpose; but being shamefully ignorant of my subject, and my husband confessing to little more knowledge than I possessed, a London bookseller was commissioned to send us everything he could procure bearing on Old Bailey trials. A great package came in response to our order, and very soon we were both absorbed—not so much in the trials as in following the brilliant career of a Mr. Garrow, who appeared as counsel in many of the cases. We sent for more books, and yet more, still intent on Mr. Garrow, whose subtle cross-examination of witnesses, and masterly, if sometimes startling, methods of arriving at the truth, seemed more thrilling to us than any novel. Occasionally other trials than those of the Old Bailey would be included in the package of books we received from London; among these my husband found and read with avidity. *The Trial of James Stewart in Ancharn in Duror of Appin, for the Murder of Colin Campbell, of Glenure, Esq., Factor for his Majesty on the forfeited estate of Ardshiel.* My husband was always interested in this period of his country's history, and had already the intention of writing a story that should turn on the Appin murder. The tale was to be of a boy, David Balfour, supposed to belong to my husband's own family, who should travel in Scotland as though it were a foreign country, meeting with various adventures and misadventures by the way. From the trial of James Stewart my husband gleaned much valuable material for his novel, the most important being the character of Alan Breck. Aside from having described him as "smallish in stature," my husband seems to have taken Alan Breck's personal appearance, even to his clothing, from the book. . . . Some time after the publication of *Kidnapped* we stopped for a short time in the Appin country, where we were surprised and interested to discover that the feeling concerning the murder of Glenure (the "Red Fox," also called "Colin Ray") was almost as keen as though the tragedy had taken place the day before. For several years my husband received letters of expostulation or commendation from members of the Campbell and Stewart clans.

Even more interesting was Stevenson's legal research into the materials for *Weir of Hermiston,*—that last and unfinished work, of which he wrote once, "Mind you, I expect it to be my masterpiece." Under the name of "The Justice Clerk" (as originally selected), it was to depict the great Hanging Judge, confronted at the last with the stern ordeal of sentencing to death his own son—a situation already in literature in Bulwer's *Paul Clifford.* The Lord Justice Clerk was the Scottish name for the head of the criminal justiciary; and Stevenson took every pains to prepare accurately the law of his case. Sidney Colvin thus reports a part of those efforts:

In a letter of Stevenson's to Mr. Baxter, of October, 1892, I find him asking for materials in terms which seem to indicate that he knew this (legal problem) quite well: "I wish Pitcairn's Criminal Trials, quam primum. Also an absolutely correct text of the Scot's judiciary oath. Also, in case Pitcairn does not come down late enough, I wish as full a report as possible of a Scot's murder trial between 1790–1820. Understand, *the fullest possible*. Is there any book which would guide me to the following facts: The Justice-Clerk tries some people capitally on circuit. Certain evidence cropping up, the charge is transferred to the Justice-Clerk's own son. Of course in the next trial the Justice-Clerk is excluded, and the case is called before the Lord Justice-General. Where would this trial have to be? I fear in Edinburgh, which would not suit my view. Could it be again at the circuit town?" The point was referred to a quondam fellow-member with Stevenson of the Edinburgh Speculative Society, Mr. Graham Murray, the present Solicitor-General for Scotland, whose reply was to the effect that there would be no difficulty in making the new trial take place at the circuit town; that it would have to be held there in the spring or autumn, before two Lords of Justiciary; and that the Lord Justice-General would have nothing to do with it, this title being at the date in question only a nominal one held by a layman (which is no longer the case). On this, Stevenson writes: "Graham Murray's note *re* the venue was highly satisfactory, and did me all the good in the world."

And so, in the hands of a master, the law of a legal novel may after all be made as true to reality as when the scribe is of the vocation of law.

✿   ✿   ✿

9. And now, at last, for our list. As here offered, it is of composite workmanship, and has grown with the accretions of ten years. It began in a manuscript list of some fifty titles, prepared by the present writer in 1898. This was then enlarged to about one hundred titles for publication in *The Brief;* and that list was then reprinted in *The Library Journal* and in *The Athenæum Monthly Bulletin.* To improve it effectively, both in the earlier classics and in the recent fiction, some co-operative effort became necessary. Accordingly, committees of my students were appointed, who kindly undertook to examine the works of one hundred selected novelists of standing.

The result of these efforts, together with the suggestions of other readers, was to increase the list by about two hundred and seventy-five titles, making some three hundred and seventy-five in all. This list was published in the ILLINOIS LAW REVIEW for April, 1908 (Vol. II, p. 574). That number of the REVIEW, and the reprint of the list, has long since been exhausted. To enlarge the list thoroughly, so as to cover the last decade, is impracticable. But a demand exists for a good reading list of standard Legal Novels. Hence the present list of One Hundred Legal Novels, selected from the former list. Two or three over the hundred are put in for good measure.

It must be added that, in making the selection, the pure detective story, however good, has been omitted; the last decade alone has seen this type of fiction multiplied, until now it forms a genre of its own.

A LIST OF ONE HUNDRED LEGAL NOVELS

Aldrich, Thomas Bailey:
Stillwater Tragedy. (C)
Allen, Grant:
Miss Cayley's Adventures. (A,D)
de *Balzac,* Honoré:
César Birotteau. (D)
Cousin Pons. (B,D)
Père Goriot. (D)
Lucien de Rubempré. (A,C)
The Lesser Bourgeoisie. (B,D)
Gobseck. (D)
Colonel Chabert. (B)
A Commission in Lunacy. (A,B)
Last Incarnation of Vautrin. (C)
Start in Life. (B)
The Marriage Contract. (D)
Becke, Louis, and *Jeffrey,* Walter:
First Fleet Family. (C)
Besant, Walter:
St. Katherine's by the Tower.
(A,B,C)
For Faith and Freedom. (A,B)
The Orange Girl. (A,B,C)
Besant, Walter, and *Rice,* James:
The Chaplain of the Fleet (Prison).
(C,D)
Blackmore, R. D.:
Lorna Doone. (A)
Bulwer-Lytton, Edward:
Eugene Aram. (A,C)
Paul Clifford. (A,C)
Burnett, Frances Hodgson:
In Connection with the De Wil-
loughby Claim. (D)
Caine, Hall:
The Deemster. (C,B)
Collins, Wilkie:
The Law and the Lady. (A,D)
Cooper, James Fenimore:
The Ways of the Hour. (A,B,C)
The Redskins. (B,C,D)
Satanstoe. (D)

The Chainbearer. (D)
Cox, E. M.:
The Achievements of John Caruthers.
(C)
Craddock, Charles Egbert (*Mary
Murfree*):
The Prophet of the Great Smoky
Mountains. (C)
Crockett, Samuel R.:
The Grey Man. (A,C)
Crawford, Francis Marion:
Sant' Ilario. (C,D)
Dickens, Charles:
Barnaby Rudge. (C)
Bleak House. (A,B)
Old Curiosity Shop. (A,B)
Oliver Twist. (A,C)
Pickwick Papers. (A,B)
A Tale of Two Cities. (A,B)
Doyle, Arthur Conan:
Micah Clarke. (A)
Dumas, Alexandre:
The Black Tulip. (C)
The Count of Monte Cristo. (A,C,D)
Marguerite de Valois. (A,C)
Twenty Years After, Part II. (A)
Eggleston, Edward:
The Mystery of Metropolisville.
(A,B,C)
The Graysons. (A)
Eliot, George:
Adam Bede. (A)
Felix Holt. (A,B,D)
Erckman, E., and *Chatrian,* A.:
The Polish Jew. (A)
Franzos, Karl Emil:
The Chief Justice. (A,B)
Fielding, Henry:
Jonathan Wild. (C)
Tom Jones. (C)
Fletcher, J. S.:
The Middle Temple Murder. (B,D)

Foote, Mary Hallock:
John Bodewin's Testimony. (A)
Ford, Paul Leicester:
The Honorable Peter Stirling. (B)
Frederic, Harold:
The Damnation of Theron Ware. (B)
French, Alice (*Octave Thanet*):
The Missionary Sheriff. (C,D)
We All. (B,C,D)
Gaboriau, Emile:
File No. 113. (C)
Monsieur Lecoq. (C)
Goldsmith, Oliver:
The Vicar of Wakefield. (C)
Gould, S. Baring:
The Broom Squire. (A,B,D)
Grant, Charles:
Stories of Naples and the Camorra.
(C)
Grant, Robert:
The Law Breakers. (D)
Eye for an Eye. (A,B,D)
Grey (or *Gray*), Maxwell:
The Silence of Dean Maitland.
(A,D)
Haggard, H. Rider:
Mr. Meeson's Will. (A,B,D)
Hale, Edward Everett:
Philip Nolan's Friends. (A)
Harte, Francis Bret:
Gabriel Conroy. (A)
Heiress of Red Dog. (A,B,D)
Hawthorne, Nathaniel:
The Scarlet Letter. (C)
Herrick, Robert:
The Common Lot. (A)
Hill, Frederick Trevor:
Tales Out of Court. (A,B)
Holland, Josiah Gilbert:
Sevenoaks. (A,D)
Howells, William Dean:
A Modern Instance. (A,D)
Hugo, Victor:
Les Misérables. (A,C,D)
Ninety-three. (C)
The Man Who Laughed. (C)
James, George P. R.:
Morley Ernstein. (B,C)

Kingsley, Henry:
Austin Elliott. (A,D)
La Ramé, Louise (*Ouida*):
Under Two Flags. (A)
Le Sage, Alain-René
Gil Blas. (C)
Mitchell, S. Weir:
Constance Trescott. (A,B,C)
O'Reilly, John Boyle:
Moondyne. (C)
Page, Thomas Nelson:
Red Rock. (D)
Parker, Gilbert:
Right of Way. (A)
Read, Opie:
A Tennessee Judge. (B)
The Jucklins. (A,B)
Reade, Charles:
Griffith Gaunt. (A)
It Is Never Too Late to Mend. (B,
C)
Hard Cash. (A,B,C)
Scott, Walter:
Anne of Geierstein. (A,C)
The Fortunes of Nigel. (C,D)
Guy Mannering. (A,B,C,D)
The Heart of Midlothian. (A,B,D)
The Fair Maid of Perth. (A)
The Antiquary. (B,D)
Ivanhoe. (A)
Peveril of the Peak. (A)
Quentin Durward. (C,D)
Redgauntlet. (B,D)
Rob Roy. (B,C)
Sienkiewicz, Henryk:
Comedy of Errors. (A)
Stevenson, Robert Louis:
Kidnapped; with its sequel,
David Balfour. (B,C)
Weir of Hermiston. (B)
Stimson, Frederic J.:
The Residuary Legatee. (D)
Stockton, Frank R:
The Late Mrs. Null. (D)
Thackeray, William Makepeace:
Pendennis. (B)
Tolstoi, Leo N.:
Resurrection. (A,B,C,D)

Train, Arthur:
  Tutt and Mr. Tutt. (A,B,C,D)
  By Advice of Counsel. (A,B,C,D)
  As It Was in the Beginning. (B)
Trollope, Anthony:
  Orley Farm. (A,B,D)
  Mr. Maule's Attempt. (A,B,C,D)
  The Vicar of Bullhampton. (A,C,D)
Twain, Mark (*Samuel Clemens*):
  Pudd'nhead Wilson. (A)

Warren, Samuel:
  Ten Thousand a Year. (B)
Weyman, Stanley:
  Francis Cludde. (A)
  My Lady Rotha. (A)
  Man in Black. (A)
Woolson, Constance Fenimore:
  Anne. (A)
Zangwill, Isaac:
  The Big Bow Mystery. (A,C)

Index by Authors

BENÉT, STEPHEN V.
The Devil and Daniel Webster, 330

BEVERIDGE, ALBERT J.
Marbury Versus Madison, 174
(From *The Life of John Marshall*)

BOWEN, CATHERINE D.
Holmes Prepares for the Bar, 26
(From *Yankee from Olympus*)
Trial of Sir Walter Ralegh, (Part I), 308
Trial of Sir Walter Ralegh, (Part II), 318
(From *The Lion and the Throne*)

BROWN, CLINTON G.
The Jim Wheat Murder Case, 58
(From *You May Take the Witness*)

BROWN, JOHN M.
Language, Legal and Literary, 562

BUCHAN, JOHN
The Judicial Temperament, 224
(From *Homilies and Recreations*)

CARDOZO, BENJAMIN N.
Law and Literature, 283

COZZENS, JAMES G.
Old Judge and Young Lawyer, 297
(From *The Just and the Unjust*)

CURTIS, CHARLES P.
The Advocate, 2
(From *It's Your Law*)

DEAN, JOSEPH
The Reputation of the Dead, 459
(From *Hatred, Ridicule, or Contempt*)

DICKENS, CHARLES
Bardell v. Pickwick, 342
(From *The Pickwick Papers*)

FORDHAM, EDWARD W.
The Baccarat Case, 392
(From *Notable Cross-Examinations*)

FRANKFURTER, FELIX
Chief Justices I Have Known, 250
(From *Of Law and Men*)

FULLER, LON L.
The Case of the Speluncean Explorers, 514

GRAY, W. FORBES
Lord Monboddo and Lord Braxfield, 137, 148
(From *Some Old Scots Judges*)

HAND, LEARNED
The Future of Wisdom in America, 277

HINE, REGINALD L.
The Solicitor and the Will, 78
(From *Confessions of an Un-Common Attorney*)

HOLDSWORTH, WILLIAM S.
Bleak House and the Procedure of the Court of Chancery, 363
(From *Charles Dickens as Legal Historian*)

HOLMES, OLIVER W.
The Profession of the Law, 494
The Path of the Law, 496

HYDE, H. MONTGOMERY
The Trial of Oscar Wilde, 403
(From *The Trials of Oscar Wilde*)

KING, WILLARD L.
Fuller's Increasing Influence on the Court, 240
(From *Melville Weston Fuller*)

KNOX, JOHN C.
Trouble with the Volstead Act, 269
(From *A Judge Comes of Age*)

MACAULAY, THOMAS B.
Jeffreys, The Hanging Judge, 120
(From *History of England*)

MACMILLAN, LORD
Law and Letters, 99
Law and Language, 106
(From *Law and Other Things*)

MARJORIBANKS, EDWARD
The Seddon Case, 418
(From *For the Defence*)

MARSHALL, JOHN
Letter to Joseph Story, 161

MASON, ALPHEUS T.
Holmes and Brandeis Dissenting, 228
(From *Brandeis: A Free Man's Life*)

MAUPASSANT, GUY de
Madame Luneau's Case
(trans. by Ernest Boyd), 388
(From *The Sisters Rondoli and Other
Stories*)

MENCKEN, H. L.
The Criminal Law, 539
(From *A Mencken Chrestomathy*)

MONTAIGNE, MICHEL de
On the Law
(trans. by E. J. Trechmann), 476
(From *The Essays*)

SANDBURG, CARL
Lincoln the Lawyer, 43
(From *Abraham Lincoln: The Prairie
Years*)

SWISHER, CARL
The New Supreme Court, 195
(From *Roger B. Taney*)

THOREAU, HENRY D.
Unjust Laws, 483
(From *On the Duty of Civil Disobedi-
ence*)

TROLLOPE, ANTHONY
Phineas Finn Awaits Trial, or Chaffan-
brass on the Law, 378
(From *Phineas Redux*)

VANDERBILT, ARTHUR T.
The Growth of Substantive Law, 545
(From *Men and Measures in the Law*)

WELLMAN, FRANCIS L.
Art in Direct Examination, 86
(From *Day in Court*)
The Manner of Cross-Examination, 438
The Cross-Examination of Mrs. Reginald
Vanderbilt, 446
(From *The Art of Cross-Examination*)

WIGMORE, JOHN H.
A List of One Hundred Legal Novels,
572

WOOLLCOTT, ALEXANDER
Knight with the Rueful Countenance
(Profile of Lloyd Paul Stryker), 71

WOOLSEY, JOHN M.
The United States of America v. One
Book Called *Ulysses*, 218